Politics and the Russian Army
Civil–Military Relations, 1689–200

Military coups have plagued many countries around the world, but
Russia, despite its tumultuous history, has not experienced a successful military coup in more than two centuries. In a series of detailed
case studies, Brian Taylor explains the political role of the Russian military. Drawing on a wealth of new material, including archives and
interviews, Taylor discusses every case of actual or potential military
intervention in Russian politics from Peter the Great to Vladimir Putin.
Taylor analyzes in particular detail the army's behavior during the political revolutions that marked the beginning and end of the twentieth
century, two periods when the military was, uncharacteristically, heavily
involved in domestic politics. He argues that a common thread unites the
late-Imperial, Soviet, and post-Soviet Russian army: an organizational
culture embodying the belief that intervention against the country's political leadership – whether tsar, general secretary, or president – is fundamentally illegitimate.

Brian D. Taylor is Assistant Professor in the Department of Political
Science at the University of Oklahoma.

Politics and the Russian Army

Civil–Military Relations, 1689–2000

BRIAN D. TAYLOR

University of Oklahoma

CAMBRIDGE
UNIVERSITY PRESS

PUBLISHED BY THE PRESS SYNDICATE OF THE UNIVERSITY OF CAMBRIDGE
The Pitt Building, Trumpington Street, Cambridge, United Kingdom

CAMBRIDGE UNIVERSITY PRESS
The Edinburgh Building, Cambridge CB2 2RU, UK
40 West 20th Street, New York, NY 10011-4211, USA
477 Williamstown Road, Port Melbourne, VIC 3207, Australia
Ruiz de Alarcón 13, 28014 Madrid, Spain
Dock House, The Waterfront, Cape Town 8001, South Africa

http://www.cambridge.org

First published 2003

Printed in the United States of America

Typeface Sabon 10/12 pt.   *System* LaTeX 2_ε [TB]

A catalog record for this book is available from the British Library.

Library of Congress Cataloging in Publication Data

Taylor, Brian D., 1964–
Politics and the Russian army : civil-military relations, 1689–2000 / Brian D. Taylor.
    p.   cm.
Includes bibliographical references and index.
ISBN 0-521-81674-2 – ISBN 0-521-01694-0 (pb.)
1. Civil-military relations – Russia – History.   2. Civil-military relations –
Soviet Union – History.   3. Civil-military relations – Russia (Federation)   4. Russia.
Armïei – Political activity – History.   I. Title.
JN6520.C58 T39   2002
322′.5′0947–dc21   2002067688

ISBN 0 521 81674 2 hardback
ISBN 0 521 01694 0 paperback

For Mark

Contents

Figures

Tables

Preface

This book is about the armed forces of one country or three, depending on how one chooses to count. Citizens of contemporary Russia certainly see a common thread uniting their history, and I proceed from a similar assumption: Imperial Russia, the Soviet Union, and the Russian Federation are treated as one country. Thus, despite the annoying fact that for seventy-four years the country had a completely different name (the Union of Soviet Socialist Republics), for the sake of brevity and simplicity I will often refer to the Russian empire/the Soviet Union/the Russian Federation as Russia. I should perhaps add that my annoyance should not be taken as a political statement, but as a more practical author's lament.

Not only did the name of the country change after the 1917 Revolution, but also the calendar. Dates in this book are given in the form in which they would have been in Russia at that time. Thus, until February 1, 1918, dates are given in Old Style according to the Julian Calendar used in Imperial Russia. The Julian Calendar lagged twelve days behind the Gregorian Calendar in the nineteenth century and thirteen days behind it in the twentieth century. After February 1, 1918, dates are given in New Style, consistent with the Gregorian Calendar used in the West.

I use the transliteration system of the U.S. Board on Geographic names, which I believe is easier for non-Russian speakers to read than the Library of Congress system (Yakovlev rather than Iakovlev, Milyukov rather than Miliukov, etc.). I also have used the familiar English form for well-known names (Trotsky rather than Trotskiy, Tsar Nicholas rather than Nikolay, etc.).

I follow conventional citation rules for Russian archival sources: the abbreviation for the archive is followed by the fond (f.), opis (op.), delo (d.), and page (l.) number.

This project began as a dissertation at the Massachusetts Institute of Technology. Inevitably I cut some of the details found in the prior version during the transition to a book. Hardcore specialists on particular topics or periods may wish to consult the thesis, *The Russian Military in Politics* (MIT, 1998), for more complete documentation and discussion of some aspects of the story. Alternatively, of course, you are welcome to contact me directly.

A very large number of individuals and organizations contributed to making this book possible. Given the amount of time I have spent on this project, and the many people who assisted me, it is almost inevitable that someone will be forgotten here. If you are in that category, please accept my apologies and thanks.

While at MIT I received financial and institutional support from multiple organizations, including the MIT Department of Political Science, the Security Studies Program of MIT (formerly DACS), the Center for International Studies at MIT (through a fellowship program supported by the MacArthur Foundation), the Harry S. Truman Scholarship Foundation, the Social Science Research Council, the Office of Net Assessment of the Department of Defense, a Foreign Language and Area Studies (FLAS) Title VI Grant, and the Institute for the Study of World Politics.

The International Research and Exchanges Board (IREX) provided support for a year in Moscow, during which most of the archival research for this book was conducted, as well as many of the interviews. I thank the IREX Moscow staff for their support. While in Moscow in 1992 and 1993–1994 I was based at the Institute of USA and Canada, Russian Academy of Sciences. I particularly thank Andrey Kortunov for his help and guidance. I also thank the staffs of the following libraries and archives for their assistance: the Russian State Military Archive, the Russian State Military History Archive, the Russian Center for the Storage and Study of Documents of Recent History, the State Archive of the Russian Federation, the Russian State Library, the Institute of Scientific Information for the Social Sciences of the Russian Academy of Sciences (INION), and the Russian-American Press Information Center.

Subsequent research trips to Moscow in 1997, 1999, 2000, and 2001 allowed me to supplement the material in the dissertation, particularly with additional interviews. Institutional support in 1999 and 2000 was provided by the Carnegie Moscow Center; I thank all of their staff, particularly Alan Rousso and Olga Chernova, for its help. The staff of the Council on Foreign and Defense Policy, and especially Aleksandr Belkin, have also been of great help during several visits. I am also grateful to many Russian military officers, politicians, scholars, and journalists for their time and assistance.

Much of the dissertation was written while on fellowship at the John M. Olin Institute at Harvard University and the Belfer Center for Science and International Affairs (BCSIA), Kennedy School of Government, Harvard University. My thanks to Samuel Huntington, Steve Rosen, and Michael Desch of the Olin Institute, as well as to Graham Allison, Steven Miller, and Michael Brown of BCSIA, for their support and contributions.

A grant from the Smith Richardson Foundation provided crucial support in the final stages of completing the book. This work was conducted at the University of Oklahoma (OU) and the University of Chicago. I particularly thank my chair at OU, Ron Peters, and Charles Glaser and John Mearsheimer of the University of Chicago for making my stay there both enjoyable and productive. Two research assistants who provided important assistance during this period were Olesia Jefferson and Tatyana Vinichenko.

Various forms of financial, institutional, and personal support have also been provided over the last several years by the Program on New Approaches to Russian Security (PONARS). Especially important in this respect has been Celeste Wallander, who created and shaped a scholarly community that is a model of erudition and collegiality.

Portions of this book appeared previously in somewhat different form in other places. I thank the publishers for permission to use this material here:

"The Russian Military in Politics: Civilian Supremacy in Comparative and Historical Perspective," Ph.D. Dissertation, Massachusetts Institute of Technology, 1998. Reprinted by permission of the Massachusetts Institute of Technology.

"Russia's Passive Army: Rethinking Military Coups," *Comparative Political Studies,* 34, 8 (2001, Sage Publications), pp. 924–952. Reprinted by permission of Sage Publications.

Portions of Chapter 7 appeared in "The Russian Military and the October 1993 Crisis," in *Russia and Eurasia Military Review Annual,* Volume 16, edited by Theodore Karasik (Academic International Press, Gulf Breeze, FL, 2002). I thank the publishers for permission to use the material here.

The map in Chapter 3 is reproduced from *Russia 1917: The February Revolution* by George Katkov. Copyright © 1967 by George Katkov. Reprinted by permission of HarperCollins Publishers Inc. and PFD on behalf of the Estate of George Katkov.

None of the above organizations, of course, is responsible for the contents of this book.

The list of individuals to whom I am grateful is even longer than the list of organizations that provided financial and institutional support. First of all I thank my dissertation committee, Don Blackmer, Barry Posen, and Steve Meyer for their enormous assistance while I was at MIT and subsequently.

I thank my many colleagues from MIT, DACS, IREX, Olin, BCSIA, PONARS, OU, the University of Chicago, and elsewhere. At the risk of leaving someone out, I thank the following individuals for their suggestions, comments, or support at various phases of this project: Golfo Alexopoulos, Graham Allison, Oksana Antonenko, Pavel Baev, Debbie Ball, Karen Ballentine, Aaron Belkin, Aleksandr Belkin, Andy Bennett, Eva Busza, Jeff Checkel, Tim Colton, Robert Cox, Kurt Dassel, James Davis, Georgi Derlugian, Mike Desch, Colin Elman, Mimi Elman, Matt Evangelista,

Peter Feaver, Jendayi Frazer, Chris Gelpi, Charlie Glaser, Hein Goemans, Steve Hanson, Eric Heginbotham, Geoff Herrera, Fiona Hill, Wade Jacoby, Pauline Jones-Loung, Charles Kenney, Beth Kier, Alexander Kozhemiakin, Jeff Legro, Dominic Lieven, Dan Lindley, Mariano Magalhaes, Tom Mahnken, Terry Martin, John Mearsheimer, David Mendeloff, Sarah Mendelson, Laura Miller, Steve Miller, Arkady Moshes, Joel Ostrow, Elena Pavlova, Alexander Pikayev, Daryl Press, Steve Rosen, Jeff Rossman, Regina Smyth, Jack Snyder, Tim Snyder, Nikolai Sokov, Valerie Sperling, John Steinberg, Ekaterina Stepanova, Brad Thayer, Trevor Thrall, Dmitriy Trenin, Astrid Tuminez, Rick Villalobos, Vadim Volkov, Mark von Hagen, Celeste Wallander, Steve Wilkinson, Boris Zhelezov, and Kimberly Marten Zisk.

Lewis Bateman of Cambridge University Press oversaw the transition from manuscript to book with great efficiency and was always a pleasure to deal with. Also essential to the production were Lauren Levin, Louise Calabro, Marielle Poss, Bob Golden, and Nancy Peterson.

I thank all of my friends in Russia – and particularly Dmitriy Babich, Boris Bednikov, Andrei and Larissa Berkenblit, Olga Dmitriyeva, Irina Dmitriyevich, Zhanna Gumenyuk, Olga Kharchenko, Nikolay Kulikovskiy, Irina Kurenkova, Vladimir Merkushev, Tatyana Nikitina, Pavel Podvig, Tatyana Vinichenko, and Aleksandr Voronin – for their friendship.

Some individuals merit special mention. Mark Kramer was of great help with many new sources on Soviet history. Kevin O'Prey has been a source of excellent advice, unwavering friendship, and tremendous personal support since the very beginning of this project. Sharon Weiner also has been extremely generous with her time, advice, and friendship for many years.

I especially thank my family, particularly my parents and my brother and sister-in-law, for their love and support over the years.

Renée de Nevers has contributed so much to this project, in countless ways big and small, that she should probably be listed as a co-author. She read every chapter on multiple occasions and provided innumerable insights and suggestions. Most of all she gave me her love, friendship, and support, for which I warmly and affectionately thank her. Anatol and Lucian should be thanked for the excellent timing of their arrival and for the many joys and distractions they provided during the final stages of this project.

Finally, it is a source of great regret and sadness that my dear friend Mark Schmoll did not live to see the completion of this book. I thank his wife Jennifer Miller and their daughter Emma for their inspiration. I miss Mark greatly, and I dedicate this book to him.

                                                              Brian D. Taylor

List of Abbreviations

ABM	Anti-Ballistic Missile
ARR	*Arkhiv russkoy revolyutsii*
CC	Central Committee
CIS	Commonwealth of Independent States
CPSU	Communist Party of the Soviet Union
FBIS-SOV	*Foreign Broadcast Information Service Daily Report: Soviet Union* and *Foreign Broadcast Information Service Daily Report: Central Eurasia*
FSB	Federal Security Service
GARF	State Archive of the Russian Federation (*Gosudarstvennyy arkhiv Rossiyskoy Federatsii*)
GDP	Gross Domestic Product
GKChP	State Committee on the Emergency Situation
GNP	Gross National Product
GPU	State Political Administration
GUO	Main Guards Directorate
INF	Intermediate Nuclear Forces
JIR	*Jane's Intelligence Review*
KA	*Krasnyy arkhiv*
KD	*Kommersant" daily*
KGB	Committee on State Security
KP	*Komsomol'skaya pravda*
KVS	*Kommunist vooruzhenikh sil*
KZ	*Krasnaya zvezda*
MK	*Moskovskiy komsomolets*
MN	*Moskovskie novosti*
MPA	Main Political Administration
MRC	Military Revolutionary Committee
MT	*Moscow Times*
MVD	Ministry of Internal Affairs

NATO	North Atlantic Treaty Organization
NCO	Non-Commissioned Officer
NEG	*Novaya ezhednevnaya gazeta*
NG	*Nezavisimaya gazeta*
NGO	Non-Governmental Organization
NKO	People's Commissariat of Defense
NKVD	People's Commissariat of Internal Affairs
NVO	*Nezavisimoye voyennoye obozreniye*
OG	*Obshchaya gazeta*
OO	Special Sections
ORA	*Oktyabr'skaya revolyutskiya i armiya*
PDPA	People's Democratic Party of Afghanistan
PMR	Transdneister Republic
PUR	Political Administration of the RKKA
PVO	Air Defense Forces
RDRA	*Revolyutsionnoye dvizheniye v russkoy armii*
RGVA	Russian State Military Archive (*Rossiyskiy gosudarstvennyy voyennyy arkhiv*)
RGVIA	Russian State Military History Archive (*Rossiyskiy gosudarstvennyy voyenno-istoricheskiy arkhiv*)
RKKA	Workers' and Peasants' Red Army
RPG	*The Russian Provisional Government 1917: Documents*
RTsKhIDNI	Russian Center for the Storage and Study of Documents of Recent History (*Rossiyskiy tsentr khraneniya i izucheniya dokumentov noveyshey istorii*)
SALT	Strategic Arms Limitation Treaty
SBP	Presidential Security Service
Stavka	Supreme Headquarters of the Russian Army (World War I)
TsAMO	Central Archive of the Ministry of Defense (*Tsentralnyy arkhiv Ministerstva Oborony*)
TsKhSD	Center for the Storage of Contemporary Documentation (*Tsentr khraneniya sovremennoy dokumentatsii*)
USSR	Union of Soviet Socialist Republics
VDV	Airborne Forces
VIZh	*Voyenno-istoricheskiy zhurnal*
VOSR	*Velikaya oktyabr'skaya sotsialisticheskaya revolyutsiya*
VV	Internal Troops
VV	*Voyenniy vestnik*

Politics and the Russian Army
Civil–Military Relations, 1689–2000

Introduction

This book is about Russian soldiers and the tsars, Communist Party bosses, and presidents they have served. The historic exploits of the Russian and Soviet armies, which crushed Napoleon and Hitler, are well known. This book tells a different, lesser known story about Russian soldiers: the role they have played in domestic politics.

As the process of Russian democratization lurches along – one step forward, two steps back, as Lenin said – Russia has at least one advantage over most post-authoritarian states. Unlike many states in transition, Russia does not have a tradition of military intervention or rule: The last successful military coup took place in 1801.

The absence of a Russian man on horseback, however, does not imply that the army has played no role in politics. Given Russia's tumultuous twentieth century, it could hardly be otherwise. The Russian Revolution and civil war, the Stalinist terror of the 1930s, the Second World War, the collapse of the Soviet Union, and the current so-called democratic transition are only the most prominent examples of political turbulence. The military has weathered revolution, imperial collapse, and mass murder of the top ranks of the officer corps by the political leadership. Such a series of intense provocations would seem to provide more than adequate grounds for military intervention in politics. Except for a few half-hearted forays, however, the Russian armed forces have remained surprisingly aloof from high politics. Indeed, since the middle of the nineteenth century the army has endeavored to remain "outside politics."[1]

The central question of the book is, What role has the Russian army played in domestic political struggles, and why? The most fruitful way to approach the question is to think of military behavior as the product of a two-step process. Armies make political choices based on both the *opportunities*

---

[1] The phrase "outside politics" is in quotes because Russian officers often used these exact words to describe their role. See especially Chapters 3 and 7.

presented by political and organizational structure and *motives* derived from their normative commitments and material interests.[2] Both opportunities (structure) and motives (agency) matter, but not in the way the previous literature suggests.

The varying strength of the Russian state is the most fundamental aspect of political opportunity. A cursory appraisal of Russian twentieth-century history shows that the army has been most involved in domestic politics during the major political crises that marked the birth and death of the Soviet Union. Periods of state weakness led to military participation in internal politics. This argument, the dominant one in the civil–military relations literature, holds up well here. But there is an important caveat: State weakness does not lead to military coups, as is traditionally claimed. Rather, a political vacuum only makes it more likely that the army will have the opportunity to seize power; whether it has the desire or ability to do so is explained by other factors.

The opportunities available for military involvement in domestic politics are also shaped by structural factors internal to the armed forces. Cleavages inside the army, sometimes deliberately fostered by civilian rulers, can make political activity more difficult. Often this component merely reinforces domestic structure and state strength. However, in several cases, cleavages within the armed forces helped determine the stance of the army. These splits were rarely decisive, but they did play a role.

At times, such as during Stalin's rule, opportunities for military activity were so limited that the influence of officers' motives on behavior was limited. In most cases, however, military motives played an important and autonomous role. The two basic types of motives are rational and cultural, or corporate interest and organizational norms.[3] It is at the level of officers' motives that this book makes its most important contribution.

Officers' norms about their proper role in politics have played a fundamental role in shaping the Russian army's behavior. A norm of civilian supremacy has deep roots in the Russian armed forces. Even in cases when other factors were pointing strongly toward a military coup, organizational culture served to restrain concerted action. An organizational culture argument has not been widely or systematically applied to the study of military intervention. I demonstrate the utility of such an approach.

At the same time, an organizational culture approach cannot stand alone. When opportunities for military involvement in domestic politics are high, such as during the Russian Revolution and the collapse of the Soviet Union

---

[2] Samuel Finer first used the categories of *opportunity* and *motive* in the study of civil–military relations, although I use them somewhat differently: S. E. Finer, *The Man on Horseback: The Role of the Military in Politics*, 2nd ed. (Harmondsworth, England: Penguin Books, 1975).

[3] Jon Elster, *Nuts and Bolts for the Social Sciences* (Cambridge, England: Cambridge University Press, 1989).

and the subsequent Russian transition, the military may be forced to play a role because other political actors will seek to use force to achieve their goals. The military can, almost quite literally, be dragged into politics. Normative commitments, however, tended to make army behavior weak, half-hearted, and consequently ineffective.

Perhaps more important than what explains Russian military behavior is what does not. Over the last 200 years the Russian military has never intervened in politics to protect its own bureaucratic interests. The Russian/Soviet military has endured severe threats to its corporate interests, such as the Stalinist purges, during which thousands of officers were murdered, and recent massive budget and force cuts that have left thousands of officers homeless and without pay for months, but these blows have not precipitated a military coup. The poor performance of the corporate interest approach is especially noteworthy given its prominence both in the comparative politics literature on military intervention and in the literature on Soviet civil–military relations. Roman Kolkowicz and Timothy Colton, the authors of the two most important books on Soviet civil–military relations, both adopted this approach.[4] Although this argument may perform better for other countries, the Russian case clearly demonstrates its limitations when employed without reference to other factors.

PLAN OF THE BOOK

Chapter 1 sets the stage for the rest of the book by providing a typology of the multiple approaches to the study of military intervention in politics. The prevalence of military coups in the 1960s and 1970s worldwide spawned an impressive body of research, with a wide range of hypotheses. I survey and systematize this literature and draw from it the four perspectives mentioned above: domestic structure, organizational structure, corporate interest, and organizational culture. Several other approaches are set aside as not relevant to the Russian cases. Chapter 8 summarizes the conclusions, and it pursues some important theoretical and policy-relevant themes brought out by the rest of the book.

The empirical chapters, Chapters 2–7, represent the heart of the book. I investigate 19 cases of actual or potential military involvement in high politics. These events run from Peter the Great to Boris Yeltsin, a period of over 300 years. The result is the only survey of Russian military behavior in sovereign power issues that covers the imperial, Soviet, and post-Soviet periods.

[4] Roman Kolkowicz, *The Soviet Military and the Communist Party* (Princeton: Princeton University Press, 1967); Timothy J. Colton, *Commissars, Commanders, and Civilian Authority: The Structure of Soviet Military Politics* (Cambridge, MA: Harvard University Press, 1979).

Not all of these chapters are created equal. Chapters 2, 4, and 5 cover large swathes of history, bringing together cases from different time periods. Chapter 2 looks at the imperial period from Peter the Great to World War I, Chapter 4 covers the period from the end of the Russian Civil War until World War II, and Chapter 5 runs from World War II to Mikhail Gorbachev's rise to power in 1985. More detailed case analysis is presented in Chapters 3, 6, and 7. Chapter 3 focuses on the Russian Revolution, Chapter 6 deals with the Gorbachev period and the collapse of the Soviet Union, and Chapter 7 examines the post-Soviet transition under Boris Yeltsin. These periods merit special attention not only because of their intrinsic historical interest, but also because the open politics of these times provide a wealth of source material. I believe the new material presented in these chapters justifies the lengthier treatment. Additionally, the comparisons between the different theories are sharpest in these cases.

Three basic comparisons form the foundation of the analysis. First, the comparison to other states is explicit in the first and last chapters and is implicit throughout. Second, I compare Russia to itself in a histori-cal (diachronic) manner. Finally, I compare different types of military be-havior to each other. The goal of these comparisons is both to explain the conduct of the Russian armed forces and to draw conclusions about when different explanations for military intervention are likely to be the strongest.

I use a wide range of sources for the empirical sections of the book. In a project of this size, some use of the Russian and English-language sec-ondary literature is inevitable.[5] When using secondary historical accounts, I have tried to distill the dominant viewpoint from the available sources and be explicit when I am taking sides in a debate.[6] A substantial chunk of the case studies is based almost entirely on primary source research, including extensive archival research and interviews. I found it necessary to consult the available primary sources either because the secondary literature did not speak directly to the questions that I am studying or because there were spe-cific debates in the existing historiography that additional primary research could help resolve.

The book is meant to be useful to a variety of readers. Social scientists will be interested in the assessment of competing explanations for military intervention. Historians will note the new evidence on some significant events from Russian history, such as the revolution, the Stalinist purges, and the

---

[5] Theda Skocpol, "Emerging Agendas and Recurrent Strategies," in Theda Skocpol, ed., *Vision and Method in Historical Sociology* (Cambridge, England: Cambridge University Press, 1984), pp. 382–383.

[6] For an excellent discussion, see Ian S. Lustick, "History, Historiography, and Political Science: Multiple Historical Records and the Problem of Selection Bias," *American Political Science Review*, 90 (1996), 605–618.

collapse of the Soviet Union. Policy makers may focus on (a) lessons for understanding the conditions that contribute to military coups and (b) what the story implies for the future of Russian democracy. In sum, the book seeks to contribute to our theoretical understanding, our historical knowledge, and our practical political judgment.

Explaining Military Intervention

Coups are the ultimate problem of civil–military relations. From ancient Rome to today's democratizing states, Juvenal's question – "but who is to guard the guardians themselves?" – has been of central political importance.

This chapter examines the range of possible explanations for military involvement in domestic politics. No single approach can by itself explain the hundreds of coups that have taken place over the years in a wide variety of countries – that is to ask too much of social science theory. Rather than posit a "golden bullet" theory that explains everything, the goals here are more modest. First, I map the lay of the land in this corner of the academic field. Second, I suggest how these different approaches may complement each other in a two-step model of military behavior. Before we turn to the different ways of explaining the phenomenon of military intervention, however, it is important to be clear what we are talking about.

MILITARY INVOLVEMENT IN SOVEREIGN POWER ISSUES

Sovereign power issues vs. de fense policy and societal choice [handwritten annotation]

The notion of a military coup evokes images of soldiers with machine guns seizing television and radio transmitters and surrounding government buildings with armored vehicles. Our stylized visions of the classic coup tend to obscure the fact that the military can have a decisive influence on determining who rules the state in many different ways. Staying in the barracks sometimes can be as influential as leaving them. When conceived of in this fashion, the notion of a coup is really shorthand for a range of military behaviors, both active and passive, that can lead to a change in the executive leadership of the state.

Timothy Colton has crafted an evocative phrase to label this class of events: *sovereign power* issues.[1] The sovereign power domain of civil–military

---

[1] Timothy J. Colton, "Perspectives on Civil–Military Relations in the Soviet Union," in Timothy J. Colton and Thane Gustafson, eds., *Soldiers and the Soviet State* (Princeton, NJ: Princeton University Press, 1990), pp. 7–11.

Military intervention vs. military
arbitration vs. military involvement

relations concerns the question of who rules and who decides who rules. Colton distinguishes this domain of civil–military relations from two others: *defense policy* and *societal choice*. Defense policy is concerned with issues directly related to the armed forces' professional concerns, such as the defense budget, military doctrine, and procurement policy. Societal choice issues are nondefense domestic political, economic, and social issues, such as macro-economic policy or education policy. Although societal choice issues are not an obvious domain of civil–military relations, military role expansion into these questions has been a common route to more extensive military involvement in politics. This book is about sovereign power issues.

There are three possible forms of military involvement in sovereign power issues. The first is the traditional focus of much of the civil–military relations literature, *military intervention*. Military intervention is the use, actual or threatened, of force by members of the military, either alone or with civilian actors, in an attempt to change the executive leadership of the state.[2]

The second possible outcome is military resolution of a civilian sovereign power dispute, or *military arbitration*. Military arbitration occurs when multiple persons or groups claim to hold legitimate state power and the military is forced to decide from whom to obey orders.[3] This is different from military intervention because the military has not made an autonomous decision to become involved in sovereign power issues, but is forced to play a role due to civilian activity. Military arbitration is a case of military *involvement* in sovereign power issues, but not one of military *intervention*.

The third possible behavior is *no military involvement* in sovereign power issues. This potential outcome is crucial and often overlooked. Much of the existing literature on military intervention studies only coups and not noncoups, thereby introducing selection bias into the research design.

---

[2] The members of the military that make a decision to intervene are almost always officers; so in most circumstances, references to the armed forces, the army, or the military apply primarily to the officer corps. The terms "military" and "armed forces" will be used interchangeably. To avoid repetition, the term "army" will on occasion be used to refer to the military as a whole; it should be clear from the context whether the term "army" is being used in this broad sense or in its more restricted meaning. A "military coup" is a special class of military intervention, an attempt to seize state power by the use of force, whereas military intervention is a broader category and includes intimidation or threats of noncooperation with the civilian leadership. For more extended definitional discussions, see S. E. Finer, *The Man on Horseback: The Role of the Military in Politics*, 2nd ed. (Harmondsworth, England: Penguin Books, 1975), pp. 20, 127–148; Edward Luttwak, *Coup d'Etat: A Practical Handbook* (Cambridge, MA: Harvard University Press, 1979), pp. 19–27; Eric A. Nordlinger, *Soldiers in Politics: Military Coups and Governments* (Englewood Cliffs, NJ: Prentice-Hall, 1977), pp. 2–3; Bruce W. Farcau, *The Coup: Tactics in the Seizure of Power* (Westport, CT: Praeger, 1994), pp. 1–9.

[3] A historical example is the December 1851 coup of French President Louis Napoleon Bonaparte; a more recent case was the Ecuadorian crisis of February 1997: David B. Ralston, *The Army of the Republic: The Place of the Military in the Political Evolution of France, 1871–1914* (Cambridge, MA: MIT Press, 1967), pp. 16–17; "Ecuador's Post-modern Coup," *The Economist*, February 15, 1997, 37.

"No involvement" may be overlooked so often because it is the "normal" state of events; military intervention and arbitration are rare occurrences. There are probably very few military officers who wake up every day and ask themselves, "Should I organize a coup today?" Although there is a natural tendency to study the event rather than the non-event, without attention to this category it is impossible to determine the bounds of applicability of a particular theory.[4]

SOVEREIGN POWER ISSUES: MODE AND LEVELS OF ANALYSIS

No one should underestimate the creativity of scholars' imaginations. A veritable cornucopia of explanations for military behavior in sovereign power issues has been advanced over the past several decades. To bring some order to this discussion, I distinguish different approaches based on their *mode* and their *level* of analysis.

By mode of analysis, I mean whether the dominant logic of the argument is structural, rational, or cultural. Structural explanations focus on the formal arrangement of units and the distribution of material capabilities across these units; the key issue is *relationships*. Rational arguments assume that actors endeavor to advance their goals or preferences; the key issue is *interests*. Cultural accounts look to peoples' subjective understandings of themselves and the world around them; the key issue is *ideas*.[5]

If looking at the mode of analysis leads to the question "What matters?," the level of analysis problem raises the question "Who matters?" In principle, there are many different plausible levels of analysis; in evolutionary biology, for example, the appropriate level could be the gene, the individual, the species, or perhaps something else. For the study of military involvement in sovereign power issues, four levels seem particularly relevant: individual, organizational, domestic, and international.[6]

Three modes of analysis and four levels of analysis gives us a grid with twelve cells (see Table 1.1). Three of these cells are logically empty, so we are left with nine basic types of explanation.

---

[4] Barbara Geddes, "How the Cases You Choose Affect the Answers You Get: Selection Bias in Comparative Politics," *Political Analysis*, 2 (1990), 131–152; Gary King, Robert O. Keohane, and Sidney Verba, *Designing Social Inquiry: Scientific Inference in Qualitative Research* (Princeton, NJ: Princeton University Press, 1994), pp. 128–139.

[5] For further discussion, see Jon Elster, *Nuts and Bolts for the Social Sciences* (Cambridge, England: Cambridge University Press, 1989); Mark Irving Lichbach and Alan S. Zuckerman, *Comparative Politics: Rationality, Culture, and Structure* (Cambridge, England: Cambridge University Press, 1997).

[6] On levels of analysis, see Robert Jervis, *Perception and Misperception in International Politics* (Princeton, NJ: Princeton University Press, 1976), pp. 13–31; Kenneth N. Waltz, *Man, the State and War: A Theoretical Analysis* (New York: Columbia University Press, 1959); J. David Singer, "The Level-of-Analysis Problem in International Relations," *World Politics*, 14 (1961), 77–92.

TABLE 1.1. *Explaining Military Intervention*

Level of Analysis	Mode of Analysis		
	Structural	Rational	Cultural
Individual		Individual self-interest	Psychological
Organizational	*(1)* Organizational structure	*(3)* Corporate interest	*(4)* Organizational culture
Domestic	*(2)* Domestic structure		Political culture
International	International structure		World culture

Not surprisingly, some of these perspectives on military involvement in sovereign power issues have received more attention than others.[7] And testing all nine of them in a book of this nature would try the patience of reader and author alike. Fortunately, some of them can be dropped out for logical, methodological, or empirical reasons, to be discussed below. Four approaches are chosen for further testing in the cases: domestic structure, organizational structure, corporate interest, and organizational culture. In the sections that follow, I go through each approach in turn, starting at the individual level and working my way up to international level explanations.

INDIVIDUAL LEVEL EXPLANATIONS

The logical place to start is with the individual officer. After all, it is General Smith or Colonel Jones who ultimately makes the decisions and potentially risks his neck. Most theoretical writing on military intervention, however, tends to downplay individual level explanations because of the difficulty of building testable and generalizable theory at this level. These concerns, as we will see, are well-founded, but this does not mean that we can ignore the individual officer in any attempt to explain army behavior. A structural approach based at this level of analysis would presumably look at genetic structures, which is beyond both my abilities and the available evidence, so we will restrict ourselves to the rational and cultural modes of analysis.

Individual Self-Interest

This type of argument stresses the rational incentives for individual military officers to either engage in or avoid participation in sovereign power issues.

---

[7] Many of the existing studies in civil–military relations combine insights from two or more of these perspectives. For heuristic reasons, however, I treat them as analytically distinct.

Given that the use of force can lead to unpleasant consequences, death being perhaps the most noteworthy of these, self-interest seemingly would enter into an officer's calculations. What a theoretical approach would predict at this level of analysis, however, is quite difficult to specify.

At first glance the well-known literature on collective action problems should be relevant here. A simple form of collective action logic seemingly would imply that coups would rarely or never take place. The collective action problem therefore is not a tenable general explanation for the absence of coups, given the more than 350 attempted military coups between 1945 and 1985, although it may help explain why they are not even *more* frequent.[8] Much of the recent literature on collective action endeavors to explain why and under what conditions it takes place, given its ubiquitous nature.[9]

Coup decisions are influenced by collective action logic, but they are not pure examples of a social dilemma.[10] Control of the state is not a pure public good, like clean air, because the benefits of it, such as power and wealth, are excludable. To the extent that material incentives motivate military intervention, the major spoils will be grabbed by the conspirators themselves, although the army in general also may benefit.

Moreover, the structure of the situation mitigates the collective action dilemma. Armies rely on coercion and hierarchy, coups arise in small conspiratorial groups, the decisions of a handful of officers often can tip the scales, and plotters are able to provide selective incentives (side payments) to other participants. Organizing a coup, then, is closer to what Donald Green and Ian Shapiro call a "quasi-dilemma" than a pure collective action problem.[11]

Other scholars working in the rational choice tradition have come to diametrically opposite conclusions about the best strategy of rational officers. Gordon Tullock, for example, argues that doing nothing, the best strategy in conventional collective action logic, is the *worst* strategy for officers during a coup attempt. Tullock reasons that neutrality will be punished by the winning side, so the trick for an individual officer is to figure out which side will win and commit to it early enough that his participation is rewarded.[12]

---

[8] This number is from Steven R. David, *Third World Coups d'Etat and International Security* (Baltimore, MD: Johns Hopkins University Press, 1987), pp. 1–2.

[9] Mark Lichbach, *The Rebel's Dilemma* (Ann Arbor, MI: University of Michigan Press, 1995); Mark Lichbach, *The Cooperator's Dilemma* (Ann Arbor, MI: University of Michigan Press, 1996); Jon Elster, *The Cement of Society: A Study of Social Order* (Cambridge, England: Cambridge University Press, 1989); Donald P. Green and Ian Shapiro, *Pathologies of Rational Choice Theory: A Critique of Applications in Political Science* (New Haven, CT: Yale University Press, 1994), pp. 72–97.

[10] The classic statement is Mancur Olson, Jr., *The Logic of Collective Action: Public Goods and the Theory of Groups* (New York: Schocken Books, 1965).

[11] Green and Shapiro, *Pathologies of Rational Choice Theory*, pp. 77–78; Olson, *Logic of Collective Action*, pp. 2, 44–46.

[12] Gordon Tullock, *The Social Dilemma: The Economics of War and Revolution* (Blacksburg, VA: University Publications, 1974), pp. 60–86.

Civil–military relations specialists also have pointed to strong personal incentives to participate in coups. Power and wealth are two possible rewards for military intervention, and they have been stressed by many scholars. Similarly, threats to an officer's position and resources could motivate a coup.[13]

Thus, the rational individual approach leads to a rather uninspiring proposition: *Officers will pursue their individual self-interest in sovereign power issues.* It is always possible post hoc to explain a particular outcome as the product of individual rational choice.[14] Clearly, there are both potential benefits and major risks involved in any military intervention, so a generalized claim about individual self-interest needs to be linked to more specific claims that can explain variation in military intervention across time and space.

The only way to make more specific predictions is to refer to other levels and modes of analysis.[15] For example, presumably military intervention is riskier (and thus less likely) when the state is strong, the military is internally factionalized, its corporate interests are being respected, and the organizational culture of the army sees military involvement in sovereign power issues as illegitimate. The opposite conditions would make coups more likely. Rational choice theorists might object to this account, but I see no other way to specify a priori under what conditions the military will play a role in sovereign power issues using this logic.

Psychological

A psychological approach to military involvement in sovereign power issues would stress the unique ideas held by particular officers. Contrary to rational choice theory, this approach expects different actors to possess different values and beliefs, and it posits that this variation can explain differences in behavior.[16]

---

[13] John Mukum Mbaku, "Military Coups as Rent-Seeking Behavior," *Journal of Political and Military Sociology*, 22 (1994), 241–284; Samuel Decalo, *Coups and Army Rule in Africa: Motivations and Constraints*, 2nd ed. (New Haven, CT: Yale University Press, 1990); Finer, *Man on Horseback*, pp. 49–52; William R. Thompson, *The Grievances of Military Coup-Makers* (Beverly Hills, CA: Sage Publications, 1973), pp. 26–28; Farcau, *The Coup*, pp. 29–32.

[14] Green and Shapiro, *Pathologies of Rational Choice Theory*, pp. 34–38; Harry Eckstein, "Social Science as Cultural Science, Rational Choice as Metaphysics," in Richard J. Ellis and Michael Thompson, eds., *Culture Matters: Essays in Honor of Aaron Wildavsky* (Boulder, CO: Westview Press, 1997), p. 39.

[15] Paradoxically, then, rational choice theory, despite the name, is arguably a structural account, because any rational individual in a particular situation would behave the same way. It is the situation that determines behavior, not preferences, because all preferences are assumed to be the same.

[16] Individual or organizational nonrational motives for intervention could include altruistic or other-regarding reasons, such as patriotism. Most scholars have looked skeptically on officers' claims that a coup was carried out for public-spirited motives, but there surely are cases when these explanations are correct; the attempt by German generals to assassinate Hitler

A common psychological argument for individual decision making is that people have distinct "operational codes" that provide them with a coherent and comprehensive world view.[17] Other scholars point to the way people create schemas to make sense of important events, and use various scripts and analogies derived from these schemas as guides to future action.[18]

Few scholars have attempted to explain military involvement in sovereign power issues using psychological arguments.[19] There are two important reasons for this. First, the data requirements for such an undertaking are rather daunting. Individual military officers have rarely created a sufficient body of public writings to be able to construct an "operational code" for them, and the task becomes even more difficult as the number of officers and cases expand. Second, and more important, militaries are "total organizations" largely cut off from wider society for extended periods and having a fairly rigid and enclosed way of life; they also indoctrinate their members from a relatively early age.[20] Organizational socialization is likely to bring about dominant organizational cultures, with at most several competing subcultures. Thus, although ideas may shape military behavior in domestic politics, it is at the organizational level that this mode of analysis offers the best payoff.

ORGANIZATIONAL LEVEL EXPLANATIONS

The organizational level of analysis is an obvious place to look for explanations of military involvement in sovereign power issues. The three perspectives that follow all focus on attributes of the armed forces themselves as a

---

in 1944 would be one example. At the same time, it is also true that military governments have been more prone to abuse their citizens' human rights than nonmilitary governments, so the tendency to see coups as "bad things" certainly has a strong basis. On the human rights comparison, see Charles Tilly, *Coercion, Capital, and European States, AD 990–1992* (Cambridge, MA: Blackwell, 1992 (1990)), p. 217.

[17] Alexander George, "The 'Operational Code': A Neglected Approach to the Study of Political Leaders and Decision-Making," *International Studies Quarterly*, 13 (1969), 190–222.

[18] Jervis, *Perception and Misperception*, pp. 235–271; Deborah Welch Larson, *Origins of Containment: A Psychological Explanation* (Princeton, NJ: Princeton University Press, 1985), pp. 50–57; Yuen Foong Khong, *Analogies at War: Korea, Munich, Dien Bien Phu, and the Vietnam Decisions of 1965* (Princeton, NJ: Princeton University Press, 1992).

[19] Tanya Charlick-Paley draws on the political psychology literature on the use of stories to examine a "post-imperial military syndrome" in France and Russia. She finds, however, that there are two different types of stories that officers tell themselves after imperial collapse, consistent with the literature on organizational cultures and subcultures. She is unable to focus on individual officers for the reasons discussed in this paragraph. See Tanya Charlick-Paley, "Accommodating to the Loss of Empire: Is There a Post-Imperial Military Syndrome?," Ph.D. Dissertation, Ohio State University, 1997.

[20] On "total organizations," see Erving Goffman, *Asylums: Essays on the Social Situations of Mental Patients and Other Inmates* (Garden City, NY: Anchor Books, 1961).

guide to their behavior. Structural, rational, and cultural modes of analysis are all relevant to understanding the military's role in domestic politics.

Organizational Structure

An organizational structure approach looks at the relationship between units within the armed forces. International and domestic structural arguments focus on the balance of power, either between states or within the state. This perspective looks at the balance of power within the military itself, as well as that between other armed state bodies, such as para-military organizations or the secret police.

One such argument states that internal divisions within the military decrease the likelihood of coups. These divisions could be, for example, between junior and senior officers, along political lines, ethnic-based, or between services (i.e., army vs. air force). Morris Janowitz, for example, contends that "armies with high internal cohesion will have greater capacity to intervene in domestic politics."[21]

Civilian leaders may deliberately create or exacerbate military cleavages as part of a "divide-and-rule" strategy, or seek ways to monitor the army from within. These strategies represent attempts to make coup-plotting more difficult. For example, Eric Nordlinger highlights "the penetration model" as a form of civilian control that relies on "the extensive use of controls, surveillance, and punishment."[22] The use of "political officers" or "commissars" by Communist regimes is the best example of this approach.[23] Although potentially a very effective means of preventing coups, Nordlinger cautions that it only works in tightly controlled dictatorships and it can actually provoke military intervention by an army protecting its autonomy.

Another common control method involving organizational structures is "counterbalancing" on the part of paramilitary or security bodies.[24] Competing armed bodies can be set up that can either deter a coup attempt or

---

[21] Morris Janowitz, *Military Institutions and Coercion in the Developing Nations* (Chicago, IL: University of Chicago Press, 1977), p. 144. See also Claude E. Welch, Jr. and Arthur K. Smith, *Military Role and Rule: Perspectives on Civil–Military Relations* (North Scituate, MA: Duxbury Press, 1974), pp. 14, 239–240; Felipe Aguero, *Soldiers, Civilians, and Democracy: Post-Franco Spain in Comparative Perspective* (Baltimore, MD: Johns Hopkins University Press, 1995), pp. 14, 30–31, 101–131, 241–242.

[22] Nordlinger, *Soldiers in Politics*, pp. 15–18. See also Farcau, *The Coup*, pp. 188–189, 194–195.

[23] Roman Kolkowicz, *The Soviet Military and the Communist Party* (Princeton, NJ: Princeton University Press, 1967); Timothy J. Colton, *Commissars, Commanders, and Civilian Authority: The Structure of Soviet Military Politics* (Cambridge, MA: Harvard University Press, 1979).

[24] James T. Quinlivan, "Coup-Proofing: Its Practice and Consequences in the Middle East," *International Security*, 24, 2 (1999), 131–165; Jendayi E. Frazer, "Sustaining Civilian Control: Armed Counterweights in Regime Stability in Africa," Ph.D. Dissertation, Stanford University, 1994; Lichbach, *Rebel's Dilemma*, 25, 181–182; Luttwak, *Coup d'Etat*, 89–104; Farcau, *The Coup*, 28, 192–193.

potentially defeat one already underway. Such a strategy by the political leadership could make plotting difficult, especially if these other bodies are large enough or perceived as particularly loyal to the government. However, as with the penetration strategy, the creation of counterbalancing forces is potentially dangerous because it represents a threat to the interests of the regular army. Moreover, Edward Luttwak reports that (as of the late 1970s) there were *no* cases of a paramilitary body actually defending the government once a coup attempt was underway.[25]

A variety of organizational structural factors, then, may influence military involvement in sovereign power issues. Sometimes these divisions can be deliberately created by civilians, whereas at other times they appear to be either accidental or the inevitable by-product of maintaining a large, complex organization. The logic of a structural approach would lead one to expect that divided militaries (including those divided by penetration or counterbalancing) would be less likely to intervene in sovereign power issues. To the extent that these divisions are ideational, however, a focus on organizational cultures and subcultures (discussed below) is more appropriate.

The organizational structure argument leads to the following propositions about military involvement in sovereign power issues: *United militaries are better able, and thus more likely, to intervene in sovereign power issues. Divided militaries are less able, and thus less likely, to intervene in sovereign power issues. During instances of military arbitration, internal splits or counterbalancing are likely when the military is divided.*[26]

Unfortunately for the organizational structure argument, the empirical basis for these propositions is rather weak. Existing research shows that coups are at least as likely when militaries are internally divided as when they have a high degree of internal cohesion, although coups carried out by more cohesive armies tend to have a longer tenure. For example, in a meta-analysis of existing quantitative studies, Ekkart Zimmerman states, "lower cohesion of the military will lead to increases in coup frequency." Thomas Cox, writing on African coups, concludes that "it is the growth of cleavages *within* armies which probably forms the basis for most coups."[27]

It may be that the logic of the organizational structure argument is only half-right, and that cohesion does make *successful* intervention more likely

---

[25] Luttwak, *Coup d'Etat*, 89–104. A recent exception could be the Basra uprising in Iraq in the spring of 1992, to the extent that military units were involved.

[26] Although the prediction on military arbitration sounds tautological and nonfalsifiable, in the cases we will see that this prediction does not fare as well as one would anticipate.

[27] Ekkart Zimmerman, *Political Violence, Crises, and Revolutions: Theories and Research* (Cambridge, MA: Schenkman Publishing, 1983), p. 278; Thomas S. Cox, *Civil–Military Relations in Sierra Leone: A Case Study of African Soldiers in Politics* (Cambridge, MA: Harvard University Press, 1976), p. 12 (emphasis in original). The best large-*N* study is William R. Thompson, "Organizational Cohesion and Military Coup Outcomes," *Comparative Political Studies*, 9 (1976), 255–276.

but that disunity makes intervention attempts more frequent. It makes sense to test the logical variant of this approach, however, while looking for evidence on both sides of the argument.

Corporate Interest

The corporate interest approach to military intervention focuses on the rational bureaucratic motives of the armed forces. Militaries are assumed to respond in a rational way to their environment, endeavoring to reduce uncertainty and to maximize the things all organizations seek: power, resources, and autonomy.[28] The most common explanation for coups at the level of the military organization is that intervention is caused by corporate motives – the desire to protect or enhance the military's resources or position.

Several important studies have advocated this viewpoint. Eric Nordlinger states, "by far the most common and salient interventionist motive involves the defense or enhancement of the military's corporate interests." Corporate interests, he argues, have played a prominent role in military intervention in such diverse states as Peru, Ghana, Egypt, and Honduras. William Thompson came to conclusions similar to Nordlinger's in his comprehensive, large-N study of all military coups between 1946 and 1970. A military coup, in Thompson's view, "is essentially a small-scale internal war fought over positions and resources."[29]

The corporate interest approach to military intervention also has received considerable attention from scholars working in a single-country context. For example, Guillermo O'Donnell emphasizes "corporate military interest as an explanatory factor in the promotion of coups" in his study of Argentina.[30] The corporate interest perspective also was the one most consistently advanced in the study of Soviet civil–military relations, particularly in the work of Roman Kolkowicz and Timothy Colton. Colton states, "officers intervene against civilian authorities when their perceived interests are being denied or threatened by civilian policy."[31]

---

[28] Anthony Downs, *Inside Bureaucracy* (Boston: Little, Brown and Company, 1967); Graham T. Allison, *Essence of Decision: Explaining the Cuban Missile Crisis* (Boston, MA: Little, Brown and Company, 1971); Charles Perrow, *Complex Organizations: A Critical Essay*, Third Edition (New York: McGraw-Hill, 1986), pp. 119–156, 219–257; Barry R. Posen, *The Sources of Military Doctrine: France, Britain, and Germany Between the World Wars* (Ithaca, NY: Cornell University Press, 1984), pp. 41–59.

[29] Nordlinger, *Soldiers in Politics*, pp. 63–78 (quote, pp. 63–64); Thompson, *Grievances of Military Coup-Makers*, p. 10. See also Bengt Abrahamsson, *Military Professionalization and Political Power* (Beverly Hills, CA: Sage Publications, 1972).

[30] Guillermo A. O'Donnell, "Modernization and Military Coups: Theory, Comparisons, and the Argentine Case," in Abraham F. Lowenthal and J. Samuel Fitch, eds., *Armies and Politics in Latin America*, revised edition (New York: Holmes & Meier, 1986), pp. 96–133.

[31] Kolkowicz, *The Soviet Military and the Communist Party*; Colton, *Commissars, Commanders, and Civilian Authority* (quote, p. 240). Colton challenged Kolkowicz's view that Soviet

The corporate interest perspective on civil–military relations leads to the following propositions about military involvement in sovereign power issues: *Militaries are likely to intervene in sovereign power issues if their corporate interests are threatened. Armies are unlikely to intervene in sovereign power issues if the government is responsive to their corporate interests. In instances of military arbitration, the armed forces will side with the contender who is most likely to advance the armed forces' corporate interests.* These rational corporate interests are defined as minimizing uncertainty and maximizing power, resources, and autonomy.

The corporate interest approach to military involvement in sovereign power issues has much to recommend it, and there is also considerable empirical evidence for this view, both from the qualitative literature and Thompson's quantitative study. An important weakness in much of this literature, however, is that it is sampled on the dependent variable (that is, only coups are studied, and not noncoups).[32] Thompson himself concludes his study by noting that the types of military grievances present in the coups in his study are also present in states that do not experience military intervention.[33] Indeed, if threats to the military's corporate interests were a sufficient condition, then coups would break out all the time all over the world.

A second and related weakness of the corporate interest approach is that all militaries are treated as having identical preferences. Armies pursue their self-interest, and these interests can be determined externally by observing a few key indicators of organizational power and well-being. Because this approach assumes that militaries subject to similar stimuli will react in the same manner, not enough attention has been paid to variation in officer corps' motives.

Organizational Culture

An organizational culture argument maintains that the beliefs and values of the officer corps explain its behavior in sovereign power issues. Organizational culture is the patterns of assumptions and values held by members of an organization that help them make sense of the world and orient their choices.[34] An organizational culture approach to military intervention does

---

civil–military relations were inherently conflictual, but he shared with Kolkowicz a focus on the interests of the armed forces as an explanation for officer corps behavior; their disagreement was more empirical than theoretical.

[32] Colton and Kolkowicz were not guilty of studying only coups; in both cases their focus was on civil–military relations in general, and not just sovereign power issues.

[33] Thompson, *The Grievances of Military Coup-Makers*, pp. 50–51.

[34] Pasquale Gagliardi, "The Creation and Change of Organizational Cultures: A Conceptual Framework," *Organization Studies*, 7 (1986), 119; Edgar H. Schein, "Coming to a New Awareness of Organizational Culture," *Sloan Management Review*, 25, 2 (1984), 3; Linda Smircich, "Concepts of Culture and Organizational Analysis," *Administrative Science Quarterly*, 28 (1983), 346.

not assume that all individuals or groups will behave in like fashion when confronted with a similar opportunity structure (i.e., political actors are not treated as having identical preferences). This approach asks the question, Why is a sufficient reason for intervention by military A not considered an appropriate one by military B?

The aspect of a military's organizational culture that is most relevant to the study of army involvement in sovereign power issues is the set of beliefs held by officers about their proper relationship to the political leadership.[35] In other words, what *norms* are held by officers on the question of who should rule the state?[36]

The organizational culture perspective stresses the unique experiences in the life of an organization as an explanation for subsequent behavior.[37] Institutional lessons learned in response to "critical events" in the life of an organization powerfully shape the outlook of an organization's members. Critical events are defined as critical due to their place in history, their role in the development of organizational beliefs, or their metaphorical power.[38] Because of the socialization processes that operate within organizations, dominant interpretations of these events tend to develop, although some subgroups and individuals will draw different lessons than the group as a whole. Organizational socialization is particularly likely to lead to a dominant interpretation in a hierarchical organization such as the military.[39]

---

[35] Culture is often treated as a single or unified concept, although in practice it is more a "meta-concept" than a single variable. Thus, it is not necessary to map all aspects of a group's culture, but only those relevant to the specific empirical question. See Ronald L. Jepperson and Ann Swidler, "What Properties of Culture Should We Measure?," *Poetics*, 22 (1994), 360–362; Sonja A. Sackmann, "Uncovering Culture in Organizations," *Journal of Applied Behavioral Science*, 27 (1991), 295–296.

[36] Norms are collective expectations about appropriate behavior. See Martha Finnemore, *National Interests in International Society* (Ithaca, NY: Cornell University Press, 1996), pp. 22–23; Peter J. Katzenstein, "Introduction," in Peter Katzenstein, ed., *The Culture of National Security: Norms and Identity in World Politics* (New York: Columbia University Press, 1996), p. 5.

[37] Good introductions to the organizational culture literature include: Schein, "Coming to a New Awareness of Organizational Culture"; Smircich, "Concepts of Culture and Organizational Analysis"; J. Steven Ott, *The Organizational Culture Perspective* (Chicago, IL: The Dorsey Press, 1989); James Q. Wilson, *Bureaucracy: What Government Agencies Do and Why They Do It* (New York: Basic Books, 1989), pp. 90–110. The concept of organizational culture recently has been applied productively to the study of military organizations by Elizabeth Kier and Jeffrey Legro, although their focus is on military doctrine: Elizabeth Kier, *Imagining War: French and British Military Doctrine Between the Wars* (Princeton, NJ: Princeton University Press, 1997); Jeffrey W. Legro, *Cooperation Under Fire: Anglo-German Restraint During World War II* (Ithaca, NY: Cornell University Press, 1995).

[38] James G. March, Lee S. Sproul, and Michal Tamuz, "Learning from Samples of One or Fewer," *Organization Science*, 2 (1991), 1–13; Daniel C. Feldman, "The Development and Enforcement of Group Norms," *Academy of Management Review*, 9 (1984), 51.

[39] March, Sproul, and Tamuz, "Learning from Samples," 3; Kier, *Imagining War*, 29.

Still, different organizational subcultures may exist within the same army.[40] For example, in Spain a younger group of officers favoring disengagement from politics represented an important organizational subculture during the transition to democracy.[41]

Restraints on military intervention will be higher before the first coup than during subsequent interventions. In a country with a tradition of military intervention or rule, officers are less inclined to doubt their right to intervene in politics. As Douglas Hibbs states, "an 'interventionist' history is likely to develop a tradition or 'culture' that makes current interventions more likely than otherwise would be the case." The same logic applies to militaries without an interventionist culture. As norms persist and are less subject to contestation, they acquire a "taken-for-granted" character. In Ann Swidler's terminology, they move from being ideologies to traditions to common sense.[42] Cultural elements with a long history become more institutionalized and take on the character of assumptions.

A failed coup attempt, or a disastrous period of military rule, also may strengthen officer corps' inhibitions against military intervention. Both the organizational learning literature and the political psychology literature suggest that failure leads to negative expectations about potential further repetitions of particular acts.[43] Militaries also learn organizational lessons from events other than coups. Such events might include wars, domestic usage for police-type missions, mutinies, and major organizational or personnel changes. All of these may take the form of "critical events."

Although some scholars have emphasized cultural and ideational factors in their historical accounts,[44] most theoretical explanations of military

[40] Sonja A. Sackmann, "Culture and Subcultures: An Analysis of Organizational Knowledge," *Administrative Science Quarterly*, 37 (1992), 140–161.

[41] Paul Preston, *The Politics of Revenge: Fascism and the Military in Twentieth-Century Spain* (London: Unwin Hyman, 1990), pp. 150, 175–202; Alfred Stepan, *Rethinking Military Politics: Brazil and the Southern Cone* (Princeton, NJ: Princeton University Press, 1988), pp. 90–92, 118–122. Although Felipe Aguero denies the importance of "attitudnal traits," his own argument highlights the importance of a liberal (i.e., apolitical) subculture within the Spanish military: Aguero, *Soldiers, Civilians, and Democracy*, pp. 21, 113–114, 128.

[42] Douglas A. Hibbs, Jr., *Mass Political Violence: A Cross-National Causal Analysis* (New York: John Wiley & Sons, 1973), pp. 106–107, 189; Ann Swidler, "Culture in Action: Symbols and Strategies," *American Sociological Review*, 51 (1986), 279.

[43] March, Sproul, and Tamuz, "Learning from Samples"; Jervis, *Perception and Misperception*, p. 278. For good examples, respectively, of a failed coup (Sri Lanka) and a disastrous period of military rule (Argentina) strengthening norms against intervention, see Donald L. Horowitz, *Coup Theories and Officers' Motives: Sri Lanka in Comparative Perspective* (Princeton, NJ: Princeton University Press, 1980), pp. 204–216; J. Samuel Fitch, *The Armed Forces and Democracy in Latin America* (Baltimore, MD: The Johns Hopkins University Press, 1998), pp. 72–75; Deborah L. Norden, *Military Rebellion in Argentina: Between Coups and Consolidation* (Lincoln, NE: University of Nebraska Press, 1996), pp. 76–77, 182–186.

[44] A good example is Donald Abenheim, *Reforging the Iron Cross: The Search for Tradition in the West German Armed Forces* (Princeton, NJ: Princeton University Press, 1988).

intervention emphasize structural and rational reasons for coups. The question of officer corps norms, however, has not been entirely ignored; although rarely, if ever, does this work draw on the organizational culture literature.[45]

J. Samuel Fitch offers the best and most comprehensive test of the importance of officer corps norms, or what he calls "role beliefs," in his work on the Ecuadorian and Argentinean armed forces. Using interviews and survey data, Fitch shows that the "role beliefs" of Ecuadorian officers changed from the 1950s to the 1960s, and he demonstrates how this changing role definition influenced military intervention in politics. Similarly, in Argentina, norms against military intervention have spread in the officer corps since the 1980s. Most interesting, perhaps, in light of the 2000 coup in Ecuador, is Fitch's finding (based on 1991 data) that "Ecuadorian officers are divided and uncertain regarding their political role, with no single dominant perspective."[46]

Samuel Huntington's argument that professionalism encourages politically passive militaries has sometimes been read as an organizational culture explanation, but his definition of professionalism is largely nonideational.[47] Moreover, empirically professionalism is not a barrier to military intervention, unless professionalism is defined in a way that makes the purported link between professionalism and voluntary subordination tautological.[48]

An organizational culture approach to military involvement in sovereign power issues, then, focuses on the norms held by officers on the question of

---

[45] Examples of brief discussions of officer corps norms include: Robert A. Dahl, *Polyarchy: Participation and Opposition* (New Haven, CT: Yale University Press, 1971), p. 50; Finer, *Man on Horseback*, pp. 22–26; Eva Busza, "Transition and Civil–Military Relations in Poland and Russia," *Communist and Post-Communist Studies*, 29 (1996), 171–172; Peter D. Feaver, *Delegation, Monitoring, and Civilian Control of the Military: Agency Theory and American Civil–Military Relations* (Cambridge, MA: John M. Olin Institute for Strategic Studies, Harvard University, May 1996), pp. 29–30; Jendayi Frazer, "Conceptualizing Civil–Military Relations During Democratic Transition," *Africa Today*, 42 (1995), 40–41.

[46] J. Samuel Fitch, *The Military Coup d'Etat as a Political Process: Ecuador, 1948–1966* (Baltimore, MD: Johns Hopkins University Press, 1977), pp. 129–145; Fitch, *Armed Forces and Democracy*, pp. 61–105 (quote, p. 72).

[47] There are several other possible ways of interpreting Huntington's argument. In addition to organizational culture, his argument can be read as one about the influence of external threat on military development (an international structure argument), the degree of fit between the military's conservative ideology and the dominant societal ideology (a political culture argument), and the methods of civilian control employed ("objective" vs. "subjective"). See Samuel P. Huntington, *The Soldier and the State: The Theory and Politics of Civil–Military Relations* (Cambridge, MA: Belknap Press/Harvard University Press, 1957), especially, pp. 80–97.

[48] Alfred Stepan, "The New Professionalism of Internal Warfare and Military Role Expansion," in Stepan, ed., *Authoritarian Brazil: Origins, Policies, and Future* (New Haven, CT: Yale University Press, 1973), pp. 47–65; Finer, *Man on Horseback*, pp. 21–24; Peter D. Feaver, "The Civil–Military Problematique: Huntington, Janowitz, and the Question of Civilian Control," *Armed Forces & Society*, 23 (1996), 160; Abrahamsson, *Military Professionalization and Political Power*; Alain Rouquie, *The Military and the State in Latin America* (Berkeley, CA: University of California Press, 1987), pp. 72–73; Fitch, *Armed Forces and Democracy*, pp. 1–35.

who should rule the state. Armies that adhere to a norm of civilian supremacy are considered *apolitical.*[49] Those that do not possess this norm are *praetorian.*[50] This leads to the following propositions: *Militaries with a strong commitment to a norm of civilian supremacy are unlikely to intervene in politics. In cases of military arbitration, militaries with a strong commitment to the norm are likely to try to remain neutral. If forced to act, the army will tend to support the most legitimate contender for power. Armies with a weak or no commitment to the norm are likely to intervene in politics. In cases of military arbitration, militaries with a weak commitment to the norm are likely to seek the arbiter role.*

An organizational culture perspective, although intuitively plausible, has not been widely or systematically applied to the study of military involvement in sovereign power issues. This book, in addition to presenting a comprehensive history of sovereign power disputes in Russia in the last three centuries, also will show the utility of an organizational culture approach. At the same time, we will see that this perspective cannot stand alone and that factors at other levels of analysis and based on different modes of explanation are also important.

DOMESTIC LEVEL EXPLANATIONS

Explanations at the domestic level of analysis look at attributes of the state and society as a whole. This is probably the dominant mode of theorizing in comparative politics. Both domestic structure and political culture are frequently invoked to explain outcomes. Rational explanations at the level of the state, although very prominent in international relations theory, make little sense in explaining state and substate outcomes and thus will be ignored here.

Domestic Structure

A domestic structure approach to military intervention highlights the armed forces' position in relation to the strength of other government institutions and other societal actors. This type of explanation is probably the dominant one in the literature, and it fits into a broader literature on political development, state strength, and political capacity. The domestic structure perspective posits that military intervention occurs because low state political capacity provides the army opportunities to become involved in politics.

---

[49] Clearly all armies have political interests, particularly in the defense politics domain. The term apolitical is meant only to apply to a military's orientation toward involvement in sovereign power issues.

[50] Classicists would complain that modern coup-prone militaries bear little resemblance to the Roman praetorians. I plead guilty to this charge. Consistent with current social science literature, I use praetorian to refer to armies that believe they have a legitimate role in sovereign power issues.

Samuel Huntington argues, "the most important causes of military intervention in politics are not military but political and reflect not the social and organizational characteristics of the military establishment but the political and institutional structure of the society." Military intervention is simply the most dramatic of extra-institutional means that actors adopt to influence policy in a weakly institutionalized, praetorian state.[51]

Subsets of this argument have focused on the structural relationship between particular societal-level units, such as social classes or ethnic groups.[52] Similarly, intervention may be less likely in more developed and complex societies.[53] There are clearly important exceptions, however, such as the coup attempts in France in 1958 and 1961 and the periods of military rule in the (arguably) most advanced Latin American states of Argentina, Chile, and Uruguay.[54]

The most general and important version of the domestic structure argument leads to the following propositions about military involvement in sovereign power issues: *Militaries in strong states are unlikely to intervene in sovereign power issues. Armies in weak states are likely to intervene in sovereign power issues. Instances of military arbitration are likely in weak states and unlikely in strong states.*[55]

---

51 Samuel P. Huntington, *Political Order in Changing Societies* (New Haven, CT: Yale University Press, 1968), especially pp. 192–263 (quote, p. 194). Two other prominent examples of this approach are: Finer, *Man on Horseback*, especially pp. 238–239; Amos Perlmutter, *The Military and Politics in Modern Times: On Professionals, Praetorians, and Revolutionary Soldiers* (New Haven, CT: Yale University Press, 1977), especially pp. 89–114. For a recent application and extension, see Kurt Dassel, "Civilians, Soldiers, and Strife: Domestic Sources of International Aggression," *International Security*, 23, 1 (1998), 107–140.

52 See, for example, Jose Nun, "The Middle-Class Military Coup Revisited," in Lowenthal and Fitch, *Armies and Politics in Latin America*, pp. 59–95; J. Craig Jenkins and Augustine J. Kposowa, "The Political Origins of African Military Coups: Ethnic Competition, Military Centrality, and the Struggle over the Postcolonial State," *International Studies Quarterly*, 36 (1992), pp. 271–292. A good multinational study rebutting the influence of social class as an explanation for military behavior is George A. Kourvetaris and Betty A. Dobratz, *Social Origins and Political Orientations in a World Perspective* (Denver, CO: University of Denver, 1973).

53 Samuel Huntington has even proposed the following law: "Countries with per-capita GNPs of $1,000 or more do not have successful coups; countries with per-capita GNPs of $3,000 or more do not have coup attempts." Samuel P. Huntington, "Reforming Civil–Military Relations," *Journal of Democracy*, 6, 4 (1995), 15. Incidentally, Russian GDP per capita the year Huntington made this statement was less than $2,500. Empirical support for Huntington's posited relationship between economic development and military coups is in John B. Londregan and Keith T. Poole, "Poverty, the Coup Trap, and the Seizure of Executive Power," *World Politics*, 42 (1990), 151–183.

54 Alain Rouquie contends that Uruguay, Chile, and Argentina are the most developed Latin American states, although on a GDP per capita basis Venezuela was the most developed state throughout the 1970s: Rouquie, *The Military and the State*, p. 6.

55 I use the terms state strength, political capacity, and political order interchangeably. For an extended discussion, see Robert W. Jackman, *Power Without Force: The Political Capacity of Nation-States* (Ann Arbor, MI: University of Michigan Press, 1993).

This explanation has considerable merit, and it has been profitably used to explain military intervention or its absence in a wide variety of states.[56] Despite this impressive literature, it has been hard to test this argument quantitatively. How the variables are operationalized plays a key role in whether multivariate analysis lends support to the political incapacity hypothesis. Even so, Ekkart Zimmerman concludes after a thorough survey of the quantitative literature on military coups that "Huntington's theory of praetorianism still seems to provide the best and most encompassing theoretical starting point."[57]

Much of the literature supporting the domestic structure argument, however, suffers from the same weakness as that advocating the corporate interest approach: It is sampled on the dependent variable. States and societies often experience structural weakness without provoking military intervention. David Goldsworthy observes, "the kinds of features said to give rise to coup-proneness are often just as characteristic of the polities where coups have *not* occurred."[58] State weakness may be a necessary condition for military intervention, then, but it is not sufficient.[59] In the cases we will see how domestic structure interacts with other variables to lead to certain outcomes.

Political Culture

Political culture explanations stress the unique beliefs and values shared by members of a particular political community, often a nation. In *The Civic Culture*, for example, Gabriel Almond and Sidney Verba pointed to diverse political cultures to explain varying outcomes in five states, particularly the degree of commitment to democratic rule.[60] A political culture explanation for military involvement in sovereign power issues, then, contends that the

---

[56] Examples are legion. For an example of state weakness being used to explain, respectively, intervention and nonintervention, see Nur Yalman, "Intervention and Extrication: The Officer Corps in the Turkish Crisis," in Henry Bienen, ed., *The Military Intervenes: Case Studies in Political Development* (New York: Russell Sage Foundation, 1968), pp. 127–144; Franklin D. Margiotta, "Civilian Control and the Mexican Military: Changing Patterns of Political Influence," in Claude E. Welch, Jr., ed., *Civilian Control of the Military: Theory and Cases from Developing Countries* (Albany, NY: SUNY Press, 1976), pp. 213–253.

[57] Zimmerman, *Political Violence, Crises, and Revolutions*, pp. 237–291. See also Hibbs, *Mass Political Violence*, pp. 93–110, 187.

[58] David Goldsworthy, "Civilian Control of the Military in Black Africa," *African Affairs*, 80, 318 (1981), 50.

[59] It is difficult to test the argument that state weakness is a necessary condition for coups without slipping into tautology. The cases show that military involvement in sovereign power issues is possible at times of considerable state strength by conventional measures, highlighting the importance of distinguishing between types of military involvement (arbitration and intervention).

[60] Gabriel A. Almond and Sidney Verba, *The Civic Culture: Political Attitudes and Democracy in Five Nations* (Princeton, NJ: Princeton University Press, 1963).

propensity for the military to play a role in politics depends on the particular values held in society at large.

This type of argument has been most frequently invoked to explain the tendency of Latin American armies to be involved in politics. Scholars point to the "Iberian military tradition" (Brian Loveman), the "Iberic-Latin tradition" (Howard Wiarda), or the "organic-statist" model of the state (Alfred Stepan) as at least partial explanations for the tradition of military strongmen.[61] Others have criticized this argument as overly deterministic and unable to account for the considerable variation in both military intervention and political culture in the region.[62]

Political culture arguments have been applied rather frequently to the study of Russian politics. The dominant tendency has been to portray Russian political culture as authoritarian and collectivist, although a minority view holds that a democratic "alternative political culture" has important roots in Russia that bodes well for current democratization efforts.[63] Neither viewpoint has much to say about the army. This is not surprising, because a political culture account would have a hard time explaining the variation in military behavior over the centuries, particularly the heavy involvement of officers in palace coups in the eighteenth century followed by a relatively passive role in the nineteenth and twentieth centuries. Thus, a political culture explanation will not be discussed further in this book.

INTERNATIONAL LEVEL EXPLANATIONS

Explaining events inside countries by reference to external factors occupies a small but important niche in the study of comparative politics. This type of argument is often referred to as a "second-image reversed" explanation.[64] Both international structure and international culture approaches have made important contributions to the study of issues at the nexus of international relations and comparative politics, although they have rarely been applied to the study of the military's role in politics. An international level rational argument would only make sense in certain variants of science fiction and hence will be ignored here. *Biting* /

[61] Brian Loveman, *For la Patria: Politics and the Armed Forces in Latin America* (Wilmington, DE: Scholarly Resources Inc., 1999); Howard J. Wiarda, *Corporatism and National Development in Latin America* (Boulder, CO: Westview Press, 1981); Alfred Stepan, *The State and Society: Peru in Comparative Perspective* (Princeton, NJ: Princeton University Press, 1978).

[62] Rouquie, *The Military and the State*, pp. 3–4.

[63] Stephen White, *Political Culture and Soviet Politics* (London: Macmillan, 1979); Nicolai N. Petro, *The Rebirth of Russian Democracy: An Interpretation of Political Culture* (Cambridge, MA: Harvard University Press, 1995).

[64] The term comes from the seminal article by Peter Gourevitch, "The Second-Image Reversed: International Sources of Domestic Politics," *International Organization*, 32 (1978), 881–911.

International Structure

Structural accounts look at the relationship between units in a system. The key units for the international structure approach are states; relations between them are ordered by anarchy, not by hierarchy. The consequence is that the system is one of self-help, and states must provide for their own well-being and survival.[65] The need for states to provide for their own security leads them to create armed forces to defend themselves. The international structure approach maintains that states with severe security threats will have armed forces with an external orientation. This external focus keeps the military from being involved in domestic politics. Similarly, in the absence of serious external threats the army is more inclined to use its force internally.[66]

According to some accounts, the divergent paths of European and post-independence Third World state building can be traced to these international structural factors. Charles Tilly argues that European state building was largely driven by the need to create an efficient war-making machine, so over time the armed forces were freed from domestic repression and policing to concentrate on external defense. In contrast, most Third World militaries rarely have a significant external threat, and therefore they play a larger role in domestic politics.[67] Samuel Huntington's theory of military professionalism is based at least in part on the observation that European states in intense rivalry with each other were compelled to create a group of full-time experts to prepare a state's military defense, who focused on that task and accordingly had no interest in domestic politics.[68] Stanislav Andreski states, "'The devil finds work for idle hands': the soldiers who have no wars to fight or prepare for will be tempted to interfere in politics."[69]

Empirical support for the international structure argument, however, is decidedly mixed. A simple quantitative test does not support the proposition.[70] The most war-prone states since World War II have had more, not

---

[65] The classic statement is Kenneth N. Waltz, *Theory of International Politics* (New York: McGraw-Hill, 1979).

[66] Michael C. Desch, *Civilian Control of the Military: The Changing Security Environment* (Baltimore, MD: Johns Hopkins University Press, 1999).

[67] Tilly, *Coercion, Capital, and European States,* especially pp. 76, 125–126, 206–207; Charles Tilly, "Reflections on the History of European State-Making," in Charles Tilly, ed., *The Formation of National States in Western Europe* (Princeton, NJ: Princeton University Press, 1975), pp. 3–83, especially pp. 75–76. See also Otto Hintze, "Military Organization and the Organization of the State," in Felix Gilbert, ed., *The Historical Essays of Otto Hintze* (New York: Oxford University Press, 1975), pp. 178–215.

[68] Huntington, *The Soldier and the State,* pp. 19–58.

[69] Stanislav Andreski, *Military Organization and Society,* 2nd ed. (Berkeley, CA: University of California Press, 1968), p. 202; Stanislav Andreski, "On the Peaceful Disposition of Military Dictatorships," *Journal of Strategic Studies,* 3, 3 (1980), 3–10.

[70] Michael Desch finds support for the proposition in several case studies, although he looks at civil–military relations in general, not only coups: Desch, *Civilian Control of the Military.*

TABLE 1.2. *War-Proneness and Military Coups, across Region Comparison*

Region	Percentage of Countries in War 1945–1980, Comparative Ranking (Actual Percentage)	Percentage of Countries with >1,000 Battle Deaths in War 1945–1980, Comparative Ranking (Actual Percentage)	Average Coups per Country 1946–1986, Comparative Ranking (Average Number)
Africa	5(8%)	5(5%)	3(2.6)
Asia	2(46%)	1(42%)	4(2.0)
Europe	3(29%)	4(7%)	5(.4)
Middle East	1(56%)	2(39%)	1(4.3)
Western Hemisphere	4(20%)	3(12%)	2(4.1)

Source: Small and Singer; Belkin and Schofer. Full citations are in footnote 71.

fewer, coups than their more peaceful counterparts. Between 1945 and 1980, 38 states were involved in an interstate war. These 38 countries had an average of 2.5 coups per country between 1946 and 1986. States not involved in an interstate war had an average of 2.37 coups per country. Of the 38 countries involved in interstate wars, only 24 of them suffered more than 1,000 battle deaths. These 24 countries had an average of 3.2 coups per country between 1946 and 1986. The remaining, more peaceful states had an average of 2.2 coups per country in the same period. Thus, it seems the devil found more work for busy than for idle hands.[71]

There is also no obvious relationship between the war-proneness of a region and the number of coups in that area in the postwar era. Table 1.2 shows the ranking of the five major world regions in terms of the percentage of countries in that region that were involved in an interstate war post–World War II, the percentage of countries in that region that experienced more than 1,000 battle deaths in interstate war, and the number of coups per country. The most war-prone regions have not had fewer coups than more peaceful regions. For example, the Middle East has been both war-prone and coup-prone since World War II. Given the prevalence of both war and coups in the Middle East, it is not surprising that Elizabeth Picard concluded that "a major cause [of] Arab military intervention in politics . . . [is] to be found in

[71] These calculations were made on the basis of two separate sets of data, one on war-proneness and one on coup attempts. The data on war-proneness are from Melvin Small and J. David Singer, *Resort to Arms: International and Civil Wars, 1816–1980* (Beverly Hills, CA: Sage Publications, 1982), pp. 165–180. The data on attempted military coups between 1946–1986 are from a database compiled by Aaron Belkin and Evan Schofer. I thank Aaron Belkin for sharing these data with me.

an external threat to state security."[72] This argument, obviously, is the exact opposite of the international structure argument.

On the other hand, if one starts counting war-proneness in 1816 and not 1946, the most war-prone states and regions do appear to have had fewer coups. The two most war-prone regions between 1816 and 1980, Europe and Asia, had the fewest number of coups between 1946 and 1986. The regions that we generally associate with military coups and rule – Africa, Latin America, and the Middle East – were also the most peaceful from 1816 to 1980. However, when states within a region are compared to each other over the same time period there is no obvious relationship between external threat and military intervention.[73] Moreover, it seems more likely that the relative absence of coups in Europe since World War II is explained by democracy and high levels of economic development and not by a past history of interstate warfare.[74]

Finally, the explanatory power of the international structure argument is also mixed in the Russian case. Russia has faced a demanding external environment for the past several centuries, and by several criteria it is one of the world's most war-prone states. The argument may play a role in explaining officer corps behavior in the late nineteenth and twentieth centuries, when military intervention has been very limited. But it has more trouble with the eighteenth and early nineteenth centuries, when Russia was engaged in many wars and the military frequently intervened in politics. Thus, this approach will not be systematically examined here.

World Culture

The recent "constructivist turn" in international relations theory has directed renewed attention to issues such as identity, norms, and values, and their potential contribution to the behavior of states and other actors in the international system.[75] Scholars have examined, for example, how international

---

[72] Elizabeth Picard, "Arab Military in Politics: from Revolutionary Plot to Authoritarian State," in Albert Hourani, Philip S. Khoury, and Mary C. Wilson, eds., *The Modern Middle East: A Reader* (Berkeley and Los Angeles, CA: University of California Press, 1993), p. 558.

[73] For a more complete discussion of the data on military intervention and war-proneness for the 1816–1980 period, see Brian D. Taylor, "The Russian Military in Politics," Ph.D. Dissertation, Massachusetts Institute of Technology, 1998.

[74] Arguably there is a relationship between intense international competition and levels of political and economic development. But if this is the case, then the relationship between international structure and military intervention is at most indirect. On the relationship between war and state strength, see, for example, Tilly, *Coercion, Capital, and European States*; Michael C. Desch, "War and Strong States, Peace and Weak States?," *International Organization*, 50 (1996), 237–268; Jeffrey Herbst, "War and the State in Africa," *International Security*, 14, 4 (1990), 117–139.

[75] Alexander Wendt, *Social Theory of International Politics* (Cambridge, England: Cambridge University Press, 1999); Jeffrey T. Checkel, "The Constructivist Turn in International

norms as embodied by a diverse range of actors, such as international organizations, nongovernmental organizations (NGOs), states, or even individuals, have influenced either domestic politics or state behavior in the international arena.[76]

A world culture approach to military involvement in sovereign power issues, then, would contend that the spread of international norms either favoring or opposing military intervention in politics is an important variable explaining military coups.[77] Through a process of "diffusion," ideas about the appropriateness of military intervention would spread from officers in one state to those in another. Richard Li and William Thompson found some statistical evidence for a "coup contagion" effect among Third World states in the 1950s and 1960s, contending that "a world subculture has taken form in which some military elites view their full participation in authoritative decision making as both correct and necessary."[78] Similarly, Samuel Huntington argues that the "third wave" of democratization "snowballed" as the example set by early democratizing states spread to those that followed.[79]

The diffusion of international norms may indeed play a role in explaining worldwide trends in the frequency of military coups. It does seem that in a growing number of countries, military intervention is seen as "politically incorrect." However, the problem with such accounts is that they tend to suggest a degree of "institutional isomorphism," or sameness, across states that is inconsistent with real-world patterns, at least in the case of military coups. What needs to be explained is how the world culture takes hold at the domestic and organizational level, and why it does in some countries and not in others. Li and Thompson state that "contagious recipiency is determined almost wholly by the degree of readiness of the recipient to be influenced."[80]

Patterns in twentieth-century Russia clearly have been out of sync with world trends. In the 1960s and 1970s, as military coups were endemic around much of the world, the Soviet military was not involved in sovereign power

Relations Theory," *World Politics*, 50 (1998), 324–348; Ted Hopf, "The Promise of Constructivism in International Relations Theory," *International Security*, 23, 1 (1998), 171–200.

[76] Finnemore, *National Interests in International Society*; Katzenstein, ed., *Culture of National Security*; Audie Klotz, *Norms in International Relations: The Struggle Against Apartheid* (Ithaca, NY: Cornell University Press, 1995).

[77] Theo Farrell, "Transnational Norms and Military Development: Constructing Ireland's Professional Army," *European Journal of International Relations*, 7 (2001), 63–102.

[78] Richard P. Y. Li and William R. Thompson, "The 'Coup Contagion' Hypothesis," *Journal of Conflict Resolution*, 19 (1975), 63–88 (quote, 82). See also Zimmerman, *Political Violence, Crises, and Revolutions*, pp. 269–272.

[79] Samuel P. Huntington, *The Third Wave: Democratization in the Late Twentieth Century* (Norman, OK: University of Oklahoma Press, 1991), pp. 100–106.

[80] Li and Thompson, "The 'Coup Contagion' Hypothesis," p. 81. See also Jeffrey T. Checkel, "Norms, Institutions, and National Identity in Contemporary Europe," *International Studies Quarterly*, 43 (1999), 83–114.

issues. In the early 1990s, however, as the international trend was in the opposite direction, the army in Russia was involved in sovereign power issues on several occasions. To the extent that international norms matter, we need to look at how they become embedded at lower levels of analysis.

NARROWING AND ORGANIZING THE FIELD

I have discussed nine different approaches, based on different modes and levels of analysis, to the study of military involvement in sovereign power issues. Testing nine different theories over several centuries would be an impossible task, at least within a reasonable time frame. Fortunately, some of the perspectives can be dropped for reasons suggested above – specifically the international structure, world culture, political culture, individual self-interest, and psychological approaches.

Dropping these theories from systematic testing does not mean that they may not be important for the study of military intervention, or for Russia in particular. To the extent that international structure and world culture matter, we need to examine how they work through structures and actors at lower levels of analysis. Moreover, these two approaches, as well as political culture, do not seem to be a good guide to explaining variation in military behavior in Russia over time. Psychological accounts can without too much damage be subsumed under the organizational culture approach. Finally, individual self-interest almost certainly plays a role in explaining military behavior. However, it can only do so in relation to the other approaches being considered, so this factor will be discussed in that context.

Thus, the four approaches that will be examined systematically are the domestic structure, organizational structure, corporate interest, and organizational culture ones.

A Two-Step Model: Opportunities and Motives

None of the multiple studies of military involvement in sovereign power issues has "proved" the inherent superiority of one approach. This book does not do so either. Indeed, the complexity of the phenomenon itself suggests that a combination of modes and levels of analysis is required to provide a complete picture.[81] The goal here, then, is not to convince skeptical readers of the preeminence of the author's preferred perspective. Scientific universalism is eschewed in favor of a more variegated account that aims to (a) assess how different approaches fit together and (b) explore why some perspectives seem to do better than others in explaining the political behavior of the Russian armed forces.

---

[81] A very clear statement on how causal complexity in the real world affects social science research is Charles C. Ragin, *The Comparative Method: Moving Beyond Qualitative and Quantitative Strategies* (Berkeley, CA: University of California Press, 1987), pp. 19–33.

Different types of approaches often illuminate different stages in a multi-step process. Specifically, domestic and organizational structural accounts help explain the *opportunities* that officers face, whereas the corporate interest and organizational culture perspectives focus on officers' *motives*. Samuel Finer used this distinction in his classic *The Man on Horseback*. This is also the basic distinction in scientific explanation between structure and agency.[82]

If we think about the two structural approaches (domestic and organizational) together, it seems likely that they will co-vary in predictable ways. A state with high political capacity should be able to maintain strong counterbalancing institutions if they choose to employ this method. Iraq under Saddam Hussein and Syria under Hafez Al-Asad are prominent examples.[83] On the other hand, when the state is weak and unable to carry out its basic functions, its institutions are likely to be incapable of effectively deterring determined coup plotters. At the same time, the military itself is more likely to be internally divided when the state is in crisis. This may explain why internally divided armies are as inclined to intervene as more unified ones.

Opportunities for intervention, then, will be lowest when the state is strong and the government has adopted a robust counterbalancing strategy. Opportunities for intervention will be highest when the state is weak, no counterbalancing institutions exist, and the military is internally unified. This last condition, however, may not obtain very often in the real world.

The two components of motives, corporate interest and organizational culture, do not logically co-vary in consistent ways.[84] There are four ideal pairings: praetorian culture/satisfied military, praetorian culture/threatened military, apolitical culture/satisfied military, and apolitical culture/threatened military. Intervention would be most likely with the combination praetorian culture/threatened military, and least likely with the combination apolitical culture/satisfied military. The two approaches compete most directly when structure is permissive of intervention, yet one perspective predicts intervention and the other predicts nonintervention. The most interesting cases for theory testing, then, will be those with one of two possible combinations: praetorian culture/satisfied military or apolitical culture/threatened military.

In this two-step model, the least interesting cases will be those when both opportunities and motives for intervention are low. In scientific language, nonintervention is overdetermined. On the other hand, when different

---

[82] For example, Jon Elster points to opportunities and desires as the two basic modes of scientific explanation, with desires consisting of two basic types, rational and normative: Finer, *Man on Horseback*; Elster, *Nuts and Bolts*.

[83] Quinlivan, "Coup-proofing."

[84] The category of motive includes both what one would conventionally think of as a motive as well as its opposite: the absence of motive (deterrent is an antonym of motive).

perspectives predict different outcomes, it is easier to test competing explanations against each other.

A key conclusion of this book is that organizational culture can often inhibit military coups, or make them weak and likely to fail, even if the opportunities are relatively high (structure is permissive) and there are strong corporate interest motives for intervention. This perspective accepts that structural and rational factors can play an explanatory role in military intervention, because they help determine the choices officers are faced with. However, actors' behavior cannot be understood simply with reference to their forward-looking utility calculations; their socially formed subjective understandings and values also must be considered.[85] Armies with different norms will respond differently (intervene or not intervene) to the same stimuli. Additionally, norms often serve as a guide to action when the outcomes of actions are uncertain.[86]

Corporate interest as an explanation performs poorly in the Russian case because of a relatively strong apolitical organizational culture from the mid-nineteenth century to the present. A historical study encompassing several centuries allows us to see the many potential coups that do not happen, yet are predicted by the corporate interest approach. This conclusion, however, does not negate the importance of this argument in explaining some coups. Intervention for corporate interest motives is more likely when the army has a more praetorian organizational culture.

A final conclusion of this book is that opportunities definitely matter. Intervention is difficult when structural barriers to coups are severe. Conversely, when opportunities for intervention are high, the military may be forced to become involved in sovereign power issues regardless of its motives, because other political actors will seek to use force to achieve their political goals. An apolitical organizational culture may keep officers off the throne, but it cannot keep them out of domestic politics if other factors make involvement likely.

METHODOLOGY AND RESEARCH DESIGN

The multicausal and two-step model outlined here will be developed in the cases through assessment of the components of both opportunity (domestic and organizational structure) and motives (corporate interest and organizational culture). This requires careful attention to adequate measures, as well as the separation of the phenomenon to be explained from what purportedly explains it. Although this last point sounds obvious, it is not as easy as it sounds.

---

[85] James G. March and Johan P. Olsen, "The New Institutionalism: Organizational Factors in Political Life," *American Political Science Review*, 78 (1984), 739; Elster, *Cement of Society*, pp. 97–99.

[86] Elster, *Cement of Society*, pp. 284–285.

In this section, then, I discuss measures and tests for each of the perspectives, how I intend to conduct the tests, and the design of the study.

Variable Measurement

The propositions derived above were stated in general terms. Here I present specific variables that I will measure when testing the different approaches.

Domestic Structure. The domestic structure perspective contends that low political capacity is the most important cause of military involvement in sovereign power issues. Political capacity, or state strength, is a difficult concept to get a handle on. A diverse range of phenomena has been proposed as the best indicator of political capacity.[87] Some of the more prominent ones subject to quantitative measurement include organizational age, political violence, political disorder (such as strikes), the size of the public sector, and the ability of the state to collect taxes. Others take a more qualitative approach to measurement, assessing legitimacy or the relationship between state power and private behavior.[88] Some of these studies are focused more on questions of public policy, such as the ability to implement economic policy, than on the more basic topic considered here, that of general system order.

Although quantitative measures have an obvious appeal as a way of providing consistent coding, in practice most of these data are not reliably available for the long period under study. The one exception is organizational age, which Robert Jackman argues has three elements: the age of the juridical state, the age of the current constitutional order, and the number of top leadership successions in that order.[89] According to Jackman, the longer the current constitutional order and the greater the number of top leadership successions in that order, the stronger the state becomes. Although organizational age may be a reasonable indicator of political capacity in a cross-country comparative study, in a single-country diachronic study it

---

[87] Uriel Rosenthal, for example, found six general ways of conceptualizing or measuring political order: (1) the absence of structural change; (2) rule-bound politics; (3) legitimate politics; (4) institutionalized politics; (5) the limitation of violence; (6) the stability of chief executive offices. Uriel Rosenthal, *Political Order: Rewards, Punishments and Political Stability* (Alphen aan den Rijn, The Netherlands: Sijthoff & Noordhoff, 1978).

[88] The literature is huge. Good places to start include Jackman, *Power Without Force*; Rosenthal, *Political Order*; Huntington, *Political Order in Changing Societies*; Stephen D. Krasner, *Defending the National Interest: Raw Material Investments and U.S. Foreign Policy* (Princeton, NJ: Princeton University Press, 1978), pp. 55–61; Joel S. Migdal, *Strong Societies and Weak States* (Princeton, NJ: Princeton University Press, 1988), pp. 279–286; Kathryn Sikkink, *Ideas and Institutions: Developmentalism in Brazil and Argentina* (Ithaca, NY: Cornell University Press, 1991), pp. 171–206; Peter B. Evans, Dietrich Rueschemeyer, and Theda Skocpol, eds., *Bringing the State Back In* (Cambridge, England: Cambridge University Press, 1985).

[89] Jackman, *Power Without Force*, pp. ix–x, 38–45, 73–93, 124–138.

TABLE 1.3. *Strength of the State vis-à-vis Society*

	Resist Private Pressure		Change Private Behavior in Intended Ways		Change Social Structure in Intended Ways	
	Yes	No	Yes	No	Yes	No
Weak		X[a]		X		X
Moderate	X		X			X
Strong	X		X		X[b]	

[a] Or sometimes.
[b] Or often only slowly.
Sources: Krasner, *Defending the National Interest*; Migdal, *Strong Societies and Weak States*.

suffers from the serious limitation of being unable to account for the decline in political capacity of an established state.

Quantitative indicators of political capacity, then, need to be supplemented with other indicators of state strength. The other major approach to measuring state strength that I use is the one originally proposed by Stephen Krasner and later modified by Joel Migdal. Krasner proposes three general categories to measure the strength of the state vis-à-vis society: the ability to resist private pressure, to change private behavior, and to change social structure.[90] Migdal's simplified version of Krasner's classification is set out in Table 1.3.

The approach of Krasner and Migdal is well designed to conduct the form of diachronic comparison used in this project. I also, where appropriate and available, will use other numerical indicators to supplement this assessment, such as deaths from political violence.

Organizational Structure. The organizational structure perspective looks at the balance of power within the military itself, as well as that between other armed state bodies, such as paramilitary organizations or the secret police. Some elements of organizational structure are seemingly relatively easy to measure. Arguments that rely on "counterbalancing" or "penetration" explanations for military behavior simply posit the presence of organizations or subunits designed to carry out this function. Thus, the existence of sizable paramilitary or security forces, or the use of groups such as political officers, is evidence of a divided military. However, as Timothy Colton demonstrated in the case of the Soviet Union, monitoring agencies often share considerable interests with their "target."[91] Questions of loyalty and the degree of civilian control over these bodies are also relevant.

[90] Krasner, *Defending the National Interest*, pp. 55–61; Migdal, *Strong Societies and Weak States*, pp.279–286.
[91] Colton, *Commissars, Commanders, and Civilian Authority*.

Other aspects of the argument are difficult to observe. Measuring "factions" within the army, such as between command levels or regions, is not easy. By definition, these internal organizational differences exist in all armies, particularly in one as large as the Russian military. The relevant question, then, would seem to be about the extent of internal cohesion. Inferring this variable from military behavior in sovereign power issues is not acceptable, but other obvious measures do not present themselves.[92] Those who study military organizational factions are forced to rely on qualitative and impressionistic evidence.[93] I will follow the same approach.

Corporate Interest. The corporate interest perspective on military involvement in sovereign power issues focuses on threats to the interests of the military organization as an explanation for army behavior. Nordlinger suggests the following military corporate interests are the most important: budgetary support, military autonomy, the absence of functional rivals (paramilitary forces), and the survival of the military. Thompson produces a similar series of organizational interests. He breaks these interests down into two separate categories: positional and resource. Positional interests include autonomy, hierarchy (the chain of command), monopoly, cohesion, honor, and political position. Resource interests are such matters as budget, pay, personnel issues (promotions, appointments, assignments, etc.), training, and interservice relations. The bureaucratic politics literature suggests that autonomy is a particularly important organizational interest. Threats to all of these interests will be important indicators used to test the corporate interest perspective.[94]

Organizational Culture. The organizational culture approach posits that the norms and beliefs of officers are a key determinant of military involvement in sovereign power issues. Evidence for the existence of norms, Martha Finnemore notes, can be found in one of two ways: either "in patterns of behavior" or "articulated in discourse." The patterns of behavior used to measure culture must be different from those that the culture purportedly explains. If the norms are articulated in discourse, they can be examined in a hermeneutic fashion (i.e., through the interpretation of texts) and using

---

[92] William Thompson, for example, looks at whether a coup was planned and led by the senior military leadership, or lower levels of the officer corps. This study, although useful, cannot say with any certainty what the effect of organizational cohesion is on military coup attempts because only coups are studied, and not noncoups. Thompson, "Organizational Cohesion and Military Coup Outcomes."

[93] Norden, *Military Rebellion in Argentina*, pp. 106–124; Aguero, *Soldiers, Civilians, and Democracy*, pp. 101–131. Note that in both of these studies the organizational factions are at least in part cultural and not structural.

[94] Nordlinger, *Soldiers in Politics*, pp. 65–78; Thompson, *Grievances of Military Coup-Makers*, pp. 12–28. On the importance of organizational autonomy, see Wilson, *Bureaucracy*, pp. 179–195.

content analysis.[95] Survey research data are also available for more recent periods.

Important sources to examine include the socialization process of officers and the beliefs, values, and assumptions of military elites. I look for statements of officers that reflect whether or not they have internalized the view that they must obey legitimate authority and that they have no role to play in the resolution of sovereign power questions. Possible sources include military journals, memoirs, interviews, survey data, and internal armed forces communications. Iain Johnston counsels the analysis of symbols, looking in particular for "frequently used idioms and phrases," "key words which appear to embody certain behavioral axioms, or which are used to describe legitimate actions," and "analogies and metaphors which function as shorthand definitions." Robert Jervis notes that the use of historical analogies by a decision maker is often a good sign of what lessons have been learned from past events.[96]

The behavior of officers also can be a good indicator of their normative orientation. I particularly will look at their behavior in domains of civil–military relations other than sovereign power issues, such as defense politics or internal usage. Whether officers submit to civilian leadership in these realms can be indicative of their degree of attachment to a norm of civilian supremacy. The amount of time that the army devotes to military preparation and training, as opposed to nondefense tasks, is another good indicator.

A potential problem is that except for archival documents and other internal military communications, officers could be using culture instrumentally – in essence, saying what they think they are supposed to say, rather than what they really believe.[97] It may be hard to distinguish between those officers who have been socialized to hold the official government view and those who do not accept the official culture but consider it unwise to say so.[98] To the extent that high-ranking officers express the same views in public, this suggests, at a minimum, that they believe these views are the appropriate ones to hold and, in that sense, reflect the dominant organizational culture. Certainly the

---

[95] Finnemore, *National Interests in International Society*, pp. 23–24.

[96] Schein, "Coming to a New Awareness of Organizational Culture," p. 13; Alastair Iain Johnston, "Thinking about Strategic Culture," *International Security*, 19, 4 (1995), 44–55 (quote, 52); Alastair Iain Johnston, *Cultural Realism: Strategic Culture and Grand Strategy in Ming China* (Princeton; NJ: Princeton University Press, 1995), pp. 32–59; Kier, *Imagining War*, pp. 30–31, 33–35; Jervis, *Perception and Misperception in International Politics*, p. 218.

[97] Kier, *Imagining War*, pp. 32–33.

[98] Finding dissenting views is particularly difficult under authoritarian regimes. This problem obviously is relevant to a study of Russia and the Soviet Union. Thus, it will be easiest to measure organizational culture for either periods of relative openness or those periods for which documentary and archival sources are available. In the periods of relative openness, such as during the Revolution or the Gorbachev and Yeltsin periods, officers engaged in open political debate on many questions, with little evidence that they were not committed to the positions that they articulated.

careful researcher has to be aware of the potential problem of manipulated culture and look for communications from a range of actors and in a variety of forms and media. This problem should not be overstated, however. Scholars of civil–military relations have been quite successful in uncovering considerable variance in officers' views, including views directly at odds with official and dominant positions.[99]

Another source of potential measurement error is the problem of divided cultures. Except in ideal cases (completely apolitical or praetorian militaries), one would expect to find evidence of competing subcultures. How does one know which is dominant, if any? To the extent that a culture is dominant, it should be reflected in materials prepared to socialize and train its members. Furthermore, those who rise to the top of an organization are more likely to reflect the dominant culture than to be adherents of a minority culture. If there is truly no dominant culture, contradictory propositions are likely to be articulated both in formal literature and in informal statements. Hierarchical organizations such as militaries also are more likely than other organizations to have a single dominant culture.

Argument Testing and Study Design

This book combines macro-historical analysis and focused case studies of actual or potential military involvement in sovereign power issues in Russian and Soviet history.[100] I survey the universe of relevant cases over the last 300 years, concentrating on the twentieth century (see Table 1.4). These observations, or cases, show variance on both the dependent variable (military involvement in sovereign power issues) and the independent variables derived from the alternative approaches.[101]

I use "process tracing" to test the theories in the focused case studies. In a process-tracing approach, according to Alexander George and Timothy

---

99 Examples include: John Steward Ambler, *Soldiers Against the State: The French Army in Politics* (Garden City, NY; Anchor Books, 1968); Stepan, *The State and Society*; Stepan, *Military in Politics*; Fitch, *Military Coup*; Fitch, *Armed Forces and Democracy*.

100 Theda Skocpol and Margaret Somers, "The Uses of Comparative History in Macrosocial Inquiry," *Comparative Studies in Society and History*, 22 (1980), 174–197; Alexander L. George, "Case Studies and Theory Development: The Method of Structured, Focused Comparison," in Paul Gordon Lauren, ed., *Diplomacy: New Approaches in History, Theory, and Policy* (New York: The Free Press, 1979), pp. 43–68; Ragin, *Comparative Method*, pp. 34–52.

101 As will be seen in Chapter 3, the coding of both the Kornilov Affair and October 1917 is not straightforward, and for October 1917 two codings best capture the army's behavior. Whether the Civil War counts as a failed intervention depends on whether the White Army is seen as representative of the army as a whole; many officers sided with the Reds after the Civil War began. The problem of divided culture and competing subcultures is directly relevant to the Revolution and Civil War case.

TABLE I.4. *Case Summary*

Chapter	Observations	Military Intervention	Military Arbitration	No Military Involvement
Chapter 2: Cultural Change in the Imperial Russian Army, 1689–1914	Eighteenth-Century Palace Coups	S		
	Decembrist Uprising	F		
	The Alexander II, Alexander III, and Nicholas II Successions			X
	1905 Revolution			X
Chapter 3: The Army and the Revolution, 1917	February Revolution/Abdication of the Tsar		X	
	Kornilov Affair	F		
	October Revolution		X	X
	Civil War	F?		
Chapter 4: From Revolution to War, 1917–1941	Post-Lenin Transition			X
	Stalinist Purges of Military			X
Chapter 5: From Victory to Stagnation, 1945–1985	The Arrest of Beria			X
	Khrushchev and the "Anti-Party Group"		X	
	The Zhukov Affair			X
	The Fall of Khrushchev			X
	The Andropov, Chernenko, and Gorbachev Successions			X
Chapter 6: Gorbachev, Perestroika and the Collapse of the Soviet Union, 1985–1991	August 1991	F		
	December 1991		X	
Chapter 7: Yeltsin and the New Russia, 1992–2000	October 1993 uprising		X	
	1994–1999			X

Note: S denotes successful intervention; F denotes failed intervention.

McKeown, "the decision-making process is the center of investigation." Not only the outcome (coup, arbitration, or noncoup) is to be explained, but also the "stream of behavior" leading up to the decision. Because decision making is a "social enterprise," actors will communicate with each other. The content of this communication is sometimes available to researchers, preferably in archives but also in interviews and memoirs. Process tracing permits the analyst, as Stephen Van Evera argues, to see if "the actors speak and behave as the theory would predict." It also allows one to increase the number of observations within each case.[102]

In addition to considering alternative explanations and the use of process-tracing, I also employ counterfactual analysis. I ask, "What would have happened if the opportunities or motives had been different?" This method supplements the study of actual cases in which there is variance in the explanatory variables.[103]

SUMMARY

Military involvement in sovereign power issues involves three possible behaviors: military intervention, military arbitration, and no military involvement. Army behavior can be explained with theories employing different modes (structural, rational, and cultural) and levels (international, domestic, organizational, individual) of analysis. No single approach can explain all coups, but a combination of theoretical approaches has the potential to increase our understanding of the phenomenon in general and Russian civil–military relations in particular. A two-step model, based on opportunities and motives, represents a promising method for explaining these interactions. The proof, I've been told, however, is in the pudding, so it is time to dig in.

---

[102] Alexander L. George and Timothy J. McKeown, "Case Studies and Theories of Organizational Decision Making," *Advances in Information Processing in Organizations*, Vol. 2 (Santa Barbara, CA: JAI Press, 1985), pp. 34–41; Stephen Van Evera, *Guide to Methodology for Students of Political Science* (Cambridge, MA: Defense and Arms Control Studies Program, Massachusetts Institute of Technology, n.d. [1996]), pp. 33–34; King, Keohane, and Verba, *Designing Social Inquiry*, pp. 85–87, 225–228.

[103] James D. Fearon, "Counterfactuals and Hypothesis Testing in Political Science," *World Politics*, 43 (1991), 169–195; Philip E. Tetlock and Aaron Belkin, eds., *Counterfactual Thought Experiments in World Politics: Logical, Methodological, and Psychological Perspectives* (Princeton, NJ: Princeton University Press, 1996).

Cultural Change in the Imperial Russian Army, 1689–1914

The Imperial period of Russian history, from the accession of Peter the Great to the abdication of Nicholas II, was a time of enormous transformation, including in the sphere of civil–military relations. Peter the Great himself rose to power with the help of military officers, and for a century after his death the involvement of the army in sovereign power issues was a normal occurrence. Only in the nineteenth century did this pattern of behavior reverse itself, and to such an extent that by the end of the Romanov dynasty military intervention was practically unthinkable.

This chapter tells the story of this shift from a praetorian to an apolitical officer corps. Two major issues dominate the discussion. The first issue is the development of the Russian state. The second major focus of this chapter is the question of military involvement in sovereign power issues. Four cases are discussed: the palace coups of the eighteenth century, the Decembrist uprising of 1825, the uneventful (and thus highly significant) successions of the second half of the nineteenth century, and the Revolution of 1905–1906.

PETER THE GREAT AND THE BUILDING OF THE RUSSIAN STATE

Peter the Great transformed Russia from Muscovy, a medieval and "eastern" polity, into the modern and European state of Imperial Russia. The creation of many highly important political and social institutions, including a standing army and navy, usually is traced to Peter. Indeed, the very notion of the "state" as something separate from and even higher than the sovereign can be traced to Peter's reign.[1]

---

[1] This is, of course, a highly abbreviated summary of the traditional historiography. For differing assessments of the importance of Peter the Great, see James Cracraft, ed., *Peter the Great Transforms Russia*, 3rd ed. (Lexington, MA: D. C. Heath and Company, 1991); Richard Pipes, *Russia Under the Old Regime* (Harmondsworth, Middlesex, England: Penguin Books, 1974), pp. 112–132; Marc Raeff, "Seventeenth-Century Europe in Eighteenth-Century Russia?,"

Peter the Great's efforts to transform Russia were driven primarily by military goals and demands. Russia was at war for the first thirty-four years of Peter's thirty-five year reign (from 1689 to 1725). Russia's geographic proximity to central Europe, as well as Peter's own travels in the West, convinced him of the need for major reform. Historians disagree about the extent to which Peter's reforms were clearly thought out and implemented, but there is little conflict about the rationale behind Peter's efforts. In the words of Michael Florinsky, "the exigencies of wars... were the moving power behind practically all Petrine reforms."[2]

The first institution subject to major reform was the armed forces. There was no clear separation of military and civilian affairs in Muscovy before the seventeenth century, and Peter the Great traditionally is given credit for the creation of the first Russian standing army. Peter's efforts to raise a standing army were neither wholly new nor completely effective, but he can properly be seen as the father of the Russian army because he created a unified force under centralized administration and established a legal basis for conscription. Most important, he was able to use the power of the autocracy and the institution of serfdom to bring a constant supply of new peasant soldiers into the army to replace those who were lost at an equally rapid rate to attrition (death, desertion, and disease). Peter's efforts eventually led to the defeat of Sweden in the Northern War (1700–1721) and Russia's arrival as an important European power.[3]

Peter's widespread reforms, although ultimately directed toward the goal of increasing the state's military power, went far beyond the armed forces. His efforts to put the state on a more firm financial basis and develop the economy were particularly important.[4] "Money is the artery of war," Peter remarked, and his government acted vigorously to extract more money from

---

with comments by Edward L. Keenan, Isabel de Madariaga, and James Cracraft, in Gary M. Hamburg, ed., *Imperial Russian History I: 1700–1861* (New York: Garland Publishing, 1992), pp. 1–28.

[2] Michael T. Florinsky, *Russia: A History and an Interpretation*, Vol. I (New York: Macmillan, 1953), p. 336. See also Pipes, *Russia Under the Old Regime*, pp. 112–122; William C. Fuller, Jr., *Strategy and Power, 1600–1914* (New York: The Free Press, 1992), pp. 35–37; John L. H. Keep, *Soldiers of the Tsar: Army and Society in Russia, 1462–1874* (Oxford, England: Clarendon Press, 1985), p. 95; Bruce D. Porter, *War and the Rise of the State: The Military Foundations of Modern Politics* (New York: The Free Press, 1994), pp. 112–113.

[3] On the conventional wisdom that Peter was responsible for the creation of a standing army, see, for example, G. H. N. Seton-Watson, "Russia," in Michael Howard, ed., *Soldiers and Governments: Nine Studies in Civil–Military Relations* (London: Eyre & Spottiswoode, 1957), p. 103. John Keep argues that considerable credit needs to be given to Peter's predecessors in the establishment of a standing army, whereas William Fuller argues, on the contrary, that Peter never succeeded in creating a regular army: Keep, *Soldiers of the Tsar*, pp. 56, 95–117; Fuller, *Strategy and Power*, pp. 35–84.

[4] Florinsky, *Russia*, I, pp. 357–364, 384–396; Pipes, *Russia Under the Old Regime*, 120–122; Fuller, *Strategy and Power*, pp. 56–64; Keep, *Soldiers of the Tsar*, pp. 129–140; Cracraft, *Peter the Great*, pp. 115–157.

the population. Peter began a process of state-led industrialization, particularly in such key sectors for the military as ship building and metallurgy. The state also took the lead in building the empire's transportation system. Finally, Peter sought to rationalize and strengthen state administration, with a series of far-reaching reforms that tied the elite more closely to the state.[5]

The traditional picture of Peter the Great as the "modernizer" and "Westernizer" of Russia, then, seems somewhat misplaced. Certainly Peter sought to make Russia an important European power. His methods, however, were similar to those used by previous Russian rulers. Peter sought to harness both the nobility and the peasantry to service for the benefit of the state and the autocracy. State power, most importantly in the form of the army, was increased, and the military served as an instrument of both internal coercion and external war fighting.[6]

Similar patterns of state development can be discerned further west in the European heartland. The rulers of France, Prussia, and Austria all sought to build a more powerful state able to extract resources from society. As in Russia, the needs of external war making and domestic control existed in a symbiotic relationship that drove the process of state building. Peter the Great and his successors were probably the least constrained of European rulers. The nobility in Russia had fewer rights than elsewhere in Europe, and the merchant class was almost nonexistent. The vast majority of the Russian population was made up of peasants, who had even fewer rights than their counterparts in western Europe. Russia's vast size and the weakness of transportation and communication links made it difficult for autocratic power to penetrate the Russian countryside. The rulers of France, Austria, and Prussia, however, faced similar problems. In general, the Russian pattern of state building was particularly coercive and was subject to fewer societal constraints than in Western Europe.[7]

RUSSIAN PRAETORIANS

A striking paradox of Peter the Great's rule is that, despite his many achievements in building a strong Russian state, he failed to establish a reliable mechanism for the transfer of supreme executive power and helped create the

[5] Florinsky, *Russia*, I, pp. 365–384, 417–423; Pipes, *Russia Under the Old Regime*, pp. 123–125; Keep, *Soldiers of the Tsar*, pp. 123–131; M. M. Bogoslovsky, "The Transformation of State Institutions," in Cracraft, *Peter the Great*, pp. 87–96.

[6] Fuller, *Strategy and Power*, 35–84; Keep, *Soldiers of the Tsar*, pp. 95–140.

[7] Charles Tilly, *Coercion, Capital, and European States, AD 990–1992* (Cambridge: Blackwell, 1992), especially pp. 137–143, 152; Porter, *War and the Rise of the State*, pp. 107–118; Pipes, *Russia Under the Old Regime*, pp. 19–24; Walter M. Pintner, "Russia as a Great Power, 1709–1856: Reflections on the Problem of Relative Backwardness, with Special Reference to the Russian Army and Russian Society," *Kennan Institute for Advanced Russian Studies, Occasional Paper*, No. 33 (1978), p. 41.

conditions for a century of palace coups.[8] In the century after Peter's death in 1725, army officers were involved constantly in questions of sovereign power, although they never seized power for themselves. The one episode that could have ended with an officer on the throne was the failed Decembrist uprising. In this section I review these instances of military intervention in politics.

The Era of Palace Coups

Peter himself had come to power with the assistance of military officers. Peter was ten years old when his father, Tsar Feodor, died in 1682. Feodor's sister Sophie, with the aid of Muscovite *strel'tsy* (musketeers), seized power and declared herself regent. In 1689 Peter organized her overthrow with the help of his so-called play regiments, which later were transformed into elite Guards regiments. An attempted revolt by the *strel'tsy* in 1698 was crushed and Peter had their units disbanded; many of them were executed. Peter then ruled without challenge until his death in 1725.[9]

In a momentous change before his death, Peter sought to make succession dependent on the wishes of the sitting tsar. Previously the oldest son generally had succeeded, but there was no set mechanism in the absence of an heir. Peter himself was unable to appoint his own successor, however, because he died suddenly in 1725. There were four pretenders to the throne in 1725: Peter's grandson, his two daughters, and his widow (Peter's only son, Alexis, had previously been charged with treason and tortured to death). All of the successions in the next century were marked by instability and officer involvement, and there were at least eight coups or attempted coups during this period. The Guards regiments established by Peter played a key role in these events. The most tumultuous period was 1725–1762, during which seven different monarchs occupied the throne. Only with the accession to power of Catherine the Great in 1762 did Russia once again have a stable leadership.[10]

The details of these succession struggles are less important for our purposes than some general points about the role of officers in these conflicts. First, these palace coups involved only a small fraction of the officer corps, elite Guards officers. These officers were members of the Imperial court, and they generally acted at the behest of and on behalf of more powerful

---

[8] Two Russian historians have recently argued that Peter the Great created the conditions for palace coups precisely because he made the state so strong vis-à-vis other societal actors that the coup was the only mechanism for aristocratic resistance: I. V. Volkova and I.V. Kurukin, "Fenomen dvortsovykh perevorotov v politicheskoy istorii Rossii XVII–XX vv," *Voprosy istorii*, No. 5–6, 1995, 43–47.

[9] Keep, *Soldiers of the Tsar*, pp. 67–72, 97–102; Florinsky, *Russia*, I, pp. 307–314; Marc Raeff, *Imperial Russia, 1682–1825: The Coming of Age of Modern Russia* (New York: Knopf, 1971), pp. 3–5.

[10] Florinsky, *Russia*, I, pp. 432–456, 496–505; Raeff, *Imperial Russia*, pp. 9–22.

members of the court. Second, these elite officers generally acted out of personal motives and grievances, not corporate ones. To the extent that corporate interests were involved, they were those of the Guards, and not the officer corps as a whole. It was only in the late eighteenth century that Guards officers began to see themselves as distinctly military, rather than as members of the broader elite. Third, the Guards officers did not try to seize power for themselves. They remained loyal to the principle of autocracy. Finally, efforts to prevent coups through the use of material incentives, political spies, changing commanders, or creating counterbalancing units were only marginally successful.[11]

The last successful military coup in Russia took place in 1801. Tsar Paul I, who had succeeded his mother Catherine the Great to the throne in 1796, was assassinated by a group comprised largely of Guards officers. Paul had alienated the military because of a purge of more than twenty percent of the officer corps, his favoritism toward elite units that he had established, and his adoption of Prussian drill and tactics. Fifty officers were involved in the coup, which made it larger than the palace coups of the eighteenth century. The coup had some support in broader society, particularly among the nobility, who were unhappy with Paul's efforts to restrict their privileges. Thus, unlike the previous interventions, which were strictly matters of the Imperial court, the intervention of 1801 had broader military and societal support. It also is important to note that Paul I had changed the law on succession, instituting the principle of primogeniture (succession of the oldest son) in 1797. The coup of 1801 was a partial challenge to this effort to establish a stable succession mechanism, although Paul's eldest son Alexander took his throne. The coup was not a challenge to the principle of autocracy itself.[12]

The Decembrist Uprising

The Russian armed forces thus had a strong tradition of involvement in sovereign power issues in the eighteenth century. At the beginning of the nineteenth century it seemed quite possible that this pattern would continue and that a military organizational culture of praetorianism would develop.

---

[11] Volkova and Kurukin, "Fenomen dvortsovykh perevorotov"; Keep, *Soldiers of the Tsar*, pp. 232–242; John L. H. Keep, "The Secret Chancellery, the Guards, and the Dynastic Crisis of 1740–1741," *Power and the People: Essays on Russian History* (Boulder, CO: East European Monographs, 1995), pp. 136–161; Seton-Watson, "Russia," p. 103; Raeff, *Imperial Russia*, pp. 9–22; P. S. Squire, *The Third Department: The Establishment and Practices of the Political Police in the Russia of Nicholas I* (Cambridge, England: Cambridge University Press, 1968), pp. 14–17.

[12] Keep, *Soldiers of the Tsar*, pp. 231–249; Keep, *Power and the People*, pp. 218–223; Florinsky, *Russia*, I, pp. 622–628; Raeff, *Imperial Russia*, pp. 27–29; Hugh Seton-Watson, *The Russian Empire 1801–1917* (Oxford: Clarendon Press, 1967), pp. 62–68; David Saunders, *Russia in the Age of Reaction and Reform 1801–1881* (London: Longman, 1992), pp. 4–10.

This section concentrates on the failed Decembrist intervention of 1825, which played an important role in changing military organizational culture toward a more apolitical stance.

Alexander I ruled Russia (1801–1825) during one of the most momentous events in modern European and Russian history, the Napoleonic Wars. The French Revolution represented a threat to dynastic rule throughout Europe, and Revolutionary France quickly became involved in wars with a coalition of European powers. From 1792 to 1815 much of Europe was at war, and these wars had profound effects on political, social, and military development in Europe. Russia played a considerable role in the defeat of Napoleon, and Russia's victory in the War of 1812 (the Fatherland War, in Russian parlance) established Russia as perhaps the dominant power in continental Europe.[13]

The force of French revolutionary ideas and arms led many European states to adopt liberalizing and modernizing reforms. Alexander I, however, who had pursued limited political reform before the Napoleonic Wars, now resisted any suggestion that further reform was necessary for Russia. The autocratic and patrimonial state of traditional Russia and its corollary institutions, particularly serfdom, were seen by the tsar as vindicated because of the Russian victory over Napoleon.[14]

Russian educated society expected that reforms similar to those taking place in western and central Europe also might be enacted at home. Discontent grew when Alexander embraced a reactionary vision for Russia, particularly because before the war the tsar had been perceived by many as relatively liberal and a reformer. Many officers shared these hopes for reform, and they were disappointed by the conservative policies of the tsar after 1815. Officers' self-confidence was high after their victories on the battlefield, and liberal elements in society looked to the army as a potential agent of change. Many officers felt the same way.[15]

---

[13] On the historical importance of the French Revolution and the Napoleonic Wars, see Michael Howard, *War in European History* (Oxford: Oxford University Press, 1976), pp. 75–115; William H. McNeill, *The Pursuit of Power: Technology, Armed Force, and Society since A.D. 1000* (Chicago: University of Chicago Press, 1982), pp. 185–222; Tilly, *Coercion, Capital, and European States*, pp. 107–114; Porter, *War and the Rise of the State*, pp. 121–145. For an excellent discussion of the influence of the French Revolution on civil–military relations, see S. E. Finer, *The Man on Horseback: The Role of the Military in Politics*, 2nd ed. (Harmondsworth, England: Penguin Books, 1975), pp. 188–200. On Russia and the Napoleonic Wars, particularly the War of 1812, see Fuller, *Strategy and Power*, pp. 177–218; Saunders, *Russia in the Age*, pp. 29–58.

[14] Fuller, *Strategy and Power*, pp. 217–218. On Alexander's reforms before 1812, see Seton-Watson, *Russian Empire*, pp. 69–83, 96–112; Raeff, *Imperial Russia*, pp. 29–32, 82–88; Saunders, *Russia in the Age*, pp. 19–25, 59–69.

[15] Marc Raeff, *The Decembrist Movement* (Englewood Cliffs, NJ: Prentice-Hall, 1966), pp. 10–15; Seton-Watson, *Russian Empire*, pp. 153, 183–184; Saunders, *Russia in the Age*, pp. 72–76, 79–84, 88–89; John L. H. Keep, "The Russian Army's Response to the French Revolution," *Power and the People*, pp. 211–238.

The origins of the Decembrist movement can be traced to the growth of a Russian "military intelligentsia" around the turn of the century. The term military intelligentsia refers to officers who, by virtue of their education, acquired a greater understanding of broader cultural, social, and political issues and, equally important, a willingness to question received ideas and to seek out new knowledge. These officers were not political radicals and they maintained the service mentality of the Russian aristocracy. At the same time, they found fault with conditions both in the army and in the larger society. A small but important element within the military intelligentsia had been to Western Europe during the Napoleonic Wars, and they shared their experiences and impressions with other officers. These officers objected to the arbitrariness of authority relations in the military and in Russia and sought greater security for the individual. The military intelligentsia, although committed to state service, also began to transfer their loyalty from the tsar to a broader notion of service to the people, the nation, or the state.[16]

In the years after 1815 the military intelligentsia began to organize itself in secret societies. These societies adopted such names as the Union of Salvation (the Society of True and Loyal Sons of the Fatherland), the Union of (Public) Welfare, and, a personal favorite, the Society of Military Men Who Love Science and Literature. The most prominent of these were the Northern Society, based in St. Petersburg, and the Southern Society, based in Tul'chin (in present-day Ukraine); these two societies came into being in 1821, after a split in the Union of Welfare. The Southern Society was dominated by Colonel P. I. Pestel', who possessed an authoritarian temperament and radical republican views. The leaders of the Northern Society, such as Captain N. M. Murav'ev, were more attracted to constitutional monarchy. Although members of the secret societies and the military intelligentsia were committed to reform, individual officers differed substantially in terms of their views of the appropriate goals. Views diverged even more substantially on the question of means, with some supporting assassination of the tsar and a military dictatorship while others seemed uncommitted to any form of action other than discussion.[17]

---

[16] Keep, *Soldiers of the Tsar*, pp. 231–272; Keep, "Russian Army's Response"; Saunders, *Russia in the Age*, pp. 97–100; Raeff, *The Decembrist Movement*, pp. 6–26; W. Bruce Lincoln, "A Re-examination of Some Historical Stereotypes: An Analysis of the Career Patterns and Backgrounds of the Decembrists," *Jahrbucher fur Geschichte Osteuropas*, 24 (1976), 357–368.

[17] Keep, *Soldiers of the Tsar*, pp. 257–267; Keep, "Russian Army's Response"; Saunders, *Russia in the Age*, pp. 98–109; Seton-Watson, *Russian Empire*, pp. 183–194; Andrzej Walicki, *A History of Russian Thought from the Enlightenment to Marxism* (Stanford, CA: Stanford University Press, 1979), pp. 57–70; O. I. Kiyanskaya, *Yuzhnyy bunt: Vosstaniye chernigovskogo pekhotnogo polka* (Moskva: RGGU, 1997). Marc Raeff's *The Decembrist Movement* reproduces many of the most important documents and writings of these societies and their members.

The event that gave the Decembrists their name was a failed military intervention launched in December 1825 after the death of Tsar Alexander I. Alexander died unexpectedly on November 19, 1825. He had no son, so according to normal succession procedures the oldest of his three brothers, Konstantin, should have taken the throne. Konstantin, however, had renounced his claim to the throne at Alexander's request in 1822 because of Konstantin's marriage to a lower-born Catholic Polish countess. According to a secret manifesto signed by Alexander in 1823, and agreed to by Konstantin, their brother Nicholas should have been the next tsar. Because this agreement had not been publicized, and contradicted the legal succession chain established by Paul I, considerable confusion accompanied Alexander's death and the throne remained unoccupied for over three weeks while Konstantin and Nicholas vacillated. The army originally swore loyalty to Konstantin, before the secret manifesto became known, and Konstantin and Nicholas each renounced the throne in favor of the other.[18]

Members of the Northern Society, based in Petersburg, saw the confused interregnum as an opportunity for action. A hasty scheme was hatched for armed opposition to the plans for the army to swear loyalty to Nicholas, scheduled for December 14. The intent was to bring troops to Senate Square in St. Petersburg on the fourteenth and declare the establishment of a dictatorship under Prince Sergey Trubetskoy, a Colonel. Trubetskoy got cold feet, however, and literally ran away and hid in the Austrian Embassy. A day-long standoff between the Decembrists and troops loyal to Nicholas ended in a rout of the Decembrists. An attempted uprising in the south also failed.[19]

Several general points are in order about what, in hindsight, was a key turning point in Russian civil–military relations. First, the rise of the military intelligentsia should be separated somewhat from the failed Decembrist intervention. Many participants in the December events were not members of secret societies, and many members of secret societies did not participate in the Decembrist uprising. They were two related but distinct phenomena, although the failure of December 1825 had considerable impact on the military intelligentsia movement, as we shall see below. Second, it seems likely that the Decembrist uprising would not have taken place if the succession had happened quickly and smoothly. At the time of Alexander's death there was no plan for a coup that could be taken off the shelf and implemented; the Decembrist uprising was an improvised response to an opportunity created by the power vacuum at the top. The act of swearing loyalty to Konstantin

[18] Raeff, *Decembrist Movement*, pp. 1–6; Seton-Watson, *Russian Empire*, pp. 194–196; Saunders, *Russia in the Age*, pp. 87–88, 110–111; Keep, *Soldiers of the Tsar*, pp. 267–269; Glynn Barratt, *The Rebel on the Bridge: A Life of the Decembrist Baron Andrey Rozen (1800–84)* (London: Paul Elek, 1975), pp. 60–82.

[19] On the failed uprising in the south, see Kiyanskaya, *Yuzhnyy bunt*.

several weeks before officers were asked to swear loyalty to Nicholas, in particular, may have encouraged many of the Decembrists to come out against Nicholas. Third, another counterfactual worth considering is whether the secret military societies would have gone on to develop a more coherent plan for military intervention if no leadership crisis had arisen in 1825, and they could have gone on scheming. This counterfactual is more difficult to resolve. The secret military societies had been detected by government informers before December 1825, with those in the south particularly compromised. On the other hand, previous reports about the societies had been largely ignored. It is certainly possible that, in the absence of the failed Decembrist uprising, secret military societies would have continued their activities and presented a potential threat to the state.[20]

Theoretical Perspectives

Arguably, none of the major perspectives on military intervention being considered – domestic structure, organizational structure, corporate interest, and organizational culture – does a good job in explaining the palace coups of the eighteenth century and the Decembrist uprising. The problem is that all of these theories were developed to explain twentieth-century civil–military relations. In the seventeenth and eighteenth centuries the major European states were still going through the process of creating permanent and professional standing armies. These changes were not fully realized until the nineteenth century and after the momentous changes in international and domestic politics brought about by the French and Industrial revolutions and the Napoleonic Wars. Thus, Russian military officers had little corporate consciousness in the eighteenth century, and they were still developing one in the early nineteenth century.

Opportunity. There clearly were ample opportunities for intervention in eighteenth- and early nineteenth-century Russia. This creates a problem for domestic and organizational structure accounts. The state's political capacity vis-à-vis society was quite high during this period, and the state still maintained considerable power to repress the population.[21] The principle of autocracy remained unquestioned. Eighteenth-century Russia does not make a good comparison with the praetorian societies of Third World states in the

---

[20] Lincoln, "A Re-examination"; Keep, *Soldiers of the Tsar*, pp. 262, 269–271; Keep, "Russian Army's Response," p. 229; Barratt, *Rebel on the Bridge*, pp. 60–67; Saunders, *Russia in the Age*, pp. 110–111; Squire, *Third Department*, pp. 44–46; Sidney Monas, *The Third Section: Police and Society in Russia under Nicholas I* (Cambridge, MA: Harvard University Press, 1961), pp. 45–48.

[21] International structure also performs poorly in this period; military interventionism and war making went hand-in-hand in eighteenth-century Russia.

twentieth century.[22] In 1825 the state also was quite strong. Indeed, Keep maintains that state strength was one reason the Decembrist intervention failed: "[T]he power of the monarchy was still absolute, its hold over the machinery of government as yet unweakened, its image untarnished by military defeat."[23] The absence of a clear succession mechanism contributed to the eighteenth-century palace coups, consistent with arguments that stress the importance of stable rules of the game. But the reestablishment of primogeniture by Paul I did not save him, stop the rise of the military intelligentsia, or prevent the Decembrist uprising.

Organizational structure is also a problematic explanation. Attempts by several tsars to employ counterbalancing techniques, such as changing commanders, creating new units, or spying by secret police, did not secure their hold on the throne. The stepped-up use of military secret police in 1821 played no role in the defeat of the Decembrist putsch, although it did contribute to the failure of the attempted uprising in the south.[24]

Motive. Military corporate interests could not serve as a motive for the palace coups of the eighteenth century because a strong collective identity did not exist in the officer corps at that time. Elite officers did not think of themselves as a distinct military caste separate from the broader elite. By the nineteenth century a greater corporate spirit did exist, and officer corps grievances did play a role in the overthrow of Paul I. This applied particularly to Guards officers. Rational self-interest also was a key motive in these coup attempts; contenders for the crown rewarded officers who provided their support, and grievances against the sitting tsar could serve as a motive for officers to join a plot. In the absence of structural barriers, these interests often translated into action.

Corporate grievances were not a major motivation for the Decembrists. John Keep argues that officer disgruntlement with military matters was a major cause of the growth of the military intelligentsia, but most historians agree that social and political concerns were the most important motivations for the Decembrists. Marc Raeff, one of the most prominent scholars of the Decembrists, draws a sharp distinction between the self-interested motives behind the palace coups of the eighteenth century and the "idealistic and moral passion that animated the Decembrists." It seems fair to say that military corporate grievances did play some role in creating a group of officers

---

[22] On state political capacity in the eighteenth century, see Florinsky, *Russia*, I, pp. 481–488, 493–495; Fuller, *Strategy and Power*, pp. 117–123; Keep, *Soldiers of the Tsar*, pp. 143, 233–239; Pipes, *Russia Under the Old Regime*, pp. 130–138, 171–190.

[23] Keep, *Soldiers of the Tsar*, p. 269.

[24] Volkova and Kurukin, "Fenomen dvortsovykh perevorotov," pp. 51–52, 56; Kiyanskaya, *Yuzhnyy bunt*, pp. 45–60; Squire, *Third Department*, pp. 44–46; Monas, *Third Section*, pp. 45–48.

inclined toward military intervention, but larger social and political goals were more important to this group of Russian officers.[25]

The organizational culture perspective is hampered by the same problem as the corporate interest approach. If there was little sense of corporate identity, then there was no possibility for a distinct organizational culture to develop. One could infer from their behavior that Guards officers in eighteenth-century Russia believed it was appropriate for them to play a role in deciding who ruled the state, but this is hardly a reliable indicator of organizational culture.

It is difficult to know to what extent the ideas of the military intelligentsia or the Decembrists were shared throughout the officer corps in 1825. There were a few generals (7) and a significant number of colonels (46) involved with the military intelligentsia (there were roughly 180 generals and 1,550 colonels in the Russian army at that time). However, no generals and only five colonels were present for the revolt on Senate Square on December 14. Although there were Decembrist sympathizers in the high command, they chose not to come out in support. Bruce Lincoln points out, "most [of those involved on December 14] were under thirty years of age, and 76 percent held the rank of captain or below." Additionally, like the coups of the previous century, the Decembrist movement was largely an affair of Guards officers and the aristocratic elite. Keep concludes, "the extent to which the armed forces had been affected by dissent and conspiratorial activity ... was modest – and anyway below the 'threshold' necessary for a successful Praetorian-type revolution."[26]

If the Decembrists had succeeded, however, it is quite possible that praetorianism would have taken hold in Russia. Russia did have a tradition of military involvement in sovereign power issues throughout the eighteenth century. Moreover, the Decembrists and the military intelligentsia of the early nineteenth century had broader concerns and more explicitly political goals than the officers involved in the palace coups of the previous century. Dominic Lieven notes, "the Decembrists drew part of their inspiration from the victories of their radical Spanish officer contemporaries and it is possible that success in 1825 might have had similar long-term consequences. These might have included the politicisation of the army and frequent subsequent

---

[25] Keep, "Russian Army's Response," pp. 229–235; Keep, *Soldiers of the Tsar*, pp. 244, 256–257; Raeff, *Decembrist Movement*, especially pp. 28–29; Saunders, *Russia in the Age*, pp. 97–100; Seton-Watson, *Russian Empire*, pp. 183–198.

[26] Lincoln, "A Re-examination," pp. 358–359, 364–365; Keep, *Soldiers of the Tsar*, pp. 259–261. For additional statistics, see V. A. D'yakov, *Osvoboditel'noye dvizheniye v Rossii 1825–1861 gg.* (Moskva: "Mysl," 1979), pp. 43–49. I estimated the number of generals and colonels based on figures provided in Walter M. Pintner, "The Burden of Defense in Imperial Russia, 1725–1914," *The Russian Review*, 43 (1984), 253; Peter Kenez, "A Profile of the Prerevolutionary Officer Corps," *California Slavic Studies*, 7 (1973), 132.

coups." Lieven points out that Russian history would have looked very different if "Spanish-style military-political traditions had taken root in Russian soil."[27]

Instead, the failure of the Decembrist uprising had the opposite effect on civil-military relations in Russia. In the words of John Keep, "praetorianism as a movement or tendency never really got off the ground in Russia."[28] In this sense, 1825 represented a "critical juncture," directing the organizational culture of the armed forces along a particular path that it would continue to follow for decades to come.[29] Although it would take some time, along with the presence of several other important factors, adherence to the norm of civilian supremacy in Russia received a considerable boost in 1825.

THE RUSSIAN STATE IN THE NINETEENTH CENTURY

Nineteenth-century Russia was a European great power struggling to maintain its position in comparison with its more wealthy and modern rivals. Changes in the state, as well as in state–society relations, were induced by the Industrial Revolution and the spread of a series of Western ideologies corrosive of the old order in Russia, particularly liberalism, nationalism, and socialism. The state attempted to cope with and manage these changes in the midst of a dangerous international environment.

Tsar Nicholas I, upon his accession to the throne in 1825, became the ruler of a powerful and secure state. Nicholas had few goals, but one of them was to maintain the status quo at home and abroad. During his thirty-year reign, W. E. Mosse notes, Nicholas imposed a "political deep freeze" not only on the Russian empire but on Central and Eastern Europe as well.[30] In an effort to deter both domestic and foreign revolutionaries, Nicholas I maintained the largest army in Europe, numbering around one million men by the 1850s. This massive force, however, was more powerful on paper than it was in the field. In the Crimean War (1854–1856), the Russian army and navy were outclassed by British and French forces. The military that had played such a

---

[27] In this instance, then, world culture tapped into a preexisting interventionist tendency in the Russian officer corps. See Dominic Lieven, *The Aristocracy in Europe, 1815–1914* (New York: Columbia University Press, 1992), pp. 192–194; Kiyanskaya, *Yuzhnyy bunt*, 27–30, 51–52.

[28] Keep, "The Origins of Russian Militarism," pp. 13–14; Keep, *Soldiers of the Tsar*, pp. 232–233, 247, 267–271.

[29] For a theoretical discussion, see Paul Pierson, "Not Just What, but *When*: Timing and Sequence in Political Processes," *Studies in American Political Development*, 14 (2000), 72–92.

[30] W. E. Mosse, *Perestroika Under the Tsars* (London: I. B. Tauris & Co. Ltd., 1992), pp. 16–22 (quote, p. 19). See also Saunders, *Russia in the Age*, pp. 116–203; Seton-Watson, *Russian Empire*, pp. 199–331; Fuller, *Strategy and Power*, pp. 219–264.

key role in bringing down Napoleon forty years earlier was no longer able to compete with its European rivals.[31]

Russia's humiliating defeat in the Crimean War is usually traced to Russian "backwardness."[32] This backwardness was technological, economic, social, and political. Russian weaponry and transportation technology had failed to keep up with advances in Europe.[33] Although Russia had begun to industrialize in the beginning of the nineteenth century, she lagged far behind her European rivals.[34] Russia's political and social institutions also suffered from stagnation and backwardness; most important in this respect was the institution of serfdom.[35]

Russia's defeat in the Crimean War and the problems of backwardness that the war made apparent served as a key impetus for the "Great Reforms" launched by Nicholas's successor, Alexander II (1855–1881). The most important of the reforms was the emancipation of the serfs in 1861. Other key reforms took place in the judicial, financial, military, administrative, and local government spheres. The Great Reforms had a complex series of motivations, but there can be little doubt that the need to remain competitive with the other European great powers played an important role in the thinking of Alexander II and many of his key officials.[36]

The Great Reforms of Alexander II marked the delayed beginning of Russia's attempt to adapt to the imperatives of the French and Industrial revolutions and to catch up with its European competitors. This process would dominate Russian history in the last fifty years of the Empire, leading

[31] Pintner, "Burden of Defense"; Pintner, "Russia as a Great Power"; Fuller, *Strategy and Power*, pp. 238–243, 252–264; John Shelton Curtiss, *The Russian Army Under Nicholas I, 1825–1855* (Durham, NC: Duke University Press, 1965).

[32] Fuller, *Strategy and Power*, especially pp. xvii–xx; Pintner, "Russia as a Great Power"; Mosse, *Perestroika Under the Tsars*, pp. 4–15. The classic treatment is Alexander Gerschenkron, "Economic Backwardness in Historical Perspective," in Bert F. Hoselitz, ed., *The Progress of Underdeveloped Areas* (Chicago, IL: University of Chicago Press, 1952), pp. 3–29.

[33] McNeill, *Pursuit of Power*, pp. 223–261; Paul Kennedy, *The Rise and Fall of the Great Powers: Economic Change and Military Conflict from 1500 to 2000* (London: Fontana Press, 1989 (1988)), pp. 218–228.

[34] Kennedy, *Rise and Fall*, pp. 218–221; Mosse, *Perestroika Under the Tsars*, pp. 19–20.

[35] Saunders, *Russia in the Age*, pp. 133–143; Mosse, *Perestroika Under the Tsars*, pp. 17–20; Keep, *Soldiers of the Tsar*, pp. 352–353; Alfred J. Reiber, "Alexander II: A Revisionist View," *Journal of Modern History*, 43 (1971), 45–51.

[36] D. C. B. Lieven, *Russia and the Origins of the First World War* (London: Macmillan, 1983), p. 5; Reiber, "Alexander II"; Jacob W. Kipp and W. Bruce Lincoln, "Autocracy and Reform: Bureaucratic Absolutism and Political Modernization in Nineteenth-Century Russia," in Hamburg, *Imperial Russian History II*, pp. 1–21; Mosse, *Perestroika Under the Tsars*, pp. 21, 51–52. Several authors have noted the similarity between the Great Reforms of Alexander II and Mikhail Gorbachev's policies of perestroika: Mosse, *Perestroika Under the Tsars*; Valerie Bunce, "Domestic Reform and International Change: The Gorbachev Reforms in Historical Perspective," *International Organization*, 47 (1993), 107–138; Dominic Lieven, *Nicholas II: Twilight of the Empire* (New York: St. Martin's Press, 1993), pp. 254–259.

up to the Revolution of 1917. The Russian political elite, and most importantly the state bureaucracy, understood that modernization was essential to Russia's standing as a great power. They also understood that modernization would lead to social, economic, and political changes that could undermine domestic order. Throughout this period the autocracy sought to both advance and control Russia's modernization.[37]

Russian industrialization had an important impact on social and class structure. It weakened the landed aristocracy and led to an explosion of the urban working class.[38] The number of factory workers and miners increased from 800,000 in 1860 to over three million in 1914. The expansion of the industrial working class, in conditions of poverty and urban squalor, was a fertile base for urban strikes and unrest. Workers' confrontations with their employers often led to confrontation with the autocracy because of the government's heavy involvement in managing labor protest and suppressing strikes. These factors contributed to the spread of revolutionary socialism among the working class and political challenges to the Tsarist state.[39]

Political modernization not only entailed changes in the economy and social structure, but also provided the basis of legitimation for the state. Russia's last tsars (Alexander II, Alexander III, and Nicholas II), however, were reluctant to change the traditional ideology of statist autocracy. The tsars believed that only they could maintain social and political order while directing the modernization effort. Liberalization and democratization were out of the question for the Romanov rulers.[40] Nationalism, which increasingly served as the basis for political legitimation and social integration elsewhere in Europe, was unable to play a comparable role in Russia. Part of the problem, of course, was the fact that at the turn of the century more than half the population of the Russian empire was non-Russian. Even more important was the mutual mistrust between educated society and the tsarist state, which deprived the regime of a potentially promising source of support.[41]

---

[37] My thinking on these issues has been greatly influenced by the work of Dominic Lieven. See Lieven, *Nicholas II*, pp. 1–21, 253–262; Lieven, *Russia and the Origins*, pp. 5–24; Dominic Lieven, *Russia's Rulers Under the Old Regime* (New Haven: Yale University Press, 1989), pp. 23–26, 277–308. See also Kipp and Lincoln, "Autocracy and Reform."

[38] On the aristocracy, see Roberta Manning, *The Crisis of the Old Regime in Russia* (Princeton, NJ: Princeton University Press, 1982); Lieven, *Nicholas II*, pp. 15–16; Lieven, *Russia's Rulers*, pp. 296–298; Pipes, *Russia Under the Old Regime*, p. 190.

[39] Peter Gatrell, *The Tsarist Economy 1850–1917* (London: B. T. Batsford Ltd., 1986), p. 86; Reginald E. Zelnick, "Russian Workers and the Revolutionary Movement: Essay Review," *Journal of Social History*, 6 (1972/73), 214–236; Gaston V. Rimlinger, "The Management of Labour Protest in Tsarist Russia, 1870–1905," *International Review of Social History*, 5 (1960), 226–248; S. A. (Stephen Anthony) Smith, *Red Petrograd: Revolution in the Factories, 1917–1918* (Cambridge, England: Cambridge University Press, 1983), pp. 37–41.

[40] Kipp and Lincoln, "Autocracy and Reform."

[41] Hans Rogger, "Nationalism and the State: A Russian Dilemma," *Comparative Study of Society and History*, 4 (1962), 253–264; Astrid S. Tuminez, *Russian Nationalism Since 1856: Ideology*

Political and economic development caused great strains on the Russian state from 1861 up to the turn of the century. Despite the state's best efforts to overcome Russia's backwardness and maintain its great power standing, the state found itself increasingly unable to compete with the powers of Western Europe, and particularly a unified Prussia after 1870. Russia's foreign failures during this period certainly did not help its standing at home; broad sectors of Russian society remained alienated from or hostile to the ruling autocracy. The state's political capacity continued to decline throughout this period, leading up to another humiliating defeat versus Japan in 1904–1905 and the Revolution of 1905–1906.[42]

The nineteenth century was a time of immense political, social, and military change for Russia. Russia's backwardness, which had been no hindrance and in some ways an advantage in its competition with its European rivals in the seventeenth and eighteenth centuries, increasingly was a major liability in the aftermath of the French and Industrial revolutions. The Great Reforms launched by Alexander II began the process of dismantling the service state and modernizing the economy, but also created new tensions and divisions in Russian society.

CIVIL–MILITARY RELATIONS AND THE END OF PRAETORIANISM

Russian civil–military relations were radically transformed in the nineteenth century. The officer corps was remade from an institution with a strong interventionist tradition into an apolitical body. How did this change happen?

Civil–military relations in Imperial Russia, of course, were in several respects very different from those in modern polities. Most important was the status of the tsar, who in many ways was more "military" than "civilian." Russian monarchs were at least formally serving colonels in an elite Guards regiment, and they conceived of themselves as the embodiment of Russian martial values. Officers swore allegiance to the tsar, and in the minds of many officers there was no real distinction between service to the nation and service to the autocracy.[43]

Although these distinctions need to be kept in mind, patterns of officer corps involvement in sovereign power issues still need to be studied and explained. After all, the military status of the tsar did not prevent palace

---

   and the Making of Foreign Policy (Lanham, MD: Rowman & Littlefield, 2000), pp. 25–171; Marc Raeff, "Some Reflections on Russian Liberalism," *Russian Review*, 18 (1959), 218–230; Michael Confino, "On Intellectuals and Intellectual Traditions in Eighteenth- and Nineteenth-Century Russia," in Hamburg, *Imperial Russian History II*, 123–155.

[42] I measure political capacity and state strength at the turn of the century in a more systematic fashion in Chapter 3.

[43] William C. Fuller, *Civil–Military Conflict in Imperial Russia, 1881–1914* (Princeton, NJ: Princeton University Press, 1985), pp. xxi–xxiii, 30–31. Fuller argues that, despite the tsar's unique status, civil–military conflict was extremely evident in the late Imperial period.

coups in the eighteenth century or the Decembrist uprising of 1825. The military was also intimately involved in the decision of Nicholas II to abdicate in 1917, as we will see in the next chapter. Sovereign power issues did not simply disappear in the nineteenth century; what changed was the role of the military in these events. Forces both internal and external to the army helped bring about this transformation in the Russian officer corps.

The failed Decembrist uprising of 1825 made the new tsar, Nicholas I, extremely attentive to the political attitudes of the officer corps. He took several steps to ensure his control over the armed forces, including a purge of the officer corps and the establishment of a secret chancellery (the Third Department) to monitor society and the bureaucracy, including the officer corps, for signs of political dissent. He also inculcated a rigid formalism in the army, with a focus on parade-ground discipline and the unthinking implementation of a superior's orders.[44]

Nicholas I's efforts to punish the military intelligentsia and impose strict discipline helped reinforce officer corps' lessons learned from the failed Decembrist uprising. The Decembrist failure led the military intelligentsia to confine its political activity to discussion clubs and to eschew revolutionary secret societies. Instead of seeking to overthrow the existing system, enlightened officers developed more moderate plans for military reform. During the 1830s and 1840s the involvement of army officers in liberal and radical underground organizations fell significantly, and the leadership of the intelligentsia passed to students and other civilians, who later spearheaded the movement against the autocracy.[45]

The reign of Nicholas I was in many ways a time of stagnation in both political and military spheres. Paradoxically, though, Nicholas helped lay the groundwork for the establishment of a more apolitical officer corps. His efforts to root out political dissent in the officer corps and compel their strict political obedience, although usually disparaged for undermining military initiative and innovation, did have salutary effects. Allen Wildman observes, "Nicholas I turned parade ground exercises, cruel discipline, and blind obedience into the foundation of the Army and of his reign. The enduring legacy was that very special aversion to politics, even to imperial politics, of the senior officers."[46]

The danger of praetorianism in Russia, although diminished during the reign of Nicholas I, was not eradicated. In the 1850s, and particularly after Russia's defeat in the Crimean War and the ascendance of Alexander II to

---

44 Curtiss, *Russian Army Under Nicholas I*, pp. 16–20, 112, 203, 368–369, *passim*; Fuller, *Strategy and Power*, pp. 238–243; Keep, *Soldiers of the Tsar*, pp. 275, 300, 314–315, 323–324, 342; Squire, *Third Department*; Monas, *Third Section*.
45 Keep, *Soldiers of the Tsar*, pp. 341–350; D'yakov, *Osvoboditel'noye dvizheniye*, pp. 19, 50–52.
46 Allan K. Wildman, *The End of the Russian Imperial Army: The Old Army and the Soldiers' Revolt*, Vol. I (Princeton, NJ: Princeton University Press, 1980), p. 11.

the throne, there was a rebirth of the military intelligentsia. This period was marked by a greater openness in Russian society and a general upsurge in excitement about the prospects for reform. Change was somewhat slow to come to the military sphere, however, as Alexander II appointed the conservative and cautious General N. O. Sukhozanet to the post of War Minister (1856–1861). His continuation of the stasis of the Nicholas period contributed to the growth of pent-up demand for change on the part of the officer corps. Defeat in the Crimean War also bolstered officers' desire for reform.[47]

The military intelligentsia of the 1850s and early 1860s were different, in several respects, from the Decembrists and the military intelligentsia under Alexander I. Most important, they were no longer the vanguard of the opposition movement; students and other civilians played this role. Professional concerns, which were not insignificant to the earlier generation, played an even larger role in the 1850s–1860s. Reformist officers sought not to remake society, but to recast the army as servants of the people and the state and not just the tsar.[48]

It is important to distinguish between two related but separate types of reform-minded officers in this period. There existed simultaneously both a younger and more radical military intelligentsia and a more senior and moderate coalition of "enlightened bureaucrats" in the officer corps. The younger group was most prominent in St. Petersburg and Warsaw. The vast majority (88%) of officers involved in the so-called revolutionary movement were junior officers, and seventy-five percent of them were twenty-five or younger in 1861.[49] These groups were also dominated by officers from the western borderlands (Poland, Belarus, Ukraine, and the Baltics); they account for seventy-three percent of the total participants. Some of these officers played a role in the Polish uprising of 1863. In general, though, these groups

---

[47] E. Willis Brooks, "Reform in the Russian Army, 1856–1861," *Slavic Review*, 43 (1984), 63–82; Keep, *Soldiers of the Tsar*, pp. 355–356; D'yakov, *Osvoboditel'noye dvizheniye*, pp. 36–37.

[48] Keep, *Soldiers of the Tsar*, pp. 357–364; Keep, "Chernyshevskii and the 'Military Miscellany'," *Power and the People*, pp. 267–292.

[49] V. A. D'yakov, "Chislennost' i sostav uchastnikov osvoboditel'nogo dvizheniya v russkoy armii v 1856–1865 gg. (opyt istoriko-sotsiologicheskogo issledovaniya)," *Istoriya SSSR*, No. 1, 1970, 27–43; V. A. D'yakov, "Peterburgskiye ofitserskiye organizatsii kontsa 50-x–nachala 60-x godov XIX veka i ikh rol' v istorii russko-pol'skikh revolyutsionnikh svyazey," in I. A. Khrenov, ed., *Iz istorii klassovoy bor'by i natsional'no-osvogoditel'nogo dvizheniya v slavyanskikh stranakh* (Moskva: "Nauka," 1964), pp. 281, 292–293, 296–297. The figure of 88 percent junior officers comes from some recalculations I made from Table 1 in "Chislennost'." Specifically, I did not count, as D'yakov does, military doctors and veterinarians, civilians in the Ministry of War, and soldiers (nonofficers) from the nobility. I also excluded officers of unknown rank on the assumption that they would be distributed in rough proportion to those of known rank. Following standard Russian usage, junior officers (ober-ofitserov) are ensigns, lieutenants, and captains.

of younger officers confined their activity to discussing liberal and radical ideas current at the time. A young officer involved in a circle in Moscow noted that the Decembrist example showed the need to keep to small, self-contained groups.[50]

Although the tendency to form "revolutionary circles" may have been confined largely to junior officers, there was broader support for military, social, and political reform in the officer corps. This reform movement was led by a group of "enlightened bureaucrats," the most important of whom was Dmitriy Milyutin, Alexander II's War Minister from 1861 until 1881.[51] Milyutin had contacts with reformers in both the army and the civilian world, and in the 1840s and 1850s he met regularly with like-minded liberal thinkers. From 1845 until 1856 Milyutin was a professor at the Nicholas Academy of the General Staff (hereafter the General Staff Academy), and he was involved with efforts to reform military education. In 1858 Milyutin played a key role in gaining approval for a military journal that he believed could help raise the educational standards of the officer corps. The journal, *Voyenniy Sbornik* [*Military Digest*], pushed the cause of military reform and had considerable support in the officer corps.[52]

When Milyutin became War Minister in 1861 he was able to enact much of the program of military reform that he had developed while at the General Staff Academy. He introduced important changes in military administration, military education, and the General Staff system. Milyutin generally is credited with laying the basis for the creation of a professional officer corps drawn from all ranks of society with a well-grounded military education. In 1874 he succeeded in pushing through the system of universal conscription, which Milyutin considered critical if Russia was to remain competitive with the other European great powers.[53]

---

[50] D'yakov, "Chislennost'"; D'yakov, "Peterburgskiye ofitserskiye organizatsii"; V. A. D'yakov and I. S. Miller, *Revolyutsionnoye dvizheniye v russkoy armii i vosstaniye 1863 g.* (Moskva: "Nauka," 1964). The junior officer is quoted in: D'yakov, *Osvoboditel'noye dvizheniye*, p. 240. See also Keep, *Soldiers of the Tsar*, pp. 357–364.

[51] W. Bruce Lincoln, *In the Vanguard of Reform: Russia's Enlightened Bureaucrats 1825–1861* (DeKalb, IL: Northern Illinois University Press, 1982); Forrest A. Miller, *Dmitri Miliutin and the Reform Era in Russia* (Charlotte, NC: Vanderbilt University Press, 1968), especially pp. 3–25.

[52] Its first editor was the civilian Nikolay Chernyshevskiy, who went on to become one of the most influential members of the radical intelligentsia. This is not as strange as it sounds, because in the 1850s Milyutin and Chernyshevskiy were united by more views than those that divided them; it was only later that their paths sharply diverged. On the founding of *Voyenniy Sbornik* and the connection between Milyutin and Chernyshevskiy, see Keep, "Chernyshevskii and the 'Military Miscellany'"; E. Willis Brooks, "The Improbable Connection: D. A. Miljutin and N.G. Cernysevskij, 1848–1862," *Jahrbucher fur Geschichte Osteuropas*, 37 (1989), 21–44.

[53] Miller, *Dmitrii Miliutin*; P. A. Zayonchkovskiy, *Voyennye reformy 1860–1870 godov v Rossii* (Moskva: Moskovskiy Universitet, 1952); Fuller, *Strategy and Power*, pp. 265–347; Keep,

Milyutin was committed to reform from above and the role of the state as an engine of progress and modernization. The fact that Milyutin occupied the top spot in the War Ministry for twenty years was crucial, because officers committed to reform could carry the struggle into the bureaucracy. To the extent that there was a possibility for a rebirth of a more praetorian military intelligentsia in the late 1850s and early 1860s, it was largely cut off by the Milyutin reforms. Milyutin himself evidently saw the need to channel young officers into professional concerns and away from the revolutionary movement. In this goal he undoubtedly succeeded; after the Polish uprising of 1863 there were few instances of officer involvement in oppositional activities.[54]

The Milyutin reforms were a belated response to the transformation of warfare and society implied by the French Revolution and the Napoleonic Wars. They were part of a general European trend toward a better educated, more professional officer corps, devoting most of its energy to planning for external warfare.[55] The Great Reforms of Alexander II and Milyutin also marked the culmination of a trend toward greater "civilianization" of the Russian state that had begun in the eighteenth century but had moved very slowly until 1855. Until this point the army had played a large role in civilian administration and local government, and it had also run a system of military settlements through which large areas of the country were placed under military administration. Under Alexander II the traditional Russian service state was largely dismantled and the military was freed to concentrate more fully on its external functions. These changes in the Russian state in the

---

Soldiers of the Tsar, pp. 351–381; Bruce W. Menning, *Bayonets Before Bullets: The Imperial Russian Army, 1861–1914* (Bloomington, IN: Indiana University Press, 1992), pp. 6–50; Carl Van Dyke, *Russian Imperial Military Doctrine and Education, 1832–1914* (New York: Greenwood Press, 1990), pp. 49–90.

[54] Perhaps the best example of a leading officer whose energies were channeled into military reform and away from more radical political activities was N. N. Obruchev, who had been involved with the revolutionary organization "Land and Freedom" in the early 1860s while a captain and refused to participate in the suppression of the Polish uprising in 1863. Obruchev became one of Milyutin's right-hand men and later served as Chief of the Main Staff. See P. A. Zayonchkovskiy, *Samoderzhaviye i russkaya armiya na rubezhe XIX–XX stoletiy* (Moskva: "Mysl," 1973), pp. 61–63, especially note 140; David Alan Rich, *The Tsar's Colonels: Professionalism, Strategy, and Subversion in Late Imperial Russia* (Cambridge, MA: Harvard University Press, 1998), pp. 45–55, 225, 243; Menning, *Bayonets Before Bullets*, pp. 17–21, 90, 96–98; Fuller, *Strategy and Power*, pp. 282–283, 317; Miller, *Dmitrii Miliutin*, pp. 142–152, 228–230; Brooks, "The Improbable Connection"; Van Dyke, *Russian Imperial Military Doctrine*, pp. 50–51, 58; Zayonchkovskiy, *Voyennye reformy*, pp. 41–44, 221–222; Keep, *Soldiers of the Tsar*, pp. 363–364.

[55] Howard, *War in European History*, pp. 75–115; Samuel P. Huntington, *The Soldier and the State: The Theory and Politics of Civil–Military Relations* (Cambridge, MA: Belknap Press/Harvard University Press, 1957), pp. 19–58.

nineteenth century were also consistent with general processes in European state building. As John Keep remarks, "a modern state needed to be ruled by officials, not by officers."[56]

After the Crimean War debacle the Russian officer corps experienced a loss of confidence and prestige. This low self-confidence made it more difficult for the army to believe that it had the competence and the right to intervene in political matters. The German army, in contrast, was emboldened to play a prominent role in domestic politics in part because of their military successes.[57] The declining prestige of the officer corps in Russia also meant that the most ambitious members of society pursued careers in the civilian world, not in the military. General M. I. Dragomirov, the Commandant of the General Staff Academy from 1878 to 1889, noted that the military attracted many "weak-charactered" young men who entered the army only because they had no other prospects and argued that there should be no place for these "losers" (*neudachniki*) in the military. The lack of prestige and self-confidence contributed to a more distant and passive attitude toward high politics and society in general, a temperament that William Fuller labels "negative corporatism."[58]

An additional factor in the decline of officer prestige, in addition to military defeat, was the worsening economic situation faced by officers. In the eighteenth and early nineteenth centuries the material position of officers was still considered respectable. Their economic situation, however, worsened in the second half of the nineteenth century. The state had more important priorities, particularly industrialization, and the general decline of the nobility made it more difficult for officers from that class to support themselves independently of their officer salary, as they had been able to do previously.[59]

---

[56] Keep, *Soldiers of the Tsar*, pp. 275–381 (quote, p. 307); Keep, "Paul I and the Militarization of Government" and "The Military Style of the Romanov Rulers," in *Power and the People*, pp. 175–209. On state making in Europe, and the process of civilianization, see Tilly, *Coercion, Capital, and European States*, especially pp. 122–126.

[57] I owe this point to Dominic Lieven. See Lieven, *Aristocracy in Europe*, pp. 181–202. On the German officer corps, see Gordon A. Craig, *The Politics of the Prussian Army, 1640–1945* (Oxford, England: Oxford University Press, 1955); Martin Kitchen, *The German Officer Corps, 1890–1914* (Oxford, England: Clarendon Press, 1968).

[58] Zayonchkovskiy, *Samoderzhaviye i russkaya armiya*, p. 176; Fuller, *Civil–Military Conflict*, pp. 26–29, 46, 216–217. See also Pintner, "The Burden of Defense," pp. 257–259; Wildman, *End of the Russian Imperial Army*, I, pp. 10–11; John Bushnell, "The Tsarist Officer Corps, 1881–1914: Customs, Duties, Inefficiency," *American Historical Review*, 86 (1981), 753–780; S. V. Volkov, *Russkiy ofitserskiy korpus* (Moskva: Voyennoye izdatel'stvo, 1993), pp. 35–36, 294.

[59] Volkov, *Russkiy ofitserskiy korpus*, pp. 241–247; Zayonchkovskiy, *Samoderzhaviye i russkaya armiya*, pp. 219–228; Fuller, *Civil–Military Conflict*, pp. 47–74; Kenez, "Profile of the Prerevolutionary," pp. 129–130.

The noble element in the officer corps declined steeply in the second half of the nineteenth century. This was consistent with Milyutin's efforts to transform the officer corps into a meritocracy based on learning and talent rather than social standing. By 1912 roughly half of the officer corps was drawn from the non-nobility. Of course, the nobility still dominated certain sectors of the armed forces, such as the elite Guards units. Although the Guards had been a major threat to the sovereign in the eighteenth century, by the late Imperial period they were a bulwark of the autocracy. The growing crisis of the Russian state underscored their common interests vis-à-vis the broad mass of Russian society. Guards units, however, represented only four percent of the armed forces, and these officers had little in common with average officers, let alone the enlisted personnel.[60]

Most of the comparative civil–military relations literature contends that class and social background are not good predictors of officer corps' political behavior. The exception has been the literature on German civil–military relations before World War I. The German army also came to be dominated by non-nobles (70% in 1913) on the eve of World War I, but the Germans were much more successful in forging a unified officer corps still committed to an aristocratic outlook. This literature, then, indirectly confirms the general finding that social background does not determine political behavior, because it argues that the officer corps retained an aristocratic outlook despite the fact that the German army recruited increasingly from the middle class. In Russia the social differences in the officer corps were so great that creating this esprit de corps was not possible.[61]

The general picture that emerges of the officer corps in the last decades of the Russian Empire is of an institution in serious decline. Military interests were less influential in the making of state policy. The officer corps suffered from falling living standards and low public prestige. They were increasingly isolated, and self-isolated, from the rest of elite society. This marks a sharp contrast with their standing at the beginning of the century, during which

---

[60] Kenez, "A Profile of the Prerevolutionary Officer Corps"; Wildman, *End of the Russian Imperial Army*, I, pp. 5–10, 19–24; Volkov, *Russkiy ofitserskiy korpus*, pp. 266–273; Zayonchkovskiy, *Samoderzhaviye i russkaya armiya*, pp. 202–214; Fuller, *Civil–Military Conflict*, pp. xxiv, 15–22.

[61] George A. Kourvetaris and Betty A. Dobratz, *Social Origins and Political Orientations in a World Perspective* (Denver, CO: University of Denver, 1973); Bengt Abrahamsson, *Military Professionalization and Political Power* (Beverly Hills, CA: Sage Publications, 1972), pp. 40–58; Alfred Stepan, *The Military in Politics: Changing Patterns in Brazil* (Princeton, NJ: Princeton University Press, 1971), pp. 30–56. A class-based explanation for officer corps behavior is a type of domestic structure argument. On the German army, see Craig, *Politics of the Prussian Army*, especially pp. 217–254; Kitchen, *German Officer Corps*; V. R. Berghahn, *Germany and the Approach of War in 1914* (New York: St. Martin's Press, 1973), pp. 3, 7–8, 13–17. For a comparison of Russia, Germany, and Britain, see Lieven, *Aristocracy in Europe*, pp. 181–202.

they were in important ways the leading element in both the state and in the state's primary opponents (the intelligentsia).[62]

The apolitical nature of the Russian officer corps in the late-imperial period is a subject of broad agreement in the existing literature. Western scholars, Soviet scholars, and post-Soviet Russian scholars have all pointed to the disinterest and even naïveté of officers concerning political matters.[63] This issue will be examined more systematically in the next chapter.

How did this crucial change come about? Several factors stand out. The "critical event" of the failure of the Decembrist uprising was an important institutional lesson. Perhaps even more important was the stewardship of Milyutin as War Minister for twenty years.[64] He created a home for reform-minded officers who previously had sought outlets in secret societies. The army began to extract itself from many internal commitments and devoted itself to preparation for external warfare. The efforts of Nicholas I to remake officer corps culture and "coup-proof" his army also contributed to this transformation.[65] Finally, consistent with the international structure approach, a challenging external threat environment, as demonstrated by the Crimean War and the Franco–Prussian War, brought home for officers the importance of greater efforts to protect the state and develop their capabilities.[66]

THE ROMANOVS AND THE ARMY, 1856–1906

The extent to which Russian civil–military relations had changed, and the army had become not a threat but a bulwark to the sitting tsar, is

---

[62] Fuller, *Civil–Military Conflict*; Zayonchkovskiy, *Samoderzhaviye i russkaya armiya*; Pintner, "Burden of Defense"; Bushnell, "Tsarist Officer Corps"; Volkov, *Russkiy ofitserskiy korpus*, pp. 97–98, 294; John L. H. Keep, *Soldiering in Tsarist Russia* (Colorado: United States Air Force Academy, 1986).

[63] Examples include: Zayonchkovskiy, *Samoderzhaviye i russkaya armiya*, pp. 75, 233–234, 317–318; Volkov, *Russkiy ofitserskiy korpus*, pp. 287–288; Kenez, "Profile of the Prerevolutionary," pp. 150–158; Oliver Allen Ray, "The Imperial Russian Army Officer," *Political Science Quarterly*, 76 (1961), 576–592; Raymond L. Garthoff, *Soviet Military Policy: A Historical Analysis* (New York: Praeger, 1966), pp. 29–41.

[64] The organizational culture literature stresses the role of organizational leaders in affecting cultural change. In addition to the discussion in Chapter 1, see Philip Selznick, *Leadership in Administration: A Sociological Interpretation* (Berkeley, CA: University of California Press, 1957).

[65] On the ability of civilian leaders to reorient military behavior, see Alfred Stepan, *Rethinking Military Politics: Brazil and the Southern Cone* (Princeton, NJ: Princeton University Press, 1988), pp. 93–102; Barry R. Posen, *The Sources of Military Doctrine: France, Britain, and Germany Between the World Wars* (Ithaca, NY: Cornell University Press, 1984), especially pp. 53–59, 74–79; Deborah D. Avant, *Political Institutions and Military Change: Lessons from Peripheral Wars* (Ithaca, NY: Cornell University Press, 1994), especially 6–18.

[66] Note, however, that a high threat environment did not have this effect in the eighteenth century.

demonstrated by an examination of two separate cases of military behavior in sovereign power issues in the second half of the nineteenth century and the early twentieth century. The first is the three Romanov successions between 1855 and 1894, and the second is the Russian Revolution of 1905–1906.

The Romanov Successions

The remarkable thing about the successions of Alexander II and III and Nicholas II is their complete unremarkability. Most studies of military coups would skate right by them. But that would be a mistake, because something had clearly changed from eighteenth-century Russia.

Nicholas I died in the middle of the Crimean War in 1855 and was succeeded without incident by his son Alexander II. Alexander II's death was even more of a potential crisis; after several failed attempts on his life, he was assassinated by a terrorist bomb in 1881. His son Alexander III assumed the throne. Finally, Nicholas II took power uneventfully in 1894 when his father died.

Prior to Alexander II, every Russian leader going back to before Peter the Great had either come to power through the use of military power or faced a successful or unsuccessful attempt to remove him or her with military force. That the armed forces were now unquestioningly swearing their loyalty to each new tsar was something new.

The Revolution of 1905–1906

The tsarist regime defeated the revolution of 1905–1906 with a combination of political concessions and coercive military force.[67] The fact that the military saved the regime could be seen as an instance of military arbitration of a civilian sovereign power dispute, although the government's opponents did not occupy any positions of state power and thus were not, in a formal sense, legitimate contenders for executive leadership. The military never was called upon to make a choice between two specific individuals or groups that both could make a serious claim to state leadership. For this reason, military behavior during the revolution of 1905–1906 is best seen as a case of military nonintervention. The army carried out, albeit reluctantly and with difficulty, the orders of their civilian leaders. Not to do so would have qualified as insubordination. The military in 1905–1906 remained loyal and obedient.

The use of the armed forces to counter domestic unrest was not a new phenomenon in Russia. The army had been involved in internal repression on behalf of the autocracy for centuries. Until the middle of the nineteenth century the army's domestic role had been confined primarily to suppressing peasant revolts. With the growth of an urban working class in the late

---

[67] For a brief overview, see Lieven, *Nicholas II*, pp. 132–160.

nineteenth century, the military was forced to become involved in strike and riot breaking as well. The army ever more frequently was summoned by civilian officials to restore order. Incidents of troops being called to the aid of civil power averaged 83 times per year for the period 1890–1894, 147 times per year for the period 1895–1899, and 312 times per year for the period 1900–1904. These missions caused increasing strain on the army.[68]

The leadership of the armed forces objected to the growing usage of the army for domestic repression. The internal mission seriously interfered with the military's primary task, namely, training and preparation for external war. The growing power of Germany was a particular concern for the military leadership. The Ministry of War, the Main Staff, and local Military District commanders all objected to the burdens of internal repression and frequently clashed with civilian officials. Army unhappiness with domestic repression, however, did not lead to officer corps' insubordination, and they remained loyal to the autocracy.[69]

This simmering conflict over the military's role came to a head in 1905. Russia suffered a humiliating defeat in the Russo-Japanese War of 1904–1905. Growing domestic turmoil, partially triggered by the defeat by Japan, burst forth as full-scale revolution in 1905. The armed forces found themselves completely overextended, with 800,000 soldiers tied down in the east and hundreds of thousands more involved in internal repression in European Russia.[70]

The army saved the government from collapse in 1905–1906. Yet it did so almost against the wishes of the military leadership and with widespread mutinies among the troops themselves. The War Ministry lost control over its commanders, who acted at the behest of local civilian officials rather than the central military administration. The Prime Minister, Sergey Witte, and the Interior Ministry devised a plan in early 1906 for frequent and decentralized deployment of army units, not only for repression of actual disorder but also deterrence. Although the War Ministry objected to this loss of control and its effect on military efficiency and even coherence, it ultimately acquiesced, with certain provisos, because of the severity of the internal threat to the regime. It was not until 1908 that the War Ministry was able to once again reassert meaningful control over its own troops.[71]

---

[68] Fuller, *Civil–Military Conflict*, pp. 81–93; John Bushnell, *Mutiny amid Repression: Russian Soldiers in the Revolution of 1905–1906* (Bloomington: Indiana University Press, 1985), pp. 31–32; Zayonchkovskiy, *Samoderzhaviye i russkaya armiya*, pp. 33–35.

[69] Fuller, *Civil–Military Conflict*, especially pp. 75–100; Bushnell, *Mutiny amid Repression*, pp. 24–32.

[70] Fuller, *Strategy and Power*, pp. 394–407; Fuller, *Civil–Military Conflict*, p. 144; Bushnell, *Mutiny amid Repression*, p. 52.

[71] Fuller, *Civil–Military Conflict*, pp. 129–168; Bushnell, *Mutiny amid Repression*.

Theoretical Perspectives

These two cases are more amenable to theoretical explanation than the previous ones. By the second half of the nineteenth century, an officer corps distinct from the ruling elite, with a reasonably strong corporate identity, had appeared in Russia. Structural opportunities for intervention existed, and there were growing corporate motives for intervention. Organizational culture seems to provide the best explanation for nonintervention in this period.

Opportunity. The domestic structure explanation is of mixed utility. The succession mechanism clearly functioned more reliably, but it is not obvious why it was more respected at the end of the century than it was at the beginning. What is striking is that military intervention declined as state political capacity weakened in the second half of the nineteenth century. The state was increasingly threatened by societal forces it could not control, which culminated in the revolution of 1905–1906. A weak state and political instability were necessary conditions for the important internal role played by the armed forces during the revolution, but, although the state was on the verge of collapse, the military showed no interest whatsoever in capturing sovereign power.

Organizational structure may have played a limited role in encouraging military passivity in this period. Specifically, the employment of secret police to monitor the officer corps may have hindered coup plotting. For example, the Ministry of Internal Affairs investigated secret societies in the General Staff Academy until 1872.[72] But there was no separate ministry with the forces capable of counterbalancing an organized military coup. Moreover, an important component of the secret police, the Gendarmes, were notionally subordinate to the Ministry of War and often headed by a military general.[73] The Ministry of Internal Affairs concentrated its efforts on the civilian opposition. A well-organized military plot would not have faced significant resistance. More to the point, perhaps, were the serious internal splits within the officer corps, although in other countries these often are a spur, not a deterrent, to military intervention.

Motive. The corporate interest perspective performs rather poorly. In the second half of the nineteenth century the Russian armed forces were experiencing significant organizational decline. Both their political power and their material resources were being curtailed at this time, yet no resistance was offered other than bureaucratic lobbying. The army's desire for organizational autonomy also was seriously undermined by frequent internal missions.

---

[72] Rich, *The Tsar's Colonels*, p. 245, note 32.
[73] Charles A. Ruud and Sergei A. Stepanov, *Fontanka 16: The Tsars' Secret Police* (Montreal: McGill-Queen's University Press, 1999), pp. 19, 23.

Organizational culture has considerable merit as an explanation for military behavior during this period. The transformation of this culture that took place in the nineteenth century from praetorian to apolitical seemingly served as a guide to army behavior. Moreover, during the revolution of 1905–1906, beliefs about the proper role of the armed forces loomed large in the considerations of leading officers. Domestic repression was seen as an interference with the military's primary task, namely, external defense. At the same time, military leaders continued to adhere to the idea that they were subordinate to the autocracy and had to carry out its wishes, even if the army did so reluctantly. To determine exactly how important the norm of civilian supremacy was in explaining military behavior would require a more concerted investigation than the one undertaken here; so far the evidence presented has been somewhat impressionistic. In the next chapter, officer corps culture for the early twentieth century is measured more systematically, and the evidence strongly supports the conclusions offered here.

CONCLUSION

This chapter has presented an overview of the development of the Russian state and civil–military relations during the Imperial period. The discussion of Russian state development highlighted the power of the Russian state from Peter the Great until Nicholas I. From the time of the Great Reforms of Alexander II, however, the political capacity of the state was challenged by the pressures of political, economic, and social modernization.

In the sphere of civil–military relations, the key development was the shift in the nineteenth century from a military that traditionally had been heavily involved in sovereign power issues to one that was largely apolitical by the beginning of the twentieth century. This change can be traced to organizational lessons learned after the Decembrist uprising, Nicholas I's efforts to create a politically obedient officer corps, and especially the military reforms of Dmitriy Milyutin. The pressures of the external environment, particularly the European great power competition, also helped reorient the armed forces toward international missions and away from a domestic political role. The change in Russian civil–military relations in the nineteenth century set the stage for the revolutions of the early twentieth century, during which the army could neither save the existing regime nor establish one of its own. The Bolshevik victory in 1917–1920, the subject of the next chapter, was the ultimate result.

3

The Army and the Revolution, 1917

The control and use of coercive power was central to the dramatic events of the Russian Revolution of 1917 and the bloody civil war that followed. The Bolsheviks would not have succeeded if they had faced concerted resistance on the part of the Imperial Russian armed forces. The army was of necessity a crucial actor in the revolution. The four sovereign power issues in which the military was involved were the February Revolution, the Kornilov affair in late August, the October Revolution, and the Civil War.

The February Revolution forced the abdication of the tsar in early March 1917. The military was thrust into the arbiter role by the three-way standoff between the tsar, the revolutionary forces, and the leaders of the political opposition in the State Duma, the Russian parliament. The military leadership refused to stand behind Nicholas II during the crisis because of their fear that if order was not soon restored the revolution would spread to the front and endanger the war effort.

The Kornilov affair refers to the conflict between the Commander in Chief of the army, General Lavr Kornilov, and the head of the Provisional Government, Alexander Kerensky. In late August, Kerensky accused Kornilov of planning a coup and treason. Kornilov had not in fact been planning to seize power, but Kerensky's accusation drove him into open rebellion, and Kornilov and several other leading officers were arrested. Most officers, however, sat out the affair.

The military leadership was again faced with a major political decision when the Bolsheviks seized power in October 1917. The military high command, with one significant exception, did initially follow Kerensky's orders to move troops to Petrograd to quash the Bolshevik uprising. However, once it became clear that the Provisional Government had collapsed, the military made no serious efforts to resist the Bolshevik take-over in Petrograd or at military headquarters a month later.

The final case is the Civil War, in which the Bolsheviks struggled to hold on to power in the face of the military challenges of the Whites, who were led by former Tsarist officers. Former officers also were well represented on the Red side, and the ability of the Soviet government to mobilize these officers on their behalf was a crucial element in the Bolshevik victory.

Table 3.1 shows that the military was a key participant in all of these events. When examined in depth, however, the most striking thing about these cases is how *passive* the military was in the face of obvious threats to its fundamental interests. Even the Kornilov affair, coded as a case of military intervention, came about only after, through a bizarre series of circumstances, the Prime Minister reneged on his commitments to the military leadership and accused its top general of treason. The military was largely a reluctant participant in the events of the revolution, up until the outbreak of civil war in 1918, at which point all officers were forced to decide which side they were on. Throughout 1917, most officers were focused on the war with Germany and the Austro-Hungarian Empire and sought to remain "outside politics."

Army behavior is best explained through a combination of opportunities and motives. The weakness of the state during the revolution created the conditions under which military involvement in sovereign power issues arose. Organizational structure is a less reliable guide to behavior; the most important factor in these terms was the divide between officers and enlisted men, a cleavage absent from theoretical discussions of military coups. Corporate interest only in a very broad sense was an important motive behind army activity – the desire to keep the army and the state from collapsing in the midst of war. Organizational culture was a fundamental determinant of officer corps behavior in 1917, but it also was violated on several occasions by some officers, who believed that without military intervention the country would collapse.

Any attempt to account for military activity in this case, then, runs up against the basic problem that theories of military involvement in sovereign power issues were not designed to explain how an army would respond to a far-reaching revolution in the midst of total war.[1] Such extreme internal and external pressures on the military are historically rare. What these cases lack in comparative similarity, however, is more than compensated for by their drama and richness.

OPPORTUNITIES FOR INTERVENTION, 1917

Opportunities for military involvement in sovereign power issues were quite broad prior to 1917. These expanded even further during and after the February Revolution. It was the extreme weakness of the Russian state that led to army participation in domestic political struggles. At the same time, internal fragmentation within the armed forces made concerted action

[1] I know of only one book on the specific question of civil–military relations and revolution: Katharine Chorley, *Armies and the Art of Revolution* (Boston, MA: Beacon Press, 1973 (1943)).

TABLE 3.1. *Chapter Summary*

| Observations | Opportunity | | Motive | | | Outcome |
	Domestic Structure	Organizational Structure	Corporate Interest	Organizational Culture		
Abdication of the Tsar	Intervention or arbitration likely.	Intervention unlikely. If arbitration, concerted action likely.	Intervention unlikely. If arbitration, will side with contender most likely to promote corporate interests.	Intervention unlikely. Praetorian subculture. If arbitration, first choice is neutrality and second choice is side with most legitimate contender.		Arbitration. Unable to remain neutral. Took position least likely to interfere with war effort. Troops and officers split.
Kornilov Affair	Intervention or arbitration likely.	Intervention unlikely.	Intervention likely.	Intervention unlikely. Praetorian subculture.		Intervention, but no coup plot.
October Revolution	Intervention or arbitration likely.	Intervention unlikely. If arbitration, internal splits likely.	Intervention likely. If arbitration, will side with contender most likely to promote corporate interests.	Intervention unlikely. Praetorian subculture. If arbitration, first choice is neutrality and second choice is side with most legitimate contender.		Nonintervention and arbitration. Internal split. Officer arbitrating took position that involvement was not military's job and would disrupt war effort.
Civil War	Intervention or arbitration likely.	Intervention unlikely.	Intervention likely.	Intervention unlikely. Praetorian subculture.		Intervention.

difficult. Most significant in this respect was the political mobilization of the rank and file after February.

Domestic Structure

The question of the political capacity of the Tsarist state on the eve of war and revolution is extremely contentious. The majority view is that the Tsarist state was quite weak in the early twentieth century; even without the war, further upheavals were likely. In this section I summarize the debate on the strength of the late-Imperial state and then turn to a closer examination of political capacity in the revolutionary year of 1917. There is quite widespread agreement that by 1917, and certainly after the February Revolution, the Russian state was extremely weak. There were clear opportunities for military activity. The domestic structure approach, then, would predict both military involvement and intervention in sovereign power issues during 1917.

The historiographical literature on the Russian Revolution asserts that until recently there was a strong consensus among Western historians that between 1905 and 1914 the Russian state had made important strides toward political and social stabilization. Only the outbreak of the war, according to the traditional view (sometimes called the "liberal" interpretation), detoured Russia's constitutional development and led to the revolution of 1917.[2]

This interpretation, however, is not as dominant as most scholars contend. Leading historians associated with the traditional view, such as Leonard Schapiro and Robert Daniels, are quite cautious in their assessment of Russian political stability. Daniels, for example, concludes that the Russian Empire on the eve of World War I was characterized by "sickness at the top and the strains of a half-developed society below."[3] Other scholars sympathetic to this view, such as Richard Pipes, Dominic Lieven, and Martin Malia, also are quite pessimistic about the prospects for the development of constitutional democracy in Russia, even in the absence of war.[4] Most agree that continued state weakness and political disorder were more likely in the coming decades than social and political stability.

---

[2] For this picture of the dominant orthodoxy, see Leopold Haimson, "The Problem of Social Stability in Urban Russia, 1905–1917 (Part One)," *Slavic Review*, 23 (1964), 619–623; Edward Acton, *Rethinking the Russian Revolution* (London: Edward Arnold, 1990), pp. 35–39, 52–55; Richard Pipes, "1917 and the Revisionists," *The National Interest*, 31 (1993), 70–72.

[3] Leonard Schapiro, *1917: The Russian Revolutions and the Origins of Present-Day Communism* (Harmondsworth, Middlesex: Penguin Books, 1984), pp. 1–14; Robert V. Daniels, *Red October: The Bolshevik Revolution of 1917* (New York: Charles Scribner's Sons, 1967), pp. 8–9.

[4] Pipes, "1917 and the Revisionists," p. 72; Richard Pipes, *The Russian Revolution* (New York: Alfred A. Knopf, 1990), pp. 193–194; Dominic Lieven, *Nicholas II: Twilight of the Empire* (New York: St. Martin's Press, 1993), pp. 186–190; Dominic Lieven, *Russia's Rulers under the Old Regime* (New Haven, CT: Yale University Press, 1989), pp. 277–308; Martin Malia, *The Soviet Tragedy: A History of Socialism in Russia, 1917–1991* (New York: The Free Press, 1994), pp. 69–70, 81–87.

Recent so-called "revisionist" history has further demonstrated that the Russian state was marked by fatal contradictions even before 1914.[5] By 1914, Russian society was dangerously polarized between the upper and lower classes in a manner that became evident in 1917. The war exacerbated but did not cause this fundamental split.[6] The peasantry demanded the redistribution of noble estates, and agricultural reforms had probably increased, rather than decreased, peasant discontent. The working class was radicalized, partially because the regime restricted the development of free trade unions and thus helped transform economic grievances into political conflicts. The middle class was weak and divided, and the rural nobility was in serious decline. Even without the war, the revisionists conclude, the autocracy was in serious trouble.[7]

World War I placed further strains on the Russian polity. Russian military defeats in 1915 led to despair among the elites, who blamed Russia's difficulties on bureaucratic incompetence. Rumors in Petersburg society about the influence of Tsarina Alexandra and the "holy man" Rasputin on government policy further weakened the autocracy. Most important, the war was causing increasing strains on the economy, evidenced by inflation, supply problems, and dangerous food shortages in the cities.[8]

By the end of 1916 the economic situation in Petrograd (the capital's name had been changed from the German-sounding St. Petersburg) had become critical. Police reports from late 1916 and early 1917 predicted that inflation and food shortages were likely to spark riots. The number of strikes in Petrograd increased sharply in the fall and winter of 1916–1917, reaching levels comparable to the massive strikes of 1914. A police report from October 1916 concluded, "the ever growing disorder in the rear, or in other words in the entire country, which is chronic and cumulative, has now attained such an extraordinarily rapid rate of growth that it now ... menaces shortly to throw the country into catastrophically destructive chaos and spontaneous anarchy."[9]

---

[5] The "revisionist" label is now something of a misnomer, since this interpretation of the Russian Revolution is currently the dominant approach. Two good introductions are Ronald Grigor Suny, "Toward a Social History of the October Revolution," *American Historical Review*, 88 (1983), 31–52; Acton, *Rethinking the Russian Revolution*.

[6] Haimson, "The Problem of Social Stability (Part One)"; Leopold Haimson, "The Problem of Social Stability in Urban Russia, 1905–1917 (Part Two)," *Slavic Review*, 24 (1965), 1–22.

[7] Acton, *Rethinking the Russian Revolution*, pp. 55–82.

[8] Lieven, *Nicholas II*, pp. 204–233; Tsuyoshi Hasegawa, *The February Revolution: Petrograd, 1917* (Seattle, WA: University of Washington Press, 1981), pp. 3–211.

[9] Quoted in D. A. Longley, "Iakovlev's Question, or the Historiography of the Problem of Spontaneity and Leadership in the Russian Revolution of February 1917," in Edith Rogovin Frankel, Jonathan Frankel, and Baruch Knei-Paz, eds., *Revolution in Russia: Reassessments of 1917* (Cambridge, England: Cambridge University Press, 1992), p. 383, note 4. See also Hasegawa, *February Revolution*, pp. 198–211; S. A. Smith, *Red Petrograd: Revolution in the Factories 1917–1918* (Cambridge, England: Cambridge University Press, 1983), pp. 44–53;

There is a fairly broad consensus, then, that by the beginning of 1917 the Tsarist regime was quite weak. Most observers attribute this weakness to deep-rooted cleavages in Russian society, while some argue that they were caused by the war. With this background in mind, I now turn to a more systematic analysis of the indicators used to measure state strength. The data are mixed on the period before the February revolution, but after that point it is not surprising that all of the measures of political capacity indicate a very weak state.

Organizational Age. Organizational age has three components: the age of the juridical state, the age of the current constitutional order, and the number of top leadership successions in that order. The exact age of the Russian state is perhaps subject to debate; but even if one starts counting from the time of Peter the Great, the state was over 200 years old by 1917. The Russian constitutional order in 1917 was only eleven years old, because the Revolution of 1905–1906 had forced Nicholas II to grant a new constitution. The tsar's official title was still "autocrat," but the Chairman of the Council of Ministers and the new legislature, consisting of the Duma and the State Council, represented potential rivals to the emperor. The tsar, however, appointed the Prime Minister, and Nicholas II was not inclined to turn executive decision-making authority over to his ministers. The new constitution also failed to create a political consensus between the state (the tsar and the bureaucracy) and society (represented by the Duma). The third measure of organizational age, the number of top leadership successions in that order, was technically zero, because Nicholas II remained the tsar under the new constitution. On the other hand, there had been four successful regime changes since the last irregular transfer of executive authority, the assassination of Paul I in 1801.[10]

Political Violence. Good statistics on the number of deaths from political violence in Russia for the period 1900–1917 are hard to come by. There were thousands of deaths during the revolution of 1905–1906; over 3,000 Jews died in pogroms alone during this period, and one source puts the number of total deaths at over 13,000. Two hundred fifty people were killed by government troops during the Lena goldfields massacre in 1912. Thousands more died during the 1917 revolution. In the civil war that followed, there were 800,000 combatant deaths, and a total of 7–10 million people died from all causes. The numbers on deaths from political violence are far from

Norman Stone, *The Eastern Front 1914–1917* (New York: Charles Scribner's Sons, 1975), pp. 284–297; Peter Gatrell, "The Economy and the War," in Harold Shukman, ed., *The Blackwell Encyclopedia of the Russian Revolution* (Oxford: Basil Blackwell Ltd, 1988), pp. 117–122.

[10] On the post-1905 constitutional order, see Geoffrey A. Hosking, *The Russian Constitutional Experiment: Government and Duma, 1907–1914* (Cambridge, England: Cambridge University Press, 1973); Pipes, *Russian Revolution*, pp. 153–194.

comprehensive; and without a good comparative basis such as that provided by the *World Handbook of Political and Social Indicators*, it is impossible to know whether political violence in Russia in the years leading up to the revolution (1907–1916) was particularly high.[11]

Internal Conflict. Various forms of internal conflict are also potential measures of low state capacity, such as strikes, peasant rebellions, and separatist movements.

Strike patterns in late-Imperial Russia were extremely erratic, and industrial conflict in general was very volatile. Three massive waves hit Russia, in 1905–1907, 1912–1914, and 1916–1917. Patterns in Russia were quite different than in the rest of Europe, where there was less fluctuation from year to year. In its dealings with the working class, just as in the case of its interaction with elite society, the Tsarist regime had failed to create legitimate and stable institutions.[12]

Peasant unrest was another sign of political disorder in 1917. Until the February Revolution there had been very few disturbances in the countryside. After the fall of the tsar, however, many peasants believed that what they saw as the unjust property structure had been overturned. Government authority collapsed, and increasingly peasants took matters into their own hands. By the time of the October Revolution the traditional social and economic order in the countryside had been turned upside down, and almost all land was in the hands of peasants.[13]

A final important form of irregular challenges to the existing political order were the national autonomy and independence movements of 1917. The collapse of the autocracy led to the spread of demands for various forms of autonomy – cultural, administrative, political – around the Russian empire. The Provisional Government refused to recognize any of these demands, maintaining that they could be resolved only after a Constituent Assembly

---

[11] Shlomo Lambroza, "The pogroms of 1903–1906," in John D. Klier and Shlomo Lambroza, eds., *Pogroms: Anti-Jewish Violence in Modern Russian History* (Cambridge, England: Cambridge University Press, 1992), pp. 227–231; A. I. Denikin, *Put' russkogo ofitsera* (Moskva: Prometey, 1990), pp. 177–178, citing the Soviet historian Pokrovskiy; Acton, *Rethinking the Russian Revolution*, p. 15; Shukman, *Blackwell Encyclopedia*, pp. 146, 201. John Keep's study of the revolution has perhaps the most information on violence during the revolution, but it is descriptive and not quantitative: John L. Keep, *The Russian Revolution: A Study in Mass Mobilization* (London: Weidenfeld and Nicolson, 1976).

[12] Diane P. Koenker and William G. Rosenberg, *Strikes and Revolution in Russia, 1917* (Princeton, NJ: Princeton University Press, 1989); Leopold H. Haimson and Charles Tilly, eds., *Strikes, Wars, and Revolutions in International Perspective: Strike Waves in the Late Nineteenth and Early Twentieth Centuries* (Cambridge, England: Cambridge University Press, 1989); Smith, *Red Petrograd*, pp. 37–38.

[13] Graeme J. Gill, *Peasants and Government in the Russian Revolution* (London: Macmillan, 1979); Keep, *Russian Revolution*, pp. 153–247, 383–471.

had been elected. These national conflicts contributed to the breakdown of state political capacity after the February Revolution.[14]

Strength of the State vis-à-vis Society. In its last decades the Tsarist regime was unable to change either social structure or private behavior in intended ways. The government was more capable of resisting private pressure, but at several points during the Revolution of 1905–1907 the tsar was forced to offer political concessions to powerful private actors. After the collapse of the autocracy the Provisional Government's authority was continually under challenge. The most important rival was the structure of local Soviets (councils), particularly the Petrograd Soviet. The inability of the Provisional Government to act without the approval of the Soviet came to be known as "dual power."[15] As 1917 progressed, the Soviets grew stronger and the Provisional Government grew weaker, which culminated in the Bolshevik rise to power in October. Bolshevik rule, however, was only consolidated after several years of ferocious civil war.

Throughout the period under study, then, state political capacity was weak or nonexistent. The domestic structure approach predicts a high degree of military involvement in sovereign power issues in 1917.

Organizational Structure

The Russian state had no robust mechanisms for counterbalancing or penetrating the army to prevent military coups. On the other hand, the military had some serious internal cleavages that did make intervention difficult. The major problem was not splits within the officer corps, although these did exist. The real obstacle to concerted military intervention in politics was the vast gulf between the officer corps and the troops.

Counterbalancing. The Tsarist government never created a security force or paramilitary organization that would have been capable of counterbalancing a military coup. The closest existing organization was the Gendarmes Corps. But the Gendarmes were more of a surveillance organization than a paramilitary one. Their entire strength was less than 10,000 personnel, and they were lightly armed. Budgetary authority rested in the hands of the Ministry of War at all times, their commander and personnel were often former army officers, and in wartime they were operationally under the

---

[14] Ronald Grigor Suny, *The Revenge of the Past: Nationalism, Revolution, and the Collapse of the Soviet Union* (Stanford: Stanford University Press, 1993), pp. 20–83; Richard Pipes, *The Formation of the Soviet Union: Communism and Nationalism 1917–1923*, Revised Edition (Cambridge, MA: Harvard University Press, 1964); Shukman, *Blackwell Encyclopedia*, pp. 194–268.

[15] On the origins of dual power, see Hasegawa, *February Revolution*, pp. 408–427.

control of the military. The Gendarmes could not have resisted a coup attempt, and they were not really designed for this role.[16]

Penetration. The government had more resources for detecting a coup than it did for preventing one underway. There were three separate but overlapping channels for collecting information on the mood of the officer corps: the Gendarmes, the Department of Police, and a separate group of agents under the Minister of War. Agents were quite active in the army after the 1905 revolution, but their usefulness is doubtful. Agents' reports primarily focused on officers' political views, such as pro-democracy leanings, or their personal conduct (gambling, womanizing, etc.). In most cases, suspicions directed against certain officers were forwarded to the military itself for handling, and in many cases the army took the side of the accused officer.[17]

There is no evidence that any of these spying networks uncovered a military coup plot. Indeed, they missed the few discussions that did take place in 1916 (see below) and played no role in any of the key episodes during the Revolution, such as the Kornilov affair. The main effect of these efforts, according to William Fuller, was to foment officer hostility against civilian bureaucrats in general and the Department of Police in particular.[18]

A new monitoring body appeared on the scene after the February Revolution. The Provisional Government, under pressure from the Petrograd Soviet, instituted political commissars to oversee the work of the military. Each army and front had a commissar appointed by the War Ministry, in consultation with the Soviet, and responsible to the War Ministry.[19] The commissars were a source of irritation between the high command and the Provisional Government, and several of them played an important role during the Kornilov affair and the October Revolution. In general, though, they did not function as a method for preventing military intervention against the government.

---

[16] William C. Fuller, Jr., *The Internal Troops of the MVD SSSR*, College Station Papers No. 6 (College Station, TX: Center for Strategic Technology, Texas A & M, 1983), p. 2; Charles A. Ruud and Sergei A. Stepanov, *Fontanka 16: The Tsars' Secret Police* (Montreal: McGill–Queen's University Press, 1999), pp. 19, 23; Lieven, *Russia's Rulers*, p. 175.

[17] William C. Fuller, Jr., *Civil–Military Conflict in Imperial Russia, 1881–1914* (Princeton, NJ: Princeton University Press, 1985), pp. 101, 212–218; Denikin, *Put' russkkogo ofitsera*, pp. 207–208; A. I. Denikin, *Ocherki Russkoy Smuty*, Vol. I, Part 1 (Moskva: "Nauka," 1991 [1921]), p. 11 (when citing *Ocherki* I use the page numbers from the original version, not the ones from the 1991 Soviet edition).

[18] Fuller, *Civil–Military Conflict*, pp. 216–218.

[19] Allan K. Wildman, *The End of the Russian Imperial Army: The Road to Soviet Power and Peace*, Vol. II (Princeton, NJ: Princeton University Press, 1987), pp. 22–24; Denikin, *Ocherki*, I(2), pp. 36–42.

Cohesion. The Tsarist officer corps on the eve of war and revolution was by all accounts extremely heterogeneous. This was true in terms of class, education levels, and conditions of service.

After the Milyutin reforms (see Chapter 2), the class make-up of the officer corps became increasingly less aristocratic. By 1912 the officer corps as a whole was almost fifty–fifty nobility and non-nobility. The very top of the officer corps was still largely noble, over eighty-five percent. Some branches of service were much more noble than others; the Guards were exclusively noble, and the Cavalry was seventy-five percent noble. The infantry, on the other hand, was a majority non-noble, with almost half of its officers being descendents of serfs.[20]

During World War I the class composition of the officer corps changed markedly. The officer corps more than tripled in size from 1914 to 1917 (from about 41 thousand to 146 thousand). Given that by 1917 the army had lost nearly 63 thousand officers, Peter Kenez estimates that almost 170 thousand young men were brought into the officer corps during the war. The majority of these new officers were non-noble. In 1916, seventy percent of junior officers were of peasant background.[21]

Class background itself was not an important predictor of political orientation.[22] Indeed, prominent White generals such as Kornilov, Anton Denikin, and Mikhail Alekseev were of humble background. More important was the fact that officers mobilized for the war were not socialized in the dominant organizational culture; this point is discussed below.

Other cleavages were also evident in the late-Tsarist officer corps. There were sharp differences between the branches of service, with the Guards at the top and the Infantry at the bottom. Education was another important division. General Staff officers (*Genshtabisty*) saw themselves as a separate and elite group. The Russian officer corps was also extremely heterogeneous in terms of wealth and conditions of service. Although part of the same officer corps, a noble Guards officer serving in St. Petersburg had little in common with a poor infantry officer from a lower-class background stationed in Siberia.[23]

[20] Peter Kenez, "A Profile of the Prerevolutionary Officer Corps," *California Slavic Studies*, 7 (1973), 128–145; Allan K. Wildman, *The End of the Russian Imperial Army: The Old Army and the Soldiers' Revolt*, Vol. I (Princeton, NJ: Princeton University Press, 1980), pp. 19–25.

[21] Kenez, "A Profile of the Prerevolutionary," 145–150; Wildman, *End of the Russian Imperial Army*, Vol. I, pp. 100–102.

[22] Kenez, "A Profile of the Prerevolutionary," 121. See also the discussion in Chapter 2.

[23] Kenez, "A Profile of the Prerevolutionary"; Wildman, *The End of the Russian Imperial Army*, Vol. I, pp. 3–24; Fuller, *Civil–Military Conflict*, pp. 15–29; Matitiahu Mayzel, "The Formation of the General Staff 1880–1917: A Social Study," *Cahiers du Monde Russe et Sovietique*, 16 (1975), 297–321.

The importance of these internal divisions is questionable. General Denikin maintained that these cleavages were no worse in the Russian army than in other militaries and that in wartime they rapidly evaporated.[24] The evidence from the cases will show that structural divisions in the officer corps were not the most important barrier to military intervention.

The one cleavage in the army that did play a significant role in 1917 was the one between the officer corps and enlisted personnel. At the beginning of 1917, soldiers outnumbered officers by roughly forty-five to one, a disparity compounded even more by the traditional weakness of the Russian non-commissioned officer structure.[25] The February Revolution gravely weakened the control officers had over their troops, who were largely of peasant background, tended to sympathize with the revolution, and desired a quick end to the war. The ability of officers to intervene after February was thus impeded by opposition from the rank and file.[26]

This split, although important, is not predicted by the organizational structure approach. The theoretical literature on military coups focuses on officer behavior and ignores conscripts, who are assumed to be irrelevant in sovereign power issues. Ordinary soldiers generally are compelled or tricked into following the lead of their commanders. Rarely will the strains of war and revolution combine in a way that makes it possible for the rank and file to play a significant political role.[27]

Prior to the February Revolution the bulk of the evidence suggests that the army was not seriously divided and that military intervention was possible. In February, however, the mutiny of the Petrograd garrison demonstrated the huge rift in the army between officers and troops. After February the military found it difficult to act in a concerted fashion because of organizational structure barriers. Given the extreme weakness of the state, culminating in its collapse, the lack of cohesion in the military is not surprising. Splits in the officer corps do not appear to have been significant enough to render it immobile, but the gap between commanders and the rank and file was a key problem. In general an organizational structure approach would predict a military able to intervene in sovereign power issues prior to February, unable to do so afterwards, and prone to split in cases of arbitration.

---

[24] Denikin, *Put' russkogo ofitsera*, p. 55.

[25] Kenez, "A Profile of the Prerevolutionary," 145; Norman Stone, "The Historical Background of the Red Army," in John Erickson and E. J. Feuchtwanger, eds., *Soviet Military Power and Performance* (London: Macmillan, 1979), 7; Wildman, *The End of the Russian Imperial Army*, Vol. I, p. 30, note 50.

[26] The two most important sources on the revolution in the army are Wildman, *The End of the Russian Imperial Army*; M. Frenkin, *Russkaya armiya i revolyutsiya 1917–1918* (Munich: Logos, 1978).

[27] Bruce W. Farcau, *The Coup: Tactics in the Seizure of Power* (Westport, CT: Praeger, 1994), p. 11; Chorley, *Armies and the Art of Revolution*, pp. 108–127, 175, 243–244.

Opportunity: Summary

The opportunity structure facing officers during the revolution, then, was a complex one. State weakness made it likely that the military would be called upon to play a role in sovereign power issues, but internal divisions would seem to suggest an inability to intervene. Officers confronted forces both pulling them into domestic politics and hindering their ability to act effectively.

MOTIVES FOR INTERVENTION, 1917

Corporate interest motives and organizational culture cut against each other in 1917. The army's interests were under severe threat after the February Revolution. Its organizational culture, however, proscribed military participation in sovereign power issues.

Corporate Interests

The conventional image of the Russian empire as an armed camp would suggest that military interests generally were satisfied by the Tsarist government. In fact, however, the army was often a loser in bureaucratic political battles in the last decades of the regime.[28] However, on the eve of the war (roughly 1910–1914) the army was a more successful bureaucratic actor. During the war the military also received considerable resources and autonomy. After the February Revolution, however, military autonomy was under serious threat, and the corporate interest perspective would predict military intervention to protect the army's interests.

The two most important indicators of an army's political standing are its budget relative to other competing state tasks and its organizational autonomy. In both of these areas the late imperial period, except on the very eve of World War I, was not a happy one for the Russian army.

Resources Pre-War. An examination of state budget expenditures from the middle of the nineteenth century until the outbreak of World War I shows a steady decline in military, particularly army, spending (Table 3.2). Spending on the army dropped from over thirty percent of government spending in 1850–1852 to less than twenty percent immediately prior to World War I. There was a growing tendency to favor the needs of other ministries over the War Ministry. Given that this same period followed the unification of Germany and coincided with a major industrialization of warfare that required additional military spending, the Russian military leadership was alarmed by its declining share of the budget.[29]

---

[28] See Chapter 2.
[29] Walter M. Pintner, "The Burden of Defense in Imperial Russia, 1725–1914," *Russian Review*, 43 (1984), 231–259; Fuller, *Civil–Military Conflict*, 47–74.

TABLE 3.2. *Distribution of State Budget Expenditures, 1850–1914*

Year	Army (%)	Navy (%)	Total Military (%)	Remainder (%)
1850–1854	31.2	6.2	37.4	62.6
1855–1859	35.6	5.4	41.0	59.0
1860–1864	30.6	5.5	36.1	63.9
1865–1869	29.0	4.3	33.3	66.7
1870–1874	28.0	4.0	32.0	68.0
1875–1879	28.8	4.2	33.0	67.0
1880–1884	26.8	3.9	30.7	69.3
1885–1889	22.8	4.4	27.2	72.8
1890–1894	23.8	4.3	28.1	71.9
1895–1899	18.7	5.5	24.2	75.8
1900–1904	17.3	5.2	22.4	77.6
1905–1909	18.9	4.4	23.3	76.7
1910–1914	19.0	6.2	25.2	74.8

Source: Pintner, "The Burden of Defense in Imperial Russia," 248.

The military's declining budget share was the result of a conscious decision on the part of the government to favor other areas of spending. The Ministry of Finance, the most powerful and influential government ministry, saw military spending as the biggest impediment to its plans for state-sponsored industrialization and railway construction. Although in principle these goals were consistent with military goals, in practice the Ministry of War had little influence over either sphere of state policy. Railways were built not for strategic reasons (i.e., the movement of troops) but for economic ones (i.e., the movement of goods). Indeed, when railways were built for strategic reasons it often was due to the pressure of the French government, and not the War Ministry. This in itself is indicative of the bureaucratic power of the army during this period.[30]

On the eve of the war the Russian military did receive a new infusion of money. Duma support for the army led to the adoption of the "Small Program" of 1910 and the "Big (or Great) Program" of 1914, both of which foresaw important increases in military expenditures and the size of the armed forces. The outbreak of war, of course, interrupted these plans for peacetime development.[31]

---

[30] Fuller, *Civil–Military Conflict*, pp. 58–71, 224; Theodore H. Von Laue, *Sergei Witte and the Industrialization of Russia* (New York: Columbia University Press, 1963); Peter Gatrell, *The Tsarist Economy 1850–1917* (London: B. T. Batsford Ltd., 1986), 150–154; D. C. B. Lieven, *Russia and the Origins of the First World War* (London: Macmillan, 1983), p. 103.

[31] David R. Jones, "Imperial Russia's Forces at War," in Allan R. Millett and Williamson Murray, eds., *Military Effectiveness. Volume I: The First World War* (Boston, MA: Allen & Unwin, 1988), pp. 257–260, 277–278; Fuller, *Civil–Military Conflict*, pp. 222–227.

Autonomy Pre-War. For most of the last several decades of the Tsarist regime, the military leadership felt that its autonomy was even more under threat than its share of the state budget. The major reason for this loss of autonomy was the increasing involvement of the army in domestic repression. Troops were called to the aid of civil power with increasing frequency from 1890 to 1904. During the revolution of 1905–1906 the army leadership basically lost control over its local commanders. The War Ministry again found itself on the losing end of a bureaucratic battle, this time with the Interior Ministry. The army's virtual loss of control over its own troops, by any measure an extreme infringement of organizational autonomy, lasted until 1908.[32]

Once the revolutionary crisis had abated, the military fought to regain control over its troops. War Minister General V. A. Sukhomlinov (1909–1915) asserted the need to free army units from domestic missions, and he was backed wholeheartedly by local commanders. Sukhomlinov gained the support of Nicholas II, and by 1914 military involvement in aid to the civil power had dropped dramatically.[33]

The picture with respect to organizational autonomy, then, was roughly similar to the budget story. From the 1880s until the 1910s the armed forces had experienced budget cuts and severe encroachments of organizational autonomy. From 1910 to 1914, however, the army had won important victories in both the budgetary and autonomy spheres. William Fuller, however, concludes that the preceding decades had seriously damaged civil–military relations. Fuller states, "in the eyes of the army leadership, the Russian state did not serve military interests before all else and did not in fact satisfy the most pressing of the army's needs."[34]

The outbreak of world war in the summer of 1914 seemingly vindicated the War Ministry's demands for increased funding and freedom from domestic missions. For the next three years all the efforts of the Russian state were directed toward the war. Did the armed forces receive the resources and autonomy they needed to wage the war effort? The two issues of resources and autonomy will be covered in turn.

Resources during War. The summer of 1915 was a debacle for Russia as it was pushed out of Galicia and Poland (the "Great Retreat"). The Great Retreat is sometimes blamed on a "shell shortage," but most historians now reject the claim that poor Russian military performance in 1915 was due to a lack of resources. By 1916, Russia's military situation seemed to be improving. The Commander of the Southwest Front, General A. A. Brusilov, even achieved a major breakthrough in late May of that year before his offensive petered

[32] Fuller, *Civil–Military Conflict*; John Bushnell, *Mutiny amid Repression: Russian Soldiers in the Revolution of 1905–1906* (Bloomington, IN: Indiana University Press, 1985).

[33] Fuller, *Civil–Military Conflict*, pp. 244–258.

[34] Fuller, *Civil–Military Conflict*, p. xxi.

out. The material shortages of the previous year had been largely overcome. Indeed, the government was pouring so much into the war economy that it was creating serious imbalances and shortages in the civilian economy. The military could not make a plausible claim that it was not being provided the necessary resources to wage the war.[35]

Autonomy during War. A major consequence of the political recriminations following the Great Retreat was Nicholas II's decision in August 1915 to assume the responsibilities of Supreme Commander. Nicholas could serve as a crucial "linchpin" connecting the military effort at the front with civilian administration in the rear. The officer corps apparently approved of Nicholas's decision. A crucial element in this support was the appointment of General M. V. Alekseev as Chief of Staff. Alekseev became de facto commander-in-chief and performed well in this role. Nicholas II, all observers agree, did not interfere in military decision making.[36]

There had been clashes between the Supreme Headquarters of the Russian Army at the front, or *Stavka*, and the civilian government over spheres of responsibility in 1914–1915, but these were caused by the regulations on wartime administration that gave the army too much power in the war zone and areas of the rear. Arguably the army had too much autonomy, not too little.[37]

If the armed forces could be basically satisfied with the degree to which their organizational autonomy was respected during the war from 1914 to 1917, this changed drastically after the February Revolution. One of the most momentous consequences of the overthrow of the government was the adoption on March 1 by the Petrograd Soviet of Workers' and Soldiers' Deputies of the justifiably famous Order No. 1. This decision completely disrupted military command authority. Order No. 1 sanctioned the formation of soldiers' committees and declared that government orders in the military sphere should only be executed if they were consistent with decisions of the Soviet. Although as written the order applied only to the Petrograd garrison, it had a highly disruptive effect on discipline at the front as well. From this point

[35] Jones, "Imperial Russia's Forces at War"; Stone, *Eastern Front*; Hasegawa, *February Revolution*, pp. 24–39; Wildman, *The End of the Russian Imperial Army*, Vol. I, pp. 80–94; Lieven, *Nicholas II*, pp. 208–217; Gatrell, "The Economy and the War."

[36] David R. Jones, "Nicholas II and the Supreme Command: An Investigation of Motives," *Sbornik: Study Group on the Russian Revolution*, 11 (1985), 47–83; Jones, "Imperial Russia's Forces at War," 291–295; Lieven, *Nicholas II*, pp. 212–215; Hasegawa, *February Revolution*, p. 31; George Katkov, *Russia 1917: The February Revolution* (New York: Harper & Row, 1967), pp. 141–142, 241; Denikin, *Put' russkogo ofitsera*, p. 289; A. A. Brusilov, *A Soldier's Notebook 1914–1918* (Westport, CT: Greenwood Publishers, 1976), pp. 170–172, 217, 226–227.

[37] Daniel W. Graf, "Military Rule Behind the Russian Front, 1914–1917: The Political Ramifications," *Jahrbucher fur Geschicte Osteuropas*, 22 (1974), 390–411.

forward the autonomy of officers to make decisions was severely compromised. The Provisional Government also became deeply involved with decisions that hitherto had been purely military matters, such as command assignments. After the February Revolution, military corporate interests were seriously threatened.[38]

In summary, the decline of government support for military interests in the last decades of the Imperial regime suggests that military intervention should be considered likely. However, from 1910 to 1917 the armed forces had fewer reasons to complain about government support for their corporate interests. Prior to February 1917, this approach would predict that military intervention was unlikely. After the February Revolution, however, this perspective clearly predicts military intervention. In instances of military arbitration the army should side with the contender for power who is most likely to support the military's corporate interests.

Organizational Culture

There is widespread agreement in the primary and secondary literature on the apolitical nature of the late-Imperial Russian officer corps. This picture of an apolitical officer corps is in general correct, but there also were troubling signs of politicization during the war and the presence of distinct, more interventionist, subcultures.

Beliefs and Socialization. The memoir literature on the late-Imperial officer corps notes the disinterest of the military not only toward sovereign power issues, but indeed toward all political issues. Denikin, for instance, stresses the complete apathy of officer candidates to political issues, in strong contrast to their politicized cohorts in civilian universities. Although there were some secret officers' organizations, they were small and insignificant because they were "foreign" to the nature of the army. Denikin maintains that the slogan "the army is outside politics (*armiya – vne politiki*)" was taken too far and was applied not only to the active participation of officers in political affairs, which Denikin considered a correct prohibition, but also to even an elementary knowledge of social and political questions. Denikin contends, "the state order was for the officer corps a predetermined fact, eliciting neither doubts nor different interpretations."[39]

Sukhomlinov paints a similar picture of army attitudes. He notes that as a military cadet in 1870–1871 he and his fellow cadets did not read

---

[38] Wildman, *The End of the Russian Imperial Army*, Vol. I, pp. 182–192; Denikin, *Ocherki*, I(1), pp. 87, 130; I(2), p. 5.

[39] Denikin, *Put' russkkogo ofitsera*, pp. 42, 52–53, 64–65 (quote, p. 52); A. I. Denikin, *Staraya Armiya*, Vol. I (Paris: "Rodnik," 1929), pp. 60, 69, 115, 142; General A. Denikin, *Staraya armiya*, Vol. II (Paris: "Rodnik," 1931), pp. 37–38, 89–91; Denikin, *Ocherki*, I(1), p. 12.

newspapers, and it was considered bad form to talk about politics. Sukhomlinov states, "I thought that a soldier, from a private to a general, should be a stranger to all forms of politics... the military is a force on which the existing state order is based."[40]

Imperial Russian army officers who went on to serve the Soviet regime also comment on the apolitical nature of the officer corps before the revolution. A. A. Ignat'ev notes that when he was an elite Guards cavalry officer no one mentioned politics at receptions and balls. He calls himself a "politically disarmed, helpless aristocrat" and emphasizes that he was "completely politically ignorant" in the pre-war period.[41]

In sum, as William Fuller puts it, "Tsarist military memoirs almost in unison insisted that the Russian officer corps was apolitical." Fuller notes that there was a small group of military intellectuals that advocated defense reform, but they had no interest in societal choice or sovereign power issues. The secret police were unable to uncover subversive officers in the army, despite persistent attempts. He concludes, "the majority of army officers were ill-educated, apathetic, and unlikely to possess coherent political ideologies." General P. O. Bobrovskiy, a leading expert in the late-Imperial officer corps on military education, noted the complete absence of political or ideological indoctrination of future officers.[42]

Behavior. Officer obedience to the tsar extended beyond the sovereign power realm. Russian military leaders stressed their subordination to the tsar in other domains of civil–military relations, including in the formation of foreign and security policy. Referring to decisions made by Russia in the July crisis of 1914, Sukhomlinov noted in his memoirs:

As War Minister I did not have a right to protest against such a decision – a move on the chessboard of power politics – even though it threatened war, because politics was not my affair. It was equally not my job as War Minister to decisively restrain the Tsar from war. I was a soldier and had to obey, because the army exists for the defense of the fatherland, and not to get involved in discussions.[43]

The Russian officer corps on the eve of World War I believed that the army's primary mission was external defense of the state. At the same time,

[40] V. A. Sukhomlinov, *Vospominaniya Sukhomlinova* (Moskva–Leningrad: Gosizdat, 1926), pp. 15, 181.

[41] A. A. Ignat'ev, *Pyat'desyat let v stroyu*, Vol. I (Moskva: Voenizdat, 1988 (1955)), pp. 84, 409.

[42] Fuller, *Civil–Military Conflict*, pp. xx, 194, 196–207, 212–218, 259–263; Yu. Galushko and A. Kolesnikov, *Shkola Rossiyskogo Ofitserstva: Istoricheskiy spravochnik* (Moskva: "Russkiy mir," 1993), pp. 127–128. See also Lieven, *Russia's Rulers*, pp. 173–175; S. V. Volkov, *Russkiy ofitserskiy korpus* (Moskva: Voenizdat, 1993), pp. 286–288; Kenez, "A Profile of the Prerevolutionary," 155–156.

[43] Sukhomlinov, *Vospominaniya Sukhomlinova*, pp. 182, 223. For a similar example, see Lieven, *Russia's Rulers*, p. 175.

soldiers in the imperial Russian army swore an oath to defend the regime against both external and internal enemies. Internal repression had been a mission of the Russian armed forces for centuries. Most officers agreed that, if properly limited, aid to the civil power was a legitimate mission. The army was used similarly elsewhere in Europe. But officers often clashed with civilian officials over the extent to which the army could be used internally.[44]

Civil–military conflict over internal usage became particularly acute during the revolution of 1905–1906. The War Minister, General A. F. Rediger, complained to the Prime Minister about excessive demands put on the troops by local civilian officials, thus taking the army away from training and external defense. Officer corps' opposition to internal missions led to a concerted effort after the revolution of 1905–1906 to free the armed forces from domestic usage. In 1911 the War Ministry imposed strict limits on the use of the army in aid to the civil power missions. By 1914 the military leadership had largely succeeded in its efforts to free the army from internal missions. Fuller concludes, "by having its attentions focused on military developments beyond Russia's borders, the Russian army was at last truly *'vne politiki'* (out of politics)."[45]

The Russian officer corps on the eve of World War I, then, had a strong commitment to an apolitical organizational culture. They believed in the importance of subordination to civilian authority, noninterference in sovereign power issues, and a focus on external defense. As Peter Kenez states, "they repeated *ad nauseam* the doctrine according to which the Army stood above politics."[46]

War and New Subcultures. The outbreak of war in 1914 obviously provided an overwhelming incentive for the armed forces to concentrate on the task of external defense. At the same time, the regulations on wartime administration did give the high command a broad range of responsibilities in the theater of military operations. This expansion of military authority into the societal choice domain during the war did lead the army into much greater involvement in traditionally civilian spheres of activity. Daniel Graf concludes, "the basis was laid for the growing politicization of the military high command, both at *Stavka* and the front headquarters."[47]

Two other important changes took place during World War I that slightly eroded the army's traditional apolitical culture. The first change involved the

---

[44] Fuller, *Civil–Military Conflict,* pp. 76–77, 106–107, 144, 267.

[45] Fuller, *Civil–Military Conflict,* pp. 155, 244–258 (quote, p. 258). See also Robert H. McNeal, *Tsar and Cossack, 1855–1914* (New York: St. Martin's Press, 1987), pp. 57–58, 72, 77; B. M. Shaposhnikov, *Vospominaniya* (Moskva: Voenizdat, 1974), p. 206; Galushko and Kolesnikov, *Shkola Rossiyskogo Ofitserstva,* p. 108.

[46] Peter Kenez, "The Ideology of the White Movement," *Soviet Studies,* 32 (1980), 61.

[47] Graf, "Military Rule," 411.

composition of the officer corps, the second was related to Russia's performance in waging the war.

Changes in the composition of the officer corps during the war came about because of the extremely high casualty rates suffered by the Russian military during the war. By 1917 less than ten percent of the officer corps were regular officers who had been in the service prior to 1914. Although the military leadership continued to be dominated by officers raised and trained in the Imperial army, most junior officers by the end of the war were not products of this environment, and they had not been socialized into the dominant apolitical organizational culture. At least some of the new wartime officers had been politically active in progressive and revolutionary organizations before the war. A secret police report from January 1917 noted ominously that there was a big difference between "cadre" and "war-time" officers and that only cadre officers could be expected to remain loyal to their oath in the event of mass demonstrations and protests.[48]

The second important change during World War I relevant to the organizational culture of the Russian armed forces was the effect of Russia's military performance on civil–military relations. Specifically, the domestic political confrontations between the autocracy and liberal members of elite society about the regime's managing of the war effort spilled over into the Russian officer corps. Rumors about the pernicious influence of the tsarina and Rasputin on the tsar and government policy spread not only in elite circles in Petersburg but also at *Stavka* and among the army, undermining the tsar's authority. A secret police report on the mood of the army in January 1917 stated that many officers were very dissatisfied with the government and complained about the influence of the "German party."[49]

Based on these rumors, the feeling began to spread among army officers, including the high command, that pro-German elements in the government were undermining the war effort. Some Duma members began to seek out officers who might participate in a palace coup to remove the tsarina from Petersburg, or even topple the tsar in favor of another member of the Romanov family. Historians disagree about how serious these plots were, but there is general agreement that the military leadership was unprepared to support a palace coup. The Grand Duke Nikolay Nikolayevich was approached, but he rejected the idea because he believed the army would not go

---

[48] Kenez, "A Profile of the Prerevolutionary," 145–149; Wildman, *The End of the Russian Imperial Army*, Vol. I, pp. 100–102, 106–107; Jones, "Imperial Russia's Forces at War," 282–284; Stone, *Eastern Front*, pp. 166–167; Hasegawa, *February Revolution*, pp. 169–170; Frenkin, *Russkaya armiya*, pp. 22, 26; Lieven, *Nicholas II*, p. 211; "Russkaya armiya nakanune revolyutsii," *Byloye*, No. 1(29), 1918, 151–152.

[49] "Russkaya armiya nakanune revolyutsii." See also Ignat'ev, *Pyat'desyat let*, Vol. I, p. 625; o. Georgiy Shavel'skiy, *Vospominaniya poslednogo protopresvitera russkoy armii i flota*, Vol. I (New York: Izdatel'stvo imeni Chekhova, 1954), p. 10. For an objective discussion of the political influence of the tsarina and Rasputin, see Lieven, *Nicholas II*, 164–170, 226–228.

along with it. The only general clearly implicated in these plots was General A. M. Krymov, who believed that the country was headed toward ruin if drastic steps were not taken. The prominent Duma deputy Aleksandr Guchkov later wrote of these plots that "I did a great deal for which I could have been hanged, but little of real achievement, because I could not succeed in involving anyone from the military." [50]

Two leading historians of the February Revolution, Tsuyoshi Hasegawa and George Katkov, agree that there was little military support for these plots. Hasegawa gives two major reasons for military unwillingness to participate in any palace coup. First, officers' primary consideration was the war effort, and they were concerned that such a momentous change in the political order would be disruptive. Second, Hasegawa states, "all the military leaders of the tsarist army were trained in the old school, which emphasized that military men were not to be involved in politics. Their inbred skepticism and disdain for domestic politics must have contributed to their refusal to join the conspiracies." [51]

Russian officer corps' commitment to a norm of civilian supremacy was very high in the late-Imperial period. Officers were socialized to believe that they had no role to play in sovereign power issues and that they should be focused on external defense. During the war, however, this commitment was somewhat eroded, because of the influx of new officers, expanded military responsibilities at home, and the threat of Russian defeat in the war. A more praetorian organizational subculture appeared, but intervention still remained unlikely. In cases of military arbitration, an apolitical army will first try to sit the conflict out; and then if forced to decide, it will side with the contender it perceives is most legitimate and thus most likely to keep the military from further involvement in politics.

Motives: Summary

The motives of the officer corps during the Revolution were mixed. Prior to February neither corporate interest nor organizational culture was an impetus to intervention. After February there were strong corporate motives for a coup, but the dominant organizational culture believed the army should be "outside politics." On the other hand, praetorian sentiments had appeared in

---

[50] Hasegawa, *February Revolution*, pp. 47, 185–197 (quote, p. 191); Katkov, *Russia 1917*, pp. 39–42, 173–177, 181–187; General Baron P. N. Vrangel', *Vospominaniya Generala Barona P. N. Vrangelya* (Frankfurt: "Posev," 1969), p. 11; Jones, "Imperial Russia's Forces at War," p. 257; Wildman, *The End of the Russian Imperial Army*, Vol. I, pp. 110–113; Frenkin, *Russkaya armiya*, pp. 21–22, 28–29; Denikin, *Ocherki*, I(1), pp. 35–39, 72, note 2.

[51] Hasegawa, *February Revolution*, p. 192; Katkov, *Russia 1917*, pp. 42, 182, 187; Shavel'skiy, *Vospominaniya*, Vol. I, p. 27; A. N. Verkhovskiy, *Rossiya na golgofe (iz pokhodnago dnevnika 1914–1918 g).* (Petrograd: 1918), p. 64.

the military leadership, and many junior officers did not share the dominant apolitical culture.

THE OFFICER CORPS AND THE FEBRUARY REVOLUTION

The February Revolution and the resultant collapse of the Romanov dynasty came with a suddenness that shocked contemporary Russian observers. Despite the many weaknesses of the regime, no one really expected what happened in February 1917. The military high command played a significant role in bringing about the abdication of the tsar.

This section has two parts. I first present a brief narrative of the key events of the February Revolution, focusing on the actions of the military leadership. I then turn to an analysis of the behavior of leading officers. Despite the disinclination of the military leadership to become involved in politics, they were thrust into the role of arbiter of a sovereign power dispute. Their behavior was strongly motivated by a desire to see order quickly restored, thus permitting the military leadership to return to the war effort.

The February Revolution and the Abdication of the Tsar

The February Revolution began on February 23 with a series of strikes and street demonstrations in Petrograd. These protests grew in intensity over the next several days, and by the twenty-fifth there was a general strike. The tsar was notified on the evening of the twenty-fifth of the disturbances, and he demanded that complete order be restored in the capital the next day. The twenty-sixth, a Sunday, was marked by violent street clashes in which around 100 people died. Troops from the Petrograd garrison (the total strength of the garrison was 180,000) were employed in the operation to repress the demonstrations. Although the government won the day on the twenty-sixth, on the twenty-seventh over 65,000 troops of the garrison mutinied. By March 1 almost the entire garrison (over 170,000 troops) had joined the insurrection.[52]

The tsar received word of the garrison mutiny on the afternoon of February 27. Nicholas decided to send an expeditionary force from the front to suppress the revolution and to leave the next morning for Tsarskoe Selo, the royal residences near Petrograd. General N. I. Ivanov was put in charge of the troops from the front, and chief of staff Alekseev began to send out orders for reinforcements. A force of several divisions was to be assembled from units of the Northern and Western Fronts in Tsarskoe Selo, which was to serve as Ivanov's headquarters when he arrived there on March 1 (see Map A of the railroads between *Stavka* and Petrograd). Nicholas, meanwhile, left *Stavka* headquarters in Mogilev for Tsarskoe Selo on the morning

---

[52] Hasegawa, *February Revolution*, pp. 215–310; Schapiro, 1917, pp. 35–44; Acton, *Rethinking the Russian Revolution*, pp. 107–128; D. A. Longley, "Iakovlev's Question."

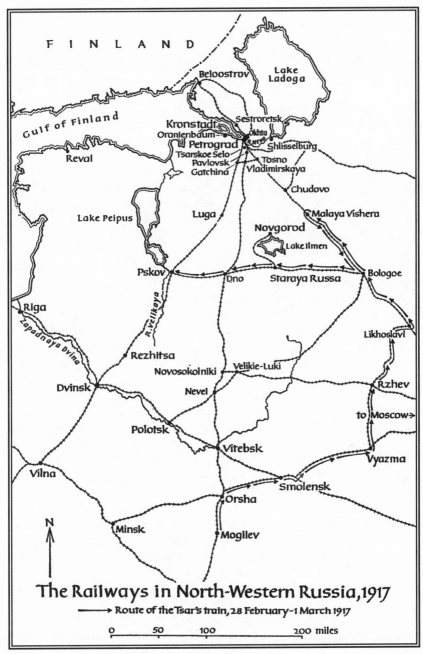

Map A. Railroads between *Stavka* and Petrograd (*Russia 1917: The February Revolution* by George Katkov).

of February 28, ignoring the suggestions of Ivanov, Alekseev, the leader of the Duma (M. V. Rodzyanko), and Grand Duke Mikhail that political concessions should accompany the military effort to restore order in Petrograd. Nicholas's effort to travel to Tsarskoe Selo, however, was greatly disrupted by reports that pro-revolutionary forces had seized key train stations en route. The tsar's train was redirected to Pskov, an intermediate point between Mogilev and Tsarskoe Selo that was the headquarters of the Northern Front. The tsar finally arrived at Pskov on the evening of March 1.[53]

The political situation had changed rapidly while Nicholas and Ivanov made their separate ways toward Tsarskoe Selo. Two new political bodies and conflicting authority structures had come into existence on February 27. The Duma had been suspended on February 26, and the next day an unofficial meeting of the Duma created a Provisional Committee of the Duma, which took responsibility for restoring order in Petrograd. On March 1 this Provisional Committee decided to form a Provisional Government (the tsar's Council of Ministers had resigned on February 27). The other body created on the twenty-seventh was the Petrograd Soviet of Workers' and Soldiers' Deputies, which came into being at the initiative of members of the socialist intelligentsia, with the support of soldiers and workers.[54]

Alekseev had been in touch with Petrograd, particularly with the War Minister, General M. A. Belyaev, the commander of the Petrograd garrison, General S. S. Khabalov, the General Staff, the Naval Staff, and Duma Chair Rodzyanko throughout the February 27–March 1 period. By the morning of February 28 it was clear that the city was in the hands of the revolutionaries and that the authorities, including Belyaev and Khabalov, had completely lost control. On March 1 Alekseev came to the conclusion that Ivanov's expeditionary force was likely to meet stiff resistance and that the Duma Provisional Committee had succeeded in establishing order in Petrograd and over the railroads. Alekseev thus telegraphed Ivanov with instructions to delay his march on Petrograd and convey this news to Nicholas. The tsar, however, never arrived in Tsarskoe Selo.[55]

Nicholas II, rather, arrived at Pskov on the evening of March 1. The Commander of the Northern Front, General N. V. Ruzskiy, met the Emperor. On the basis of information he had received from Alekseev, Ruzskiy met with the tsar for several hours and tried to persuade Nicholas of the futility of trying to put down the revolution with force and the need for political compromise with the Duma. A telegram from Alekseev to Nicholas arrived at about 11 P.M., in which Alekseev urged the tsar to issue a manifesto granting a constitutional monarchy with a government formed by the Duma. Nicholas eventually agreed.

---

[53] Hasegawa, *February Revolution*, pp. 431–441, 459–473.
[54] Schapiro, *1917*, 44–47; Hasegawa, *February Revolution*, pp. 313–427.
[55] Hasegawa, *February Revolution*, pp. 442–486.

On the morning of March 2, however, Ruzskiy had a four-hour "conversation" with Duma leader Rodzyanko over the Hughes apparatus, a kind of primitive teleprompter. By this point Rodzyanko had lost control of the Duma, and the Provisional Government was established on March 1 without his participation. Rodzyanko told Ruzskiy that the tsar's manifesto was too late and that the monarchy itself was in question. Ruzskiy sent a copy of the conversation to Alekseev, who polled all the front commanders. They unanimously endorsed the solution of Nicholas's abdication in favor of his son, Aleksey, with a regency headed by Grand Duke Mikhail. Nicholas agreed to this on March 2, but later that day he decided that his son should abdicate as well and that his brother Mikhail should become emperor. Mikhail, however, refused the throne the following day, March 3, after a lengthy discussion with the Provisional Government and the Duma Committee. The Romanov dynasty had come to an end.[56]

Explaining the High Command's Behavior during the February Revolution

Why did the military high command seemingly change its behavior so quickly, moving from support for repressing the Petrograd uprising on February 27–28 to endorsement of the tsar's abdication a mere two days later? This rapid change in stance is sometimes explained as the product of some sort of conspiracy between the leading generals and the Duma Committee. The evidence for this interpretation is extremely weak, however. I follow the general conclusion put forward by Hasegawa in his comprehensive account of the February Revolution: "[T]he actions and policies of the Duma Committee leaders and the military leaders are presented, not as conspiracies, but as their reaction to the over-all revolutionary situation in the capital." The high command was forced to respond to the events in Petrograd and the news they received from there as best they could, and they played a largely reactive role throughout the crisis. This conclusion is supported by primary sources that are available for process tracing the thoughts and actions of the army leadership.[57]

---

[56] Hasegawa, *February Revolution*, pp. 487–515, 546–568.

[57] Hasegawa, *February Revolution*, p. xvi. Two major sources form the backbone of this section. First, all the key documents of communications between *Stavka*, the Northern Front, and Petrograd have been published. See "Fevral'skaya revolyutsiya 1917 goda," *Krasnyy arkhiv* [hereafter *KA*], Nos. 21 and 22, 1927, 3–78, 3–70. I have verified the completeness of these records in the Russian State Military History Archive (RGVIA) in Moscow: fond 2003 (*Stavka*), opis 1, dela 1751–1754. Hereafter I follow conventional citation rules: i.e., RGVIA, f. 2003, op. 1, d. 1751, followed by the page (l.) number. The other major source, which includes some of the key telegraphs as well as some relevant memoir excerpts, is P. E. Shchegolev, ed., *Otrecheniye Nikolaya II: Vospominaniya ochevidtsev, dokumenty*, 2nd ed. (Moskva: Sovetskiy pisatel', 1990 [1927]).

Perhaps the most extreme version of the conspiracy theory is put forward by Matitiahu Mayzel. Mayzel asserts, "the high command (and the officers behind it) wished to get rid of the tsar."[58] Yet it is clear that on February 27th and 28th the high command, under Nicholas's orders, took a series of important steps toward putting down the revolution in Petrograd. On the twenty-seventh Alekseev communicated the need to send four ("the most solid and reliable") divisions to hook up with Ivanov, adding that "we must do everything to speed the arrival of solid forces. Our future depends on it." A similar number of forces were sent from the Western Front. On the afternoon of the 28th, Alekseev telegraphed the front commanders, "on all of us lies our sacred duty to the Emperor and the motherland to maintain loyalty to their duty and oath among the troops of the front armies, to secure the movement of the railways and the flow of food supplies." Alekseev also ordered Brusilov, the commander of the Southwestern Front, to prepare additional troops as a reserve force if necessary.[59]

To the extent the military leadership took a political stance on February 27–28, it was the recommendation of Generals Alekseev, Ruzskiy, and Brusilov to Nicholas not only to rely on force to restore order in Petrograd, but also to grant the concession of a cabinet that enjoyed the support of the Duma. This course of action had been urged on the tsar many times before from a wide range of political actors, and it was also recommended to Nicholas by Rodzyanko and Grand Duke Mikhail on the twenty-seventh. At the same time, the military leadership continued to follow the tsar's orders on sending troops. The high command was most concerned that order be restored in Petrograd and on the railways, since continued disorder threatened to disrupt the war effort.[60]

Alekseev's determination to use force was curtailed by news he received from Petrograd on the evening of the twenty-eighth. The Naval Staff informed *Stavka* that the Duma was trying to return the troops to the barracks, but that a government decision appointing a cabinet enjoying public confidence was necessary, and that without such a decision soon there was a danger that a worker–socialist organization could come to power. Alekseev also received news that a Provisional Government headed by Rodzyanko had been formed. Finally, Alekseev received a telegram dispatched to all railway stations by the Duma member A. A. Bublikov, who had seized control of the Ministry of Transport and arrested the former Minister. The "Bublikov telegram," as it came to be known, declared that the State Duma had taken power into its hands. From the point of view of *Stavka*, the essential part of

---

[58] Matitiahu Mayzel, *Generals and Revolutionaries: The Russian General Staff during the Revolution: A Study in the Transformation of Military Elite* (Osnabruck: Biblio-Verlag, 1979), p. 73.

[59] "Fevral'skaya revolyutsiya," *KA*, No. 21, 9–10, 22–24.

[60] Hasegawa, *February Revolution*, 459–463; "Fevral'skaya revolyutsiya," *KA*, No. 21, 7, 13.

the Bublikov telegram was that it called for all railway workers to stay at their posts and double their efforts to keep the trains moving.[61]

At around 1 A.M. on March 1 Alekseev telegraphed General Ivanov at Tsarskoe Selo, although Ivanov actually did not arrive there until nine o'clock that night. Alekseev stated that he had information that the Provisional Government was reasserting control and that a compromise based on the "stability of the monarchical principle" and new elections and a new government was possible. Alekseev advised Ivanov to "change his methods of action" and that negotiations could lead to "conciliation" and the "avoidance of shameful civil strife, so desired by our enemy." Alekseev asked Ivanov to report all of this to the tsar and expressed his wish that Nicholas would accept such an outcome, which would strengthen Russia. Alekseev's evident optimism has confounded historians, since it was apparently based on very little reliable information about the state of affairs in Petrograd. Alekseev, in particular, had not received any information about the "stability of the monarchical principle." The most likely explanation for Alekseev's change of mood is that he seized upon a couple of indicators of a change for the better, particularly the news about the railroads, and filled in the blanks in a manner consistent with his own thinking. He also knew that the tsar had not yet arrived in Tsarskoe Selo, that Ivanov's reinforcements were not in place, and that the garrison in Petrograd was completely unreliable. It is not surprising that Alekseev asked Ivanov not to proceed until news about the changed situation in Petrograd had been communicated to Nicholas.[62]

When the tsar finally arrived in Pskov on the evening of March 1, things finally came to a head. The high command continued to hold the view, as expressed by Quartermaster General A. S. Lukhomskiy, that "it is impossible to conduct a war while a revolution is taking place in Russia" and that the tsar should "issue an act that can calm the population." Alekseev sent a telegram to the tsar in Pskov on the afternoon of the first, to be delivered

---

[61] "Fevral'skaya revolyutsiya," *KA*, No. 21, 29, 32–33, 35.

[62] "Fevral'skaya revolyutsiya," *KA*, No. 21, 31. Several prominent historians, including Allan Wildman and George Katkov, have suggested that Alekseev was verging on insubordination by sending such a telegram to Ivanov. We are now into the realm of counterfactuals, but I do not find this argument persuasive. There is no reason to think that Alekseev would have disobeyed a direct order from Nicholas if Nicholas had insisted that Ivanov continue his mission. Given the extent of Alekseev's authority as Chief of Staff, the fact that he had not communicated with the tsar all day, and that the situation in Petrograd had apparently radically changed, Alekseev's decision that a highly risky repressive operation against Petrograd, with unclear prospects for success, should be delayed until the tsar could assess the situation for himself was not unreasonable. It is also somewhat of a moot point, since Nicholas himself telegramed Ivanov asking him to halt his operation at midnight on March 1 (a mere three hours after Ivanov arrived in Tsarskoe Selo), and Ivanov's reinforcements had not yet arrived. This telegram is "Fevral'skaya revolyutsiya," *KA*, No. 21, 53. For Wildman and Katkov's views, see Wildman, *The End of the Russian Imperial Army*, Vol. I, pp. 205–207; Katkov, *Russia 1917*, pp. 302–305, 313–317.

by Ruzskiy when Nicholas arrived. Alekseev pointed out that the disorder had spread to Moscow and that it would be impossible to keep the railroads running and deliver supplies to the front in such a condition. This would be "fatal" for Russia and could lead to "a shameful conclusion of the war, with all the corresponding difficult consequences for Russia." It would be impossible, Alekseev argued, to isolate the army from revolution in the rear. He considered it his duty to inform the emperor that it was "necessary to take immediate measures to calm the population and restore normal life in the country." Alekseev believed that without such a decision by the tsar it was possible that extremist elements would come to power. He said, "I beg your highness, for the sake of saving Russia and the dynasty," to appoint a prime minister enjoying public confidence with the authority to form a cabinet.[63]

Northern Front commander Ruzskiy was entrusted by Alekseev with the task of persuading the tsar to accept a political compromise. Originally Rodzyanko had planned to come from Petrograd to negotiate with Nicholas, but he had failed to do so. Ruzskiy met with Nicholas on the evening of March 1 in Pskov. Ruzskiy later remarked that he understood that the most serious hour of his life had arrived, "when from a front commander-in-chief he was turned into a purely political actor." Ruzskiy began his conversation with the tsar by noting "that it was difficult for him to speak, because his report was beyond the limits of his competence" and he asked Nicholas to bear in mind that because the decisions to be made dealt "not with military questions, but those of state administration," he would understand if the tsar found it objectionable to listen to his report. Nicholas told Ruzskiy to speak with complete openness. Ruzskiy then set to work to persuade the emperor of the need to form a cabinet that would be responsible to the Duma. Ruzskiy eventually was able to persuade the tsar to grant the political concession of a responsible ministry.[64]

About this time a second telegram arrived from Alekseev also urging this concession. Alekseev reminded the tsar of "the growing danger of the spread of anarchy across the entire country, the further disintegration of the army,

---

[63] "Fevral'skaya revolyutsiya," *KA*, No. 21, 36–37, 39–40. See also Nicolas de Basily, *Diplomat of Imperial Russia 1903–1917: Memoirs* (Stanford, CA: Hoover Institution Press, 1973), 103–148.

[64] The details of this meeting are based on Ruzskiy's recollections, available in two second-hand accounts (of S. N. Vil'chkovskiy and A. V. Romanov) and one brief newspaper interview. See General S. N. Vil'chkovskiy, "Prebyvaniye Nikolaya II v Pskove 1 i 2 marta 1917 g.," in Shegolev, *Otrecheniye Nikolaya II*, pp. 146–168; General N. V. Ruzskiy, "Beseda s zhurnalistom V. Samoylovym ob otrechenii Nikolaya II," in Shegolev, *Otrecheniye Nikolaya II*, pp. 142–145; "Iz dnevnika A. V. Romanova," *KA*, No. 1(26), 1928, 201–208. See also "V dni otrecheniya (Iz dnevnika Nikolaya II)," in Shegolev, *Otrecheniye Nikolaya II*, p. 34; "Fevral'skaya revolyutsiya," *KA*, No. 21, 41–42; Hasegawa, *February Revolution*, pp. 450–458; Katkov, *Russia 1917*, pp. 318–321.

and the impossibility of continuing the war" under these conditions. He "implored" the emperor to grant a responsible ministry headed by Rodzyanko. Alekseev had tasked the Foreign Ministry representative at *Stavka*, Nicolas de Basily, with preparing the text of such an act. Nicholas agreed to the text without changes. Nicholas seemed so indifferent that Ruzskiy asked again "if he would be acting against the wishes of the emperor if he were to inform *Stavka* and Petrograd of Nicholas's agreement to the manifesto." The tsar replied that it was a difficult decision for him but that he took it in the best interests of Russia.[65]

Most historians have concluded that, in the words of George Katkov, Ruzskiy "gave the emperor no choice" but to agree to these political concessions. It is impossible to know what Nicholas was thinking, but it should be stressed that neither Ruzskiy nor Alekseev ever suggested to the tsar that they would not follow his orders if he decided differently. In the crucial Alekseev telegram that arrived in the middle of Ruzskiy's discussion with Nicholas, Alekseev wrote, "I zealously implore your Imperial Majesty, if you please," to agree to the manifesto prepared at *Stavka*, hardly a coercive choice of words. The pressure of the circumstances certainly forced Nicholas's decision as much as any threat of military insubordination, which would have been quite out of character for either the tsar or the high command to contemplate.[66]

Ruzskiy's relief at persuading Nicholas to accept this political concession was quickly dissipated when he contacted Rodzyanko the morning of March 2 to tell him of the tsar's decision. Rodzyanko replied that Ruzskiy and Nicholas II were obviously not aware of the most recent developments in Petrograd, where "the most frightening revolution" was taking place. He stated that "the dynastic question has been put point blank," and that Nicholas needed to abdicate in favor of his son. Ruzskiy replied by noting the threat of anarchy to the country in general and the war effort in particular. He emphasized, "the crisis needs to be liquidated as soon as possible, in order to give back to the army the possibility of looking only forward in the direction of the enemy...if the anarchy of which you are speaking spreads to the army and commanders lose the authority of power – think, what will become of our motherland then?"[67]

The army, having already been forced to arbitrate between the Duma Committee and the tsar on the question of a responsible ministry, was immediately thrust again on to center stage. The contents of the Ruzskiy-Rodzyanko conversation were immediately relayed to *Stavka*. Around noon on March 2, Alekseev began to inform the other front commanders about

[65] "Iz dnevnika A. V. Romanova," 204; "Fevral'skaya revolyutsiya," *KA*, No. 21, 53–54; de Basily, *Diplomat of Imperial Russia*, pp. 116–117; Vil'chkovskiy, "Prebyvaniye Nikolaya II," 153–154.

[66] Katkov, *Russia 1917*, p. 324; Hasegawa, *February Revolution*, pp. 494–495.

[67] "Fevral'skaya revolyutsiya," *KA*, No. 21, 55–59.

the previous night's developments. Alekseev communicated his opinion that there was no other option than for the tsar to abdicate in favor of his son, under the regency of Grand Duke Mikhail. Alekseev argued that there was no other choice because the Provisional Government in essence had control over the functioning of the railways and the future of the army. "It is necessary to save the army in the field from collapse," Alekseev stressed, "to continue the struggle with the external enemy to the end and save the independence of Russia." De Basily later remarked that Alekseev endorsed abdication because "to oppose it would have been to add civil war to external war." Alekseev asked all of the front commanders, if they agreed with his views, to send them to the tsar as soon as possible. Alekseev concluded:

Among the high command of the front armies there needs to be a unity of views and goals and thus save the army from wavering and possible instances of betrayal of duty. The army should with all of its might struggle with the external enemy, and decisions about internal affairs should free it from the temptation to take part in the revolution, which can be more painlessly accomplished with a decision from the top.[68]

All of the front commanders supported Alekseev's position. In the afternoon of March 2, Alekseev telegraphed Nicholas with the replies of the front commanders. The Grand Duke Nikolay Nikolayevich, commander of the Caucasian Front, wrote that victory in the war was necessary for both Russia and the future of the dynasty and thus required extraordinary measures. The other commanders replied in similar terms, stressing the importance of the war effort. The one dissonant note came from General V. V. Sakharov, the commander of the Romanian Front, who denounced the Duma in extremely bitter terms. Sakharov concluded, however, that there seemed to be no other choice but to submit to the Duma's demands if the war were to be continued. Alekseev concluded his telegram to Nicholas by noting, "the army's contact with matters of internal politics will signify the inevitable end of the war, shame for Russia, her collapse."[69]

On March 2, Ruzskiy once again met with the emperor, this time on the question of the tsar's abdication. He found this discussion with the tsar much easier than the one on granting a responsible ministry the previous evening. Nicholas had already crossed the Rubicon the night before by agreeing to a constitutional monarchy with a strong parliament, thereby giving up on the ideal of autocracy that he had adhered to since his childhood. Moreover, the combined opinions of the military leadership, including his trusted chief of staff Alekseev and his uncle the Grand Duke Nikolay, certainly carried great weight. According to the diplomat de Basily, Alekseev was a "faithful soldier [who] had never failed in his loyalty to his sovereign and supreme commander," but Alekseev saw no other way out without risking internal

---

[68] "Fevral'skaya revolyutsiya," *KA*, No. 21, 67–70; de Basily, *Diplomat of Imperial Russia*, 120.
[69] "Fevral'skaya revolyutsiya," *KA*, No. 21, 67–75. See also: Denikin, *Ocherki*, I (1), pp. 56–57.

disorder and military defeat and collapse. Hasegawa sums up the stance of Alekseev, and the entire high command, in similar terms: "The best course of action seemed to Alekseev to take the posture of noninterference in internal politics, while putting pressure on the [t]sar to sacrifice himself for a peaceful settlement of the crisis." Katkov offers a similar assessment, rejecting the view that the abdication of the tsar came about because of a "general's revolution." "Throughout the war," Katkov concludes, "the generals adopted a strictly non-political attitude."[70]

The decision of the tsar to abdicate in favor of his brother, Grand Duke Mikhail, rather than his son Aleksey instantly threw the entire revolutionary settlement into an additional round of turmoil. Evidently, Alekseev and leading Duma liberals such as Rodzyanko, Aleksandr Guchkov (who became the first Minister of War in the Provisional Government), and Pavel Milyukov (who became Minister of Foreign Affairs) expected that the abdication in favor of a child would end the revolutionary upheaval in Petrograd while maintaining the Romanov dynasty. Katkov states, "even when the abdication had been decided upon the generals still believed that they were taking part in an action to save the monarchy and maintain the dynasty." Grand Duke Mikhail's accession to the throne was more problematic from both a political and legal point of view.[71]

Rodzyanko contacted Alekseev early on the morning of March 3 and asked that Alekseev delay the announcement of the abdication of Nicholas II. Rodzyanko explained his desire to hold up the news on the basis of his judgment that Grand Duke Mikhail was an unacceptable candidate as emperor who had no popular support. Rodzyanko said that the Duma Committee and the Provisional Government would rule until a Constituent Assembly could be called. Alekseev was extremely unhappy with this news. He considered both the uncertainty about the dynastic question and the calling of a Constituent Assembly during the middle of the war harmful from the point of view of the army. Alekseev noted that "all the thoughts and endeavors of command personnel of the field army" are directed toward keeping the army focused on the war and not allowing it to come into contact with "the unhealthy internal condition that part of Russia is experiencing." He concluded by emphasizing, "I am a soldier, and all of my thoughts are directed west, towards the front and the enemy."[72]

This latest news from Petrograd apparently convinced Alekseev that he had been played for a fool by Rodzyanko during their negotiations over the

[70] Vil'chkovskiy, "Prebyvaniye Nikolaya II," 160–163; "Iz dnevnika A.V. Romanova," 206–207; de Basily, *Diplomat of Imperial Russia*, p. 120; Hasegawa, *February Revolution*, 501–507 (quote, p. 501); Katkov, *Russia 1917*, pp. 323, 326–344, 356, 427–430 (quote, p. 428).

[71] De Basily, *Diplomat of Imperial Russia*, pp. 125–132; "Iz dnevnika A.V. Romanova," 207; Hasegawa, *February Revolution*, p. 546; Katkov, *Russia 1917*, p. 429.

[72] "Fevral'skaya revolyutsiya," *KA*, No. 22, 25–29.

last several days. Alekseev first had been led to believe that the granting of a constitutional monarchy by the tsar, and then Nicholas II's abdication, would end the revolution and allow the army to concentrate on the war. Now he was being told that the entire dynastic principle was in question. The afternoon of March 3 Alekseev telegraphed all of the front commanders. He summarized the current situation and then laid out a series of conclusions. He maintained that the Duma Committee was divided and that left-wing elements had gained influence over Rodzyanko. He noted that the Petrograd garrison had become "harmful and dangerous for everyone." The entire situation, Alekseev argued, was full of grave danger for the front armies and could undermine Russia's fighting capacity, leading to military defeat, the loss of territory, and the triumph of extreme leftist elements in Russia's remaining territory. Alekseev considered it necessary to insist to Rodzyanko that the tsar's abdication manifesto be realized, and that there be a conference at *Stavka* of all the front commanders "to establish unity in all cases and circumstances." He suggested that the conference should be March 8 or 9. Alekseev concluded, "the collective voice of the army's highest ranks and their conditions...should become known to all and influence the course of events."[73]

This March 3 telegram of Alekseev often has been interpreted as a possible prelude to military intervention. Hasegawa states, "the proposal for a conference of commanders in chief clearly indicated his [Alekseev's] intention to revive the plan of military intervention against Petrograd." There are several problems with this interpretation. It is true that this is the strongest language Alekseev had used on the need for the military to influence a sovereign power question. He was clearly frustrated about first being forced into the arbiter role, only to end up with the least desirable outcome from his point of view. At the same time, it seems an overstatement to claim that a potential coup was in the offing. If Alekseev was interested in using force against the Provisional Government, he would have had to take bolder steps than calling for a conference a week later. Additionally, the very day (March 3) that Alekseev was allegedly contemplating military intervention he ordered General Ivanov to return to *Stavka*. The previous day (March 2) the movement of troops from the front to hook up with Ivanov was halted. This would indeed be a strange coup, then, because troops were being ordered to move away from Petrograd and the planning for it was to take place a week later. Allan Wildman's characterization of Alekseev's March 3 telegram seems more accurate: "This was the first glimmer of the impulse to suspend the traditional view of the Army as 'above politics' for the sake of reestablishing authority and discipline." Alekseev had no plan to intervene, but a "glimmer of [an] impulse."[74]

73 "Fevral'skaya revolyutsiya," *KA*, No. 22, 22–24.
74 Hasegawa, *February Revolution*, p. 552; Wildman, *End of the Russian Imperial Army*, Vol. I, p. 213. Katkov, similarly, speaks of "the formation of a military *junta*" as a possible result

Regardless of Alekseev's intent, the suggestion of a conference at *Stavka* of the front commanders was rejected by the commanders themselves. Ruzskiy noted that the best way to maintain unity among the high command was for *Stavka* to be in direct contact with the government, and for *Stavka* to then issue government orders to the commanders of the fronts. Several of them stressed the need for the commanders to remain at the front in order to maintain discipline. Brusilov stressed the need to appeal to the troops with the message that they were to defend Mother Russia and that the army "cannot get involved in politics now." Only Sakharov gave an unqualified endorsement to Alekseev's proposal.[75]

On the evening of March 3, Alekseev had a final series of conversations with Guchkov and Rodzyanko during which he learned of Grand Duke Mikhail's decision to abdicate. Alekseev reacted with despair to this news, which he thought would have a negative impact on the armed forces. He stated, "the current army in the field needs to be preserved and spared from all kinds of passions about internal questions.... The ferocious struggle [with the enemy] is still far from over, and the fatherland needs every fighter." Alekseev requested that the new government do its utmost for the defense effort and the maintenance of unity and discipline in the armed forces.[76]

The two abdication manifestoes were distributed throughout the armed forces on March 4. There were only a few reported instances of senior commanders refusing to announce the abdications. Many of them left the task of explaining the abdications to their junior officers. Wildman notes that this reluctance may have been due to their fears that their authority as commanders had been undermined, but he explained their hesitation as a product of something else: "Perhaps more fundamental was their total unfamiliarity with 'politics': when suddenly thrust into the role of explaining a political act of the first magnitude (one, moreover, that went to the heart of their own loyalties), they were at a complete loss."[77]

Summary

The outcome of the February Revolution hinged importantly on the political stance of the military leadership. The army became the arbiter of the sovereign power dispute that the revolution provoked. The army high command was far from eager to play this role, but it had no choice. Throughout

---

of Alekseev's proposed conference: Katkov, *Russia 1917*, p. 350. Hasegawa reconstructs the movement of Ivanov's units in considerable detail, and he shows that Ivanov's mission was not canceled because of unreliable troops, as some (particularly Soviet) scholars have argued, but due to a change in policy: Hasegawa, *February Revolution*, pp. 478–486.

75 "Fevral'skaya revolyutsiya," *KA*, No. 22, 24–25, 32–33, 42–44.

76 "Fevral'skaya revolyutsiya," *KA*, No. 22, 36–42.

77 Wildman, *The End of the Russian Imperial Army*, Vol. I, pp. 217–219; Peter Kenez, *Civil War in South Russia, 1918* (Berkeley, CA: University of California Press, 1971), pp. 20–21.

the revolutionary crisis, leading Russian officers were guided by their concern that the war effort continue without disruption. The desire of the military leadership to stay "outside politics" and focused on external defense was consistent with their organizational culture. The domestic structure explanation also is essential for understanding why the military was thrust into the arbiter role, although it does not account for the extreme reluctance of the military to become more directly involved, let alone to try and seize power for itself. Cleavages within the officer corps (organizational structure) were not important: Despite allegedly serious internal splits, it remained unified throughout the crisis. The troops of the Petrograd garrison, on the other hand, were a fundamental contributor to the revolution, which represented the first, but by no means the last, appearance of the army rank and file on the political stage in 1917. The corporate interest approach may help explain why the army was willing to come to terms with the Duma leadership, which it thought could help advance the war effort. More important, though, was the fact that the military leadership wanted political stability so it could continue the war. It did not behave as a rational bureaucratic actor seeking to gain for itself a more powerful role as a result of the revolutionary chaos. The Russian army in February 1917 was not predisposed toward a virtual military dictatorship, similar to the arrangement in Germany under Hindenburg and Ludendorff.[78] In the next section we will see to what extent the organizational culture of the Russian officer corps had changed as a result of the disintegration of the armed forces in the aftermath of the February Revolution.

THE PROVISIONAL GOVERNMENT AND THE KORNILOV AFFAIR

The February Revolution, in the eyes of most segments of Russian society and the Russian political elite, was supposed to usher in a new era in the country's political life, a bold departure from the old regime. There was little agreement, however, on the terms of the new order. The sharpest clash was between elite society and the bulk of the Russian population. If the February Revolution had abruptly ended the polarization between the government and the elites, the polarization between the upper and lower classes was as sharp as ever. The war effort was perhaps the most contentious issue dividing Russian society.

This polarization of Russian society was clearly reflected in the army. The officer corps believed in a continuation of the war until victory was achieved. The soldiers, on the other hand, were ready for peace. The February Revolution marked the beginning of the disintegration of the Russian armed forces, which severely strained relations within the army and between the military and the government.

---

[78] Gordon A. Craig, *The Politics of the Prussian Army 1640–1945* (Oxford, England: Oxford University Press, 1955), pp. 299–341.

Efforts by the military leadership to fight disintegration within the country and the army eventually led to a confrontation between General Kornilov, appointed Supreme Commander in July, and the Provisional Government headed by Alexander Kerensky. In late August, Kornilov was denounced as a plotter by Kerensky and dismissed as commander. Kornilov at this point raised the flag of revolt and sent troops to march on Petrograd, but he had little backing and his putsch was quickly defeated. Whether Kornilov had been planning a military coup before Kerensky's denunciation of him is a hotly contested issue. I find little evidence that a military coup against the Provisional Government was being planned, although the idea did have some support in the officer corps. Military action against the Petrograd Soviet was intended, but in conjunction with Kerensky. Kornilov is undoubtedly guilty of insubordination, but only after Kerensky decided to dismiss him.

In this section I discuss the key political developments between the February Revolution and the Kornilov affair. I concentrate on the attitude of the high command toward developments in the armed forces and the thinking of leading officers about the role of the army in sovereign power issues. I then explain the behavior of the armed forces during the Kornilov affair.

Dual Power: The Provisional Government, the Soviets, and the War

After the smoke of the February Revolution had cleared, two authority structures emerged as contenders for influence in the formation of state policy. The Provisional Government was formed on the basis of the Duma, and bourgeois liberals dominated the first government. The revolution in Petrograd, however, had largely been accomplished by workers and soldiers, and the Petrograd Soviet represented their interests. The Soviet rejected the prospect of either (a) trying to establish a revolutionary government of its own or (b) entering into a coalition with the bourgeois liberals, and adopted a policy of conditional support for the Provisional Government.[79]

The entire period of Provisional Government rule was marked by a series of crises, confrontations, and accommodations between the government and the Soviet. Perhaps the most vexing question of all was the war. The first Provisional Government was brought down in April by a disagreement with the Petrograd Soviet over Russia's war aims, accompanied by massive protests in support of the Soviet (the "April Crisis"). In May a "coalition government" based on the liberal Kadet party and moderate socialist elements from the Petrograd Soviet came into being.[80]

The new coalition government and its War Minister, the socialist Kerensky, decided that a Russian military offensive was necessary to force

---

[79] Acton, *Rethinking the Russian Revolution*, pp. 22–27, 129–166; Schapiro, *1917*, pp. 55–119.

[80] Rex A. Wade, *The Russian Search for Peace: February–October 1917* (Stanford, CA: Stanford University Press, 1969), pp. 9–50.

the allies to take them and their program for an immediate peace seriously. The military leadership thought that an offensive was the only way to stop the disintegration of the armed forces. The "Kerensky offensive" was launched on June 18 and collapsed almost immediately. The problem of the war had not been solved. A separate peace was ruled out on the grounds that it could lead to German victory in the war, which would probably be fatal for the revolution. Yet the army was obviously in no state to fight, and its disintegration gathered speed after the failure of the Kerensky offensive.[81]

The war was by no means the only problem faced by the Provisional Government. Equally vexing issues were the state of the economy, the demand of the peasantry for land, the rise of national autonomy movements, and the need to call a Constituent Assembly to provide the government with greater legitimacy. All of these issues, however, were bound up with the war; and they were difficult, if not impossible, to solve until the war was over. Most relevant from the point of view of the army, it was difficult to solve the land question during the war. The redistribution of land could not take place without risking a complete collapse of the front, since many peasant-soldiers would return to their native villages to get their fair share. Most soldiers thought that the February Revolution signaled the end of the war and the distribution of land, and the inability of both the government and the Soviets to solve either problem contributed significantly to the drift of the army masses to the Bolsheviks, who promised to satisfy immediately the soldiers' desire for peace and land.[82]

The High Command and the Revolution

The adoption by the Petrograd Soviet of Order No. 1 caused the collapse of the old authority relations in the Russian military. Dual power quickly became a fact of life at the front as well as in the rear. The polarization in Russian society between the elites and the masses was reproduced in the army, with an often unbridgeable gulf separating officers from the troops. Soldiers' committees sprang up at the front to represent rank-and-file interests, and they were already well-institutionalized by April. These committees were a clear symbol of dual power in the army.[83]

The high command was dismayed to discover that the revolution had seriously undermined officer control over the troops. Equally distressing to

[81] Wade, *Russian Search for Peace*, pp. 51–117; Frenkin, *Russkaya armiya*, pp. 341–384; Wildman, *The End of the Russian Imperial Army*, Vol. II, pp. 73–111.

[82] Wade, *Russian Search for Peace*, pp. 142–143; Gill, *Peasants and Government*; Frenkin, *Russkaya armiya*; Wildman, *The End of the Russian Imperial Army*.

[83] Wildman, *The End of the Russian Imperial Army*, Vol. I, pp. 202–290; Frenkin, *Russkaya armiya*, pp. 53–181.

the high command was the fact that the Provisional Government was dependent on the Petrograd Soviet. The Soviet pursued an internally contradictory policy toward the army, striving both to maintain it as a fighting force to defend the revolution from the Central Powers and to undermine it as a possible base for counterrevolution. The officer corps found itself under attack from below and lacking real support on the part of either the Provisional Government or the Soviet.[84]

Most troops and officers accepted the abdication of Nicholas II "calmly" (*spokoyno*). Many officers were apparently optimistic, seeing the fall of the autocracy as marking the end of the pernicious influence of the "German lobby" (the tsarina, Rasputin, and their "circle") on state policy. General V. I. Selivachev enthused in his diary, "Is not this the beginning of the end for Germany??" Within a week, however, Selivachev had become extremely pessimistic and was predicting "a time of terror and civil war."[85]

The high command already had lost considerable faith in the Provisional Government during the negotiations over the abdication; and as the revolution spread to the front, their alarm was readily apparent. Between March 4 and March 7 Alekseev, who was appointed Supreme Commander by the Provisional Government, fired off a series of telegrams to Prime Minister G. E. L'vov and Defense Minister Guchkov. Alekseev noted that complaints were coming in from front commanders – particularly from the Northern and Western fronts (the ones closest to Petrograd and Moscow) – regarding the appearance of "delegates" from the capital in the army, claiming to speak for the workers or the Soviet. Alekseev stressed that all orders to military commanders should come through *Stavka* and only from the Provisional Government; the army did not recognize the Petrograd Soviet as a governing body authorized to make pronouncements on military matters. The arrest and even murder of officers by their own troops was seriously undermining officer morale and military discipline. The high command, only a few days after the abdication, began to warn of the possible collapse of the army and the threat to the country from Germany if the military disintegrated.[86]

The military high command had no interest in having the army, including both officers and soldiers, involved in politics. This stance is clear from their reaction to a decision of the Provisional Government to allow military personnel to participate in politics. Order No. 114, issued on March 5, introduced several major changes in the army's service regulations. The

---

[84] Wildman, *The End of the Russian Imperial Army*, Vol. I, pp. 374–375; Schapiro, *1917*, p. 89.

[85] RGVIA, f. 2003, op. 1, d. 1755, ll. 14–50; "Verkhovnoye komandovaniye v pervye dni revolyutsii," *KA*, No. 5, 1924, 233–235; "Iz dnevnika gen. V. I. Selivacheva," *KA*, No. 9, 1925, 108–114; Verkhovskiy, "Rossiya na golgofe," 67–74.

[86] RGVIA, f. 2003, op. 1, d. 1756, ll. 50, 83–87, 100–101; "Verkhovnoye komandovaniye," *KA*, No. 5, 225–228; "Fevral'skaya revolyutsiya," *KA*, No. 22, 50–52, 57–58.

change that elicited the biggest outcry from the officer corps was the one permitting military personnel to become members of organizations with political
goals.[87]

Alekseev protested that a fundamental change in the service regulations
allowing military personnel to participate in political groups during wartime
would be "disastrous" for the war effort and military discipline. He predicted
an "inevitable split" in the army. Alekseev reminded the government that
the army was currently at war and that "turning it into an arena of political
struggle will inevitably entail catastrophic consequences."[88]

A detailed reply to Order No. 114 on behalf of *Stavka* was drafted by
Quartermaster-General Lukhomskiy. Lukhomskiy declared that the permission for soldiers to get involved in politics is "completely intolerable" and a
"violation of the one true principle – the non-interference of the army in politics." "History teaches us," Lukhomskiy continued, "that an army dragged
into politics will always take part in coup d'états." Lukhomskiy stressed
that the army recognized the revolution and the new government, and that
it should be left alone and not become occupied with political questions. If
the army was dragged into politics, he warned, its "currently calm voice"
would possibly become "threatening" and that it was hard to say what political position the army would take. Lukhomskiy perceptively predicted that
the consequences of involving the army in politics would be dire, including
military defeat by the Germans and a "lengthy civil war" in Russia.[89]

Other officers, from front commanders on down, also protested Order
No. 114 and its potentially pernicious effects on the military. General
Brusilov protested:

Allowing soldiers to participate in political organizations is undoubtedly harmful,
because it undermines the basic foundations of military service and introduces into
military units a political element, when an army should be outside it. The interference of the army in politics is a destructive influence on its necessary discipline and
inevitably distracts the military from its direct goal, and this will always be a threat
to the firmness of state power and will weaken the stability of the state organism.
The army is isolated from political influences and overtures in all states, even those
with the most liberal political systems.[90]

An avalanche of complaints poured into *Stavka* about the proposed
changes. Corps Commander Mishchenko considered the changes concerning
political activity in Order 114 "completely incompatible with the military

---

[87] For the text of Order No. 114, see L. S. Gaponenko et al., eds., *Velikaya oktyabr'skaya
sotsialisticheskaya revolyutsiya* [hereafter *VOSR*]: *Revolyutsionnoye dvizheniye v Rossii posle
sverzheniya samoderzhaviya. Dokumenty i materialy* (Moskva: Izdatel'stvo Akademii Nauk
SSSR, 1957), p. 424.

[88] RGVIA, f. 2003, op. 1, d. 1758, l. 95; RGVIA, f. 2003, op. 1, d. 1760, l. 23 .

[89] RGVIA, f. 2003, op. 1, d. 1758, ll. 131–137.

[90] RGVIA, f. 2003, op. 1, d. 1760, ll. 32–35.

spirit." General M. F. Kvetsinskiy, the Chief of Staff of the Western Front, noted that officers had been raised under the old system and were thereby politically "inert," but other groups were already active among the troops and working successfully to bring them over to their side. Kvetsinskiy predicted that if prohibitions were not reinstated, officers also would start to become involved in politics. A Major-General and a Colonel telegraphed the War Ministry from the Far East to protest Order No. 114, arguing that all officers should be "outside politics" and that those who could not adhere to such a stance should retire. Similar views were expressed by other officers.[91]

The innovations of the Provisional Government encapsulated in Order No. 114 sharply contradicted the organizational culture of the Russian officer corps. Nevertheless, the Provisional Government let the order stand and went one step further, setting up a commission to work out a "Declaration of Soldiers' Rights." Military personnel of all ranks were given the right to join any political organization and to express their political views when off duty either in print or orally. Alekseev objected strongly to Guchkov about the provisions in the draft declaration. Alekseev wondered if there was any distinction between free speech and treason, noting sarcastically that under the new declaration apparently one could work for, say, the restoration of the monarchy or "solicit donations for the German navy."[92]

On May 1, Guchkov resigned from the Provisional Government. The Declaration of Soldiers' Rights was issued by the new War Minister, Kerensky, on May 8. Kerensky had been the only socialist to join the first Provisional Government and was a lawyer with no military or foreign policy experience. Alekseev had no faith whatsoever in Kerensky, deriding him as a "nincompoop, buffoon and charlatan" in his diaries. Most historians have been equally unkind to Kerensky, accusing him of engaging in "banal theatrics" and being "hysterical" and noting that he "was doubtless a poseur and a windbag." Kerensky engineered the dismissal of Alekseev as Supreme Commander, presumably because of Alekseev's support for the allied war aims and his opposition to the Declaration of Soldiers' Rights. Kerensky had Brusilov, the commander of the Southwestern Front, appointed in Alekseev's place.[93]

The collapse of the June Kerensky offensive was both a consequence of the disintegration of the army and a further catalyst to its breakdown. The despair of the high command plummeted to new depths. Their mood was

---

[91] For the officers cited here, plus additional ones not cited, see RGVIA, f. 2003, op. 1, d. 1760, ll. 41–49, 60; RGVIA, f. 366, op. 1, d. 11, ll. 170–173, 308–311. See also Denikin, *Ocherki*, I (1), p. 63; I (2), p. 24.

[92] RGVIA, f. 2003, op. 1, d. 1760, ll. 79–81.

[93] George Katkov, *The Kornilov Affair: Kerensky and the Break-up of the Russian Army* (London: Longman, 1980), pp. 11, 19–21; Wildman, *The End of the Russian Imperial Army*, Vol. II, p. 27; Schapiro, 1917, p. 55; Acton, *Rethinking the Russian Revolution*, p. 131.

expressed well by General P. S. Baluyev, commander of the Eleventh Army on the Southwestern Front. Baluyev telegraphed Kerensky and Brusilov on July 12, claiming that he was "horrified (*v uzhase*) at the shame and ruin that threatens Russia and the revolution." Many units, he reported, have become "undisciplined armed crowds." Baluyev considered it necessary to restore the commanders' full powers that had existed before the revolution, to reintroduce the death penalty, and to halt all meetings and political discussions in the army until the war was over. Supreme Commander Brusilov telegraphed Kerensky on July 13 with a list of similar demands, including: granting commanders full disciplinary powers; forbidding political meetings; reducing the role of committees to advisory status, dealing only with questions of the soldiers' daily life; and "categorically forbidding soldiers' participation in any political societies or organizations during the war."[94]

Kerensky, in response to the failure of the June offensive and the clamor from the officer corps for stricter discipline, called a conference at *Stavka* on July 16 that included all of the Front commanders plus several other prominent generals. The military leadership called for discipline to be restored, the raising of the authority of the commander, the abolition or curtailment of committees and commissars in the army, the cancellation of the Declaration of Soldiers' Rights, and the abolition of politics from the army. On July 12 the government had approved the restoration of the death penalty at the front for military personnel guilty of certain crimes, and it was proposed that it be extended to the rear. The conference had little effect, since, as Leonard Schapiro notes, the military leadership was "demanding the impossible – that the clock be turned back, and that the effects of the revolution on the army be wiped out."[95]

The most important change to come out of the July 16 *Stavka* conference was the appointment of a new Supreme Commander. General Lavr Kornilov had been Commander of the Petrograd garrison during the April Crisis, but resigned after his intention to use force in support of the government against demonstrators was countermanded by the Petrograd Soviet. He was made Commander of the Eighth Army on the Southwestern Front. Kornilov made a name for himself by applying summary execution to deserters and with a toughly worded telegram (which was leaked to the press) calling for harsh measures on the part of the government to restore discipline in the army.

---

[94] RGVIA, f. 2003, op. 1, d. 1786, ll. 192–197; RGVIA, f. 366, op. 1, d. 81, ll. 50–53. For Alekseev's reports from March, April, and May on the state of the army, see L. S. Gaponenko, ed., *Revolyutsionnoye dvizheniye v russkoy armii 27 fevralya–24 oktyabrya 1917 goda: sbornik dokumentov* (Moskva: "Nauka," 1968), pp. 35–38, 61–63, 111. Officers' letters during the summer of 1917 also reflected their despair about their loss of authority and the disintegration of the army: RGVIA, f. 2003, op. 1, d. 1786, ll. 5–23.

[95] Schapiro, *1917*, p. 103. For a complete transcript, see "Protokol Soveshchaniya Ministra-Predsedatelya A.F. Kerenskogo s generalitetom v STAVKE 16 iyulya 1917 goda," *Russkiy arkhiv*, No. 3, 1993, 139–184.

Kornilov had not attended the July 16 conference, but a telegram he sent to the meeting was more conciliatory toward committees and commissars than the views expressed by the rest of the high command. Kerensky apparently found Kornilov more acceptable than the other top generals, despite Kornilov's reputation as a stern disciplinarian.[96]

Kornilov, the Provisional Government, and the Question of Dictatorship

Kornilov's appointment as Supreme Commander came at a time when the mood in the country had shifted somewhat toward the right. The collapse of the June offensive had demonstrated the desperate position of the army. The violence of the "July Days," in which radical workers, soldiers, and sailors, with definite Bolshevik participation if not leadership, tried to force the Petrograd Soviet to push aside the Provisional Government and take power for itself, was also seen by some elements of society as proof that firm state power was needed. During the July Days the Provisional Government announced that they had information demonstrating that Lenin and other Bolsheviks were working for Germany. The military leadership, having witnessed the effects of Bolshevik propaganda on the troops, supported a crackdown on the Bolsheviks and strong state power.[97]

One of Kornilov's conditions for accepting the post of Supreme Commander was that the government apply stern measures like the death penalty for military crimes in the rear as well as the front. Throughout the month of August, Kornilov was involved in negotiations with Kerensky and the Deputy War Minister, B. V. Savinkov, to get government agreement to his program, which included not only the death penalty but also raising the power and authority of commanders and curtailing the responsibilities of soldiers' committees and government commissars. Government pursuit of such policies would put it on a collision course with the Petrograd Soviet.[98]

Kornilov was the most visible symbol of the desire among some sectors of society for a "strong hand." He thus garnered the support of a wide range of groups who had been agitating throughout the summer for a strong

---

[96] Jorgen Larsen Munck, *The Kornilov Revolt: A Critical Examination of Sources and Research* (Aarhus, Denmark: Aarhus University Press, 1987), pp. 49–69; Katkov, *Kornilov Affair*, pp. 30–31, 39–46; Wildman, *The End of the Russian Imperial Army*, Vol. II, pp. 156–157.

[97] Alexander Rabinowitch, *Prelude to Revolution: The Petrograd Bolsheviks and the July 1917 Uprising* (Bloomington, IN: Indiana University Press, 1968); Pipes, *Russian Revolution*, pp. 419–438; Semion Lyandres, *The Bolsheviks' "German Gold" Revisited*, The Carl Beck Papers in Russian and East European Studies, No. 1106 (Pittsburgh: Center for Russian and East European Studies, February 1995); Alexander Rabinowitch, *The Bolsheviks Come to Power: The Revolution of 1917 in Petrograd* (New York: W. W. Norton & Co., 1976), pp. 14–20; Schapiro, *1917*, pp. 83–84, 94–95.

[98] Katkov, *Kornilov Affair*, pp. 41–64; Rabinowitch, *Bolsheviks Come to Power*, pp. 100–109; Munck, *Kornilov Revolt*, pp. 69–92. For the text of the Kornilov program submitted to the Provisional Government on August 10, see *Krasnaya letopis'*, No. 1(10), 1924, 207–217.

government, a restriction on the authority of the Soviets, and a prosecution of the war effort to victory over the Germans. Although it is clear that these groups supported Kornilov's program, there is less convincing evidence on whether they supported a military dictatorship and the extent of Kornilov's contacts with these groups.[99]

Several military organizations have been accused of conspiring with these organizations and Kornilov to establish a military dictatorship. These include the Union of Officers, the Military League, the Union of Cossack Troops, the Union of St. George Cavaliers, and the Union of Military Duty. The most important of these groups was the Union of Officers, which had been formed in May. Kerensky and the Deputy War Minister Savinkov saw the Union of Officers as "a nest of reaction." Kerensky's brother-in-law, Colonel V. L. Baranovskiy, who was a key assistant to Kerensky in the War Ministry, disagreed with this assessment, but his voice was evidently a minority one. Savinkov asked the chief commissar at *Stavka*, Captain M. M. Filonenko, to monitor the activities of the Main Committee of the Union.[100]

That there were praetorian sentiments among some members of the Russian officer corps, and that these sentiments increased between March and August, is clear. Denikin reports growing dismay among officers about the weakness of the state and the potential collapse of Russia. Officer support for a coup, however, apparently was not widespread, and little concrete evidence of plotting has appeared. Top commanders who apparently talked about the need for a military dictatorship included General P. N. Vrangel', General A. M. Krymov, and Admiral A. V. Kolchak. Military censors noted in June an officer's letter that said that "some officers say that only a military dictatorship can save us." By August the desire for a strong hand was widespread among officers, but this view must be dissociated from support for a military coup. Wildman accepts the claims that the Union of Officers was plotting against the government, but rejects the idea that its views represented the majority of officers.[101]

A second minority subculture was that of the so-called democratic officers, who supported the revolution and endeavored to work closely with the

[99] William G. Rosenberg, *Liberals in the Russian Revolution: The Constitutional Democratic Party, 1917–1921* (Princeton, NJ: Princeton University Press, 1974), pp. 205–224; James D. White, "The Kornilov Affair – A Study in Counter-Revolution," *Soviet Studies*, 20 (1968), pp. 187–205; Katkov, *Kornilov Affair*, pp. 136–144; Munck, *Kornilov Revolt*, pp. 126–134.

[100] RGVIA, f. 366, op. 2, d. 38, l. 7; RGVIA, f. 2003, op. 1, d. 1786, ll. 176–179; RGVIA, f. 366, op. 1, d. 67, ll. 19-30; RGVIA, f. 366, op. 2, d. 38, l. 16. For background, besides the sources in the previous note, see Katkov, *Kornilov Affair*, pp. 11–19; Allan Wildman, "Officers of the General Staff and the Kornilov Movement," in Frankel, Frankel, and Knei-Paz, *Revolution in Russia*, pp. 92–94.

[101] Denikin, *Ocherki*, I(1), pp. 88–89, 123; II, pp. 25, 28–30; Vrangel', *Vospominaniya*, pp. 32–34; Wildman, "Officers of the General Staff," pp. 84, 93–94; RGVIA, f. 2003, op. 1, d. 1773, ll. 203–217.

soldiers' committees. A good example of this type of officer was Colonel Verkhovskiy, the Commander of the Moscow Military District from June until August and War Minister after the Kornilov affair. Verkhovskiy believed that officers needed to work with "the most conscious" soldiers to convince them of the need to restore military discipline for the good of the war effort, and he opposed any return to the more strict and physical type of discipline favored by other Russian officers.[102]

It seems that the majority of officers, and particularly the high command, occupied a position somewhere between the "praetorian" and "democratic" subcultures. These officers were apolitical patriots who were distressed by the disintegration of the army and believed that politics should be removed from the army and that the military should concentrate on the war effort.

Prince G. N. Trubetskoy, Director of the Diplomatic Chancellery at *Stavka* from March until the Kornilov affair, remarked that Russian generals had an "exclusively military world view, discussing all current events from that point of view." Despite their opposition to involvement in politics, Trubetskoy contends, they were somewhat forced into it by the collapse of the army. As for Kornilov, Trubetskoy stated: "[H]e is first of all a soldier and he little understands complex political questions. In this sense he clearly reflects the properties of the entire command staff of the army." Most subsequent historians have shared this assessment. Alexander Rabinowitch states, "Kornilov remained very much an officer of the old school; national political issues interested him only insofar as they affected the primary task of restoring the army."[103]

General I. P. Romanovskiy, the Quartermaster-General at *Stavka* at the time of the Kornilov affair, summarizes the outlook of the military leadership well. Politics, Romanovskiy asserts, was "completely foreign" to him. The disintegration of the army in 1917 was a cause of much suffering, and Romanovskiy says he came to the conclusion that strong power was necessary to save the army and Russia: "[W]hat kind of power it was essentially was all the same to me, as long as it was strong." These views reflected an organizational culture based on opposition to military involvement in sovereign power issues combined with the sentiment that the potential collapse of the army and the state should not be permitted.[104]

---

[102] Verkhovskiy, *Rossiya na golgofe*, pp. 84, 87; Wildman, "Officers of the General Staff," pp. 87–90.

[103] Gosudarstvennyy arkhiv Rossiyskoy Federatsii (GARF), f. 1780, op. 1, d. 11, l. 1; Rabinowitch, *Bolsheviks Come to Power*, p. 97. See also General E. I. Martynov, *Kornilov (popytka voyennogo perevorota)* (Leningrad: Voyennaya tipografiya uprav. delami NKVM i RVS SSSR, 1927), pp. 20, 47; General N. N. Golovin, *Rossiyskaya kontr-revolyutsiya v 1917–1918 gg.*, Part I, Book 2 (Tallinn: "Illyustrirovannaya Rossiya," 1937), pp. 9–12; Verkhovskiy, *Rossiya na golgofe*, pp. 89–90, 106. See also "Iz dnevnika gen. V. I. Selivacheva."

[104] GARF, f. 1780, op. 1, d. 14, l. 87.

By August 1917, then, there was a widespread feeling in the officer corps and among significant elements of the nonsocialist political elite that a firm hand was needed to conduct the war and prevent government collapse. General Kornilov was the most prominent symbol of this sentiment. Some of those who longed for a strong hand believed that a military coup would be required for it to come about, and they looked to Kornilov as the potential "man on horseback." For a plot to succeed, however, it needed a leader, and it is far from clear that Kornilov saw himself as a putschist. To better answer this question, we need to look in more detail at the Kornilov affair.

The Kornilov Affair

Kornilov took over as Supreme Commander in late July 1917. He urged the Provisional Government to adopt his program of tough military measures to restore the fighting capacity of the army. His disillusionment grew after two trips to Petrograd on August 3 and 10 produced no results. Most shocking, perhaps, to Kornilov was the discovery that a possible traitor was a member of the Provisional Government; both Kerensky and Savinkov told him not to go into too much detail during his operational report because they suspected a minister of passing information to the Germans (the suspected member, probably unfairly, was Agriculture Minister V. M. Chernov, the leader of the Socialist Revolutionary [SR] Party). The fall of Riga to the Germans on August 20 was another major demoralizing event.[105]

After his August 3 trip to Petrograd, Kornilov ordered the movement of the Third Cavalry Corps to an area about 250 miles from Petrograd. This troop movement could be justified by the threat to Riga and potentially Petrograd from the Germans, but the deployment also had a political purpose. Kornilov's Chief of Staff, General Lukhomskiy, suspected as much and asked Kornilov his reasons. Kornilov answered that according to available reports the Bolsheviks were planning an action in Petrograd for the end of August (the six-month anniversary of the February Revolution), intimating that these troops might be used to suppress demonstrations. Kornilov went on to state that it was necessary to introduce firm measures to save the army and Russia. He added that he was not a counterrevolutionary, but that the Provisional Government, although it contained strong people, also had members who were fatal for Russia. Thus, Kornilov said, it might be necessary to put pressure on the government. Kornilov said that he counted on broad support and that a reconstituted government would have to include

---

[105] There are two detailed studies in English of the Kornilov affair: Katkov, *Kornilov Affair*; Munck, *Kornilov Revolt*. I have been able to draw on the materials of the Investigative Commission established to study the Kornilov affair, which are stored at GARF in Moscow and were unavailable to Katkov and Munck. See also Martynov, *Kornilov*; White, "The Kornilov Affair"; Rabinowitch, *Bolsheviks Come to Power*, pp. 94–150; Wildman, "Officers of the General Staff"; Wildman, *The End of the Russian Imperial Army*, Vol. II, pp. 184–223.

people like Kerensky and Savinkov. Lukhomskiy states that he had no doubt that Kerensky and Kornilov would come to an agreement. Kornilov was certainly, though, entertaining the idea of pressuring the government, although he had no concrete plan to do so.[106]

Savinkov and Filonenko, respectively the Deputy Defense Minister and the government commissar at *Stavka*, played a key role in the Kornilov affair. Savinkov, Filonenko, and Kerensky were all members of the SR Party, and Savinkov basically ran the War Ministry as Kerensky's deputy from the end of July. Filonenko had served as commissar under Kornilov in the Eighth Army, and he replaced Savinkov as government commissar at *Stavka* when Savinkov moved to Petrograd at the end of July. Savinkov and Filonenko worked closely with Kornilov in drafting his program for military reform, and played a key role in negotiating between Kerensky and Kornilov over the contents of the reform program.[107]

Kerensky was wavering about whether to adopt Kornilov's program. He certainly understood that by siding with Kornilov he would be breaking his ties with the Soviet, his original base of support after the February Revolution. In mid-August, Kerensky evidently decided to press ahead with the Kornilov program, and he tasked Savinkov to go to *Stavka* to come to a final agreement with Kornilov. Kerensky told Savinkov on August 17 that he had accepted Kornilov's demand that the death penalty be extended to the rear and that the Petrograd Military District, with the exception of Petrograd itself, be placed under the authority of the Supreme Commander. The plan to create a separate Petrograd Army had been proposed as early as April and had been put in motion by Kornilov in early August. Kerensky also instructed Savinkov to agree with Kornilov on the dispatch of the 3rd Cavalry Corps to Petrograd at the end of August to repress the projected Bolshevik demonstration and any disturbances provoked by the announcement by the Provisional Government of the adoption of Kornilov's program and the placement of Petrograd under martial law.[108]

Savinkov discussed these plans with Kornilov at *Stavka* on August 23–24. Kornilov complained to Savinkov about Kerensky's indecisiveness, but

---

[106] See Lukomskiy's deposition to the Investigative Commission, which is probably the best single source on military command thinking during the Kornilov affair, even more informative than Kornilov's own deposition: GARF, f. 1780, op. 1, d. 14, ll. 50–54. See also General Loukomsky, *Memoirs of the Russian Revolution* (London: T. Fisher Unwin Ltd., 1922), pp. 95–101. For Kornilov's deposition, see "General L. G. Kornilov pered chrezvychaynoy komissiey vremennogo pravitel'stva," *Kentavr*, Nos. 5–6, 1995, 105–120, 101–113.

[107] Katkov, *Kornilov Affair*, pp. 47, 57, 66–67, *passim*; Munck, *Kornilov Revolt*, pp. 64–67; Rabinowitch, *Bolsheviks Come to Power*, pp. 99–108; Wildman, *The End of the Russian Imperial Army*, Vol. II, pp. 191–192, note 13; Martynov, *Kornilov*, pp. 24–25, 43, *passim*.

[108] Katkov, *Kornilov Affair*, pp. 65–67; GARF, f. 1780, op. 1, d. 31, l. 35; Martynov, *Kornilov*, p. 79; RGVIA, f. 366, op. 1, d. 127, ll. 26–27; GARF, f. 1780, d. 1, op. 14, ll. 50–53, 82–83; "General L. G. Kornilov," *Kentavr*, No. 6, 105–106.

Savinkov convinced Kornilov of Kerensky's indispensability and told him that Kerensky had agreed to introduce the death penalty in the rear. Savinkov also negotiated, on Kerensky's order, the demarcation between the area of the Petrograd Military District under Kornilov's command and the area under the control of the Petrograd Military Governor. This agreement was immediately communicated to the War Ministry in Petrograd, and Kerensky issued a telegram to Kornilov confirming the subordination of the Petrograd Military District to the Supreme Commander. Finally, Savinkov requested, under Kerensky's authority, the dispatch of the 3rd Cavalry Corps to Petrograd. Kornilov informed Savinkov before Savinkov's departure that he believed the government was moving in the right direction and he asked Savinkov to tell Kerensky that he would support Kerensky for the good of the fatherland. All those at *Stavka* thought that Kornilov's program had finally been accepted and that firm power was soon to be introduced in the country that would halt the collapse of the army.[109]

At this point the Kornilov affair becomes rather strange, if not downright surreal. On August 22 V. N. L'vov, who had been the Procurator of the Holy Synod in the first two provisional governments, went to see Kerensky in Petrograd. L'vov had apparently decided, either on his own volition or because of political conversations in Moscow, that Kerensky needed to be persuaded to change the make-up of the government. L'vov told Kerensky that a powerful group of people stood behind his demand to change the government, and Kerensky evidently empowered L'vov to negotiate on his behalf with this "powerful group."[110]

L'vov returned to Moscow, where he told several people that he had been sent by Kerensky to negotiate with Kornilov, and then went on to *Stavka* on August 24. L'vov met with Kornilov on August 25. L'vov told Kornilov that he had come on Kerensky's behalf to discuss the composition of the new government. L'vov laid out three options: (1) a new government formed by Kerensky, (2) a directorate that would include Kornilov, and (3) a dictatorship. Kornilov replied that he favored the third option, that he would not reject the role of dictator if offered to him, and that regardless he

---

[109] "General L. G. Kornilov," *Kentavr*, No. 5, 115–117; GARF, f. 1780, op. 1, d. 31, ll. 37, 56; GARF, f. 1780, op. 1, d. 14, ll. 54–56, 82–84; GARF, f. 1780, op. 1, d. 11, l. 3; D. A. Chigayev, ed., *VOSR: Revolyutsionnoye dvizheniye v Rossii v avguste 1917 g: Razgrom kornilovskogo myatezha. Dokumenty i materialy* [hereafter *VOSR: Razgrom*] (Moskva: Izdatel'stvo Akademii Nauk SSSR, 1959), pp. 421–425, 451; RGVIA, f. 366, op. 1, d. 67, ll. 45–51; Katkov, *Kornilov Affair*, pp. 67–72; Munck, *Kornilov Revolt*, pp. 100–105.

[110] V. N. L'vov should not be confused with the Prime Minister of the First Provisional Government, G. E. L'vov. All contemporary observers and later historians have regarded L'vov as unreliable if not delusional. L'vov gave no fewer than four different versions of his story to the Investigative Commission between August 27 and October 5. See GARF, f. 1780, op. 1, d. 31, ll. 5–18, 97; N. Ukraintsev, "The Kornilov Affair: Observations by a Member of the Extraordinary Commission of Inquiry," *Soviet Studies*, 25 (1973), 294–295; Katkov, *Kornilov Affair*, pp. 74–82; Munck, *Kornilov Revolt*, pp. 30–32.

considered the participation of Kerensky and Savinkov in the government desirable. Kornilov also told L'vov to relay to Kerensky and Savinkov his desire that they come to *Stavka*, since he could not guarantee their safety in Petrograd and the composition of the new government could be agreed in Mogilev.[111]

Lukhomskiy maintains that one of the major sources of the subsequent disagreement was over the term dictatorship, which he maintains implied for Kornilov a collective, and not a personal, dictatorship. Lukhomskiy's account is backed by other sources, and on August 25 and 26 there were several discussions about the composition of a future government. Lukhomskiy and Kornilov testified that on the 26th the opinion at headquarters had centered around the notion of a Council of National Defense *(Sovet Narodnoy oborony)* with Kornilov as its head and Kerensky as its deputy. The fact that no firm decision had been made by Kornilov about the most desirable composition of a future government is clear from the fact that on the 26th he telegraphed several leading political figures, asking that they come to *Stavka* to discuss the composition of a new government.[112]

While L'vov was in Mogilev, Savinkov had returned to Petrograd to report his agreements with Kornilov to Kerensky. Despite the fact that Kerensky had agreed to accept Kornilov's proposals at the time he sent Savinkov to *Stavka* (August 17), he now hesitated to adopt them. Savinkov tried several times on August 25 and 26 to persuade Kerensky to sign the new laws and bring them before the cabinet. Kerensky eventually agreed to submit them to the government on the night of the twenty-sixth.[113]

L'vov, meanwhile, returned to Petrograd on August 26 to report to Kerensky the results of his discussion with Kornilov. Until this meeting, Kerensky had no idea who L'vov allegedly was representing. L'vov now said that he had come on behalf of Kornilov, although L'vov had told everyone else that Kerensky had sent *him* to Kornilov, and not the other way around. L'vov told Kerensky that Kornilov had presented him with the ultimatum that Kerensky and the entire government resign and that all military and civil power be transferred to Kornilov, and L'vov also stated Kornilov's desire for Kerensky and Savinkov to go to Mogilev. Katkov correctly notes that "the word 'ultimatum' is the pivot on which the whole Kornilov affair revolves." Kornilov believed that he had merely told L'vov his preferences about the shape of a future government, reiterated his belief that the measures worked out with Savinkov be immediately introduced, and asked that

---

[111] Munck, *Kornilov Revolt*, pp. 106–109; Katkov, *Kornilov Affair*, pp. 77–81. The relevant primary sources are cited in the following note.

[112] "General L. G. Kornilov," *Kentavr*, No. 6, 101–104; GARF, f. 1780, op. 1, d. 31, ll. 5–18, 26, 67–69; GARF, f. 1780, op. 1, d. 14, ll. 56–57; GARF, f. 1780, op. 1, d. 11, l. 3–5; GARF, f. 1780, op. 1, d. 14, l. 37; *VOSR: Razgrom*, 450.

[113] Katkov, *Kornilov Affair*, pp. 83–84; Munck, *Kornilov Revolt*, p. 111.

Kerensky and Savinkov come to *Stavka* to discuss the composition of the future government and for their own safety.[114]

Kerensky decided to double-check L'vov's report of Kornilov's "demands" by conducting a conversation with Kornilov over the Hughes apparatus that night (August 26). Kerensky asked Kornilov to confirm the message he had sent with L'vov, without stating the message's content. Kornilov verified that he had asked L'vov to transmit a message and that he requested that Kerensky and Savinkov come to *Stavka*. Neither Kerensky nor Kornilov, however, said anything specific about the content of Kornilov's message to Kerensky. Kornilov's very phrasing, however, suggests he had not sent an ultimatum; Kornilov referred only to "the outline that I had sketched for Vladimir Nikolayevich [L'vov] with the request that he report it to you [i.e., Kerensky]." Kornilov's failure to state explicitly the nature of his message to Kerensky was, as Lukhomskiy stated, "a very serious mistake." Kerensky's failure to ask is equally culpable.[115]

Kerensky had L'vov arrested and telegraphed Kornilov, ordering him to give up his post to the Chief of Staff, Lukhomskiy. Kerensky then reported to the cabinet that Kornilov had sent L'vov with an ultimatum that he be given dictatorial power. Kerensky received from the cabinet extraordinary powers to deal with the crisis. Kerensky refused Savinkov's request that he be allowed to clear up the misunderstanding with Kornilov, arguing that it was not a misunderstanding but a "crime." Kerensky had his own reasons for not wanting to come to an agreement with Kornilov, both because he feared him as a rival for power and because going along with Kornilov's program would mean breaking with his socialist allies in the Soviet.[116]

At *Stavka* the Hughes apparatus discussion between Kornilov and Kerensky was taken as clear evidence that Kerensky would take the steps agreed with Savinkov. Kornilov telegraphed Savinkov the previously agreed telegram on the movement of the Third Cavalry Corps to Petrograd and the introduction of martial law beginning on August 29. The arrival of the telegram dismissing Kornilov, Trubetskoy reports, was like an "exploding bomb." Kornilov and others close to him at *Stavka* concluded that either (a) Kornilov was the victim of some provocation (some blamed L'vov, others Kerensky, others Savinkov and Filonenko) or (b) leftist elements in the government and the Soviet had pressured Kerensky to break with Kornilov.[117]

[114] Katkov, *Kornilov Affair*, pp. 86–88; Munck, *Kornilov Revolt*, pp. 108–109; GARF, f. 1780, op. 1, d. 14, l. 57; *VOSR: Razgrom*, p.441–442.

[115] *VOSR: Razgrom*, p. 443; GARF, f. 1780, op. 1, d. 14, l. 57.

[116] Katkov, *Kornilov Affair*, pp. 91–95, 157; Munck, *Kornilov Revolt*, pp. 110–114; Martynov, *Kornilov*, p. 100.

[117] "General L. G. Kornilov," *Kentavr*, No. 6, 104; GARF, f. 1780, op. 1, d. 31, ll. 98–99; GARF, f. 1780, op. 1, d. 14, ll. 57–59, 84; GARF, f. 1780, op. 1, d. 11, ll. 4–5.

Lukhomskiy refused the post of Supreme Commander and said that it was too late to go back on the agreement between Kerensky and Kornilov. Lukhomskiy maintained that only the program proposed by Kornilov could save the army from collapse and save Russia from a humiliating defeat. Both Filonenko at *Stavka* and Savinkov in Petrograd believed that a huge misunderstanding had taken place, and Savinkov had a long conversation with Kornilov over the Hughes apparatus on the afternoon of August 27 to try to ameliorate the situation. By this point, however, neither Kerensky nor Kornilov was interested in backing down. Kerensky issued a public telegram on the twenty-seventh accusing Kornilov of "attempting to encroach on supreme power in the state" and ordering Kornilov to give up the post of Supreme Commander to General V. N. Klembovskiy, the commander of the Northern Front. Kornilov responded with an inflammatory appeal to the population accusing the Provisional Government of being under the influence of "the Bolshevik majority of the Soviets [the Bolsheviks did not in fact have a majority in the Soviet at this time – B. T.] acting in complete agreement with the plans of German General Staff" and proclaimed, "Russian people, your great motherland is dying!" [118]

The fact that the Kerensky–Kornilov dispute was now out in the open made it impossible for it to be resolved in a way satisfactory to both sides. Klembovskiy, like Lukhomskiy, also refused to take over the position of Supreme Commander. Kornilov sent word to General Krymov to continue his advance on Petrograd, on foot if the railroads were disrupted, but then lost communication with him. As Kornilov told the Investigative Commission, he had made no alternative arrangements to stay in touch with Krymov because the operation was being carried out in agreement with the government and he did not foresee that the very same government would order communications between the two of them cut off. [119]

The chaos in the high command was mirrored by chaos in the ruling circles in Petrograd. The former Supreme Commander, Alekseev, was brought in to help resolve the crisis. He appealed to Kerensky to compromise with Kornilov, but Kerensky said that was impossible. On August 29, telegrams continued to arrive at the War Ministry from the front commanders asking to whom they were subordinate. Alekseev decided that the situation was too dangerous and could be exploited by the Germans, so he agreed to become Chief of Staff under Kerensky as Supreme Commander and to work with Kornilov to defuse the crisis. [120]

[118] *VOSR: Razgrom*, pp. 445–452; ; GARF, f. 1780, op. 1, d. 31, ll. 28; Katkov, *Kornilov Affair*, pp. 92–93, 97–99; Munck, *Kornilov Revolt*, pp. 7–8, 112–113.

[119] *VOSR: Razgrom*, pp. 453, 455–456; "General L. G. Kornilov," *Kentavr*, No. 6, 107.

[120] *VOSR: Razgrom*, pp. 466–467; GARF, f. 1780, op. 1, d. 12, ll. 2–3; Munck, *Kornilov Revolt*, pp. 113–114; Katkov, *Kornilov Affair*, pp. 100–103.

Alekseev and Kornilov "spoke" on the Hughes apparatus several times on August 30. It was agreed that Alekseev would come to *Stavka* as soon as possible and that until he arrived the Provisional Government would issue a statement that all of Kornilov's orders relevant to operational matters should be obeyed. As Kornilov sarcastically remarked in a letter to Krymov dispatched on August 30, "thus came about an episode unique in world history: a supreme commander, accused of treason and betrayal of the motherland and handed over to justice for it, received an order to continue to command the armies." Alekseev arrived at Mogilev on the afternoon of September 1. That evening Alekseev arrested Kornilov, Lukhomskiy, and Romanovskiy. Alekseev was forced to take this step to avoid further confrontation.[121]

Krymov's expedition, in the meantime, had petered out on the outskirts of Petrograd. Initially on August 27 both Kerensky and Kornilov believed that Kornilov was likely to succeed. Some accounts attribute Krymov's failure to the countermobilization of the Soviets, soldiers' committees, and other mass organizations. Other analysts emphasize the confusion faced by Krymov, his officers, and his troops upon learning that there was no Bolshevik uprising in Petrograd and that Kerensky had accused Kornilov of mutiny. Both accounts undoubtedly contain an element of truth and are not mutually inconsistent. Regardless, as George Katkov points out, "not a single shot was fired on either side."[122]

Explaining the High Command's Behavior during the Kornilov Affair

The fact that Kornilov refused to submit to the Provisional Government on August 27 means that the Kornilov affair must be coded as a case of military intervention. There is no doubt that after August 27 Kornilov was insubordinate and took steps to change the executive leadership of the state. Kornilov's insubordination, however, is not proof of a previous plot to overthrow the government.

---

[121] Katkov, *Kornilov Affair*, pp. 105–114; *VOSR: Razgrom*, pp. 466–469; Martynov, *Kornilov*, pp. 191–193; "General L. G. Kornilov," *Kentavr*, No. 6, 108.

[122] Katkov, *Kornilov Affair*, pp. 100–101, 105–106, 197 (quote, p. 197); Rabinowitch, *Bolsheviks Come to Power*, pp. 127–150; Munck, *Kornilov Revolt*, pp. 114–118; Martynov, *Kornilov*, pp. 129–151; Wildman, *The End of the Russian Imperial Army*, Vol. II, pp. 184–202; Pipes, *Russian Revolution*, pp. 461–462. Incidentally, it appears that there was in fact no planned Bolshevik demonstration in Petrograd and that the information was based on an unreliable counterintelligence report. Regardless, there can be no doubt that Kornilov believed the report, and he also expected opposition from the Bolsheviks and the Petrograd Soviet when the law on applying the death penalty in the rear was announced. It was not simply a "cock-and-bull story," as Allan Wildman asserts. See "General L. G. Kornilov," *Kentavr*, No. 5, 120, note 22; Loukomsky, *Memoirs of the Russian Revolution*, p. 105; Rabinowitch, *Bolsheviks Come to Power*, p. 117; Wildman, *The End of the Russian Imperial Army*, Vol. II, p. 195.

As should be clear from the previous section, the evidence for a Kornilov conspiracy is weak. The Investigative Commission established by the Kerensky Government to examine the affair found no evidence for a previous conspiracy. The only witness who claimed to have direct evidence for the existence of a plot was L'vov, and his testimony on this issue was contradicted by three other witnesses – and L'vov himself on two occasions. Kerensky insisted that there was a plot, and indeed spent a considerable portion of the rest of his life trying to prove its existence. He was unable to produce any evidence for the Commission, however, and his claim that he had information from counterintelligence was directly contradicted by N. D. Mironov, a counterintelligence officer who was sent by Savinkov in August to *Stavka* to check on potential plotters in the Officers' Union. Mironov was unable to uncover any evidence for a plot and was completely surprised by the Kornilov "uprising." The Commission also found no evidence for a plot among the high command or the Officers' Union, basing their conclusion on extensive interviews with all of the relevant parties and searches of their premises. No documents supporting the existence of a plot were uncovered. Similarly, none of the officers of the Third Cavalry Corps believed that they were acting against the Provisional Government. Everyone at *Stavka*, the Commission concluded, believed that Kornilov and Kerensky were working together.[123]

Some scholars point to the dispatch of a group of officers to Petrograd to assist Krymov's Third Cavalry Corps in putting down the anticipated Bolshevik demonstration as evidence of the existence of a plot.[124] The problem is that, at the time the officers were sent (August 25–26), Kornilov had every reason to think he was acting in accordance with the Provisional Government. The officers were told that they were to be at the disposal of Krymov and assist him in putting down a Bolshevik uprising. No action against the Provisional Government was discussed.[125]

Other information pointing to the existence of a Kornilov plot appeared in the years following the revolution in various émigré memoirs and newspapers. Many of these accounts were published years or decades after the event and contradict each other on key points. It does seem true, nevertheless, that various individuals and organizations, including some officers, took concrete steps to assist Kornilov at the end of August. Clear links between these individuals and groups and Kornilov, however, have not been well established. No plans were made to maintain contacts between these groups and *Stavka*.

---

[123] GARF, f. 1780, op. 1, d. 31, ll. 5–41, 48–57, 97–102. See also Ukraintsev, "The Kornilov Affair," a 1956 article by a member of the Commission. The two major Western studies of the Kornilov affair both conclude that Kornilov did not conspire to overthrow the Provisional Government: Katkov, *Kornilov Affair*; Munck, *Kornilov Revolt*.

[124] Martynov, *Kornilov*, pp. 90–91; Rabinowitch, *Bolsheviks Come to Power*, p. 117.

[125] GARF, f. 1780, op. 1, d. 21; GARF, f. 1780, op. 1, d. 11, ll. 146, 173–175; GARF, f. 1780, op. 1, d. 14, l. 63; GARF, f. 1780, op. 1, d. 31, ll. 42–48, 101–102; Denikin, *Ocherki*, I(2), pp. 210–211; II, pp. 40, 53–54; *VOSR: Razgrom*, pp. 420, 452–453.

Most important, the goal of these various plots seemed to be directed toward suppressing the Bolsheviks and the Petrograd Soviet, and not the Provisional Government itself.[126]

The best evidence for any praetorian leanings on Kornilov's part is found in Lukhomskiy's testimony. Several times in August, Kornilov had considered pressuring the government to adopt his reform plans and expel the members that he believed were traitors, such as Chernov. The relevant counterfactual is whether Kornilov would have tried to overthrow the government if it had decided not to adopt his proposed measures. Denikin suggests that such an outcome was very possible.[127] My reading of the available evidence is that Kornilov had no actual plan to move against the government in late August if his reforms were rejected, but that some of his associates were urging him on and that Kornilov may have undertaken such an effort later if he became convinced that the external military threat to the army and the country was severe enough. Another possibility is that Kornilov would have moved against the Petrograd Soviet without the authorization of the Provisional Government, hoping to win its assent after the fact. Kornilov and many other top officers had come to the conclusion that the disintegration in the army was inextricably linked to (a) political and economic developments in the rear and (b) the failure of the government to cope with the crisis.

Kornilov justified his own behavior as motivated by national interest reasons, in particular the disintegration of the army and the possible loss of the war. His appeals to the people on August 27 and 28 argued that the Provisional Government's actions "are killing the army and shaking the country from within" and undermining "the very independent existence of the state." In his testimony to the Investigative Commission, Kornilov also stressed his goals of forcing "traitors to the Motherland" from the cabinet and pressuring the government to create "strong and firm power" in the country.[128]

General Lukhomskiy, Kornilov's chief of staff, admitted openly that by supporting Kornilov on August 27 his stance was, in a formal sense, criminal. Lukhomskiy argued that to understand his decision of August 27 one needed to understand the situation in the army and the country. If the measures proposed by Kornilov were not adopted rapidly, Lukhomskiy believed, then in the next 2–3 months the army would collapse, leading to the "death of Russia." The commanders of the various fronts were also placed in a difficult position. All of them had endorsed the measures proposed by Kornilov for

---

[126] For varying treatments of this material, see White, "The Kornilov Affair"; Katkov, *Kornilov Affair*, pp. 136–144; Munck, *Kornilov Revolt*, pp. 37–38, 126–134; Denikin, *Ocherki*, Vol. II, pp. 25–34, 40, 43, 54; N. G. Dumova, "Maloizvestnye materialy po istorii Kornilovshchiny," *Voprosy istorii*, No. 11, 1968, 69–93.

[127] Denikin, *Ocherki*, I(1), p. 69; I(2), pp. 197–198; II, pp. 29–30, 36, 39.

[128] *VOSR: Razgrom*, p. 446; Martynov, *Kornilov*, pp. 116–117, 122; "General L. G. Kornilov," *Kentavr*, No. 6, 105; RGVIA, f. 366, op. 2, d. 99, ll. 27–32.

restoring discipline and the fighting capacity of the army. Generals Baluyev (Western Front), Shcherbachev (Rumanian Front), and Klembovskiy (Northern Front) telegraphed to *Stavka* and Petrograd their support for Kornilov and his program, but without taking a stand against the Provisional Government. The commander of the Caucasian Front, General Przheval'skiy, telegraphed his support of the Provisional Government and stated that "any split in the army and its participation in a civil war will be fatal for the fatherland." General Denikin of the Southwestern Front, on the other hand, took a stance of open defiance to the government, arguing that the dismissal of Kornilov would lead to the collapse of the army and the death of the country, and that "I will not go with it [the government] along that path." [129]

In the end only Denikin refused to submit to the Provisional Government. He undertook no military efforts to support Kornilov, however, and was arrested by a commissar and a crowd of troops. Once the "paper war" between Kornilov and Kerensky broke into public view on August 28, Baluyev and Shcherbachev sided openly with the Provisional Government. Klembovskiy was in a trickier spot, because he had refused the Supreme Command when so instructed by Kerensky. Klembovskiy adopted a stance of neutrality and made no effort to support either side. Klembovskiy explained his behavior to the Investigative Commission in the following manner:

In general I adhered to the policy that the military should not interfere in politics, and should exclusively devote its efforts to operational questions. If I had started to interfere in politics and written various appeals then it could have been harmful to military operations. To divert the army from its most important tasks at such a serious moment was impossible. [130]

Kornilov received the most support at *Stavka*, whose officers knew of Kornilov's prior agreement with the government and believed that L'vov had acted as Kerensky's emissary. These officers evidently felt a certain obligation of military honor to stay by the Supreme Commander's side in light of what they perceived as his shabby treatment by the government. Even the Officers' Union, often portrayed as a nest of reactionary officers, was not four-square behind Kornilov. For example, Lieutenant Colonel Govorov, head of the Officers' Union in the 10th Army on the Western Front, appealed to all members of the Union to remain subordinate to the Provisional Government and remain focused on their "only task, to raise the fighting capacity of the army for saving the Motherland from foreign invasion." He reminded Officers' Union members that the first

[129] GARF, f. 1780, op. 1, d. 14, ll. 57–68, 71–74; Loukomsky, *Memoirs of the Russian Revolution*, p. 112; *VOSR: Razgrom*, pp. 447–448; Martynov, *Kornilov*, pp. 102, 114–116.

[130] GARF, f. 1780, op. 1, d. 31, l. 1; GARF, f. 1780, op. 1, d. 83, l. 20; GARF, f. 1780, op. 1, d. 83, ll. 14–17; RGVIA, f. 366, op. 2, d. 99, ll. 172–179; Wildman, *The End of the Russian Imperial Army*, II, pp. 193–202; Wildman, "Officers of the General Staff," pp. 95–96.

clause of their regulations stated that the Union was a purely professional organization with no political platform.[131]

Summary

The Kornilov affair was a case of military intervention in politics, but it hardly conforms to any reasonable definition of a military coup. This in no way resembled a well-planned military conspiracy. Kornilov's intervention came only after his agreement with the Provisional Government broke down because of a bizarre series of circumstances. To the extent there was intervention by Kornilov, it was stimulated by his belief that the government's policies were leading to the disintegration of the armed forces and inevitable military defeat. Domestic structure in that sense represented not just an opportunity, but a motive in itself. When the state is disintegrating, it is impossible for the armed forces to remain completely aloof from sovereign power issues.

The other aspect of opportunity, organizational structure, was less important. The commissar at *Stavka* was part of the negotiations between Kornilov and Kerensky, and the counterintelligence officer there found no evidence of a plot. Internal divisions within the army, particularly between officers and troops, played a role in the outcome of the affair after Kerensky denounced Kornilov, but equally important was the fact that when Krymov started his mission it was in agreement with the government, and neither he nor his troops were prepared for the sudden turn in events. There is little evidence that the rest of the officer corps was deterred from supporting Kornilov by the prospect of failure, because initially both the government and *Stavka* thought that Kornilov was likely to succeed.

A corporate interest account is consistent with those historians who contend that there was a military conspiracy behind Kornilov, because the encroachments on officer autonomy in 1917 represent a clear grounds for military intervention from this perspective. I found the evidence for a Kornilov plot weak, and thus I see the corporate interest explanation as not compelling.

Kornilov clearly violated organizational norms against military intervention when he revolted on August 27. The repeated protests by Kornilov and his defenders, such as Denikin, that Kornilov had no personal ambitions and no political goals, and that he only sought the preservation of Russia, were an attempt to justify the violation of an existing norm of civilian supremacy. In Kornilov's defense, the circumstances under which he revolted on August 27 were extreme. But culture was clearly overridden in this case by other concerns related to domestic structure.

---

[131] GARF, f. 1780, op. 1, d. 14, l. 61; GARF, f. 1780, op. 1, d. 24, l. 11.

The failure of the rest of the officer corps to act in support of Kornilov can be explained by their organizational culture. Given the chaos and disintegration around them, the relative *inactivity* of the officer corps is best explained by norms that inhibited military intervention. Their apolitical stance is shown even more clearly in the next section, in which the October Revolution and the Bolshevik rise to power are discussed.

THE OFFICER CORPS AND THE OCTOBER REVOLUTION

The Bolshevik party took power in Petrograd on the night of October 25–26. Was this a revolution or a coup d'etat? Most observers at the time apparently saw it as a reckless coup, and they predicted that the Bolsheviks would be unable to hold power. In the end, it took a bloody civil war for the Bolsheviks to consolidate their rule. On the other hand, there are strong grounds for calling the October events a revolution, given the considerable popular support the Bolsheviks had in late 1917 in the major cities of the country. Allan Wildman's description of the "so-called 'October Revolution' of 1917" strikes me as the most apt; he notes that October "was concurrently a *social upheaval* and a *contest for power*."[132]

The officer corps and the high command, like the rest of Russian society, had to define their stance toward the Bolshevik assumption of power in Petrograd. To many officers the Bolsheviks were little more than German agents trying to undermine the Russian state from within. Lenin had called for the abolition of the army, and the Bolsheviks had made their hostility toward the officer corps clear. Given the Bolsheviks' positions on the war and the army, one might have expected a more forceful and consistent reaction on the part of the military leadership to the October events. Although the high command at *Stavka* did try to send troops to Petrograd in support of the Provisional Government, these efforts were somewhat half-hearted, and the commander of the vital Northern Front acted to impede the dispatch of troops to Petrograd. Even more remarkably, perhaps, *Stavka* capitulated to the Bolsheviks without resistance a month later. This passive stance can be explained partially by the calculation that there was no opportunity for action given the uncontrollability of the troops, but also by officer corps' beliefs that domestic political activity was inappropriate and that their primary mission was to remain at the front and defend the state. In October and November 1917, officers were not prepared to launch a civil war to defeat the Bolsheviks; this action would come later, and it only really gathered steam once the war was over.

---

[132] Wildman, *The End of the Russian Imperial Army*, II, p. 262 (emphasis in original). On this debate, see Pipes, *Russian Revolution*; Pipes, "1917 and the Revisionists"; Acton, *Rethinking the Russian Revolution*, pp. 167–209; Suny, "Toward a Social History" Ronald Grigor Suny, "Revision and Retreat in the Historiography of 1917: Social History and its Critics," *Russian Review*, 53 (1994), 165–182.

In this section I examine the October Revolution (if I can be permitted this loaded term), the Bolshevik take-over at *Stavka*, and the response of the armed forces. I first discuss the relevant political and military developments, and then I provide an explanation for officer corps' behavior.

The Bolshevik Victory and the Military

The Kornilov affair further undermined the tottering Provisional Government and was a fillip for the Bolshevik party. Conservative elements in society felt betrayed by Kerensky, and the masses lost faith in him and turned even more to the Soviets to represent their interests. The Bolsheviks gained most of all, as they were most responsive to mass demands for immediate peace and land.[133]

The effects of the Kornilov affair in the armed forces were devastating. The split between the officer corps and the troops became more pronounced than ever. More arrests of officers by their troops took place, and on the Northern Front one commander reported that "there is complete distrust towards the high command staff and there are voices among the soldiers that the entire command staff should be raised on bayonets." Similar reports came in from other fronts. Verkhovskiy, who had been promoted to General and War Minister due to his perceived service to the revolution during the Kornilov affair, noted in his diary that "the masses look at their officers like a convict looks at his chain." A sharp growth in support among the soldiers for the Bolsheviks was noted by multiple observers, particularly on the Northern and Western Fronts.[134]

The "social upheaval" in the country, as Wildman notes, was accompanied by a "contest for power." Dual power had given way to a general feeling of powerlessness, particularly on the part of the Provisional Government. The Socialist Revolutionary S. Mstislavskiy later remarked that "power was in essence lying on the ground. In order to pick it up . . . it was enough to bend over." Lenin not only grasped this fact but was determined to act on it. In September the Bolsheviks secured a majority in the Petrograd Soviet, and on September 25 a Bolshevik-dominated Presidium was elected with Trotsky as chair. At about the same time the Central Executive Committee of the Soviet decided, under Bolshevik prompting, to call a nationwide (Second)

[133] Schapiro, *1917*, pp. 118–119; Rabinowitch, *Bolsheviks Come to Power*, pp. 165–167; Wildman, *The End of the Russian Imperial Army*, Vol. II, pp. 223–226; Frenkin, *Russkaya armiya*, pp. 435–446, 546, 557; Katkov, *Kornilov Affair*, pp. 121–124.

[134] The two direct quotes in this paragraph are from: RGVIA, f. 2003, op. 1, d. 1800, ll. 379–380; Verkhovskiy, *Rossiya na golgofe*, p. 127. Additional support for these conclusions include: RGVIA, f. 366, op. 1, d. 66, ll. 104–110; RGVIA, f. 2003, op. 1, d. 1800, ll. 386–400, 430–435; Verkhovskiy, *Rossiya na golgofe*, pp. 111–112, 114, 123, 125–127; "Iz dnevnika gen. V. G. Boldyreva," *KA*, No. 23, 1927, 263; Wildman, *The End of the Russian Imperial Army*, Vol. II, pp. 224–290; Frenkin, *Russkaya armiya*, pp. 435–557.

Congress of Soviets in Petrograd for late October. Lenin worked throughout October to persuade the rest of the Bolshevik leadership to seize power prior to the Second Congress of Soviets in order to present the Congress with a *fait accompli.*[135]

The seizure of power in the capital required an armed force to carry out the operation. On October 9 the Petrograd Soviet formed a Military Revolutionary Committee (MRC) to defend the capital against "counterrevolution." The specific catalyst for the formation of the MRC was the announcement, in the second week of October, that the Provisional Government intended to move troops from the Petrograd garrison to the front. The Commander of the Northern Front, General V. A. Cheremisov, opposed this step, convinced that more unreliable troops were the last thing he needed. The government went ahead anyway, and the fear that they might be sent to the front inclined most of the Petrograd garrison to either remain neutral or side with the Bolsheviks during the seizure of power. Kerensky seemed unaware that he had very few reliable troops to resist a Bolshevik attempt to seize power, the prospect of which by the second half of October was an open secret.[136]

The Bolshevik take-over really began on October 21–23, when the MRC made a largely successful bid to wrest political control over the Petrograd garrison from the Provisional Government. On October 23 the MRC gained control over the Peter and Paul Fortress, overlooking the Winter Palace, and the neighboring Kronwerk Arsenal. By October 24, Bolshevik efforts to grab key government buildings were well underway, and the government finally woke up to the fact that it had few reliable troops in the capital. The main force on the government side consisted of military school cadets and the Women's Battalion; even Cossack units in the capital refused to support the Provisional Government. Much of the military activity on the Soviet side, meanwhile, was carried out by Baltic Fleet sailors and Red Guards, sometimes acting independently of the MRC.[137]

The final act in the struggle for Petrograd, as during the February Revolution, was played out at the front. Efforts to order troops from the front began in earnest on October 25. Kerensky ordered Cheremisov, the Northern Front commander, to dispatch two Cossack divisions and several other units to Petrograd; Cheremisov immediately carried out this order. Kerensky himself fled Petrograd the morning of the 25th in search of reliable troops from the

[135] Mstiskavskiy is quoted in Frenkin, *Russkaya armiya*, p. 577. On Bolshevik party politics in September and October, see Schapiro, *1917*, pp. 121–128; Rabinowitch, *Bolsheviks Come to Power*, pp. 168–208.

[136] Rabinowitch, *Bolsheviks Come to Power*, 224–248; Schapiro, *1917*, pp. 128–132; Wildman, *The End of the Russian Imperial Army*, Vol. II, pp. 290–294; Frenkin, *Russkaya armiya*, pp. 559–578.

[137] Rabinowitch, *Bolsheviks Come to Power*, pp. 241–272; Rex A. Wade, "The Red Guards: Spontaneity and the October Revolution," in Frankel, Frankel, and Knei-Paz, *Revolution in Russia*, pp. 65–69.

front. By the evening of October 25 more than an entire corps had been dispatched toward Petrograd.[138]

Cheremisov was in touch with officers at the General Staff in Petrograd, located across Palace Square from the Winter Palace, several times on the 25th. He was told that even the most disciplined units were abandoning their posts, that "the government is deprived of the remnants of power," and that the Cossacks were disobeying orders and refusing to leave the barracks. Chaos reigned at the General Staff, the situation was regarded as hopeless, and a conversation between Cheremisov and the staff broke off when it was reported that the building was being seized by the MRC and that the staff was stopping work and leaving immediately. Cheremisov also undoubtedly knew that the Bolsheviks had made considerable inroads among the troops of his front in September and October; Bolsheviks represented a plurality of Northern Front delegates to the Second Congress of Soviets, and with their allies the Left SRs were a majority.[139]

At 10:00 P.M. on October 25, Cheremisov ordered that all forces dispatched from the Northern Front toward Petrograd should come to a halt. Cheremisov had been skeptical about the use of front troops in Petrograd from the beginning. On October 23 he received an order to have troops ready to send to Petrograd if necessary; Cheremisov handed the order to his commissar, W. S. Voytinskiy, stating, "This is political and has nothing to do with me.... You can try to execute it if you think it can be done." The news from Petrograd obviously reinforced his prior belief that the front army should not be used in what he called the "political scrape" in Petrograd. When a demoralized Kerensky arrived at Pskov on the evening of the 25th, Cheremisov apparently persuaded Kerensky that further resistance was futile, and Cheremisov later insisted that the order to halt the troops moving on Petrograd came from Kerensky. Kerensky even suggested at one point that he would name Cheremisov as Supreme Commander in his stead.[140]

Kerensky reversed himself the morning of October 26 and decided to continue his bid to march on Petrograd with troops from the front. Kerensky was persuaded to continue by front commissar Voytinskiy, Quartermaster

---

[138] Many of the key telegrams and documents on the high command and the October Revolution have been published. See, in particular, G. N. Golikov, ed., *VOSR: Oktyabr'skoye vooruzhennoye vosstaniye v Petrograde. Dokumenty i materialy* [hereafter *VOSR: Vosstaniye*] (Moskva: Izdatel'stvo Akademii Nauk SSSR, 1957), especially. pp. 277–278, 399–426, 593–663; "Oktyabr' na fronte," *KA*, Nos. 23–24, 1927, 149–194, 71–107; "Stavka 25–26 Oktyabrya 1917 g.," *Arkhiv russkoy revolyutsii* [hereafter *ARR*], Vol. 7, 1922, 279–320. On these specific orders, see *VOSR: Vosstaniye*, pp. 399, 593–594; "Stavka 25–26 Oktyabrya," 286–291.

[139] *VOSR: Vosstaniye*, pp. 403, 407–408; Wildman, *The End of the Russian Imperial Army*, Vol. II, p. 286.

[140] Wildman, *The End of the Russian Imperial Army*, Vol. II, pp. 294–298 (quote, p. 294); Katkov, *Kornilov Affair*, pp. 128–129; *VOSR: Vosstaniye*, pp. 411–413, 603–609.

General of the Northern Front Baranovskiy (Kerensky's brother-in-law), and General P. N. Krasnov, the commander of the Third Cavalry Corps. All of them thought that Cheremisov was being overly pessimistic and thereby dooming the Provisional Government's real chances for success. Kerensky and Krasnov set off to rejoin Krasnov's units, which had been halted in transit the night before on Cheremisov's order. Krasnov really only commanded a division, and not a corps, since the other two divisions in the corps were scattered across the Northern Front and unable to join up with him, and even the First Don Cossack Division under his command was far from full strength.[141]

Kerensky continued to order additional units from *Stavka* and the Northern Front as he and Krasnov moved on Petrograd. General N. N. Dukhonin, the Chief of Staff at Mogilev, believed that plenty of troops were en route and that Krasnov and Kerensky would have a more than adequate force. Most of these units suffered from resistance of the troops and delays imposed by the railroad workers en route. Cheremisov believed that sending more troops from the Northern Front was dangerous because it would cause the army to split into competing factions. He persuaded Dukhonin on October 27 to halt the movement of troops from the 12th Army under his command. Cheremisov noted that two of his three front army committees were pro-Bolshevik, and various units had discussed going to Petrograd to assist the revolution. Cheremisov believed that all troop movements in support of either side should stop, since otherwise the situation "could lead to a civil war at the front and to the collapse of the front." Thus when Krasnov went into battle against pro-Bolshevik forces (mainly sailors and Red Guards) on October 30 on the outskirts of Petrograd he was heavily outgunned. Krasnov in fact had only about 1,000 troops compared to the 10–20 thousand armed men (I hesitate to call them troops) on the Bolshevik side. Krasnov's Cossacks opted to negotiate, and a cease-fire was worked out. Kerensky fled the scene before he could be handed over to the Bolshevik side, and the whole affair was over.[142]

Soviet Power and the Capitulation of Stavka

The Bolsheviks had now temporarily secured power in Petrograd. Their seizure of power had received the backing of the Second Congress of Soviets, which opened in Petrograd on October 25. Many Bolsheviks and all Mensheviks and SRs, as well as most army units, believed that the Congress's call for a Soviet-based government implied the formation of a broad-based

[141] *VOSR: Vosstaniye*, pp. 603–609; Wildman, *The End of the Russian Imperial Army*, Vol. II, pp. 295–298.

[142] Wildman, *The End of the Russian Imperial Army*, Vol. II, pp. 298–307; "Oktyabr na fronte," *KA*, No. 23, 155–156, 166–167, 171–173, 176–182; *VOSR: Vosstaniye*, pp. 610–613, 638–640.

socialist government. The most important policy decisions of the Second Congress were the decrees on land and peace, which called for an immediate peace and the transfer of private lands to peasant committees without compensation for the landlords.[143]

The Bolsheviks also successfully seized power in Moscow by November 2. The Moscow Soviet, which had a Bolshevik majority, formed a Military Revolutionary Committee on October 25. Resistance, including from the military, was much more fierce than in Petrograd, and more than 1,000 people died in a week of fighting. It seems that much of the military opposition came from students at military academies and that many officers did not participate on either side. The Western Front, which was the closest to Moscow, was experiencing difficulties similar to those of the Northern Front, and the Chief of Staff of the front, General R. F. Val'ter, feared the consequences among the troops of trying to send reinforcements to either Petrograd or Moscow.[144]

Despite Bolshevik victories in the two most important cities, many Russian elites, including the military leadership, remained convinced that the Bolsheviks' days were numbered. Dukhonin, now the acting Supreme Commander, continued to command the troops at his own discretion while he waited for the political situation to become more clear. He ordered all troops to remain at the front and continue to fulfill their "duty to the motherland" while political negotiations on the formation of a new government were conducted.[145]

A key card in the Bolshevik deck was their effort to secure an immediate peace and thus further undermine the high command. On November 7, Lenin directed Dukhonin to begin negotiations immediately with the enemy on a cease-fire, to be followed by peace talks. The next day Lenin, Stalin, and N. V. Krylenko, on behalf of Sovnarkom, contacted Dukhonin and asked him what steps he was taking to implement the government's instructions. Dukhonin replied that only a government supported by the country and the army would have enough weight with the enemy to be able to achieve meaningful results.[146]

---

[143] Schapiro, *1917*, pp. 133–134; Rabinowitch, *Bolsheviks Come to Power*, pp. 291–298, 301–304, 306; Frenkin, *Russkaya armiya*, pp. 616–617, 643–645.

[144] Schapiro, *1917*, pp. 154–155; John L. H. Keep, "The Spread of Bolshevism to the Interior: 1917–1918," in Shukman, *Blackwell Encyclopedia*, p. 201; A. G. Kavtaradze, *Voyennye spetsialisty na sluzhbe Respubliki Sovetov 1917–1920 gg.* (Mosvka: "Nauka," 1988), pp. 33–34; "Oktyabr na fronte," *KA*, No. 23, 173–176; A. Shlyapnikov, "Oktyabr'skiy perevorot i stavka," *KA*, No. 8, 1925, 166–167.

[145] Schapiro, *1917*, pp. 139–142; Wildman, *The End of the Russian Imperial Army*, Vol. II, pp. 297, 302–303; David R. Jones, "The Officers and the October Revolution," *Soviet Studies*, 28 (1976), 212–216; *VOSR: Vosstaniye*, p. 805.

[146] The story of the Bolshevik peace campaign of November 1917 is told in detail by Wildman: Wildman, *The End of the Russian Imperial Army*, Vol. II, pp. 379–405. Most of the relevant

The Bolsheviks responded to Dukhonin's refusal by dismissing him as Supreme Commander and appointing in his place Krylenko, a Bolshevik activist with limited military experience and no command experience who held the rank of ensign (*praporshchik*). Dukhonin replied that he could only give up power to a government that had the support of the majority of the people. "I am completely unconcerned with the political face of that authority," Dukhonin stated, "since at the current moment merely an authority as such is necessary." Dukhonin continued to concern himself with operational matters and trying to maintain some semblance of authority at the front.[147]

Krylenko, in the meantime, was doing his best to make Dukhonin's position untenable. Krylenko set out for the Northern Front on November 11, announcing that he was going to the front to secure peace. He summoned Cheremisov to meet him. Cheremisov refused, asking Krylenko to come to him so he could tell Krylenko why his peace efforts were "impracticable." Krylenko did not go to see Cheremisov but pushed on to the Fifth Army on the Northern Front, where the commander, General V. G. Boldyrev, also refused to meet with Krylenko. The morning of November 12, Krylenko addressed a meeting of the Fifth Army Committee at which he declared his intention to secure peace, over the "corpses" of the "counterrevolutionary command staff" if necessary.[148]

The Bolsheviks had considerable support in the Fifth Army and on November 13 Boldyrev was arrested. Cheremisov asked Dukhonin to be relieved of his command. Dukhonin urged him to remain "for the good of the motherland," but by November 15 Cheremisov's Chief of Staff, General S. G. Lukirskiy, was acting front commander. General V. V. Antipov, who had been a corps commander, assumed the command of the Fifth Army. Lukirskiy contacted Antipov on November 15 to find out if Antipov was a "Krylenko protégé." Antipov stated that he had told Krylenko that he considered politics in the army to be "completely intolerable" and that he had never involved himself in politics and would not do so. Lukirskiy seemed satisfied and thereby "appointed" Antipov as Commander of the Fifth Army. The next day, however, Antipov asked to be removed "for health reasons."[149]

The situation on the Western Front was similarly chaotic and difficult for the command staff. On December 12 the Minsk MRC asked General Baluyev

documents on *Stavka* and the Bolshevik campaign are published as "Nakanune peremiriya," *KA*, No. 23, 1927, 195–249. On the specific points here, see "Nakanune peremiriya," 197–201; L. S. Gaponenko, ed., *Oktyabr'skaya revolyutskiya i armiya: 25 oktyabrya 1917 g.–mart 1918 g. Sbornik dokumentov* [hereafter *ORA*] (Moskva; "Nauka," 1973), pp. 83–85.

[147] *ORA*, pp. 85–86; "Nakanune peremiriya," 206; Shukman, *Blackwell Encyclopedia*, pp. 335–336.

[148] "Nakanune peremiriya," 208, 223–227; *ORA*, pp. 110–111.

[149] "Nakanune peremiriya," 223–227; *ORA*, pp. 110–111; RGVIA, f. 2003, op. 1, d. 1802, ll. 77–87, 157.

to enter into armistice negotiations with the Germans. Baluyev replied that he did not take orders from the MRC and would not enter into negotiations; he also said that if the MRC resorted to force, he would resign. Despite Dukhonin's protests and suggestion that the Western Front military leadership resist the MRC with force, virtually the entire top command staff of the front resigned. The Chief of Staff of the front, General Val'ter, told *Stavka* that it would be impossible to resist the MRC, "on whose side are all the troops of the front." Much of the Western Front staff decided to stay in place, however, arguing that the situation was temporary and that they could not leave administrative control either to "completely inexperienced people" or to "the winds of fate." They agreed to stay in their posts on the condition that they be removed from politics and that they play no role in the peace negotiations, a position that *Stavka* endorsed.[150]

Dukhonin continued to believe that the Bolshevik position was weak and that *Stavka* could hold out. The peace negotiations would fail, Dukhonin argued, because neither the Germans nor the allies took the Bolsheviks seriously. Dukhonin also made arrangements to resist with force any attempt by Krylenko to move on *Stavka*. He appealed to all political parties to solve the question of state authority and asked the troops to not be fooled by promises of peace, warning them of Russia's possible enslavement to imperial Germany.[151]

Dukhonin's position, however, was becoming more tenuous by the day. Already he had lost control over the Northern and Western Fronts. The Bolsheviks were weaker on the Southwestern and Rumanian Fronts, but their peace proposals resonated with the troops there also. The political situation on these latter two fronts was even more chaotic because on November 6 the Ukrainian Rada (Council) had declared the founding of the Ukrainian People's Republic and on November 7 the Cossack Ataman General Kaledin proclaimed a Don Republic and invited the Bolsheviks' opponents to come to the region to organize resistance. The Germans, moreover, had proved quite happy to enter into negotiations on a cease-fire directly with Russian units at the local level, since a separate peace on the Eastern Front would free up resources for the war in the west.[152]

By November 18, Dukhonin and *Stavka* had apparently decided that further resistance was pointless. The All-Army Committee based at *Stavka*, which had remained loyal to Dukhonin while many of the front committees were becoming pro-Bolshevik, stated its desire to avoid bloodshed and

[150] "Nakanune peremiriya," 215–218; ORA, 116–120; RGVIA, f. 2003, op. 1, d. 1812, ll. 246–253.
[151] "Nakanune peremiriya," 218–220, 223, 226, 229–231; RGVIA, f. 2003, op. 1, d. 1802, ll. 31–37.
[152] Wildman, *The End of the Russian Imperial Army*, Vol. II, pp. 350–397; Frenkin, *Russkaya armiya*, 618–644; Pipes, *Formation of the Soviet Union*, pp. 53–73, 114–126; Suny, *Revenge of the Past*, pp. 43–51; Shukman, *Blackwell Encyclopedia*, pp. 205–207, 220–223.

come to an agreement with the Sovnarkom. On the night of November 18 the Mogilev Soviet established a MRC and recognized Krylenko as commander-in-chief. Dukhonin tried to persuade the commander of the Rumanian Front, General Shcherbachev, to take over his position, because he wanted to transfer his command without Bolshevik participation, which would imply "obedience." Shcherbachev begged off, and he even suggested that the new commander-in-chief be elected by the front and army committees! Dukhonin and the rest of the military leadership also considered moving headquarters to Kiev, but negotiations with the Ukrainian Rada went nowhere and the high command could not decide among themselves.[153]

Krylenko arrived at *Stavka* on November 20, by which point Dukhonin had decided to submit peacefully. Although there were still some units willing to fight, Dukhonin allowed himself to be arrested without incident. One of his last decisions was to order the release of Kornilov and the other officers implicated in the Kornilov affair, who made their way to the Don region to begin organizing what would become the White Volunteer Army. A mob of soldiers, driven perhaps by the release of Kornilov or simple blood lust, attacked Krylenko's railroad car where Dukhonin was being held, dragged him out, and viciously beat and murdered the last commander-in-chief of the Russian Empire.[154]

Explaining Officer Behavior after the October Revolution

The coding of the October Revolution case is a tricky question. The officer corps's behavior clearly was not a case of military intervention. It is hard to code it as a case of military arbitration, since the military leadership did not really choose anyone as their preferred contender for supreme executive power. The Chief of Staff, Dukhonin, remained loyal to the recognized Supreme Commander, Kerensky, until after Kerensky ran away for good. But the military leadership did not hold to a consistent line, since Cheremisov clearly worked against sending troops to support the Provisional Government. For this reason I have coded this case as *both* military arbitration and military noninvolvement. The military high command was unwilling to recognize the Bolshevik government as legitimate for several weeks, but eventually there were no other viable contenders and the Bolsheviks won by default.

Dukhonin's stance when the October Revolution broke out is perhaps the easiest to understand. He took orders from the Supreme Commander, Kerensky, and carried them out as best he could until the defeat of Kerensky

---

[153] "Nakanune peremiriya," 236–238; Wildman, *The End of the Russian Imperial Army*, Vol. II, pp. 399–400; Kenez, *Civil War in South Russia*, p. 52.

[154] Wildman, *The End of the Russian Imperial Army*, Vol. II, pp. 400–401; Kenez, *Civil War in South Russia*, pp. 52–53.

and Krasnov's forces. The Provisional Government, Dukhonin remarked in a telegram to the population on October 27, was the "authorized organ of democracy" until the Constituent Assembly convened, and he noted that the front army was prepared to defend the government with force.[155]

The activity of Cheremisov, the Northern Front commander, is more difficult to explain. General Krasnov and Cheremisov's front commissar, Voytinskiy, suggest that Cheremisov was a Bolshevik sympathizer and actively working to undermine Kerensky's position. This is clearly not true, since when Krylenko arrived at the Northern Front on November 12 Cheremisov refused to see him. In fact on several occasions Cheremisov made quite disparaging remarks about the Bolsheviks, and he went into emigration after the revolution.[156]

Cheremisov justified his opposition to sending troops to Petrograd on three grounds: the need to maintain the front, his opposition to interference in politics, and the futility of the effort. Cheremisov told Dukhonin: "[A]n overwhelming number of front troops and the entire fleet [Baltic] stand for noninterference in the Petrograd political scrape and demand that the army fulfill only its direct task, i.e. the defense of the front...." "The political struggle should not concern us," Cheremisov remarked, and noted that he had restrained units from going to Petrograd to support the Bolsheviks, telling them that "I personally consider the active interference of the army in politics intolerable and therefore I consider it inexpedient in general to send troops to the support of one or the other of the warring parties." Only by taking such a position, Cheremisov said, "have I succeeded so far in preserving the front from collapse. I am pursuing an exclusively operational task, i.e. first of all and only strive to prevent the front from collapsing."[157]

Dukhonin's response demonstrates clearly the dilemma faced by the military command. Dukhonin noted the need to maintain the front, but also to follow orders from the existing government. Dukhonin said, "Undoubtedly, the principal task is to firmly maintain the front.... On the other hand, I have to be concerned about the attempt of a separate group of the population to seize legitimate power in their hands and impose their will, which could in the most decisive manner affect the defense of the motherland and her vital interests." Dukhonin, however, eventually relented to Cheremisov's protests

[155] *VOSR: Vosstaniye*, p. 609.

[156] P. N. Krasnov, "Na vnutrennem fronte," *ARR*, Vol. 1, 1922, 143; Wildman, *The End of the Russian Imperial Army*, Vol. II, p. 294, note 64; *VOSR: Vosstaniye*, p. 611; "Oktyabr na fronte," *KA*, No. 23, 184; "Nakanune peremiriya," 224.

[157] *VOSR: Vosstaniye*, pp. 611–612. The order in which communications between *Stavka* and the Northern Front took place is confusing based on the published documents. Based on my archival research, the documents should be read in the following order: *VOSR: Vosstaniye*, pp. 614–615; "Oktaybr na fronte," *KA*, No. 23, 163–166; *VOSR: Vosstaniye*, pp. 610–613. See RGVIA, f. 2003, op. 1, d. 1807, ll. 259–274. See also Cheremisov's comments in "Oktyabr na fronte," *KA*, No. 23, 176–182.

that sending troops from the Northern Front "inevitably will lead to civil war and the collapse of the front," and he agreed that no units would be sent except for the Third Cavalry Corps (Krasnov's forces).[158]

Cheremisov's stance is perfectly understandable, but he did skirt the boundaries of insubordination. For example, around midnight on October 25 he contacted the commander of the Western Front, Baluyev, and told him that "the Provisional Government in its previous form essentially does not exist" and noted that his front committee had decided to stand neither with the government nor the Bolsheviks. Cheremisov suggested that he and Baluyev "unite their activity and views." Baluyev replied, "It's a pity that your forces are participating in politics; we have sworn an oath to the Provisional Government." Baluyev also noted that military policy was determined by *Stavka*, and not by commanders deciding to unite their views. Cheremisov replied that the Provisional Government no longer existed and that under the circumstances "we do not have the right to evade politics and not take into consideration the political mood of the masses; we are obligated to consider this mood, so that the front does not open up for the enemy." Baluyev's position was that "as a soldier, at the current time I recognize only one policy for us – to save the Motherland from the Germans, and on that point I am in solidarity with you." Baluyev concluded, "It is decisively all the same to me who is in the Provisional Government as long as it exists and it eliminates the ruin that is reigning in Russia."[159]

Cheremisov did not, it appears, ever ignore or disobey a direct order, but he did his best to maneuver Kerensky, Dukhonin, and Baluyev around to his point of view that it would be catastrophic for the army to send troops from the front to deal with the "political squabble" in Petrograd. Dukhonin, Krasnov, Baluyev, Voytinskiy, and Baranovskiy all became suspicious of Cheremisov's actions and considered his behavior inappropriate if not downright treasonous. Cheremisov was hardly at the mercy of the front committees and MRCs, though, as is sometimes suggested. Cheremisov told the chair of the MRC in Reval that he had taken from the beginning a stance of the army's noninterference in Petrograd politics, but that Kerensky had nonetheless decided to send troops. Cheremisov noted that because the army must be "an organized army, and not a disorganized crowd," the orders of the Supreme Commander (Kerensky) and *Stavka* had to be "unquestionably carried out."[160]

It turned out that Cheremisov was right about the difficulty that the military would have in moving troops from his front to Petrograd, and several

[158] *VOSR: Vosstaniye*, pp. 612–613.
[159] *VOSR: Vosstaniye*, pp. 415–417.
[160] *VOSR: Vosstaniye*, pp. 603–609, 611–613; "Stavka 25–26 Oktyabrya 1917 g.," 300, 302–303; "Oktyabr na fronte," *KA*, No. 23, 182–186; "Oktyabr na fronte," *KA*, No. 24, 98–105.

of his subordinates, including his Chief of Staff and his army commanders, agreed with him on this point. The Provisional Government's claim to legitimacy was quite weak, both because of the manner in which it took power and because of the nature of "dual power" and the popularity of the Soviets. Cheremisov also felt, along with most other observers, that the Bolsheviks would not last. Despite all of these caveats, Cheremisov's very determination to not interfere in Petrograd politics was a form of political arbitration, because he did not unflinchingly implement government orders.[161]

The behavior of top generals such as Dukhonin, Baluyev, and Krasnov, on the other hand, should be coded as military noninvolvement in a sovereign power dispute because they carried out orders of the existing government up to the point when that government de facto ceased to exist. These officers did so even though there was no love lost between the officer corps and Kerensky, who was blamed for bringing the army to ruin and despised for his duplicitous dealings with Kornilov. Krasnov later reflected on why he had supported Kerensky during the October Revolution, summarizing his thoughts the night of October 25–26 when he went to meet Kerensky: "Yes, I am going. Because it is not to Kerensky I go, but to the Motherland, to great Russia, which I cannot disavow. And if Russia is with Kerensky, then I too will go with him. I will hate and curse him, but I will go and serve and die for Russia."[162]

The difference between the behavior of Cheremisov and the other top generals, although coded differently, should not be exaggerated. All of the high command cared little about which government ruled in Petrograd, as long as they could end the anarchy in the country and army and continue the war effort. The difference in the behavior of different officers was based more on tactical considerations, in conditions of chaos and poor information, than on strategic differences about the proper role of the army.

Once Krasnov's expedition had failed, it became clear to the top military command that there was no sense in offering further resistance. Dukhonin and the front commanders believed that their single task was to attend to operational matters, maintaining order in the army until a legitimate government came into being. The Provisional Government's acting War Minister and the General Staff Chief in Petrograd, Generals A. A. Manikovskiy and V. V. Marushevskiy, agreed to serve the Soviet regime on the condition that they focus entirely on "the daily needs of the army." Marushevskiy noted, "we categorically are removing ourselves from involvement in internal

---

[161] "Oktyabr na fronte," *KA*, No. 23, 163, 168, 176–182, 192–194; "Oktyabr na fronte," *KA*, No. 24, 71–79; *VOSR: Vosstaniye*, 601; "Iz dnevnika gen. V. G. Boldyreva," 263.

[162] Krasnov, "Na vnutrennem fronte," 149, 163. See also Jones, "Officers and the October Revolution," 210–212.

politics." Manikovskiy and Marushevskiy, however, were arrested by the Bolsheviks on November 19.[163]

Dukhonin complained bitterly to General Shcherbachev, "the situation is, of course, extremely difficult, complicated by the complete bankruptcy in state relations of the political parties, who cannot in any way come to an agreement, leaving the army, primarily the command staff, to disentangle the mess they've created." Despite these bitter feelings, Dukhonin and the rest of *Stavka* capitulated without a fight to Krylenko. The General-Quartermaster at *Stavka*, General M. K. Diterikhs, argued on November 18 that the fact that the allies had communicated their views on a separate peace to Sovnarkom was an "oblique recognition by the allies of Petrograd [i.e., Bolshevik] authority." Thus, *Stavka* should cancel its plans to evacuate to the South because, "being a strictly military organ, Stavka cannot concern itself with the political struggle for power." Diterikhs persuaded Dukhonin to "save the dignity of a non-political Stavka" and submit to arrest when Krylenko arrived. Most of the officers from the various departments at *Stavka* continued to work under Krylenko.[164]

Indeed, the willingness of some officers to submit to Bolshevik authority, despite the extreme hostility of the Bolsheviks to the officer corps, was evident even in these early days of Soviet power. On November 19 the new commander of the 12th Army, General V. F. Novitskiy, urged Dukhonin to come to an agreement with the Sovnarkom. Noting that his army committee was pro-Sovnarkom, Novitskiy argued that the only way to "weaken the anarchy that exists in the army" is to come to "an agreement with the new authority." Even if the command staff disperses, he concluded, "surely Russia and the army will remain and they need in these great and difficult historical minutes courageous, firm, and experienced leadership, which can save them from complete disintegration."[165]

The new temporary commander of the Southwestern Front after the fall of *Stavka*, General N. N. Stogov, complained about the large number of political questions with which he was being forced to deal. The Southwestern Front was particularly chaotic, with the Ukrainian Rada, the Cossacks, and various pro-Sovnarkom Military Revolutionary Committees trying to assert their authority and move troops about in their own political interests. "In relation to politics I stand on the point of view I have stated more than once," Stogov stressed, "the noninterference in the conflict of political tendencies.... Despite that from all sides the appearance of demands about giving this or

[163] "Oktyabr na fronte," *KA*, No. 24, 75–79; Shlyapnikov, "Oktyabr'skiy perevorot i stavka," 166–167; M. N. Pokrovskiy and Ya.A. Yakovlev, eds., *Razlozheniye armii v 1917 godu* (Moskva–Leningrad: Gosizdat, 1925), pp. 167–168; "Nakanune peremiriya," 197–201; RGVIA, f. 2003, op. 1, d. 1812, ll. 23–24; Kavtaradze, *Voyennye spetsialisty*, pp. 60–62.

[164] "Nakanune peremiriya," 228–231, 239–240; Wildman, *The End of the Russian Imperial Army*, Vol. II, p. 400; Kavtaradze, *Voyennye spetsialisty*, p. 58.

[165] *ORA*, pp. 144–145.

that order with a political tinge has not stopped." Stogov added that given these conditions he would have a hard time taking moral responsibility for further developments, despite his "desire to carry out his soldierly duty to the motherland to the end."[166]

The historian David Jones discerns three main types of officer corps behavior in the aftermath of the October Revolution, and his conclusions are perfectly consistent with the evidence discussed in this section, and throughout the entire chapter, about the existence of a dominant organizational culture and two subcultures in the Russian officer corps during the revolution. One subculture that Jones highlights is the group of officers such as Kornilov, Denikin, and Alekseev, who after the October Revolution went south to try to organize an anti-Bolshevik resistance. Jones maintains that this group was a small one consisting of "the most embittered" officers. A second small group was made up of officers such as Novitskiy, who decided that the Bolsheviks represented the best chance to restore strong power in the state. Jones concludes:

A third group (at first by far the most numerous) tried, like Boldyrev, to remain politically neutral in conditions of growing internal strife.... These officers usually attempted to hold the front while a front remained, and then sought to retire temporarily from military life as a means of preserving their neutrality amidst the conflicting claims, appeals and demands of both Whites and Reds.[167]

Summary

The opportunity structure for military intervention in October was mixed. State weakness remained a severe problem and presented a real opportunity to seize power, which the Bolsheviks exploited. On the other hand, organizational barriers to army activity were strong due to support for the Bolsheviks among the troops of the Petrograd garrison and the Northern and Western Fronts. It was not counterbalancing, penetration, or officer-corps cleavages that prevented intervention, though, as organizational structure accounts would predict.

In terms of motives, it is hard to imagine a more decisive threat to the military's corporate interests than the Bolshevik take-over. The Bolshevik party had called for Russia's defeat in the war, was suspected of working for Germany, and favored the abolition of the armed forces. The military high

---

[166] RGVIA, f. 2003, op. 1, d. 1803, ll. 92–101, 142–143, 187–191.

[167] Jones, "Officers and the October Revolution," 223. See also John Erickson, "The Origins of the Red Army," in Richard Pipes, ed., *Revolutionary Russia* (Cambridge, MA: Harvard University Press, 1968), p. 230. A. G. Kavtaradze demonstrates convincingly that the standard Soviet view that the "overwhelming majority" of the officer corps was actively anti-Soviet power in October 1917 is false. At a maximum, Kavtaradze writes, less than three percent of the officer corps was openly against the October Revolution. The majority took a wait-and-see attitude: Kavtaradze, *Voyennye spetsialisty*, pp. 37–38.

command's passive behavior during the October Revolution thus gives additional weight to the organizational culture interpretation. Process tracing of this case has demonstrated that officers were guided in their behavior by their beliefs about the army's proper role in politics, specifically the norm that the military was "outside politics" and should not interfere in party political disputes. This factor combined with organizational structure barriers to intervention to immobilize the officer corps in October.

THE CIVIL WAR

Theories of military coups are not designed to explain such a complex political phenomenon as revolution, and thus at times they have not adequately captured the multiple and mixed opportunities and motivations of officers. This observation applies even more to the ability of these theories to explain military behavior in a civil war. The Russian Civil War lasted three years and cost millions of lives. Military officers were of course key actors on both sides of the lines. In this section I briefly discuss the motivations of officers who fought for the Reds and the Whites.[168]

The new Bolshevik regime achieved an armistice with the Germans on December 2, and peace talks opened at Brest-Litovsk on December 9. The Soviet government was initially unwilling to agree to the harsh terms demanded by the Central Powers, and it tried to adopt the policy proposed by Trotsky of "Neither War nor Peace." In the meantime, the new government was busy consolidating Soviet rule at home. By February 1918 most of the old Russian Empire was under Soviet control. The Ukrainian Rada fell in January, and in February the Don Cossack resistance collapsed and the Volunteer Army under the leadership of Generals Alekseev, Kornilov, and Denikin was forced to abandon Rostov and head out onto the steppe.[169]

The Volunteer Army was the first and ultimately most important source of resistance to Soviet rule. General Alekseev, the former Supreme Commander who was in retirement after his dismissal, had begun work to create an organization of conservative officers even before the October Revolution, and after the Bolsheviks seized power he endeavored to congregate anti-Bolshevik officers in the Don Cossack region in the south of Russia. Peter Kenez notes, "Alekseev was the first to recognize that in order to fight the Bolsheviks it was necessary to form a new army rather than try to save units of the old one." Very few officers answered Alekseev's call in November 1917, and even many officers in the region (in the Don and Kuban) did

---

[168] Good general introductions are Evan Mawdsley, *The Russian Civil War* (Boston, MA: Allen & Unwin, 1987); Diane P. Koenker, William G. Rosenberg, and Ronald Grigor Suny, eds., *Party, State, and Society in the Russian Civil War: Explorations in Social History* (Bloomington, IN: Indiana University Press, 1989).

[169] Mawdsley, *Russian Civil War*, pp. 3–29; Schapiro, *1917*, pp. 151–169.

not join the Volunteer Army. The entire army was only 4,000 men strong by February 1918 (the size of the Russian officer corps in November 1917 was 250,000).[170]

The Volunteer Army was composed of the most bitter officers from the old army. They were ardent patriots and nationalists who believed that the Bolsheviks were leading Russia to ruin. The leaders of the Volunteer Army were committed to continuing the war against Germany. They believed that the Bolsheviks were German agents; thus to continue the war against the enemy, one had to fight both the Bolsheviks and the Germans. Kenez, the major Western historian of the Volunteer army, remarks, "to ask the generals to give up fighting the foreign enemy was to ask them to be something other than they were."[171]

While Alekseev, Kornilov, and Denikin were trying without much success to raise a force capable of opposing the Bolsheviks, the new Soviet government continued its efforts to undermine the old army. Evan Mawdsley observes, "by mid-November no one controlled the army." The Front commanders did their best to hold the army together, but many soldiers and officers drifted away. The Sovnarkom decision in mid-December to introduce elections for commanders further accelerated the collapse, and on January 29 Krylenko announced the demobilization of the entire army. When Trotsky on February 10 (new style; the Russian calendar was synchronized with the Western one on February 1) at Brest-Litovsk declared the end of the war, even though no formal peace treaty had been signed, the Soviet government had no real army to defend the country. Germany attacked on February 18 and took Minsk on February 21 and Kiev on March 2. The Soviet government at that point accepted extremely harsh terms from the Central Powers and signed the Treaty of Brest-Litovsk on March 3.[172]

The most important consequence of the German onslaught on Russia in late February, the so-called Eleven Days War, was the impetus it provided to the Soviet regime to establish a regular army. Utopian plans for a workers' and peasants' militia had to be scrapped. The Soviet government appealed to old officers to come to the defense of the motherland, and thousands of officers answered this call; A. G. Kavtaradze, the leading specialist on this question, puts the number at more than 8,000. Mawdsley stresses, "A central fact about the Red Army, one often forgotten, is that it was originally intended for use not against counterrevolutionaries but against the Germans and the Austrians."[173]

---

[170] Kenez, *Civil War in South Russia*, pp. 57–71; Mawdsley, *Russian Civil War*, pp. 20–21; Kavtaradze, *Voyennye spetsialisty*, p. 28.

[171] Kenez, *Civil War in South Russia*, p. 71; Mawdsley, *Russian Civil War*, pp. 20–21, 165; Kenez, "Ideology of the White Movement," pp. 74–75.

[172] Mawdsley, *Russian Civil War*, pp. 31–37.

[173] Kavtaradze, *Voyennye spetsialisty*, pp. 70, 166; Mawdsley, *Russian Civil War*, p. 59.

Many of these old army officers that came to the defense of the Soviet regime, labeled "military specialists" by the Bolsheviks, were quite explicit about their patriotic motives and the fact that they had not decided to join the Red Army out of love for Bolshevism. These officers stated their opposition to any involvement in civil war, but they were prepared to work for the defense of the country from external attack, which they saw as their duty to the motherland. One early recruit to the Red Army in February 1918 was General D. P. Parskiy, who told General M. D. Bonch-Bruyevich, head of the Soviet Supreme Military Council, "I am far from this socialism that your Bolsheviks preach. But I am ready to work honorably not only with them, but with anyone, even the Devil and his disciples, if only to save Russia from German slavery."[174]

Thus, many of the officers fighting for both the Reds and the Whites saw themselves as defending the fatherland against external invaders. This was a particularly important motivation for the "military specialists," but even the Volunteer Army officers, who were quite clearly focused on fighting inside Russia, saw the war against the Bolsheviks as a continuation of and inextricably linked to the war against Germany. Many who supported the Whites apparently saw Brest-Litovsk as further proof that the Bolsheviks were German spies. For the "military specialists," as Mawdsley points out, the enlistment in the Soviet army in February 1918 to fight against Germany served "as a bridge – a one-way bridge – to the service of the Soviet regime and to battles on the 'internal' front." Once they had enlisted in the Red Army for patriotic reasons, it was easier to redirect them internally once the German threat had passed. The Soviet regime probably would not have survived without the assistance of the "military specialists," who filled an overwhelming majority of the top command and staff positions in the Red Army during the Civil War.[175]

It is important to stress that, although thousands of officers joined the Soviet and Volunteer armies in late 1917–early 1918, hundreds of thousands of officers remained neutral. The vast majority of the old officer corps had no stomach for civil war. As David Jones puts it, these officers believed that "their duty was to defend the 'Fatherland,' not decide who best represented it." The former Supreme Commander, General Brusilov, was asked by younger officers in early 1918 what they should do. According to Jones, "he [Brusilov] repeatedly reminded them that governments could come and go, but Russia would remain; an officer should therefore remain aloof from the civil strife, and wait until he could again honorably serve the nation against

[174] Kavtaradze, *Voyennye spetsialisty*, pp. 65, 69–70; Mawdsley, *Russian Civil War*, pp. 60–61 (including the Parskiy quote); Erickson, "Origins of the Red Army," pp. 243, 253.

[175] V. M. Voynov, "Ofitserskiy korpus belykh armiy na vostoke strany (1918–1920 gg.)," *Otechestvennaya istoriya*, No. 6, 1994, 53; Mawdsley, *Russian Civil War*, p. 61; Kavtaradze, *Voyennye spetsialisty*, pp. 198–226.

its external foes." Brusilov himself, like many other officers, eventually joined the Soviet army only after the Polish invasion of April 1920.[176]

As the Civil War continued, it became more difficult for officers, as for the rest of the Russian population, to remain completely outside the conflict. Both the Reds and the Whites introduced conscription in the second half of 1918. Many of the officers drawn into the civil war ended up on one side or the other because of nonpolitical motives, such as where they and their families lived or with whom they had personal or professional ties. Even many of those who ended up in the Red Army from the very first days of the October Revolution did so not because of commitment to the Bolshevik cause but out of a sense of patriotism, duty, and what Jones calls "professional inertia." Kavtaradze stresses that many officers that ended up serving the Whites did so because they lived in regions under White control and the pressure of material circumstances; a similar observation could be made about those fighting on the Soviet side.[177]

A striking and strange aspect of the Russian Civil War is that most of the officers fighting and dying on both sides seemed to care little about the political and ideological issues that were allegedly central to the conflict. This is seen most clearly on the Soviet side. Bonch-Bruyevich noted in the summer of 1918 that many of the officers living in the area controlled by the Bolsheviks were reluctant to join the Red Army because they saw it as a narrow class- and party-based force more for fighting counterrevolution than for defense of the state against external enemies. Those who did volunteer, who represented less than ten percent of the officers living in the Soviet zone, did so out of patriotism and the habit of military service, and perhaps economic necessity. Material circumstances and coercion certainly played a role for those old army officers that were enlisted in the Red Army once conscription of officers started in the second half of 1918. Kavtaradze, quoting an unnamed "military specialist," says that most of them upheld the "basic principle of no involvement in politics and service exclusively in military affairs." As the Bolshevik regime endured, many old tsarist officers came to accept it as the legitimate Russian government. One reason for the Bolshevik victory, Mawdsley emphasizes, was that "the Bolsheviks were able and willing to make use of much of the apolitical debris of the Tsarist state, including the army officer-corps."[178]

---

[176] David R. Jones, "The Officers and the Soviets, 1917–1920: A Study in Motives," in David R. Jones, ed., *Soviet Armed Forces Review Annual*, Vol. I (Gulf Breeze, FL: Academic International Press, 1977), pp. 177–178, 181; Kavtaradze, *Voyennye spetsialisty*, p. 169; Voynov, "Ofitserskiy korpus belykh armiy," 62; Brusilov, *Soldier's Notebook*, pp. 326–327; Kenez, *Civil War in South Russia*, p. 71; Kenez, "Ideology of the White Movement," p. 66.

[177] Jones, "Officers and the Soviets," pp. 178–180; Kavtaradze, *Voyennye spetsialisty*, p. 49; Kenez, *Civil War in South Russia*, p. 278.

[178] Kavtaradze, *Voyennye spetsialisty*, pp. 95–97, 211, 220–221; Jones, "Officers and the Soviets"; Mawdsley, *Russian Civil War*, p. 285.

It is less true of the Whites that they did not care about politics. The White political leadership, unlike on the Soviet side, was dominated by officers; the territory under White control was essentially under the rule of military dictatorship. The White leadership, though, seemed to have no clear ideology other than a conservative, patriotic nationalism. For the White leadership, the Bolsheviks were not compatriots but an evil and alien force that had taken over their country; for many White officers this feeling expressed itself as a paranoid and vociferous anti-Semitism. The White military leadership continued to express the old maxim of the Imperial army, that the military is "outside politics." Denikin, the leader of the Volunteer Army for most of its existence, argued that the White officers had little interest in political or class warfare. They were, he argued, fighting for the very existence of Russia. The Whites put forward no clear political program, arguing that they did not want to predetermine the future state system, which was a question to be addressed by the Russian people. General N. N. Yudenich, the commander of the White Northwestern Army, adopted the slogan, "Against the Bolsheviks, without Politics." The leader of the Russian Army in the East, Admiral A. V. Kolchak, adopted a similar attitude toward politics.[179]

Kenez notes the absurdity of trying to be "above politics" during a civil war. But there is no reason to doubt the sincerity of the White officers on this point. They were not, as Kenez makes clear, the reactionary monarchists of Soviet demonology, although there were clearly both monarchists and reactionaries on the White side. Most leading White officers were patriots and nationalists, fighting for the idea of "Russia" more than any other idea. Kenez concludes that the primary reason for the White failure was not military but political: "The leaders of the Volunteer Army were such poor politicians that they did not understand the nature of the war they were fighting. They misunderstood politics to such an extent that they believed it could simply be avoided. Such ostrich-like behavior invited disaster."[180]

Summary

The Russian Civil War clearly represents a case of military intervention in politics, the largest in Russian history. Which side represented the legitimate government of Russia is a political and ideological question that will not be resolved here.

---

[179] *Denikin. Yudenich. Vrangel': Revolyutsiya i grazhdanskaya voyna v opisaniyakh belogvardeytsev* (Moskva: Otechestvo, 1991), pp. 15, 18, n. 1; Denikin, *Ocherki*, I(2), pp. 10, 111; II, p. 14; Mawdsley, *Russian Civil War*, pp. 95–99, 107–110, 135–136, 165, 197, 280; Kenez, "Ideology of the White Movement"; Kenez, *Civil War in South Russia*, pp. 204, 210–211, 280; Voynov, "Ofitserskiy korpus belykh armiy."

[180] Kenez, *Civil War in South Russia*, p. 280; Kenez, "Ideology of the White Movement."

The four civil–military relations theories being tested are not well equipped to explain behavior during a civil war, but several of them contain important insights. The domestic structure approach highlights how various social groups, including the military, got drawn into sovereign power issues during a period of state collapse. Lack of military cohesion clearly was not a barrier to military involvement in sovereign power issues. Consistent with the empirical literature, but in opposition to the logic of the organizational structure perspective, army disunity was more a contributor to intervention than a barrier to it.

In terms of motives, the corporate interest approach fares poorly as an explanation for military involvement in the civil war, since much bigger issues were at stake than narrow military ones. The organizational culture perspective also encounters problems. Many officers violated previous apolitical group norms, while simultaneously defending their actions in terms of this culture. Most officers maintained that they were supposed to protect the country from external enemies and remain aloof from domestic politics. These officers did their best to sit out the Civil War. For most officers of the Imperial Russian Army, the Civil War was not an opportunity to grab power but a national tragedy that, like the rest of the population, they were unable to avoid.

CONCLUSION

The armed forces were a key player during the Russian Revolution and Civil War. The officer corps encountered a contradictory mix of structural opportunities and barriers, of motives to intervene and norms against intervention. Weighing the evidence is complicated by the fact that some of the theories are wrong for the right reasons, while others are right for the wrong reasons.

Domestic structure is an essential part of the explanation. The extreme weakness of the Russian state created a situation in which the army could not avoid participation in domestic politics. In February and October the military was almost quite literally dragged into politics against its will. The Kornilov affair and the Civil War were both in part efforts by a small group of officers to take action to prevent army and state collapse, although the Kornilov affair would not have happened without a bizarre series of events that is impossible to describe as a planned coup attempt. Military *involvement* in sovereign power issues, if not intervention, was clearly a product of low state political capacity.

Organizational structure was only a partial guide to military behavior, and when correct it was right for the wrong reasons. Counterbalancing was never an issue, and penetration by police spies and political commissars had little effect on officer behavior. The internal divisions in the officer corps that mattered were more ideational than structural. The one way in which lack of cohesion mattered in the army was the split between troops and officers, a factor overlooked in the literature.

From the time of the February Revolution there were strong corporate interest motives for military intervention. And sections of the military did intervene during both the Kornilov affair and the Civil War. But it would be incorrect to describe either of these efforts as motivated by threats to the army's resources, position, or autonomy. Officers were pulled into high politics against their will because of state collapse. Threats to the military's autonomy and even existence were not defended by vigorous efforts to intervene in politics. This is seen most clearly in the case of the October Revolution and its aftermath, when the military put up little resistance to the seizure of power by a revolutionary party completely hostile to military interests. When the corporate interest approach does correctly predict intervention, it is right for the wrong reasons.

Organizational culture, on the other hand, was often wrong for the right reasons. Prior to 1917 the dominant culture stressed the importance of civilian supremacy and the impermissibility of military involvement in sovereign power issues. This norm was violated by leading officers on several occasions. But organizational culture still provides a very good account for many of the decisions made by officers. Throughout the revolution, officers were motivated by their previously held beliefs about their proper role in politics, particularly a commitment to external defense and of remaining "outside politics." Even when officers violated this norm of civilian supremacy, particularly during the Civil War, it continued to shape their thinking and behavior. Perhaps the most surprising aspect of the revolution and Civil War is how long it took to push the officer corps to intervene, despite the collapse of the state, the prospect of military defeat, and the serious threats to their interests that the revolution entailed. In many countries it takes much less to bring about a military coup.

In general, the combination of external war, revolution, and civil war makes this case a difficult one for civil–military relations theory. Officers groped their way ahead in unfamiliar territory under contradictory and severe pressures. Ultimately, they were no match for Lenin and the Bolsheviks.

4

From Revolution to War, 1917–1941

The Red Army of the new Soviet state was founded in the midst of civil war. Despite the ideological nature of the new regime and the unique circumstances of the army's creation, there was considerable basis for the apolitical organizational culture of the Tsarist army to be passed on to the Red Army. Moreover, the combination of growing state strength and robust organizational control mechanisms severely constricted the possibility of military intervention. Structure and culture, in terms of the two-step model of opportunity and motive set out in Chapter 1, combined to make a military coup extremely unlikely.

This chapter examines the post-Lenin succession and the Great Purges of the military under Stalin (see Table 4.1). In both of these cases the military did not become involved in sovereign power issues. The Great Purges receive the most extended treatment both because of their theoretical and intrinsic interest (why did the officer corps not do more to protect itself?) and because of new sources available from Soviet archives. There were definite corporate interest motives for military intervention in 1937–1938, but a combination of organizational culture and structural obstacles prevented any potential military coup. Before turning to these cases, however, I briefly discuss the origins of the Soviet army and the building of the Soviet state, in order to understand the organizational and political context in which officers' decisions were made.

A NEW SOVIET ARMY?

Was the Soviet military an army "of a new type," as the Bolshevik regime claimed? In fact there were significant continuities from the old Imperial army, in terms of both personnel and organizational culture. The Bolsheviks undertook strenuous efforts to change the military's culture, but most of these endeavors served to reinforce a norm of civilian supremacy inherited from the Imperial officer corps.

138

TABLE 4.1. *Chapter Summary*

Observations	Opportunity		Motive		Outcome
	Domestic Structure	Organizational Structure	Corporate Interest	Organizational Culture	
Post-Lenin Succession	Intervention or arbitration likely.	Intervention unlikely.	Intervention likely.	Intervention unlikely.	No intervention.
Great Purges	Intervention unlikely.	Intervention unlikely.	Intervention likely.	Intervention unlikely.	No intervention.

The Bolsheviks, like other European socialist parties, had an antipathy toward professional standing armies and were ideologically committed to a militia system for national defense. The exigencies of civil war, however, led them quickly to abandon these ideals in 1918 in favor of a traditional military system. The existence of a standing army separate from the people implied that civil–military relations would remain an important political issue in the Soviet Union, just as it was in capitalist states.[1]

The Bolshevik leadership was particularly nervous about the question of control over the armed forces. Their Marxist world view and their tendency to draw analogies from European revolutionary history led them to attribute special importance to the problem of "Bonapartism." The fact that the overwhelming majority of Red Army officers during the Civil War were ex-Tsarist officers (referred to as "military specialists") made many Bolsheviks extremely suspicious of the army high command. At the same time, the Bolsheviks had little choice but to rely on military specialists because they lacked trained officers of their own.[2]

During the Civil War the command staff of the Red Army consisted overwhelmingly of military specialists. After the war the Bolsheviks tried to reduce their reliance on ex-Tsarist officers, but they dominated two key institutions, the General Staff and the General Staff Academy. The officers who designed the Soviet staff system were educated in Tsarist military academies, and the structure and functions of the Red Army Staff closely mirrored those of the Imperial system. Military specialists were more than ninety percent of the teaching and administrative staff of military academies and schools. Not surprisingly, the methods and in many ways even the curriculum were copied from the Imperial General Staff Academy. Indeed, in most cases the same buildings were used.[3]

In the mid-1920s, during the so-called military reform period, efforts were made to cut back the Red Army's reliance on military specialists by shrinking the officer corps and training new officers. More than half of the officer corps

---

[1] Mark von Hagen, *Soldiers in the Proletarian Dictatorship: The Red Army and the Soviet Socialist State, 1917–1930* (Ithaca, NY: Cornell University Press, 1990), pp. 13–180; Francesco Benvenuti, *The Bolsheviks and the Red Army, 1918–1922* (Cambridge, England: Cambridge University Press, 1988); John Erickson, *The Soviet High Command: A Military–Political History, 1918–1941* (London: Macmillan, 1962), pp. 3–138.

[2] A. G. Kavtaradze, *Voyennye spetsialisty na sluzhbe Respubliki Sovetov 1917–1920 gg.* (Mosvka: "Nauka," 1988); von Hagen, *Soldiers in the Proletarian Dictatorship*, pp. xi, 59–61, 145, 327; Benvenuti, *Bolsheviks and the Red Army*, pp. 35, 93, 96–97, 180–181, 218.

[3] Kavtaradze, *Voyennye spetsialisty*, pp. 198, 222–224; Erickson, *Soviet High Command*, p. 194; John Erickson, *The Russian Imperial/Soviet General Staff*, College Station Papers No. 3 (College Station, TX: Center for Strategic Technology, Texas A & M University, 1981), pp. 50–103; John Erickson, "The General Staff: Theory and Practice from the Tsarist to the Soviet Regime," in Robert L. Pfaltzgraff and Uri Ra'anan, eds., *National Security Policy: The Decision-Making Process* (Hamden, CT: Archon Books, 1984), pp. 31–46; Philip A. Bayer, *The Evolution of the Soviet General Staff, 1917–1941* (New York: Garland Publishing, 1987).

at this time had been educated as officers in the Imperial Army, and even the thirty-seven percent that had been trained in Soviet military establishments were instructed by former Tsarist officers. One reason among many for Leon Trotsky's ouster as head of the Soviet armed forces in early 1925 was his heavy reliance on ex-Tsarist officers. Mikhail Frunze, the leader of the armed forces after Trotsky, cut large numbers of military specialists from the army. By the end of the decade, ex-Tsarist officers represented around ten percent of the Soviet officer corps.[4]

Military specialists, however, continued to dominate the military intelligentsia. Seventy-nine of the 100 authors of the 1929 *Field Service Regulations* were ex-Tsarist officers, and more than eighty percent of contributors to military journals that year were also military specialists. The Red Army (later General) Staff was headed by former Imperial army officers from 1926 until World War II: Mikhail Tukhachevskiy, Boris Shaposhnikov, and Aleksandr Yegorov. Military specialists played a dominant role in military education. Leading theorists such as Shaposhnikov and Aleksandr Svechin had been educated at the Imperial General Staff Academy. Svechin was one of the most influential instructors at the General Staff Academy in the 1920s and had little time for Marxist jargon in his classroom.[5]

Throughout the 1920s, ex-Tsarist officers represented a significant, albeit progressively shrinking, contingent within the Red Army officer corps. More important than their quantitative influence was their qualitative influence on military education, the General Staff, and military thought. Thus, despite the Bolshevik claim to have created an "army of a new type," there were considerable continuities from the Imperial Army to the Red Army. Key elements of the organizational culture of the Tsarist armed forces were carried into the Soviet army by military specialists.

The most important change from the old period to the new was the vigorous effort by the Bolsheviks to ensure the political reliability of the officer corps. This policy had three components. First, political commissars were attached to military officers and countersigned their orders under the policy of dual command (*dvoyenachaliye*) instituted during the Civil War. Starting in 1924, dual command was gradually phased out in favor of one-man command (*edinonachaliye*). Commissars were maintained, however, and made responsible for political instruction. The second policy used to ensure officer corps loyalty was the political instruction of the officer corps in Bolshevik

---

[4] Dale R. Herspring, *Russian Civil–Military Relations* (Bloomington, IN: Indiana University Press, 1996), pp. 66–67; von Hagen, *Soldiers in the Proletarian Dictatorship*, pp. 210–220; Erickson, *Soviet High Command*, pp. 318–319; Raymond L. Garthoff, *Soviet Military Policy: A Historical Analysis* (New York: Frederick A. Praeger, 1966), p. 34, note 15.

[5] Erickson, *Soviet High Command*, pp. 318–319; Garthoff, *Soviet Military Policy*, p. 34; Herspring, *Russian Civil–Military Relations*, pp. 3–20, 57; Vitaly Rapoport and Yuri Alexeev, *High Treason: Essays on the History of the Red Army, 1918–1938* (Durham, NC: Duke University Press, 1985), pp. 124–138, 171–176.

party ideology. The regime desired that officers would be consciously committed to the party's policies and goals, rather than apolitical with respect to domestic politics. Third, the Bolsheviks adopted a policy of "affirmative action" in favor of workers and poor peasants as officer candidates and discriminated against former nobles, bourgeoisie, Cossacks, and so-called *kulaks* (wealthier peasants). The party believed that workers and poor peasants would be more sympathetic to Bolshevik rule.[6]

These innovations in some respects reinforced, and in other ways undermined, an apolitical organizational culture. The Bolsheviks were committed firmly to the principle of civilian supremacy and believed that the military should play no role in sovereign power issues. The difference from the previous regime was that in the Red Army military obedience was to be maintained by the conscious (i.e., pro-communist) political views of the officers, rather than their disinterest toward politics. Bolshevik policy represented an alternative approach to civilian control, then, rather than a repudiation of the principle. To the extent that officers were rewarded for their political commitment or class background, though, the notion that the military was "outside politics" was undermined. Indeed, such a slogan would be an anathema to the party leadership. In 1924 the military leadership under Frunze warned against the "spirit of apoliticism" in party political education in the armed forces. Frunze was probably right to be concerned, because there is evidence that regular officers and soldiers were less than committed to political education and that military training often took precedence.[7]

There was one final check on the Red Army officer corps if these efforts to ensure their political reliability failed: the secret police.[8] Secret police units, called Special Departments (*Osobye otdely*, or OO), were established in the armed forces during the Civil War. Special Departments, with the aid of informants, conducted political surveillance over military personnel.[9]

Throughout most of the interwar period the secret police also controlled the Internal Troops and the Border Troops. In principle these groupings

[6] von Hagen, *Soldiers in the Proletarian Dictatorship*; Erickson, *Soviet High Command*; Herspring, *Russian Civil–Military Relations*, pp. 55–70; Roger R. Reese, *Stalin's Reluctant Soldiers: A Social History of the Red Army, 1925–1941* (Lawrence, KS: University Press of Kansas, 1996).

[7] von Hagen, *Soldiers in the Proletarian Dictatorship*, p. 253; Zbigniew Brzezinski, ed., *Political Controls in the Soviet Army: A Study Based on Reports by Former Soviet Officers* (New York: Research Program on the U.S.S.R., 1954), pp. 20, 40–41, 47–48, 87–88; Reese, *Stalin's Reluctant Soldiers*, pp. 79–80.

[8] The secret police went through multiple name changes throughout Soviet history; the names perhaps best known are Cheka, NKVD, and KGB, but there were several others. For details on these organizational changes, see Amy W. Knight, *The KGB: Police and Politics in the Soviet Union* (Boston, MA: Unwin Hyman, 1988), pp. 10–52, 315.

[9] Knight, *KGB*, pp. 221–275; Brzezinski, *Political Controls*, pp. 54–83; George Leggett, *The Cheka: Lenin's Political Police* (Oxford, England: Clarendon Press, 1981), pp. 90–98, 205–213, 224–229, 232.

could act as an armed counterbalance to the armed forces, but in practice their principal mission involved internal repression and border control. These bodies, which numbered tens of thousands of personnel, helped free the armed forces from internal missions after the Civil War. These internal missions included suppressing local disturbances and fighting partisans and armed detachments, particularly in unstable border regions (collectivization will be discussed below). The army apparently was able to focus largely on external defense once the Civil War was over. William Fuller suggests that "former Tsarist 'military specialists' may have impressed the importance of emancipating the regular army from internal service on their new Soviet masters." In this sense, also, there was considerable continuity from the old regime.[10]

One final way in which the Red Army differed from the Imperial Army was the emphasis placed by the political leadership on using the armed forces as a "school of the nation." Such a role, of course, was not unique to the Soviet Union; since the nineteenth century all European states had to varying degrees used the armed forces to spread literacy and nationalism. The Bolsheviks, however, were the most committed to using the armed forces to, paraphrasing Eugen Weber, turn peasants into Soviet men. The bulk of the army came from the peasantry, and military service was seen as the ideal vehicle for exterminating the pernicious influences of village life on young peasants and enlisting them in the cause of "building socialism." The military leadership was ambivalent about these goals. Although they recognized the importance of building support among the peasantry, the military leadership was reluctant to divert the armed forces too much from the task of preparing for war.[11]

The Red Army, then, was only partially an "army of a new type." Many members of its officers corps were educated in Tsarist military institutions and had served in the Imperial Army. The Red Army Staff and the Military Academy were especially important "transmission belts" of the old organizational culture into the new army, and they also served as an institutional home for advocates of traditional forms of military organization and doctrine and a focus on external warfare as the army's primary task. On the other hand, the Bolsheviks introduced several important innovations into military life, most importantly a series of political controls and efforts to use

[10] William C. Fuller, Jr., *The Internal Troops of the MVD SSSR*, College Station Papers No. 6 (College Station, TX: Center for Strategic Technology, Texas A & M University, 1983), pp. 13–22 (quote, p. 20); Knight, *KGB*, pp. 222–229.

[11] von Hagen, *Soldiers in the Proletarian Dictatorship*, especially pp. 231–325; Reese, *Stalin's Reluctant Soldiers*, especially pp. x, 1–3, 71, 80–99. On Europe in general, see Eugen Weber, *Peasants into Frenchmen: The Modernization of Rural France, 1870–1914* (Stanford, CA: Stanford University Press, 1976), pp. 292–302; Barry R. Posen, "Nationalism, the Mass Army, and Military Power," *International Security*, 18 (1993), 80–124; Michael Howard, *War in European History* (Oxford, England: Oxford University Press, 1976), pp. 94–115.

the army to develop conscious support for regime goals among both officers and enlisted men. Thus, the Red Army in the interwar period was an amalgamation of old and new. Most important, perhaps, it was an institution whose sense of identity was in the process of being created.

REBUILDING THE RUSSIAN STATE, OR BUILDING THE SOVIET STATE

The Soviet state established after the October Revolution, like the Red Army, had important continuities with its Imperial predecessor, despite its revolutionary goals. An important change, however, was the ability of the Bolsheviks to alleviate the weaknesses that had plagued the Tsarist government in its last decades. Driven by international and domestic pressures, the ideology of the ruling party, and the personality of Joseph Stalin, by the mid-1930s a quite powerful state apparatus had been built.

The Bolsheviks won the Civil War at least in part because they were more successful than their political and military opponents at creating functioning government institutions. That the Reds proved more proficient than the Whites at state building is a paradox, given that Lenin had vowed to "smash" the bourgeois state in Russia and the Whites were "statists." In reality the Bolsheviks essentially took over the old state apparatus, including its structures and many personnel. T. H. Rigby observes, "the structural changes were scarcely greater than those sometimes accompanying changes of government in Western parliamentary systems.... The conditions were thus propitious for the transfer not only of specialist knowledge and administrative techniques, but also of less tangible behaviors and attitudes."[12]

The Bolsheviks' success in building a strong centralized state has been touted as one of their most important achievements by historians and social scientists. Theda Skocpol, for example, contends that the Soviet government had a much higher political capacity than the Tsarist one and was able to accomplish its social and political goals much better than the old regime. She shows that the state apparatus grew considerably in the 1920s and 1930s, perhaps by as much as five times.[13]

---

[12] T. H. Rigby, *Lenin's Government: Sovnarkom 1917–1922* (Cambridge, England: Cambridge University Press, 1979), p. 64. See also Diane P. Koenker, William G. Rosenberg, and Ronald Grigor Suny, eds., *Party, State, and Society in the Russian Civil War: Explorations in Social History* (Bloomington, IN: Indiana University Press, 1989), especially the chapters by Lewin, Fitzpatrick, and Orlovsky; Robert Service, *The Bolshevik Party in Revolution 1917–1923: A Study in Organisational Change* (London: Macmillan, 1979); Graeme Gill, *The Origins of the Stalinist Political System* (Cambridge, England: Cambridge University Press, 1990), pp. 23–110.

[13] Theda Skocpol, *States and Social Revolutions: A Comparative Analysis of France, Russia, and China* (Cambridge, England: Cambridge University Press, 1979), especially pp. 226–233; Theda Skocpol, "Social Revolutions and Mass Military Mobilization," *World Politics,*

The notion of an all-powerful Soviet state was the basis for one of the most prominent theoretical approaches to the study of the Soviet Union, totalitarianism. The totalitarian school depicted the Soviet state as an extremely powerful actor, able to act seemingly at will to change social structure and private behavior in far-reaching ways. Revisionist social historians have attacked this picture of Soviet society in the 1930s as directed from an all-powerful center. These historians, writing "from below" (i.e., focusing on groups other than the national political elite), argue that the state was much weaker in the 1930s than the traditional picture pretends. Although in many ways overstated, this new literature does underscore the degree to which the ruling Bolshevik party felt itself to be isolated and under threat. The Bolsheviks felt isolated both in the country, as a "worker's party" in an overwhelmingly peasant society, and internationally, as a "socialist" state in a world of capitalist ones. The Communist Party had made few inroads into the countryside in the 1920s, where its organizational structure was weak everywhere and in many places nonexistent.[14]

Stalin responded to this sense of isolation by going on the offensive, launching a "revolution from above" marked by the collectivization and industrialization campaigns of the late 1920s-early 1930s. From 1929 until 1933 "a veritable civil war," in the words of Moshe Lewin, raged in the Soviet countryside. But the battle was unequal, and most resistance by peasants to the collectivization drive was passive. Despite the weakness of the party and the state in the countryside, there was little chance that the regime would be directly threatened. Organized political opposition had been eliminated in the country in the early 1920s, and the secret police were a reliable element of state power that were capable of defeating any organized acts of resistance or violence. If the state was weak, the society that it was attacking was even weaker.[15]

---

40 (1988), 147–168; Theodore H. von Laue, "Stalin in Focus," *Slavic Review*, 42 (1983), 373–389.

[14] Carl J. Friedrich and Zbigniew K. Brzezinski, *Totalitarian Dictatorship and Autocracy* (Cambridge, MA: Harvard University Press, 1956); Stephen F. Cohen, *Rethinking the Soviet Experience: Politics and History Since 1917* (Oxford: Oxford University Press, 1985), pp. 3–37; Abbott Gleason, *Totalitarianism: The Inner History of the Cold War* (Oxford, England: Oxford University Press, 1995); Jane Burbank, "Controversies over Stalinism: Searching for a Soviet Society," *Politics & Society*, 19 (1991), 325–340; *Russian Review*, 45, 4 (1986) and 46, 4 (1987); Gill, *Origins of the Stalinist Political System*, especially pp. 113–114, 177, 203–204, 209–218, 259–261, 267–268, 307–312.

[15] Robert C. Tucker, "Stalinism as Revolution from Above," in Robert C. Tucker, ed., *Stalinism: Essays in Historical Interpretation* (New York: W. W. Norton, 1977), pp. 77–108; Moshe Lewin, *Russian Peasants and Soviet Power: A Study of Collectivization* (New York: W. W. Norton, 1968), p. 19; Michal Reiman, *The Birth of Stalinism: The USSR on the Eve of the "Second Revolution"* (Bloomington, IN: Indiana University Press, 1987); Knight, *KGB*, pp. 13–22; O. V. Khlevnyuk, *1937-y: Stalin, NKVD, i sovetskoye obshchestvo* (Moskva: "Respublika," 1992), pp. 10–31.

Measuring state political capacity in terms of organizational age or political violence, as Robert Jackman proposes, is thus in this case quite misleading. The Soviet order was only a decade or two old and had undergone only one transition of the supreme political leadership, which in most cases would suggest weak institutions. Similarly, political violence during the 1920s and especially during the 1930s was outrageously high, although the exact figures are the subject of considerable dispute. Recent work suggests that the total "excess" deaths (famine, repression, etc.) for the period 1927–1938 were in the 9–11 million range. Regardless of the exact figures, the Soviet state in this period clearly was one of the most murderous in history.[16]

Jackman contends that regimes that must rely on the use of force do not generate either legitimacy or political capacity. He specifically acknowledges, however, that in cases like the Stalinist period in the Soviet Union "severe repression can demobilize potential challengers for long periods." Stalin's "revolution from above" could not have been successful without the apparent belief of a critical mass of party and secret police officials that once the regime had decided to use physical coercion there was no turning back until the regime had carried the policies of collectivization and industrialization through to the end. The Great Terror of 1936–1938 was Stalin's final, and successful, bid to establish himself as the uncontested dictator of the Soviet Union. Stalin's political opponents – past, present, and future, real and imagined – were all labeled enemies and marked for destruction. Repeatedly throughout the 1930s Stalin was able to mobilize sufficient elite support for his policies, relying heavily on coercion, to ensure that no viable alternatives to his rule persisted. Contrary to Jackman's general argument, Stalin's use of repression was a decisive factor in increasing the political capacity of the Soviet state.[17]

Stephen Krasner's approach to state strength leads to different conclusions than Jackman's about the interwar Soviet Union. The Soviet Union for Krasner is a prime example of what he calls a "dominant" state: It was able to resist private pressure, change private behavior in intended ways, and change social structure in intended ways. Krasner's view is thus consistent

---

[16] Alec Nove, "Victims of Stalinism: How Many?" and Stephen G. Wheatcroft, "More Light on the Scale of Repression and Excess Mortality in the Soviet Union in the 1930s," both in J. Arch Getty and Roberta T. Manning, eds., *Stalinist Terror: New Perspectives* (Cambridge, England: Cambridge University Press, 1993), pp. 261–290; V. P. Popov, "Gosudarstvennyy terror v sovetskoy Rossii 1923–1953 gg. (istochniki i ikh interpretatsiya)," *Otechestvennye arkhivy*, No. 2, 1992, 20–31; N. A. Aralovets, "Poteri naseleniya sovetskogo obshchestva v 1930-e gody: problemy, istochniki, metody izucheniya v otechestvennoy istoriografii," *Otechestvennaya istoriya*, No. 1, 1995, 135–146.

[17] Robert W. Jackman, *Power without Force: The Political Capacity of Nation-States* (Ann Arbor, MI: University of Michigan Press, 1993), pp. 30–31, 35–38, 98–99, 109–114 (quote, p. 113); Gill, *Origins of the Stalinist Political System*, pp. 223, 246–255, 275–306; Khlevnyuk, *1937-y*; Robert Conquest, *The Great Terror: A Reassessment* (Oxford, England: Oxford University Press, 1990).

with the totalitarian school discussed above. Although revisionist scholarship has provided a much more complex portrait of Soviet politics in the 1930s, ultimately Stalin's success in carrying out the "revolution from above" seems to validate the conclusion of the totalitarian school that the Soviet regime was very powerful in the 1930s. Krasner is thus right to stress the dominant power of the Soviet state.[18]

The political capacity of the Soviet state, then, grew progressively stronger during the interwar period. During the Civil War chaos reigned in the country, but ultimately the Bolshevik regime was able to re-create a functioning state apparatus and restore political order in the country. In the 1920s the Soviet state faced no serious political challenges to Bolshevik rule, but its influence throughout the country was quite weak. Stalin's "revolution from above" and the subsequent purges solidified both his personal rule and the dominant position of the Soviet state.

SOVEREIGN POWER ISSUES AND THE MILITARY: FROM LENIN TO STALIN

In this section I look at two crucial periods for civil–military relations in the interwar period: the post-Lenin power struggle and potential resistance to Stalin's "revolution from above." First, though, I briefly discuss whether there was such a thing as "civil–military relations" in the Soviet Union.

Most scholars assumed that civil–military relations existed in Soviet politics.[19] Civil–military relations as a general topic examines the interaction between civilian political elites and the armed forces. The two most important studies in the literature on Soviet civil-military relations, by Roman Kolkowicz and Timothy Colton, both argue that military intervention in sovereign power issues is caused by corporate interest motives. Colton states, for example, "officers intervene against civilian authorities when their perceived interests are being denied or threatened by civilian policy."[20]

---

[18] Stephen D. Krasner, *Defending the National Interest: Raw Materials Investments and U.S. Foreign Policy* (Princeton, NJ: Princeton University Press, 1978), pp. 56–57.

[19] Because of my interest in the more general social science literature on military behavior in sovereign power issues, I have made no attempt to address the entire body of literature on Soviet civil–military relations. In addition to those studies cited below, important contributions include: Herspring, *Russian Civil–Military Relations*; Dale R. Herspring, *The Soviet High Command 1967–1989: Personalities and Politics* (Princeton, NJ: Princeton University Press, 1990); Thomas M. Nichols, *The Sacred Cause: Civil–Military Conflict over Soviet National Security, 1917–1992* (Ithaca, NY: Cornell University Press, 1993); Condoleezza Rice, "The Party, the Military, and Decision Authority in the Soviet Union," *World Politics*, 40 (1987), 55–81; Edward L. Warner, III, *The Military in Contemporary Soviet Politics: An Institutional Analysis* (New York: Praeger Publishers, 1977).

[20] Roman Kolkowicz, *The Soviet Military and the Communist Party* (Princeton, NJ: Princeton University Press, 1967); Roman Kolkowicz, "Interest Groups in Soviet Politics: The Case of the Military," in Dale R. Herspring and Ivan Volgyes, eds., *Civil–Military Relations in*

Where Kolkowicz and Colton differed was in (a) their assessment of the extent to which the Communist Party had satisfied military interests and (b) their conclusions about the importance of organizational structure for military behavior. Kolkowicz argued that the military was often dissatisfied but that political officers, or commissars, inside the armed forces prevented army intervention. Colton concluded that political officers were not an effective monitoring agency, and he asserted that the absence of a military coup could be explained by party support for army interests.

William Odom, in contrast, maintained that "civil–military relations is a flawed concept for the Soviet case." Odom argued that the army is the "administrative arm of the party, not something separate from and competing with it," and that generals were simply "executants." If there was a conflict over military policy, Odom noted, party figures and military officers could be found on both sides of the issue. Thus, army intervention in sovereign power issues is simply not a concern for Odom, because "the marshals . . . are in the same political boat" with the Communist Party.[21]

Odom's observation that disputes over military policy were not purely party–military disputes is true, but less significant than he imagines. It is almost always true, whether in democratic or authoritarian states, that policy disputes do not break down on strictly military–civilian lines. The study of coups is not simply about a unified army overthrowing a similarly united civilian government; in almost all cases there will be some overlap.[22] So long as it is possible for some members of the armed forces, alone or with other political actors, to attempt to seize state power or to become involved in arbitrating a sovereign power dispute, then studying sovereign power issues as a civil–military relations issue is necessary and important. Although civil–military relations in communist systems have their unique features, the impossibility of military involvement in sovereign power issues is not one of them.

Communist Systems (Boulder, CO: Westview Press, 1978), pp. 9–25; Timothy J. Colton, *Commissars, Commanders, and Civilian Authority: The Structure of Soviet Military Politics* (Cambridge, MA: Harvard University Press, 1979), quote, p. 240; Timothy J. Colton, "The Party–Military Connection: A Participatory Model," in Herspring and Volgyes, eds., *Civil–Military Relations*, pp. 53–75; Timothy J. Colton, "Perspectives on Civil–Military Relations in the Soviet Union," in Timothy J. Colton and Thane Gustafson, eds., *Soldiers and the Soviet State* (Princeton, NJ: Princeton University Press, 1990), pp. 3–44.

[21] William E. Odom, *The Collapse of the Soviet Military* (New Haven, CT: Yale University Press, 1998), pp. 218–222, 456 (quote, note 59); William E. Odom, "The Party–Military Connection: A Critique," in Herspring and Volgyes, eds., *Civil–Military Relations*, pp. 27–52 (quotes, pp. 41, 44, 48).

[22] Richard K. Betts, *Soldiers, Statesmen, and Cold War Crises* (Cambridge, MA: Harvard University Press, 1977), pp. 4–5; Michael C. Desch, *Civilian Control of the Military: The Changing Security Environment* (Baltimore, MD: Johns Hopkins University Press, 1999), p. 3; Bruce W. Farcau, *The Coup: Tactics in the Seizure of Power* (Westport, CT: Praeger, 1994), p. 35.

The Post-Lenin Power Struggle

The early and mid-1920s was a difficult time for Soviet civil–military relations. The post–Civil War demobilization and the general economic crisis in the country had a deleterious effect on the Red Army. The officers and soldiers that remained in the military felt adrift, with no clear sense of purpose and subject to the hostility of many in the party. In addition, the succession struggle touched off by Lenin's prolonged poor health and eventual death in January 1924 was a potential opportunity for military intervention in politics, particularly since Trotsky, the War Commissar, was a major contender for power. The succession struggle involved, most prominently, Trotsky, Joseph Stalin, Nikolay Bukharin, Lev Kamenev, and Grigoriy Zinoviev. Very briefly, Trotsky was defeated by Stalin, Kamenev, and Zinoviev in 1923–1924, Kamenev and Zinoviev were beaten by Stalin and Bukharin in 1924–1925, the "United Opposition" of Trotsky, Kamenev, and Zinoviev was defeated by Stalin and Bukharin in 1926–1927, and finally the "Right Opposition" led by Bukharin was ousted by Stalin in 1928–1929.[23] Why did the military remain quiescent during this period, given perceived attacks on its corporate interests (resources and autonomy) and the potential for greater influence implied by the weakness of Bolshevik rule and the leadership power struggle?

There are several reasons for this behavior. The most common explanation is that the army was prevented from intervening in politics by Communist Party penetration into the military in the form of commissars (the Political Administration). Roman Kolkowicz calls the commissar system "the Party's crucial instrument of control." Timothy Colton, who is in general quite critical of Kolkowicz's argument, also notes that party penetration of the military was important in the earliest years of the Soviet state.[24]

A second common explanation is that Trotsky made no attempt to involve the army in high politics. Isaac Deutscher, for example, argues that Trotsky restrained his supporters in the armed forces who wanted to mobilize support for him in the army. Instead, Trotsky accepted Politburo authority over the military and believed that it was impermissible in a socialist state to use the armed forces for political gain.[25]

Both of these arguments provide part of the explanation for the military's political quiescence in the early 1920s. It is certainly true that the party leadership was concerned about controlling the armed forces and that Trotsky made no attempt to appeal to the military for support. But this is only part of the story. At the height of the struggle between Trotsky and the ruling

[23] For details see Leonard Schapiro, *The Communist Party of the Soviet Union*, 2nd ed. (London: Eyre & Spottiswoode, 1970), pp. 271–381.
[24] Kolkowicz, *Soviet Military*, p. 123; Colton, "Perspectives on Civil–Military Relations," p. 17.
[25] Isaac Deutscher, *The Prophet Unarmed: Trotsky: 1921–1929* (London: Oxford University Press, 1959), pp. 160–162; Erickson, *Soviet High Command*, p. 166.

triumvirate of Stalin, Zinoviev, and Kamenev in the fall and winter of 1923, the Political Administration was in the hands of a Trotsky ally, Vladimir Antonov-Ovseenko. Antonov-Ovseenko suggested that Trotsky had the support of Bolsheviks in the army, and there is some evidence for this view. The triumvirate demonstrated its concern about the political leanings of army communists by replacing Antonov-Ovseenko in January 1924. Thus, party control of the military through the Political Administration is at best only a partial explanation, since the Political Administration was not controlled by the ruling group.[26]

It is true that Trotsky believed it was illegitimate to appeal to the army in a sovereign power issue. He also had good reason to believe, as Roy Medvedev argues, that the army was not a "docile instrument" in his hands.[27] Army officers were of two basic types: either (a) committed Bolsheviks who had started in the party and made their military career during the Civil War or (b) former Imperial officers. The first group was committed to the idea that the party, not the military, should decide who rules, and the second group saw the army as an apolitical body that should serve whichever group captured power. Thus, neither group would be inclined to support Trotsky in a bid for power.

An important additional barrier to military intervention in this period is that the armed forces leadership, including Trotsky and his successors Mikhail Frunze and Kliment Voroshilov, was dominated by Bolsheviks who had their initial experience with the military during the Civil War. Civil–military relations during this period was largely a contest between competing groups of militarized Bolsheviks for control over the armed forces in the aftermath of the civil war.[28] The only officers with more than a few years of experience were the military specialists, and they defined their role as apolitical.

As the 1920s went on, there was a conscious effort to separate more clearly the civilian and military spheres. Frunze, Trotsky's successor as head

---

[26] Whether Antonov–Ovseenko obliquely threatened a coup against the party leadership by invoking the specter of using the army's "peasant masses" to call the party leaders "to order" is still unclear. In Dmitriy Volkogonov's recent biography of Trotsky, based on archival sources, he makes no mention of this alleged threat, noting only Antonov–Ovseenko's claim that military communists were discussing the need to support Trotsky "as one." On the role of Antonov–Ovseenko and the Political Administration in the 1923 power struggle, see Dmitriy Volkogonov, *Trotskiy: politicheskiy portret*, Vol. II (Moskva: Novosti, 1992), pp. 32–33, 45; Roy Medvedev, *Let History Judge: The Origins and Consequences of Stalinism*, revised edition (Oxford, England: Oxford University Press, 1989), pp. 133–136; Boris Orlov, "Nakanune bol'shogo terrora: armiya i oppozitsiya," *Cahiers du Monde russe et sovietique*, 32 (1991), 411–412; von Hagen, *Soldiers in the Proletarian Dictatorship*, pp. 198–205; Erickson, *Soviet High Command*, pp. 142–143, 164–165, 168; Deutscher, *Prophet Unarmed*, pp. 160–162.

[27] Medvedev, *Let History Judge*, pp. 133–136.

[28] William Odom's description of a unified party–military leadership is thus most apt in these early years, but even then the party leadership itself worried about the possibility of military involvement in sovereign power issues.

of the Red Army, launched a program of reform that included a policy of "militarization." Militarization, Mark von Hagen argues, "actually meant the remilitarization of an institution that was perceived to have lost its distinctive military spirit because civilian organizations and practices had so penetrated the army's way of conducting its affairs." The reformers sought tighter discipline and introduced unity of command (*edinonachaliye*), so officers were no longer required to have their orders countersigned by political commissars. Although Frunze died mysteriously in 1925 during surgery, his successor Voroshilov, a Stalin ally, continued the policy of militarization.[29]

This trend toward a more traditional and separate military is evidenced by the appearance in 1928 of the so-called Inner-Army Opposition. The Inner-Army Opposition, in fact, had no ties whatsoever to Stalin's political opponents on the Left (Trotsky et al.) or the Right (Nikolay Bukharin et al.). The Inner-Army Opposition was composed of a group of military commissars, associated mainly with the Tolmachev Main Military–Political Academy in Moscow and the Political Administration of the Belorussian Military District. The complaints of this grouping were confined to the question of party control over the army; this group was in no way involved in the post-Lenin power struggle. Specifically, the Inner-Army Opposition was concerned about how *edinonachaliye* was being introduced and believed the role of party organs in the military had been reduced too far. They favored strengthening the role of the party in the armed forces.[30]

The political leadership reacted harshly to the appearance of the Inner-Army Opposition. Many members of this group were forced from both the army and the party. The political leadership's reaction is explained more by their insecurities due to the recent political situation – the continuing battles with the Right and Left Opposition and the beginning of collectivization – than by any threat posed by the Inner-Army Opposition. The group had no ties with the "real" opposition (in fact, they never used the word opposition) and had nothing to do with sovereign power issues.[31]

The United (or Left) Opposition of Trotsky, Zinoviev, and Kamenev of 1926–1927 did have some backing in the army. The Deputy Commissar of War in 1925–1926, Mikhail Lashevich, was an ally of Zinoviev and was removed for his participation in a secret opposition meeting in 1926. There are also unsubstantiated allegations that in 1927, at roughly the same time that Trotsky was criticizing the party leadership for not adequately providing

---

[29] Von Hagen, *Soldiers in the Proletarian Dictatorship*, pp. 210–220 (quote, p. 211). On Frunze's death, which remains a mystery, see Medvedev, *Let History Judge*, pp. 155–159; Dmitriy A. Volkogonov, *Triumf i tragediya: Politicheskiy portret I.V. Stalina*, Vol. I (Moskva: Novosti, 1989), pp. 127–128.

[30] Steven J. Main, "The Red Army and the Soviet Military and Political Leadership in the Late 1920s: The Case of the 'Inner-Army Opposition of 1928'," *Europe-Asia Studies*, 47 (1995), 337–355.

[31] Main, "Red Army and the Soviet Military."

for the country's defense, a group of officers submitted a secret memorandum to the Politburo questioning Voroshilov's competence as War Commissar. A Secret Police (GPU) report from November 1927 also refers to sympathy for the United Opposition in the armed forces, although the GPU may have exaggerated this support.[32]

The most recent examination of military behavior in the post-Lenin power struggle concludes that neither the Left nor the Right Opposition had much military backing. Boris Orlov provides several reasons for weak army support for the United Opposition. First, personnel changes in the officer corps in the 1920s removed potential supporters. Second, the nationalist orientation of Stalin's policy of "socialism in one country" resonated more with officers than did Trotsky's internationalist stance. Third, officers feared persecution for publicly opposing the Stalinist leadership. Support for the Right Opposition of Bukharin, Aleksey Rykov, and Mikhail Tomsky was even weaker in the armed forces. None of these party leaders had many ties with the officer corps, even from the civil war period.[33]

There were, of course, officers such as Lashevich who supported the opposition to Stalin within the party. There is no evidence, however, that attempts were made either by commanders or by party oppositionists to involve the army as a political force. To the extent that there were officers who supported the opposition, they worked within party channels for their political beliefs. The military did not involve itself as a corporate actor. Moreover, none of the most prominent military leaders of the Red Army, such as Tukhachevskiy or Shaposhnikov, was ever discussed as pretenders to power.[34]

The Military and Stalin's "Revolution from Above"

The military leadership in the late 1920s and early 1930s devoted their energies to the sphere of defense politics. They had little interest in questions of sovereign power, which was a matter for the Bolshevik Party. Top officers also were concerned about the effect that involvement in societal choice issues had on military training and readiness. This concern is demonstrated most clearly with respect to the military's reaction to the collectivization of agriculture, which began in the winter of 1927–1928.

The civilian political leadership expected the armed forces to play an active role in the collectivization campaign. Party organs in the military were called on to prepare peasant soldiers for positions in the collective farms upon

[32] *VKP(B) v resolyutsiyakh i resheniyakh s"ezdov, konferentsiy i plenumov TsK*, Vol. 2, 5th ed. (Moskva: Partizdat, 1936), pp. 114–121; Lars T. Lih, Oleg V. Naumov, and Oleg V. Khlevniuk, eds., *Stalin's Letters to Molotov, 1925–1936* (New Haven, CT: Yale University Press, 1995), pp. 100–101, 113–118; Erickson, *Soviet High Command*, pp. 201–202, 286; Deutscher, *Prophet Unarmed*, p. 350; Reiman, *Birth of Stalinism*, pp. 19–36, 123–126.

[33] Orlov, "Nakanune bolshogo terrora," 414–415.

[34] Orlov, "Nakanune bolshogo terrora," 414–415.

demobilization. Army personnel organized in special brigades were also used to repress peasant resistance, although these brigades were organized by secret police Special Sections (OO) and were led by the OO outside the normal military chain of command. Elements within the military leadership, however, became increasingly unhappy with the impact that collectivization was having on military training and troop morale. Officers feared the detrimental impact that widespread participation in collectivization and other societal choice issues could have on military readiness. Mark von Hagen demonstrates convincingly that the opposition of top officers led to a slowdown in the pace of collectivization in 1930, with renewed attention devoted to military training and readiness.[35]

Stalin expressed displeasure with officers' reactions to collectivization. He instructed several commanders from the Ukrainian Military District that "the military should occupy themselves with their own business and not discuss things that do not concern them."[36] Military resistance to collectivization was, oddly enough, based on a similar premise: that the army should concentrate on military preparation and training, and not be diverted by domestic tasks. Officers protested against collectivization precisely because it was interfering with their efforts to strengthen national defense. Army objections to collectivization were limited to written and verbal protests. Roger Reese suggests that there was "a very real potential for cooperation between the high command and Bukharin against Stalin." Reese bases this conclusion on evidence of opposition, particularly among soldiers, to forced collectivization. Reese admits, however, that there is no evidence that the military leadership believed that Stalin should be replaced as party head, or that Bukharin ever thought of appealing to the military leadership for support. Military opposition to collectivization implies neither officer corps opposition to Stalin as party leader nor a willingness to intervene in sovereign power issues.[37]

In the mid-1930s the armed forces were able to concentrate on further professional development. The Red Army Staff was renamed the General Staff, the rank of Marshal was introduced, the Commissariat of Defense was reorganized, the armed forces were considerably expanded, and officers were granted more privileges and autonomy. The growing military threat from both Germany and Japan seemed to warrant these reforms.[38]

---

[35] Von Hagen, *Soldiers in the Proletarian Dictatorship*, pp. 308–328, 342–343; Reese, *Stalin's Reluctant Soldiers*, pp. 84–92; Roger R. Reese, "Red Army Opposition to Forced Collectivization, 1929–1930: The Army Wavers," *Slavic Review*, 55 (1996), 24–45; Orlov, "Nakanune bolshogo terrora," 415.

[36] Colton, *Commissars, Commanders*, pp. 254–255, 346–347, note 11; Jonathan Haslam, "Political Opposition to Stalin and the Origins of the Terror in Russia, 1932–1936," *The Historical Journal*, 29 (1986), 399.

[37] Reese, "Red Army Opposition."

[38] Erickson, *Soviet High Command*, pp. 366–403; Rapoport and Alexeev, *High Treason*, pp. 177–193.

This considerable progress was wiped out, however, along with much of the top officer corps, during the Great Purges, which hit the armed forces in 1937–1938.

THE GREAT PURGES AND THE MILITARY

Stalin's purge of the Red Army officer corps on the eve of World War II has long puzzled observers. Condoleezza Rice states, "Stalin's willingness to launch extensive purges in the midst of a war scare is difficult to understand." Thousands of officers were repressed (killed or arrested). The highest levels of the military were hit the hardest: For example, all military district commanders were removed, and 76 of 85 members of the Military Soviet, the country's top military body, were repressed. The military catastrophe of 1941 often is attributed directly to the purges.[39]

Many observers have wondered why Stalin purged his officer corps on the eve of a major war.[40] An even more interesting question is why they let him get away with it. The purges clearly were a massive threat not only to the corporate interests of the armed forces, but also to the very lives of its officers. Given the massive power that the army possessed, why did it not offer resistance to the purges? Why was there no military coup? Although much has been written about the purges of the Soviet military, only recently has access to the Russian archives allowed one to explore in detail the thinking of officers about the purges.[41]

This section has three parts. First, I provide a basic description of the prelude to and implementation of Stalin's purge of the army. Second, I examine officer corps' thinking during the purges and discuss some of the political views held by officers that may have placed them under suspicion. Third, I

---

[39] Condoleezza Rice, "The Making of Soviet Strategy," in Peter Paret, ed., *Makers of Modern Strategy: from Machiavelli to the Nuclear Age* (Princeton, NJ: Princeton University Press, 1986), p. 670; Volkogonov, *Triumf i tragediya*, Vol. II, p. 52; *Izvestiya TsK KPSS*, No. 4 (1989), 74–80; Nikita Khrushchev, *Khrushchev Remembers* (Boston: Little, Brown and Company, 1970), p. 591; John Erickson, *The Road to Stalingrad: Stalin's War with Germany* (London: Weidenfeld and Nicolson, 1975), pp. 5–7. Cf. Reese, *Stalin's Reluctant Soldiers*.

[40] With very few exceptions, no one takes the official justification for the military purges seriously: that there were a large number of "enemies of the people" inside the officer corps. Nor can the claim that there was a military plot to overthrow Stalin be sustained, as I demonstrate below.

[41] I have relied on material from the former Communist Party archive, now known as the Center for the Storage and Study of Documents of Recent History [hereafter by its Russian acronym, RTsKhIDNI], and the major military archive for this period, the Russian State Military Archive [RGVA]. Both of these archives, particularly RGVA, have much useful material available, but access is still restricted. Moreover, full access is not available either to the secret police archive or the Presidential Archive, where the most valuable material on the purges of the military undoubtedly is held. For the most recent archivally based account of the purges in the army, see O. F. Suvenirov, *Tragediya RKKA: 1937–38* (Moskva: Terra, 1998).

offer an explanation for military behavior during the purges. Although there were obvious corporate motives for intervention, the opportunity for a coup was very limited due to the strength of the Stalinist state and a variety of organizational control measures. Additionally, the organizational culture of the army held that intervention was illegitimate.

Purge of the High Command

The main blow against the armed forces high command came in May–June 1937, when Marshal Mikhail Tukhachevskiy and other top officers were arrested and shot, accused of working for foreign governments and plotting against Stalin. Before discussing these events, however, we must go back to 1936 and look at the period leading up to Stalin's attack on the military leadership. Several leading officers took small-scale steps in the autumn of 1936 to resist the escalating purges. By the time of the February–March 1937 Central Committee Plenum, which signaled the launching of wide-scale terror directed against the party, there were ominous signs that the military would not be exempted from the purges. The most likely period for military resistance was some time in late 1936 or early 1937.

During previous purges of the party in 1929 and 1933–1934 the military had been less affected than the party as a whole. Five percent of military communists were purged in 1929 and 4.3 percent in 1933, compared to 11.7 and 17 percent, respectively, for the party as a whole (unlike in 1937–1938, those purged were not threatened with the euphemistic "highest measure of punishment," i.e., execution). For the period 1924–1936 the military dismissed around 47,000 officers, 22,000 of them in the years 1933–1936; apparently five thousand of them were former oppositionists. As noted above, the military had not been a prominent player in Stalin's disputes with his party opponents in the 1920s, and in the campaign against "specialists" in the late 1920s the military suffered less than other agencies. Thus, up to 1936 the military leadership had little reason to think that Stalin's campaign against "internal enemies" was directed at them.[42]

The arrest of high-ranking officers began in the summer of 1936. In July Division Commander Dmitriy Shmidt of the Kiev Military District was arrested. In August the Deputy Commander of the Leningrad Military District, Corps Commander V. M. Primakov, and the military attaché in London, Corps Commander V. K. Putna, were arrested.[43] Shmidt, Primakov, and

---

[42] Conquest, *Great Terror*, p. 185; Erickson, *Soviet High Command*, pp. 315, 374; RTsKhIDNI, f. 17, op. 2, d. 612, vyp. (*vypusk*) II, l. 82; *Voyennye arkhivy Rossii*, No. 1, 1993, 20.

[43] Ranks in the Soviet officer corps in the interwar period carried different titles for officers of general rank. The titles and their current equivalents, in descending order, were: Marshal (Marshal), Army Commander First Class (General of the Army), Army Commander Second Class (Colonel General), Corps Commander (Lieutenant General), Division Commander (Major General), and Brigade Commander (Major General or Colonel, depending on responsibilities). From the rank of Colonel down there is no difference from current practice.

Putna all had to some degree been involved with the Trotskyist opposition in the 1920s. Thus, those officers who had remained loyal to the party's "general line" (i.e., Stalin's position) probably did not see themselves as vulnerable at this point.[44]

The Commander of the Kiev Military District, Army Commander First Rank Ion Yakir, was a civil war hero and a full member of the Central Committee. Yakir's response to the arrest of Shmidt and several other officers from his district took two forms, both of which suggested he was not a whole-hearted proponent of Stalin's campaign against enemies. First, in July 1936, a few weeks after Shmidt's arrest, he sent a long order to officers and party organs in his district calling on them to pay more attention to the "political–moral condition" of their units. What is most notable about this order is what it did not say: There were no calls for "unmasking" enemies of the people, appeals for "greater vigilance," or references to "wrecking" activities. Yakir's mildly worded decree could have been issued at any time in the history of the Red Army.[45]

A second signal that Yakir was a potential opponent to a spread of the purges into the army was his encounter with the powerful head of the secret police, Nikolay Yezhov, over the Shmidt case. Yakir traveled to Moscow, where Shmidt was being held by the NKVD (the secret police). Previous reports claim that Yakir went to intercede on behalf of Shmidt, but a recent Russian account asserts that Yakir went to Moscow after finding out that Shmidt had implicated Yakir himself in planning a military uprising. Needless to say, "extraordinary methods" had been used to extract this "confession" from Shmidt. Regardless of Yakir's motive for the trip, Shmidt repudiated his previous forced testimony in Yakir's presence and wrote a note to defense minister Voroshilov to this effect. However, after Yakir returned to Kiev he was contacted by Voroshilov, who told him that under additional questioning Shmidt had confirmed his earlier confession. Shmidt was eventually executed in May 1937.[46]

Other top officers also were obstructing the spread of Stalin's purge into the armed forces. One of the most important was Corps Commander

---

[44] Conquest, *Great Terror*, pp. 188–190; Robert C. Tucker, *Stalin in Power: The Revolution from Above, 1928–1941* (New York: W. W. Norton & Company, 1990), pp. 379–380; "Delo o tak nazyvayemoy 'antisovetskoy trotskistskoy voyennoy organizatsii' v krasnoy armii," *Izvestiya TsK KPSS*, No. 4, 1989, 43–45. This last source draws heavily on the report of the Shvernik commission formed under Khrushchev, which had complete access to all the relevant archives; large excerpts from this report have now been published. See: "M. N. Tukhachevskiy i 'voyenno-fashistskiy zagovor': Spravka o proverke obvineniy," *Voyennye arkhivy Rossii*, No. 1, 1993, 29–113; "O masshtabakh repressiy v krasnoy armii v predvoyennye gody," *Voyenno-istoricheskiy zhurnal* [hereafter *VIZh*], Nos. 2–3, 5, 1993. Further references to these reports will cite only the journal name and the issue and page number.

[45] RGVA, f. 25880, op. 4, d. 39, ll. 384–407. See also RGVA, f. 25880, op. 4, d. 39, l. 481.

[46] Conquest, *Great Terror*, p. 192; Tucker, *Stalin in Power*, pp. 380–381; Rapoport and Alexeev, *High Treason*, p. 240; Valentin Kovalev, *Dva stalinskikh narkoma* (Moskva: "Progress," 1995), pp. 218–219; A.M. Larina, "Nezabyvayemoye," *Znamya*, No. 12, 1988, 135.

B. M. Feldman, who was head of the cadres department of the defense ministry (the People's Commissariat of Defense, or NKO). In October 1936 Feldman sent a memorandum to Voroshilov noting that many military district commanders had been sending in packets calling for various officers to be expelled because of Trotskyist activity in the past or relations with former Trotskyists. Feldman reported that he had checked many of these cases himself and found an insufficient basis for dismissal. He called these incidents "shameful" and suggested that all recent dismissal orders be returned to the local level for reconsideration. Voroshilov wrote "correct" on Feldman's report, and four days later Feldman notified Voroshilov that the number of officers dismissed had been reduced from 1,000 to 300. In November 1936 Voroshilov prepared an order in which he called for officers to bring this "irresponsibility" to an end and to take a more "bolshevik attitude" toward cadres instruction (by "bolshevik attitude" Voroshilov meant more of an effort to work with and politically educate officers with suspect backgrounds). Throughout the second half of 1936 and the beginning of 1937, Feldman intervened on behalf of various officers accused of politically suspect backgrounds or views and suggested that they be kept in the army and worked with, rather than dismissing them.[47]

There are rumors that Feldman was the only top officer to consider military action against Stalin to stop the purges. Allegedly Feldman raised the issue with both Tukhachevskiy and Yakir in late 1936–early 1937, and both of them rebuffed this suggestion. Feldman is quoted as saying to Tukhachevskiy, "Do you really not see where this is leading? He will suffocate us all one by one like baby chicks. We must do something." Tukhachevskiy reportedly replied, "What you are suggesting is a coup. I will not do that." Obviously it is impossible to verify this story, but it is clear that Feldman was concerned about the growing purge in the army. Vitaliy Rapoport and Yuri Alexeev (a pseudonym for Yuri Geller) contend that this episode "is the only attempt to organize resistance to terror in the Army that we know took place."[48]

The real signal for the launching of the Great Terror of 1937–1938, in addition to several major show trials, was the February–March 1937 Central Committee Plenum. Stalin, Yezhov, and Vyacheslav Molotov (Chair of the Council of People's Commissars) all gave major reports on the topic of enemies of the people and called for greater vigilance on the part of all party members in unmasking spies, wreckers, Trotskyists, and so on.[49]

---

47 The Voroshilov order in the archives has no date or number on it, so it is possible that this order was not issued. See RGVA, f. 37837, op. 21, d. 88, ll. 160–165; RGVA, f. 37837, op. 21, d. 99, ll. 90–91, 116; RGVA, f. 37837, op. 21, d. 109, l. 126.

48 Rapoport and Alexeev, *High Treason*, p. 282; Boris Sokolov, *Mikhail Tukhachevskiy: Zhizn' i smert' krasnogo marshala* (Smolensk: "Rusich," 1999), pp. 395–396.

49 The complete stenogram of the February–March 1937 Plenum was published in the journal *Voprosy istorii*, 1992–1995; I cite the archival version. For background, see Khlevnyuk, *1937-y*, pp. 72–152.

Both Voroshilov and the head of the Political Administration, Commissar First Rank Yan Gamarnik, made reports to the Plenum on "wrecking" in the armed forces. Voroshilov reported to the Plenum on the activity of "Trotskyists and spies" in the armed forces. He noted that so far they had uncovered "not very many" enemies, and he stated his hope that the Red Army would not have many because the party "sends its best cadres to the army." Voroshilov's general tone was less threatening than that of Yezhov or Molotov, and he said little about the need for greater vigilance and the unmasking of enemies. Although there is some evidence, such as his support for Feldman in late 1936, that Voroshilov initially opposed the purges in the army, he was a loyal Stalin crony and thus was highly unlikely to stick his neck out.[50]

Gamarnik reported to the Plenum on the insufficiencies of party-political work in the armed forces. He was rather short on specific examples, however, and confined himself largely to mundane matters. For example, he talked about the feeding of soldiers, noting that "the food is not always prepared clean and tasty" and chastised commanders for "insufficient vigilance" in this matter. Molotov and Stalin interrupted Gamarnik during his speech and asked for more specific details, with Molotov complaining that "we still need one concrete instance of criticism of political work."[51]

Molotov, in an ominous sign, went out of his way in his closing speech to single out the military for criticism. He noted the importance of the armed forces for the country and the efforts that enemies would go to in order to infiltrate the military with spies and wreckers. Molotov criticized the army's political organs for their insufficient vigilance both in unmasking enemies in the armed forces and in the Political Administration itself.[52]

One of the focal points of the February–March 1937 Plenum was the question of the fate of the former Right oppositionists Nikolay Bukharin and Aleksey Rykov. Army Commander First Rank I. P. Uborevich, commander of the Belorussian Military District, allegedly went over to Bukharin and "pressed his hand" in a show of sympathy, publicly suggesting that he did not believe Bukharin was an enemy of the people. There are also reports that Yakir was suspicious of the charges against former oppositionists.[53]

After the February–March Plenum it was clear to party members that the purge was gathering strength and that resistance was highly dangerous.

---

[50] RTsKhIDNI, f. 17, op. 2, d. 612, vyp. II, ll. 76–85; Rapoport and Alexeev, *High Treason*, p. 275.

[51] RTsKhIDNI, f. 17, op. 2, d. 612, vyp. III, ll. 41–45.

[52] RTsKhIDNI, f. 17, op. 2, d. 612, vyp. II, ll. 89–90.

[53] Conquest, *Great Terror*, pp. 173–174, 192; Volkogonov, *Triumf i tragediya*, I, p. 488; Larina, "Nezabyvayemoye," 166–167. For an example of Uborevich's lack of "vigilance" in dealing with politically suspect officers, see RGVA, f. 37837, op. 21, d. 109, l. 122.

Nonetheless, several generals continued to speak out on behalf of arrested associates and drag their feet on implementing the purges. In April Corps Commander I. I. Garkavy, the Commander of the Urals Military District (and a relative of Yakir's: they were married to sisters), was arrested. Again Yakir interceded on his behalf, going to Stalin himself. Several lower-ranking officers accused Gamarnik of foot-dragging on implementing the directives of the February–March Plenum. Gamarnik, these officers asserted, approached the question of saboteurs "in a purely formal manner" and "without teeth."[54]

None of these small-scale efforts by top military leaders such as Feldman, Uborevich, Yakir, and Gamarnik had any chance of stopping Stalin's juggernaut. Robert Conquest notes that Stalin apparently distrusted the military, not least because they had failed "to show enthusiasm for the increasing tempo of the purge." Stalin's blow against the military came at the very point when he was moving from attacks on former political opponents to a more widespread purge among those who had previously been loyal to his line. The army, as a hypothetical threat to Stalin's rule due to its control over coercive power, was preemptively beheaded to clear the way for the Great Purge.[55]

Stalin, with the willing assistance of the NKVD, turned up the pressure on the armed forces after the February–March Plenum. In April and May, former NKVD and military officers were coerced to implicate leading officers, including Tukhachevskiy, Yakir, and Uborevich, in counterrevolutionary activity. Accusations against the military leadership included plotting to overthrow the Soviet government and spying on behalf of various foreign powers, particularly Germany. Stalin also made threatening noises about enemies in the armed forces at a military dinner at Voroshilov's apartment after the May Day parade.[56]

A series of personnel shuffles in April and May kept top commanders off guard and in some cases isolated them from familiar troops. Among those either reassigned or scheduled for transfer were Tukhachevskiy, Yakir, Uborevich, Feldman, and Gamarnik, as well as several of their deputies. Tukhachevskiy, for example, was demoted from his position as Deputy People's Commissar of Defense to the command of the insignificant Volga Military District.[57] The major arrests among the high command were made in May. Army Commander Second Rank A. I. Kork, the head of the Frunze

---

[54] Conquest, *Great Terror*, p. 193; Larina, "Nezabyvayemoye," 135; RGVA, f. 37837, op. 21, d. 100, ll. 168–172; RGVA, f. 9, op. 29, d. 320, ll. 36–47, 52–60; Zoya Eroshok, "Ego znala vsya strana," in A. Proskurin, ed., *Vozvrashchennye imena: Sbornik publitsisticheskikh statey*, Book I (Moskva: Novosti, 1989), pp. 142–143.

[55] Conquest, *Great Terror*, pp. 186, 192–193 (quote, p. 186).

[56] *Voyennye arkhivy Rossii*, No. 1, 1993, 31–41; *Izvestiya TsK KPSS*, No. 4, 1989, 45–49.

[57] These actual or planned changes are from Politburo protocols: RTsKhIDNI, f. 17, op. 3, d. 986, ll. 10, 18; RTsKhIDNI, f. 17, op. 3, d. 987, ll. 27, 37, 69–70.

Academy, was taken in on May 14 and Feldman was detained on May 15. Tukhachevskiy allegedly referred to Feldman's arrest as a "monstrous provocation." A week later, on May 22, Tukhachevskiy himself was arrested, shortly after he took up his new post. Also taken in on May 22 was Army Commander Second Rank R. P. Eydeman, the head of Osoaviakhim (a civil defense organization). Eydeman earlier that spring had expressed his bewilderment that good party people were being arrested as enemies of the people.[58]

The final group of "plotters" was detained by the NKVD at the end of May. Yakir and Uborevich were arrested on May 28 and May 29, respectively. The last key figure to go down at this time was Gamarnik, but his fate was somewhat different. Gamarnik shot himself on May 31. Different versions, not necessarily incompatible, of Gamarnik's suicide exist. His daughter maintains that Marshal V. K. Blyukher, the commander of the Far East, came to visit on May 30 and told Gamarnik that either he would have to sit in judgment of Tukhachevskiy and the others or be tried himself. According to the official Soviet commission established under Khrushchev, Gamarnik killed himself on May 31 after being informed that he was being dismissed from his post for his ties with Yakir, who had been implicated in the "military-fascist plot."[59]

All of the leading officers upon detention denied any participation in plots against the government or cooperation with Germany or other foreign powers. However, confessions were eventually beaten out of them. Tukhachevskiy's deposition is spattered with blood. Other means of coercion were habitually used as well, including various psychological pressures and threats against the accused's family. Yezhov played an active role in the questioning of several of the key "plotters," including Tukhachevskiy and Yakir. Stalin was heavily involved in the process, receiving copies of the prisoners' depositions daily and meeting with Yezhov and other top NKVD officials involved in the "investigation" almost daily. Copies of the confessions were circulated among other key Politburo members, particularly Voroshilov, Molotov, and another pro-Stalin hard-liner, Lazar Kaganovich.[60]

It seems superfluous to say so, but it is worth stressing that no convincing evidence of a military plot against Stalin has ever been found, nor is there

---

[58] *Voyennye arkhivy Rossii*, No. 1, 1993, 38–45; *Izvestiya TsK KPSS*, No. 4, 1989, 49; Conquest, *Great Terror*, p. 199.

[59] *Voyennye arkhivy Rossii*, No. 1 (1993), 45–47; *Izvestiya TsK KPSS*, No. 4, 1989, 49–52; Conquest, *Great Terror*, pp. 200–201; Volkogonov, *Triumf i tragediya*, I, pp. 539–540; Eroshok, "Ego znala vsya strana," pp. 143–144.

[60] *Voyennye arkhivy Rossii*, No. 1, 1993, 36–46; *Izvestiya TsK KPSS*, No. 4, 1989, 47–51; Volkogonov, *Triumf i tragediya*, Vol. I, pp. 541–542; Dmitriy Volkogonov, *Sem' vozhdey*, Vol. I (Moskva: Novosti, 1996), p. 205. On NKVD methods, see Conquest, *Great Terror*, pp. 121–130; Tucker, *Stalin in Power*, pp. 466–474.

any proof that they were fascist spies.[61] Nonetheless, to this day, scholars occasionally argue that a real military plot against Stalin existed, most recently the American historian Robert Thurston. Thurston relies on the report of an ex-NKVD colonel (in fact, a border guards officer) and a junior-ranking army officer from the Far East. Why either of these officers would have known about the thinking of military leaders such as Tukhachevskiy and Yakir is unclear, and their accounts either are contradicted by available evidence or are utterly fantastic; the conspiracy in the Far East, for example, was supposed to begin with an uprising in Khabarovsk, which is 6,000 miles from Moscow. Moreover, the account of the officer from the Far East, according to Robert Tucker, "has been persuasively exposed by an ex-Soviet source as a forgery."[62]

Official investigations into the Tukhachevskiy affair carried out under Khrushchev and Gorbachev turned up no evidence of such a plot. The reports from these investigations demonstrate with considerable material from the most secret archives in Russia that the "evidence" against the military command was falsified, internally contradictory, and based on forced confessions. Other scholars with unimpeded access to the archives, such as the former General Dmitriy Volkogonov, also found no evidence of a military conspiracy. I looked for months in party and army archives in Moscow and found no evidence of a plot at any level in the armed forces. An NKVD officer who monitored Tukhachevskiy for years was unable to uncover any compromising material on him. Of course, it is impossible to definitively prove a negative, but there is no serious evidence for a "Tukhachevskiy plot."[63]

Whether Stalin believed in the existence of a military plot is impossible to say. Stalin's closest Politburo colleagues, such as Molotov and Kaganovich,

---

[61] Recent archival evidence also suggests that there was no secret "red file" prepared in Nazi Germany, with or without NKVD instigation, that implicated Tukhachevskiy in spying. For varying accounts of this issue, see: Conquest, *Great Terror*, pp. 195–199; Donald Cameron Watt, "Who Plotted Against Whom? Stalin's Purge of the Soviet High Command Revisited," *Journal of Soviet Military Studies*, 3 (1990), 46–65; "Sovetskaya razvedka i russkaya voyennaya emigratsiya 20-40-x godov," *Novaya i noveyshaya istoriya*, No. 3, 1998, 123–124; Pavel Sudoplatov and Anatoli Sudoplatov, *Special Tasks: The Memoirs of an Unwanted Witness – A Soviet Spymaster* (Boston: Little, Brown and Company, 1994), pp. 90–93; Sokolov, *Mikhail Tukhachevskiy*, pp. 441–485; Nikolay Abramov, "Delo Tukhachevskogo: novaya versiya," in G. V. Smirnov, ed., *Krovavyy marshal: Mikhail Tukhachevskiy, 1893–1937* (Sankt-Peterburg: "KORONA print," 1997), pp. 67–78.

[62] Robert W. Thurston, *Life and Terror in Stalin's Russia 1934–1941* (New Haven, CT: Yale University Press, 1996), pp. 50–58; A. Svetlanin, *Dal'nevostochnyy zagovor* (Frankfurt: Posev, 1953); Isaac Deutscher, *Stalin*, revised edition (Harmondsworth, Middlesex, England: Penguin Books, 1966), pp. 375–376; Robert C. Tucker, "Problems of Interpretation," *Slavic Review*, 42 (1983), 80, note 2. For a recent Russian work arguing that there was a real plot, see Smirnov, *Krovavyy marshal*, pp. 338–377.

[63] *Voyennye arkhivy Rossii*, No. 1, 1993 (the NKVD officer who monitored Tukhachevskiy is cited on p. 101); *Izvestiya TsK KPSS*, No. 4, 1989; Volkogonov, *Triumf i tragediya*, Vol. I, pp. 530–555; Volkogonov, *Sem' vozhdey*, Vol. I, p. 205.

evidently believed that Tukhachevskiy represented a real threat to the Soviet leadership. Molotov reportedly remarked late in life that "Tukhachevskiy was a very dangerous military plotter" and that "we even knew the date of the coup." At a minimum, as Beria allegedly believed, the Politburo thought the military leadership was too independent. But the fact that the political leadership distrusted its generals is hardly proof of a military plot, nor an adequate explanation for the murder of thousands of officers.[64]

From June 1 to June 4 an expanded session of the Military Soviet of the USSR met with the participation of Politburo members to pass judgment on those officers arrested by the NKVD. Already twenty members (out of eighty-five) of the Military Soviet had been arrested. The first day the Military Soviet heard the report of Voroshilov on "the uncovering by the NKVD organs of a counter-revolutionary conspiracy in the RKKA (the Workers' and Peasants' Red Army)."[65]

On June 2 Stalin himself addressed the assembly. Stalin stressed the work of the Tukhachevskiy group as German spies and had little to say about a plot against the Soviet government; when he mentioned the alleged plot, it was something that the Germans had urged on the group and not something they had planned themselves. The one specific accusation that has a ring of plausibility to it was Stalin's claim that "they felt sorry for the peasants," a reference to military unhappiness with collectivization. In the second half of his speech, Stalin concentrated on the failure of "signalization" (i.e., informing) in the armed forces. "Every member of the party," Stalin stressed, "every honest, non-party, citizen of the USSR not only has the right but the duty to inform about insufficiencies that he notices.... You are obligated to send a letter to your People's Commissar, with a copy to the Central Committee." He also emphasized the need to promote younger cadres to leading positions. Stalin's message was not subtle and could hardly fail to be noticed by the officers present: A purge was being unleashed in the armed forces, and it was time for officers to unmask the enemies in their midst.[66]

In the week following the Military Soviet meeting, preparations were made for a military trial of eight top officers: Tukhachevskiy, Yakir, Uborevich, Kork, Feldman, Eydeman, Putna, and Primakov. Stalin met regularly that week with Yezhov, his chief prosecutor Andrey Vyshinskiy, Voroshilov, and other top Politburo members (Molotov and Kaganovich) to prepare the trial, which was held on June 11. The trial was not held in public, like the show trials; presumably the NKVD had not had enough time

[64] F. Chuyev, *Sto sorok besed s Molotovym* (Moskva: "Terra," 1991), pp. 418, 442; Feliks Chuyev, *Tak govoril Kaganovich: Ispoved' stalinskogo apostola* (Moskva: "Otechestvo," 1992), pp. 45–46, 100–101; Sudoplatov, *Special Tasks*, p. 89.

[65] *Voyennye arkhivy Rossii*, No. 1, 1993, 47–49.

[66] "'Nevol'niki v Rukakh Germanskogo Reykhsvera': Rech' I. V. Stalina v Narkomate oborony," *Istochnik*, No. 3, 1994, 72–88.

to work on the officers and ensure that they would play their designated roles. Stalin created a special military tribunal consisting of top officers to sit in judgment on their former colleagues. The verdict, of course, was predetermined, and by the end of 1938 six of the eight commanders in the tribunal were themselves dead.[67]

Although Stalin received the verdict he expected (the defendants were all shot), the trial did not go completely as planned. Tukhachevskiy, Yakir, and especially Uborevich denied some of the accusations against them. At one point a one-hour break had to be declared because Uborevich was not cooperating, and Vyshinskiy and Ulrikh never returned to questioning him. Two members of the tribunal, Marshal Blyukher and Commander Second Rank P. E. Dybenko, asked for specific details of the accused officers' wrecking and spying activities, which Yakir and Uborevich said they could not provide. The main focus of the trial was the accusation that the group had worked for Nazi Germany. The one charge that probably had a factual basis was the claim that the group had lobbied for the removal of Voroshilov as People's Commissar of Defense, although in the trial this mutated into a charge of planning a "terrorist act" against Voroshilov. Tukhachevskiy and other professional officers had no respect for Voroshilov's knowledge of military affairs. Yezhov reported to Stalin after the trial that of the members of the military court only Semen Budennyy, the head of the cavalry and a long-time Stalin ally, had participated actively, and that most of them had sat silently throughout the trial.[68]

The Tukhachevskiy affair marked the beginning of a wide-scale purge of the Soviet officer corps. Within 10 days of the Tukhachevskiy trial, 980 command and political officers had been arrested, including 80 of general rank. Thousands of officers were shot as counterrevolutionaries in 1937–1938, and thousands more were discharged from the army in this period. The purges wound down at the end of 1938, but not before tremendous damage had been done to the armed forces.[69]

The toll was the most severe at the very top of the Red Army. Three of five marshals (Tukhachevskiy, Blyukher, and Yegorov), three of four army

---

[67] *Voyennye arkhivy Rossii*, No. 1, 1993, 49–52; *Izvestiya TsK KPSS*, No. 4, 1989, 54–56.

[68] *Voyennye arkhivy Rossii*, No. 1, 1993, 47, 51–57, 63, 65; *Izvestiya TsK KPSS*, No. 4, 1989, 53, 56–57; Volkogonov, *Triumf i tragediya*, Vol. I, pp. 540–543; Aleksey Khorev, "Kak sudili Tukhachevskogo," *Krasnaya zvezda*, April 17, 1991, 4. The Shvernik Commission uncovered evidence that the stenogram of the trial was falsified, so the exact course of the trial probably will never be known. On the views of Tukhachevskiy, Yakir, and other professional soldiers on Voroshilov, see N. M. Yakunov, "Stalin i krasnaya armiya (Arkhivnye nakhodki)," *Istoriya SSSR*, No. 5, 1991, 175; Boris Viktorov, "Kak my reabilitirovali 'zagovorshchikov'," in Smirnov, *Krovavyy marshal*, pp. 16–17; Sudoplatov, *Special Tasks*, pp. 89–90. Marshal Georgiy Zhukov relates how Tukhachevskiy once told Voroshilov to his face that he was incompetent: K. M. Simonov, "Zametki k biografii G. K. Zhukova," *VIZh*, No. 12, 1987, 42.

[69] *Izvestiya TsK KPSS*, No. 4, 1989, 57; *VIZh*, No. 2, 1993, 72; Conquest, *Great Terror*, pp. 427–441.

commanders first rank (Yakir, Uborevich, and I. P. Belov), and all nine army commanders second rank were killed. Seventy-six of eighty-five members of the Military Soviet were repressed, and seventy-two of these seventy-six were killed or committed suicide. In the years 1937–1940, as a result of Stalin's terror, all military district commanders, ninety percent of district chiefs of staff and deputies, and eighty percent of corps and divisional commanders were removed. Over ninety percent of those of general's rank, and over eighty-five percent of colonels, were repressed.[70]

The total number of officers purged during the Great Terror was in the tens of thousands. The number 40,000 has often been taken as a reliable estimate, based on a speech made by Voroshilov in November 1938 and several published Soviet sources. It now seems clear that the 40,000 figure refers to the number of those dismissed from the armed forces in 1937–1938, and not the number killed, as some historians have interpreted these figures. Over 10,000 of those dismissed were later reinstated. Current best estimates suggest that around 20,000 officers were permanently discharged from the officer corps and thousands of them were killed.[71]

What Was a Counterrevolutionary? Political Beliefs of the Soviet Officer Corps

This section investigates the types of officers' statements that attracted the attention of the secret police and political officers. Reports filed by NKVD and Political Administration (PUR) officers represent the best source we have on the organizational culture of the Soviet armed forces for this crucial period. Of course, these reports tend to stress "political insufficiencies" uncovered in the officer corps, so they are not a representative sample. Those officers who did not attract the attention of the secret police or commissars evidently either adhered to the regime line or were sufficiently discreet. A Soviet officer who emigrated after the war later remarked that because of monitoring by the NKVD and PUR he "avoided all talks which would bring out my

---

[70] *Izvestiya TsK KPSS*, No. 4, 1989, 58–60, 74–80; *VIZh*, No. 2, 1993, 73; Volkogonov, *Triumf i tragediya*, Vol. II, p. 52; O. Suvenirov, "Narkomat oborony i NKVD v predvoyennye gody," *Voprosy istorii*, No. 6, 1991, 30; Lt. Col. A. Gerasimov, "Prava i obyazannosti," *Voyenniy vestnik*, No. 3, 1990, 7; Rapoport and Alexeev, *High Treason*, pp. 276–277.

[71] A. T. Ukolov and V. I. Ivkin, "O masshtabakh repressiy v krasnoy armii v predvoyennye gody," *VIZh*, No. 1, 1993, 56–59; "O rabote za 1939 god: Iz otcheta nachal'nika Upravleniya po nachal'stvuyushchemu sostavu RKKA Narkomata Oborony SSSR E.A. Shchadenko," *Izvestiya TsK KPSS*, No. 1, 1990, 186–192; M. I. Mel'tyukhov, "Repressii v krasnoy armii: itogi noveyshikh issledovaniy," *Otechestvennaya istoriya*, No. 5, 1997, 115–116; Reese, *Stalin's Reluctant Soldiers*, pp. 132–162; Roger R. Reese, "The Impact of the Great Purge on the Red Army: Wrestling with Hard Numbers," *The Soviet and Post-Soviet Review*, 19 (1992), 71–90; Roger R. Reese, "The Red Army and the Great Purges," in Getty and Manning, *Stalinist Terror*, pp. 198–214.

antigovernmental views or my views on the party."[72] Still, many officers did express views that attracted unwanted attention and much can be learned by an examination of the thinking of those who expressed "counterrevolutionary" ideas. The most important finding is that there is very little evidence that officers believed that the armed forces should play a role in sovereign power issues, or that a military coup was an appropriate response to the purges. Much more common was the view that the military should stay out of politics and focus on strictly military affairs.

Many officers, of course, were denounced for reasons having nothing to do with their views on military training and the role of the political organs. Some common grounds for being condemned included: having a relative or close colleague who was an "enemy of the people"; having lived abroad, or having relatives who lived abroad; having concealed one's social origins (i.e., aristocratic or bourgeois ancestors); nationality; having served in the Tsarist army; having lived in territory under White control during the Civil War. Certainly we should not look too hard for logic in the decisions to purge certain officers. Military districts were given quotas for unmasking "enemies of the people," and overfulfilling the plan was highly encouraged.[73]

The military purges were not motivated by any genuine fears of praetorianism. Nonetheless, a couple of junior officers did make comments in 1937 about the possibility of military intervention or suggested that the army should play a more prominent role in politics. In early 1937 a Lieutenant Revels from the Moscow Military District commented on the show trials of the old opposition: "If the Trotskyists carried out a coup and killed Stalin, Voroshilov, and others, probably many from the Red Army would support them. They would probably even find commanders [who would support them]." Revels concluded that many people are "unhappy with Soviet power"; he was arrested shortly thereafter. Another junior officer, T. N. Kravchuk, said in late 1936 that the army should play a bigger role in government because it is "the most prepared for leading government." Kravchuk was also arrested as a "Trotskyist." Finally, in June 1937, less than a week after the execution of the Tukhachevskiy group, a PUR officer informed that he heard an officer remark that the large number of arrests "could lead to a military coup." These comments are the most explicit I found that referred to the possibility of military intervention, or called for a larger role for the armed forces in politics. It is thus possible that a more praetorian subculture existed in the armed forces in the 1930s, although none of these statements refers to any specific plans, but rather to a general mood of disenchantment. This mood apparently was inspired by unhappiness with Soviet policies, such as collectivization and the purges.[74]

---

[72] Reese, *Stalin's Reluctant Soldiers*, p. 96.

[73] RGVA, f. 9, op. 29, d. 372; RGVA, f. 4, op. 18, d. 46, l. 99; Mel'tyukhov, "Repressii v krasnoy armii," 118.

[74] RGVA, f. 9, op. 39, d. 29, ll. 122–123, 184–188; RGVA, f. 9, op. 30, d. 56, ll. 112–113.

The most common reaction to the news of the uncovering of the "anti-Soviet Trotskyist military organization" was not the thought of military intervention, but bewilderment and incomprehension. Political officers reported that many soldiers and officers felt that now they did not know whom to trust. A Pacific Fleet officer remarked, "Who can you trust now? Now all orders from superiors are placed in doubt because no one can guarantee that the orders are not wrecking. Now, having received an order, I'll first think – should I carry it out or not?" There were frequent instances of expressions of doubt about whether Tukhachevskiy, Gamarnik, and the others were guilty. Some military personnel criticized Stalin or the NKVD.[75]

Memoirs of former Soviet officers, including the World War II hero Georgiy Zhukov, also note the confusion reigning in the officer corps at the time. L. S. Skvirskiy, an instructor at the Frunze Academy in 1937, observes that he and his colleagues were "bewildered," "horrified," and "stunned" by the announcement regarding Tukhachevskiy, Yakir, and the others. Although the accusations did not make sense, Skvirskiy adds, it was also dangerous to express doubts aloud.[76]

Key figures in the military leadership had been unenthusiastic implementers of the purges. Similar foot-dragging was evident at lower levels. Indeed, the most common denunciation in NKVD and PUR reports was that officers did not take political work in the armed forces seriously. Discussions in the central administration of the NKO (Defense Ministry) in the spring of 1937 showed a disturbing lack of "vigilance" among military personnel. One officer saw the calls for greater vigilance as a political fad. Another objected to the study of Marxism–Leninism, suggesting that it could be carried out at home. Entire party bureaus in the armed forces decided to make party-political study voluntary, and in some sections party-political study had not been conducted for an entire year.[77] Other directorates were accused of "apoliticism," with low attendance at party meetings and demonstrations. Thirty or forty people knew a copy of *Mein Kampf* was circulating at the Central House of the Red Army, a major cultural enlightenment center for Moscow-based military personnel, without reporting it to the proper authorities. Thus it is not surprising that in July 1937 the political organs of the central administration of the NKO noted considerable "obstructionism" among

---

[75] RGVA, f. 33879, op. 1, d. 234, ll. 1–18, 34–48, 166–192, 214–238, 298–308, 317–347, 366–379 (quote l. 2); RGVA, f. 33879, op. 1, d. 233, ll. 24–38, 39–57; RGVA, f. 4, op. 19, d. 37, ll. 148–149; RGVA, f. 9, op. 30, d. 56, ll. 128–130, 140–147.

[76] G. I. Zhukov, *Vospominaniya i rasmyshleniya*, 11th ed., Vol. I (Moskva: Novosti, 1992), pp. 229–230; L. C. Skvirskiy, "V predvoyennye gody," *Voprosy istorii*, No. 9, 1989, 61; Petro G. Grigorenko, *Memoirs* (New York: W. W. Norton and Company, 1982), p. 69.

[77] The troops had around five to six hours a week of political training, and officers had two to four hours per week of political lessons. Roger Reese shows how haphazardly political instruction was carried out. See Brzezinski, *Political Controls*, pp. 40–42, 51–53; Colton, *Commissars, Commanders*, pp. 72–73; Reese, *Stalin's Reluctant Soldiers*, pp. 79–80, 92–93.

the central apparat, concluding that Gamarnik, Tukhachevskiy, and Feldman had "implanted enemies of the people in all branches of the Red Army."[78]

Reports on the apolitical views of officers came in from other parts of the country as well. Kravchuk, the junior officer mentioned above, refused to allow the political officer to read party announcements to the troops during marches because it would "spoil the soldiers' mood." He also complained about the NKVD, referring to them as "parasites." A lieutenant was dismissed in November 1936 for arguing for the abolition of political organs in the army. Major L. V. Maksimov, a regimental chief of staff, got into trouble with the NKVD in April 1937 for criticizing the amount of party material being published by the army and comparing the Red Army unfavorably with the Tsarist army. Soviet officers were "illiterate," remarked Maksimov, "and also stuffed with Marxism–Leninism. All that is disagreeable to me." Lieutenant P. I. Zimin of the Kiev Military District lauded Trotsky for his use of military specialists during the civil war and his efforts to limit the role of the political apparatus of the Red Army, and also complained about the constant monitoring of people's political views in the armed forces.[79]

In fact, complaints about the role of the PUR and the NKVD were among the most common grounds for being suspected of counterrevolutionary activity in late 1936 and early 1937. One junior officer, a Lieutenant T. T. Bure of the Moscow Military District, was particularly blunt in stating his views. Asked by a commissar if he had read a summary of Stalin's report on the new Soviet constitution, Bure replied: "Why are you pestering me about Stalin's report? I need to know combat affairs, and you political workers need to know reports and the history of the party, it's your bread-and-butter. I don't have time to study party history and Stalin's reports."[80]

Other grounds for being suspected of counterrevolutionary views included a series of statements that were factually true but still politically dangerous. Pronouncements that could get one into trouble included: comments about the poor conditions for workers in the Soviet Union, observations that Trotsky played an important role in the revolution and civil war or that Stalin played a lesser role in the same events, or suggestions that it was impossible to build socialism in one country. Remarks critical of collectivization could also attract NKVD attention.[81]

After the February–March Plenum some members of the high command endeavored to convince their subordinates of the need for greater attention

---

[78] RGVA, f. 9, op. 30, d. 56, ll. 8, 46–47, 55–60, 83, 93, 111, 120–127, 131–134. One soldier, in a saracastic comment on the state of the Soviet armed forces, remarked about the *Mein Kampf* incident, "in two years we are going to be reading that book anyway."

[79] RGVA, f. 9, op. 39, d. 29, ll. 184–188, 202–205; RGVA, f. 37837, op. 21, d. 109, l. 59; RGVA, f. 37837, op. 22, d. 1, ll. 258–261; RGVA, f. 9, op. 39, d. 30, ll. 49–51.

[80] RGVA, f. 9, op. 39, d. 29, ll. 91–92.

[81] RGVA, f. 37837, op. 21, d. 109, passim; RGVA, f. 9, op. 39, d. 39, ll. 147–148.

to political matters. Gamarnik, for example, criticized party members for the belief that party work interferes with military training. Many officers, he maintained, were politically "backward." Gamarnik noted that he had witnessed several commanders complain to Voroshilov that too much time was wasted on Marxist–Leninist indoctrination. Gamarnik did not save himself by these comments, but they probably reflected real "deficiencies" in the officer corps at the time.[82]

The spring of 1937 was probably the worst time ever for an officer to base his claim to service on his apolitical views. At a meeting of NKO party aktiv in June, after the execution of Tukhachevskiy and his co-defendants, speaker after speaker stressed that military personnel should look for the political basis for even professional disagreements. The armed forces were thrown into turmoil by the campaign to weed out "enemies of the people." The entire method of evaluating the political reliability of officers was changed. Before April 1937 Gamarnik (the head of the PUR) and Feldman (department head for cadres) worked closely together in deciding personnel questions. After June 1937 Voroshilov played a much bigger role in cadres' decisions, in conjunction with the NKVD. The department for cadres, now headed by E. A. Shchadenko, simply received long lists of personnel subject to arrest from Voroshilov's office.[83]

Despite this all-out campaign, however, officers continued to get into trouble for comments about their distaste for political work in the armed forces, or politics in general. An Air Force officer, A. V. Zamyatin, noted in July 1937 that he had not read the report of Politburo member Andrey Zhdanov to the February–March Plenum, because "I'm not subordinate to the party and it doesn't have anything to do with me." Another officer, this time from the ground forces, remarked in July, "I'm a non-party person, politics doesn't interest me." A Lieutenant Shavshan remarked that it was hard to know who to believe [after the Tukhachevskiy affair] and "I am now outside politics (*vne politiki*)." The head of a military educational institute for tank officers was expelled from the party and army for stating, "I don't need party work, but service." The belief of officers that they should be "outside politics" had apparently persisted from the prerevolutionary period, but now such sentiments, if expressed openly, could subject officers to arrest by the NKVD.[84]

Denunciations and arrests for apolitical beliefs and statements continued into 1938 and 1939. A lieutenant in the Transbaikal Military District was denounced in March 1938 for avoiding political lessons, about which

[82] RGVA, f. 9, op. 29, d. 319, ll. 2–19, 22–52, 285–293; RGVA, f. 9, op. 30, d. 85, ll. 422–428.
[83] RGVA, f. 4, op. 18, d. 61; RGVA, f. 37837, op. 21, d. 99; RGVA, f. 37837, op. 21, d. 109; RGVA, f. 37837, op. 22, d. 1.
[84] RGVA, f. 33879, op. 1, d. 234, ll. 318, 336–337, 367; RGVA, f. 9, op. 39, d. 29, ll. 279–280; RGVA, f. 9, op. 29, d. 372, ll. 216–217; RGVA, f. 37837, op. 22, d. 7, l. 218; RGVA, f. 9, op. 29, d. 340, l. 447.

he reportedly said, "you can't eat politics." Colonel Vladimirov of the Far Eastern Army was denounced by a PUR officer in June 1938 for similar views. The PUR officer wrote, "Vladimirov is hardly at all interested in the political life of the country, the army, or his division. In my opinion he even reads newspapers very irregularly. He has served in the party for a long time, but he doesn't feel the weight of it, like a communist." Captain Somov from the Central Asian Military District was denounced by a OO officer in May 1939 for his attitude toward political work. Somov said, "I will not engage in party-political work, the regulations do not require it. Let the political officer do it, it's his bread-and-butter." Other officers were also denounced for ignoring party work.[85]

Some officers were so hostile to political work that it is difficult to see how they survived as long as they did. Brigade Commander F. N. Zelentsov, the head of the Moscow Railroad Military School, was denounced by two PUR officers in April 1939. The political officers complained that Zelentsov completely ignored party-political work, because he believed that it did nothing to prepare lieutenants for war. Reportedly when Zelentsov found out in June 1937 that Gamarnik had committed suicide, he marched into the commissar's office and said sarcastically: "Well, comrade regimental commissar, now we all understand just what was going on in the army – the institution of commissars, self-criticism, etc. – all that was the work of the enemy Gamarnik."[86]

Thus, one of the most frequent grounds for dismissal that I encountered in the archives was statements by officers that belittled party work in the army, and conversely stressed the attention that should be devoted to military training and more narrow professional tasks. Statements that suggested widespread adherence to an apolitical organizational culture were common in the Soviet officer corps in the late 1930s. Conversely, as noted above, I found very few instances of expressions of praetorian views, despite the interest that OO and PUR officers undoubtedly would have shown in such statements. Several major NKO and PUR conferences held in 1937–1938 produced no concrete reports of praetorian sentiments held by officers. In contrast, complaints about the inattention of regular commanders to political affairs often were expressed.[87]

It is impossible to determine on the basis of archival evidence if the apolitical organizational culture was the dominant one. There were certainly many officers who were committed communists and party members and did not chafe at party-political work.[88] It seems that there were two competing

---

[85] RGVA, f. 4, op. 19, d. 29, l. 118; RGVA, f. 9, op. 39, d. 69, ll. 247–254; RGVA, f. 9, op. 39, d. 75, ll. 83–85; RGVA, f. 9, op. 36, d. 2892, ll. 93–95.

[86] RGVA, f. 9, op. 36, d. 2892, ll. 73–76.

[87] RGVA, f. 9, op. 29, d. 340; RGVA, f. 4, op. 14, d. 2020, ll. 79–92.

[88] Petro Grigorenko, for instance, who later became a famous dissident, was a true believer in the 1930s: Grigorenko, *Memoirs*, pp. 36, 77. See also V. Zabrodin, interview with

subcultures in the Soviet officer corps in the 1930s: the apolitical one and the pro-Bolshevik one. The communist organizational culture was dominant in the sense that it was the one articulated by the military leadership, but a quantitative assessment of dominance is not possible. What is clear is that both of these organizational cultures were noninterventionist, and that there were few adherents to a praetorian military culture at this time.[89] Many officers with more interventionist tendencies had selected themselves out of the country by siding with the Whites in the Civil War, and the NKVD and the PUR were unable to uncover more than a handful of officers with praetorian sentiments. Most important, there is no reliable evidence of a potential or actual military plot during the Great Terror.

Explaining Military Behavior during the Purges

Military nonintervention to halt the purges is best explained by the absence of an opportunity, given the strength of the state and its control mechanisms over the military. An apolitical organizational culture also meant that motives were mixed, with corporate interest reasons for intervention confronted by normative beliefs that saw such behavior as inappropriate.

Domestic structure presented obvious obstacles to military intervention. The Stalinist state had a high degree of political capacity and was able to crush any potential domestic sources of opposition. The regime had shown its ability to withstand severe trials, such as collectivization. From the 1920s on, no serious opposition to party rule had come forward. There were no obvious alternatives to Stalin's government. Any military officers with praetorian tendencies were likely to see the opportunity for successful intervention as low.

Stalin effectively used a variety of control mechanisms to further deter plotting. That these barriers worked so effectively is further testament to the power of the state. The presence of both secret police officers and commissars in every military unit was a powerful deterrent. An additional danger was that one would be reported as an "enemy of the people," even by regular line officers. There was also the possibility of counterbalancing by secret police armed units (the internal troops). In 1936 control over the Kremlin regiment had been transferred to the NKVD. An American military attaché, reporting on the Tukhachevskiy affair, noted that "treasonable plans have less chance of success in the Soviet Union than in any other country." A military coup, then, would have been a very risky enterprise.[90]

Colonel-General (retired) A. S. Zheltov, "'Odna nepravda nam v ubytok...'," *Kommunist vooruzhenikh sil*, No. 12, 1989, 76–78.

[89] For a similar conclusion by a Russian historian, see Mel'tyukhov, "Repressii v krasnoy armii," 112.

[90] Yu. N. Zhukov, "Tak byl li 'zagovor Tukhacheskogo'?" *Otechestvennaya istoriya*, No. 1, 1999, 178; Sokolov, *Mikhail Tukhachevskiy*, pp. 376, 396–397; "Attaché Assessments of the

On the other hand, there were definite corporate interest motives for military intervention during the Terror. It is hard to imagine a greater infringement on the autonomy of the armed forces than Stalin's purges. The political leadership of the country delivered the army into the hands of secret police thugs. The behavior of NKVD officers, and the monitoring by NKVD special sections, was a frequent source of complaint by the military. During the purges many officers wrote to top military and party officials, including Voroshilov and Stalin, to protest against NKVD excesses.[91]

Another potential corporate motive for intervention was the influence of the purges on the ability of the armed forces to carry out its professional tasks. The purges contributed to substantial shortfalls in officer corps manning levels, particularly at the highest ranks. The commander of the Transcaucasian Military District, N. V. Kuybyshev, reported in November 1937 that he had three divisions currently commanded by captains. The Armenian Division was commanded by a captain who before that had commanded neither a regiment nor a battalion; he had commanded only a battery. In June 1938 the commander of the Kharkov Military District, I. K. Smirnov, noted that junior lieutenants were commanding battalions (which are normally commanded by lieutenant colonels). Roger Reese points out that the shortfall in officers was caused not only by the purges but by the rapid expansion of the officer corps at this time. By neglecting to mention that the purges hit hardest at the very top of the military leadership, however, Reese's argument understates the purges' importance. Those officers most competent to implement such an expansion of the officer corps were wiped out, along with the leading figures responsible for the development of military doctrine, technology, and organization.[92]

The purges also severely disrupted training and relations among military personnel. Zhukov reports that military and political training suffered as a result of the purges, and that discipline was severely undermined. At major military conferences in November 1937 and June 1938 there were many complaints about the disruption of training. The purges made officers afraid to

---

Impact of the 1930s Purges on the Red Army," *Journal of Soviet Military Studies*, 2 (1989), 425.

91 O. F. Suvenirov, "Za chest' i dostoinstvo voinov RKKA," in A. V. Afanas'ev, ed., *Oni ne molchali* (Moskva: Politizdat, 1991), pp. 372–373, 379–380; RGVA, f. 9, op. 39, d. 69, ll. 334–336; Grigorenko, *Memoirs*, pp. 70, 73–77, 84–85; Suvenirov, "Narkomat oborony i NKVD"; Knight, *KGB*, pp. 249–275; Brzezinski, *Political Controls*, pp. 54–83.

92 For numbers on the shortfall in the officer corps, see the work of Roger Reese, cited above. See also: "O rabote za 1939 god"; F. B. Komal, "Voyennye kadry nakanune voyny," *VIZh*, No. 2, 1990, 21–28. On the other points in this paragraph, see RGVA, f. 4, op. 18, d. 54, ll. 92–93; Yakunov, "Stalin i krasnaya armiya," 170–173; RGVA, f. 4, op. 14, d. 2020, ll. 152–153; Skvirskiy, "V predvoyennye gody," 59; Zhukov, *Vospominaniya i rasmyshleniya*, Vol. I, p. 240; Seweryn Bialer, ed., *Stalin and His Generals: Soviet Military Memoirs of World War II* (New York: Pegasus, 1969), pp. 84–86.

maintain normal professional contacts due to the fear that a colleague might be denounced as an enemy of the people, making one guilty by association. The carrying out of one's professional duties was also fraught with danger. Grigorenko relates how he was accused of "wrecking" by an inspector of the Minsk fortified area who used incorrect procedures to check installations for their ability to resist a chemical weapons attack. The inspector, not Grigorenko, was arrested when it was revealed that he had made a mistake in his inspection. Colonel General A. T. Stuchenko tells the classic story of the arrest of Army Commander I. I. Vatsetis, a military specialist who was a leading lecturer at the Frunze Academy. During the break between a two-part lecture, the class commissar announced, "Comrades! The lecture will not continue. Lecturer Vatsetis has been arrested as an enemy of the people." Such an environment was hardly conducive to either effective military training or the building of esprit de corps within the officer corps.[93]

There were clearly, then, serious corporate interest motives that could have provoked a military intervention during Stalin's terror. Yet no coup attempt took place. In addition to the structural obstacles mentioned, the apolitical organizational culture nullified the rational corporate motives. The officer corps was focused on professional issues and endeavored to minimize nondefense tasks (such as collectivization or internal repression). Military specialists from the old regime helped instill the notion that the military should be "outside politics." Although the party leadership undertook serious efforts to weed out such views, it is clear from NKVD and PUR reports that they persisted into the 1930s. The bulk of the available evidence suggests a strong commitment to a norm of civilian supremacy among the Soviet officer corps in the 1930s.

Given the combination of structural barriers to intervention and the lack of a praetorian organizational culture, resistance to the purges by officers came only in the form of individual or small-group response. Future World War II heroes such as Zhukov and Marshal I. S. Konev (a Corps Commander in 1937–1938) were among those officers who defended their colleagues accused of being enemies of the people. Konev even attracted the attention of the head of PUR at the time, L. Z. Mekhlis, who denounced him to Stalin and Beria in December 1938. Mekhlis wrote that Konev "acted against the unmasking and arrest of counter-revolutionary elements" and noted that Konev had defended Uborevich at a party conference in the Belorussian Military District after Uborevich's execution. Officer memoirs note instances of officers defending colleagues from attacks against them, and the historian

---

[93] Zhukov, *Vospominaniya i rasmyshleniya*, Vol. I, pp. 229–230, 234, 246; RGVA, f. 4, op. 18, d. 54; RGVA, f. 4, op. 14, d. 2020; RGVA, f. 4, op. 18, d. 47; Grigorenko, *Memoirs*, pp. 74–84, 88, 91; Bialer, *Stalin and his Generals*, pp. 65–83; Edmund Iodkovskiy, interview with Lieutenant-General N. G. Pavlenko, "Istoriya voyna eshche ne napisana," *Ogonyek*, No. 25, 1989, 7.

Oleg Suvenirov has uncovered dozens of examples of the resistance of military personnel to the purges.[94]

Resistance obviously was not the only strategy available for trying to survive the purges. Timothy Colton and other analysts have highlighted three basic strategies: withdrawal, offense, and active defense (resistance). Withdrawal involved the attempt to "hide" as much as possible from the surrounding purge process, while an offensive strategy consisted of denouncing others in either a sincere attempt to uncover enemies or a cynical attempt to save one's skin. Both Colton and the major Russian expert on the purges, Oleg Khlevnyuk, conclude that withdrawal was the most common strategy adopted.[95]

A necessary corollary of the purges, and the offensive strategy of denunciation, was that many people moved up in status very quickly. The phenomenon of captains commanding divisions and junior lieutenants in charge of battalions has already been discussed. For those benefiting from the purge, there was an element of self-interest in *not* resisting the purges, but riding the wave and seeing how high it would take you. This strategy, of course, was risky, but it is another part of the explanation of why there was not more resistance to the purges.[96]

One final reason why some officers did not resist the purges, of course, is that they *believed* that the country and the armed forces were full of enemies of the people. How widespread these beliefs were is difficult to say. There is plenty of testimony from people who believed in the presence of enemies, those who doubted such stories, and those who were confused and did not know what to think. Grigorenko states that at the time he believed that most of those accused were enemies of the people; by 1938, however, he had learned of the use of torture and forced confessions. Zhukov, on the other hand, had doubts about many of the cases when people were accused of being enemies, and he states flatly that "no one" believed the accusation that the commander of the Belorussian Military District after Uborevich, Commander First Rank Belov, was an enemy (Belov was shot in 1938).

[94] RGVA, f. 9, op. 29, d. 405, ll. 4–8; Zhukov, *Vospominaniya i rasmyshleniya*, I, pp. 233–236; Grigorenko, *Memoirs*, 88–90; Bialer, *Stalin and his Generals*, p. 81; Suvenirov, "Za chest' i dostoinstvo"; Oleg Suvenirov, "Protiv repressiy v krasnoy armii (1937–1940 gody)," *Kommunist*, No. 17, 1990, 67–75; Colton, *Commissars, Commanders*, pp. 147–150; Skvirskiy, "V predvoyennye gody," 62–63.

[95] Colton, *Commissars, Commanders*, pp. 144–150; Khlevnyuk, *1937-y*, p. 153.

[96] Stalin, Voroshilov, and the rest of the leadership made a virtual fetish out of the process of promoting younger cadres in 1937–1938, thereby making a virtue out of necessity. The party and military archives for this period are replete with references to the need to promote younger, "faithful to the Motherland and the Lenin–Stalin Party" cadres. See, for example, RGVA, f. 4, op. 15, d. 13, ll. 231–237. See also Colton, *Commissars, Commanders*, pp. 150–151; Reese, *Stalin's Reluctant Soldiers*, pp. 147–158; Sheila Fitzpatrick, *The Cultural Front: Power and Culture in Revolutionary Russia* (Ithaca, NY: Cornell University Press, 1992), pp. 11–15, 141–182.

Stuchenko also states his doubts about many of the accusations. To the extent that there were officers who sincerely believed that the armed forces had been infiltrated by enemies of the people, though, this both abetted Stalin's purge and made resistance more difficult. Moreover, some of those who did not believe in the widespread presence of enemies in the country still believed that Stalin himself was not aware of NKVD excesses in carrying out the purges.[97]

CONCLUSION

This chapter has examined Soviet civil–military relations during the first two and a half decades of Soviet rule. This period was a time of flux in civil–military relations. There were significant continuities from the Imperial army and state, as well as substantially new elements of both military organizational culture and state structure and performance.

During this period the armed forces did not play a role in sovereign power politics. The most startling case of military inactivity was the Great Purges, during which clear corporate motives existed for military intervention. I have argued that a combination of reasons explains this behavior. The officer corps had a relatively high commitment to a norm of civilian supremacy, due to both (a) influences from the Tsarist army, transmitted by military specialists, and (b) political indoctrination by the new regime. Even if there had been a more praetorian culture, however, a military coup would have been extremely difficult because of the power of the Stalinist state and its organizational control mechanisms. The one organization in society that had the best chance of resisting the Great Terror had neither the desire nor the opportunity to take up arms against Stalin.

[97] Grigorenko, *Memoirs*, pp. 76, 85; Zhukov, *Vospominaniya i rasmyshleniya*, Vol. I, pp. 230–232, 239; Bialer, ed., *Stalin and his Generals*, p. 82; Khlevnyuk, *1937-y*, pp. 207–216.

5

From Victory to Stagnation, 1945–1985

The victory over Nazi Germany was the crowning achievement of the Soviet state in its seventy-four years of existence. This chapter examines civil–military relations in the period from the military victory in the Great Patriotic War to the rise to power of Mikhail Gorbachev in 1985. The war established the Soviet Union as a global superpower, and the victory helped legitimize Soviet rule in a way that more than twenty years of "building socialism" had been unable to do. The four major theories – domestic structure, organizational structure, corporate interest, and organizational culture – all predict that the military was unlikely to be involved in sovereign power issues. Opportunities for intervention were low because the domestic political order was fairly solid and multiple military and security bodies existed capable of counterbalancing each other. There also were few motives for intervention for most of this period, because the army's corporate interests generally were respected by the post-Stalin leadership and the officer corps remained attached to an apolitical organizational culture.

This chapter investigates five sovereign power episodes in the postwar period, first in the Khrushchev era and then in the period from Brezhnev to Gorbachev (see Table 5.1). In the Khrushchev period there was one instance of military arbitration due to disputes in the political leadership. The army also played an implementation role in one power struggle, but under strict party control and not as an independent actor. The armed forces never sought an expanded political role; and aside from these two episodes, they played no role in resolving the sovereign power issues that arose.

SOVEREIGN POWER ISSUES DURING THE KHRUSHCHEV ERA

Stalin made clear after the war that the system he had built would not be changed. The revolutionary phase of Stalinism that predominated in the 1930s

TABLE 5.1. *Chapter Summary*

	Opportunity		Motive		
Observations	Domestic Structure	Organizational Structure	Corporate Interest	Organizational Culture	Outcome
The Arrest of Beria	Intervention unlikely.	Intervention unlikely.	Intervention unlikely.	Intervention unlikely.	No intervention.
Khrushchev and the "Anti-Party Group"	Intervention or arbitration unlikely.	Intervention unlikely. If arbitration, counterbalancing likely.	Intervention unlikely. If arbitration, will side with contender most likely to promote corporate interests.	Intervention unlikely. If arbitration, first choice is neutrality and second choice is side with most legitimate contender.	Arbitration. Side with contender most likely to promote corporate interests.
The Zhukov Affair	Intervention unlikely.	Intervention unlikely.	Intervention unlikely.	Intervention unlikely.	No intervention.
The Fall of Khrushchev	Intervention unlikely.	Intervention unlikely.	Intervention likely.	Intervention unlikely.	No intervention.
The Andropov, Chernenko, and Gorbachev Successions	Intervention unlikely.	Intervention unlikely.	Intervention unlikely.	Intervention unlikely.	No intervention.

came to an end, and the postwar Soviet state was marked by highly conservative tendencies. Stalin preserved all of the most important aspects of the system: personal dictatorship, mass terror, a powerful police state, and a secondary role for the Communist Party. If terror never again achieved the levels of 1937–1938, the smaller purges carried out by Stalin in the postwar period were an obvious reminder of the previous terror and served to stifle any oppositionist tendencies within either the regime or society at large. Several leading officers were removed in the "mini-purges" of the postwar period, including the commanders of the Air Force (Alexander Novikov) and Navy (Nikolay Kuznetsov). Marshal Zhukov, the most prominent of Stalin's World War II generals, was also demoted and disgraced. Stalin went to great lengths to demonstrate that the military's achievements in the Second World War did not warrant a larger political role for the armed forces. Moreover, Stalin's authority was extremely high and there were no civil–military conflicts of significant magnitude that an intervention in sovereign power issues was likely or feasible. The post-Stalin transition, however, opened up several opportunities for greater military involvement in high politics.[1]

This section discusses four such episodes during the years 1953–1964. These four incidents are: the arrest of Beria (1953), Khrushchev's struggle with the so-called anti-party group (1957), The Zhukov affair (1957), and the fall of Khrushchev (1964). The armed forces were a significant player in most of these events, but in none of these cases did the army show an interest in acquiring political leadership in the state. The army played a role due to the reliance of the party leadership, particularly Khrushchev, on military support during key crises. He turned to the army for help in the arrest of Beria and also received support from Zhukov in the conflict with the anti-party group. Khrushchev was quick to cut the military back down to size by summarily dismissing Zhukov as defense minister four months later. Despite severe disagreements over military policy in the intervening years, the armed forces were not involved in planning the ouster of Khrushchev in 1964 and chose to remain aloof from the entire affair.

---

[1] The best discussion of the postwar Stalinist political order is Seweryn Bialer, *Stalin's Successors: Leadership, Stability, and Change in the Soviet Union* (Cambridge, England: Cambridge University Press, 1980), pp. 9–27. On the "mini-purges" and Zhukov, see Richard Woff, "Stalin's Ghosts," in Harold Shukman, ed., *Stalin's Generals* (New York: Grove Press, 1993), p. 367; John Erickson, "Novikov," in Shukman, *Stalin's Generals*, pp. 173–174; Geoffrey Jukes, "Kuznetsov," in Shukman, *Stalin's Generals*, p. 114; Vladimir Karpov, "Rasprava Stalina nad Marshalom Zhukovym," *Vestnik PVO*, Nos. 7–8, 1992, 62–75; I. S. Konev, *Zapiski komanduyushchego frontom* (Moskva: voyennoye izdatel'stvo, 1991), pp. 594–597; G. N. Pavlenko, "Razmyshleniya o sud'be polkovodtsa," *Voyenno-istoricheskiy zhurnal* [hereafter *VIZh*], No. 12, 1988, 29–32; William J. Spahr, *Zhukov: The Rise and Fall of a Great Captain* (Novato, CA: Presidio Press, 1993), pp. 200–202.

The Arrest of Beria, 1953

Stalin's death in March 1953 touched off a power struggle at the top of the Soviet leadership. The three major players were: Georgiy Malenkov, the Chair of the Council of Ministers; Lavrentii Beria, a Vice-Chair of the Council of Ministers and the head of the Ministry of Internal Affairs (MVD); and Nikita Khrushchev, the senior member of the Central Committee Secretariat. The first round of the power struggle ended with Beria's arrest in June 1953. He was executed in December 1953.[2]

Khrushchev was the key organizer of the arrest of Beria. The arrest was a difficult undertaking because of Beria's position as head of the MVD, which combined the functions of the interior ministry and the secret police. Beria controlled political surveillance, Kremlin security, and two MVD divisions in Moscow. Khrushchev turned to a group of military officers to carry out the mission, and units of the Moscow Military District were mobilized to prevent pro-Beria actions by MVD troops. This is the only known instance of counterbalancing in Soviet history, and there is no evidence that MVD troops tried to mobilize.

The role of the military in Beria's arrest, then, was crucial. Strobe Talbott, the editor of Khrushchev's memoirs, argued that "it is likely that some of the marshals . . . were far more active in the preliminary plotting than is suggested here [by Khrushchev]." Amy Knight, using recent revelations from the Soviet press, also maintains that military support was the key to Khrushchev's victory. She contends that the military "demanded a tougher line" in foreign policy in return for their support, and that "a say in party politics . . . was the quid pro quo exacted from Khrushchev by the generals in return for their support."[3]

The available evidence, however, shows no military involvement in planning Beria's arrest; their role was one of implementation. Moreover, there is no evidence that the military asked for policy changes or a greater political role in return for their support. In fact, the available testimony makes clear that the officers involved, with the possible exception of Zhukov, had no idea what their mission was until the morning of the arrest. These officers responded to a direct order from the party and government leadership to carry out the arrest – no bargaining was involved. Despite the army's key role, then, this case is coded as an instance of noninvolvement because the

---

[2] For overviews, see William J. Tompson, *Khrushchev: A Political Life* (New York: St. Martin's Press, 1995), pp. 114–142; Amy Knight, *Beria: Stalin's First Lieutenant* (Princeton, NJ: Princeton University Press, 1993), pp. 176–224; Dmitriy Volkogonov, *Sem' vozhdey*, Vol. I (Moskva: Novosti, 1996), pp. 343–358; V. P. Naumov, "Byl li zagovor Berii?", *Novaya i noveyshaya istoriya*, No. 5, 1998, 17–39; Yu. V. Aksyutin and A. V. Pyzhikov, *Poststalinskoye obshchestvo: problema liderstva i transformatsiya vlasti* (Moskva: Nauchnaya Kniga, 1999), pp. 21–55.

[3] Nikita Khrushchev, *Khrushchev Remembers* (Boston: Little, Brown and Company, 1970), pp. 321–322; Knight, *Beria*, pp. 196, 211.

military simply carried out the orders of the political leadership. A review of the relevant events demonstrates that the military was not involved in organizing Beria's arrest.

The most important task for Khrushchev was to get Malenkov, a perceived ally of Beria's, on his side. According to Khrushchev, over a period of time he was able to convince Malenkov that Beria was dangerous and had to be removed from power. Khrushchev also had the support of Nikolay Bulganin, the Minister of Defense. Bulganin was a career party official and a former political officer; he was not a professional soldier. Khrushchev and Malenkov then enlisted the support of Vyacheslav Molotov, who was a Vice-Chair of the Council of Ministers and highly influential. Eventually Khrushchev gained the support of a majority of the members of the Communist Party Presidium (the name at the time for the Politburo).[4]

The arrest of Beria was complicated by the fact that he was in charge of Kremlin security and two MVD divisions in Moscow. For this reason, Khrushchev turned to several military officers to carry out the arrest. The head of the Moscow Military District, Colonel-General P. A. Artem'ev, had been an interior ministry commander before the war and was potentially an ally of Beria. Bulganin arranged for Artem'ev to be sent to Smolensk to observe exercises. Khrushchev and Bulganin turned to General K. S. Moskalenko, commander of Moscow's Air Defense Forces (PVO), to carry out the arrest.[5]

Khrushchev called Moskalenko at 9 A.M. on June 26th, the day of the scheduled Presidium meeting at which Beria was to be arrested. Moskalenko was told to prepare a group of loyal officers for a special mission. He chose four officers either currently or previously under his command in the Moscow PVO. Bulganin called Moskalenko and told him to bring this group, armed, to the Ministry of Defense. Moskalenko saw Bulganin alone and was told that they were to arrest Beria at the Kremlin. According to Moskalenko, he and Bulganin decided to add Zhukov and several other officers to the group because it was too small.[6]

Several versions exist of Zhukov's role in the plot to arrest Beria. These accounts differ somewhat in terms of the details of Zhukov's involvement: whether he became involved the day of or the day before the operation, whether he was contacted by Khrushchev, Khrushchev and Malenkov, or Bulganin, whether he knew what his mission was before he arrived at the

[4] *Khrushchev Remembers*, pp. 322–335; F. Chuyev, *Sto sorok besed s Molotovym: Iz dnevnika F. Chuyeva* (Moskva: Terra, 1991), pp. 343–346; Knight, *Beria*, pp. 194–196.

[5] A. Antonov-Ovseenko, "Ka'era Palacha," in V. F. Nekrasov, ed., *Beriya: konets kar'ery* (Moskva: Politizdat, 1991), p. 133; Anatoliy Sul'yanov, *Arestovat' v Kremle: O zhizni i smerti marshala Beriya: Povest'* (Minsk: MP "Slavyane," 1991), pp. 306–307.

[6] K. S. Moskalenko, "Kak byl arestovan Beriya," *Moskovskie novosti*, June 10, 1990, 8; Nekrasov, *Beriya*, pp. 283–289; *Khrushchev Remembers*, p. 336; N. S. Khrushchev, "Aktsiya," in Nekrasov, *Beriya*, p. 277.

Kremlin, and so on. All of these versions, however, agree on one key point: that Zhukov played no role in preparing the plot against Beria, but merely carried out the will of the political leadership.[7]

The designated group of officers proceeded to the Kremlin in Bulganin's car and one separate car. They went in Bulganin's car because as a member of the Presidium, his car was not required to stop when going into the Kremlin, and at that time officers had to give up their weapons upon entering the Kremlin. Bulganin took them into a waiting room adjacent to where the Presidium meeting was to take place. Khrushchev and Bulganin (and perhaps Malenkov and Molotov) came in to tell the group their mission. It was explained to the officers that they were to wait outside the Presidium meeting until they received a signal from Malenkov to come in and arrest Beria. According to Moskalenko and Colonel I. G. Zub, another participating officer, not all members of the Presidium had been informed of the manner of Beria's arrest and they were startled when the officers came in. The officers arrested Beria without much difficulty.[8]

The officers had to wait until that night to remove Beria from the Kremlin. A group of PVO officers was brought in to replace the Kremlin guard. Units of the Moscow PVO and the Kantemirov and Taman divisions were mobilized to prevent MVD armed units from supporting Beria. Beria was detained by Moskalenko and eventually transferred to an underground military bunker, where he was held until his trial and execution in December 1953.[9]

The arrest of Beria represented the greatest military involvement in a sovereign power issue in Russia since the civil war. The incident, however, does not demonstrate any praetorian ambitions on the part of the Soviet military. All of the eyewitness accounts agree that the officers involved in the arrest of Beria played a purely operational role. The armed forces were not involved in the plot, which was organized by Khrushchev and other Presidium members.

---

[7] Vasiliy Sokolov, "Slovo o marshale Zhukove," in S. S. Smirnov et al., *Marshal Zhukov: Kakim my ego pomnim* (Moskva: Politizdat, 1988), pp. 247–250; V. I. Semin, "Vstrecha zemlyakov," in A. D. Mirkina and B. S. Yarovikov, eds., *Marshal Zhukov: Polkovodets i chelovek*, Vol. II (Moskva: Novosti, 1988), pp. 43–46; F. Burlatskiy, "Khrushchev. Shtrikhi k politicheskomu portretu," in Yu. V. Aksyutin, ed., *Nikita Sergeevich Khrushchev: Materialy k biografii* (Moskva: Politizdat, 1989), p. 14; Pavel Sudoplatov and Anatoli Sudoplatov, *Special Tasks: The Memoirs of an Unwanted Witness – A Soviet Spymaster* (Boston: Little, Brown and Company, 1994), p. 371; Naumov, "Byl li zagovor Berii?," 27–28, 30.

[8] Captain S. Bystrov, "Zadanie osobogo svoystva," *Krasnaya zvezda* [hereafter *KZ*], March 18–20, 1988. See also the accounts of Khrushchev, Moskalenko, Zhukov, and Molotov cited above.

[9] Knight, *Beria*, pp. 198–201; Bystrov, "Zadanie osobogo svoystva"; Moskalenko, "Kak byl arestovan Beriya"; Roy Medvedev, *N. S. Khrushchev: Politicheskaya biografiya* (Moskva: "Kniga," 1990), pp. 71–72; A. Skorokhodov, "Kak nas 'gotovili na voynu' s Beriey," in Nekrasov, *Beriya*, pp. 289–295.

The handful of officers involved in the arrest had every reason to see the order as a legitimate one handed down by the party and the government. Moskalenko states that because he had orders from Khrushchev and Bulganin, he believed it was sanctioned by the Communist Party, its Central Committee, and its Presidium. Moskalenko had never met Beria and had no reason to dislike him personally. Zub also claims that he was only fulfilling his military duty.[10]

Knight attributes military participation partially to "the long-standing animosity between the military and the police." There was indeed considerable hostility toward the secret police on the part of the armed forces due to the purges and police interference in military affairs during World War II. Zhukov maintained that he blamed Beria for the plots against him in the postwar period. Even if this was a motive for Zhukov, however, it could not have been for the other officers, who had little time to think about their orders before they were called on to implement them. Once inside the Kremlin, moreover, they knew that if they failed they would be arrested or killed by Beria's Kremlin guards.[11]

Additional evidence that the military was not a major player in the planning of the Beria arrest, and that they had made no political demands in return for their support, is found in the transcript of the July 1953 Central Committee Meeting at which Beria's arrest was sanctioned. No professional officers (there were twenty-eight in the Central Committee) were invited to speak. Military matters were mentioned by only one speaker, Defense Minister Bulganin, who argued that the MVD should be "demilitarized" and made a purely civilian ministry. This issue received one paragraph in a printed transcript that runs to 142 pages. It was not mentioned in the formal Central Committee resolution on Beria. The resolution and the Plenum focused on Beria's domestic and foreign policy positions, his alleged personal vices, and his purported intent to seize power. The one signal of party gratitude to the army was Zhukov's promotion from candidate to full Central Committee member. If the military had been a key player, one would have expected a higher profile position at the Plenum.[12]

Thus, there is no basis for concluding from the arrest of Beria that the military was an influential independent actor in sovereign power issues. The role

[10] Moskalenko, "Kak byl arestovan Beria"; Bystrov, "Zadanie osobogo svoystva"; Volkogonov, *Sem' vozhdey*, Vol. I, p. 356.

[11] Knight, *Beria*, p. 196; Sokolov, "Slovo o Marshale Zhukove"; Burlatskiy, "Khrushchev," 14; Bystrov, "Zadanie osobogo svoystva."

[12] "Plenum TsK KPSS: iyul' 1953 goda: stenograficheskiy otchet," *Izvestiya TsK KPSS*, Nos. 1–2, 1991. Sergey Khrushchev, Nikita Khrushchev's son, also contends that there was no bargaining over the military's role in the arrest of Beria: Author's interview, February 2000. The data on military Central Committee membership are from: Timothy J. Colton, *Commissars, Commanders, and Civilian Authority: The Structure of Soviet Military Politics* (Cambridge, MA: Harvard University Press, 1979), p. 27.

of the armed forces was crucial in the affair, but strictly as an implementer of a party decision. The arrest of Beria was not a case of military intervention or military arbitration. The military acted at the behest of the legitimate party leadership, and Beria never claimed to be the legitimate executive leader in the state. The Soviet military saluted and followed orders when commanded to arrest Beria.

Khrushchev and the "Anti-Party Group"

The power struggle at the top of the Presidium did not end with the arrest of Beria. Malenkov was forced to resign as Premier in early 1955. Unhappiness with Khrushchev's growing power and opposition to some of his policies, however, led to an attempt to remove him in June 1957 by the so-called anti-party group headed by Malenkov, Molotov, and Lazar Kaganovich. Zhukov helped Khrushchev defeat the anti-party group, and he became the first professional soldier in Soviet history to serve as a full member of the Politburo. Zhukov's rise was short-lived, however, and he was removed from the Presidium (Politburo) and dismissed as Defense Minister four months later, in October 1957 (the so-called Zhukov affair, which will be discussed next).

The anti-party group made its move against Khrushchev at a June 18, 1957 Presidium meeting.[13] Malenkov, Molotov, and Kaganovich had planned carefully for the attempt to oust Khrushchev, lining up a majority of seven of eleven Presidium members behind them. They proposed that Khrushchev be removed from the chair and replaced by Bulganin, the Chair of the Council of Ministers. They attempted to remove Khrushchev as Party First Secretary. However, three members of the Presidium were absent, as well as two candidate Presidium members, and Khrushchev argued that it was necessary for all Presidium and Secretariat members to be present for a decision to be made.

The Presidium and Secretariat met again on June 19, with all members present. The anti-party group still had a majority of the Presidium (seven vs. four), but they were a minority of all of those present (eight vs. twelve) because Khrushchev had the support of most candidate Presidium and Secretariat members. Khrushchev and his allies argued that only the Central

---

[13] The most valuable source is the complete transcript of the June 1957 Central Committee Plenum: "Poslednyaya 'antipartiynaya gruppa'," *Istoricheskiy arkhiv*, Nos. 3–6, 1993, and Nos. 1–2, 1994 [hereafter cited as "Poslednyaya . . . ," with the issue and page number]. For summaries, see N. Barsukov, "Proval 'antipartiynoy gruppy'," *Kommunist*, No. 8, 1990, 98–108; Tompson, *Khrushchev*, pp. 178–183; Sergey Khrushchev, *Nikita Khrushchev: Krizisy i rakety*, Vol. I (Moskva: Novosti, 1994), pp. 306–319. For the losing side's perspective, see Lazar Moiseyevich Kaganovich, *Pamyatnye zapiski* (Moskva: Vagrius, 1996), pp. 510–524. Apparently, there is no stenogram of the crucial Presidium meetings that took place June 18–21: Volkogonov, *Sem' vozhdey*, Vol. I, p. 437.

Committee (CC) could remove the Party First Secretary. The Presidium continued to meet for four days, until June 21. A CC meeting was forced by the arrival at the Kremlin of a group of twenty CC members demanding that the Presidium call a Plenum. The anti-party group was forced to relent and the matter went to the full CC, which fully supported Khrushchev.

The pressure of Central Committee members on the Presidium played a decisive role in Khrushchev's victory. Several CC members argued at the Plenum that they had become aware that the Presidium had been meeting for several days and that Khrushchev had been deprived of the chair, and thus they spontaneously organized themselves.[14] Even if this explanation is true for those CC members working in Moscow, it does not explain the arrival in Moscow of CC members from all over the country. Khrushchev had used his control over the party apparatus, the KGB, and the armed forces to organize the arrival in Moscow of Central Committee members. Marshal Zhukov, the Minister of Defense and a Candidate Presidium member, organized the dispatch of Air Force planes to fly some CC members to Moscow. Molotov particularly highlights the role of CC Secretary Suslov and KGB head Serov and their control of the technical apparatus in calling CC members to Moscow.[15]

The arrival of the delegation of Central Committee members at the Presidium meeting on June 21 caused a stormy reaction by the anti-party group. Presidium member Saburov, one of the anti-party group, reportedly exclaimed that tanks had been sent to surround them. The fact that Marshal I. S. Konev was one of the CC members who arrived at the Presidium meeting to request a Plenum certainly contributed to the impression that the army had been called out in support of Khrushchev. CC Secretary A. B. Aristov said that when the names of officers were mentioned as part of the delegation, "a quick transformation of several comrades from lions to rabbits took place. I saw how the faces of Malenkov, Kaganovich, and [Presidium candidate member] Shepilov changed."[16]

The exact role Zhukov played in Khrushchev's victory remains unclear. There is no doubt that he sided with Khrushchev from the beginning, and that some CC members arrived in Moscow on Air Force planes. There is some evidence that he played an even larger role by threatening in the Presidium to call on the army if it tried to remove Khrushchev, but this point remains in dispute. According to some accounts, Zhukov said, "the army is against this decision, and not one tank will move from its place without my order." Other

---

[14] One speaker making this claim was Marshal Konev, who argued that Zhukov's absence from the Ministry of Defense for four days naturally raised questions: "Poslednyaya...," No. 4, 1993, 52. See also the comments of Dmitriy Ustinov: "Poslednyaya...," No. 6, 1993, 33.

[15] Chuyev, *Sto sorok besed*, pp. 354–355; Kaganovich, *Pamyatnye zapiski*, p. 521; Khrushchev, *Nikita Khrushchev*, Vol. I, pp. 310–313.

[16] This incident is mentioned by many of the speakers, including Khrushchev, Zhukov, Saburov, Shepilov, Aristov, Kapitonov, Ignatov, and Konev: "Poslednyaya...," No. 3, 1993, 12, 14, 58; No. 4, 1993, 17, 60; No. 5, 1993, 20, 72–73.

accounts say that Zhukov said he would appeal to "the army and people" and that they would support him. Zhukov claims he said he would appeal to party organs in the army and tell them what was happening. Zhukov also maintains he made this statement on June 18; none of the other accounts is specific about the date.[17]

Other accounts, however, directly or indirectly challenge the claim that Zhukov threatened to call on the army. Neither Kaganovich nor Molotov mentions this seemingly critical incident in their versions of these events. Anastas Mikoyan, a full Presidium member, denies that Zhukov made any such statement to the Presidium, suggesting that Zhukov later bragged about it to inflate his role. Mikoyan contends that what Zhukov actually said to the Presidium was that no tanks would move without his order, in response to Saburov's outburst that tanks had been sent to surround them. According to Mikoyan, then, Zhukov was not threatening to call out the army in defense of Khrushchev, but denying that such a thing had happened. This is also the version reported by Viktor Grishin (a Central Committee member at the time) and Khrushchev's son, Sergey Khrushchev, who denies that Zhukov threatened to call out tanks or that either side would have thought of appealing to the army to solve an intraparty dispute.[18]

Whether Zhukov's behavior during the showdown with the anti-party group warrants the label "military arbitration" is thus not obvious. I have chosen to code the case this way because, at a minimum, Zhukov's decision to provide material support to Khrushchev by flying CC members to Moscow helped tip the scales. Both sides of the dispute thought Zhukov was a key figure in the events. The anti-party group had sounded out Zhukov's position before the Presidium meeting, with both Kaganovich and Malenkov hinting to Zhukov that he could become a full Presidium member if he supported them. Many of the speakers suggest that the key institutions over which the struggle ensued were, in order of importance, the First Secretary position and the CC Secretariat, the KGB, and the Armed Forces. Zhukov and Khrushchev both later pointed to the importance of Zhukov securing the army's support for Khrushchev.[19]

---

[17] Burlatskiy, "Khrushchev," p. 15; "Khrushchev protiv Zhukova," *Glasnost*, October 3, 10, 17, 1991; Petro G. Grigorenko, *Memoirs* (New York: W. W. Norton, 1982), p. 224.

[18] Kaganovich, *Pamyatnye zapiski*, pp. 510–524; Chuyev, *Sto sorok besed*, pp. 354–355; Tsentr khraneniya sovremennoy dokumentatsii [hereafter TsKhSD], f. 2, op. 1, d. 269, l. 56; V. V. Grishin, *Ot Khrushcheva do Gorbacheva: Politicheskiye portrety pyati gensekov i A. N. Kosygina* (Moskva: Aspol, 1996), pp. 23–24; Khrushchev, *Nikita Khrushchev*, Vol. I, pp. 308–309; Author's interview with Sergey Khrushchev. I thank Mark Kramer for making a copy of the Zhukov Affair Plenum stenogram available to me.

[19] "Poslednyaya...," No. 3, 1993, 53; No. 4, 1993, 31, 58; No. 5, 1993, 33, 38, 71; No. 6, 1993, 6; A. D. Mirkina, "Ne skloniv golovy," in Mirkina and Yarovikov, *Marshal Zhukov*, Vol. II, p. 70; N. K. Khrushchev, *Khrushchev Remembers: The Last Testament* (Boston: Little, Brown and Company, 1974), p. 14.

It is clearly the case that Zhukov's stance in June 1957 was crucial to Khrushchev's victory. How the role of the armed forces as an institution should be evaluated, however, is less straightforward. Could Zhukov have called out the army in support of Khrushchev? The dissident General Petro Grigorenko maintains that the army would not have followed Zhukov. On the other hand, several military members of the CC may have participated in the so-called group of twenty that arrived at the Presidium to demand a Plenum. Only the participation of Marshal Konev is clearly indicated in the transcripts of the June 1957 Plenum, but Marshal Moskalenko and several others also may have been present. It is quite possible that Zhukov encouraged their actions, although no references to discussions within the Ministry of Defense during the crisis were made at a meeting of military party members in the Moscow area on July 2.[20]

An important motivation for Zhukov's pro-Khrushchev stance was the issue of the mass repressions in the army organized by Stalin and unmasked by Khrushchev in his "secret speech" at the Twentieth Party Congress in 1956. Zhukov raised the issue of the responsibility of Molotov, Malenkov, and Kaganovich for the Great Purges, particularly in the armed forces, in both the Presidium and at the Plenum. Zhukov personally had been threatened by Molotov, both during the war and in the postwar period, and Molotov had been the most active opponent of destalinization. Khrushchev had succeeded in covering up his involvement in the purges (by having documents destroyed) and gaining credit for the "secret speech" and destalinization, even though he was heavily involved in the Great Purges and Malenkov and others had supported the destalinization campaign. Zhukov also had information that Malenkov had continued to use the secret police to spy on the top military leadership after Stalin's death. He evidently feared a return to repressions in the army if the "anti-party group" were victorious.[21]

The Zhukov Affair

Does Zhukov's stance in June 1957 demonstrate a praetorian mood in the Soviet armed forces? The strongest evidence that Zhukov's behavior did not reflect a greater desire for political power on the part of the military is the fact that four months later Zhukov was removed as Defense Minister and tossed out of the Presidium, with no opposition from the armed forces.

[20] Grigorenko, *Memoirs*, p. 224; Tsentralnyy arkhiv Ministerstva Oborony [hereafter TsAMO], f. 32, op. 701323c, d. 38, especially l. 52 (Volkogonov Archive, Harvard University); Poslednyaya...," No. 4, 1993, 60.

[21] "Poslednyaya...," No. 3, 1993, 13–20; No. 4, 1993, 52–54, 57; TsaMO, f. 32, op. 701323c, d. 38, ll. 10–11, 13–18, 52, 56, 86; K. M. Simonov, "Zametki k biografii G. K. Zhukova," *VIZh*, No. 10, 1987, 57; Vladimir Naumov, "'Utverdit' dokladchikom tovarishcha Khrushcheva'," *Moskovskiye novosti*, February 4, 1996, 34; Aksyutin and Pyzhikov, *Poststalinskoye obshchestvo*, pp. 91–139.

Neither Zhukov nor any other member of the military leadership made any effort to mobilize army support for Zhukov; his standing in the Politburo clearly was dependent on Khrushchev's continuing good will. A brief review of this episode demonstrates the subservience of the military to party rule.

On October 5, 1957, Zhukov left Moscow for a three-week visit to Yugoslavia and Albania. In his absence a campaign was launched to remove him. On October 19 the Presidium met to discuss "party-political work in the Armed Forces," and a report was presented by General A. S. Zheltov, the head of the Main Political Administration (MPA), the Communist Party organization in the armed forces. On October 22–23 a meeting of party members of the Moscow garrison and Ministry of Defense was held at which Zheltov and Khrushchev both gave reports attacking Zhukov. Similar meetings were held in military districts around the country. On October 26, Zhukov returned to Moscow and was taken immediately to a Presidium meeting, at which he was removed as Minister of Defense. On October 28–29 the Central Committee met and dismissed Zhukov from the Presidium and the Central Committee.[22]

There were a host of accusations against Zhukov, including weakening Communist Party control over the military, creating a Zhukov "cult of personality" in the army, and, most seriously, trying to acquire unlimited political power and of "Bonapartism." Khrushchev told the October CC Plenum, "in Zhukov's understanding there is no place for the party . . . he was counting on the power of the army. . . . This is nothing other than a military dictatorship, a military junta." Khrushchev was even more direct in his memoirs, stating that "Zhukov was striving to seize control . . . we were heading for a coup d'etat. . . . We couldn't let Zhukov stage a South American-style military takeover in our country."[23]

Other speakers echoed Khrushchev's claim about the political danger Zhukov represented. Presidium member Mikhail Suslov noted the impermissibility in a socialist state of a "general on a white horse 'saving' the country." General M. V. Zakharov accused Zhukov of "Napoleonic aspirations" and "Bonapartism."[24]

---

[22] The most important source on Zhukov's removal is the transcript of the October 1957 CC Plenum: TsKhSD, f. 2, op. 1, d. 261, 266, 268, 269. Key excerpts were published as "Khrushchev protiv Zhukova," *Glasnost*, October 3, 10, 17, 1991 [cited hereafter as *Glasnost* with the appropriate date]. Also useful are Vladimir Karpov, "Taynaya rasprava nad marshalom Zhukovym," *Pravda*, August 17 and 19, 1991; Khruschev, *Nikita Khrushchev*, Vol. I, pp. 325-334. For English-language accounts, see: Spahr, *Zhukov*, pp. 235-252; Colton, *Commissars, Commanders*, pp. 175-195.

[23] *Glasnost*, October 3, 1991, 7; TsKhSD, f. 2, op. 1, d. 269, l. 73; Khrushchev, *Last Testament*, pp. 14-17.

[24] TsKhSD, f. 2, op. 1, d. 269, l. 9; TsKhSD, f. 2, op. 1, d. 268, ll. 73-74. See also TsKhSD, f. 2, op. 1, d. 268, l. 18; TsKhSD, f. 2, op. 1, d. 269, l. 56.

Khrushchev also claims that Moskalenko accused Zhukov of planning to seize power. According to Khrushchev, Zhukov replied, "How can you accuse me? You yourself told me many times, 'Take power in your own hands. Just take it! Take power!'" Khrushchev states that he believed Zhukov that Moskalenko had said this. He contends that no action was taken against Moskalenko because of his assistance in the arrest of Beria in 1953. Sergey Khrushchev and Viktor Grishin also believe this story. Sergey Khrushchev maintains that no action was taken against Moskalenko because he was known as a sycophant, who was quite capable of trying to suck up to Zhukov by telling him to take power and then turning around and accusing Zhukov of planning a coup to please Khrushchev.[25]

Still, it is hard to believe that Moskalenko would be allowed to remain the commander of the crucial Moscow Military District until 1960 if he had stated praetorian tendencies. He was later appointed head of the Strategic Rocket Forces. Moreover, as the Russian military historian V. A. Anfilov points out, Zhukov had nothing bad to say about Moskalenko in his memoirs; in fact, he said good things about Moskalenko.[26] Zhukov presumably would have been more critical of Moskalenko if Moskalenko had accused him of planning a military coup in October 1957. Regardless, there is no evidence that, if Moskalenko did make such a statement to Zhukov, that Zhukov took the suggestion seriously.

No evidence that Zhukov had any intention of trying to seize power was presented at the October Plenum. The best piece of evidence that Khrushchev could produce for the alleged plot was that Zhukov had taken steps to set up a central school for special forces (Spetsnaz) and had informed only two other officers, without acquiring CC approval. Khrushchev said accusingly, "Beria also had his group of commandos." In fact, every Military District had established Spetsnaz companies. Zhukov argued he simply was trying to create a better training method for the special forces, maintaining that he did not consider this a new question that needed party approval. Moreover, it is untrue that only Zhukov and two other officers knew of the existence of the school; plans for establishing the school were conducted through regular Ministry of Defense channels.[27]

The fact that Zhukov was not trying to seize power also is evident from how he was treated at the time. Zhukov was not arrested, reduced in rank, or dismissed from the party. After Khrushchev's removal from power

[25] N. K. Khrushchev, *Khrushchev Remembers: The Glasnost Tapes* (Boston: Little, Brown and Company, 1990), pp. 62–63, n. 8; Khrushchev, *Nikita Khrushchev*, Vol. I, pp. 329–330; Author's interview with Sergey Khrushchev; Grishin, *Ot Khrushcheva do Gorbacheva*, p. 24.
[26] V. A. Anfilov, "N. S. Khrushchev: 'Sam ya ne slyshal, no mne govoril...'," *VIZh*, No. 4, 1994, 89.
[27] *Glasnost*, October 3, 10, and 17; S. Khrushchev, *Nikita Khrushchev*, Vol. I, pp. 328–333; Karpov, "Taynaya rasprava"; Leonid Mlechin, *Predsedateli KGB: Rassekrechennye sud'by* (Moskva: Tsentrpoligraf, 1999), pp. 414–415.

in 1964 the accusations of "Bonapartism" against Zhukov were dropped. Recent archival revelations show that Zhukov remained distressed for years about this accusation. In private conversations with his wife, reported to Khrushchev by the KGB, Zhukov said he "couldn't make peace" with the allegation. "What facts are there? None," Zhukov complained. "If I had been trying to seize power," he noted, "why wasn't I arrested?"[28]

Although there is no evidence that Zhukov had any intention or desire to seize power, he apparently was trying to reduce party influence over the army and increase military autonomy. The danger of a weakening of Communist Party control over the armed forces was a constant refrain at the October 1957 Plenum. Zhukov had proposed downgrading the status of Military Soviets, joint army-party bodies established at multiple levels to resolve mutual problems. Allegedly he had also sought to have army generals placed in charge of the KGB and the MVD, presumably to reduce secret service influence over the armed forces. Khrushchev stated at the Plenum that Zhukov was trying to create a situation in which "military communists would have contact with the party only through him."[29]

There also was a real clash between the MPA and the professional officer corps, and Zhukov in particular. Zheltov, the head of the MPA, took advantage of Zhukov's absence in October to discuss with the political leadership his objections to how Zhukov was conducting party-political work. Khrushchev called a Presidium meeting (on October 19) at which Zheltov outlined his objections to how the MPA was treated. Marshals Konev and Malinovskiy were asked to attend the Presidium meeting and give their reaction; they argued that Zheltov was settling a personal score with Zhukov. Allegedly other Presidium members suggested that members of the party leadership be sent to investigate the question at the local level, which led to the series of meetings held immediately prior to Zhukov's dismissal.[30]

Zhukov's statement at the October 1957 Plenum demonstrated that his views on army-party relations were out of step with those of the party leadership. Zhukov admitted that he underrated the role of the political organs and overrated the role of commanders. He argued that he believed that commanders should also lead political work, because almost all professional officers were by this point educated, committed communists. He noted that many of them held positions in party bodies at the appropriate level. Zhukov said, "these commanders should now be looked at in a different light than they were 20–25 years ago." In other words, the need for political commissars overseeing the work of professional officers had diminished since the early days of the Soviet state. Although he still saw a role for party bodies in

---

[28] Colton, *Commissars, Commanders*, pp. 178–184; "G. K. Zhukov: neizvestnye stranitsy biografii," *Voyennye arkhivy rossii*, Vol. I, 1993, pp. 237–238.

[29] TsKhSD, f. 2, op. 1, d. 269, ll. 5, 9, 33, 55 73; TsKhSD, f. 2, op. 1, d. 266, ll. 81–82.

[30] For Zheltov's account, see Captain S. Bystrov, "V oktyabre 1957-go," *KZ*, May 21, 1989, 4.

the armed forces, it is clear that Zhukov wished to change substantially the nature of the relationship between the MPA and the regular army.[31]

There were, then, real policy differences behind Zhukov's dismissal. As Zhukov remarked later, he was not entirely innocent in his dismissal – "there is no smoke without fire." Most of the policy differences, however, were not new, and were used primarily as pretexts for Zhukov's dismissal. The most likely reason for the sacking was the fear of Khrushchev and other Presidium members that Zhukov, with all his popularity and prestige, had been allowed to become too powerful.[32]

This fear of Zhukov on the part of Khrushchev and other members of the political leadership was rooted in the struggle with the anti-party group in June 1957. Sergey Khrushchev contends that there was a direct link between the June and October events, and that in the absence of the earlier crisis the political differences with Zhukov would have been handled differently. "Recent events," he continues, "willy-nilly made [my father] cautious." Zhukov's role during the intraparty struggle, and his alleged statements after the crisis about threatening to appeal to the army and people, led Nikita Khrushchev to cut the army back down to size. Zhukov later argued that he was dismissed by Khrushchev because Khrushchev feared competition. Zhukov said:

There was a moment when he staggered, and I secured for him the support of the army. At the time he sincerely thanked me, but he drew completely opposite conclusions: what if I suddenly wished to sit in his place? . . . Wrongly! I never wanted state power – I'm a soldier, and the army is my concern.[33]

Other members of the political leadership also distrusted and feared Zhukov. Allegedly some Presidium members would look to Zhukov to see how he was voting when they were not certain of how to vote. At the October Plenum, Zhukov commented that he was surprised to learn that other members of the Presidium were alarmed because of his character and authority, that they were afraid of him and did not trust him. Zhukov's bearing was intimidating, and his rudeness and conceitedness were remarked on by many of his colleagues. Zhukov apparently remained proud until the end. He later told former comrades, "all this could have been managed differently if I could have bowed down low enough, but I couldn't bow down. And why

---

[31] *Glasnost*, October 10, 1991, 6–7.

[32] Roman Kolkowicz, then, was partially correct that a conflict between the party, particularly the MPA, and the army played a role in Zhukov's dismissal. Timothy Colton, however, is also correct in seeing the allegation about Zhukov's underappreciation of political work as a pretext, with other motives being more important. See Roman Kolkowicz, *The Soviet Military and the Communist Party* (Princeton, NJ: Princeton University Press, 1967), pp. 113–135; Colton, *Commissars, Commanders*, pp. 175–195. For the Zhukov quote, see: Simonov, "Zametki k biografii," *VIZh*, No. 12, 1987, 46.

[33] Khrushchev, *Nikita Khrushchev*, Vol. I, pp. 325, 330; Mirkina, "Ne skloniv golovy," p. 70.

should I bow? I don't feel guilty of anything that I should have had to beg for."[34]

Recent revelations about the Zhukov affair strongly confirm earlier conclusions that Zhukov himself had no designs on power, and that his dismissal was rooted in a combination of defense politics, personality clashes, and timing. Neither in June nor October 1957 did the Soviet army demonstrate praetorian ambitions.

The Fall of Khrushchev, 1964

Khrushchev clashed seriously with the military leadership during his rule, particularly in the later years. In 1960 he announced plans to reduce the armed forces by more than one million men, including 250,000 officers. Recent archival evidence shows how Khrushchev ran roughshod over military concerns and interests with these cuts. Khrushchev also pushed a "single-variant" military doctrine that placed almost exclusive reliance on nuclear missiles, significantly downgrading the importance of the army, navy, and air force. In August 1964 Khrushchev eliminated the ground forces' separate command structure and subordinated it directly to the General Staff. Prominent marshals were dismissed at various points during these political battles, such as Chief of the General Staff V. D. Sokolovskiy (1960), First Deputy Minister of Defense I. S. Konev (1960), and Chief of the General Staff M. V. Zakharov (1963).[35]

These well-documented civil–military fights have led to speculation that the military played an important role in Khrushchev's ouster in October 1964.[36] In fact, evidence that has come to light in recent years demonstrates convincingly that the army was not a major player in Khrushchev's ouster. Indeed, even though a group within the Presidium had been planning to

---

[34] Karpov, "Taynaya rasprava," *Pravda*, August 17, 1991, 4; *Glasnost*, October 10 and 17, 1991; Pavlenko, "Razmyshleniya," *VIZh*, No. 12, 1988, 34–35; Burlatskiy, "Khrushchev," p. 16; Colton, *Commissars, Commanders*, pp. 187–188; "G. K. Zhukov," 233.

[35] Matthew Evangelista, *Unarmed Forces: The Transnational Movement to End the Cold War* (Ithaca, NY: Cornell University Press, 1999), pp. 90–122; Vladislav M. Zubok, "Khrushchev's 1960 Troop Cut: New Russian Evidence," *Cold War International History Project Bulletin*, Issues 8–9 (1996/1997), 416–420; Khrushchev, *Nikita Khrushchev*, Vol. II, pp. 422–429; Victor Gobarev, "Khrushchev and the Military: Historical and Psychological Analyses," *Journal of Slavic Military Studies*, 11, 3 (1998), 141–142; Kolkowicz, *Soviet Military*; Edward L. Warner, III, *The Military in Contemporary Soviet Politics: An Institutional Analysis* (New York: Praeger Publishers, 1977), pp. 99–100, 137–146; Thomas M. Nichols, *The Sacred Cause: Civil–Military Conflict Over Soviet National Security, 1917–1992* (Ithaca, NY: Cornell University Press, 1993), pp. 57–90; Dale R. Herspring, *The Soviet High Command, 1967–1989: Personalities and Politics* (Princeton, NJ: Princeton University Press, 1990), pp. 32–40.

[36] Kolkowicz, *Soviet Military*, pp. 151, 289–300; Herspring, *Soviet High Command*, p. 36; Nichols, *Sacred Cause*, p. 84.

topple Khrushchev since the spring of 1964, apparently the military high command was not notified until several days before the plot was carried out.[37]

The persons responsible for initiating the effort were Leonid Brezhnev and Nikolay Podgornyy, who both held senior leadership positions and were considered by Khrushchev as possible successors. Brezhnev and Podgornyy carefully lined up support among other members of the Presidium, the Secretariat, and the Central Committee. It was particularly important that they attract to their side A. N. Shelepin, a key CC Secretary, and V. E. Semichastnyy, the head of the KGB. With Shelepin and Semichastnyy on their side they could be fairly confident that word of their plotting would not get back to Khrushchev. Brezhnev worked his way through a list of CC members, carefully sounding out them or their associates, putting a plus or minus next to each name.[38]

The armed forces leadership played a completely passive role. The Minister of Defense, Malinovskiy, was, according to Semichastnyy, notified only two days before the Presidium meeting at which Khrushchev was ousted. According to Petr Shelest, the Ukrainian Party Secretary and a Presidium member, Malinovskiy told the group of plotters that the military was "outside politics" and would support neither side. First Deputy Minister of Defense Marshal A. A. Grechko allegedly "became very frightened" when told of the plot by Brezhnev and avoided giving any direct answer about his stance. Neither Malinovskiy nor any other officer sat on the Presidium, and no officers were present at the key Presidium meeting of October 12 at which the conspirators got formal support for the removal of Khrushchev. The commander of the Moscow Military District also had not been informed, but KGB special departments in the district had orders to report to Semichastnyy any suspicious troop movements.[39]

Khrushchev was called back to Moscow from holiday on October 13 by the rest of the Presidium and was formally removed by a CC Plenum

[37] The most important sources are "Zapisi V. Malina na zasedanii Prezidiuma TsK KPSS," *Vestnik Arkhiva Prezidenta Rossiyskoy Federatsii*, No. 2, 1998, 125–135; "Kak snimali N. S. Khrushcheva: Materialy plenuma TsK KPSS. Oktyabr' 1964 g.," *Istoricheskiy arkhiv*, No. 2, 1993, 3–19; Sergey Khrushchev, *Khrushchev on Khrushchev: An Inside Account of the Man and His Era* (Boston, MA: Little, Brown, and Company, 1990), pp. 45–162; Khrushchev, *Nikita Khrushchev*, Vol. II, pp. 470–509; V. I. Semichasntyy [head of the KGB in 1964], interview, "Kak smeshchali N. S. Khrushcheva," *Argumenty i fakty*," May 20, 1989, 5–6. For recent summaries, see: Aksyutin and Pyzhikov, *Poststalinskoye obshchestvo*, pp. 315–373; Tompson, *Khrushchev*, pp. 268–277; Volkogonov, *Sem' vozhdey*, Vol. I, pp. 441–446.

[38] Aksyutin and Pyzhikov, *Poststalinskoye obshchestvo*, pp. 316–320; Tompson, *Khrushchev*, p. 268; Khrushchev, *Khrushchev on Khrushchev*, pp. 45–47, 68–70, 82; Semichastny, "Kak smeshchali N. S. Khrushcheva."

[39] Aksyutin and Pyzhikov, *Poststalinskoye obshchestvo*, p. 349; "Kak snimali N. S. Khrushcheva," 3; Khrushchev, *Khrushchev on Khrushchev*, p. 136; Tompson, *Khrushchev*, pp. 270–271; "Zapisi V. Malina."

on October 14, 1964. Khrushchev had alienated almost all major sectors of the Soviet political elite by this time. Most of the criticism leveled at Khrushchev by other Presidium members had to do with his imperious and rude leadership style and policies that threatened the interest of party officials, the most important constituency in the CC. Brezhnev's speech to the CC on October 14 attacked Khrushchev's "rude violation of Leninist norms of party leadership" and his policies in the spheres of agriculture and local party organization. Brezhnev did not mention defense policy once in the entire speech. William Tompson notes, "remarkably little attention was paid to the complaints of the military, which further confirms the belief that the armed forces were not involved in the plot."[40]

The fall of Khrushchev is a case of military nonintervention. Although there were two contenders for supreme executive power at the time (Khrushchev, and the Presidium and Central Committee majority behind Brezhnev and Podgornyy), neither side appealed to the army for support. The army remained completely neutral and let the Communist Party decide the matter. The stance taken by the armed forces leadership shows that they had no desire or inclination to become involved in sovereign power disputes.

The Soviet military's passive role in the ouster of Nikita Khrushchev suggests that corporate motives alone are not a sufficient cause of military intervention. Khrushchev directly and increasingly attacked the military's prerogatives in the last years of his rule, but the armed forces did not participate in the extensive conspiracy to overthrow him and stated that the army would not become involved when it finally was informed of the plot. A rational bureaucratic actor would have been willing, even eager, to join the anti-Khrushchev group. The military's passive stance in October 1964 further strengthens the viewpoint that Zhukov's key influence in June 1957 derived from his personal standing in the party leadership, and not from any institutionally powerful role for the Soviet armed forces.

SOVEREIGN POWER ISSUES FROM BREZHNEV TO GORBACHEV

It has become commonplace to refer to the Brezhnev era, in a phrase coined by Jeremy Azrael, as the "golden age" of Soviet civil–military relations. Leonid Brezhnev's reign as General Secretary of the Communist Party from 1964 until 1982 is seen as a period in which the armed forces were granted most of their wishes and in which there was extraordinary harmony between the military and civilian leaderships.[41]

---

[40] "Kak snimali N. S. Khrushcheva," 6–15; Tompson, *Khrushchev*, pp. 257–277 (quote, p. 272); N. A. Barsukov, "Oktyabr' 64-go," *Svobodnaya mysl'*, No. 10, 1994, 24–27.

[41] Jeremy R. Azrael, *The Soviet Civilian Leadership and the Military High Command, 1976–1986*, R-3521-AF (Santa Monica, CA: Rand Corporation, June 1987).

What accounts for this "golden age"? Two very different interpretations have been provided. One approach stresses either "congruent values" (William Odom) or "compatible objectives and crosscutting interests" (Timothy Colton) between the military and party leadership. An alternative view, put forward by Thomas Nichols, is that the "golden age" came about due to the abdication of civilian control – the political leadership simply chose not to challenge a politically powerful military.[42]

This debate cannot be resolved here. Indeed, it is somewhat tangential to the main thrust of this book, which focuses on military participation in sovereign power issues. Discussions about the reasons for the "golden age" revolve around issues of defense policy. Moreover, even in the realm of defense policy, the entire Brezhnev period was not one of civil–military harmony. Azrael's original piece on the topic restricted the term "golden age" to the first ten years of the Brezhnev leadership. Azrael and others have demonstrated growing civil–military conflict in the late 1970s and early 1980s. These conflicts took place over such major defense policy issues as arms control, the defense budget, military doctrine, the Ministry of Defense leadership, weapons procurement, and Afghanistan. The military failed to carry the day in many of these disputes, several of which will be discussed below.[43]

The one defense policy issue that often is depicted as bearing directly on sovereign power issues is the firing of Chief of the General Staff Marshal Nikolay Ogarkov in 1984. Ogarkov had been involved in a multiyear dispute with the civilian leadership about the scale of the Soviet military effort. Many Western commentators attribute his eventual dismissal to

---

[42] William E. Odom, "The Party–Military Connection: A Critique," in Dale R. Herspring and Ivan Volgyes, eds., *Civil–Military Relations in Communist Systems* (Boulder, CO: Westview Press, 1978), pp. 27–52; Colton, *Commissars, Commanders,* especially pp. 279–281; Timothy J. Colton, "The Party–Military Connection: A Participatory Model," in Herspring and Volgyes, *Civil–Military Relations,* pp. 53–75; Nichols, *Sacred Cause,* pp. 90–129.

[43] Some of the more important works on these questions, in addition to the previously cited work by Azrael, Colton, Herspring, Kolkowicz, Nichols, and Odom, are Evangelista, *Unarmed Forces*; Timothy J. Colton and Thane Gustafson, eds., *Soldiers and the Soviet State* (Princeton, NJ: Princeton University Press, 1990); Stephen M. Meyer, "The Political Power of the Soviet Military Establishment," Occasional Paper No. 15 (Tokyo: Research Institute for Peace and Security, 1989); Condoleezza Rice, "The Party, the Military, and Decision Authority in the Soviet Union," *World Politics,* 40 (1987), 55–81; Jiri Valenta and William Potter, eds., *Soviet Decision-Making for National Security* (London: Allen & Unwin, 1984); David Holloway, *The Soviet Union and the Arms Race* (New Haven, CT: Yale University Press, 1983); Abraham S. Becker, *Sitting on Bayonets: The Soviet Defense Burden and the Slowdown of Soviet Defense Spending,* JRS-01 (Santa Monica, CA: RAND/UCLA Center for the Study of Soviet International Behavior, 1985); Kimberly Marten Zisk, *Engaging the Enemy: Organizational Theory and Soviet Military Innovation, 1955–1991* (Princeton, NJ: Princeton University Press, 1993); Andrew Bennett, *Condemned to Repetition?: The Rise, Fall, and Reprise of Soviet-Russian Military Interventionism, 1973–1996* (Cambridge, MA: MIT Press, 1999).

the coming succession struggle related to the serious illnesses of General Secretary Konstantin Chernenko and Minister of Defense Dmitriy Ustinov. These analysts argue that Ogarkov would have been the major candidate for Defense Minister upon Ustinov's death, and thus would be in a strong position to influence the post-Chernenko succession, because since 1973 the Defense Minister had been a member of the Politburo and it would be hard to deny Ogarkov this post. Thus, it is suggested, Ogarkov had to be dismissed.[44]

New evidence suggests a different explanation for Ogarkov's dismissal as Chief of the General Staff. Former Politburo member Vitaliy Vorotnikov has recounted how Ogarkov came to speak with him after Ustinov had recommended transferring Ogarkov to the head of the Western TVD (theater command) at a meeting of the Defense Council. The Defense Council was chaired by the General Secretary and was the Politburo's top advisory body on defense issues. Ogarkov told Vorotnikov that he and Ustinov had clashed for many years over various questions of military policy, including military development, tactics, procurement, and social support for officers and soldiers. Ogarkov added that Ustinov did not like his directness and authority. Ogarkov also met with Mikhail Gorbachev, another Politburo member, to voice his complaints. He wished to meet with General Secretary Chernenko, but Vorotnikov told him that this would serve no purpose because of Chernenko's closeness to Ustinov. The influential chair of the Council of Ministers, Nikolay Tikhonov, raised the possibility of keeping Ogarkov as Chief of the General Staff at a Politburo meeting, and he was supported by Vorotnikov and Gorbachev. But Chernenko looked at Ustinov, who reiterated the need to shift Ogarkov to a new post, and, according to Vorotnikov, "that was that."[45]

In Vorotnikov's view, Ogarkov's dismissal arose purely due to a conflict between Ogarkov and Ustinov. His account does not suggest that Ogarkov was seen as a growing political threat, and the political leadership certainly was not unanimous in seeking his removal. Rather, other Politburo members were willing to defer to Ustinov's judgment on a matter directly under his supervision. The uniformed military was in no way involved and was powerless to protect Ogarkov in a matter that fell under the party leadership's authority. Vorotnikov's description of the Ogarkov incident is consistent with other reports that suggest that Ustinov and Ogarkov often clashed over defense policy, particularly procurement issues. Ustinov was a civilian party official with a long background in the military–industrial sector, and

[44] Azrael, *Soviet Civilian Leadership*, pp. 10–37; Nichols, *Sacred Cause*, pp. 119–124; Herspring, *Soviet High Command*, pp. 119–214; Bruce Parrott, "Political Change and Civil–Military Relations," in Colton and Gustafson, *Soldiers and the Soviet State*, pp. 62–75.

[45] V. I. Vorotnikov, *A bylo eto tak . . . : Iz dnevnika chlena Politbyuro TsK KPSS* (Moskva: Sovet veteranov knigoizdaniya, SI-MAYA, 1995), pp. 45–48.

his institutional loyalties were to the party and military industry, not the officer corps.[46]

It is crucial to bear this point in mind when discussing the post-Brezhnev successions. Ustinov was an influential member of the Politburo when Yuriy Andropov became General Secretary in November 1982 and when Chernenko became General Secretary in February 1984. Ustinov had been a candidate member of the Politburo since 1965 and a full member since 1976, which made him one of the longest-serving Politburo members. Ustinov certainly played an important role in the Andropov and Chernenko successions. But he did so as a leading member of the Politburo, and not as Defense Minister. In particular, Ustinov did not have a "military vote" in succession decisions, especially because he represented the views of the party leadership and not the uniformed military.[47]

By the time of Brezhnev's death the succession procedure had become somewhat institutionalized. The recent memoir literature agrees that Andropov and Chernenko acceded to the head of the party without much difficulty. Both Andropov and Chernenko were the head of the Secretariat and the second person in the party behind the General Secretary prior to their respective successions. Their elevation to the top job was therefore to be expected, barring unforeseen contingencies. Andropov's alleged attempt before his death to leapfrog Gorbachev over Chernenko into the number two

---

[46] Georgi Arbatov, the former director of the USA–Canada Institute, asserts that "Ustinov...matched Brezhnev in his sycophancy toward the military. It seemed as if he were trying to prove that a civilian minister could get even more for the military than a professional officer could." Georgi Arbatov, *The System: An Insider's Life in Soviet Politics* (New York: Times Book/Random House, 1993), p. 195. However, recent evidence makes it clear that the military–industrial sector, and not the armed forces, dominated the so-called military–industrial complex. See Peter Almquist, "Soviet Military Acquisition: From a Sellers' Market to a Buyers'?," in Susan L. Clark, ed., *Soviet Military Policy in a Changing World* (Boulder, CO: Westview Press, 1991), pp. 133–151; Peter Almquist, *Red Forge: Soviet Military Industry Since 1965* (New York: Columbia University Press, 1990), pp. 110–112, 126–131; Matthew Partan, "Who Controlled the Former-Soviet Military Industry?," *Soviet Defense Notes*, 4, 1 (1992), 1–5.

[47] On Ustinov, the military, and the post-Brezhnev successions, see Parrott, "Political Change and Civil-Military Relations," 69–75, 90–91; Amy Knight, "The KGB and Civil–Military Relations," in Colton and Gustafson, *Soldiers and the Soviet State*, pp. 104–107. Arbatov suggests that Ustinov played the key role in choosing Chernenko as the successor to Andropov, and he contends that Ustinov was so powerful because "he had many military divisions at his disposal." Arbatov, *The System*, p. 278. This view is problematic for four reasons. First, with the exception of the incidents under Khrushchev discussed above (the arrest of Beria and perhaps the June 1957 Plenum), the threat or use of force was never raised in Soviet succession struggles. Second, as mentioned, Ustinov did not represent the professional military. Third, as I discuss next, the post-Brezhnev successions took place in a much more straightforward manner than implied by Arbatov's reference to "military divisions." Fourth, according to Gorbachev, Ustinov thought Gorbachev, not Chernenko, should be named General Secretary after Andropov's death: Mikhail Gorbachev, *Zhizn' i reformy*, Vol. I (Moskva: Novosti, 1995), pp. 248–249.

spot was no more successful than that of any previous Soviet leader to anoint his successor without broader agreement in the Politburo. Other Politburo and Secretariat members at the time agree that the Gorbachev faction was too weak in 1984 to challenge Chernenko.[48]

It also was expected that the new General Secretary would put forward a candidate for the second position in the party soon after taking power. The so-called "second secretary" chaired the Secretariat's meetings and also chaired the Politburo in the absence of the General Secretary. Andropov put forward Chernenko for second secretary, who at the time was considered the second most authoritative figure in the party and the only possible challenger to Andropov for the top job. Similarly, Chernenko advocated Gorbachev for the second spot, even though he had hitherto shown no noticeable sympathy for Gorbachev. But Gorbachev was an authoritative figure in the party with considerable support, and he was probably the strongest possible competitor to Chernenko for the position of General Secretary in 1984. In both cases it appears that the new general secretary offered an olive branch to the second strongest Politburo faction by appointing the leader of that group to the position of second secretary.

Some of the old guard in the Politburo, however, opposed Gorbachev's elevation to the second position. In particular, Soviet Premier Tikhonov strongly objected. He received the support of Viktor Grishin and Grigoriy Romanov, who saw themselves as contenders for that position. All Politburo members knew that Chernenko was very sick and that therefore whoever became second secretary had a strong chance of succeeding to the top job in the near future. Ustinov supported Chernenko's proposal, and Gorbachev's other supporters also fought back against Tikhonov. In the end, it seems (accounts differ slightly on this point), no firm Politburo decision was made, although Gorbachev de facto became second secretary and moved into the office traditionally reserved for that person. Gorbachev took the chair the first time Chernenko was unable to chair a Politburo meeting. The difficulty that Gorbachev had in winning the second position demonstrates that there was little chance of his claiming the top job in 1984.[49]

---

[48] Gorbachev, *Zhizn' i reformy*, Vol. I, 213–222, 244–252; Vorotnikov, *A bylo eto tak*, p. 37; E. K. Ligachev, *Zagadka Gorbacheva* (Novosibirsk: Sibirskiy tsentr SP "Interbuk", 1992), pp. 27, 57; Nikolay Ryzhkov, *Perestroyka: istoriya predatel'stv* (Moskva: Novosti, 1992), pp. 57–59; Grishin, *Ot Khrushcheva do Gorbacheva*, pp. 69–70; Angus Roxburgh, *The Second Russian Revolution: The Struggle for Power in the Kremlin* (London: BBC Books, 1991), pp. 5–23; Arbatov, *The System*, pp. 278–279; David Remnick, *Lenin's Tomb: The Last Days of the Soviet Empire* (New York: Vintage Books, 1994), pp. 191–192. A good overview of the Andropov, Chernenko, and Gorbachev successions is Archie Brown, *The Gorbachev Factor* (Oxford, England: Oxford University Press, 1996), pp. 53–88.

[49] Gorbachev, *Zhizn' i reformy*, Vol. I, pp. 250–252; Vorotnikov, *A bylo eto tak*, pp. 39–40; Ligachev, *Zagadka Gorbacheva*, p. 27; Ryzhkov, *Perestroyka*, pp. 59–60; Roxburgh, *Second Russian Revolution*, pp. 18–19.

Dmitriy Ustinov died in December 1984. He was replaced as Minister of Defense by Sergey Sokolov, a career officer. Sokolov was not made either a full or candidate member of the Politburo at that time (this shows, incidentally, that Ogarkov's removal was almost certainly not related to apprehension in the Politburo about having to appoint Ogarkov to head the Ministry of Defense and make him a Politburo member in the event of Ustinov's death). Although Ustinov and his predecessor Marshal Grechko had been full Politburo members, the fact that Sokolov did not become even a candidate Politburo member until after Gorbachev's succession confirms that there was no automatic "military slot" in the Politburo.

General Secretary Chernenko died in March 1985, having served in that position for only thirteen months. Memoir accounts differ over whether Gorbachev's victory was a close shave or not, although most accounts contend that Gorbachev's potential opponent Grishin decided in the end that his position was untenable and therefore he offered no opposition. Regardless, the armed forces played absolutely no role in Gorbachev's succession. The decision was made in the Communist Party inner circle, from which they were at the time shut out.[50]

EXPLAINING MILITARY BEHAVIOR IN POSTWAR SOVEREIGN POWER ISSUES

From 1953 to 1985 there were a series of sovereign power issues in Soviet politics in which the armed forces potentially could have intervened. In none of these cases was there military intervention. On one occasion the military played the arbiter role in a party conflict. During Khrushchev's struggle with the anti-party group the Minister of Defense, Marshal Zhukov, played a key role in his capacity as a candidate member of the Presidium. This incident, however, does not indicate a military leadership bent on grabbing for itself a larger role in domestic politics. In all other sovereign power disputes in this period the military played either an implementation role or no role at all.

The low level of military involvement in sovereign power issues in this period is not too surprising, despite the fact that there was considerable speculation by Western experts about the potential threat of the army to civilian rule in the Soviet Union. In fact, for most of the period both the opportunities and motives for intervention were rather low.

[50] For the various memoir accounts, none of which mention the participation of any military personnel in the succession question, see Gorbachev, *Zhizn' i reformy*, Vol. I, pp. 262–272; Ligachev, *Zagadka Gorbacheva*, pp. 57–66; Vorotnikov, *A bylo eto tak...*, pp. 56–59; Ryzhkov, *Perestroyka*, pp. 78–81; Grishin, *Ot Khrushcheva do Gorbacheva*, pp. 70, 305; Roxburgh, *The Second Russian Revolution*, pp. 5–9; "'Nam ne nuzhno menyat' politiku' – zayavil M.S. Gorbachev pri vydvizhenii ego na post General'nogo sekretarya TsK KPSS," *Istochnik*, No. 0/1, 1993, 66–75.

Opportunity: Domestic Structure

The Soviet Union after World War II had a very high degree of political order. The ability of the system to weather the stress of the war and emerge victorious was perhaps the most important source of the regime's legitimacy in the postwar period. The post-Stalin political leadership introduced several important changes in the political system without taking any steps that would endanger Communist Party hegemony. Key changes included the switch from personal dictatorship to oligarchy, the end of mass terror, the reining in of the secret police, and the development of a more regularized bureaucratic structure and decision-making institutions.[51]

Thus, the regime undertook a series of reforms that partially dismantled the Stalinist system and brought about some important improvements in the quality of life for Soviet citizens. Victor Zaslavsky refers to the post-Stalin system as one based on an "organized consensus" in which society accepted the existing political system and the regime granted greater physical and economic security to those who did not challenge it.[52]

One striking aspect of the post-Stalin political system was the domination of the regime by a group of political leaders, such as Nikita Khrushchev and Leonid Brezhnev, who had risen to prominence at a young age due to the opportunities for advancement created by the great purges of 1937–1938. The postwar political elite, unlike the early Bolshevik leaders, had no real desire to change the social structure of the country. They placed their emphasis on maintaining the existing system and preserving strong government and political order. Although there were pressures for reform throughout the period, any changes introduced were limited and carefully controlled. The political leadership was willing to sacrifice economic efficiency for the more important goal of internal stability. The essential conservatism of the post-Stalin leadership meant that more sweeping reform would have to wait until this generation left the political stage. Although the consequences of such a policy in the long run were pernicious, in the short run it guaranteed that the state would remain sufficiently powerful to deter and repress any potential opposition.[53]

The factors discussed here suggest that the Soviet state continued to have a high degree of political capacity in the postwar period. After Stalin, perhaps the state was no longer what Stephen Krasner would call a "dominant state"; there was no revolutionary impulse to remake the social structure of the country. The regime was quite content to ensure, in Bialer's

---

[51] Bialer, *Stalin's Successors*, pp. 30, 45–46, 50–52, 184.

[52] Victor Zaslavsky, *The Neo-Stalinist State: Class, Ethnicity, and Consensus in Soviet Society* (Armonk, NY: Sharpe, 1994 (1982)), pp. 130–164.

[53] Bialer, *Stalin's Successors*, pp. 53–61, 86–126; Robert V. Daniels, "Political Processes and Generational Change," in Archie Brown, ed., *Political Leadership in the Soviet Union* (Bloomington, IN: Indiana University Press, 1989), pp. 96–126.

words, "the indefinite reproduction of the basic existing social relations." In Krasner's classification, the Soviet state from the 1950s to the 1980s was a strong state, able to resist private pressure and change private behavior in intended ways.[54]

In terms of organizational age, however, the Soviet state had an important weakness. By the time of Stalin's death in 1953 the Soviet regime had been in power for thirty-six years. During that period there had been only one leadership succession. The Soviet state had no formal institutional mechanism for choosing a successor to the top leadership position, which introduced an element of instability to an otherwise highly stable political system and also created the possibility either for the military to insert itself into the process or for contending factions to appeal to the armed forces for support. Military intervention or arbitration, then, was a built-in possibility with respect to Soviet sovereign power issues. This was an important change in the political system after Stalin's death.

Despite this weakness of the system, in comparative terms the Soviet political order was highly stable.[55] Thus, a domestic structure perspective on military involvement in sovereign power issues would predict no military intervention in the postwar Soviet period. This approach, then, performs fairly well. The episodes during which the Soviet military became involved in sovereign power issues, once as an arbiter and once as an executor, were due to the absence of an institutionalized mechanism for the transfer of power. However, in neither case did the army try to take advantage of the opportunity presented by this institutional weakness to gain a larger political role, as the domestic structure approach might expect. The army's reluctance to be involved in sovereign power issues was due to other considerations.

Opportunity: Organizational Structure

The Soviet political system had several different power structures that in principle could be called upon to counterbalance one another. The armed forces controlled the greatest amount of military force. The KGB and the MVD, which for almost all of the postwar period were two separate bodies, also had some military forces at their disposal and had responsibility for internal security.

The possibility of direct counterbalancing came about during only one of the postwar sovereign power crises, the arrest of Beria in 1953. As head of the MVD, which at the time was merged with the KGB, Beria controlled both

---

54 Stephen D. Krasner, *Defending the National Interest: Raw Materials Investments and U.S. Foreign Policy* (Princeton, NJ: Princeton University Press, 1978), pp. 54–58; Bialer, *Stalin's Successors*, p. 55.

55 Samuel P. Huntington, *Political Order in Changing Societies* (New Haven, CT: Yale University Press, 1968), especially pp. 78–92.

the Kremlin guards and the Internal Troops. Thus Khrushchev had to call on several top army officers to arrest Beria, and the military played an important role in detaining and trying him as well. There is no evidence, however, that any MVD troops tried to mobilize. In the remaining sovereign power issues in this period there was no counterbalancing, particularly during the anti-party group episode in 1957 and Khrushchev's ouster in 1964.

The KGB had some forces at its disposal for counterbalancing a military coup attempt. The KGB controlled the Kremlin regiment and was responsible for the security of all top party and government figures, including the General Secretary. It does not appear, however, that these KGB troops possessed heavy weaponry such as tanks or armored personnel carriers. The leading Western expert on the KGB, Amy Knight, concluded that these troops probably could not successfully counterbalance the regular army and that the party leadership did not see KGB troops as a deterrent to military intervention.[56]

The Ministry of Internal Affairs (MVD) controlled an armed body known as the Internal Troops (*Vnutrenniye Voyska*, or VV). The Internal Troops in the Soviet period consisted of several hundred thousand personnel, and generally took on the job of suppressing internal resistance to the regime if the use of force was necessary, although the army was occasionally called on for support. William Fuller argues that this was the primary mission of the Internal Troops, and that serving as an armed counterweight to the army was a less important function. Fuller bases this conclusion on the number and type of VV units near Moscow, as well as on an examination of VV functions.[57]

Perhaps more important than counterbalancing was the presence of two organizations capable of monitoring the officer corps, the MPA and the so-called special sections of the KGB. The MPA in theory represented the "eyes and ears" of the Communist Party inside the armed forces. Many professional officers resented the MPA, but after Zhukov's failed attempt to reduce its influence, no efforts were made to touch it until the late-1980s. In many ways the MPA was successfully integrated into the Ministry of Defense, and the monitoring role played by political officers in the early Soviet period lessened, with more emphasis given to maintaining morale and educating the troops in Marxism–Leninism.[58]

The KGB special sections placed officers in the armed forces, and they also had a web of informers throughout the military. Although their main function was military counterintelligence, special section officers

---

[56] Amy W. Knight, *The KGB: Police and Politics in the Soviet Union* (Boston, MA: Unwin Hyman, 1990), pp. 221–227 (especially p. 226), 249; M. S. Dokuchayev, *Moskva. Kreml'. Okhrana.* (Moskva: Bizness-press, 1995), p. 67.

[57] William C. Fuller, Jr., *The Internal Troops of the MVD SSSR*, College Station Papers No. 6 (College Station, TX: Center for Strategic Technology, Texas A & M University, 1983); Knight, *KGB*, p. 226.

[58] Colton, *Commissars, Commanders.*

undoubtedly also monitored the political attitudes of officers. They were believed to be both more independent and more powerful than the MPA political officers. The combination of MPA oversight and KGB monitoring meant that army officers had strong incentives to refrain from sensitive discussions on any political issue, and particularly of course potential plots.[59]

Although each of these structures by itself may not have been sufficient to prevent or deter a coup, the combination of all of them meant that organizational structure barriers to military intervention were rather high in the Soviet Union. The deterrent effect of these bodies was reinforced by, and indeed was an important part of, the high political capacity of the Soviet state in general. Domestic and organizational structure combined made the prospect of military intervention low.

Motives: Corporate Interest

The Soviet armed forces were treated well by the political leadership during most of the post-Stalin period. The degree of government commitment to the military is indicated by the size and economic burden of the Soviet military. The Soviet armed forces in 1985 were the largest in the world (5.3 million), and fifteen to twenty-five percent of Gross National Product was devoted annually to military spending.[60] The one exception to this general picture of government support for the army is the latter half of Khrushchev's rule. During this period, as noted above, Khrushchev clashed with the military over such issues as the size of the armed forces and military doctrine.

The corporate interest perspective, then, would predict the likelihood of military intervention in one period from 1953 to 1985: the early 1960s. In fact, the armed forces leadership played virtually no role in the plot that led to the removal of Khrushchev in 1964. They were informed of the plot almost on the eve of its implementation, and they showed no desire to become involved. The corporate interest approach would predict greater military involvement in Khrushchev's ouster. On the other hand, the general noninvolvement of the army in sovereign power issues in the postwar period can be attributed partially to its satisfaction with its power, resources, and degree of autonomy. Additionally, Zhukov's support for Khrushchev in June 1957 probably was due to his belief that the anti-party group was implicated in the military purges under Stalin and thus were a potential threat to military autonomy.

---

[59] Knight, *KGB*, pp. 249–275; Zbigniew Brzezinski, ed., *Political Controls in the Soviet Army: A Study Based on Reports by Former Soviet Officers* (New York: Research Program on the U.S.S.R., 1954).

[60] *The Military Balance 1985–86* (London: International Institute for Strategic Studies, 1985), p. 21; U.S. Department of Defense, *Soviet Military Power 1990* (Washington, D.C.: U.S. Government Printing Office, 1990), p. 3; James Noren, "The Controversy over Western Measures of Soviet Defense Expenditures," *Post-Soviet Affairs*, 11 (1995), 238–276.

Motives: Organizational Culture

An organizational culture approach is the hardest one to test for this period. The controlled nature of the Soviet political system precluded officer corps statements that would provide a reliable picture of the organization's internal norms about sovereign power issues. Military archives for this period, unlike for the earlier periods studied, remain largely closed. Thus, the conclusions discussed here are highly tentative.

In the previous chapter we saw how the apolitical organizational culture of the late-Imperial officer corps was transmitted to the Red Army. The purges, the war, and the postwar experience under Stalin probably strengthened this apolitical organizational culture. Stalin's efforts to "keep the military in its place" reinforced the institutional lessons the armed forces had learned during the purges. Marshal Zhukov, for example, noted that officers understood that it was dangerous to contradict Stalin on general political questions, because "everyone still remembered the recent past." Assertions that Stalin was incorrect, Zhukov noted, could lead immediately to an invitation to "drink coffee with [secret police chief] Beria."[61] During the war the armed forces learned that the military profited the most when it stayed focused on defense issues under the general guidance of Stalin and the party leadership. After the war was over, Stalin again went to considerable lengths to demonstrate his mastery over the armed forces. All of these episodes probably strengthened the army's commitment to a norm of civilian supremacy.

Communist Party dominance over the military was part of the training of all officers. Many steps were taken to ensure that the principle of civilian and party control embedded in the Constitution and Party Program was transmitted to officers. The Soviet *Officer's Handbook*, for example, stressed, "the decisive role of the supervisory, organizing, and educational activities of the Communist Party in Soviet military development is emphasized in the Program of the CPSU, in resolutions adopted at Party meetings, Plenary meetings of the Central Committee, and other Party Documents." The primacy of the civilian political leadership in determining national security policy and military strategy was taught at the General Staff Academy and other military academies.[62]

Party supervision over the armed forces was quite robust. For example, Marshal Sergey Akhromeyev, the Chief of the General Staff from 1984 to 1988, notes that the Administrative Organs Department of the Central Committee had to sign off on every speech given by the Minister of Defense,

---

[61] Simonov, "Zametki k biografii," *VIZh*, No. 9, 1987, 54.

[62] Major-General S. N. Kozlov, ed., *The Officer's Handbook*, United States Air Force translation (Washington, D.C.: U.S. Government Printing Office, 1971), pp. 4–38, especially p. 5; Ghulam Dastagir Wardak and Graham Hall Turbiville, Jr., *The Voroshilov Lectures: Materials from the Soviet General Staff Academy*, (Washington, D.C.: National Defense University Press, 1989/1990), pp. 58, 61, 406 (Volume I), pp. 27–29 (Volume II).

even if given to a closed military audience. Frequently the CC would make changes in the text with which, Akhromeyev observes, "it was useless to argue."[63]

The extent to which Soviet officers accepted Marxist–Leninist ideology is difficult to know, although General Aleksandr Lebed reports that he and his fellow officers had a lackadaisical attitude toward Marxism–Leninism and party-political work in the army. Regardless, there were few officers who went into open dissent. One general who did challenge the Communist Party was Petro Grigorenko. He eventually was stripped of his rank and party membership, imprisoned, and eventually exiled. Grigorenko never questioned the notion of civilian control or the need for army subordination. He did not seek to organize officers against the Communist Party. When he was called before the party collegium of the Party Control Commission, he wore a civilian suit to underline the fact that he was there as a party member and not as an officer.[64]

The Soviet military's behavior in disputes with the political leadership over defense policy is also illustrative. Although the military was expected to articulate their views on defense policy and had considerable authority in this sphere, the civilian leadership was able to order the military to implement positions with which it disagreed. Civilian supremacy applied both in sovereign power and in defense politics issues.

Khrushchev, as we have seen, was able to impose a series of defense policy decisions extremely disadvantageous to the armed forces. Despite the more harmonious relations under Brezhnev, the political leadership could impose its views on the army when it wanted to. Two examples, arms control policy and the Soviet intervention in Afghanistan, demonstrate military subordination to civilian control.

Arms control is one sphere in which the military leadership occasionally clashed with their civilian counterparts. Minister of Defense Marshal Andrei Grechko believed arms control was a ploy by the United States to gain unilateral advantages. Grechko fought against aspects of SALT I, SALT II, and the ABM Treaty. According to Arkady Shevchenko, a former high-ranking official in the Ministry of Foreign Affairs, "Grechko remained permanently apoplectic during SALT." Grechko was suspicious that Georgiy Korniyenko, the former First Deputy Minister of Foreign Affairs, was an American agent because he was such an advocate of the ABM Treaty. Although the Soviet military's influence in arms control negotiations was very large, Brezhnev

---

[63] S. Akhromeyev and G. Korniyenko, *Glazami marshala i diplomata: kriticheskiy vzglyad po vneshnyuyu politiku SSSR do i posle 1985 goda* (Moskva: "Mezhdunarodnye otnosheniya," 1992), pp. 33–34.

[64] Aleksandr Lebed, *Za derzhavu obidno…* (Moskva: Redaktsiya gazety "Moskovskaya pravda," 1995), pp. 93, 163, 175–176, 182–185, 216, 218–224; Grigorenko, *Memoirs*, pp. 210–212, 258.

and the rest of the Politburo occasionally overrode Grechko's objections and adopted positions opposed by the military.[65]

The military intervention in Afghanistan was one of the most consequential Soviet national security decisions during the Cold War. Georgiy Arbatov, former head of the USA–Canada Institute, claims that "the Ministry of Defense actively supported the intervention." Thomas Nichols endorses Arbatov's view, stating that "the high command and the Party leadership shared the blame for the Afghan decision."[66] In fact, every professional officer consulted on the decision, including General Staff Chief Ogarkov, opposed the intervention. Minister of Defense Dmitriy Ustinov was one of the key party leaders who made the decision, but, as explained above, Ustinov was a career Communist Party official and not a professional officer.

Officer opposition to the intervention in Afghanistan is evident not only from the personal testimony of the officers involved but also civilian participants and archival evidence. In April 1978 the People's Democratic Party of Afghanistan (PDPA) seized power. Although the PDPA received considerable support from the Soviet Union, the Soviet government rebuffed requests for direct military intervention from March 1979 until the decision to intervene in December 1979. Throughout this period, Soviet military officers advised against direct military involvement. Key officers that opposed military intervention included the following: Chief of the General Staff Ogarkov; his first deputy, Akhromeyev; the Chief of the Main Operations Directorate of the General Staff, General V. I. Varennikov; Commander of the Ground Forces, General I. G. Pavlovskiy; and the chief of the military advisory group in Afghanistan, Lieutenant General L. N. Gorelov.[67]

This military opposition was expressed on multiple occasions. In April 1979, Ogarkov advised against sending Soviet helicopter pilots to

---

[65] Arkady N. Shevchenko, *Breaking with Moscow* (New York: Alfred Knopf, 1985), pp. 202–205; Akhromeyev and Korniyenko, *Glazami marshala i diplomata*, p. 41; Arbatov, *The System*, pp. 195–196; Anatoly Dobrynin, *In Confidence: Moscow's Ambassador to America's Six Cold War Presidents (1962–1986)* (New York: Times Books/Random House, 1995), pp. 248, 330, 394; Aleksandr G. Savel'yev and Nikolay N. Detinov, *The Big Five: Arms Control Decision-Making in the Soviet Union* (Westport, CT: Praeger, 1995), pp. 35, 46–47; Raymond L. Garthoff, *Detente and Confrontation: American-Soviet Relations from Nixon to Reagan*, Revised Edition (Washington, D.C.: The Brookings Institution, 1994), pp. 517–518.

[66] Arbatov, *The System*, p. 192; Nichols, *Sacred Cause*, p. 106.

[67] Garthoff, *Detente and Confrontation*, pp. 977–1046; Odd Arne Westad, "*Concerning the Situation in "A": New Russian Evidence on the Soviet Intervention in Afghanistan*," *Cold War International History Project Bulletin*, Issues 8–9 (1996/1997), 128–184; G. N. Sevost'yanov, "Dokumenty sovetskogo rukovodstva o polozhenii v Afganistane. 1979–1980," *Novaya i noveyshaya istoriya*, No. 3, 1996, 91–99; B. V. Gromov, *Ogranichennyy kontingent* (Moskva: Progress, 1994), pp. 17–104; G. M. Korniyenko, "Kak prinimalis' resheniya o vvode sovetskikh voysk v Afganistan i ikh vyvode," *Novaya i noveyshaya istoriya*, No. 3, 1993, 107–112; Akhromeyev and Korniyenko, *Glazami marshala i diplomata*, pp. 162–174; Colonel-General V. A. Merimskiy, "Kabul-Moskva: Voyna po zakazu," *VIZh*, Nos. 10–12, 1993, and No. 1, 1994.

Afghanistan. Pavlovskiy opposed an Afghan request for a brigade of Airborne Forces during a fact-finding mission in August. Most important, when the political leadership decided in early December 1979 to send in Soviet troops, Ogarkov and Varennikov told Brezhnev, Ustinov, Andropov, and Gromyko (the four key decision makers) that military intervention would be a mistake. When Ogarkov told Ustinov that the decision was "reckless," Ustinov retorted, "are you trying to instruct the Politburo? You only have to carry out orders."[68] Ustinov, of course, was right: The armed forces had to carry out orders, and they did so.

Evidence on the organizational culture of the Soviet army in the postwar period is quite limited, because there are few available sources that provide an uncensored look at military organizational culture in the pre-Gorbachev postwar period. The available evidence, combined with the evidence from the previous chapter, suggests that the army maintained a rather strong commitment to a norm of civilian supremacy. Process tracing of key events such as the arrest of Beria, the Zhukov affair, and the fall of Khrushchev seems to reinforce these conclusions and shows the role that officers' beliefs played in their behavior during these episodes. During the arrest of Beria, officers simply carried out party orders and played no independent political role. The accusations of "Bonapartism" leveled against Zhukov in 1957 have been shown to be false. And Defense Minister Malinovskiy told the plotters against Khrushchev in 1964 that the army was "outside politics," the same phrase used by officers in the Imperial Russian army during the Revolution. The one exception in the postwar period was Khrushchev's struggle with the anti-party group in 1957, when Presidium member Zhukov played a key role. However, Zhukov and the armed forces leadership had no intention to act independently against the party.

CONCLUSION

This chapter has examined Soviet civil–military relations in the postwar period, up to Mikhail Gorbachev's rise to power in 1985. The stability of the mature Stalinist and post-Stalinist political system set the foundation for generally trouble-free civil–military relations. On those occasions when the army clashed with the party leadership over defense politics, as in the late-Khrushchev period, this did not lead to military intervention in sovereign power issues. The one episode of military arbitration arose as a result of the weakness of the Soviet succession mechanism and not from a desire by officers to be involved in high politics. In general, both the opportunities and motives for intervention were low. That was considerably less true under Mikhail Gorbachev.

---

[68] Gromov, *Ogranichenniy kontingent,* 78; Sevost'yanov, "Dokumenty sovetskogo rukovodstva," pp. 93–95.

6

Gorbachev, Perestroika, and the Collapse of the Soviet Union, 1985–1991

The sudden and unexpected disintegration of the powerful Soviet empire, even in retrospect, is not easy to understand and explain.[1] The role of the armed forces in this collapse is perhaps the most baffling element. The prominent Sovietologist Jerry Hough wrote in 1992 that he did not think the Soviet Union would fall apart because he assumed that countries do not just collapse unless their army has been destroyed or gravely weakened in war. "It was inconceivable," Hough maintains, that the military would let the Soviet Union collapse "without even being seriously bloodied. Simply inconceivable. I still don't believe it."[2]

The Soviet armed forces were involved in two sovereign power issues at the end of Mikhail Gorbachev's rule: the failed August 1991 hard-liner coup and the collapse of the Soviet Union in December 1991 (see Table 6.1). Several leading officers, including the Minister of Defense, were involved in the August 1991 coup, but key subordinates refused to follow orders and the putsch rapidly collapsed. The army was thrust into the arbiter role in December 1991, but chose not to intervene to prevent the collapse of the Soviet Union.

The effects of Gorbachev's perestroika policies greatly increased both the opportunity and motives for military intervention. The substantial weakening of the political capacity of the Soviet state played a key role in opening up an opportunity for military involvement in sovereign power issues. Under these circumstances the organizational structural barriers set up to inhibit coups, specifically counterbalancing and penetration, were not effective mechanisms to prevent coups. Internal splits in the army may have played an inhibiting role, but the most important cleavages were ideational.

---

[1] For a good, short analysis see Alexander Dallin, "Causes of the Collapse of the USSR," *Post-Soviet Affairs*, 8, 4 (1992), 279–302.
[2] Jerry Hough, "The Fall of Gorbachev," *Politics of Soviet Economic Reform*, 2, 1 (1992), 2.

TABLE 6.1. *Chapter Summary*

Observations	Opportunity		Motive		Outcome
	Domestic Structure	Organizational Structure	Corporate Interest	Organizational Culture	
August 1991 Coup Attempt	Intervention or arbitration likely.	Intervention unlikely.	Intervention likely.	Intervention unlikely.	Intervention.
December 1991 and the Collapse of the USSR	Intervention or arbitration likely.	Intervention unlikely. If arbitration, counterbalancing or internal splits likely.	Intervention likely. If arbitration, will side with contender most likely to promote corporate interests.	Intervention unlikely. If arbitration, first choice is neutrality and second choice is side with most legitimate contender.	Arbitration. Took passive position, supporting the most legitimate contender and allowing the state to collapse.

Gorbachev's domestic and foreign policies substantially threatened the corporate interests of the Soviet military. The failed coup, however, was motivated not by the army's internal problems, but by the threat to the state's territorial integrity brought about by state weakness. The army's core organizational culture remained committed to noninvolvement in sovereign power issues, although there was also a more praetorian subculture. The August 1991 coup, then, was a violation of dominant military norms, although the foot-dragging and half-measures exhibited by key officers did condemn the coup to failure. Military passivity in December 1991 when the Soviet Union collapsed is also partially explained by organizational culture.

The two-step model of military involvement in sovereign power issues helps us understand how factors at different modes and levels of analysis can be combined to explain military behavior. Before investigating the events of late 1991 in detail, I discuss what each of the four approaches would predict for the two cases.

OPPORTUNITIES FOR INTERVENTION

Opportunities for military involvement in sovereign power issues were quite broad by the end of the Gorbachev period. It was the extreme weakness of the Soviet state that led to army participation in domestic political struggles. Counterbalancing and penetration of the armed forces should have made intervention difficult, but in practice these concerns had little effect. Internal splits within the armed forces became more prominent in the late 1980s, but the most significant ones were ideational and not structural.

Domestic Structure and the Gorbachev Revolution

Political order declined significantly during the last years of the Soviet state. Gorbachev's reform efforts, rather than invigorating the decrepit Soviet system, deepened the crisis of the regime. All indicators of state strength and system stability show that the state was very weak and that the military had a clear opportunity to intervene in the last years of the Soviet Union.

Gorbachev's policies of glasnost (openness) and democratization, which opened up the political arena to competition and open debate, were the key steps leading to the weakening of the Soviet state. Alexander Dallin points out that these policies had two devastating effects on regime legitimacy. First, in Dallin's words, the opening of the political system "brought about a remarkable sense of having been lied to." The (many) dark spots of Soviet history were exposed and the Communist Party's claim to universal authority was rendered hollow. Second, glasnost and democratization had an explosive effect on the ethnic republics and national consciousness.[3]

[3] Dallin, "Causes of the Collapse," pp. 296–299.

The declining political capacity of the Soviet regime is demonstrated clearly by many different indicators of state strength. The basic organizational structures of Soviet power were dismantled, political violence and internal conflict increased, and the power of the state was weakened relative to society.

Organizational Age. The state's organizational age formally remained unchanged during this period. The Soviet Union had survived for over seventy years and had gone through eight leadership successions. This provided a certain sense of inertia to Soviet rule. At the same time, Gorbachev's political reforms largely dismantled Communist Party rule, which had formed the basis of the previous political order.

Starting in 1989 the fundamentals of Soviet rule were completely changed. In 1989 a legislature (the Congress of People's Deputies and its sub-body, the Supreme Soviet) based on competitive elections was created. A year later, Article 6 was removed from the Constitution, which had established the "leading and guiding" role of the Communist Party. A Soviet presidency was instituted in March 1990, and Gorbachev had himself elected to the post by the parliament. Further constitutional changes were introduced at the end of 1990, including the creation of the post of vice-president and an increase in the status of the Federation Council (the USSR president and the heads of the fifteen Soviet republics). The rules of the game established over decades of Communist Party rule were upended in the space of a few years. These multiple institutional changes in the Soviet political system led to a serious weakening of the state.[4]

Political Violence. Deaths from political and ethnic violence escalated sharply in the last years of Soviet rule (see Table 6.2). The number of deaths from political and ethnic violence in the last five years of the Soviet states was over 1,200. In contrast, according to a recently declassified KGB report, there were no deaths from political violence between 1968 and 1985. Although unofficial sources report slightly higher numbers, and there was a greater degree of political violence in the late 1950s and early 1960s, the increase under Gorbachev is still striking.[5] The huge increase in political violence in the last

---

[4] Jack F. Matlock, Jr., *Autopsy on an Empire: The American Ambassador's Account of the Collapse of the Soviet Union* (New York: Random House, 1995), pp. 201–226, 288–294, 306–321, 331–337, 359–362, 388–390, 421–434; Archie Brown, *The Gorbachev Factor* (Oxford, England: Oxford University Press, 1996), pp. 155–211.

[5] On the Khrushchev and Brezhnev periods, see "O massovykh Bezporyadkakh s 1957 goda," *Vestnik arkhiva Prezidenta Rossiyskoy Federatsii*, No. 6, 1995, 146–153; V. A. Kozlov, *Massovye besporyadki v SSSR pri Khrushcheve i Brezhneve* (Novosibirsk: Sibirskiy khronograf, 1999). The data for 1986–1991 were compiled by the author from multiple sources: Radio Free Europe/Radio Liberty publications, particularly *Report on the USSR* and *RFE/RL Research Report*; Open Media Research Institute, *Daily Digest*; SIPRI Yearbook; Zvi Gitelman, "The

TABLE 6.2. *Deaths from Political and Ethnic Violence,
Soviet Union, 1986–1991*

1986	1987	1988	1989	1990	1991
2	0	91	200	605	328

Source: See footnote 5.

years of the Soviet state is indicative of a regime that was rapidly losing its ability to demand compliance from its subjects and maintain political order.

Internal Conflict. The sharp decline of the Soviet regime's capacity was evidenced also by the rise of autonomy and independence movements in the republics. A "parade of sovereignties" began during which republican laws were declared preeminent over Union laws and the decisions and instructions of central institutions were ignored by republican governments in the "war of laws." The push for independence was particularly strong in the Baltic states, Moldova, Armenia, and Georgia. Most remarkably, the new political leadership in Russia *de facto* endorsed the claims of the republics against the center by launching its own sovereignty drive and challenging central institutions. The decline in Union legitimacy forced Gorbachev to negotiate a new Union Treaty with the republics that would have granted them sovereign status; the August 1991 coup was launched a day before the treaty's scheduled signing.[6]

Strike activity also increased markedly during the late-Gorbachev years. From the period 1956–1983 there were an average of about four strikes per year, although for obvious reasons this unofficial data may underreport actual strike activity. In contrast, by 1991 there were strikes in over 1,700 enterprises in the Russian Federation alone. Of course, strikes are not *prima facie* political events, but many of these strikes were in fact motivated by ethnic or political demands. The miners' strikes of 1989–1991 played a particularly crucial role in challenging the Soviet political order.[7]

Nationalities," in Stephen White, Alex Pravda, and Zvi Gitelman, eds., *Developments in Soviet Politics* (Durham, NC: Duke University Press, 1990), pp. 137–158; "Chronology of Noteworthy Events," in Edward A. Hewett and Victor H. Winston, eds., *Milestones in Glasnost and Perestroyka: Politics and People* (Washington, D.C.: Brookings Institution, 1991), pp. 499–536; data provided by the Division of Ethnopolitical Research, Analytical Center, Council of the Federation, Russia; and data gathered by the author from the Soviet/Russian press.

[6] Viktor Zaslavsky, "Nationalism and Democratic Transition in Postcommunist Societies," *Daedalus*, 121, 2 (1992), 97–121; Ronald Grigor Suny, *The Revenge of the Past: Nationalism, Revolution, and the Collapse of the Soviet Union* (Stanford, CA: Stanford University Press, 1993), pp. 127–160; Lubomyr Hajda and Mark Beissinger, eds., *The Nationalities Factor in Soviet Politics and Society* (Boulder, CO: Westview Press, 1990); John Dunlop, *The Rise of Russia and the Fall of the Soviet Empire* (Princeton, NJ: Princeton University Press, 1993).

[7] Walter D. Connor, *The Accidental Proletariat: Workers, Politics, and Crisis in Gorbachev's Russia* (Princeton, NJ: Princeton University Press, 1991), pp. 249–257, 271–312; Linda J. Cook, *The*

Strength of the State vis-à-vis Society. By the late-Gorbachev period the government had lost the ability to change private behavior, as the centrally planned economy broke down and the Party's authority to give enforceable directives was removed. The Soviet state did have the ability to resist private pressure, in the sense that state policy had not been hijacked by private actors. But this was largely because the policies of the central government were increasingly irrelevant. There was no point in capturing the state if the state had no power. The state did still have the ability to change the social structure, but again by default: As the state weakened, new actors rushed in to fill the vacuum, in both the economic and political spheres.[8]

These categories also understate the weakness of the Soviet state from 1989 to 1991 because they do not incorporate the federal element. The most important actors undermining the Soviet state were not private but were, instead, the political leadership in the fifteen republics, who refused to follow directives from Moscow or contribute resources to the center, including young men for the draft and payments to the central budget. Gorbachev turned to the right in late 1990 and allied himself with statists and conservatives, including the police and the military, who were willing to use force to enforce central rule. By the spring of 1991, however, it had become clear to Gorbachev that he could not accomplish anything without the support of the republics, and he launched negotiations with republican leaders to reform the union.[9]

All of these factors point to a profound weakening of the state's political capacity in the last years of Soviet rule. The domestic structure perspective predicts that military intervention and arbitration become likely when the state is weak and the opportunity for intervention rises.

Organizational Structure

The Soviet state had at its disposal, at least on paper, considerable forces available for penetrating and counterbalancing the armed forces. Indeed,

---

Soviet Social Contract and Why It Failed: Welfare Policy and Workers' Politics from Brezhnev to Yeltsin (Cambridge, MA: Harvard University Press, 1993), pp. 70–73, 150–179, 187–200; Linda J. Cook, "Workers in the Russian Federation: Responses to the Post-communist Transition, 1989–1993," *Communist and Post-Communist Studies*, 28 (1995), pp. 19–27; Elizabeth Teague, "Ethnic Tensions Remain Main Cause of Work Stoppages," *Report on the USSR*, 2, 41 (1990), 21–22; Elizabeth Teague and Philip Hanson, "Most Soviet Strikes Politically Motivated," *Report on the USSR*, 1, 34 (1989), 1–2.

[8] U.S. Central Intelligence Agency and Defense Intelligence Agency, "Beyond Perestroyka: The Soviet Economy in Crisis," in Alexander Dallin and Gail Lapidus, eds., *The Soviet System: From Crisis to Collapse*, revised edition (Boulder, CO: Westview Press, 1995), pp. 322–336; Dawn Mann, "Nongovernment by Decree," *Report on the USSR*, 2, 35 (1990), 1–4; Steven L. Solnick, *Stealing the State: Control and Collapse in Soviet Institutions* (Cambridge, MA: Harvard University Press, 1998).

[9] Matlock, *Autopsy on an Empire*, pp. 421–517.

the number of forces that could be dedicated to preventing a coup actually increased in the last years of the Soviet Union. However, the crisis of the state meant that in practice these agencies also were potential threats to the executive leadership of the state, not reliable deterrents. On the other hand, the Soviet army became less cohesive in its last years, although the most important splits were more ideational than structural.

Counterbalancing. Both the KGB and the Ministry of Internal Affairs (MVD) possessed forces capable of counterbalancing a coup attempt. The largest group of KGB forces were the Border Troops, numbering several hundred thousand personnel, but they were not trained or deployed for counter-balancing missions. More relevant were the Kremlin regiment and the Ninth Directorate of the KGB, which was responsible for the security of top government leaders. The KGB also possessed several elite special assignment (*spetsnaz*) groups, such as the renowned Alpha Group. In 1990–1991 the KGB acquired around 24,000 troops from the regular armed forces: a para-trooper division, two motorized rifle divisions, and a motorized rifle brigade. Most relevant for counterbalancing was the 27th motorized rifle brigade, which was based in the Moscow area.[10]

The Internal Troops (*Vnutrenniye Voyska*, or VV) of the MVD were also potential counterweights to army intervention. The VV numbered several hundred thousand personnel, but most of these were static guards and not mobile troops. The roughly 36,000 "operational forces" were doubled in size in the late-Gorbachev period to encompass 72,000 troops. The most impor-tant of the operational forces were the 10,000 troops of the Dzerzhinsky Motorized Rifle Division, based in Moscow.[11]

This expansion of the armed power of the KGB and the MVD VV in the last years of Gorbachev's rule could suggest a deliberate attempt to strengthen forces capable of counterbalancing a military coup. All analysts agree, however, that the transfer of some units from the army to the KGB, along with the expansion of the VV, was due to increased ethnic violence in various "hot spots" of the Soviet Union. The army objected to being used for

[10] Amy W. Knight, *The KGB: Police and Politics in the Soviet Union* (Boston, MA: Unwin Hyman, 1990), pp. 221–227; Yevgenia Albats, *The State within a State: The KGB and Its Hold on Russia – Past, Present, and Future* (New York: Farrar, Straus, & Giroux, 1994), pp. 24–25; Mikhail Boltunov, *Al'fa ne khotela ubivat'* (Sankt-Peterburg: "Shans," 1995); Leonid Mlechin, *Predsedateli KGB: Rassekrechennye sud'by* (Moskva: Tsentrpoligraf, 1999), p. 606.

[11] William C. Fuller, Jr., *The Internal Troops of the MVD SSSR*, College Station Papers No. 6 (College Station, TX: Center for Strategic Technology, Texas A & M University, 1983); Mark Galeotti, "Perestroika, Perestrelka, Pereborka: Policing Russia in a Time of Change," *Europe-Asia Studies*, 45 (1993), 769, 777; Louise I. Shelley, *Policing Soviet Society: The Evolution of State Control* (New York: Routledge, 1996), pp. 69–70.

internal security missions, so the other so-called power ministries had to be beefed up.[12]

On paper, then, there were considerable counterbalancing forces available to deter a coup. The real situation was more complex. First, most of these KGB and MVD forces were not trained and deployed in a way that made them optimally suited for this role. Second, and more important, the serious weakening of the state rendered these forces less reliable. The growing disorder threatened the KGB and the MVD as much as the army, and made them more likely to carry out a coup than to thwart one. However, from a straightforward structural perspective, one would still conclude that the presence of multiple agencies with troops capable of resisting a coup made the opportunity for intervention relatively low.

Penetration. The Soviet armed forces were also penetrated by two monitoring organizations that would complicate the planning of a coup. The better known of these two groups was the Main Political Administration (MPA), which controlled the "commissars" of the Communist Party. The MPA over time played a less important role in monitoring the regular army. They became closely bound together with the Ministry of Defense and focused more on indoctrination and political education than on internal spying.[13]

The more important monitoring agency was the Third Directorate of the KGB, which was responsible for military counterintelligence. The KGB had its own "special section" officers spread throughout the armed forces, who also worked with informers who spied on their fellow army officers. The KGB special sections were perhaps the most reliable organizational structure capable of preventing a coup.[14]

The MPA and the KGB, however, were, like the MVD and the armed forces, threatened by Gorbachev's policies and the weakening of the state. In structural terms they made the opportunity for intervention low, but in practice they would prove to be less reliable.

Cohesion. The Soviet armed forces in the mid-1980s were considered extremely cohesive by most observers. Large and well-funded, they were the most important source of Soviet power in the international arena. Prior to the Gorbachev era, the one structural factor that was seen as a potential

---

[12] Galeotti, "Perestroika, Perestrelka, Pereborka," 777; Shelley, *Policing Soviet Society*, pp. 69–70; Albats, *State within a State*, 24–25; Vadim Bakatin, *Doroga v proshedshem vremeni* (Moskva: Dom, 1999), pp. 287–288.

[13] Timothy J. Colton, *Commissars, Commanders, and Civilian Authority: The Structure of Soviet Military Politics* (Cambridge, MA: Harvard University Press, 1979).

[14] Knight, *KGB*, pp. 249–275; Zbigniew Brzezinski, ed., *Political Controls in the Soviet Army: A Study Based on Reports by Former Soviet Officers* (New York: Research Program on the USSR, 1954).

source of divisiveness in the military were the large numbers of draftees from the Central Asian republics (around twenty percent by 1990).[15]

This ethnic split became exacerbated as nationality conflicts erupted around the Soviet Union in the late 1980s. The multiethnic nature of the army created tensions between conscripts. Moreover, republics began to adopt laws that challenged the Ministry of Defense's conscription and basing policies. Some republics sought to create their own armed forces.[16]

The officer corps was more homogeneous than the rank-and-file. More than ninety percent of the officer corps was Slavic, although estimates of the Russian percentage vary widely, from sixty-one percent to eighty-five percent. As support for Ukrainian independence grew, the danger to the Soviet army that its Ukrainian officers (estimates range from ten to twenty-five percent) would become less reliable increased.[17] This only became a serious problem, however, after the August 1991 coup failed.

A potentially more important split was a generational/ideational one in the officer corps. Junior- and middle-level officers were much more inclined to support political and military reform than were their older and more senior colleagues. Military deputies in the Russian parliament ranged across the political spectrum, with rank being one of the best predictors of these differences.[18] Conscripts were also less likely to share the conservative political views held by many in the high command.

Thus, the political crisis of the state had consequences for the internal cohesion of one of its key bulwarks, the army. These splits, some structural and some ideational, also undermined the ability of the army to act as a cohesive player in sovereign power issues.

In general, then, an organizational structural perspective would predict that the threat of military intervention was low. Counterbalancing and penetration structures remained in place; indeed, the KGB and the MVD had been strengthened. The cohesion of the army had begun to decline, further complicating coup plotting.

---

[15] Deborah Yarsike Ball, "Ethnic Conflict, Unit Performance, and the Soviet Armed Forces," *Armed Forces & Society*, 20 (1994), 239–258; Teresa Rakowska-Harmstone, "Nationalities and the Soviet Military," in Hajda and Beissinger, *Nationalities Factor*, pp. 79–80.

[16] Matthew A. Partan, "The Military Fails to Act: Explaining Soviet Ministry of Defense Responses to Domestic Challenges, 1985 to 1991," Ph.D. dissertation, Massachusetts Institute of Technology, 1993, pp. 234–306, 340–366; Susan L. Clark, "Ethnic Tensions and the Soviet Military" and "Appendix: Sovereignty and Republic Armed Forces," in Susan L. Clark, ed., *Soviet Military Power in a Changing World* (Boulder, CO: Westview Press, 1991), pp. 205–239, 301–305; William E. Odom, *The Collapse of the Soviet Military* (New Haven, CT: Yale University Press, 1998), pp. 280–304.

[17] Partan, *Military Fails to Act*, p. 142, note 14.

[18] Partan, *Military Fails to Act*, pp. 324–325; Stephen M. Meyer, "How the Threat (and the Coup) Collapsed: The Politicization of the Soviet Military," *International Security*, 16, 3 (1991/1992), 19–20, 27–29.

Opportunity: Summary

The opportunity structure facing Soviet officers during the perestroika period was mixed. State weakness made it easier for the military to play a role in sovereign power issues. On the other hand, the structure of the armed forces should have made putting a coup together a difficult undertaking. Officers confronted forces both pulling them in to domestic politics and hindering their ability to act effectively.

MOTIVES FOR INTERVENTION

Corporate interest motives and organizational culture cut against each other in the late-Soviet period. The army's interests were under severe threat starting around 1988. On the other hand, the dominant organizational culture proscribed military participation in sovereign power issues.

Corporate Interests

Gorbachev's policies at both the foreign and domestic level seriously threatened the organizational interests of the Soviet armed forces and created a clear motive for a military coup. Both the power and resources of the military were under threat, their autonomy was impinged, and organizational uncertainty increased. By the end of the Gorbachev period, the very existence of a unified Soviet military was under question.

Autonomy. Gorbachev's first key move against the army's interests was his effort to reduce the high degree of military autonomy over defense policy. Gorbachev empowered civilian actors, such as the Ministry of Foreign Affairs and policy specialists, and gave them more influence over military doctrine and national security policy. A rollback in military autonomy in the defense policy sphere was necessary for Gorbachev to further his policies of perestroika and new thinking, which were designed at least in part to allow the transfer of resources from the defense sector to the civilian economy.[19]

Gorbachev's far-reaching political reforms, discussed above, further endangered Soviet military interests. The democratically empowered parliament elected in 1989 began to seek influence over a range of defense and security policies. The legislature sought to exert more control over the defense budget, manpower policies, and other military issues.[20]

---

[19] Stephen M. Meyer, "The Sources and Prospects of Gorbachev's New Political Thinking on Security," *International Security*, 13, 2 (1988), 124–163.

[20] Committee on Armed Services, House of Representatives, *The New Soviet Legislature: Committee on Defense and State Security* (Washington, D.C.: Government Printing Office, 1990); Jeffrey Checkel, "Improved Oversight of National Security Policymaking?," *Soviet Defense*

Resources. In 1988 Gorbachev stepped up his efforts to reduce the military burden on the economy. Gorbachev announced unilateral cuts in conventional forces totaling half a million men at the United Nations in December 1988. He also launched a highly visible program to convert defense industries to civilian production; and beginning in 1989, defense procurement orders were cut back by thirty percent per year.[21]

Liberalization in the Soviet Union also led to political change in Eastern Europe. In 1989 all of the Soviet-backed Communist regimes collapsed, with the acquiescence of Moscow. The dramatic revolution in Eastern Europe fundamentally damaged military interests. More than twenty highly capable Soviet divisions, involving hundreds of thousands of personnel, had to be withdrawn from Eastern Europe in the space of a few years. This rapid retreat not only seriously weakened the Soviet military's position in Europe, but also created severe headaches for the high command because they had to organize the withdrawal and rebasing of these troops at a speed much greater than the General Staff considered possible. The collapse of the Warsaw Pact and its deleterious effects on the Soviet armed forces was a cause of bitter complaint by the Soviet officer corps.[22]

The rise of republican political power and independence movements severely threatened the armed forces. The Baltic and Transcaucasian republics and Moldova were particularly aggressive in challenging the military draft. By the summer of 1991, over thirty laws or acts had been passed by republican parliaments or governments that interfered with the all-Union draft, and the number of draft evaders grew dramatically in the last years of the Soviet state. Several republics also began to establish their own armed formations.[23]

Notes, 1, 4 (1989), 7–8; Mikhail Tsypkin, "The Committee for Defense and State Security of the USSR Supreme Soviet," *Report on the USSR*, 2, 19 (1990), 8–11; Matthew Partan, "Military Reform Proposals in the Soviet Union," *Soviet Defense Notes*, 2, 5 (1990).

[21] A. S. Chernyaev, *Shest' let s Gorbachevym: Po dnevnikovym zapisyam* (Moskva: "Progress" – "Kultura," 1993), pp. 253–260; "'Po samym optimisticheskim prognozam, mne dayut god-poltora' – zayavil M.S. Gorbachev v dekabre 1988 goda," *Istochnik*, Nos. 5–6, 1993, 130–147; Kevin P. O'Prey, *A Farewell to Arms?: Russia's Struggles with Defense Conversion* (New York: The Twentieth Century Fund Press, 1995), pp. 27–33.

[22] Raymond L. Garthoff, *The Great Transition: American–Soviet Relations and the End of the Cold War* (Washington, D.C.: The Brookings Institution, 1994), pp. 598–622; S. F. Akhromeyev and G. M. Korniyenko, *Glazami marshala i diplomata: kriticheskiy vzglyad po vneshnyuyu politiku SSR do i posle 1985 goda* (Moskva: Mezhdunarodnye otnosheniya, 1992), pp. 69–71, 226–233; I. Mikulin, "Mir ne mozhet pokoit'sya na fundamente slabosti," in M. K. Gorshkov and V. V. Zhuravlev, eds., *Nesokrushimaya i legendarnaya: v ogne politicheskikh batatiy 1985–1993 gg.* (Moskva: Terra, 1994), pp. 142–144; Viktor Baranets, *Poteryannaya armiya: Zapiski polkovnika genshtaba* (Moskva: Sovershenno sekretno, 1998), pp. 142–144; Leonid Ivashov, *Marshal Yazov (Rokovoy avgust 91-go)* (Vel'sk, Russia: MP "Vel'ti," 1993), pp. 50–52.

[23] I. Sas, "Ot prizyva uklonilsya," *Glasnost*, May 16, 1991, 4; I. Matveyev, interviewed by V. Litovkin, "Prizyv zakonchen – sluzhit' nekomu," *Izvestiya*, July 22, 1991, 2;

The corporate interest perspective on military intervention contends that the army intervenes when its interests are threatened. In the late 1970s, Timothy Colton elaborated a scenario under which the Soviet armed forces might intervene in politics:

The only inducement to full-scale intervention would be the conflux of a number of policy choices highly unfavorable to military interests. One can envisage, for example, a reformist civilian leadership embarking upon policies of ideological revision, military demobilization, shifting of investment priorities, and accommodation with foreign adversaries such as would alarm military leaders.[24]

These conditions were clearly met by at least 1988. After that date, further developments impinged even further on the armed forces' corporate interests. This perspective leads to the prediction that the Soviet army would intervene in politics to protect itself against these threats. In cases of military arbitration the army would side with the contender most likely to defend its interests.

Organizational Culture

The dominant culture of the Soviet army had a relatively strong commitment to a norm of civilian supremacy in the late 1980s. However, there is also evidence for the appearance of a more praetorian subculture in the armed forces.

Beliefs and Socialization. A core belief of the Soviet military was that its primary mission was external defense of the state, not internal policing or involvement in domestic politics. This orientation is clear from the content of military journals, surveys of the officer corps, and the statements of the military leadership. Several critical events during this period also served as institutional lessons that reinforced the focus on external defense.

The Soviet military's focus on external defense missions is demonstrated clearly by an analysis of army publications. The main journal of the Ground Forces was *Voyenniy Vestnik* [*Military Herald*]. *Voyenniy Vestnik* [hereafter *VV*] was the primary journal for the forces that would most likely be used for internal missions, including the Airborne Forces and mechanized and infantry units. A comprehensive review of *VV* for the period 1980–1991 shows a strong commitment to external defense as the army's key mission, and little or no attention to internal security or societal choice issues. This is in sharp contrast with the French military in the 1950s and the Brazilian army in the 1950s and 1960s, which began to focus more on internal threats and "counterrevolutionary war" in their journals, a shift in orientation

K. Bayalinov et al., "Skol'ko armiy v nashey strane?," *Komsomol'skaya pravda* [hereafter *KP*], March 12, 1991, 3.

[24] Colton, *Commissars, Commanders*, p. 288.

that pointed to a changing organizational culture with a more praetorian outlook.[25]

Each article in *VV* was coded as pertaining to one of seven categories: Political Indoctrination, Societal Choice, Tactics and Training, Personnel Issues, Military History, Foreign Militaries, and Internal Security.[26] The results are presented in Figures 6.1 and 6.2. Figure 6.1 covers all articles except lead or featured pieces. Figure 6.2 comprises lead or featured articles.

Tactics and Training was the topic of a majority of *VV*'s articles, although the amount of coverage dropped starting in 1989. Personnel Issues, Military History, and Foreign Militaries were also frequent topics. Nonmilitary issues received little coverage in *Voyenniy Vestnik*. There was a slight increase in the number of articles on Societal Choice issues and a slight decrease in Political Indoctrination pieces in the last years of Soviet power. The most interesting change, perhaps, is that in 1990 the first articles on Internal Security in the decade under study appeared. There were three articles (one percent) on Internal Security in 1990 and four articles (one percent) on Internal Security in 1991. These articles dealt either with the use of the military for internal missions, particularly in Baku in January 1990, or independence movements in the republics. There were no articles on the use of army units in Tbilisi in April 1989 or in Vilnius in January 1991, events for which the Soviet army was vilified. The insignificant coverage of Internal Security issues in *VV* as the Soviet state was on the verge of collapse is indicative of a resilient organizational culture focused on narrow military issues.

The changing orientation of *VV* editorials is also telling (see Figure 6.2). Political Indoctrination, which had been a major topic of lead and featured articles pre-Gorbachev, received much less attention after 1987. In 1989 the number of lead articles dropped in half, and *VV* used interviews rather than articles as their feature pieces. These interviews focused mainly on Tactics

---

[25] John Steward Ambler, *Soldiers Against the State: The French Army in Politics* (Garden City, NY: Anchor Books, 1968), pp. 180–218, 333–365; Alfred Stepan, *The Military in Politics: Changing Patterns in Brazil* (Princeton, NJ: Princeton University Press, 1971), pp. 172–187.

[26] Political Indoctrination refers to Communist Party or leadership propaganda, material on the foreign and defense policy of the state, and official Soviet holidays. Societal Choice issues are domestic economic and social issues and includes military involvement in or discussion of matters outside the realm of defense policy. Tactics and Training covers a range of narrow military issues, including training, tactics, operational art, military education, and military organization. Personnel Issues are such matters as officership, human relations, morale and discipline, legal questions, officers' living conditions, and so on. Military History encompasses articles about World War II and other past Soviet and Russian wars. Foreign Militaries pertains to articles written about the armed forces of other states. Internal Security refers to pieces on internal threats to the state and military internal activity. Many articles, of course, covered more than one theme. For each article I determined what I believed the dominant topic of the article was. For example, a quote from Lenin was not enough for an article to be coded as "political indoctrination" if the main thrust of the piece was on a different topic.

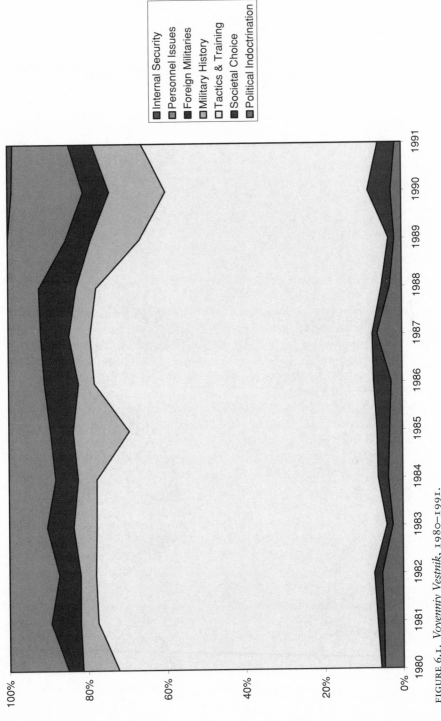

FIGURE 6.1. *Voyenny Vestnik*, 1980–1991.

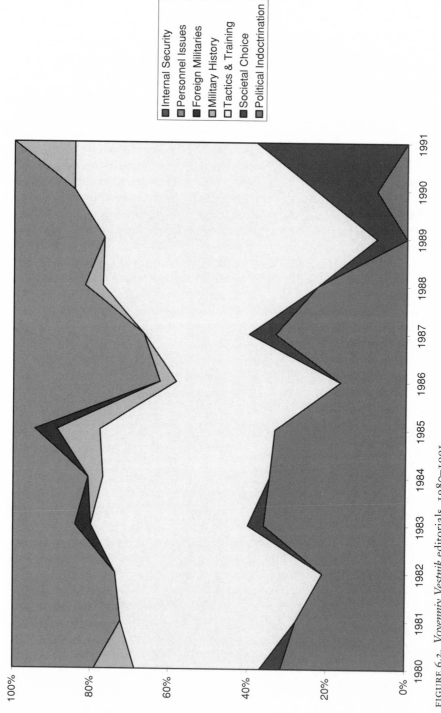

FIGURE 6.2. *Voyenniy Vestnik* editorials, 1980–1991.

and Training. In 1990 and 1991, however, there was a big jump in discussion of Societal Choice issues. If the content of regular articles demonstrates a remarkable fixation on narrow military issues, the focus of lead interviews provides a more mixed picture.

The most prominent contending task, other than external defense, that faced the Soviet military was internal policing, due to the increase in ethnic violence. *VV* conducted two polls on this issue. The first, conducted in the Moscow Military District, showed that fifty-two percent of officers and soldiers believed that the military should not be used to "support social order." More than a third said the military could be used for such a task, but only in extreme situations. All of those polled agreed that there should be a decision of the Supreme Soviet if the army were to be used internally. A poll of its readers showed similar results, with sixty-four percent against internal usage and a third supporting it if there was a corresponding decision of the Supreme Soviet. Poll results published in the military newspaper *Red Star* showed even more striking results. Ninety-six percent of officers polled said external defense was the main task of the armed forces. Only twenty-four percent believed the army had a role in dealing with natural disasters and major accidents. Officers were "categorically against" using the military for maintaining social order, stopping interethnic conflicts, and carrying out economic tasks.[27]

Kommunist vooruzhenykh sil [Communist of the Armed Forces – hereafter *KVS]* published a series of articles in late 1989 on the issue of internal missions. Five of the six officers writing on the topic stressed that the major task of the army was external defense and expressed their disapproval of internal missions. Colonel K. Vorob'ev, for example, maintained that dealing with internal disorder was a function of the Internal Troops and the police, not the Armed Forces. Although the authors acknowledged that the government might call on the army to perform internal tasks, they evinced no enthusiasm for these missions.[28]

Minister of Defense Marshal Dmitriy Yazov similarly stressed that the army had a single, external function. The use of army units for internal missions was possible only in extreme situations. Yazov argued that as the MVD was strengthened it would become unnecessary for the armed forces

---

[27] Captain G. Loza and Lt.-Col. R. Nadeyev, "Byulleten' obshchestvennogo mneniya," *VV*, No. 8, 1989, 15–16; Lieutenant Colonel I. Barkovskiy, "Byulleten' obshchestvennogo mneniya," *VV*, No. 3, 1990, 10; Lieutenant-Colonel K. Polyakov, "O chem govorit statistika," *Krasnaya zvezda* [hereafter *KZ*], August 31, 1990, 2. Unfortunately, as is often the case with polls published in the Soviet/Russian press, complete data on the poll, its size, and the exact questions asked were not provided.

[28] Colonel K. Vorob'ev, "Mera krayne nezhelatel'naya," *KVS*, No. 18, 1989, 27. These articles from *KVS* are discussed in more detail in Brian Taylor, "Internal Function of Soviet Army Discussed," *Soviet Defense Notes*, 1, 6 (1989), 4–6; Stephen Foye, "Domestic Role of Soviet Armed Forces Debated," *Report on the USSR*, 2, 3 (1990), 7–9.

to provide internal support. Yazov concluded, "this will allow the army and navy to more fully do the job for which it is intended – securing a high and unceasing readiness to defend the Motherland." Other leading officers, such as Sergey Akhromeyev, the Chief of the General Staff from 1984 to 1988 and Gorbachev's chief military adviser from 1989 to 1991, also made clear their view that the mission of the armed forces was external defense and that the army should eschew domestic policing or economic tasks.[29]

The well-known Russian General Aleksandr Lebed returns again and again in his memoirs to his view that the military should not be involved in internal missions. Lebed was commander of the Tula Airborne Division from 1988 to 1990, and elements of his division were on several occasions sent to "hot spots" around the former Soviet Union. Lebed declares:

I thought then and I think now: it's not the army's job to deal with internal disorder. . . . Placing police functions on the army in general, and on the airborne forces in particular, is the greatest humiliation for the army. The army is not psycho-logically prepared for that sort of activity, and if it is still forced to undertake it this will lead to only one result – wild bitterness and difficult and unbearable insults on the part of the crowd towards the army.[30]

The influential General Boris Gromov, who in 1990 was head of the Kiev Military District and in 1991 was the Deputy Minister of the MVD, also stated his opposition to the internal use of the military. Asked about the possibility of using the military internally, Gromov replied: "I am categori-cally against that, if the situation is connected to inter-nationality relations. Everyone should stick to their own affairs." Gromov also dismissed rumors about the possibility of a military coup as "unfounded nonsense."[31]

Consistent with the organizational culture approach, there was a key event during the Gorbachev period that significantly shaped officer corps thinking about their proper role. A defining moment for the Soviet Armed Force's attitude towards internal missions came on April 9, 1989, when military units, along with MVD Troops, were used to disperse a political meeting in Tbilisi, Georgia. Nineteen people died in the ensuing violence.

The key institutional lesson drawn from the Tbilisi events was that it was detrimental to the prestige and integrity of the armed forces for the army to play a role in internal political disputes. This lesson came to be known as the "Tbilisi syndrome." Minister of Defense Yazov said that officers were psy-chologically "fettered" by the "Tbilisi syndrome," which caused hesitation

---

[29] D. T. Yazov, *Voyennaya Reforma* (Moskva: Voyennoye Izdatel'stvo, 1990), pp. 40–41; In-terview with D. Yazov by N. Burbyga, "Vesenniy prizyv," *Izvestiya*, March 12, 1990, 3; Akhromeyev and Korniyenko, *Glazami marshala i diplomata*, pp. 175–190.

[30] Aleksandr Lebed, *Za derzhavu obidno . . .* (Moskva: "Moskovskaya Pravda," 1995), pp. 231, 235, 249, 291–292, 297, 301, 366 (quote, p. 249).

[31] B. Gromov, "Slukhi o voyennom perevorote raspuskayut ne ot bol'shogo uma," in Gorshkov and Zhuravlev, *Nesokrushimaya i legendarnaya*, pp. 116–117.

in carrying out their orders and duties in emergency situations. The use of the army in Baku in January 1990 and in Vilnius in January 1991 strengthened the "Tbilisi syndrome" and confirmed the lessons learned from that event about internal involvement.[32]

Soviet military officers also believed that they were obligated to follow orders from civilian political leaders. Officers continuously stated their commitment to remain subordinate to civilian power. At a Politburo meeting in March 1988 Yazov stated, "the army should be united with the people and should work under the leadership of the Communist Party." The Chief of the General Staff, General of the Army Mikhail Moiseyev, said, "we are prepared to carry out any order of the Motherland in defense of the Soviet people." When the post of president was introduced in March 1990, General Moiseyev noted that according to the recent constitutional amendments the president was commander-in-chief and the president was responsible for the defense of the state and the development of the armed forces.[33]

Akhromeyev also made clear his commitment to the view that the military should be subordinate to civilian rule. In August 1990 he maintained:

[T]he Army has been and will be with the people and will steadfastly carry out the instructions and orders issued by the legally elected highest organs of power and its own supreme commander in chief – the USSR president – and the USSR Supreme Soviet to which the people have given that right.

Akhromeyev made a similar point in his memoirs:

Officers understood that the Armed Forces are not a political force and that they should not participate in political struggles. Their job – punctually carry out the decisions of the supreme organs of state power and the President of the USSR.[34]

This position of the top military leaders was echoed by other officers. In the discussion in *Communist of the Armed Forces* (*KVS*) on the internal use of the military, Colonel Bel'kov wrote:

The army is an instrument of the state. The forms and limits of its usage are defined by state power as embodied by her legislative and executive organs. They, precisely they and only they, are empowered to take decisions about the use of the army.

---

[32] Yazov, *Voyennaya Reforma*, p. 52; Captain V. Yermolin, "Tbilisskiy sindrom," *KZ*, April 9, 1991, 1.

[33] Mikhail Gorbachev, *Zhizn' i reformy*, Vol. I (Moskva: Novosti, 1995), p. 385 (Yazov quote); Interview with General M. A. Moiseyev, "Zadachi u nas odni," *KZ*, February 10, 1990, 1; Interview with General M. A. Moiseyev, "Vazhnyy shag v voyennom stroitel'stve," *KZ*, March 15, 1990, 1–2.

[34] Marshal S. F. Akhromeyev et al., "Ne syp'te sol' na rany…" *KP*, August 4, 1990, 2; Akhromeyev and Korniyenko, *Glazami marshala i diplomata*, pp. 73–75, 317. See also Marshal S. Akhromeyev, "Napadki na vooruzhenye sily SSSR. Pochemu?" *KZ*, April 8, 1990, 2, 4; Marshal S. Akhromeyev, "Kakiye vooruzhennye sily nuzhny Sovetskomu Soyuzu," *Ogonyek*, No. 50, 1989, 8.

In a law-governed state the army should be subordinate to a democratically elected government.[35]

A skeptic would argue that these statements do not reflect these officers' "true" views. However, there were other officers who expressed more praetorian views (they will be discussed below), so officers did have some leeway in their public pronouncements. Another test of the sincerity of officers' statements is the behavior of the army in nonsovereign power issues.

Behavior. The Soviet military often was depicted as having almost unbridled control over security policy.[36] In Chapter 5 I showed how this view is mistaken, and how the armed forces submitted to party decisions on such matters as arms control and the invasion of Afghanistan.

The Gorbachev period provides the most persuasive imaginable test of who had the final word in Soviet national security policy. The changes introduced by Gorbachev in security policy led to budget and force cuts, far-reaching arms control treaties, and the collapse of the Warsaw Pact, with the subsequent withdrawal of Soviet forces from Eastern Europe. The military resisted these changes, but were unable to stop them. In the end they saluted and carried out orders.

When Gorbachev came to power, there was already an established interagency mechanism for developing Soviet security policy. Gorbachev notes that Foreign Minister Eduard Shevardnadze often became frustrated with the military in these discussions, so Gorbachev would intervene in the process and they would "work everything out." The "final prerogative" in deciding foreign policy, Gorbachev adds, belonged to the Politburo and the General Secretary. Akhromeyev states that sharp discussions were often carried out and that Gorbachev was often critical of military views, but concludes that "he [Gorbachev] conducted the work democratically, but the last word was, of course, his own."[37]

Akhromeyev and the rest of the military leadership were forced to accept many decisions with which they disagreed, including those they played little or no role in formulating. His memoirs at times become a virtual litany of Soviet policies to which the army was opposed: the unilateral moratorium on nuclear testing, leaving naval forces out of conventional arms control negotiations, leaving French and British nuclear weapons out of nuclear arms

---

[35] Colonel O. Bel'kov, "Armiya dolzhna delat' svoye delo," *KVS*, No. 19, 1989, 18.

[36] See, for example, Thomas M. Nichols, *The Sacred Cause: Civil–Military Conflict over Soviet National Security, 1917–1992* (Ithaca, NY: Cornell University Press, 1993); Georgi Arbatov, *The System: An Insider's Life in Soviet Politics* (New York: Times Books/Random House, 1993), pp. 194–195.

[37] Gorbachev, *Zhizn' i reformy*, Vol. II, pp. 12–14; Akhromeyev and Korniyenko, *Glazami marshala i diplomata*, pp. 71–74, 90–91; Aleksandr G. Savel'yev and Nikolay N. Detinov, *The Big Five: Arms Control Decision-Making in the Soviet Union* (Westport, CT: Praeger, 1995).

control negotiations, and including the SS-23 in the Intermediate Nuclear Forces (INF) Treaty. Akhromeyev and his co-author, former Deputy Foreign Minister Georgiy Korniyenko, were particularly irritated with how German reunification and the decision to withdraw Soviet forces from Eastern Europe were handled.[38]

The issues that caused the most debate about whether the military remained subordinate to civilian authority were several episodes of internal usage of the army. The two events that have attracted the most attention are the Tbilisi events of April 1989 and the crackdown in Vilnius in January 1991. Much ink has been spilled by both the principals involved and outside analysts, with no clear resolution of the central question: "What did Gorbachev know and when did he know it?" I have discussed the contradictory evidence on this question for the Tbilisi and Vilnius events at length elsewhere.[39] Here I would like to discuss one episode that has received considerably less attention, the coup scare of September 1990, and provide some general conclusions on Gorbachev's involvement in these events.

In September 1990 Moscow was gripped by a massive coup scare.[40] The sudden and suspicious movement of several airborne (VDV) regiments toward Moscow on September 9 caused a scandal in the press, and the Supreme Soviet established an investigatory commission. Minister of Defense Yazov was called before the Supreme Soviet, where he testified that some of the units were engaged in maneuvers, some were preparing for a parade, and some were picking potatoes. Many listeners, particularly in the democratic camp, did not find his answers persuasive.

It turns out that these observers had good reason to be suspicious. There was no coup attempt in September 1990, but President Gorbachev had ordered the VDV to move toward Moscow in anticipation of the opening of the Supreme Soviet and a planned democratic rally on September 16. After the scandal broke out, Gorbachev kept silent and dissociated himself from the decision.

---

[38] Akhromeyev and Korniyenko, *Glazami marshal i diplomata*, pp. 61–64, 69–71, 73–74, 95–98, 109, 130–133, 193–194, 226–233, 255–264. See also Baranets, *Poteryannaya armiya*, pp. 109–112; Ivashov, *Marshal Yazov*, pp. 25–28, 50–52; Michael R. Beschloss and Strobe Talbott, *At the Highest Levels: The Inside Story of the End of the Cold War* (Boston: Little, Brown, and Company, 1993), pp. 118, 289–290, 363–370; Savel'yev and Detinov, *The Big Five*, pp. 117, 133–135.

[39] Brian D. Taylor, "The Russian Military in Politics: Civilian Supremacy in Comparative and Historical Perspective," Ph.D. dissertation, Massachusetts Institute of Technology, February 1998, pp. 469–483; Brian D. Taylor, "The Soviet Military and the Disintegration of the USSR," *Journal of Cold War Studies*, 5, 1(winter 2003).

[40] Kevin P. O'Prey, "Anatomy of a Coup Scare," *Soviet Defense Notes*, 3, 1 (1991); Lebed, *Za derzhavu obidno . . .*, pp. 343–350; Interview with Colonel-General E. Podkolzin [Commander of the VDV] by D. Makarov, "VDV, kak vsegda, na strazhe," *Argumenty i fakty*, No. 12 (March), 1993, 1, 6.

The fact that no coup attempt was underway is clear from the movement of troops. In particular, as was pointed out at the time, the most likely units to be involved in a coup attempt, the Taman and Kantemirov Divisions based near Moscow, had not moved, nor had several other special units based in the Moscow area. The movement of VDV regiments, on the other hand, suggests preparation for civil disorder, since the VDV had been called on to deal with these situations on several occasions under Gorbachev.[41]

Colonel-General E. Podkolzin was Chief of Staff of the VDV in 1990. Podkolzin later explained that Gorbachev had ordered the movement of troops into Moscow. When the outcry erupted, a cover-up was ordered and Podkolzin, as Chief of Staff, was put in charge of drawing up materials (maps, orders, etc.) showing that the troop movements were part of a training exercise. Lebed was commander of the Tula Airborne Division at the time and he also was involved in the cover-up. He was ordered to cooperate with Podkolzin by the Commander of the VDV, General Vladislav Achalov, who was put in charge of the cover-up by Yazov. Both Podkolzin and Lebed dismiss the idea that Yazov could have ordered the troop movements himself. Yazov testified in the trial of the August 1991 coup plotters that three or four times in 1990–1991 he had received verbal orders from Gorbachev to move troops to Moscow, usually before the opening of the Supreme Soviet or on holidays. Although Yazov is not specific about the dates, the two most prominent such events were in September 1990 and March 1991.[42]

Yazov, one might say, had obvious reasons to lie about these events. But there was little motivation for either Podkolzin or Lebed to lie, particularly three to five years after the fact. Gorbachev remained silent at the time of the coup scare, and neither he nor any of his top aides mention this incident in their memoirs. The most telling fact is that no one lost his job because of this episode. It is hard to believe that the president would have been either so silent or so serene about such a scandal if the military had been operating behind his back. The evidence is quite strong that Gorbachev ordered these troop movements.

The fact that Gorbachev almost certainly was behind the September 1990 events does not, of course, necessarily mean that he was involved in the Tbilisi and Vilnius decisions. But in these two cases there is very strong evidence that Gorbachev knew of and approved the movement of troops, although what exact orders Gorbachev authorized for the troops is less clear. He has acknowledged approving the dispatch of troops to Tbilisi a day and a half before the violence, and in the Vilnius case the U.S. Central Intelligence

[41] O'Prey, "Anatomy of a Coup Scare," 5; "Vzglyad," *Moscow TV*, October 19, 1990 [*Foreign Broadcast Information Service Daily Report: Soviet Union* [hereafter FBIS-SOV]-90-204, October 22, 1990, 88–89].

[42] Aleksandr Pel'ts, "Kakie ukazaniya daval Mikhail Gorbachev?," *KZ*, January 29, 1994, 2.

Agency, which would have had access to signals intelligence, concluded that Gorbachev had ordered the deployment of VDV troops to the area, even if he had not given a direct order to shoot, and had thus set the tragedy in motion. Gorbachev, the CIA said, "was strategically, if not tactically," responsible for the January 1991 events in Vilnius.[43]

In my view the most plausible explanation of how much Gorbachev knew prior to Tbilisi and Vilnius is that he ordered troop deployments and gave general instructions to "restore order," without approving more specific operational commands. Thus, when things went badly or there was a scandal he was in a position to deny responsibility. In other words, Gorbachev was always careful to maintain "plausible deniability."

This is certainly the view held by leading officers. Podkolzin contends that Gorbachev was behind the use of the army in many "hot spots" but that Gorbachev "always pretended that he did not know anything." General Leonid Ivashov, who worked in one of the Ministry of Defense Directorates under Yazov, also asserts that Gorbachev knew what was going on but had a "style" of claiming that he did not give any orders. Lebed also refers scathingly to "Gorbachev's style of work," which he describes as the provision of vague, oral orders of the nature, "fly where they have sent you and make everything okay. What is considered okay and how you achieve it is your problem." The head and deputy head of the KGB under Gorbachev, Vladimir Kryuchkov and Filip Bobkov, make similar accusations.[44]

Of course, several of these individuals, particularly Kryuchkov, had an interest in blaming Gorbachev. But even Gorbachev's own civilian advisers are critical of him for not taking responsibility for events such as Tbilisi or Vilnius, regardless of whether he gave specific orders. His close adviser Anatoliy Chernyaev strongly implies that Gorbachev supported the actions in Vilnius and only dissociated himself because he had promised U.S. President George Bush that he would not use force. Gorbachev ally Vadim Bakatin, who headed the MVD in 1988–1990 and the KGB after the failed August coup, goes further and asserts that Gorbachev had to know what the KGB and army had planned in Vilnius. Yegor Kuznetsov, an assistant to Gorbachev's top aide Shakhnazarov, remarked that Gorbachev in cases like Vilnius would order the armed forces to "restore order" but refuse to authorize specific activities, telling the military leadership to work things out

---

[43] A. B. Veber et al., eds., *Soyuz mozhno bylo sokhranit': Belaya kniga: dokumenty i fakty o politike M. S. Gorbacheva po reformirovaniyu i sokhraneniyu mnogonatsional'nogo gosudarstva* (Moskva: "Aprel'-85," 1995), p. 50; Beschloss and Talbott, *At the Highest Levels*, pp. 307–309.

[44] Podkolzin, "VDV, kak vsegda"; Ivashov, *Marshal Yazov*, pp. 60–61; Lebed, *Za derzhavu obidno...*, pp. 230, 280, 288; Vladimir Kryuchkov, *Lichnoye delo*, Vol. II (Moskva: Olimp, 1998), pp. 30–31; F. D. Bobkov, *KGB i vlast'* (Moskva: Veteran MP, 1995), pp. 343, 346.

for themselves. Kuznetsov added, "they [the military leadership] hated him for that."[45]

It also should be noted that, with the exception of General Igor Rodionov, who was moved from command of the Transcaucasus Military District to the directorship of the General Staff Academy after the Tbilisi events, no one was ever fired or even transferred or demoted for allegedly, in Gorbachev's own account, disobeying the commander-in-chief. Gorbachev may be telling the truth that he did not order the specific military actions that led to bloodshed in Tbilisi and Vilnius, but there are strong reasons to believe that he was less innocent than he has claimed.

Subcultures. The Soviet military generally retained its apolitical organizational culture in the last years of Gorbachev's rule. However, there was a slight shift toward more attention to internal missions and societal choice issues as the Soviet Union approached collapse. A subculture developed in the officer corps that argued for greater military involvement in politics.

In the *KVS* forum on internal usage discussed above, a minority view was advanced by retired Colonel P. Skorodenko. He argued that the army still plays an important internal role in defending socialism against counterrevolution, praising the introduction of martial law in Poland in 1981.[46] Skorodenko maintained that defense of socialism, and not just the state, was the purpose of the Soviet army.

The most open manifestation of political activity by officers was their involvement in parliamentary politics. The old Supreme Soviet always had military members, but when the body was strictly a rubber stamp for Communist Party decisions, their presence was mandated by the Party and did not reflect officer corps' culture. After 1989, however, the Congress of People's Deputies and the Supreme Soviet began to reflect a diversity of opinions. The political leadership did not take steps to bar serving officers from running for parliament.[47] Eighty-two deputies in the Soviet Congress elected in 1989 had ties to the military. Although less than four percent of the 2,250 deputies, the military members had a high profile. Moreover, if one counts

[45] Anatoliy Chernyaev, *1991 god: Dnevnik pomoshchnika Prezidenta SSSR* (Moskva: TERRA; Respublika, 1997), pp. 69–79; Chernyaev, *Shest' let s Gorbachevym*, p. 409; V. I. Boldin, *Krusheniye p'edestala: Shtrikhi k portretu M. S. Gorbacheva* (Moskva: Respublika, 1995), pp. 348–349; Bakatin, *Doroga v proshedshem vremeni*, pp. 234–235; Author's interview with Yegor Kuznetsov, July 18, 1994.

[46] Colonel (Retired) P. Skorodenko, "V tselyakh zashchity sotsializma," *KVS*, No. 19 (October), 1989, 19–20.

[47] *Zakon Soyuza Sovetskikh Sotsialisticheskikh Respublik o vyborakh narodnykh deputatov SSSR* (Moskva: Izvestiya sovetov narodnykh deputatov SSSR, 1988). Despite the negative consequences of permitting officers to serve in parliament, Gorbachev praised their efforts, referring to military deputies as "fighters for social consolidation": "Priyem v Kremle," *Pravda*, June 27, 1990, 1–2.

military legislators at all levels of government (republic, oblast, city, etc.), more than 9,000 military deputies (less than two percent of the officer corps) were serving by April 1991.[48]

Military deputies ranged across the political spectrum, and as deputies they had the right to criticize government policy. The sight of uniformed officers attacking the political leadership from the floor of the parliament helped undermine the view that the military should not play a role in sovereign power issues.[49] Military deputies did not present a united front, however, and officers such as the radical democrat Vladimir Lopatin and the reactionary "black Colonel" Viktor Alksnis stood at opposite ends of the political spectrum. Yazov made clear that he thought that military deputies should concentrate on defense issues and explaining Supreme Soviet decisions to their units. When Alksnis went too far in his criticisms of Gorbachev, Yazov publicly noted that Alksnis "does not represent the Soviet Army." Yazov also called in Alksnis and told him that he was "compromising the army" by his actions.[50]

Yazov made clear in his public statements that he saw the military's mission as external defense, and his censuring of Alksnis demonstrates that he did not seek an expanded political role for the military. At the same time, Yazov was faced with a genuine dilemma, because the national independence movements were impairing the ability of the armed forces to carry out their mission. The collapse of the draft in many republics calls for the removal of Soviet army bases from certain regions, and efforts to set up republican militias and armies were a direct threat to the fighting capacity of the armed forces.[51]

Gorbachev and the military leadership saw eye to eye on the need to maintain the Soviet Union. By the last years of his reign, though, many officers had lost faith in Gorbachev's ability to hold the state together. This

---

[48] "Doveriyem oblechennye: biograficheskiye dannye o narodnykh deputatakh SSSR – predstavitelyakh vooruzhennykh sil SSSR," *KVS*, No. 10, 1989, 3–29 and No. 12, 1989, 3; John W. R. Lepingwell, "Military Deputies in the USSR Congress," *Report on the USSR*, 2, 20 (1990), 19–22; Colonel-General N. I. Shlyaga, "Splachivat' partiynye ryady," *KZ*, March 30, 1991, 1–2.

[49] For further discussion, see Meyer, "How the Threat (and the Coup) Collapsed," 14–16, 28–29.

[50] Vladimir Lopatin, "Armiya i politika," *Znamya*, No. 7, 1990, 147–159; Interview with Major Vladimir Lopatin by S. Aleksandrov, "'Sluzhit' narodu, a ne partiyam'," *Nedelya*, May 28, 1990, 1, 3; "Armiya i politiki," in Gorshkov and Zhuravlev, *Nesokrushimaya i legendarnaya*, pp. 203–206; *Moscow Domestic Service*, December 20, 1990 [FBIS-SOV-90-246, December 21, 1990, 19–20]; A. Stepova and S. Chugayev, "Predlozheniye Prezidenta," *Izvestiya*, November 15, 1990, 1; Yazov, *Voyennaya reforma*, p. 51; James H. Brusstar and Ellen Jones, *The Russian Military's Role in Politics* (Washington, D.C.: National Defense University, 1995), p. 45, n. 21.

[51] D. Yazov, "Dlya presecheniya antiarmeyskikh deystviy budut prinyaty vse neobkhodimye mery," in Gorshkov and Zhuravlev, *Nesokrushimaya i legendarnaya*, pp. 196–197; Yazov, *Voyennaya reforma*, pp. 30–35.

caused a profound dilemma for the officer corps, which was committed both to an apolitical focus on external missions and to defending the territorial integrity of the Soviet state. Soviet ideology had long taught that the internal role of the military had disappeared, but to all appearances it was back.[52]

These pressures on the army led some officers not only to argue that the military had to play an important internal role, but also to suggest that the army could act independent of the civilian leadership. For example, Colonel Alksnis declared to the Supreme Soviet:

> They [presumably, the "democrats" – B.T.] are frightening the people with threats of a military coup. The army will not go against the people, but the army has been pushed to the limit by the nationalists' activities. If the necessary measures are not taken, the people with weapons will take to the streets. This will not be a military coup. The military will be defending their human rights.[53]

Although Alksnis was clear to say he was not talking about a military coup, he was referring to autonomous activity by the military, even if on an individual basis. His views were inconsistent with those of the military leadership, but they did reflect a minority subculture that believed the military needed to act on its own to defend the armed forces, and potentially the integrity of the state.

The prospect of a military coup apparently was discussed at the highest levels of the military leadership. General Ivashov, one of Yazov's close assistants, remarked in 1995 that he and other officers had "begged Yazov to lead a coup" but that Yazov refused. Ivashov does not mention such discussions in his own book on Yazov and the August coup, referring only to an effort in June 1991 by the hard-line commander of the Volga–Urals Military District, Colonel-General Albert Makashov, to get the Military Collegium, the army's top body, to declare "no confidence" in Gorbachev. Yazov apparently strongly objected, exclaiming, "are you trying to turn me into a Pinochet?" The crisis in the country was leading top officers to question their belief that the army had no internal role.[54]

---

[52] "O nekotorykh aktakh po voprosam oborony, prinyatykh v soyuznykh respublikakh," in Gorshkov and Zhuravlev, *Nesokrushimaya i legendarnaya*, pp. 198–199; Akhromeyev and Korniyenko, *Glazami marshala i diplomata*, p. 293; Ivashov, *Marshal Yazov*, pp. 55–58; Stephen Foye, "Gorbachev, the Army, and the Union," *Report on the USSR*, 2, 49 (1990), 1–3.

[53] Stepova and Chugayev, "Predlozheniye Prezidenta," 1.

[54] Odom, *Collapse of the Soviet Military*, p. 339; Ivashov, *Marshal Yazov*, p. 66. Odom is incorrect that Ivashov was an MPA officer; he was head of the General Staff Administrative Affairs Department under Yazov and is a ground forces officer. No officer I have asked about Ivashov's statement subsequently, including those in the Ministry of Defense leadership and the General Staff apparatus at the time, could confirm such discussions. Retired Colonel Petr Romashkin believes that such discussions did take place, but were more general than Ivashov's account, along the lines of "we must do something to save the army and the country." He added that August 1991 showed that the army was not prepared for forceful measures. Author's interview with Romashkin, June 8, 2000.

The changes introduced in Soviet political institutions, particularly the switch from Communist Party to presidential rule, also introduced confusion into the question of to whom the military was subordinate. The top military leadership, such as Moiseyev and Akhromeyev, were careful to be explicit about the switch in subordination to the President. Others, such as Makashov, were not prepared to switch their allegiance from the Communist Party so quickly. Makashov noted that officers were indoctrinated in the principles of "patriotism, internationalism, and Leninism" and claimed that communists in the armed forces "are not planning on ideological surrender.... We are decisively against any attempt to depoliticize the armed forces."[55]

In general, the Soviet officer corps exhibited a rather strong attachment to a norm of civilian supremacy in the late-Gorbachev period. They insisted that the army's primary function was external defense and that the military was subordinate to civilian rule. There was, however, a weakening of this attachment in the last years of the Soviet state. This weakening is best explained by the army's greater involvement in domestic order operations, the switch of civilian control from party to presidential rule, and, more generally, the crisis of the state. These changes served to slightly undermine the strong commitment to an apolitical organizational culture. Still, military intervention remained unlikely, according to this perspective.

Motives: Summary

There were strong corporate motives for a military coup in the last years of Soviet rule. On the other hand, the dominant norms of the army proscribed military intervention in sovereign power issues, although a more praetorian subculture also existed.

THE AUGUST 1991 COUP

In August 1991 a small clique of top-ranking, hard-line government officials attempted to depose Soviet President Mikhail Gorbachev and institute emergency rule in the country. Defense Minister Dmitriy Yazov was one of the eight members of the State Committee on the Emergency Situation (GKChP). Military units were brought into Moscow to enforce the state of emergency. The coup collapsed, however, when resistance developed within the armed forces to a planned storming of the Russian White House, the headquarters of the resistance to the putsch led by Russian President Boris Yeltsin.[56]

---

[55] Makashov, "O chem tokuyut nashi uchenye-tetereva?", *Izvestiya*, March 16, 1990, 6. Depoliticization refers to the debate about the status of Communist Party bodies in the armed forces. See Stephen Foye, "Gorbachev and the Depoliticization of the Army," *Report on the USSR*, 2, 37 (1990), 1–3.

[56] For a good general overview in English, see Dunlop, *Rise of Russia*, pp. 186–255; On the military, see Taylor, "Soviet Military and the Disintegration"; John W. R. Lepingwell, "Soviet

Before turning to the narrative, however, I must briefly deal with the claim that no coup attempt in fact took place in August 1991, and that the whole event was a charade staged by Gorbachev himself. Even before the coup had collapsed rumors began to circulate that Gorbachev was behind the GKChP. Many of the conspirators, for obvious reasons, have endorsed this view, but it had not received much credit in American accounts until Amy Knight endorsed it in her 1996 book *Spies without Cloaks*. A full discussion of this issue would take us too far afield, but I will note that I find this interpretation of the August coup unconvincing. It is true that Gorbachev had on previous occasions discussed with his top officials the possibility of introducing a state of emergency, and the GKChP did hope that he would endorse their efforts. But they also had decided to remove him from power and isolate him if he did not go along, as their prior preparations and the subsequent testimony of several participants makes clear. Although Gorbachev is at fault for surrounding himself with figures like Kryuchkov and his chief of staff Valeriy Boldin, the evidence for the claim that he himself was behind the GKChP is weak and unpersuasive. Similarly, William Odom's argument that August 1991 was not a failed coup attempt, but a successful one by Boris Yeltsin, focuses strictly on consequences and not on the decision to intervene; by any conventional definition, August 1991 was a failed coup.[57]

Civil–Military Relations and the August Coup," *World Politics*, 44 (1992), 539–572; Odom, *Collapse of the Soviet Military*, pp. 305–346; Robert V. Barylski, *The Soldier in Russian Politics: Duty, Dictatorship, and Democracy Under Gorbachev and Yeltsin* (New Brunswick, NJ: Transaction Publishers, 1998), pp. 97–125. The most valuable Russian sources on the coup are: V. Stepankov and Ye. Lisov, *Kremlevskiy zagovor: versiya sledsviya* (Moskva: Ogonek, 1992); "Obvinitel'noye zaklyucheniye sledstviya po delo GKChP," *Novaya ezhednevnaya gazeta* [hereafter *NEG*], July 30, August 4, 6, 25, 27, September 1, 1993; Georgiy Urushadze, *Vybrannye mesta iz perepiski s vragami: Sem' dney za kulisami vlasti* (Sankt-Peterburg: Izdatel'stvo Evropeyskogo Doma, 1995), especially pp. 309–408. Both the Stepankov and Lisov book and the *NEG* materials are based on the prosecutor's case against the GKChP. Urushadze is a St. Petersburg journalist who was an expert on the Russian Supreme Soviet's commission on the coup. He uses and provides lengthy citations from many party and KGB documents. Many of the major participants have provided memoir accounts on the coup: Boris Yel'tsin, *Zapiski prezidenta* (Moskva: Ogonek, 1994), pp. 67–133; Gorbachev, *Zhizn' i reformy*, Vol. II, pp. 555–581; M. S. Gorbachev, *Avgustovskiy putch: prichiny i sledstviya* (Moskva: Novosti, 1991); Kryuchkov, *Lichnoye delo*, Vol. II, pp. 130–214. Some of the other memoir accounts are cited below. For a good discussion of Yazov's role by one of his top assistants, see Ivashov, *Marshal Yazov*. Lebed's account is also very useful: Aleksandr Lebed, *Spektakl' nazyvalsya putch: neizvestnoye ob izvestnom* (Tiraspol, Moldova: Lada, 1993). This material was also published as part of his memoirs: Lebed, *Za derzhavu obidno...*, pp. 383–411.

57 Amy Knight, *Spies Without Cloaks: The KGB's Successors* (Princeton, NJ: Princeton University Press, 1996), pp. 12–37; Odom, *Collapse of the Soviet Military*, 341. Odom is wrong that there was no legal procedure for leadership succession in the Soviet Union in 1991. The GKChP removed Gorbachev as President in August 1991, not as General Secretary of the Communist Party, and there was a procedure both for presidential removal and for declaring a state of emergency, acts which required a parliamentary decision.

The coup attempt took place on the eve of the intended signing of the new Union Treaty that Gorbachev had negotiated with nine of the fifteen republics. The plotters believed that this treaty would lead to the break-up of the Soviet Union. Minister of Defense Yazov was the key military plotter, without whom the coup almost certainly would not have taken place. Yazov told investigators the day after the coup's collapse that the proposed Union Treaty, which was to have been signed August 20, would have led to the collapse of the USSR, and that this fact motivated the urgency with which the plot was implemented. Two of his assistants also attribute Yazov's participation in the plot to his concern about the fate of the Union. At the same time, all observers agree that Yazov acted half-heartedly. When Gorbachev was told that Yazov was a member of the GKChP, he did not believe it, saying they must have put Yazov's name down without asking him. Major-General A. V. Tsal'ko (in August 1991 he was a Colonel and a USSR People's Deputy) explains that Yazov was going through an internal struggle, as if between two people, throughout the coup. On the one hand, Yazov was agitated by the collapse of the state; on the other hand, he did not want to send the army against the people. Thus, Yazov did not make clear decisions and took half measures. Yeltsin later stated that Yazov "played a passive role the whole time."[58]

The most resolute military supporter of the coup was General Valentin Varennikov, Commander of the Ground Forces. Varennikov was the military representative at the famous meeting with Gorbachev in the Crimea on August 18, and he was the only military figure involved in planning the storming of the White House who seemed to have no doubts about undertaking it. At his trial in July 1994, Varennikov maintained that his only desire in joining the coup attempt was to "disrupt the signing of the Union Treaty, dismantling the USSR, scheduled for August 20." Varennikov compares his participation in the failed coup attempt with his service during the Great Patriotic War, stating that "in August 1991 I also came forward in defense of our Motherland – against the collapse of the Soviet Union." Deputy Minister of Defense Vladislav Achalov, the third member of the top military leadership intimately involved in the coup attempt, also maintains that preserving the USSR was a proper goal of the GKChP, even if they adopted improper means. Gromov, a career army officer who was serving as Deputy Interior

---

[58] "ChP v dele GKChP: Dopros Dmitriya Yazova," *Izvestiya*, October 10, 1991, 7; Ivashov, *Marshal Yazov*, p. 70; A. Krayniy, "Kak i pochemu marshal Yazov okazalsya zagovorshchikom?," *KP*, August 27, 1991, 3; Chernyaev, *1991 god*, p. 191; Author's interview with Major General A. V. Tsal'ko, July 28, 1994; Yeltsin, *Zapiski prezidenta*, p. 77. See also Stepankov and Lisov, *Kremlevskiy zagovor*, pp. 25–29, 132–133, 180, 186–187; M. K. Gorshkov and V. V. Zhuravlev, eds., *Krasnoye ili beloye? (Drama Avgusta-91: fakty, gipotezy, stolknoveniye mneniy)* (Moskva: Terra, 1992), pp. 249–252; Yuriy Luzhkov, *72 chasa agonii. Avgust 1991 g.: Nachalo i konets kommunisticheskogo putcha v Rossii* (Moskva: Magisterium, 1991), pp. 53, 84.

Minister in August 1991, has also justified the coup as an effort to "maintain the Soviet Union."[59]

Despite this seemingly compelling rationale for the coup, the imminent collapse of the state that officers were sworn to defend, the putsch fizzled out after three days. As we will see, military activity, or more accurately inactivity, played a key role in bringing the coup down.

Storming the White House

On the morning of August 19, Yazov convened a meeting of the Military Collegium at which he informed them of Gorbachev's "illness" and the introduction of a state of emergency. He sent an order to the commanders of all of the military districts, informing them of the state of emergency and ordering heightened military readiness and strengthened security measures. The heads of the Moscow and Leningrad military districts were named military commandants of those cities.[60]

The extent to which military officers around the Soviet Union would have been prepared to enforce a state of emergency was never really tested. Nine deputy ministers, ten military district and fleet commanders, eight heads of central departments, and three lower-level commanders were removed from the high command for activity in support of the GKChP, which usually involved either adopting statements in support of the GKChP or taking measures against soldiers who opposed the GKChP. A total of 316 officers were removed for their activities. On the other hand, there were acts of resistance to the GKChP within the military from Leningrad to the Far East. According to American intelligence officials who intercepted Soviet military communications during the coup, the majority of commanders "weren't taking the calls [from the Ministry of Defense]." Many officers came to the defense of the Russian White House on their own volition. Other officers responded to appeals from civilian officials; for example, Lieutenant-General N. Zimin removed his troops from around the Moscow mayor's office after he was asked to do so by Deputy Mayor Yuriy Luzhkov. It is difficult to predict how officers would have reacted if more active measures would have been ordered. Extrapolating from events in Moscow, it appears that military behavior

---

[59] Valentin Varennikov, *Sud'ba i sovest'* (Moskva: Paleya, 1993); Viktor Khamrayev, "Valentin Varennikov uveren, chto evo opravdayut v avguste," *Segodnya*, July 26, 1994, 2; Author's interview with General (retired) V. A. Achalov, July 26, 1994; Boris Soldatenko, "'Shturm belogo doma ne planirovalos," *KZ*, July 15, 1994, 3.

[60] The material in this section is based largely on the following sources, which are in fundamental agreement on the key details: Stepankov and Lisov, *Kremlevskiy zagovor*; Ivashov, *Marshal Yazov*; "Obvinitel'noye zaklyucheniye," *NEG*; "GKChP: Armiya privlekalas', no ne uchastovala" *Armiya*, Nos. 6–8, 1992 [Russian Supreme Soviet hearing on military participation in the coup, hereafter cited as *Armiya* with the issue and page number]; Lebed, *Spektakl' nazyvalsya putch*; "Pochemu 'Grom' ne gryanul," (depositions of Boris Gromov and Pavel Grachev), *Moskovskiye novosti*, July 17, 1994, 8.

would have been highly dependent on the activities of the local population and civilian political leadership. Most officers seemed to adopt a "wait and see" attitude; on the one hand, they had orders from the Minister of Defense but, on the other hand, doubts had begun to grow about the legitimacy of these orders.[61]

The key event in the three-day drama was the resistance to the coup led by Russian President Boris Yeltsin and the possibility that the Russian government headquarters, the so-called White House, would be stormed by force. A joint operation to storm the White House by army, MVD, and KGB forces was planned and scheduled for the night of August 20–21. The story of why the storming did not take place demonstrates the thinking of Russian officers about their role in resolving sovereign power questions and the crucial role that organizational culture played in determining the outcome of the crisis.

Two Ground Forces divisions, the Taman Motorized Rifle Division and the Kantemirov Tank Division, were introduced into Moscow on August 19. They were placed at various locations around Moscow, but given no specific tasks. Also brought into Moscow was the 106th Tula Airborne Division. Units of this division were responsible for guarding such key installations as the State Bank and radio and television stations. The behavior of this division would turn out to be decisive. Lieutenant-General Pavel Grachev was the commander of the Airborne Forces (VDV) in August 1991; and his deputy, Major-General Lebed, was tasked by Grachev with operational control of the Tula Division, which Lebed had previously commanded. At around noon on August 19, Grachev ordered Lebed to take the second battalion of the Tula Division's Ryazan regiment to "organize the guarding and defense" of the White House. Lebed was told to enter into negotiations with the head of White House security about the placement of the battalion. Why did Grachev send this battalion to the White House?[62]

This episode is one of the most mysterious of the putsch. Two completely opposing explanations have been offered for this episode. One explanation is that Grachev sent the battalion to the White House at Yeltsin's request – that is, that this unit went over to the "defenders" of the White House.[63]

---

[61] "GKChP," *Armiya*, No. 6, 16, 24; Dunlop, *Rise of Russia*, pp. 234–236, 250; Lepingwell, "Soviet Civil–Military Relations," 563–565; "GKChP," *Armiya*, No. 7–8, 27–28; Seymour M. Hersh, "The Wild East," *Atlantic Monthly*, June 1994, 85–86; Luzhkov, *72 chasa agonii*, pp. 49–50.

[62] This battalion should not be confused with the company of the Taman Division, commanded by Major Sergey Evdokimov, that undoubtedly went over to the White House. For Evdkomikov's story, see *V avguste 91-go: Rossiya glazami ochevidtsev* (Moskva–Sankt-Peterburg: Limbus-Press, 1993), pp. 14–16, 106–107; Stepankov and Lisov, *Kremelvskiy zagovor*, pp. 152–153, 177–178.

[63] Yeltsin phoned Grachev early on August 19 from his dacha to ask what was going on. He told Grachev that he believed the GKChP was unconstitutional and asked for Grachev's

The second explanation is that Grachev sent the unit at Yazov's order, to take the White House under control.[64]

Lebed's account of these events is revealing, but it provides no clue to Grachev's motivation. Lebed himself was completely in the dark about his mission; he had an order to "guard and defend" the White House, but he had no idea from whom he was defending it. Indeed, it was only on the evening of the 19th, while meeting with Yeltsin's representatives, that Lebed learned of the existence of the GKChP! Lebed's political deputy, Lieutenant-Colonel O. Ye. Bastanov, told Colonel Sergey Yushenkov, a Russian People's Deputy present at the White House, that they had orders to defend the facility but not the people, and that they would not have resisted an attack with force.[65]

Ultimately, only Pavel Grachev knows for certain his motivations at the time. Although he tended to stress his pro-Yeltsin stance in subsequent interviews, the most likely explanation for his behavior is that he was adopting a wait-and-see attitude. He was able to say "yes" to both Yazov and Yeltsin without committing firmly to either camp. In one revealing interview at the time, Grachev gave the following explanation for his behavior:

Question: Thus rumors about a split in the army and that the airborne troops went over to Yeltsin's side do not correspond to reality?
Grachev: Of course. If I had allowed my forces to split, then at that minute I would have been replaced. And who would have taken my place and what orders they would have given is difficult to say. Understand properly: Yazov ordered me to take under guard ... the RSFSR Supreme Soviet. And Yeltsin ordered that I provide him with

---

support. Grachev, after some hesitation, agreed to send a battalion to the White House and, apparently, a company of troops to Yeltsin's dacha. Yeltsin turned to his wife after this discussion and said, "Grachev is ours." Yel'tsin, *Zapiski prezidenta*, pp. 83–85; Urushadze, *Vybrannye mesta is perepiski s vragami*, pp. 353–354; Aleksandr Korzhakov, *Boris Yel'tsin: ot rassveta do zakata* (Moskva: Interbuk, 1997), pp. 83–88; *Izvestiya*, September 4, 1991, 8; *KZ*, August 31, 1991, 3.

[64] This is the conclusion the prosecutor came to after weighing all the evidence: "Obvinitel'noye zaklyucheniye," *NEG*, August 25, 1993. General Konstantin Kobets, then the chair of the Russian Supreme Soviet Committee on Defense Reform, who was in charge of the defense of the White House, was not persuaded that the unit had come over to the Russian side: *Korichnevyy putch krasnykh: Avgust '91* (Moskva: Tekst, 1991), p. 75. Yazov later claimed that Grachev and Lebed's conduct was satisfactory during the putsch: Dmitrii Yazov, interviewed by Aleksandr Prokhanov, "Armiya – vershina politiki," *Zavtra*, No. 21 (June), 1994. See also Viktor Baranets, *Yel'tsin i ego generaly: Zapiski polkovnika genshtaba* (Moskva: Sovershenno sekretno, 1997), pp. 388–390.

[65] Although Lebed's claim about his lack of knowledge about the GKChP sounds fantastic, it is quite plausible, because since early morning Lebed had been organizing the movement of the 106th Tula Division to Moscow and he had not had an opportunity to watch TV or listen to the radio. Lebed's account is an excellent description of the enormous chaos present in the military during those three days, although he explains this chaos as a product of some larger conspiracy: Aleksandr Lebed, *Spektakl' nazyvalsya putch*. Author's interview with Sergey Yushenkov, July 20, 1994.

security. Therefore about the *nonfulfillment* of an order there was no discussion in the beginning: I tried to tack between the army leadership and the Russian government.[66]

Regardless of Grachev's motives, the units were not allowed to place their armored vehicles next to the White House. Lebed had agreed on the approach of these units with the Russian leadership, but Colonel Tsal'ko became suspicious and persuaded the crowd to stop the column. Given that Grachev and Lebed's motives were unclear, and that the Airborne Troops would most likely play a key role in any attempt to storm the White House by force, Tsal'ko's caution was appropriate.[67]

On August 20 the GKChP decided to attempt to storm the White House by force. KGB head Vladimir Kryuchkov, MVD chief Boris Pugo, and Yazov tasked their deputies with drawing up a plan for a joint operation to seize the White House. Achalov, Varennikov, Grachev, Lebed, and Gromov were present at the planning meeting. At Grachev's request, Lebed was asked to report on the situation at the White House. Lebed stated that there was a crowd of up to 100,000 people at the Russian Supreme Soviet, that there were extensive fortified barricades, and that there was a well-armed security force in the building. The use of force, Lebed predicted, "would lead to a grandiose blood-letting." Varennikov criticized Lebed for his report, saying that he was "obligated to be an optimist, and you have introduced pessimism and lack of confidence here."[68]

Grachev and Gromov both made moderate efforts at this meeting to delay the storming. Grachev claimed that the Airborne Troops had insufficient forces to fulfill the tasks assigned to them; Achalov ordered that two additional regiments be flown to Moscow. Gromov suggested that his troops enter Moscow only in wheeled, not tracked, vehicles and that they not carry weapons during the operation. According to Gromov, when the meeting ended, Grachev stated that the operation would lead to much bloodshed, but no one reacted to this statement. The operation was given the code name "Thunder."

Both Grachev and Gromov took a series of steps to impede the operation later that evening. After another trip to the White House for reconnaissance, Lebed reported to Grachev that the operation was senseless and

---

[66] Emphasis in original. Interview with Colonel-General Pavel Grachev by Sergey Romanovskiy, "'My vse okazalis' zalozhnikami Yazova'," *Sobesednik*, No. 36 (September), 1991, 7.

[67] The Russian military analyst Pavel Fel'gengauer believes that Tsal'ko's move was crucial: Author's interview, July 7, 1994; Gorshkov and Zhuravlev, *Nesokrushimaya i legendarnaya*, pp. 231–233. Tsal'ko credits his decision to an "internal feeling." Author's interview. Lebed maintains that Tsal'ko was motivated by his offense at rough treatment by one of Yeltsin's bodyguards, who was accompanying Lebed at the time: Lebed, *Spektakl' nazyvalsya putch*, pp. 20–22.

[68] See the citations in note 60 for this and subsequent paragraphs.

that he would not participate. Grachev "beamed" and replied, according to Lebed, "I always believed in you, and it is excellent that I was not mistaken." Grachev sent Lebed to the White House to warn them of the planned attack and assigned him the task of receiving the two regiments being flown in at Achalov's orders. Two of Lebed's regimental commanders from the 106th Tula Division also reported to Achalov that storming the White House would be impossible, and it appears that the reinforcing regiments did not arrive as planned.

Gromov protested the planned operation to Pugo, but Pugo told him that orders were to be followed. Nevertheless, Gromov told the commander of the elite MVD Dzerzhinsky division not to move his forces without a direct order from Gromov, even if he received an order from Pugo. Gromov also took steps to inform the White House about the GKChP's plans. Gromov and Grachev also spoke by phone and agreed that their units would not take part in the storming. Grachev and Air Force Commander Yevgeniy Shaposhnikov also agreed that their forces would not participate.[69]

The KGB special forces were experiencing similar opposition to the storming.[70] Thus, Operation "Thunder" collapsed before it ever began. Although the operational plans had been worked out, all of the key units seemed to be waiting both for direct orders from the top and for activity by the forces of the other ministries. Grachev and his deputies joked bitterly that all the plotters were sleeping and "hoping that we would start the massacre."[71] In any event, Grachev had already pledged to Yeltsin, Gromov, Shaposhnikov, and his deputies that the VDV would not take part in the storming. Gromov also was determined to resist the operation.

Achalov, in the early morning of August 21, about thirty minutes before the planned storming, called Grachev to check on the situation. Grachev told Achalov that there was a huge group of people in front of the White House

---

[69] I have not discussed Shaposhnikov's role in any detail because the behavior of the army, and not the air force, was the key to the failure of the coup. The most important step Shaposhnikov took from an operational standpoint was to delay the movements of other units by the Military Transport Aviation. See Shaposhnikov, *Vybor*, pp. 9–50. See also Baranets, *Yel'tsin i ego generaly*, pp. 81–88, 321.

[70] The KGB is covered in detail in: Stepankov and Lisov, *Kremlevskiy zagovor*; "Obvinitel'noye zaklyucheniye," *NEG*; Boltunov, *Al'fa ne khotela ubivat'*, pp. 346–367.

[71] Because Kryuchkov and Yazov did not give a direct order in the early morning on August 21 to start the storming, the plotters have subsequently claimed that they did not plan to storm the White House. But orders had been given the previous evening, and they fully expected the storming to go ahead as planned, but the inactivity of Grachev and Gromov prevented the storming. The head of the KGB's Alpha unit, General Karpukhin, did intend to carry out the assault but his deputies and the rest of the unit resisted. At that point he told Grachev that his unit would not participate. In addition to the interviews with Grachev cited above, see Boltunov, *Al'fa ne khotela ubivat*, pp. 357–363; also see the interviews with the relevant KGB officers in Gorshkov and Zhuravlev, *Krasnoye ili beloye?*, pp. 108–111.

and that he was going to withdraw his forces. Achalov went to the White House himself to inspect the scene. Seeing the large crowd and hearing of the deaths of three civilians, Achalov decided that the operation should be called off. He reported this to Yazov, who after some hesitation gave the command to halt the movement of all forces. Achalov informed Grachev and Gromov of Yazov's decision.[72]

Yazov refused to attend the meeting of the GKChP on the morning of August 21, informing them that he was "leaving this game." Yazov called a meeting of the Military Collegium, at which it was agreed that all armed forces should be withdrawn from Moscow. The other members of the GKChP came to the Ministry of Defense to try to change Yazov's mind, but, relying on the decision of the Collegium, Yazov refused to rescind his order to withdraw the troops. He told them, "What, did we launch this thing in order to start shooting? We screwed up, now we have to answer [for what we did]." Yazov proposed that they fly to the Crimea to see Gorbachev, and thus the coup attempt collapsed.

Explaining Military Behavior during the August Coup

The serious weakening of the Soviet state, and the threat of its collapse into multiple republics, was the key motivation for Yazov's decision to join the plotters (the key role in organizing the plot, all observers agree, belonged to KGB chief Kryuchkov). Low state political capacity, as in 1917, created not just an opportunity for intervention but a motive of its own – the need to halt the collapse of the state. Corporate interest, although on the face of it a compelling motive for intervention, actually played almost no role in the coup decision. The timing of the coup does not fit with an interpretation based on corporate interests. Serious attacks on the army's autonomy, power, and resources had all taken place by 1988. By 1990, with the collapse of the Warsaw Pact and the reunification of Germany, these processes had gone far beyond what an interest-based explanation would suggest was the threshold for military intervention.

Why did the Soviet military fail to take decisive measures to carry out the coup? The paradox of the August 1991 coup attempt, as noted by Russian People's Deputy Lev Ponomarev, was that without the participation of the military the coup would not have taken place, but that it was precisely the

---

[72] In an otherwise compelling account of the coup, John Dunlop argues that the three civilians who died were killed at the beginning of the attempt to storm the White House. However, the units involved were from the Taman Division, who had no designated role in Operation "Thunder," and were moving *away* from the White House at the time of the incident. These units were involved (unsuccessfully) in trying to enforce the curfew: Dunlop, *Rise of Russia*, pp. 244–245; Stepankov and Lisov, *Kremlevskiy zagovor*, pp. 176–177; Kobets, in *V avguste 91-go*, p. 166; Lebed, *Spektakl' nazyvalsya putch*, pp. 38–39.

"passive participation" of both the armed forces leadership and the troops they commanded that led to the coup's collapse.[73]

There are three possible explanations for this passivity. The first is that officers were passive because of counterbalancing or internal splits (organizational structure). The second is that officers foresaw the possibility of the coup's failure and did not want to be on the losing side (individual self-interest). The third explanation is that the particular beliefs held by Soviet officers inhibited them from acting decisively (organizational culture). All three factors played some role, but I argue that the third reason was the most important for the coup's failure.[74]

Organizational structure in the form of penetration or counterbalancing was not important for the simple reason that the KGB, the MVD, and the army leadership were all on the same side. Trying to coordinate the activities of units of three different agencies might have somewhat complicated the effort, but one could just as easily argue that having the three major power ministries involved should have deterred any possible resistance.

Internal cleavages in the military were a potential hindrance to an effective coup.[75] But the nationality splits in the army played little role, at the level of either officers or enlisted personnel, because the major action during the coup took place in Moscow, where most soldiers were Russian. Whether the rank-and-file would have carried out orders for more decisive action was never tested because the military's leading officers halted the coup.

The most important split in the officer corps during the August coup was an ideational one, not a structural one. Key officers did not believe that the activities of the GKChP were legitimate, and therefore they engaged in active or passive resistance. Junior and middle-ranking officers were especially likely to oppose the coup on these grounds.[76] Thus, organizational structure was at best a secondary factor in the collapse of the coup.

There is more evidence for the view that individual officers tried to protect themselves by using a fence-sitting strategy.[77] The fence-sitting behavior

---

[73] *Armiya*, No. 6, 15. See also: N. Gul'binskiy and M. Shakina, *Afganistan...Kreml'...* *"Lefortovo"...?: Epizody politicheskoy biografii Aleksandra Rutskogo* (Moskva: Lada-M, 1994), p. 114.

[74] As Jon Elster points out, both self-interested and normative reasons may be present in any particular action, but this does not mean that norms are not autonomous or important: Jon Elster, *The Cement of Society: A Study of Social Order* (Cambridge, England: Cambridge University Press, 1989), pp. 97, 106–107, 125–151.

[75] For this argument, see Odom, *Collapse of the Soviet Military*, pp. 305–346; Meyer, "How the Threat (and the Coup) Collapsed."

[76] An officer serving in the General Staff in August 1991 claims that most General Staff officers remained neutral during the coup, although privately senior officers (generals) tended to support the coup and mid-level officers (Colonels) tended to oppose it. Author's interview with Colonel (retired) Valeriy Yarynich, October 28, 1994.

[77] For a collective action explanation for military behavior, see Jerry F. Hough, *Democratization and Revolution in the USSR 1985–1991* (Washington, D.C.: Brookings Institution, 1997), pp. 443–448.

exhibited by officers such as Grachev, who tried to "tack between" Yazov and Yeltsin, is in part explained by self-interested calculation. Adopting a wait-and-see attitude is a sensible course when an officer is uncertain about the validity of orders. The Russian military analyst Pavel Fel'gengauer noted that officers always follow an order, for otherwise they can face a military tribunal. But when contradictory orders start to come from different sources and the legality of these orders is unclear, Fel'gengauer continued, "any normal, not too politicized officer will try to act cautiously, slowly, and, if possible, confusedly...activity seems significantly more severe than inactivity. The majority of officers acted along these lines."[78]

This explanation has a great deal of merit. It benefits considerably, however, from hindsight. As Mikhail Boltunov points out in his book on the KGB Alpha unit, what if the coup had lasted three weeks and not three days? At the time that Grachev, Gromov, Lebed, and Shaposhnikov had decided to disobey orders, it was not at all clear that the coup would collapse so suddenly. Indeed, it was only the failure of the military to carry out orders that caused the putsch's failure, as Gorbachev himself noted later. Shaposhnikov and his deputies thought that he might be arrested when he was summoned to Yazov's office on August 20, and Grachev stated that he knew that he could face a tribunal for insubordination. Shaposhnikov and Grachev both have noted that open opposition would lead to their being replaced by people more willing to carry out any orders. Grachev later remarked, "you civilians can squabble, but we have regulations."[79]

Something other than self-interested calculation had to be present for top officers to resist orders and drag their feet, because not carrying out orders was potentially as risky as implementing them. This inhibiting factor was the army's organizational culture. Organizational norms were clearly violated by Yazov and several other top officers who participated in organizing the coup, due to their concern about possible state collapse. At the same time, many officers believed that the military should not be involved in sovereign power issues and that they should remain subordinate to civilian control. Thus, these officers faced an internal struggle, and Yeltsin and his allies successfully used these military beliefs to disrupt the coup.

The August 1991 events also showed the presence of two subcultures within the armed forces. One subculture was embodied by Varennikov, who was one of the few top officers who was willing, even eager, to use harsh measures to achieve their goals. Varennikov sent five telegrams on August 19 and 20 from Kiev, where he went after Foros to talk with Ukrainian President Leonid Kravchuk, to complain about "indecisiveness and half-measures" and to urge "immediate measures to liquidate the group of B. N. Yeltsin's

---

[78] Fel'gengauer, in Gorshkov and Zhuravlev, *Nesokrushimaya i legendarnaya*, pp. 231–232.
[79] Gorbachev, *Avgustovskiy putch*, p. 21; Shaposhnikov, *Vybor*, pp. 28–37; Interview with Grachev by Romanovskiy, "'My vse okazalis' zalozhnikami Yazova.'"

adventurists." Varennikov ordered, seemingly on his own initiative, the deployment of army aviation and three additional tank companies from the Taman Division to assist the storming. The head of army aviation, Pavlov, did not fulfill Varennikov's order, and the commander of the Taman Division, Marchenko, refused the order because it was not delivered in writing.[80]

The other subculture was the one embodied by officers such as Tsal'ko, Yushenkov, and General Kobets, who immediately supported Yeltsin. Junior officers, in particular, seemed more inclined to embrace the Russian pro-democracy movement.[81]

The dominant military organizational culture, however, was the one adhered to by Shaposhnikov, Gromov, Grachev, and Lebed. They faced a situation in which they had orders from the Minister of Defense to fulfill and the consequences for insubordination were potentially severe, but also the growing knowledge that the military was deeply involved in a sovereign power dispute. In such a situation the question of who holds legitimate power can play a key role in determining military behavior. Officers that adhere to a norm of civilian supremacy will tend to support those politicians who will be able to rule without the need to rely on military force, because involvement in domestic politics is not considered a proper function of the armed forces.

Boris Yeltsin and his advisers clearly understood this military dilemma between following orders and staying out of politics, and they worked hard to exploit it to their advantage. Yeltsin possessed enormous legitimacy and authority. Two months prior to the coup he had been elected President of Russia with fifty-seven percent of the vote in the first popular presidential election in Russian history. Yeltsin, his Vice-President Alexander Rutskoy (an Air Force Colonel and an Afghanistan war hero), and General Kobets made several appeals to the armed forces not to participate in unconstitutional activity. Yeltsin also declared himself commander-in-chief of the Russian Federation, since the legal commander-in-chief, Gorbachev, was isolated from power. They used various channels, such as personal contacts and parliamentary deputies, especially from the military, to explain their position to key officers. Understanding that he could not ask these officers to disobey direct orders, Kobets appealed to commanders to delay the implementation

---

[80] Stepankov and Lisov, *Kremlevskiy zagovor*, pp. 149–150; *Armiya*, No. 7–8, 24–25. Another adherent to this "hardliner" subculture was the infamous General Makashov. On his activity during the coup, see *Armiya*, No. 7–8, 28; A. Tarasov, "Chem byl zanyat vo vremya perevorota general Makashov?" *Izvestiya*, September 21, 1991, 8; Interview with Albert Makashov by Vladimir Voronov, "'Menya uvol'nyali Gorbachev, El'tsin, Bush i papa rimskiy!'," *Sobesednik*, No. 33 (August), 1992, 10.

[81] Meyer, "How the Threat (and the Coup) Collapsed"; Yu. I. Deryugin, I. V. Obraztsov, V. V. Serebryannikov, *Problemy sotsiologii armii* (Moskva: Institut sotsial'no-politicheskikh issledovaniy, 1994), pp. 45, 50.

of orders until he had time to organize countermeasures. Kobets states that Colonel-General Kalinin, the Commander of the Moscow Military District who was named the Military Commandant of Moscow, in essence fulfilled both Yazov's and Yeltsin's orders. Moscow Deputy Mayor Yuriy Luzhkov also noted Kalinin's foot-dragging.[82]

Popular legitimacy, evidenced by the large and resolute crowd at the White House, also played a crucial role. Some commentators have argued that the presence of the crowd made little difference and that the White House could have been stormed easily. But it is clear from the account of key figures such as Lebed, Grachev, Gromov, and even Achalov that they were not morally prepared for the massacre that would have taken place in the event of a storming. Yeltsin states, "the 'massive bloodletting' [quoting Lebed] would have been a most serious blow to the military, from which they would not have recovered. Therefore they only imitated the preparation for a storming, imitated military activity, wasted time."[83]

Gorbachev, despite his general unpopularity at the time, was the legitimate leader of the Soviet Union, and this fact also had an effect on officers. Most officers would have gladly voted against him in a free election, but his displacement by the GKChP was clearly unconstitutional. Shaposhnikov maintains that he "felt uncomfortable" when Yazov announced at the Collegium meeting on August 19 that Gorbachev was ill and that Vice-President Gennadiy Yanayev had taken on the president's duties. Yushenkov notes that Shaposhnikov and Grachev were helped in their "difficult decision" by the fact that the Soviet president had been "effectively denied power."[84]

If Gorbachev was unpopular but legitimate, the members of the GKChP were unpopular and illegitimate. The GKChP clearly were concerned about the appearance of legality. They forced the leading role in the State Emergency Committee on Vice-President Yanayev because of constitutional reasons, even though he was too weak a personality to be the

[82] Yeltsin, *Zapiski prezidenta*, pp. 103–116; Kobets, in *V avguste 91-go*, pp. 10–14, 103–106; Ivashov, *Marshal Yazov*, pp. 90–91; Dunlop, *Rise of Russia*, pp. 213–215; Odom, *Collapse of the Soviet Military*, p. 340; Gul'binskiy and Shakina, *Afganistan ... Kreml' ... "Lefortovo" ...?*, pp. 118–120; Ruslan Khasbulatov, *The Struggle for Russia: Power and Change in the Democratic Revolution* (New York: Routledge, 1993), pp. 131–169; Sergey Filatov, *Sovershenno nesekretno* (Moskva: Vagrius, 2000), p. 128; Luzhkov, *72 chasa agonii*, pp. 50–51, 55, 76. Colonel Anatoliy Volkov, who was the assistant of General Dmitriy Volkogonov, Yeltsin's military adviser in the presidential administration, was sent by Kobets to the Taman and Kantemirov Divisions and the Moscow Military District headquarters with Yeltsin's orders to the military. Author's interview with Volkov, July 20, 1994.

[83] Yeltsin, *Zapiski prezidenta*, pp. 113, 116. Incidentally, when the considerably less well defended White House was stormed in October 1993, about 100 people lost their lives. Many more would have died if an attempt had been made in August 1991.

[84] Interview with Shaposhnikov in *KP*, August 27, 1991, 3; Shaposhnikov, *Vybor*, pp. 18–19; Author's interview with Yushenkov.

lead figure (he earned the nickname "shaking hands" for his performance at the GKChP's press conference). Yanayev tried to persuade them that Anatoliy Lukyanov, the speaker of the Supreme Soviet, should take on Gorbachev's responsibilities, but Lukyanov refused to become acting president or a formal member of the GKChP because it was an executive body, and he represented the legislative branch. Few people were fooled by these legal maneuverings, though, and the members of the GKChP did not have the popularity or charisma to command support either among the populace or in the army.[85]

The efforts of Yeltsin to convince officers that the GKChP was illegitimate and that Gorbachev and he were the rightful leaders of the Soviet Union and Russia played an important role. No longer did officers face the simple task of carrying out orders; they were put in a position in which the military was involved in a sovereign power dispute. Even Yazov's behavior suggests that he understood he had violated his own conception of the military's role and position by becoming involved in the coup. Yazov pursued half measures almost from the beginning, and he gave the order to withdraw the troops – his refusal to order force caused the coup to collapse. Moreover, Yazov did not take punitive steps against Shaposhnikov and others who were obviously not complying with orders in a timely fashion. The day after the coup collapsed Yazov remarked, "I was an old fool to participate in this adventure."[86]

Akhromeyev also violated organizational norms, even though he had sworn for years that the military was subordinate to civilian leadership and would not intervene in politics. Akhromeyev did not take part in planning the coup, but he supported it and provided his assistance to the plotters. Norms are sometimes violated, but the violator usually feels a sense of shame for having transgressed.[87] Although it is impossible to know for sure, this sense of shame probably played a role in Akhromeyev's decision to commit suicide after the coup failed. The day after the coup collapsed he wrote to Gorbachev:

I understand that as a Marshal of the Soviet Union I violated the Military Oath and committed a military crime. I also committed no less of a crime as an adviser to the President of the USSR. Nothing remains for me now except to take responsibility for my actions.[88]

---

[85] Stepankov and Lisov, *Kremlevskiy zagovor*, pp. 101–102; "Obvinitel'noye zaklyucheniye...," *NEG*, July 30, August 4, 1993; Yeltsin, *Zapiski prezidenta*, p. 108; Urushadze, *Vybrannye mesta iz perepiski s vragami*, p. 344; Albats, *The State within a State*, pp. 288–293.

[86] "ChP v dele GKChP," *Izvestiya*, October 10, 1991, 7.

[87] Elster, *Cement of Society*, pp. 99–100, 105.

[88] Stepankov and Lisov, *Kremlevskiy zagovor*, pp. 240–242.

Axioms and events particular to the Soviet military, consistent with the organizational culture approach, played a key role. For example, the Soviet military often expressed the maxims that "the army and people are united" and "the army will never go against the people." Shaposhnikov noted that these words had become a "hackneyed stereotype, and were treated as such. The extreme situation of August 19–21 suddenly showed that these were not words, they were reality!"[89]

The lessons of Tbilisi, Baku, and Vilnius were prominent in the minds of those involved. On each of these prior occasions the army had been blamed for the consequences of poor decisions made by political leaders. Shaposhnikov recalled how immediately after the Collegium meeting on August 19 he remembered the events in Tbilisi, Baku, and Vilnius. He thought, "Why should our poor soldier, our miserable officer, our hoodwinked general pay for the mistakes and ambitions of politicians?" Ivashov argued that one of the factors leading Yazov to act indecisively was the "sad experience" of these incidents and the "dark stain" they had cast on the army. Grachev maintained that every soldier and officer began to feel special responsibility for his activity after these events and also began to think about for what purpose he was being asked to "spill the blood of peaceful citizens, compatriots." He said, "in essence it was precisely the army that was able to stop the bloodletting that could have taken place the night of August 20–21. You see, the army learned its lesson from the January events in Vilnius."[90] The importance of these critical events in the organization's history give additional weight to the organizational culture view.

The low political capacity of the Soviet state in 1991, which threatened the existence of the Union, was the key reason that some members of the officer corps violated organizational norms and took part in the August 1991 coup. At the same time, when push came to shove, the Soviet armed forces exhibited few praetorian tendencies. Even Defense Minister Yazov, who got the military involved in the first place, showed no enthusiasm for a role in high politics. With few exceptions, most officers in positions of responsibility did everything they could to avoid decisive actions. Their "passive participation" was testimony to a military organizational culture with an attachment to a norm of civilian supremacy. Individual self-interest and, to a lesser extent, internal splits in the military also led to the coup's failure. Corporate interests, on the other hand, were not an important motive for the coup and did not have a major effect on officer behavior during the putsch.

---

[89] Interview with Marshal E. I. Shaposhnikov, "Vozrodit' avtoritet armii," *KZ*, August 30, 1991, 1.

[90] Shaposhnikov, *Vybor*, p. 19; Ivashov, *Marshal Yazov*, p. 70; Grachev, interview in *KZ*, August 31, 1991, 3; Grachev interviewed by Lashkevich, *Izvestiya*, October 14, 1991, 8.

THE COLLAPSE OF THE USSR

The failed August 1991 coup gave a sharp impetus to the process of the disintegration of the Soviet Union. By the end of the year the USSR had collapsed. Why did the armed forces not intervene to halt the breakdown of the state they were sworn to defend? Military behavior is explained by three considerations. First, the coup and its aftermath increased splits in the armed forces, particularly along ethnic lines. Second, the belief that a coup attempt would fail and that the instigators of a military putsch would be punished influenced officers. Third, the normative view that the military should not intervene in high politics was reinforced by the August 1991 failed coup.

Although the military did not intervene in December 1991, they did play an arbiter role. After Yeltsin and the leaders of Ukraine and Belarus declared the Soviet Union dissolved, both Gorbachev and Yeltsin met with the high command and asked for support. The military refused to intervene, which de facto meant that they had acquiesced to Yeltsin's position and the collapse of the Soviet Union.

The Effect of the August 1991 Coup on the Military

The rapid collapse of the hard-liner coup effort had serious consequences for the armed forces. The minister of defense, the chief of the general staff, nine deputy ministers, ten military district and fleet commanders (including the commander of the Moscow Military District), and eight heads of central departments were dismissed for support of the failed putsch. Some officers compared the house cleaning to the purges under Stalin. Additionally, Communist Party organs inside the armed forces were abolished, while the party itself was banned. The removal of Communist Party bodies was strongly supported by the new Minister of Defense, Yevgeniy Shaposhnikov, and by a large majority (over ninety percent) of the officer corps. Russian military analyst Pavel Fel'gengauer contends that the military used the failure of the August coup to destroy party bodies in the armed forces, which they had never liked. After over seventy years of party domination, however, this change certainly contributed to the post-coup upheaval in the armed forces.[91]

---

[91] Baranets, *Poteryannaya armiya*, pp. 158–162; Shaposhnikov, *Vybor*, pp. 97–101; Interview with Shaposhnikov, "Vozrodit' avtoritet armii," *KZ*, August 30, 1991, 1; Author's interview with Fel'gengauer, July 7, 1994. Ninety-four percent of officers and warrant officers supported the "departyization" of the armed forces (the removal of Communist Party cells). Seventy-one percent supported the removal of political organs, which were responsible for political education. This number was over eighty percent for regular line officers (i.e., not counting political workers). V. Serebryannikov, *Zagadka perevorota: Kak razygryvali armeyskuyu kartu* (Moskva: "Pravda Severa," 1992), p. 39.

Those officers who actively opposed the coup were rewarded. The new Minister, Shaposhnikov, and his new first deputy, Grachev, had distinguished themselves during the August days for their resistance to the GKChP. The rise of an air force officer to the top job and the appointment of an Airborne Forces general to be his top deputy was a remarkable change for an army that had always been dominated by Ground Forces commanders. The new Chief of the General Staff, General Vladimir Lobov, was head of the Frunze Military Academy at the time of the coup and had refused an appointment by the GKChP as military commandant of a region of Moscow. General Kobets, who had helped organize Yeltsin's defense of the White House, was named the chair of the Russian Federation commission on military reform.[92]

The new military leadership stressed repeatedly in interviews after their appointments the principle that the army should not be involved in politics. Shaposhnikov stated, "the army cannot be and should not be an arena of party or political confrontation, nor a means for the satisfaction of someone's ambitions. Serving the people, upholding the Constitution, defending the Fatherland – these are the three foundations for military service." Shaposhnikov later remarked in his memoirs that he saw ending the army's internal involvement as one of his key tasks upon becoming Defense Minister. General Staff Chief Lobov said, "the military should, of course, be largely under the control of civilian authorities, and the military should not interfere in politics." The Defense Ministry ordered local military commanders not to become involved in ethnic conflicts in a clear attempt to prevent the use of the military for resolving internal missions.[93]

The effect of these changes on the officer corps was clear. First, much of the top military leadership was changed, thereby disrupting personal and institutional ties within the highest ranks of the officer corps. Second, a clear message was communicated that officers with praetorian leanings were not wanted in the Soviet officer corps. Third, an equally stark message was sent that those who resist following dubious orders are likely to be rewarded. Finally, the new military leadership stated plainly their commitment to a norm of civilian supremacy. All of these changes strengthened the determination of many officers, including the top leaders, to keep the army out of politics at all costs. This firmness was required for the military to weather the chaos of the coming months.

---

[92] Stephen Foye, "El'tsin Begins Housecleaning in the Defense Ministry," *Report on the USSR*, 3, 36 (1991), 31–34.

[93] Interview with Shaposhnikov, "Vozrodit' avtoritet armii"; Shaposhnikov, *Vybor*, pp. 66, 72; Interview with General Vladimir Lobov by Yuliy Semenov, "Mayak Morning Panorama," *Mayak Radio*, September 26, 1991 [FBIS-SOV-91-189, September 30, 1991, 41]; TASS, "Protivostoyaniye narastayet," *KZ*, September 25, 1991, 1.

The Collapse of the USSR and the Military's Reaction

The first states to break free from the Soviet Union were the Baltic states of Estonia, Latvia, and Lithuania. Their independence was recognized by the new Soviet State Council (Gorbachev plus the heads of the other republics) on September 6. After the coup collapsed, an avalanche of independence declarations came out, the first and most significant being the August 24 declaration by Ukraine. By the end of September Belarus, Moldova, Azerbaijan, Uzbekistan, Kirgiziya, Georgia, Tajikistan, and Armenia had all announced their independence in one form or another.

These independence declarations had a somewhat symbolic character, and the future of the Soviet state was still undetermined. Gorbachev entered into negotiations with the leaders of the remaining republics (except Moldova and Georgia) on a new treaty for a "union of sovereign states." These negotiations dragged on for several months, but they eventually reached a dead end after over ninety percent of Ukrainians voted for independence on December 1. There could be no serious talk of a union without Ukraine's participation. Shortly after the Ukrainian vote, on December 7–8, Yeltsin, newly elected Ukrainian President Leonid Kravchuk, and chair of the Belarussian Supreme Soviet Stanislav Shushkevich met in the Belovezhskaya Forest in Belarus and declared the death of the Soviet Union and the founding of the Commonwealth of Independent States (CIS). Other former Soviet republics were invited to join, and the deal was clinched on December 12 when the five Central Asian states asked to join. The Commonwealth Declaration was signed by the leaders of eleven republics (all except Georgia) on December 22 in Alma Ata, Kazakhstan. Gorbachev resigned as Soviet leader on December 25, and the Soviet Union ceased to exist.[94]

The fate of the military was a major topic of the post-August negotiations. In fact, by November nearly all of the all-union ministries had been disbanded; the Soviet presidency and legislature and the defense and foreign affairs ministries were about the only significant institutions remaining. The State Council decided in November that, whatever the ultimate shape of the future union, the armed forces would remain unified and under a single command. There were considerable grounds for skepticism, however, because several of these same republics were hard at work "privatizing" the

---

[94] Dunlop, *Rise of Russia*, pp. 256–284; Matlock, *Autopsy on an Empire*, pp. 605–647. The accounts of Gorbachev and Yeltsin, although largely a mutual exercise in finger pointing, are still useful: Yeltsin, *Zapiski prezidenta*, pp. 143–169; Gorbachev, *Zhizn' i reformy*, Vol. II, pp. 582–602; *Soyuz mozhno bylo sokhranit'*, 201–338; Mikhail Gorbachev, *Dekabr'-91: Moya pozitsiya* (Moskva: Novosti, 1992). Gorbachev's aides have also left accounts: Andrey Grachev, *Dal'she bez menya: Ukhod prezidenta* (Moskva: "Progress-Kul'tura," 1994); Georgii Khosroevich Shakhnazarov, *Tsena svobody: reformatsiya Gorbacheva glazami ego pomoshchnika* (Moskva: Rossika: Zevs, 1993), pp. 276–309; Chernyaev, *Shest' let s Gorbachevym*, pp. 488–517.

Soviet military units on their territory. The key player, again, was Ukraine, which had declared its control over these units in August and had appointed its own Minister of Defense, Major General Konstantin Morozov. By October the Ukrainian Supreme Soviet had established much of the legal basis for their own armed forces.[95]

Events in the military sphere moved at a breathtaking pace in December. On December 6, just after the referendum on independence, Ukraine's Supreme Soviet adopted a new military oath of allegiance to Ukraine and Morozov became the first officer to take the oath. The agreement between Yeltsin, Kravchuk, and Shushkevich on the CIS did not call for a unified military, but only unified control over nuclear weapons, with "joint" command over the "common military-strategic space" of the Commonwealth. On December 13 Kravchuk declared himself Commander-in-Chief of the Ukrainian Armed Forces and decreed that the Ukrainian military would be formed from Soviet forces stationed in the country. Although Morozov said on December 17 that the forces in Ukraine were still subordinate to Moscow and that the transfer of control would take place "in stages," the direction in which Ukraine was heading was clear.[96]

The threat of the collapse of the armed forces generated considerable anxiety among officers. In late November a General Staff department issued a protest against the collapse of the state and the army. The head of the department, Major-General Leonid Kozhendayev, stressed that they were not "putschists" or "mutineers." The army, he said, "does not want to and will not force the people to do something." The military, according to Kozhendayev, was ready to help politicians stop the "active civil war" taking place in the country. Another officer, Captain V. Shurygin, published an open letter to Shaposhnikov in the hard-line paper *Den'*. Shurygin complained bitterly and sarcastically about the collapse of the state and the army, asking rhetorically, "in what army do we serve?"[97]

95 Shaposhnikov, *Vybor*, 101–154; Major A. Yegorov, "Gossovet SSSR skazal 'da' edinym vooruzhennym silam," *KZ*, November 6, 1991, 1; P. Kalashnikov, "Vooruzhennye Sily SSR: vo skol'ko oboydetsya ikh edinstvo?," in Gorshkov and Zhuravlev, *Nesokrushimaya i legendarnaya*, pp. 249–250; Kathleen Mihalisko, "Laying the Foundations for the Armed Forces of Ukraine," *Report on the USSR*, 3, 45 (1991), 19–22; Kathleen Mihalisko, "Ukraine Asserts Control over Nonstrategic Forces, *RFE/RL Research Report*, 1, 4 (1992), 50–53; Bohdan Pyskir, "The Silent Coup: The Building of Ukraine's Military," *European Security*, 2 (1993), 140–161.

96 Mihalisko, "Ukraine Asserts Control"; *Soyuz mozhno bylo sokhranit'*, 304–305; Colonel A. Polyakov, "Ukazy ob oborone," *KZ*, December 13, 1991, 1; Interview with Colonel-General K. Morozov by A. Polyakov, "Voyska na Ukraine podchinyayutsya ministru oborony SSSR," *KZ*, December 18, 1991, 1.

97 Interview with Major-General Leonid Kozhendayev by A. Khokhlov, "Ofitsery Genshtaba protiv vsekh prezidentov srazu," *KP*, November 30, 1991, 2; Captain V. Shurygin, *Den'*, November 17, 1991, in Gorshkov and Zhuravlev, *Nesokrushimaya i legendarnaya*, pp. 250–252.

Rumors of an impending military coup once again circulated in the Soviet and Western press. Lobov was removed without warning on December 7, allegedly for "health reasons." John Dunlop subsequently linked these rumors and Lobov's dismissal to the formation of the CIS, arguing that it was necessary for Yeltsin to "act quickly and decisively to head off a military-police putsch."[98]

No evidence has emerged to substantiate these rumors of an impending putsch, and Shaposhnikov categorically rejected them. The reason for Lobov's removal was completely commonplace – he lost a turf battle with Shaposhnikov. Since his appointment in August, Lobov had been promoting a reform plan that would have removed the General Staff from the Defense Ministry and subordinated it directly to the president. The Defense Ministry in Lobov's plan would have been headed by a civilian, and its jurisdiction would have been limited to personnel and supply issues; the General Staff would have had control over military training and operations. Shaposhnikov stated that Lobov was dismissed because he continued to agitate for this reorganization of the armed forces even after the Military Collegium and President Gorbachev had rejected it. Shaposhnikov's version of Lobov's dismissal was endorsed by other officers and military analysts. Yeltsin noted in his memoirs that rumors of a military coup circulated at the time, but he gives them no credit, and none of the other civilian memoirs, including Gorbachev's, even mentions the possibility of a military coup.[99]

There is no evidence that a plot was hatched in the armed forces to stop the collapse of the Soviet state. On the contrary, apparently Shaposhnikov even resisted an invitation from the commander-in-chief, Gorbachev, for the military to take power. Gorbachev called Shaposhnikov in November 1991 and told him that there was only one remaining solution: The military should take power in its hands, restore order, install a government agreeable to it, and then step aside. Shaposhnikov told Gorbachev that they would both end up in prison with Yanayev and Yazov if the military tried to seize power. Yeltsin's authority is very high, said Shaposhnikov – such a decision could lead to a civil war. Politicians have created this mess (*kasha*), he concluded, and they should clean it up. Gorbachev replied that he had just been thinking out loud.[100]

---

[98] Dunlop, *Rise of Russia*, pp. 271–274.

[99] Interview with General V. N. Lobov by Pavel Fel'gengauer, "Novyy nachal'nik Sovetskogo Genshtaba," *Nezavisimaya gazeta* [hereafter *NG*], September 3, 1991, 1–2; O. Vladykin, "Armiya vne politicheskikh igr," *KZ*, December 14, 1991, 1; Shaposhnikov, *Vybor*, pp. 115–116; Yu. Teplyakov, "Generaly ukhodyat. Pochemu?," *Moskovskiye novosti*, December 15, 1991; Interview with Colonel V. Lopatin, *NG*, January 7, 1992; Yeltsin, *Zapiski prezidenta*, p. 240.

[100] Marshal Yevgeniy Shaposhnikov, appearance at Harvard University, October 17, 1994. Shaposhnikov left this incident out of the first edition of his memoirs, but it appears in the second edition: Evgeniy Shaposhnikov, *Vybor*, second edition (Moskva: PIK, 1995),

The Belovezhskaya Forest agreement creating the CIS again put before Shaposhnikov the need to decide his political stance. Shaposhnikov knew that Yeltsin, Kravchuk, and Shushkevich were discussing the position of the three Slavic states (Russia, Ukraine, and Belarus) toward the future union, but it was only when Yeltsin called him on the evening of December 8 that he learned of the CIS agreement. Shaposhnikov was heartened by the news that the three leaders had agreed on unified control over nuclear weapons. Yeltsin admitted that they had not reached agreement yet on conventional forces, but reiterated his support for unified armed forces. Shaposhnikov supported the establishment of the CIS because he believed the Union had reached a "dead end" and that the CIS provided some concreteness to a hitherto completely amorphous situation. He also thought there was still a chance for a common approach to defense and security. Morozov, the Ukrainian Defense Minister, opposed Ukrainian participation in the CIS because he believed it hindered the process of officers transferring their loyalty to Ukraine. Morozov, however, like Shaposhnikov, was not consulted on his views about the CIS beforehand and was not present at the Belovezhskaya meeting.[101]

Gorbachev made another bid for the support of the high command after the Belovezhskaya Forest agreement creating the CIS was announced. He met with the senior military leadership on December 10 and asked them to help save the Union. Gorbachev's performance was not well received, however, particularly because he began the meeting by "repenting," as Shaposhnikov put it, for not paying more attention to army problems in the past. Moreover, there was little that Gorbachev could offer the military. Russia was already in charge of state finances, and Yeltsin had promised a pay increase to officers because of burgeoning inflation. Yeltsin met with the high command on December 11, the day after Gorbachev, and stated his support for unified armed forces and his belief that the CIS offered a solution to the impasse the union treaty negotiations had reached. Yeltsin's presentation reportedly was received more favorably than Gorbachev's by the top officer corps.[102]

pp. 137–138. Shaposhnikov said in 1999 that he still does not know whether it was a "serious proposal" or whether Gorbachev indeed was just "thinking aloud": Author's interview with Evgeniy Shaposhnikov, September 29, 1999. This incident was also alluded to during Varennikov's trial. See Arkadiy Zheldykov, "Sobralsya li Gorbachev vvesti voyennoye polozheniye?," *Izvestiya*, June 22, 1994, 2.

[101] Shaposhnikov, *Vybor*, pp. 120–128; General Konstantin Morozov, appearance at Harvard University, February 16, 1995. Gorbachev accuses Shaposhnikov in his memoirs of having discussions with Yeltsin "over his head" and dissembling about how much he knew about the Belovezhskaya agreement, a charge Shaposhnikov denies: Gorbachev, *Zhizn' i reformy*, Vol. II, pp. 598–599; Author's interview with Shaposhnikov.

[102] Shaposhnikov, *Vybor*, p. 137; Pavel Fel'gengauer, "V bor'be za armiyu, pokhozhe, pobezhdayet Boris Yel'tsin," *NG*, December 12, 1991, 1; V. Yuzbashev, *Izvestiya*, December 12, 1991, excerpted in Gorshkov and Zhuravlev, *Nesokrushimaya i legendarnaya*, pp. 258–259; Stephen Foye, "From Union to Commonwealth: Will the Armed Forces Go Along?," *Report on the USSR*, 3, 51 (1991), 4–7. Gorbachev staffer Yegor Kuznetsov claims that after Yeltsin

This, then, was the extent of military arbitration in December 1991. Military support for Gorbachev would have necessarily entailed the use of armed force to prevent the collapse of the Soviet Union. Given the very high standing of Yeltsin in Russia, as well as Kravchuk at the time, the army would have been forced to act decisively to resist the Belovezhskaya accord. The high command had no desire to undertake such a mission, particularly after the August 1991 experience. This refusal to use force meant that the Belovezhskaya agreement would stand and the Soviet Union would collapse, but the army was not prepared to support the discredited Gorbachev against the highly popular Yeltsin. There also was still hope that a unified military would be maintained.

The future of the armed forces was discussed by the CIS heads of state in Minsk on December 30. The right of each state to form its own army was affirmed, but "strategic forces" were to remain under joint control. The Minsk agreement seemed to include all but ground forces under the term "strategic forces," but the Ukrainian leadership took the position that only nuclear forces were strategic. The military high command accused Ukraine of acting in bad faith and maintained that all forces required for the common defense of the CIS were strategic. Regardless, Ukraine moved immediately in early January 1992 to resubordinate the general purpose forces on its territory to Kiev. Officers were required to swear a new oath and the General Staff communications links from Moscow were shut off. A major brouhaha erupted between Moscow and Kiev, particularly over the Black Sea Fleet.[103]

The last gasp of the Soviet military was heard in Moscow on January 17, 1992, at the All-Army Officers' Assembly. Five thousand officers attended the conference and angrily protested the collapse of the Soviet Union and the armed forces. Shaposhnikov, whose new title was that of Commander-in-Chief of the CIS Armed Forces, angrily stalked out when one officer called for

---

and the leaders of Ukraine and Belarus announced the creation of the Commonwealth of Independent States on December 8, Gorbachev was "desperate" to do something to stop the agreement. A speech was prepared calling for the support of the army and patriotic forces. However, that version was rejected because it was clear by that point that Gorbachev had no power. Top Gorbachev aide Georgiy Shakhnazarov recounts a meeting of Gorbachev advisers held on December 10 at which their response to the Belovezhskaya agreement was discussed. At this meeting Yevgeniy Primakov, a top Gorbachev associate, stated that Gorbachev would not be able to rely on the army. Author's interview with Kuznetsov, July 18, 1994; Shakhnazarov, *Tsena pobedy*, pp. 304–306.

[103] Shaposhnikov, *Vybor*, pp. 140–142; Pavel Fel'gengauer, "Kak delit' armiyu – po chestnomu ili po spravedlivosti?," *NG*, December 31, 1991, 1–2; P. Chernenko, "Soglasheniye podpisano, voprosy ostayutsya," *KZ*, January 1, 1992, in Gorshkov and Zhuravlev, *Nesokrushimaya i legendarnaya*, pp. 269–271; Captain V. Chupakhin, "'Ya obrashchayus' k narodam, parlamentam, rukovoditelyam suverennykh gosudarstv…'," *KZ*, January 7, 1992, 1, 3; Viktor Litovkin, "Armiya ne dolzhna byt' kozyrem v politicheskoy igre," *Izvestiya*, January 16, 1992, 3; Stephen Foye, "CIS: Kiev and Moscow Clash over Armed Forces," *RFE/RL Research Report*, 1, 3 (1992), 1–3; Pyskir, "Silent Coup."

his resignation. After a unanimous vote asking for Shaposhnikov to return, he came back to a standing ovation. Shaposhnikov pointed out that the CIS heads of state had agreed that each state had the right to form its own army, and Shaposhnikov reiterated his view that this transition should take place gradually. He concluded emotionally:

I believe that all the questions should be settled without tears and suffering for your families and yourselves. Can't you understand? What else can be done? What do you expect me to do – order the troops to turn their guns and tanks on Moscow? We have had all that already, but that is precisely what they [those who called for his resignation – B.T.] were hinting at. I know what this would mean. We are not Thailand. We represent one-sixth of the earth's surface. We are being looked upon, comrades, as sick. I beg your forgiveness.[104]

The Assembly came to an abrupt end less than thirty minutes after this impassioned confrontation. The officers adopted a declaration to the "peoples, parliaments, and heads of government of the Commonwealth of Independent States," asking them to maintain a unified armed forces. Many observers at the time believed the conference was evidence of the praetorian leanings of the Soviet army, and Fel'gengauer argued that the conference indicated that a military coup was likely. Polls conducted at the meeting also showed that the officers were in a dangerous mood, with seventy-one percent supporting the restoration of a unified government in the Soviet Union's former borders and seventy-nine percent of those polled believing that the armed forces themselves should decide the future of the military.[105]

The All-Army Officers' Assembly certainly was evidence of a disgruntled officer corps. Given the collapse of the state and the disintegration of the armed forces, as well as political and ethnic violence in several different parts of the former Soviet Union, the officers' mood is hardly surprising. Adopting a declaration, however, is a restrained reaction to the collapse of a superpower and its armed forces. Indeed, the officers ended the declaration by noting that they did not aspire to interfere in politics and decide the question of the structure of power in the independent states, which is a matter for the people. They were concerned, they said, about their fates and the fate of the armed forces.[106]

The armed forces continued to disintegrate over the next several months. By the end of March, in Shaposhnikov's view, the officer corps had come to accept that there would not be unified armed forces and that some form of joint command had to be worked out in the CIS. The final nail in the coffin

---

[104] FBIS-SOV-92-012, January 17, 1992, 11–18; FBIS-SOV-92-013, January 21, 1992, 15–27 (quote 19).

[105] *KZ*, January 21, 1992; *NG*, January 21, 1992; *NG*, February 5, 1992; Gorshkov and Zhuravlev, *Nesokrushimaya i legendarnaya*, pp. 279–306; Shaposhnikov, *Vybor*, pp. 142–147; Baranets, *Yel'tsin i ego generaly*, pp. 103–106.

[106] *KZ*, January 21, 1992.

was driven on May 7, 1992, when Russia established its own armed forces. Technically the Joint Armed Forces of the Commonwealth of Independent States continued to exist, but the fact that the Soviet armed forces had utterly collapsed was apparent to everyone.[107]

Explaining Military Behavior and the Collapse of the USSR

Jerry Hough, as noted at the beginning of this chapter, believed it was "inconceivable" that the military would let the Soviet Union collapse without offering serious resistance. Hough was right to be baffled. There were extremely strong corporate interest motives for intervention, given the consequences for the armed forces of their own collapse and dismemberment, and power was virtually lying in the streets, ready to be seized by the most decisive actor. This actor turned out to be Boris Yeltsin, though, and not the Soviet army.

The most obvious reason that there was no coup effort in December 1991, or an intervention on Gorbachev's behalf to hold the Soviet Union together, is the fact that the August 1991 hard-liner coup had failed so spectacularly. A failed coup attempt strengthens officers' inhibitions about military intervention. The August 1991 coup reinforced officers' commitment to a norm of civilian supremacy. As Yazov told the prosecutor the day after the coup collapsed, "this example should serve as a lesson to all of us."[108] Additionally, the August failure suggested that intervention was highly risky and that potential plotters would be punished. Thus, nonintervention in December 1991 had two basic motives: organizational culture and self-interested calculations of the prospects of success.

There were several reasons to think that a coup in December was even less likely to succeed than the August attempt. Many top officers had been removed after the failed putsch, so potential plotters would have less faith in their associates if they had only served together a short time. The removal of Communist Party bodies from the military also had a disruptive effect on the army. The key organization behind the August effort, the KGB, had been put in the hands of a committed reformer and divided up into several parts. The central government had lost control of most all-Union structures, including financial ones, which further complicated the tasks of a takeover effort. Finally, some officers had already transferred their loyalty to the republic governments, which undermined the assurance that orders from Moscow would be carried out. For example, in Ukraine about forty percent of the military was ethnic Ukrainian, including about twenty percent of the officer corps, and seventy percent of personnel in the Black Sea Fleet voted for

---

[107] Shaposhnikov, *Vybor*, pp. 148–149; Gorshkov and Zhuravlev, *Nesokrushimaya i legendarnaya*, pp. 379–381.
[108] *Izvestiya*, October 10, 1991, 7.

Ukrainian independence. All of these changes can be seen as organizational structural barriers to a coup attempt.[109]

It is also important to remember that the collapse of the state and the armed forces was a gradual process. There was no clear, decisive moment when it would have been easy for plotting officers to agree that they should intervene. Many of the former republics declared their independence in the month after the August coup, and in October and November the central government was steadily stripped of its powers. The Ukrainian independence referendum was on December 1. The period between December 8, when the CIS was formed, and December 25, when Gorbachev resigned, was probably the most likely period for an intervention. In many ways, however, the CIS was preferable to Gorbachev's amorphous union, particularly because it included Ukraine. A majority of officers at the All-Army Officers' Assembly supported the establishment of the CIS.[110] Moreover, it was not until January 1992 that it became clear that a united armed forces would not be maintained. The drawn-out nature of the Soviet collapse probably helped inhibit those officers with praetorian ambitions, because it would have been hard to persuade a core group of plotters that the time for action had definitely come.

These reasons for nonintervention in December 1991 are important, but not a complete explanation. Hough was right to point out that the Soviet military was not even "seriously bloodied." Armies often intervene, even when they risk failure (coups by their very nature are risky undertakings), if there is a sufficiently strong motivation. An additional important deterrent to intervention was the organizational culture of the Soviet armed forces.

The aftermath of the August 1991 coup, as noted, led to the dismissal of many of those officers adhering to a more praetorian subculture. Additionally, the dominant culture that held a relatively strong attachment to a norm of civilian supremacy was bolstered. The belief that the military should not intervene in politics was embodied most clearly by the new Defense Minister, Marshal Shaposhnikov. Less than a week after the failed coup, Shaposhnikov stated that he had a "positive attitude" toward Baltic, Ukrainian, and Belarussian independence. "If the parliaments of the republics decide that they want to secede from the Union," Shaposhnikov said, "they must be allowed to do so. I am against forcibly holding back those who want to break away."[111]

---

[109] Foye, "CIS: Kiev and Moscow Clash," 2; Pyskir, "Silent Coup," 146–147; Brian Taylor, "Ukrainian Security: Dilemmas of Ukrainianization," *Soviet Defense Notes*, 5, 3 (1993), 2–3.

[110] "A nastroyeniye ofitserov takoye," *KZ*, January 22, 1992, 2.

[111] Interview with Marshal Shaposhnikov by Raimund Loew, *Vienna Oesterreich Eins Radio Network*, August 26, 1991 [FBIS-SOV-91-166, August 27, 1991, 58].

Shaposhnikov held rigorously to his view that the military should not be used in sovereign power disputes and to hold the union together by force throughout his tenure as Soviet Defense Minister and Commander-in-Chief of the CIS Armed Forces. He demonstrated this by his categorical rejection of Gorbachev's suggestion that the military step in to hold the state together. After the formation of the CIS was announced, Shaposhnikov declared, "we need to get away from a situation in which soldiers have to choose between someone. This is a job for politicians, it's for them to define. The job of the minister of defense of the USSR is to not permit dragging the army into political games." He made a similar assertion at the All-Army Officers' Assembly:

As commander in chief of the CIS armed forces I state yet again that I will never allow our Armed Forces to be used against our own people in the resolution of interethnic and political conflicts. I think I will express the will of everyone if I say that we will never sink so low as to dethrone someone or to enthrone someone with the aid of our bayonets. This is not our task.[112]

The Chief of the General Staff between August and December, General Vladimir Lobov, also was a strong adherent to a norm of civilian supremacy. In January 1992, after his dismissal, he noted bitterly that the army was in a "tragic situation," because it did not know to whom it was subordinate and which state it belonged to and should defend. Lobov criticized the planned officers' assembly, commenting that it would only "rub salt in the wounds" and drag the already politicized army into a "dangerous game." Lobov added, "a political decision is needed, but one taken not by soldiers but by politicians." A commentator in the military newspaper *Red Star* advocated a similar viewpoint, stating that "it is not the army's job to participate in political games . . . the army should serve the Fatherland. That is its sole and definitive choice."[113]

The determination of Shaposhnikov and the rest of the top officer corps to keep the military out of politics was challenged verbally by some participants of the All-Army Officers' Assembly. When Shaposhnikov threatened to resign, however, he received the support of the meeting. More important, there was no attempt by other officers to take matters into their own hands, either alone or with civilian actors, to try to hold the Soviet Union together. Ultimately the Soviet officer corps accepted the collapse of the state because their organizational culture inhibited military intervention, and this normative constraint was reinforced by the failed August 1991 coup. In this respect,

---

[112] O. Vladykin, "Armiya vne politicheskikh igr," *KZ*, December 14, 1991, 1; *Ostankino Television*, January 17, 1992 [FBIS-SOV-92-012, January 17, 1992, 14–15]; Shaposhnikov, *Vybor*, pp. 127, 145.

[113] Interview with General Vladimir Lobov by Nikolay Burbyga, "Budet li edinaya armiya na territorii odinnadtsati gosudarstv?," *Izvestiya*, January 13, 1992, 2; Vyacheslav Lukashevich, "Kak nas teper' nazyvat' – SSG, SNG, ili vse zhe SSSR?," *KZ*, December 12, 1991, 1.

Shaposhnikov was right – the Soviet Union was not Thailand. Even motives of the highest national interest, the collapse of the country officers were sworn to defend, could not motivate an intervention after that experience.

CONCLUSION

Top officers, from Marshal Yazov on down, denied repeatedly that a military coup was possible in the Soviet Union. The ineffective coup attempt of August 1991 was actually the worst of all possible courses of action, since it led to the very event it was supposed to forestall – the collapse of the Soviet Union. Yazov and Akhromeyev proved no more adept than Alekseev and Kornilov did in 1917 in averting disaster for their organization.

The common thread between 1917 and 1991 was that political capacity was so low that the state itself was in danger of disintegration. It was almost inevitable that the armed forces, as one of the key attributes of statehood, would become involved in efforts to prevent state collapse. Domestic structure, then, stands out as a key factor leading to military participation in sovereign power issues.

Organizational structure was a less decisive factor in influencing the opportunity for military intervention, but it also played a role. Counterbalancing and penetration, the two most commonly recommended strategies for reducing the opportunity for coups, were not significant factors. Indeed, the KGB, one of the key organizations responsible for monitoring the army and preventing plotting, was the instigator of the August 1991 coup. Internal splits in the army were the most important organizational structure factor, but these divisions were themselves a product of extreme state weakness.

The corporate interest perspective on military intervention performs the worst. The Soviet armed forces' corporate interests came under attack by Gorbachev long before the August 1991 coup. The military weathered a series of sharp challenges to their prerogatives and interests beginning in 1986–1987 and lasting throughout the period. A corporate interest explanation would have predicted earlier and more resolute intervention. Corporate interest motives were not the reason for military intervention in August 1991; more weighty issues were at stake. Finally, the collapse of the state represented a severe blow to the military's organizational interests, but the army acquiesced in this decision.

The August 1991 coup was a clear violation of organizational norms that opposed military participation in sovereign power issues. Thus, this explanation on its own is not a satisfactory guide to army behavior. On the other hand, organizational culture plays a large role in explaining the armed forces' half-hearted participation in the 1991 coup. The refusal of key officers to support the intervention in August 1991 caused its failure. Although attachment to a norm of civilian supremacy was weakened during the Gorbachev period, particularly from 1989 to 1991, it still remained strong enough to inhibit effective military intervention.

Organizational culture also helps explain why the military failed to intervene in December 1991 to prevent the collapse of the Soviet Union. The organizational lessons learned from the failed August 1991 coup attempt strengthened the position of apolitical officers and reinforced a norm of civilian supremacy. This led the military high command to take a passive stance in December 1991 and support the most legitimate political leaders, even if this meant that the state collapsed around them.

7

Yeltsin and the New Russia, 1992–2000

The Red Army, strangely enough, managed to outlive the Soviet Union it-self by a few months as the armed forces of the Commonwealth of Inde-pendent States. In May 1992, however, this fiction was abandoned when Russian President Boris Yeltsin decreed the establishment of the Russian armed forces. Unlike in 1917, when there were both continuities and dis-continuities from the Imperial to the Soviet period, there was no question that the new Russian army was the direct descendent of the Soviet armed forces and the inheritor of most of its personnel, equipment, institutions, and culture.

The Russian military under Yeltsin experienced a period perhaps even more politically tumultuous than the Gorbachev era. In October 1993 the armed forces were once again thrust into the role of political arbiter in the conflict between President Yeltsin and the Supreme Soviet. The Russian army also has been involved in its largest internal war since the civil war in the bloody conflict with Chechnya. These events have strained Russian civil–military relations, as have the continuing economic and social problems faced by the armed forces.

The significant difficulties of the Russian state and its army brought about speculation about the possibility of military intervention in poli-tics.[1] In a 1997 poll, sixty-three percent of Russians said that "the threat

---

[1] A striking example are the results of an informal poll taken of American and Russian specialists at an early 1997 meeting in Monterey, California. The Russian participants thought that the probability of "a coup, chaos, or disintegration of the Russian military within the next 12 to 18 months" was 60 percent, with some putting the probability at 100 percent. The Americans were only slightly less pessimistic, concluding that the probability of one of these bleak outcomes was 30–40 percent. See Douglas Stanglin et al., "Washington Whispers: Behind Closed Doors," *U.S. News & World Report*, April 14, 1997, 23–24. For other predictions of a Russian military coup, see, for example, Peter Reddaway, "Desperation Time For Yeltsin's Clique," *New York Times*, January 13, 1995, 31; "Russia's Crisis: Could it Lead to Fascism?" *The Economist*, July 11, 1998.

of military dictatorship" was one of their concerns. Indeed, even Yeltsin himself remarked in his memoirs after retirement that in the early 1990s there was a "real threat of a military putsch." Yeltsin saw this as one of the possibilities arising out of state collapse and the resulting political and economic turmoil, explicitly making comparisons to Yugoslavia and the Russian civil war.[2]

The armed forces, however, have continued to show little interest in being a significant player in sovereign power issues. In October 1993 the military only with great reluctance was sucked into the political arbiter role. Since that date, despite the continuing hardships and disorder, the armed forces have remained "outside politics."

This chapter analyzes civil–military relations in the Yeltsin period and offers an explanation for the army's behavior (see Table 7.1 for a summary). The situation facing the army was similar to that during Mikhail Gorbachev's rule. An extremely weak state created opportunities for intervention, but multiple military and security bodies and divisions within the armed forces hindered conspiratorial activity. Motives for intervention were also mixed. Severe blows to the army's interests were an impetus to intervention, but the officer corps' norms continued to inhibit praetorianism.

Thus, although there were significant changes in Russian civil–military relations in the 1990s, the predictions made by the alternative theories do not change much. I therefore keep the review of evidence for the different perspectives prior to the October 1993 political crisis, the key civil–military event of the period, relatively brief. The final major section of the chapter discusses developments after October 1993, explaining the army's passivity during this period.

OPPORTUNITIES FOR INTERVENTION

Opportunities for military involvement in sovereign power issues remained substantial during the early Yeltsin years. The new Russian state was extremely weak after the collapse of the Soviet empire. Counterbalancing continued to present a barrier to intervention, particularly after the break-up of the KGB into multiple agencies, but penetration of the armed forces declined. The army continued to be riven by internal splits, but as before the most significant ones were ideational and not structural.

---

[2] Stephen White, *Russia's New Politics: The Management of a Postcommunist Society* (Cambridge: Cambridge University Press, 2000), p. 188; Boris Yel'tsin, *Prezidentskiy marafon: Razmyshleniya, vospominaniya, vpetchatleniya...* (Moskva: AST, 2000), pp. 62–63, 79. See also the views of one of his top advisers, Georgiy Satarov: Yuriy Baturin et al., *Epokha Yel'tsina: Ocherki politicheskoy istorii* (Moskva: Vagrius, 2000), p. 636.

TABLE 7.1. *Chapter Summary*

Observations	Opportunity		Motive		Outcome
	Domestic Structure	Organizational Structure	Corporate Interest	Organizational Culture	
October 1993 Events	Intervention or arbitration likely.	Intervention unlikely. If arbitration, counterbalancing or internal splits likely.	Intervention likely. If arbitration, will side with contender most likely to protect corporate interests.	Intervention unlikely. If arbitration, first choice is neutrality and second choice is side with most legitimate contender.	Arbitration. Sided with most legitimate contender after initial neutrality.
1994–1999	Intervention or arbitration likely.	Intervention unlikely.	Intervention likely.	Intervention unlikely.	No Intervention.

TABLE 7.2. *Deaths from Political Violence, 1986–1993*

1986	1987	1988	1989	1990	1991	1992	1993
2	0	91	200	605	326	583	225

Note: Figures are for the Soviet Union (through 1991) and Russia (1992–1993).
Sources: See footnote 5.

Domestic Structure and the New Russian State

The weakness of the Soviet state in its last years was dramatically confirmed by its collapse in December 1991. The successor Russian state was plagued by similar problems, and many observers predicted that Russia was likely to disintegrate as well.[3] The basic indicators of state strength and political order suggest that the Russian state was very weak and that the military had a clear opportunity to intervene in sovereign power issues.

Organizational Age. Although in practice the old Soviet Constitution remained in effect until a new one was adopted in December 1993, in essence a new constitutional order began in 1992 with Boris Yeltsin as the first chief executive of the new period. This "liability of newness" facing the Russian state led to sharp political conflicts between the executive and legislative branches of power, which occasionally involved the judiciary as well. The rules, norms, and divisions of power governing these relations were highly uncertain and the object of intense struggle.[4]

Political Violence. The continuation of rather high levels of political violence also reflected the political disorder of Russia. The trend that started in the second half of the Gorbachev period continued in 1992 and 1993 (see Table 7.2). This violence reflected the inability of the Russian state to create legitimate institutions for managing political conflict.[5]

[3] Jessica Eve Stern, "Moscow Meltdown: Can Russia Survive?," *International Security*, 18, 4 (1994), 40–65; Peter Reddaway, "Russia Comes Apart," *New York Times*, January 10, 1993, E23.

[4] Michael McFaul, "Russia's 'Privatized' State as an Impediment to Democratic Consolidation," *Security Dialogue*, 29 (1998), 191–199, 315–332.

[5] The data for 1986–1993 were compiled by the author from multiple sources: Radio Free Europe/Radio Liberty publications, particularly *Report on the USSR* and *RFE/RL Research Report*; Open Media Research Institute, *Daily Digest*; *SIPRI Yearbook*; Zvi Gitelman, "The Nationalities," in Stephen White, Alex Pravda, and Zvi Gitelman, eds., *Developments in Soviet Politics* (Durham, NC: Duke University Press, 1990), pp. 137–158; "Chronology of Noteworthy Events," in Edward A. Hewett and Victor H. Winston, eds., *Milestones in Glasnost and Perestroyka: Politics and People* (Washington, D.C.: Brookings Institution, 1991), pp. 499–536; data provided by the Division of Ethnopolitical Research, Analytical Center, Council of the Federation, Russia; and data gathered by the author from the Soviet/Russian press.

Resource Extraction. Another indicator of state capacity is the ability of the government to compel the transfer of resources to the government.[6] The performance of the Russian federal government in this respect shows the inability of the state to enforce compliance with its directives. For example, federal revenues declined from 16.2 percent of GDP in 1992 to 11.9 percent in 1993. Several regions – Bashkortostan, Chechnya, Sakha-Yakutia, and Tatarstan – unilaterally declared themselves fiscally sovereign and halted all or most revenue transfers to the federal government (taxes are collected at the local level). According to one World Bank study, in 1992 about twenty regions unilaterally halted full payment to the center, and this number increased to around thirty regions, although it is not clear that many of these efforts lasted more than a few weeks. Still, this pattern was a worrisome repeat of the processes of republic self-assertion that had doomed the Soviet system. In late 1993 the Russian Finance Minister, Boris Fedorov, accused regional governments of trying to kill the central state through "financial asphyxiation."[7]

Political Parties. Political parties are one of the most prominent and reliable mechanisms for the creation of legitimate institutions through which political conflict can be resolved.[8] After the collapse of the Soviet Communist Party, however, there were no institutionalized parties in independent Russia. At most what existed in 1992–1993 were "proto-parties." The institutional design of the legislature, the Supreme Soviet, allowed no role for political parties and the "factions" that existed had little influence over their members. The president, Boris Yeltsin, also lacked a party institutional base upon which he could rely.[9]

[6] Joel S. Midgal, *Strong Societies and Weak States: State–Society Relations and State Capabilities in the Third World* (Princeton, NJ: Princeton University Press, 1988), pp. 281–284.

[7] The World Bank, *Fiscal Management in Russia* (Washington, D.C.: The World Bank, 1996), p. 3; The World Bank, *Russian Federation: Toward Medium-Term Viability* (Washington, D.C.: The World Bank, 1996), pp. 7, 32–33; Chrisine I. Wallich, *Russia and the Challenge of Fiscal Federalism* (Washington, D.C.: The World Bank, 1994), p. 248; Daniel Treisman, "The Politics of Intergovernmental Transfers in Post-Soviet Russia," *British Journal of Political Science*, 26 (1996), 300.

[8] Samuel P. Huntington, *Political Order in Changing Societies* (New Haven, CT: Yale University Press, 1968).

[9] M. Steven Fish, *Democracy From Scratch: Opposition and Regime in the New Russian Revolution* (Princeton, NJ: Princeton University Press, 1995), pp. 204, 210–218, 232–233; Michael McFaul, *Post-Communist Politics: Democratic Prospects in Russia and Eastern Europe* (Washington, D.C.: Center for Strategic and International Studies, 1993), pp. 63–84; Joel Ostrow, "Institutional Design and Legislative Conflict: The Russian Supreme Soviet – A Well-Oiled Machine, Out of Control," *Communist and Post-Communist Studies*, 29 (1996), 413–433.

Strength of the State vis-à-vis Society. The government was able to launch the transition to a market economy by freeing prices and eschewing government planning, but this ability to change social structure was more a reflection of state weakness than strength. The changes in private behavior that took place were in some ways consistent with state desires, as entrepreneurs rushed to make money in the new economic order. However, the government was unable to control, regulate, tax, or police the new private economy in a consistent manner. It also was not able to achieve its goal of monetary stabilization. Finally, the government was not able to resist private pressure, because it constantly was forced to change and in some cases abandon its reform policies in response to the pressures of private actors. Enterprise managers were able to hijack the state's privatization program in pursuit of their own interests.[10]

The domestic structure approach predicts that military involvement in sovereign power issues becomes likely when the state is weak. Instances of military arbitration are more likely to appear, and the armed forces may try to take advantage of state weakness to seize state power.

Organizational Structure and the Power Ministries

The August 1991 coup attempt demonstrated that the multiple structures put in place by the Soviet political leadership with at least the partial mission of preventing coups failed to perform properly. The KGB, rather than monitoring for praetorian moods in the army, actually played the lead role in organizing the putsch. The Internal Troops of the Ministry of Internal Affairs (VV MVD), similarly, joined in the coup. Communist Party organs in the army also were of no use to Gorbachev – the Communist Party also backed the coup. Thus, several of these structures were either abolished or reformed under Yeltsin. Russia, however, continued to possess a diverse array of "power ministries," the umbrella term for armed state bodies such as the armed forces, the police, and the secret police. At least on paper, organizational structural barriers after 1992 remained fairly robust.

Counterbalancing. The most significant change was the splitting of the KGB into multiple agencies. Most of the KGB's domestic functions were housed in the new Ministry of Security, including military counter-intelligence, which controls the special sections in the army. In terms of counterbalancing, the most important change was the transfer of the Ninth Directorate of the KGB, which had been responsible for the physical security of top government officials, to the Kremlin and the president. The Main Guard Directorate controlled the Kremlin regiment and also housed the Presidential Security

---

[10] Michael McFaul, "State Power, Institutional Change, and the Politics of Privatization in Russia," *World Politics*, 47 (1995), 210–243.

Service. This change served to complicate a coup launched by the KGB by removing the president's bodyguards from its control. The Alpha anti-terrorist unit, which refused to storm the White House in August 1991, also was made part of the Main Guard Directorate.[11]

The Internal Troops of the MVD also remained in existence after the collapse of the Soviet Union. The Moscow-based Dzerzhinsky division was the most significant MVD force that could play a counterbalancing role.

Thus, as was the case under Soviet rule, there were several agencies that possessed forces capable of resisting a military coup attempt. Whether these recently reformed bodies would prove more reliable than their Soviet predecessors, particularly during a period of low state capacity, remained to be seen.

Penetration. One of the two monitoring agencies at least notionally devoted to observing the Soviet officer corps for praetorian beliefs, the Main Political Administration (MPA) of the Communist Party, was in effect abolished after the August Coup. Many "commissars" were reassigned to education and morale work among the troops, but these officers were completely subordinate to the Ministry of Defense. The MPA lost its raison d'être after the collapse of Communist rule. The other monitoring agencies, the "special sections," were made part of the Ministry of Security and continued to watch over the officer corps. Their ideological role of watching for "dissident thought" was played down after the end of one-party rule, and most of their work involved fighting espionage and crime in the armed forces.[12]

Cohesion. The collapse of the Soviet Union eliminated one of the most significant potential sources of division within the armed forces, the ethnic heterogeneity of the troops. After the collapse of the Soviet Union, both the officer corps and the rank-and-file became overwhelmingly ethnic Russian.

The Russian officer corps still contained notable internal splits. The one that was the most significant for sovereign power issues, however, was political/ideational and not really structural.[13] Thus, these divisions will be discussed under organizational culture.

Although organizational structural obstacles to military intervention were probably less severe in 1992–1993 than in the Soviet period, there still remained significant counterbalancing and penetration structures. This approach would contend that opportunities for intervention were low and that

[11] Amy Knight, *Spies Without Cloaks: The KGB's Successors* (Princeton, NJ: Princeton University Press, 1996), pp. 34–37; Ol'ga Semenova, "Znamenitoy gruppe "Al'fa" – chetvert' veka," *Nezavisimoye voyennoye obozreniye* [hereafter NVO], September 3, 1999, 7.

[12] Author's interview with Dmitriy Trenin, Carnegie Moscow Center, October 5, 1999.

[13] David Mendeloff, "Explaining Russian Military Quiescence: The 'Paradox of Disintegration' and the Myth of a Military Coup," *Communist and Post-Communist Studies*, 27 (1994), 237–243.

in the event of military arbitration there was the possibility of counterbalancing activity or internal splits.

Opportunity: Summary

Low state political capacity seemingly made military intervention or arbitration likely. Organizational structural factors, however, did present obstacles to concerted military action in sovereign power issues.

MOTIVES FOR INTERVENTION

The cuts in the army's budget and size begun under Gorbachev escalated rapidly in the first years of Yeltsin's rule. The army was in severe crisis. On the other hand, there still remained a strong commitment to the notion that the army should not participate in sovereign power issues.

Military Corporate Interests and Yeltsin

The Russian military continued to suffer a loss of power and resources in the post-independence period. Indeed, the cuts experienced under Gorbachev look like child's play compared to those of the Yeltsin era. The dual pressures of state collapse and economic reform had particularly negative consequences for the armed forces.

Autonomy. The one area in which life did not get worse for the army under Yeltsin was organizational autonomy. Contrary to the demands of some civilian reformers, the Russian Ministry of Defense continued to be led by and dominated by professional officers, although one civilian was appointed Deputy Minister. The military had substantial authority over questions such as military reform and doctrinal change. Communist Party oversight was removed, of course, while parliamentary control over the armed forces remained limited. On the other hand, democratization meant that the press was free to investigate and criticize army decisions and behavior, which it did with vigor. Yeltsin as president and his assistant on national security affairs, Yuriy Baturin, also kept close tabs on the armed forces.[14]

---

[14] John Lepingwell, "The Russian Military in the 1990s: Disintegration or Renewal?," in Douglas W. Blum, ed., *Russia's Future: Consolidation or Disintegration?* (Boulder, CO: Westview Press, 1994), pp. 121–123; Kimberly Marten Zisk, "Civil–Military Relations in the New Russia," *Mershon Center Occasional Paper* (Columbus, OH: The Mershon Center, The Ohio State University, March 1993), 12–13; Vyacheslav Kostikov, *Roman s prezidentom: Zapiski press-sekretarya* (Moskva: Vagrius, 1997), pp. 18, 21.

Resources. Two of the most straightforward measures of corporate interest, organizational size and budget, dropped markedly in 1992–1993. The size of the armed forces fell dramatically, from around 2.8 million at the time the Russian military was created in May 1992 to less than two million by 1994. Military spending also dropped substantially, from over ten percent of GNP in the late Soviet period to around five percent of GNP in the first years of the Russian state, and this took place at a time when the size of the economy had shrunk dramatically.[15]

These aggregate figures on downsizing trends actually understate the difficulties faced by the armed forces. More than 100 thousand officers and warrant officers did not have an apartment, and more than 400 thousand more officers and retired or reserve officers would need housing in the next few years. Over seventy percent of military personnel were dissatisfied with their living conditions, and more than sixty percent thought that poor housing affected discipline and readiness. The situation with manpower policy was equally bleak. The Law on Military Service exempted more than eighty percent of draft-age men from military service. Some reports suggested that the armed forces were short of around 700–900 thousand personnel because of difficulties with the draft and the departure of tens of thousands of junior officers unsatisfied with their conditions of service. Salary increases failed to keep up with inflation, and officers often had their pay delayed by months at a time.[16]

The threat to the military's corporate interests across a range of indicators, then, was severe in 1992–1993. Organizational uncertainty also was extremely high, given the difficulties in coping with state collapse,

---

[15] Roy Allison, *Military Forces in the Soviet Successor States*, Adelphi Paper 280 (London: International Institute for Strategic Studies, 1993), p. 20; *The Military Balance 1992–1993* (London: International Institute for Strategic Studies, 1992), 92; *The Military Balance 1993–1994* (London: International Institute for Strategic Studies, 1993), pp. 98–99; *The Military Balance 1994–1995* (London: International Institute for Strategic Studies, 1994), p. 111; Colonel-General Vasiliy Vorob'ev, interviewed by Colonel Ivan Ivanyuk, "Voyennyy byudzhet bez abstraktsiy i illyuzii," *Krasnaya zvezda* [hereafter *KZ*], March 12, 1994, 1–2.

[16] S. V. Yanin, "Faktory sotsial'noy napryazhennosti v armeyskoy srede," *Sotsis*, No. 12, 1993, 36–50; Lt.-Gen. N. I. Kotylev, "...Esli voz'metsya vsya Rossiya," *Armiya*, No. 19, 1993, 20–23; Vitaliy Strugovets, "Armiya mozhet ostat'sya bez popolneniya," *KZ*, April 23, 1993, 3; Sergey Stepashin, interviewed by Sergey Sektretov, *Nezavisimaya gazeta* [hereafter *NG*], July 2, 1993, 1, 3; Oleg Vladykin, "Prizyvnikov ne khvatayet," *KZ*, July 17, 1993, 1; Col. S. Solovev and S. Yanin, "Naskol'ko zashchishchen zashchitnik otechestva," *Armiya*, No. 19, 1993, 17–19; Vladimir Yermolin, "Pochemu plokho 'rabotayut' zakony, prizvannye zashchishchat' voyennosluzhashchego?," *KZ*, August 10, 1993, 3; V. V. Serebryannikov, "Voyennaya sotsiologiya: opyt i problemy," *Sotsis*, No. 12, 1993, 20–32; Tsentr voenno-sotsiologicheskikh, psikhologicheskikh i pravovykh issledovaniy Vooruzhennykh Sil Rossiyskoy Federatsii, *Spravochno-Analiticheskiy material po itogam sotsiologicheskikh issledovaniy moral'no-psikhologicheskogo sostoyaniya lichnogo sostava Vooruzhennykh Sil Rossiyskoy Federatsii* (Moskva: December 1993).

radical economic reform, and political turmoil. The majority of officers believed that the army was under siege, and Yeltsin had no illusions about his lack of support in the army because of these hardships.[17] The crisis in the Russian armed forces led many observers to suggest that a coup was possible. Kimberly Marten Zisk, for example, argued in March 1993:

An anti-Yeltsin coup may thus become likely if Yeltsin proves either unwilling to meet military demands, or unable to solve the social, economic, and corporatist problems officers now face. Yeltsin must demonstrate, continually, both sympathy toward the military and competence as the crisis in Russian society continues. If he does not, the patience of the Russian General Staff may very well snap.[18]

The corporate interest approach leads to the prediction that the military would be likely to intervene in politics to defend its organizational interests. In cases of military arbitration the armed forces should side with the contender for power most sympathetic to military concerns.

Organizational Culture

The Soviet armed forces had a very strong commitment to the norm of civilian supremacy, but there was a slight drop in this attachment during the late Gorbachev period and a small praetorian subculture appeared. In the Yeltsin era the dominant organizational culture retained a commitment to a norm of civilian supremacy. However, there were some indications that this attachment had weakened still further, and the praetorian subculture that became apparent under Gorbachev persisted into the post-Soviet period.

Beliefs and Socialization. The Russian armed forces continued to adhere to the idea that their main mission was external defense and they should not be involved in sovereign power issues. The military journal *Voyenniy Vestnik* [*VV*], as in the period 1980–1991, continued to devote the large majority of its coverage to narrow military issues.[19] In 1992–1993 *VV* dedicated more than ninety percent of its coverage to various military issues. Nonmilitary issues continued to get little coverage in *VV*. Indeed, there were no articles

[17] Yanin, "Faktory sotsial'noy napryazhennosti"; Serebryannikov, "Voyennaya sotsiologiya"; *Spravochno-Analiticheskiy material*; Baturin et al., *Epokha Yel'tsina*, p. 326; Mendeloff, "Explaining Russian Military Quiescence," 227–231.

[18] Zisk, "Civil–Military Relations," 17.

[19] On the coding rules and categories used here, see the discussion in Chapter 6. For reasons of space, and because the results did not differ significantly from those discussed in the previous chapter, I have omitted a more detailed discussion. For a full analysis, see Brian D. Taylor, "The Russian Military in Politics: Civilian Supremacy in Comparative and Historical Perspective," Ph.D. Dissertation, Massachusetts Institute of Technology, February 1998, 544–547.

on Internal Security in 1992–1993, and there was also a drop in materials on Societal Choice issues.

Minister of Defense Grachev reiterated continuously in his first years in office that the military should be "outside politics" and subordinate to civilian rule. He remarked, "as a military man, I am accountable to civilians and I implement the will of the president, the Supreme Soviet, and the government." He noted that President Yeltsin's order to "departyize" and "depoliticize" the army would be carried out "strictly." Grachev added, "whoever cannot get along without politics, let him engage in it. But first of all he is obligated to resign from the ranks of the Armed Forces of Russia." Grachev clearly stated the Ministry of Defense position in December 1992:

The army should be outside politics, and the leadership of the Armed Forces will not permit it to be dragged into politics. Soldiers do not want to become hostages, or even more so participants in any political games. A ban on political activity in the army was declared in the Law on Defense. Hence our attitude towards those people who want to involve the office corps in politics, to politicize soldiers.[20]

The role of the military in sovereign power issues was frequently discussed in Russia in 1992–1993 because of the power struggle between President Yeltsin and the Russian parliament (the Congress of People's Deputies and the Supreme Soviet). Grachev and the military leadership consistently took the line that the army was not on the "side" of any particular branch of government, but "on the side of law and the Constitution." Moreover, they appealed to leading civilian elites to eschew attempts to get the army involved in political struggles. In March 1993, during a serious clash between Yeltsin and the legislative branch during which Yeltsin threatened to impose "special rule," the Main Military Collegium, the military's top body, issued a statement that "the dragging of the army into political confrontations is intolerable." The Collegium warned against appeals to the officer corps by competing political forces and attempts to split the army. The Collegium had issued a similar pronouncement in October 1992.[21]

---

[20] "Vystupleniye ministra oborony Rossiyskoy Federatsii generala armi P. S. Gracheva na VII S"ezde narodnykh deputatov Rossii 5 Dekabrya 1992 goda," *O polozhenii v vooruzhennykh silakh i oboronnoy politike (Po materialam VII S"ezda narodnykh deputatov Rossiyskoy Federatsii)* (Moskva: Glavnoye upravleniye po rabote s lichnym sostavom ministerstva oborony Rossiyskoy Federatsii, 1992), pp. 4–5; "General armii pavel Grachev: 'Kto khochet zanimat'sya politikoy, pust' snimet pogony'," *KZ*, September 1, 1992, 1; Lieutenant-Colonel Anatoliy Dokuchayev, "Vooruzhennye Sily Rossii – na storone Zakona i Konstitutsii," *KZ*, December 18, 1992, 1, 3.

[21] "Vystupleniye ministra oborony," 4–5; "Obrashcheniye Kollegii Ministerstva oborony RF k lichnomu sostavu Vooruzhennykh Sil Rossii," *KZ*, March 26, 1993, 1; "U armii dolzhen byt' nadezhnyy immunitet k politicheskim stressam," *KZ*, March 26, 1993, 1; "Rukovodstvo vooruzhennykh sil podtverzhdayet konstitutsionnuyu vernost' prezidentu," in M. K. Gorshkov and V. V. Zhuravlev, eds., *Nesokrushimaya i legendarnaya: v ogne politicheskikh bataliy 1985–1993 gg.* (Moskva: Terra, 1994), pp. 448–450.

The position of the armed forces toward civilian authority was summed up by Aleksandr Gol'ts, the lead political commentator of *Red Star*, the army newspaper. Gol'ts asserted that the army "has no intention to intervene in a political skirmish." The very question about whose side the army is on, Gol'ts said, was "humiliating" for the officer corps. It suggests that politicians distrust the military and think them capable of a "state crime." Gol'ts wondered what was the source of these suspicions: "Indeed we, thank God, do not live in a 'banana republic,' where military coups take place with the periodicity of monsoon rains. There is no tradition in the Russian army of it taking on itself the role of a decisive force in a struggle among politicians." Gol'ts further noted that the events of August 1991 showed that the military does not aspire to this role.[22]

Institutional lessons learned in the late Soviet period, as Gol'ts suggests, played an important role in shaping officer corps norms about involvement in sovereign power issues. The "Tbilisi syndrome" was strengthened by the failure of the August 1991 coup attempt. In December 1992 Grachev told the Congress of People's Deputies, "Today the overwhelming majority of soldiers do not want to get pulled into any sort of political battles or games. They learned well the lessons of the dramatic events of the perestroika period and August 1991." Colonel-General M. Burlakov, the commander of Russian forces based in a unified Germany during their withdrawal, observed in March 1993 that Russian soldiers had learned some important lessons in the last few years. The most important one, Burlakov stated, was that the army should be "secured from the influence of political battles, in order to prepare for battles of a different kind in a planned and systematic way." *Red Star* similarly emphasized institutional lessons and their influence on the officer corps:

In the last few years it [the army] has learned a great deal. So many times it has been set up and betrayed. There was Afghanistan, and Tbilisi, and Vilnius, and the August putsch of 1991. The bitter experience received in the burden of these dramas, of course, had its effect. And if there are some political forces or leaders that even theoretically consider the use of military force in the resolution of internal political problems, they need to think about this.[23]

Officers in military publications stressed the tradition of subordination to civilian authority in the Russian and Soviet armed forces. Colonel Oleg Belkov noted that the Russian army "does not have putschist traditions, and also no putschist inclinations." Colonel V. M. Rodachin, writing in the General Staff journal *Military Thought*, noted that prerevolutionary Russia and the Soviet Union had a loyal and subservient army and that these

---

[22] Aleksandr Gol'ts, "Mozhet byt', khvatit dergat' armiyu?", *KZ*, March 27, 1993, 2.
[23] "General armii Pavel Grachev"; "General-Polkovnik M. Burlakov: My delayem delo, a simpatii i antipatii ostavlyayem doma," *KZ*, March 31, 1993, 1; "U armii dolzhen byt'." See also Anatoliy Stasovskiy and Aleksandr Pel'ts, "Byl afganskiy sindrom, tbilisskiy ... Avgustovskogo byt' ne dolzhno," *KZ*, August 20, 1992, 1–3.

traditions influenced the current stance of the officer corps. Major-General of Justice V. G. Strekozov set out the Ministry of Defense position in a pamphlet to be used in officer corps training:

The army is often the object of politics, but it cannot be, must not be, its subject. The army cannot define policy, either external or internal. The army is an instrument for the realization of policy determined by the highest legislative and executive organs of the state.... Civilian control over the army is an indispensable condition of the normal functioning of a civilized state.[24]

Available polling data indicates that a large majority of officers opposed military involvement in sovereign power issues. In February 1992, in a poll of 1,200 officers and warrant officers from all different services, ninety percent stated their opposition to military rule and their belief that civilian professionals should run the state. A poll conducted in June 1992 among attendees of a meeting of the coordinating council of the Officers' Assembly (and therefore those officers most likely to be interested in politics) showed that seventy-five percent of respondents said it was not the job of the military to take power; the responses of the remaining twenty-five percent were not reported. Data on the size of the coordinating council (126 members) and the number of respondents (eighty percent) suggests that only 100 people were involved in this poll. Regardless, in both cases a clear majority expressed anti-praetorian views.[25]

The unwillingness of Russian officers to be involved in sovereign power issues extended to a general distrust of orders with a political tinge to them. Twenty percent of officers polled in 1993 stated that they might not fulfill orders in a crisis situation if they were not certain of their legality. Another twenty-eight percent did not have a clear position on the question. These results were a clear reflection of the "Tbilisi syndrome" and the institutional lessons learned by the military in events such as Tbilisi, Vilnius, and the failed August 1991 coup. As the military observer Pavel Fel'gengauer put it, "the sad experience of the last few years has fully convinced many soldiers of the veracity of old army wisdom: never hurry to carry out orders, especially oral ones."[26] The intriguing possibility suggested by these data is

---

[24] Colonel O. Bel'kov, "Armiya i politicheskaya bor'ba (zametki politologa)," *Armiya*, No. 20, 1992, 26; Colonel V. M. Rodachin, "Armiya i politicheskaya vlast'," *Voyennaya mysl',* No. 5, 1993, 13–14; Gen.-Major V. G. Strekozov, "Konstitutsionnye osnovy Rossiyskoy Federatsii. Mesto Vooruzhennykh Sil v gosudarstve," *Posobiye po obshchestvenno-gosudarstvennoy podgotovke ofitserov, generalov i admiralov Vooruzhennykh Sil Rossiyskoy Federatsii* (Moskva: Glavnoye upravleniye po rabote s lichnym sostavom Ministerstva Oborony Rossiyskoy Federatsii, 1993), p. 9.

[25] Lieutenant-Colonel F. Makarov, "84 protsenta voyennosluzhashchikh schitayut, chto sotsial'naya napryazhennost' narastayet," *KZ*, March 6, 1992, 1; Major P. Zalesskiy, "Chto segodnya trevozhit ofitserov," *Armiya*, No. 15, 1992, 13.

[26] Serebryannikov, "Voyennaya sotsiologiya," 29; Yu. I. Deryugin, I. V. Obraztsov, and V. V. Serebryannikov, *Problemy sotsiologii armii* (Moskva: Institut sotsial'no-politicheskikh

that, because of the institutional lessons learned in the late Soviet period, the Russian officer corps might refuse to follow *any* orders in a political crisis.

Behavior. The armed forces continued to be on the losing side of many national security decisions, and they implemented these policies, sometimes grudgingly, but always remaining subordinate. The military had to accept huge cuts in its budget and its size. The military also had no choice but to accept civilian decisions to exempt more than eighty percent of young men from the draft.[27]

The armed forces leadership disagreed with the timetable for withdrawal of Russian troops from the Baltic states, but implemented Yeltsin's decision to carry out these troop movements in the space of a few years. Their primary concern was the need for adequate housing for returning officers. There were several interruptions in the withdrawal, but these were due to political decisions. The withdrawals were completed on schedule by the end of August 1994. Between 1989 and 1994 more than 700,000 military personnel returned to Russia from Eastern Europe and the Baltic states, as well as 500,00 dependents, many of them without adequate housing in Russia.[28]

On other security issues the military's voice was heard. For example, military opposition to a deal with Japan over the Kurile Islands played a role in hardening the Russian position on this issue. In 1992 General Staff Chief Colonel-General Viktor Dubynin lobbied behind the scenes, particularly with sympathetic Supreme Soviet members, to build support for retaining the islands. Military pressure alone was not responsible for Yeltsin's unwillingness to give up the islands, however – a large majority of the population (seventy-two percent) supported retaining the islands. Defense Minister Grachev made clear his opposition to a withdrawal of Russian military forces from the Kuriles, but also noted that "if there is a political decision within the framework of a reduction of the army, I will carry out the order." It is not unusual that the military would have a large say on issues related to changing the boundaries of the state, but the army's

---

issledovaniy RAN, 1994), pp. 199–200; Pavel Fel'gengauer, "Armiya poka neytral'na," *NG*, October 30, 1992, 2.

[27] Vladykin, "Prizyvnikov ne khvatayet"; Strugovets, "Armiya mozhet ostat'sya bez popolneniya."

[28] *INTERFAX*, August 27, 1994 [Foreign Broadcast Information Service, *Daily Report: Central Eurasia*, No. 94–169, August 29, 1994, 22 (hereafter cited as FBIS-SOV with issue number and date)]; Douglas L. Clarke, "Former Soviet Armed Forces in the Baltic States," *RFE/RL Research Report*, 1,16 (1992), 43–49; Stephen Foye, "Russian Politics Complicates Baltic Troop Withdrawal," *RFE/RL Research Report*, 1, 46 (1992), 30–35; Dzintra Bungs, "Progress on Withdrawal from the Baltic States," *RFE/RL Research Report*, 2, 25 (1993), 50–59.

position was within the context of their overall subordination to civilian rule.[29]

Insubordination at the top ranks was not a problem, and the military leadership remained under Yeltsin's control on key foreign and security policy questions. However, the collapse of the Soviet armed forces did create problems with controlling many officers based on the periphery of the old empire. The Soviet armed forces were known for their iron discipline, but in the great uncertainty of 1992, as new armies were being formed and lines of authority were confused, some of these habits of obedience were undermined.

From January to May 1992 there was no clear government structure over most officers. The command of the Joint Armed Forces of the CIS technically was subordinate to the CIS Council of Heads of State, which met infrequently and could hardly exercise effective oversight. Some states, most notably Ukraine, acted decisively to resubordinate units on their territory to their control. In other cases the legal status of forces based outside Russia was ambiguous, and Yeltsin was forced to issue a series of decrees in the spring of 1992 bringing troops in the Baltics, the Transcaucasus, and Moldova under Russian control. Only when the Russian army was formed in May 1992, and Russia took responsibility for some units based in the former Soviet republics, was this uncertainty ended.[30]

The first half of 1992 was particularly tense for soldiers based in the Transcaucasus. In the newly independent states of Armenia, Azerbaijan, and Georgia, as well as the break-away region of Chechnya, military bases came under frequent attack as various paramilitary formations sought to "privatize" the equipment held in the region. Sixteen servicemen were killed in the region from January 1 to March 11 of 1992, and dozens more were wounded, attacked, or taken hostage. Armored vehicles, small arms, and ammunition were stolen, starting in 1990 and continuing into the post-Soviet period. In June 1992 Grachev issued an order allowing units based in "hot spots" to defend themselves without consulting with Moscow each time. Given these conditions, it was difficult for Moscow to maintain strict control over its troops.[31]

---

[29] Viktor Baranets, *Yel'tsin i ego generaly: Zapiski polkovnika genshtaba* (Moskva: Sovershenno Sekretno, 1997), pp. 272–307; Bates Gill, "North-East Asia and multilateral security institutions," *SIPRI Yearbook 1994* (Oxford, England: Oxford University Press, 1994), p. 153, note 11; FBIS-SOV-92-107, 33; Stephen Foye, "The Struggle over Russia's Kuril Islands Policy," *RFE/RL Research Report*, 1, 36 (1992), 34–40.

[30] Allison, *Military Forces*, 9–12, 18–21; Gorshkov and Zhuravlev, *Nesokrushimaya i legendarnaya*, pp. 343–344; Sergey Parkhomenko, "Bezhentsy s oruzhiyem v rukakh," *NG*, June 30, 1992, 1.

[31] *POSTFACTUM*, March 20, 1992 [FBIS-SOV-92-056, March 23, 1992, 19–20]; Colonel-General G. G. Kondratyev, interviewed by Mikhail Leshchinskiy, "Topical Interview" Program, *Ostankino*, June 24, 1992 [FBIS-SOV-92-125, June 29, 1992, 8–12]; Pavel K. Baev, "Russian Military Thinking and the 'Near Abroad'," *Jane's Intelligence Review* [herafter *JIR*],

The role of Russia in general, and the Russian armed forces in particular, in several disputes in the former Soviet space has been a subject of considerable debate. I briefly examine the Russian military's role in three disputes: the debate with Ukraine over control of the Black Sea Fleet, the war between Georgia and the Abkhazian region, and the fight between Moldova and the break-away region of Transdniester.

BLACK SEA FLEET. The dispute between Russia and Ukraine over the Black Sea Fleet began immediately after the collapse of the Soviet Union in December 1991. When Ukraine began the process of swearing loyalty to Ukraine among fleet personnel in early January 1992, Yeltsin announced that he had instructed Admiral Chernavin, the commander of the CIS Navy, to tell his troops that they should not swear an oath to Ukraine and that they had Yeltsin's protection. Yeltsin declared, "The Black Sea Fleet was, is, and will be Russian."[32]

The failure of the political leadership of the two states to arrive at a definitive settlement of the issue increased the uncertainty of officers serving in the fleet. From the ultimate issue of loyalty and subordination, to more quotidian (but equally important) concerns such as pay, the Black Sea Fleet was in a state of limbo. The fleet's two commanders in 1992 and 1993, Admirals Igor Kasatonov and Eduard Baltin, at various times expressed their support for maintaining a unified fleet under Russian control. The Officers' Assembly of the Black Sea Fleet also spoke out in favor of such a solution. Furthermore, on several occasions, crises were sparked by decisions of ships' crews to raise either the Ukrainian or Russian flag. The officers and crew of the Black Sea Fleet became more politicized as the dispute continued to fester and their fate remained unresolved.[33]

Still, the dispute over the Black Sea Fleet was primarily a political conflict between Russia and Ukraine and not a question of military insubordination. Indeed, combat vessels did not participate in the hoisting of Russian flags during several of the crises, and Admiral Baltin specifically ordered the flying of the regular flag (the old Soviet flag) during one tense period. Finally, although the final resolution of the Black Sea Fleet dispute did not take place until 1997, it is clear that the Black Sea Fleet officer corps was in no position to block a political settlement, including one in which Russia had to compromise more than Ukraine. Thus, there is no reason to consider the Ukrainian–Russian dispute over the fleet an indicator that

6,12 (1994), 531–533; Allison, *Military Forces*, pp. 63–71; Elizabeth Fuller, "Paramilitary Forces Dominate Fighting in Transcaucasus," *RFE/RL Research Report*, 2, 25 (1993), 74–82.

[32] *Ostankino Television*, January 9, 1992 [FBIS-SOV-92-008, January 13, 1992, 41]; Douglas L. Clarke, "The Saga of the Black Sea Fleet," *RFE/RL Research Report*, 1, 4 (1992), 45–49; Douglas L. Clarke, "The Battle for the Black Sea Fleet," *RFE/RL Research Report*, 1, 5 (1992), 53–57.

[33] Lieutenant-Colonel Vladimir Mukhin, "Pochemu chernomorskiy flot ostalsya nerazdelennym," *NG*, September 14, 1993, 2.

Russian military officers rejected the principle of subordination to civilian control.[34]

ABKHAZIA. Abkhazia is a region in the republic of Georgia that has a long history of tense relations with its larger and more populous Georgian neighbors. Tensions between Georgia and Abkhazia grew as the Soviet Union unraveled, particularly due to the nationalist policies of Georgian President Zviad Gamsakhurdia.[35] The Georgian–Abkhaz conflict became militarized when Georgian Defense Minister Tengiz Kitovani launched an attack on the Abkhazian capital of Sukhumi in August 1992. Throughout 1992 and 1993 a war raged in Abkhazia, and in September 1993 the Abkhazians succeeded in pushing the Georgians out of Sukhumi. A Russian-mediated cease-fire was achieved in December 1993 after Georgian President Eduard Shevardnadze gained Russian intervention by agreeing to become a member of the CIS, and in 1994 Russian peacekeepers were deployed between the two sides.[36]

Many observers believe that Russian military involvement was crucial to the Abkhaz victory. However, an Abkhaz victory without Russian support is not the incredible prospect that many observers have claimed. It was in Georgia's interest to (a) inflate the importance of Russian efforts in order to excuse their own poor performance and (b) obfuscate the fact that Georgia started the war. Shevardnadze himself admitted in April 1993 that Georgia really did not have an army and that discipline was "very weak." There was also considerable volunteer and mercenary activity (probably assisted by Moscow) in support of Abkhazia from Russian Cossacks and the peoples of the North Caucasus, particularly Chechens, who consider themselves ethnic kin of the Abkhazians.[37]

Still, there are good reasons to believe that the Russian military was not completely neutral in the conflict. Evidence on the use of Russian aircraft on several occasions, for example, is fairly well documented. It also seems that

34 John W. R. Lepingwell, "The Black Sea Fleet Agreement: Progress or Empty Promises?," *RFE/RL Research Report*, 2, 28 (1993), 52–54; Sherman W. Garnett, *Keystone in the Arch: Ukraine in the Emerging Security Environment of Central and Eastern Europe* (Washington, D.C.: Carnegie Endowment for International Peace, 1997), pp. 72–76; Il'ya Bulavinov, "Posledneye mnogotochiye," *Kommersant" daily* [hereafter *KD*], May 29, 1997, 1–2.

35 For background, see John Colarusso, "Abkhazia," *Central Asian Survey*, 14, (1995), 76–82; Shireen T. Hunter, *The Transcaucasus in Transition: Nation-Building and Conflict* (Washington, D.C.: Center for Strategic and International Studies, 1994), pp. 124–126; Catherine Dale, "Turmoil in Abkhazia: Russian Responses," *RFE/RL Research Report*, 2, 34 (1993), 48–49.

36 Colarusso, "Abkhazia"; Kevin O'Prey, "Keeping the Peace in the Borderlands of Russia," in William J. Durch, ed., *UN Peacekeeping, American Policy, and the Uncivil Wars of the 1990s* (New York: St. Martin's Press, 1996), pp. 423–429; John W. R. Lepingwell, "The Russian Military and Security Policy in the 'Near Abroad'," *Survival*, 36, 3 (1994), 75–76.

37 Fuller, "Paramilitary Forces," 81; Dale, "Turmoil in Abkhazia"; Colarusso, "Abkhazia"; O'Prey, "Keeping the Peace," pp. 424–426; Baturin et al., *Epokha Yel'tsina*, p. 588; Dodge Billingsley, "Georgian-Abkhazian security issues," *JIR*, 8, 2 (1996), 65–68; Dodge Billingsley, "Confederates of the Caucasus," *JIR*, 9, 2 (1997), 65–68.

Abkhazian heavy equipment being held by Russian forces as a condition of a July 1993 cease-fire later reappeared with the Abkhazian forces. A former Russian officer, reserve Lieutenant-Colonel Sergey Leonenko, who fought on the Abkhaz side (his wife was Abkhazian), maintained that Russian officers provided advice on planning military operations, while suggesting that Russian units were not directly involved in the fighting. Thus, it does appear that there was some Russian military support for Abkhazia.[38]

The question, then, is whether Russian military support for Abkhazia, regardless of its exact scale, was government policy or due to military insubordination. There is definite evidence of "free-lancing" on the part of local commanders. One problem was illegal arms sales or transfers. The Ministry of Defense leadership, including Grachev, admitted on several occasions that illegal arms sales had taken place. There is also evidence that both Georgia and Abkhazia received assistance from Russian soldiers and officers, which suggests the absence of a clearly coordinated policy. Leonenko intimated that he would get active-duty Russian officers in trouble if he gave too many details of their involvement, given Grachev's orders on noninterference.[39]

Some observers, including Georgian President Shevardnadze, suggested that the Russian Ministry of Defense leadership was pursuing a policy without Yeltsin's approval. The bulk of evidence, however, indicates that, to the extent the General Staff controlled its units in the area, the Russian military was acting largely with Yeltsin's blessing. First, official rules of engagement approved by Yeltsin allowed the military to defend themselves with deadly force when under attack. Second, there was never an instance of a Russian officer being fired for unauthorized activity in support of Abkhazia. Third, there are reports that the Russian Foreign Intelligence Service and the Ministry of Security also were involved, which, if true, suggests the existence of a central government policy being implemented by multiple agencies. Fourth, United States' intelligence analysts concluded that Yeltsin was

---

[38] Igor' Rotar', interview with Andrey Kozyrev, "Voyennye dolzhny ovladed' iskusstvom mirotvorchestva," *NG*, November 24, 1993, 1, 3; Aleksandr Zhilin, interview with Lieutenant-Colonel (reserve) Sergey Leonenko, "Za pravoye delo?", *Moskovskiye novosti* [hereafter *MN*], July 18, 1993, A4; Dale, "Turmoil in Abkhazia"; O'Prey, "Keeping the Peace," pp. 424–426; Lepingwell, "Russian Military and Security Policy," 75–76; Fiona Hill and Pamela Jewett, *"Back in the USSR": Russia's Intervention in the Internal Affairs of the Former Soviet Republics and the Implications for United States Policy Toward Russia* (Cambridge, MA: Strengthening Democratic Institutions Project, Harvard University, January 1994), pp. 48–60.

[39] Colonel-General Boris Gromov, interviewed by Sanobar Shermatova, "Boris Gromov," *MN*, July 25, 1993, A11; *Ostankino Television*, September 27, 1992 [FBIS-SOV-92-192, October 2, 1992, 4–5]; Igor' Georgadze, interviewed by Sergey Chernykh, "Gruziya obeshchayet vzyat' Rossiyu v razvedku," *Komsomolskaya pravda* [hereafter *KP*], November 11, 1993, 2; Leonenko, "Za Pravoye delo?"; Billingsley, "Georgian–Abkhazian security issues."

behind Russian military policy in the "near-abroad," and they could point to particular meetings between Yeltsin and Grachev as evidence.[40]

Most important, there was a growing Russian consensus for a strong role in the "near-abroad" starting about mid-1992 and continuing into 1993. Although the Ministry of Foreign Affairs had initially articulated a liberal foreign policy line à la Gorbachev and Shevardnadze's "new thinking," this position was gradually hardened under concerted attack from the parliament and other foreign policy elites. The outbreak of several violent conflicts along Russia's borders played an important role in convincing the Russian elite that Russia needed to play a larger role in maintaining order in the "near-abroad." Yeltsin began to speak out more on Russia's special responsibility "as the guarantor of peace and stability in the region."[41]

The Russian military leadership was one of the important institutions arguing for a central Russian role in the region. The armed forces also were the first institution to have to confront this issue because of the large number of troops based in the "near-abroad." The army almost certainly were an influential voice, but, as John Lepingwell notes, "there is little evidence... of extensive civil–military conflict over the military's role in security policy." At most, in the words of Fiona Hill and Pamela Jewett, "Yeltsin had... turned over Moscow's management of the [Abkhaz–Georgian] conflict to the military." It does not seem, however, that the Ministry of Defense operated without Yeltsin's approval in the Abkhaz crisis.[42]

In the Georgian–Abkhaz war, then, there is no good evidence of systematic military insubordination at the top level. There is evidence, however, that some local officers and soldiers did engage in "free-lancing," particularly on behalf of the Abkhaz side of the conflict. Although this activity was in no way a direct challenge to civilian rule, it does indicate that insubordination was becoming a problem in the Russian officer corps.

TRANSDNIESTER. Transdniester is a region within Moldova that historically (since 1793) has belonged to the Russian/Soviet empire. The rest of Moldova (Bessarabia), on the other hand, has close historical ties with Romania. During the Gorbachev period, Moldovan nationalist elites strove

---

[40] *Ostankino Television* and *INTERFAX*, October 5, 1992 [FBIS-SOV-92-194, October 6, 1992, 54–55]; Hill and Jewett, *"Back in the USSR,"* p. 46; Hunter, *Transcaucasus in Transition*, p. 131; Stanislav Lunev, "Russian Military Policy in the Transcaucasus," *Prism: A Bi-Weekly on the Post-Soviet States* (Jamestown Foundation electronic publication), April 19, 1996; Knight, *Spies Without Cloaks*, p. 134; Paul Quinn-Judge, "Russia trying to regain grip over republics, U.S. aides say," *Boston Globe*, January 5, 1994, 1, 16.

[41] Dale, "Turmoil in Abkhazia," 53; O'Prey, "Keeping the Peace"; Andrew Bennett, *Condemned to Repetition?: The Rise, Fall, and Reprise of Soviet–Russian Military Interventionism, 1973–1996* (Cambridge, MA: MIT Press, 1999), pp. 295–347.

[42] Lepingwell, "Russian Military and Security Policy," 70; Hill and Jewett, *"Back in the USSR"*, p. 52.

either for independence or for reunification with Romania. Transdniester's population was about fifty-three percent Slavic (twenty-five percent Russian and twenty-eight percent Ukrainian) and forty percent Moldovan, and the political and economic elite in the region leaned toward Moscow. The self-proclaimed Transdniester Republic (PMR) came into existence in September 1990 and sought to separate from Moldova proper.[43]

Fighting between Transdniester and Moldova began after the collapse of the Soviet Union. The conflict remained at a low level until around March 1992, when Moldovan President Mircea Snegur declared a state of emergency throughout Moldova. The fighting escalated until June 1992, when the Russian 14th Army based in the PMR briefly sided openly with the Transdniester government and enforced a peace that maintained PMR control over the region. This peace has endured, without resolution, since 1992.[44]

The 14th Army was based in Ukraine and Moldova, and Russia and the PMR also laid claim to some of its resources. The headquarters of the Army was Tiraspol, the capital of the self-declared PMR. The PMR decided in January 1992 to form its own military on the basis of units in the republic, and it had the support of Lieutenant General Gennadiy Yakovlev, the Commander of the 14th Army, until he sided with the PMR and briefly became head of its Defense and Security Department. Yakovlev was replaced by Major General Yuriy Netkachev.[45]

Netkachev had considerable difficulty in the winter and spring of 1992 in maintaining control over his troops. More than half of the command personnel were from the Transdniester region, and the percentage was even higher among junior and mid-level officers. These officers sympathized with the local population. Although the 14th Army was officially neutral, some of its officers engaged in fighting on the PMR side and also transferred weapons to PMR irregular forces and the Russian Cossacks fighting with them. President Yeltsin's decision to bring the 14th Army under Russian

---

[43] PMR stands for Pridniestrovian (i.e., Transdniestrian) Moldovan Republic. For background, see Eduard Ozhiganov, "The Republic of Moldova: Transdniester and the 14th Army," in Alexei Arbatov, Abram Chayes, Antonia Handler Chayes, and Lara Olsen, eds.,*Managing Conflict in the Former Soviet Union: Russian and American Perspectives* (Cambridge, MA: MIT Press, 1997), pp. 147–209; Charles King, "Moldovan Identity and the Politics of Pan-Romanianism," *Slavic Review*, 53 (1994), 345–368; Pal Kolsto and Andrei Edemsky with Natalya Kalashnikova, "The Dniester Conflict: Between Irredentism and Separatism," *Europe-Asia Studies*, 45 (1993), 973–988; Stuart J. Kaufman, "Spiraling to Ethnic War: Elites, Masses, and Moscow in Moldova's Civil War," *International Security*, 21, 2 (1996), 119–128.

[44] On the events of 1992, in addition to the sources in the previous note, see Brian D. Taylor, "Commentary on Moldova," in Arbatov et al., *Managing Conflict*, pp. 211–218; O'Prey, "Keeping the Peace," pp. 436–440.

[45] For details, see Taylor, "Commentary on Moldova."

control in April 1992 slowed the process of disintegration in the army, but personnel continued to aid the Transdniester separatists.[46]

There is good evidence, then, that the participation of Russian military personnel in the Transdniester conflict was the result of local free-lancing. Unlike in Abkhazia, where Russian military personnel had few ties to the local population, in Transdniester the majority of officers were from the area and supported the PMR independence movement. Under these conditions the 14th Army command was unable to maintain control over the army.

To reassert Russian control over the 14th Army, Moscow sent a new commander considered reliable by Minister of Defense Grachev. The new commander was Major-General Aleksandr Lebed, who distinguished himself during the August 1991 events in Moscow and who had been close to Grachev for more than a decade. Lebed successfully reestablished Moscow's control over the 14th Army and brought an end to the fighting by his outspoken verbal attacks on the Moldovan leadership and his more restrained, but effective, use of artillery against the Moldovan side. This turn of events forced Moldovan President Snegur to sign a peace agreement with Yeltsin in July 1992 that resulted in the deployment of peacekeeping troops.

There is considerable evidence that Lebed acted with Moscow's blessing, including that of the political leadership, during his initial actions in Moldova. He was specifically sent to reassert control over the 14th Army, and he succeeded. However, he soon fell out with Grachev and became a thorn in the side of Yeltsin because of his outspoken behavior. In particular, Lebed got into trouble for statements to the press on July 4, 1992, in which he labeled the Moldovan government and President Snegur "fascist" and urged the Yeltsin government to stop going around the world "like a goat after a carrot." Grachev telegraphed Lebed the next day, ordering him to stop making statements to the press. "Evaluating the activities and decisions of the government of Moldova is the prerogative of the government and Supreme Soviet of Russia," emphasized Grachev. "Your task is to successfully lead the 14th Army and not to permit attacks on its military objects, and to protect the lives of its soldiers."[47]

Lebed telegraphed Grachev that all of his statements to the press "correspond to reality." Grachev replied the same day that whether Lebed's statements were true or not was irrelevant; Lebed had an order to not talk to the press, and he should stick to his professional tasks and "stop engaging in political populism."

---

[46] "14-ya armiya vmeshivayetsya v sobytiya pod davleniyem 'snizu'," in Gorshkov and Zhuravlev, *Nesokrushimaya i legendarnaya*, pp. 361–364; Kaufman, "Spiraling to Ethnic War," 131.

[47] For the Lebed-Grachev telegrams quoted here, see: Aleksandr Lebed', *Za derzhavu obidno . . .* (Moskva: "Moskovskaya pravda," 1995), pp. 450–463.

Lebed and Grachev engaged in another war of telegrams in September 1992, in which Grachev again stated his position that officers should not engage in politics and made clear that he had discussed Lebed's activities with Yeltsin. Grachev said that he and Yeltsin had not completely given up hope in Lebed's "loyalty and reliability for Russia." Grachev emphasized again that "politics is the affair of the political leadership and to a certain extent the Minister of Defense, and that's it." Grachev reminded Lebed that he was "a military officer and not a former employee of the CC CPSU [Central Committee of the Communist Party of the Soviet Union]."

Lebed remained Commander of the 14th Army until he was removed in June 1995. Despite his political grandstanding, evidently Yeltsin and Grachev decided he was a useful figure who could control the 14th Army. Equally important, he was less of a threat to either of them in Tiraspol than in Moscow, where he would have even more opportunities to engage in politics.

Thus, in Moldova we have the clearest case of Russian military insubordination. First, elements of the 14th Army assisted the PMR without the approval of their commander or Moscow. This took place during the period of greatest uncertainty for officers, before the Russian army was established in May 1992 and when the military was ostensibly under the control of the CIS. Second, the new commander of the Army, General Lebed, flaunted his political popularity to directly challenge the Minister of Defense and the president. At the same time, it is clear that the Ministry of Defense was not conducting a policy separate from the government's, and that Grachev endeavored to uphold the principle that the military should be subordinate to civilian control and not engage in politics.

Subcultures. Polling data cited above showed that there was a minority subculture in the Russian armed forces after the collapse of the Soviet Union favoring a more active role in high politics. Many of the more praetorian-minded officers were familiar figures from the late Soviet period. In most cases these individuals were now retired, but they continued to speak out on issues of civil–military relations. The infamous "Black Colonel," Viktor Alksnis, in February 1992 denounced the collapse of the Soviet Union and its armed forces. Alksnis's position is worth quoting at length, because it shows how extreme state weakness leading to state collapse can call into question officer corps attachment to a norm of civilian supremacy and make intervention possible:

If one starts from the logic of a normal political struggle in a civilized state, then the Armed Forces, of course, should be outside politics. It makes no difference to the army who is in power – communists, democrats, or the representatives of some other political tendency. That is not the army's concern. The army stands on guard of statehood. But since today in our country we are talking about not simply the change of the regime, but about the collapse of the state and practically about the annihilation of its most important institution – the Armed Forces – then political neutrality in this case is hardly possible. . . . If all problems had been decided within the framework of a united USSR, then the "politicization" of the Armed Forces would have been out of the question. But in as much as destroying the state also destroys the army, it cannot remain inactive.[48]

The more praetorian military subculture was informally represented by the "Union of Officers." The Union of Officers attacked the Yeltsin regime and the Ministry of Defense under Grachev as "unconstitutional" and called on all officers to "serve the people, and not the current mafioso groupings." The head of the Union of Officers was Stanislav Terekhov, a Lieutenant-Colonel who had been dismissed from the armed forces. Terekhov asserted that his organization represented seventy to eighty percent of the armed forces, and on at least one occasion he said they had the support of ninety-nine percent of officers. Despite these bold claims, most observers concurred that the Union of Officers did not have much influence in the officer corps.[49]

The dominant culture of the post-Soviet Russian military continued to believe that the army should not be involved in sovereign power issues. After the negative experiences of the late Gorbachev years, particularly the failed August 1991 coup, the army leadership was intent on staying out of domestic political disputes. At the same time, the collapse of the Soviet army led to an erosion in the army's traditionally iron discipline. Although episodes such as Abkhazia and Moldova were corrosive of the army's traditional apolitical culture, they were not necessarily harbingers of a military coup. Indeed, the polling data above on the wariness of officers about potentially political orders showed that the officer corps had little desire to participate in sovereign power issues. While there was evidence that commitment to the principle of subordination had declined, it is not obvious that this created a risk of military involvement in politics. Praetorian views were held by only a relatively small subculture.

Motives: Summary

Purely material motives served as a potential impetus for a military coup, as the army's organizational interests were under threat in the early Yeltsin years. The dominant ideas of the officer corps, however, viewed such a step as impermissible.

---

[48] "Stanet li armiya razmennoy kartoy?," *Armiya*, Nos. 3–4 (1992), 16–17.
[49] "Tovarishchi ofitsery, ob"edinyaytes'!" and "Interv'yu bez replik kommentariyev" in Gorshkov and Zhuravlev, *Nesokrushimaya i legendarnaya*, pp. 425–427, 471–472; Fel'gengauer, "Armiya poka neytral'na"; Viktor Baranets, *Genshtab bez tayn*, Vol. II (Moskva: Politbyuro, 1999), p. 163; Mendeloff, "Explaining Russian Military Quiescence," 234–235; Stephen Foye, "Russia's Fragmented Army Drawn into the Political Fray," *RFE/RL Research Report*, 2, 15 (1993), 4–6.

THE OCTOBER 1993 CRISIS

The Russian political system was under severe stress throughout most of 1992–1993. After the euphoria following the August coup passed, the collapse of the Soviet Union and the launching of radical economic reform quickly polarized the political landscape. President Yeltsin fell out with two key former allies, his vice-president, the Air Force General Alexander Rutskoy, and the speaker of the Russian Supreme Soviet, Ruslan Khasbulatov. In March 1993 Yeltsin stepped to the brink of open confrontation by threatening to introduce direct presidential rule, but then pulled back. His next gambit was more successful; in April 1993 a nationwide, nonbinding referendum was conducted in which the voters expressed their support for Yeltsin and his policies, and they also voted for early parliamentary elections but not presidential ones.[50]

The political conflict over government policies was exacerbated greatly by the lack of clear rules of the game and the contested nature of political institutions. The Russian Constitution was based on the heavily amended and internally contradictory Constitution of the Russian Federation from 1978. The political system combined both an executive presidency and a parliamentary system. The Constitution stated that Russia's government order was based on the separation of powers, while at the same time asserting that the Congress of People's Deputies was the "highest organ of state power." The Congress was able to amend the Constitution virtually at will, which it did over 300 times in 1992–1993 alone. Parliamentary speaker Khasbulatov had set himself the goal of either impeaching Yeltsin or reducing him to a mere figurehead. It was obvious that something had to give.[51]

Yeltsin took the fateful step on September 21, 1993, when he issued a decree (No. 1400) disbanding the parliament and calling for a new constitution and fresh elections. He based this decision on his election to the presidency in 1991, the results of the April 1993 referendum, and his constitutional responsibility for the security of the country. Yeltsin did not have the constitutional authority to dismiss the parliament, however, and the Constitutional Court, led by its Khasbulatov-leaning Chairman Valeriy Zorkin, quickly declared Decree 1400 unconstitutional and concluded that there were grounds for removing Yeltsin from the presidency. The Supreme Soviet did not wait for the Constitutional Court's ruling, however, and moved to displace Yeltsin

---

[50] David Remnick, *Resurrection: The Struggle for a New Russia* (New York: Random House, 1997), pp. 37–56.

[51] Leonid Polyakov, "Otzovite svoye resheniye, poka ne pozdno...," *NG*, September 30, 1993, 2; Robert Sharlet, "Russian Constitutional Crisis: Law and Politics Under Yel'tsin," *Post-Soviet Affairs*, 9 (1993), 314–327.

from the presidency and swear in Rutskoy as "acting president" only a few hours after Decree 1400 was released.[52]

The constitutional crisis of September 1993 forced the armed forces into the role of arbiter. They were faced with two political leaders who claimed the role of commander-in-chief. This section examines the behavior of the armed forces during the events of September–October 1993. There are three major parts to this section. First, I look at the behavior of the armed forces from September 21 to October 2, the nonviolent phase of the conflict. Second, I examine in detail the decision made by the armed forces on the night of October 3–4 to support Yeltsin once the conflict became violent. Third, I explain military behavior in light of the evidence and in reference to the competing perspectives on military involvement in sovereign power issues.[53]

The Crisis in Moscow and the Army: September 21–October 2

The first officer to learn of Yeltsin's plan to dismiss the parliament was, not surprisingly, Grachev. Yeltsin informed Grachev, along with several other top ministers, on September 12. According to Yeltsin, Grachev had been in favor of such a step for a while. Grachev insisted that the army was ready for a possible confrontation, although he had taken no concrete steps to prepare for various contingencies, believing that the troops of the Ministry of Internal Affairs (MVD) should be responsible for internal order.[54]

The rest of the military leadership, the Military Collegium, was informed on September 20. Before that date, Grachev had not informed any other top generals, including the Chief of the General Staff, Mikhail Kolesnikov. Grachev tried to persuade the Collegium that no Ministry of Defense troops were required, but that nonetheless he had to inform Yeltsin that

[52] In fact, the Supreme Soviet did not have the constitutional authority to remove Yeltsin, which resided with the Congress of People's Deputies. For the text of Yeltsin's decree and the decisions of the Supreme Soviet and the Constitutional Court, see A. P. Surkov, ed., *Moskva. Osen'-93: Khronika protivostoyaniya* (Moskva: Respublika, 1994), pp. vii–xii, 7–17.

[53] For two very different journalistic accounts, see Remnick, *Resurrection*, pp. 54–83; Jonathan Steele, *Eternal Russia: Yeltsin, Gorbachev, and the Mirage of Democracy* (Cambridge, MA: Harvard University Press, 1994), pp. 371–387. Two thorough chronicles of the affair, with accompanying interviews and articles, are Surkov, *Moskva. Osen'-93*; and a special issue of the journal *Vek XX i Mir*, released under the title *93-Oktyabr', Moskva: Khronika tekushchikh sobytiy*, 1993. The most important memoirs are Boris Yel'tsin, *Zapiski prezidenta* (Moskva: "Ogonek," 1994); R. I. Khasbulatov, *Velikaya rossiyskaya tragediya* (Moskva: TOO SIMS, 1994); Aleksandr Rutskoy, *Krovavaya osen': Dnevnik sobytiy 21 sentyabrya – 4 oktyabrya 1993 goda* (Moskva: [s.n.], 1995); Aleksandr Korzhakov, *Boris Yel'tsin: Ot rassveta do zakata* (Moskva, 1997); Yegor Gaidar, *Dni porazhenii i pobed* (Moskva, 1997). A similar account to Rutskoy's and Khasbulatov's, although even more hard-line, is Ivan Ivanov (pseudonym), *Anafema: Khronika gosudarstvennogo perevorota: zapiski razvedchika* (Sankt-Peterburg: "Paleya," 1995).

[54] Yel'tsin, *Zapiski prezidenta*, pp. 349–352; Korzhakov, *Boris Yel'tsin*, pp. 155–157; Baranets, *Yel'tsin i ego generaly*, pp. 201–202.

the army supported the commander-in-chief. A majority of the Collegium argued, however, for a position of neutrality, contending that this stance was consistent with the Law on Defense and Grachev's own slogan about the army being "outside politics."[55]

News of the Collegium meeting almost immediately leaked to the Supreme Soviet leadership. Colonel-General Konstantin Kobets, a Deputy Minister of Defense, Supreme Soviet Deputy, and Yeltsin loyalist, went to Khasbulatov, apparently to persuade him that the parliament needed to settle with Yeltsin. Khasbulatov called Grachev and asked him to come to the Supreme Soviet building, known colloquially as the White House, but Grachev refused and sent General Staff chief Kolesnikov. Kolesnikov apparently confirmed that the Collegium had decided to adopt a stance of neutrality in the conflict between Yeltsin and the parliament.[56]

Rutskoy made a fatal blunder the first night (September 21–22) of the conflict. At a session of the Supreme Soviet he announced that he was appointing the former Deputy Minister of Defense, Colonel-General (retired) Vladislav Achalov, his "Minister of Defense" and that Grachev was to be dismissed. Rutskoy also appointed new ministers of security and internal affairs (MVD). The appointment of Achalov had several negative consequences for Rutskoy. Most important, it raised the possibility of a split in the armed forces. This was the outcome that the military leadership was most intent on avoiding. The appointment of Achalov, then, drove the high command into Yeltsin's arms. There was no chance that the military leadership would subordinate themselves to Achalov. From an operational point of view the step was meaningless, because Achalov had no means available to communicate with or control forces outside the walls of the White House. The move was also a personal affront to Grachev, who had served under Achalov in the Airborne Forces in the past. Achalov later claimed that he knew the move was a mistake and that Rutskoy had not even asked him in advance about the appointment.[57]

Once Rutskoy had appointed his own defense minister, Grachev and the military leadership had to make clear that only Yeltsin was the lawful

[55] Author's interview with Pavel Fel'gengauer, July 7, 1994; Baranets, *Yel'tsin i ego generaly*, p. 201; Viktor Baranets, *Poteryannaya armiya: Zapiski polkovnika genshtaba* (Moskva: Sovershenno Sekretno, 1998), pp. 171, 174–175; Aleksandr Rutskoy, "Podgotovka," in *Neizvestnyy Rutskoy: Politicheskiy portret* (Moskva: Obozrevatel', 1994), p. 95; Khasbulatov, *Velikaya rossiyskaya tragediya*, Vol. I, pp. 186–189; Yuriy Voronin, *Svintsom po Rossii* (Moskva: Paleya, 1995), pp. 183–184; Ivanov, *Anafema*, p. 15; Ravil' Zaripov, interview with General (retired) Vladislav Achalov, "Po tu storonu 'barrikadnoy'," *KP*, October 7, 1994, 6; Unattributed, "Silovye vedomstva ne khoteli by vmeshivat'sya v konflikt," *KD*, September 23, 1993, 3.

[56] Rutskoy, "Podgotovka," pp. 95–96; Khasbulatov, *Velikaya rossiyskaya tragediya*, Vol. I, pp. 189–190; Voronin, *Svintsom po Rossii*, pp. 187–188; Veronika Kutsyllo, "V Rossii vvedeno prezidentskoye pravleniye," *KD*, September 22, 1993, 1, 3.

[57] *Moskva. Osen'-93*, p. 40; Author's interview with Vladislav Achalov, July 26, 1994; Ivanov, *Anafema*, pp. 40–41, 70.

commander-in-chief and only Grachev had the authority to give orders as Minister of Defense. A stance of strict neutrality would have raised doubts in the minds of commanders about whose orders should be obeyed and would have led to the very split in the officer corps that Grachev and the high command were working to avoid. Grachev announced that the entire command staff had affirmed that they followed only the orders of Grachev and Yeltsin. Kolesnikov, who only a few days before had told Khasbulatov that the military would remain neutral, stated on September 23, "I obey the Minister of Defense, the Minister of Defense obeys the Supreme Commander. The army is strong and mighty because of its linchpin, and its linchpin – unity of command."[58]

Rutskoy, Khasbulatov, and others in the parliament called for officers and soldiers to come to their defense. On September 22 Rutskoy sent an order to the head of the Airborne Troops and the Commander of the Moscow Military District demanding that units be sent to the White House. He also appealed to the commanders of four of the five military services (army, navy, air force, and air defense forces – evidently he was not yet in need of the help of the strategic rocket forces) to not remain "outside politics" and take an "active position." He continued to send appeals to various units throughout the crisis, and he called on officers not to fulfill orders of Yeltsin and Grachev. Khasbulatov and other parliamentarians claim to have expected that the army would be on their side and that units loyal to them would arrive within a day or two.[59]

There was some reason to think that Rutskoy and the Supreme Soviet might be successful in their efforts to gain the support of the officer corps. Rutskoy was a general and a Hero of the Soviet Union due to his service in Afghanistan. Rutskoy and the parliament had throughout 1992 and 1993 sought to show their support for the armed forces and blamed Yeltsin for the collapse of the Soviet Union and the impoverishment of the army. The military correspondent of *Moscow News*, Aleksandr Zhilin, cited polls showing that sixty-two percent of officers supported Rutskoy. Other polling data from the spring and summer of 1993 found that sixty to seventy percent of officers and warrant officers were for Rutskoy, while only twelve to fourteen percent were for Yeltsin. At the same time, allegedly seventy percent of generals were pro-Yeltsin. Regardless of the exact accuracy of this polling data (as is often the case with Russian military polling data, the complete results were

---

[58] Pavel Fel'gengauer, "Rukovodsto armii sdelalo vybor," *Segodnya*, September 23, 1993; Petr Karapetyan, "Tamantsev ispytyvayet poligon," *KZ*, September 24, 1993.

[59] Rutskoy, *Krovavaya osen'*, pp. 31–34, 184–186, 231, 232–233, 286–287, 302; Khasbulatov, *Velikaya rossiyskaya tragediya*, Vol. I, pp. 184–185, 194, 297; Sergey Filatov, *Sovershenno nesekretno: Kulary Rossiyskoy vlasti* (Moskva: Vagrius, 2000), pp. 289–290; *Moskva. Osen'-93*, pp. 58, 99, 101–102; *93-Oktyabr'*, Moskva, pp. 12, 50; *Listovki belogo doma: Moskovskiye letuchiye izdaniya 22 sentyabrya–4 oktyabrya 1993* (Moskva: [s.n.], 1993), pp. 14, 20.

not published), there was certainly reason to believe that Rutskoy might be able to bring some units over to his side.[60]

In fact, the White House had almost no active support from the army. Although at the time the pro-parliamentary forces made exaggerated claims about the backing they had from various officers, Rutskoy later admitted that these statements were disinformation and that not a single unit came to their defense. Rutskoy's support was limited to individual officers and private armed organizations, such as Cossack groups and the fascist Russian National Unity. The maximum number of active-duty officers that came to the White House was 200, and it was probably far less. Grachev claimed that only fifteen officers went to the White House, Lieutenant-General (retired) V. V. Serebryannikov, an adviser to Khasbulatov, put the number at sixty; and during the crisis itself, Achalov said they had the support of eighty officers. The Union of Officers led by Lieutenant-Colonel (retired) Terekhov also supported Rutskoy, but many of these officers were retired, and there were only 100–200 of them present at the Supreme Soviet building. This is a minuscule amount of support in a multimillion-man army.[61]

Rutskoy and Achalov had colleagues throughout the armed forces, including in the high command, and they worked to gain additional support during the crisis. Rutskoy claimed that both Air Force Commander Petr Deynekin and Deputy Minister of Defense Boris Gromov had offered moral support, but were unwilling to go further. Voronin states that Kolesnikov and Deputy Defense Minister General V. Mironov took a similar stance. Yeltsin and Grachev later claimed that Deynekin and the other members of the high command who spoke with Rutskoy rebuffed his appeals for help and told him that there was only one President (Yeltsin) and one Minister of Defense (Grachev). Rutskoy also maintained that he had two meetings with a representative from the Moscow Military District who said that they were considering sending units to support the White House; allegedly on October 2 Rutskoy was told that a regiment would arrive on October 3. However, elsewhere in his account,

[60] Alexander Zhilin, "Who is to Blame," *Moscow Guardian*, 3/38, October 15, 1993, 4–7; Deryugin, Obraztsov, and Serebryannikov, *Problemy sotsiologii armii*, pp. 82, 122.

[61] Rutskoy, *Krovavaya osen'*, pp. 156–157, 218, 514–517; Aleksandr Gamov, interview with Major-General Aleksandr Rutskoy, "Nadeyus', chto na etot raz moy parashyut raskroyetsya," *KP*, May 20, 1994, 5; Dmitriy Kholodov, "Oktyabr' tsveta khaki," *Moskovskiy komsomolets* [hereafter *MK*], October 8, 1, 4; Aleksandr Pel'ts, "Armiya byla vynuzhdena deistvovat' reshitel'no," *KZ*, October 8, 1; Deryugin, Obraztsov, and Serebryannikov, *Problemy sotsiologii armii*, p. 82; Stepan Kiselev et al., "Moskva. Subbota, 2 Oktyabrya. Khronika smutnogo vremeni (den' pervyy)," *MN*, October 10, 1993, 2; Nikolay Burbyga, "Tragediya u shtaba OVS SNG,"*Izvestiya*, September 29, 1993, 2; Aleksandr Gorbunov and Andrey Kolesnikov, "Iz 'belogo doma' – chernym khodom," *MN*, October 31, 1993, 11; Baranets, *Poteryannaya armiya*, pp. 187–188.

Rutskoy states that in response to all of his appeals to the army for help the only reply he received was that officers promised to "consider the matter."[62]

Despite these intensive efforts and considerable public bluster, allegedly in private Achalov had no illusions about his prospects. He told his associates on the second night of the crisis that they could not count on the army if the conflict became violent. On September 25 Khasbulatov asked Achalov where the promised military units were, to which Achalov sarcastically replied, "the same place your promised workers' collectives are."[63]

The one active step involving armed force taken by pro-Rutskoy forces in the early days of the crisis was an attack on the military headquarters of the Commonwealth of Independent States (CIS) in Moscow. The attack took place the night of September 23 and was organized by Terekhov from the Officers' Union. Rutskoy, Khasbulatov, and Achalov denied any involvement in the attack and said it had not been sanctioned by the White House. Indeed, Rutskoy later suggested that it was a provocation organized by Yeltsin to discredit the pro-Rutskoy forces. However, Terekhov himself later admitted, indeed bragged, about his role in planning the attack. Moreover, government sources reported that Achalov's "Deputy Minister of Defense," the retired Colonel-General Albert Makashov (who had been a vociferous supporter of the August 1991 coup), had taken an armed group to the State Committee on Emergency Situations on September 23 and demanded that it be turned over to the White House. It is probably true that Rutskoy and Khasbulatov had not sanctioned these efforts (Rutskoy's former top aide, Andrei Fedorov, maintains that Terekhov thought up the attack himself), but they were indicative of the extremist orientation of some of their supporters. Khasbulatov later castigated those who carried out the attack against the CIS military headquarters as "light-headed" people who, while claiming to defend the Constitution, had done great damage to the pro-parliamentary side.[64]

While Rutskoy and Achalov were making concerted efforts to gain the support of the officer corps, Yeltsin and Grachev continued to stress that

[62] Rutskoy, *Krovavaya osen'*, pp. 211, 232–233, 381; Kiselev et al, "Moskva. Subbota, 2 Oktyabrya"; Voronin, *Svintsom po Rossii*, p. 190; Yeltsin, *Zapiski prezidenta*, p. 373; Igor' Chernyak, "Ministr Grachev utverzhdayet," *KP*, October 8, 1993, 2; Ivanov, *Anafema*, pp. 72–73.

[63] Ivanov, *Anafema*, pp. 40–41; Khasbulatov, *Velikaya rossiyskaya tragediya*, Vol. I, p. 297; Rutskoy, *Krovavaya osen'*, pp. 157, 331–332.

[64] Pavel Fel'gengauer, "V gorod vvedeny dopolnitel'nye sily," *Segodnya*, September 25, 1993, 2; Vladimir Zaynetdinov, Igor' Chernyak and Ol'ga Saprykina, "V vooruzhennoy predvybornoy skhvatke navsegda poteryany dva golosa," *KP*, September 25, 1993, 1; Burbyga, "Tragediya u shtaba OVS SNG"; *Moskva. Osen'-93*, pp. 100, 102–104, 109–110; *93-Oktyabr', Moskva*, pp. 48, 54, 70–72; Rutskoy, *Krovavaya osen'*, pp. 91–101, 173; Ivanov, *Anafema*, pp. 58–61; Aleksandr Shadrin, "Ya ne ponimayu…, " *Argumenty i fakty*, No. 40, 1994, 1; Author's interview with Andrey Fedorov, December 13, 1997; Khasbulatov, *Velikaya rossiyskaya tragediya*, Vol. I, pp. 233–235.

the army should not be involved. Yeltsin appealed to the armed forces on September 22 to remain calm and to stay focused on military training and the defense of the state. He urged them not to respond to provocations that tried to draw them into politics. On September 25 Yeltsin issued an order that officers making political speeches would be dismissed. Throughout the period after September 21, Grachev reiterated his oft-stated maxim that the army should be "outside politics." He emphasized that the MVD had responsibility for internal order, that the army would stick to its own affairs, and that military units would not be introduced to Moscow. Grachev stated, "the army will not meddle in political activity. . . . Leave the army alone." General Staff Colonel Viktor Baranets reports that this statement of Grachev's was widely supported in the armed forces. To curtail Rutskoy's and Achalov's attempts to drag the army in, Grachev imposed a harsh communications regime in the Ministry of Defense, shutting off most telephones in the building. He ordered that military units reinforce their security, not allow unauthorized personnel on to their territory, and not distribute weapons to personnel. Only orders from Grachev and Kolesnikov were to be obeyed.[65]

A large majority of officers hoped that the political crisis could be resolved peacefully, without military involvement. In an opinion poll conducted on September 25, eighty percent of military personnel surveyed maintained that the army should remain neutral in the conflict. The figure for the general population on the same question was sixty-two percent for army neutrality, twenty percent for military support for Yeltsin, and only five percent for army support for the parliament.[66]

Khasbulatov and his deputy Voronin maintain, probably correctly, that much of the officer corps supported the so-called zero option, which proposed a return to the pre-September 21 status quo and simultaneous presidential and parliamentary elections. Colonel Baranets also argues that most officers expressed their support for a return to the status quo and feared the outbreak of violence or even civil war. On October 2, officers from the key Moscow Taman and Kantemirov divisions were adamant that they would not get involved. Analysts for the paper *Kommersant" daily* argued early in the crisis that neither side could count on military support.[67]

---

[65] Boris Yel'tsin, "Obrashcheniye Prezidenta Rossiyskoy Federatsii – Glavnokomanduyu-shchego Vooruzhennymi Silami Rossii," *KZ*, September 24, 1993, 1; *93-Oktyabr'*, *Moskva*, p. 100; "Parlament klyunul na prezidentskuyu blesny," *MN*, October 17, 1993, 4–5; "'Vertushki' Minoborony uzhe vklyucheny," *KP*, October 6, 1993, 2; Fel'gengauer, "Rukovodsto armii sdelalo vybor"; Fel'gengauer, "V gorod vvedeny dopolnitel'nye sily"; Vladimir Maryukha, "General armii Pavel Grachev," *KZ*, September 23, 1993, 1; Zaynet-dinov, Chernyak and Saprykina, "V vooruzhennoy predvybornoy skhvatke"; *93-Oktyabr'*, *Moskva*, pp. 5, 14, 16, 50; Baranets, *Poteryannaya armiya*, pp. 172–173.
[66] *93-Oktyabr'*, *Moskva*, p. 129.
[67] Khasbulatov, *Velikaya rossiyskaya tragediya*, Vol. I, p. 337; Voronin, *Svintsom po Rossii*, p. 190; Sergey Turchenko, "Chernaya pobeda," *Sovetskaya rossiya*, December 18, 1993, 4; Baranets,

Red Star commentator Aleksandr Gol'ts articulated the military's hopes for a peaceful solution on October 2. Gol'ts invoked the experiences of Tbilisi, Baku, Vilnius, and August 1991 as proof that the military wanted to be "outside politics," as it is in "civilized" states. Due to these episodes, Gol'ts argued, the military has "developed an immunity to political games." Russian soldiers understand that their personal political views can only be expressed "in the voting booth" and that these views are not relevant to the carrying out of one's military duties. Army commanders, Gol'ts stated, should not have to "work out political riddles" or "analyze legal details regarding the legitimacy of this or that person." The military, he argued, was very fearful of the possibility of a split in the armed forces and the prospect of civil war. For this reason, "irresponsible orders" to disobey commanders and bring units to the White House were ignored. The president, Gol'ts concluded, had won a "definite moral and political victory" by asking the military to remain calm and go about its business. Gol'ts hoped that both sides would continue to show such restraint.[68]

Bloodshed in Moscow and the Army: October 3–4

The armed forces, by all accounts, were determined to not get involved directly in the political confrontation between Yeltsin and the Supreme Soviet. Why, then, did the military leadership agree to attack the White House on October 4? Only the outbreak of widespread violence in Moscow the night of October 3–4 was seen as sufficient cause to bring in the army, and the military leadership wavered considerably before agreeing to send in several units. It took a personal visit from President Yeltsin and Prime Minister Viktor Chernomyrdin to the Ministry of Defense, along with a direct, public, and written order from Yeltsin, to persuade Grachev and the military leadership to storm the White House. Ultimately the military's subordination to the commander-in-chief trumped their extreme reluctance to play the arbiter role.

Violence in Moscow broke out on the afternoon of October 3. On the previous day there had been sharp clashes between the police and several thousand pro-parliament demonstrators at a meeting not far from the White House called by the hard-line "Worker's Russia" and the National Salvation Front. October 3 was a Sunday and was unseasonably warm, and a large crowd (probably around 4,000–10,000 people) gathered for a demonstration at October Square, several miles from the White House. The crowd marched toward the White House and overwhelmed the special police units

Poteryannaya armiya, pp. 177–178, 180–181, 190; Deryugin, Obraztsov, and Serebryannikov, *Problemy sotsiologii armii*, p. 82; Unattributed, "Silovye vedomstva ne khoteli."

[68] Aleksandr Gol'ts, "Armiya ostayetsya garantom grazhdanskogo mira," *KZ*, October 2, 1993, 2.

that tried to block their way. The demonstrators continued toward the White House, and they succeeded in breaking through the police encirclement of the building that had been put in place on September 24, after the attack on the CIS headquarters.[69]

Rutskoy, after having been isolated in the White House for almost two weeks, reacted rashly to this apparent turn in his fortunes. At about four in the afternoon on October 3, Rutskoy addressed his supporters from the balcony of the White House, asking them to form fighting detachments "to take by storm the Mayor's and Ostankino [the television center]." The Mayor's office was located across the street from the White House, and the crowd and pro-parliamentary forces succeeded in driving out the remaining police and taking control of the building. Ostankino was several miles across town, and the pro-parliamentary demonstrators set out for their next goal, led by General Makashov. Khasbulatov also addressed the crowd, declaring, "I call on our valiant soldiers to bring troops and tanks here in order to take the Kremlin by storm, where the usurper is holding power, former president Yeltsin, the criminal."[70]

Rutskoy, Khasbulatov, and their supporters claim that the failure of the police to stop the crowd en route to the White House on October 3 was a planned provocation by the authorities. There is much that remains murky about the violence in Moscow on October 3–4, but what remains undisputed is that the two leaders of the opposition, Rutskoy and Khasbulatov, called on their supporters to storm key government buildings, and that Rutskoy's "Deputy Minister of Defense," Makashov, played a key role in the attack on both the Mayor's and Ostankino. Yeltsin's alleged conspiracy would not have worked if Rutskoy, Khasbulatov, and Makashov had not taken these actions. The conspiracy theory also looks ridiculous in light of the army's stance during the affair; Yeltsin could not have known in advance what position the army would take if violence erupted, given its declared neutrality, and thereby would have been running a huge and unnecessary risk by escalating the conflict.[71]

Yeltsin had been taking the day off at his dacha outside Moscow when the violence broke out in the city. He signed a decree introducing emergency rule

[69] 93-Oktyabr', Moskva, pp. 211–212, 224–225; Moskva. Osen'-93, pp. 302–305, 359–363, 424–430; Vadim Belykh, "Moskva, 3 Oktyabrya. Krovavoye voskresen'e," Izvestiya, October 5, 1993, 2; Kolya Kachurin, "Ministry Admits Troops Were Poorly Prepared," Moscow Times [hereafter MT], October 5, 1993, 5; Vladimir Larin, ed., Vse o chernom oktyabre (Moskva: Komsomolskaya Pravda, October 1993); MN, October 10, 1993; Kuranty, October 5, 1993.
[70] Moskva. Osen'-93, p. 365; Khasbulatov, Velikaya rossiyskaya tragediya, Vol. II, p. 112.
[71] The literature on the details of the fighting of October 3–4 that bears on the conspiracy question is enormous; I cite only a few major sources here. For the pro-Yeltsin treatment, see Moskva. Osen'-93; Remnick, Resurrection, pp. 54–83. For the version of the pro-parliament forces, see Khasbulatov, Velikaya rossiyskaya tragediya; Rutskoy, Krovavaya osen'; Ivanov, Anafema; Steele, Eternal Russia, pp. 371–387.

in Moscow and returned to the Kremlin around six in the evening. The governments of Russia and Moscow, in conjunction with the ministers of internal affairs, security, and defense, were instructed to restore order in the city.

Orders from Grachev to bring troops into Moscow went out around 5:00 P.M. However, these orders were carried out with considerable confusion and delay. It appears that the commander of the Moscow Military District, Colonel-General Leontiy Kuznetsov, gave a series of orders to his subordinates, who had direct orders from Grachev, that were designed to slow their movement into the city. For example, the commander of the Taman Division, Major-General V. G. Yevnevich, was ordered to halt his troops at the city limits to "check equipment, weapons, and personnel." Yevnevich eventually sent an officer directly to Grachev to verify the orders and did not arrive at the Ministry of Defense headquarters until midnight.[72]

Although in the days after October 3–4 Grachev made confident claims about the reliability of his troops, at the time he was quite anxious. He asked the head of the Main Guard Directorate, Mikhail Barsukov, for troops from the Kremlin Guard in case the Ministry of Defense was stormed by pro-parliament demonstrators. The traffic police reported to the Kremlin that all army troops were waiting by the city limits. Kolesnikov reportedly cursed out one commander for his tardiness by proclaiming, "I could have gone there and back on my bicycle in two hours!"[73]

The failure of the army to come out promptly and decisively to suppress the parliamentary forces caused panic among some members of the Yeltsin administration. An operational staff for putting down the uprising was created under the Presidential Administration and headed by Deputy Defense Minister Kobets, with Yeltsin's adviser on military affairs, retired General Dmitriy Volkogonov, as his deputy. Former Minister of Defense Marshal Yevgeniy Shaposhnikov also participated. Kobets allegedly called Yeltsin several times to argue that the White House be stormed during the night. Kobets' operational staff ultimately played no role in planning and carrying out the attack on the White House, but it did organize the defense of other key objects in the city and coordinated the work of the various power ministries.[74]

[72] Baranets, *Poteryannaya armiya*, pp. 196–200.

[73] Korzhakov, *Boris Yel'tsin*, pp. 163–166; Yeltsin, *Zapiski prezidenta*, p. 382; Baranets, *Poteryannaya armiya*, pp. 196, 201–202. Relevant press accounts from the time are Kholodov, "Oktyabr' tsveta khaki"; Pel'ts, "Armiya byla vynuzhdena deistvovat' reshitel'no"; Nikolay Burbyga, "Belyy dom ya videl skvoz' pritsel," *Izvestiya*, October 6, 1993, 2; Pavel Fel'gengauer, "Army's Role: Less than Certain," *MT*, October 12, 1993, 1–2; Zhilin, "Who Is to Blame"; *93-Oktyabr'*, *Moskva*, p. 229; *Moskva. Osen'-93*, pp. 435, 451.

[74] Author's interview with Colonel A. A. Volkov, Assistant to Dmitriy Volkogonov, July 20, 1994; Author's interview with General (retired) A. I. Vladimirov, military adviser in Presidential Administration, September 21, 1999; Turchenko, "Chernaya pobeda"; Dmitriy Volkogonov and Evgeniy Kiselev, "Itogi," *NTV*, October 17, 1993; Dmitriy Volkogonov,

The Internal Troops of the MVD were able to defeat the efforts of Makashov and the pro-parliamentary forces to take control of the Ostank-ino television center, at a cost of forty-six deaths. At that point, Makashov returned with his forces to the White House. Rutskoy and his allies then pre-pared for a government storming of their headquarters at the White House.[75]

The decisive moment that determined the further conduct of the armed forces was the visit of President Yeltsin and Prime Minister Chernomyrdin to the Ministry of Defense in the middle of the night (around 2:00 A.M.) on October 4. It was at this meeting that Grachev and the Ministry of Defense leadership agreed to use the army to storm the White House. Before this meeting the army leadership had been unable to come to any firm decision. Many top officers believed that storming the White House was not the army's job and that the MVD and other special units could handle the matter. Deputy Minister of Defense Gromov, in fact, refused to show up for work that night. Moreover, Grachev apparently insisted that the operation not take place at night, as some of Yeltsin's advisers wished, but in the morning. Grachev was concerned both about government units firing on each other in the darkness and about the crowd that was still outside the White House during the night.[76]

Yeltsin and Chernomyrdin were received in awkward silence by the coun-try's top generals. The officers present had no concrete proposals on the oper-ation until a member of Yeltsin's Presidential Security Service was introduced by Korzhakov. This officer suggested a plan for storming the White House. Once there was a concrete plan, according to Yeltsin, it became much easier for all present. Chernomyrdin asked if there were any objections. Grachev turned to Yeltsin and asked, "Boris Nikolayevich, are you giving me sanc-tion to use tanks in Moscow?" Chernomyrdin exploded at Grachev, asking why the president should have to decide exactly how Grachev would carry out the operation. Grachev insisted on a written order. Yeltsin promised to

---

"U posledney cherty," in *Moskva. Osen'-93*, pp. 605–607; Filatov, *Sovershenno nesekretno*, p. 315; Baranets, *Poteryannaya armiya*, pp. 186–187.

[75] *Moskva. Osen'-93*, pp. 381–415, 530–531, 582–590; Rutskoy, *Krovavaya osen'*, pp. 406–431; Ivanov, *Anafema*, pp. 234–305, 467–468; Thomas de Waal, "Elite Unit Key to TV Victory," *MT*, October 7, 1993, 3; Igor' Andreyev, "Oborona teletsentra: vzglyad iznutri," *Izvestiya*, October 12, 1993, 2; Vladimir Novikov, "Vystrel iz granatometa reshil vsye," *MK*, October 3, 1995, 2.

[76] There are multiple accounts of the decisive meeting at the Ministry of Defense. Although sources disagree about who was present and whether it was a Security Council or Military Collegium session, or just a meeting of relevant officials, the basic details are known. See Yeltsin, *Zapiski prezidenta*, pp. 384–386; Korzhakov, *Boris Yel'tsin*, pp. 167–170; Baturin et al., *Epokha Yel'tsina*, p. 369; Filatov, *Sovershenno nesekretno*, p. 315; Baranets, *Poteryannaya armiya*, pp. 207–208, 214–215; Baranets, *Yel'tsin i ego generaly*, pp. 26, 202–203, 326; Pavel Fel'gengauer, interview with Colonel-General Mikhail Kolesnikov, "Mikhail Kolesnikov," *Segodnya*, December 29, 1993, 9; Ivanov, *Anafema*, pp. 317–323; Fel'gengauer, "Army's Role"; Turchenko, "Chernaya pobeda"; Burbyga, "Belyy dom ya videl."

send Grachev a written order, and he had one drawn up as soon as he returned to the Kremlin; the order was hand-delivered to Grachev. This decree underlined Yeltsin's responsibility for the decision and authorized the use of the military in an internal conflict.[77]

Grachev delegated command of the operation to Deputy Minister of Defense Colonel-General G. G. Kondrat'ev. Units were brought in from the Taman and Kantemirov divisions, the 119th airborne-parachute regiment, the 27th Motorized Rifle Brigade, the Tula Airborne Division, and a company of separate Airborne Troops special forces (*spetsnaz*). Grachev and Kondrat'ev still had some difficulties bringing in the designated units. Reportedly some officers from the Kantemirov division refused orders to participate. Additionally, apparently the operational staff around Kobets sent several officers from their group, including Kobets himself, as "presidential emissaries" to persuade officers that it was necessary for the army to put an end to mass disorder in Moscow.[78]

The operation began around 7:00 A.M., a time when there were very few people in front of the White House. Tank fire was used against the building, and the fighting lasted until that afternoon, when Rutskoy and Khasbulatov finally capitulated. MVD units were also involved. A key role in the operation was played by members of the Union of Afghan Veterans, who were substituted for conscripts in several units and rode in on the top of armored personnel carriers, cleared the barricades, and participated in the firing on the White House.[79]

Yeltsin had even more trouble with his own Kremlin guard than he did with the Armed Forces. Two special anti-terrorist units, "Alpha" and "Vympel," which previously had been part of the secret police (KGB/Ministry of Security), resisted participating in the storming of the White House. At 5:00 A.M. on October 4, Yeltsin was asked to meet with about thirty officers from the group. Yeltsin addressed them directly: "Are you ready to carry out the order of the president?" None of the officers replied. Yeltsin tried again: "Then I will ask you in a different way – do you

---

[77] In addition to the sources in the previous note, see *Moskva. Osen'-93*, 601–605; Boris Yeltsin, "Sem' blizhayshikh dney," *NG*, October 5, 1993, 2.

[78] Pel'ts, "Armiya byla vynuzhdena"; Kholodov, "Oktyabr' tsveta khaki"; Zhilin, "Who Is to Blame"; Colonel-General G. G. Kondrat'ev, interviewed by Aleksey Surkov, "Armiya ostalas' predannoy svoyemu narodu, svoyemu verkhovnomu glavnokomanduyushchemu!", in *Moskva. Osen'-93*, p. 598; Baranets, *Poteryannaya armiya*, pp. 201–202, 208; Turchenko, "Chernya pobeda"; Author's interview with Volkov; Author's interview with Vladimirov; Author's interview with anonymous active-duty officer, fall 1999.

[79] Burbyga, "V armii predatelei shchitayut na edinitsy," *Izvestiya*, October 7, 1993, 3; Yelena Korotkova, "Afghantsy otpushcheniya," *MK*, October 3, 1995, 2; Interview with General Yevnevich, "Pust' sudyat politikov," *MK*, October 3, 1996, 2; Major-General V. G. Yevnevich, interviewed by Aleksey Surkov, "Nerzberikha nenuzhnoy voyny," in *Moskva. Osen'-93*, p. 596; Author's interview with Fedorov.

refuse to carry out the order of the president?" Again there was no response. Yeltsin stormed out, telling their commander that the order must be carried out. The commander of the "Alpha" group, General Zaytsev, reportedly was on the verge of suicide due to embarrassment over the insubordination of his troops. Eventually several volunteers from "Alpha" were persuaded to go near the White House for "reconnaissance." One of their personnel was shot, and only at that point did the entire unit agree to participate. "Alpha" and "Vympel" did not storm the White House, but entered into negotiations with Rutskoy and Khasbulatov, who agreed to capitulate. "Alpha" and "Vympel" did not fire a single shot.[80]

Rutskoy continued to appeal for military support up to the moment when he surrendered. In one radio transmission, Rutskoy yelled, "I implore military comrades!... Immediately to the aid of the Supreme Soviet building! Pilots, if you hear me! Bring out combat vehicles!" He was shown on CNN that afternoon cowering under a desk, yelling into a transmitter, "I appeal to military pilots, I implore you, I demand: send the planes into the air!" Khasbulatov states that until the end, Rutskoy and Achalov kept insisting that forces would come to rescue them. Makashov argued against surrendering even after "Alpha" and "Vympel" had come into the building and agreed with Khasbulatov and Rutskoy on their surrender. In fact, hardly any military officers tried to bring units over to the White House on October 4. Two officers (a colonel and a naval captain-lieutenant) tried to bring over small groups of soldiers (around seventeen or eighteen men), but both groups were intercepted en route. Another lieutenant-colonel also tried to organize a group to defend the White House, but received no support. There were also a handful of students from Moscow area military academies who supported the White House on an individual basis. The highest published estimate of troops that went to support the White House is 80. One of Achalov's deputies remarked, "in Moscow there was not one battalion that remained faithful to its oath [i.e., to 'President Rutskoy']." Rutskoy notes how he appealed to the army, the police, and the workers, but "no one came to our defense."[81]

On October 5, the day after the storming, Defense Minister Grachev claimed that the armed forces had "rallied like never before, become more

---

[80] Yeltsin, *Zapiski prezidenta*, pp. 11–13; Korzhakov, *Boris Yel'tsin*, pp. 171–176, 193–196; Aleksandr Gorbunov and Andrey Kolesnikov, "Shturm 'belogo doma': 'Al'fa' ne khotela krovi," *MN*, November 7, 1993, 11; Leonid Nikitinskiy, "Katya i 'Al'fa,'" *Izvestiya*, October 19, 1993, 1, 5.

[81] *Moskva. Osen'-93*, p. 461; "Poslednyaya komanda Aleksandra Rutskogo," *KP*, October 6, 1993, 2; Khasbulatov, *Velikaya rossiyskaya tragediya*, Vol. I, pp. 389, 398; Burbyga, "V armii predatelei shchitayut na edinitsy"; Pel'ts, "Armiya byla vynuzhdena"; Vasiliy Starikov, "Starshiy leitenant Ostapenko zastrelilsya tak," *Novaya ezhednevnaya gazeta*, March 24, 1994, 1–2; Baranets, *Poteryannaya armiya*, p. 215; Ivanov, *Anafema*, p. 416; Rutskoy, *Krovavaya osen'*, p. 500.

united and manageable." This statement was obvious hyperbole. It must be stressed, however, that despite the fears of a split in the armed forces and some hesitation the night of October 3–4, the army played a key role in blockading and storming the White House less than twenty-four hours after Yeltsin had declared a state of emergency in Moscow. This took place at a time when over 20,000 soldiers in the Moscow Military District were away from their units picking potatoes. The Russian armed forces successfully carried out one of its first missions, one for which it was not designed, not prepared, and had no desire to carry out.[82]

Explaining Military Behavior during the October Events

Grachev and the armed forces leadership claimed throughout 1992 and 1993 that the army was "outside politics." They took the exact same stance from September 21 to October 2. Why, then, did the military shell the parliament building with 125-mm shells on October 4? Three aspects of the army's involvement must be explained. First, why was it necessary to call in the army the night of October 3–4? Second, why did the army initially hesitate to become involved? Third, why did it eventually carry out the suppression of the pro-parliamentary forces at the White House on October 4?

Military Involvement. The fact that the army was dragged into the political dispute between Yeltsin and the Supreme Soviet was due to the low political capacity of the new Russian state. The ambiguities and contradictions in the design of the political system led to open conflict. Both sides to the dispute share the blame for allowing the crisis to reach this point. Ultimately Rutskoy, Khasbulatov, and their supporters are primarily responsible for the violence, because it was their actions the evening of October 3 that pushed the political conflict into its bloody denouement.

The domestic structure approach best explains why the armed forces became involved in a domestic political crisis. The October 1993 events were not, however, the classic military coup that the major works in this tradition consider likely in periods of political disorder. October 1993 was not a case of military intervention. Otto Latsis, political commentator for the newspaper *Izvestiya*, noted after the October events:

The *use* of the army in internal conflicts is no gift, it signifies the failing of politics.... But this in principle shouldn't be confused with the *intervention* of the army in politics, that is an independent political decision of the military.... It would

---

[82] Igor' Chernyak, "Vliyaniye krupnogo kalibra," *KP*, October 7, 1993, 2; Fel'gengauer, "Po otsenkam spetsialistov"; Kholodov, "Rokovoy urozhay"; Yeltsin, *Zapiski prezidenta*, p. 385.

have been intervention if the army had *not* stormed in October 1993, having an order from the legal president and commander-in-chief.[83]

Military Hesitation. Many of President Yeltsin's most ardent supporters criticized the military leadership after the October events for being slow to come to the defense of the Yeltsin regime the night of October 3–4. Reportedly some members of Yeltsin's team even used the word "treason" to describe Grachev's behavior that night. Deputy Prime Minister Gaidar made plans to arm private citizens in case the army did not bring in troops to support Yeltsin.[84]

Clearly there was no lack of opportunity for involvement in a sovereign power issue the night of October 3–4 – both Yeltsin and Rutskoy were begging for support. State weakness, then, explains the fact that the military was forced to act, but not its extreme hesitancy to do so. Similarly, organizational structure was not a major obstacle to military behavior. Penetration and counterbalancing were not an issue, because all the power ministries were on the same side. Internal divisions in the army is a more plausible explanation for army hesitancy, but the most important split here was ideational and not structural.

Corporate interest represented a potentially powerful motive for army participation. The post-Soviet Russian army had fared extremely poorly as an organization in its first few years of existence. The political crisis of September–October 1993 could have been a golden opportunity to promote the military's interests. Rather than seeking a larger role in politics, however, the army hoped to avoid any involvement and wished simply, as Grachev put it in Garbo-esque fashion, to be "left alone." Furthermore, despite speculation to the contrary, there is no evidence that the military gained any concessions from Yeltsin the night of October 3–4 as a way of winning its support.[85]

The best explanation for the hesitancy of the Russian army to storm the White House is its organizational culture. There were two interrelated aspects of the organizational culture that were important and reflected both long-standing traditions and recent organizational lessons. First, there was the "Tbilisi syndrome," which had been further strengthened by the August 1991 coup effort; the army had learned that it should avoid internal missions because it was often made the scapegoat when

---

[83] Otto Latsis, "U drakona ne odna golova," *Izvestiya*, October 13, 1993, 5 (emphasis in original).

[84] Baturin et al., *Epokha Yel'tsina*, pp. 449–450; Sokolov, "Dazhe ministr pod podozreniyem"; Gaidar, *Dni porazheniy i pobed*, pp. 284–294; Yegor Gaidar, "Krasnaya osen' 93-go," *Izvestiya*, September 28 and September 29, 1994, 5.

[85] Brian D. Taylor, "Russian Civil–Military Relations After the October Uprising," *Survival*, 36, 1 (1994), 3–29.

things went wrong. Second, there was Grachev's favorite axiom, "the army is outside politics," which had been adopted as a direct consequence of events such as Tbilisi and August 1991 and heavily promoted by Grachev and the government. These were deeply rooted components of Russian military organizational culture, and they had been reinforced in recent years.

These cultural barriers to military participation in a sovereign power dispute were well known to both sides of the conflict. Yeltsin wrote in his memoirs that they all (the government, the military, and society) "had become hostages of a pretty formula: the army is outside politics." Gaidar, Yeltsin's Deputy Prime Minister, made the same point:

In the course of recent years we repeated many times that the army is outside politics, that it should never be used to decide internal political aims. It had become in a certain sense an article of faith, convincingly confirmed in August 1991 and from that time acquiring a special durability. None of us had ever discussed the possibility of using the army in an internal political struggle.[86]

Members of the opposition also recognized that the army's institutional culture was a barrier to involvement. Khasbulatov notes that Grachev was hoping to the end that the army would not have to be used. The general mood in the armed forces the night of October 3–4, writes Khasbulatov, was "do not get involved, avoid bloodshed."[87]

Officers pointed to the military's norms about internal politics as an explanation for their reluctance to get involved. General Volkogonov, who was communicating with officers in Moscow and around the country, noted, "until the last moment, literally until Monday night (October 4), this slogan was heard everywhere, that the army is outside politics." Deputy Minister of Defense Mironov observed that the slogan "the army is outside politics... undoubtedly, made a definite imprint both on societal perceptions and on the psychology of soldiers." *Red Star* ran a long piece responding to complaints in the liberal press that the army had been slow to act during the crisis. Vladimir Leonidov asserted that the maxim "the army is outside politics... is the law by which the armed forces live in all civilized states." Leonidov stated:

"The army outside politics" is the formula which, if you like, has entered into the souls of the military, sincerely accepted by them. Taught by the bitter experience of August 1991, the military, frankly speaking, came to believe that never again do they need to send their tanks and BTRs [Armored Personnel Carriers] along the streets of Moscow. And if a dramatic spiral of

---

[86] Yeltsin, *Zapiski prezidenta*, p. 384; Gaidar, "Krasnaya osen' 93-go," September 29, 1994, 5. See also Aleksey Arbatov, "Fashizm ne proshel, no demokratiya poterpela porazheniye," *NG*, October 22, 1993, 5.

[87] Khasbulatov, *Velikaya rossiyskaya tragediya*, Vol. I, pp. 341, 344.

events leads to that, then an extremely responsible and detailed explanation is necessary.[88]

These behavioral maxims in several instances had acquired the force of law. General Leonid Ivashov noted that after Tbilisi, Vilnius, and the August 1991 coup "there were heard demands to call to account soldiers who carried out criminal orders. This norm was even written into the draft military regulations." Moreover, Ivashov observed, the Law on Defense permitted the use of the army inside the country only on the basis of a law or decree adopted by the Supreme Soviet. *Segodnya*'s military correspondent, Pavel Fel'gengauer, notes that because of the provisions of the Law on Defense the military leadership was not certain it had the legal right to attack the White House. For this reason the written, public order of Yeltsin to Grachev the morning of October 4 was crucial. Retired Colonel Vladimir Lopatin states, "Yeltsin took on himself the responsibility for going outside the law, in the name of putting down mass disorder and securing the stability of the state."[89]

It is not surprising that the armed forces were very hesitant to become involved in the conflict between Yeltsin and parliament the night of October 3–4. The notion that the army is "outside politics" was central to their organizational culture. They had no desire to play the arbiter role. Moreover, although Yeltsin was the commander-in-chief, the legality of several of his steps, including Decree 1400 and his order to use the army on October 4, were dubious. Given these constraints on military activity, why did the armed forces leadership eventually agree to storm the White House?

Military Subordination. The decisive factor propelling the army into action on October 4 was a direct, written order from Yeltsin. When asked what it was that eventually moved the military leadership, General Volkogonov replied without hesitation, "the order of the Commander-in-Chief, which was given in the presence of the Prime Minister." Yeltsin later reflected, "I took the view that the Defense Minister should have acted himself, but he did not. That is why I had to give the order." When push came to shove, the military leadership's unwillingness to be involved in sovereign power issues was trumped by the need to carry out the orders of the legitimate head of state.[90]

---

[88] Volkogonov and Kiselev, "Itogi"; Colonel-General V. I. Mironov, interviewed by Aleksey Surkov, "Raskol armii ne grozil," in *Moskva. Osen'-93*, p. 591; Vladimir Leonidov, "Okazyvayetsya, Rossiyu spasla Akhedzhakova!" KZ, October 7, 1993, 3.

[89] Lieutenant-General Leonid Ivashov, interviewed by Igor' Chernyak, "Kogda nad 'Belym domom' rasseyalsya dym," KP, October 20, 1993, 2; Fel'gengauer, "Army's Role"; Vladimir Lopatin, "O roli sily v ispolnenii zakona," NG, October 19, 1993, 1–2.

[90] As Igor' Chernyak, the defense correspondent for *Komsomolskaya pravda* remarked, it was "rather strange" for the commander-in-chief to complain that Grachev had not acted without orders. See Volkogonov and Kiselev, "Itogi"; Unattributed (AFP-Reuters), "President

This is not to say that the military leadership would have carried out any order of Yeltsin's. If it took one blunder of Rutskoy's, the appointment of Achalov, to drive the military into Yeltsin's arms, it was his catastrophic mistake of ordering the storming of Ostankino and the Mayor's office that was decisive on October 3–4. The *Red Star* commentator Leonidov argued, "[the] fact that we were already talking not about political competition, but the threat of bloody chaos, fearsome unlimited criminality, marauding, civil war in the country, in the end, was the single legal basis for the introduction of forces into Moscow." The former Minister of Defense, Marshal Yevgeniy Shaposhnikov, drew a sharp distinction between events like Tbilisi and Vilnius and the October 1993 episode. In October 1993, Shaposhnikov maintained, "the army was not sent against a peaceful demonstrating people, but against armed thugs. There is a big difference."[91]

Any claim to legitimacy that Rutskoy had was lost in the eyes of the military leadership on October 3. Even before that date, only a small minority of the officer corps took his claim to be president and commander-in-chief seriously. Yeltsin commanded greater legitimacy as the existing president and commander-in-chief who had won a major referendum in April 1993. A poll conducted on September 22 found that eighty percent of Russians considered Yeltsin their president, compared to twenty percent for Rutskoy. A poll conducted in Moscow the night of October 4, after the violence, was even more definitive: Seventy-one percent of respondents supported Yeltsin, while only four percent supported Rutskoy and Khasbulatov. Seventy-eight percent of those polled supported the use of force to restore order in the capital.[92]

The armed forces had several reasons, then, to carry out Yeltsin's orders. Still, many, perhaps most, officers considered the use of the army a violation of their oath. This was true even of many liberal and moderate officers. For example, Major-General Aleksandr Tsal'ko, the Head of the Presidential Commission for the Social Protection of Soldiers and their Families, who made his name as a proreform deputy in the Soviet parliament, was critical of the military's behavior in October 1993. Tsal'ko said that both the president and the army acted unlawfully and that the crisis should have been resolved with other methods. He declared, "one cannot do such things (*Nel'zya tak delat*)." The retired General V. V. Serebryannikov, although he

---

Criticizes Grachev on TV," *MT*, November 13, 1993, 1–2; Igor' Chernyak, "Koney i generalov na pereprave ne menyayut," *KP*, November 25, 1993, 2.

[91] Leonidov, "Okazyvayetsya, Rossiyu spasla Akhedzhakova!"; Yevgeniy Shaposhnikov, interviewed by Yelena Dikun, "Armiya v gorode–posledniy argument prezidenta," *Obshchaya gazeta*, October 15, 1993, 8. This view also was endorsed by Major-General (retired) Vladimir Slipchenko, the former head of scientific research at the General Staff Academy, and Colonel Sergey Yushenkov, who was head of the Duma Defense Committee from 1993 until 1995. Author's interviews.

[92] *Moskva. Osen'-93*, pp. 63, 488–489.

worked for Khasbulatov, was seen as relatively liberal on civil–military relations issues and wrote several important pieces on the strengthening of civilian control. Serebryannikov argued that the army's storming of the White House was a violation of its oath to uphold the Constitution and that the military should have supported neither side. Serebryannikov maintained that "an army that only follows the order of its commander is a criminal army," adding that the military needs to be taught respect for the law and the Constitution.[93]

More hard-line officers were even more critical of the military's behavior in October 1993. A Colonel A. N. Ivanov (presumably a pseudonym) wrote an open letter to the newspaper *Nezavisimaya Gazeta* denouncing the Yeltsin regime in the strongest terms. He called the shelling of the White House "monstrous" and said that the main feeling of the army toward the government was "HATRED, ALL-CONSUMING BLUNT HATRED, HATRED." Ivanov said he was "ashamed" for the army and that he was embarrassed to wear his uniform in public anymore. Colonel Baranets, the former General Staff officer, also states that many officers felt ashamed to wear their uniforms after October 4. Most officers, he claimed, opposed the storming of the White House and argued that the conflict should have been resolved peacefully.[94]

Of course, none of these officers were in the position of Grachev and the military leadership, who received a direct order of the commander-in-chief. Nor were they in the position of those unit commanders who had to bring in their troops. Those who had to carry out such orders, such as General Yevnevich, the commander of the Taman Division, remarked later that it was "emotionally and morally difficult," but that "no one has the right to not carry out" an order of one's commander. Similarly, *Red Star* observed on the first anniversary of the October events, "the military, as befits it, carried out the order. Many men in uniform felt the tragedy of the events more sharply and painfully than anyone else." The sense of shame felt by many officers was certainly genuine, and alluded to even by those who supported Grachev's decision. Shaposhnikov stated, "it seems to me that a normal officer or soldier regrets that he was drawn into this conflict and now desires only one thing, that it not be repeated.

---

93 Author's interview with Major-General Aleksandr Tsal'ko, July 28, 1994; Author's interview with Lieutenant-General (retired) V. V. Serebryannikov, July 6, 1994. Tsal'ko stressed that his views were his "personal opinion." For more on Serebryannikov's views, see Serebryannikov, "Osnovnoy zakon i oborona"; Deryugin, Obraztsov, and Serebryannikov, *Problemy sotsiologii armii*, pp. 55–130.

94 Colonel A. N. Ivanov [MO employee], "K neschast'yu, ostalas' sovest' (letter)," *NG*, November 2, 1993, 8 (emphasis in original); Turchenko, "Chernaya pobeda"; Baranets, *Poteryannaya armiya*, pp. 211–212, 216. For a reply to Ivanov from a junior officer, see Junior Lieutenant V. D. Tarasov, "Gde pryatalas' sovest'?" *NG*, November 16, 1993, 8.

This is a black mark on the White House, and a mark on all of us, on Russia."[95]

Thus, the best explanation for the military's behavior in October 1993 is the organizational culture approach. The domestic structure approach also provides an important part of the story by pointing to the conditions that make military involvement in sovereign power issues likely. The combination of these two factors suggests that militaries with a relatively strong adherence to a norm of civilian supremacy will opt for *arbitration*, and not *intervention*, when extreme state weakness forces military involvement in sovereign power issues.

RUSSIAN CIVIL–MILITARY RELATIONS, 1994–1999

The rest of the Yeltsin years, from the October events up until his surprise retirement on New Year's 1999, were as tumultuous as his first two years in power. Financial collapse, bitterly contested elections, multiple power shuffles, and civil war against the break-away republic of Chechnya on two occasions were just a few of the highlights of these years. For the army the Yeltsin decade was a disaster in almost every respect, starting with the collapse of the Soviet army and including the October 1993 events and the failed intervention in Chechnya from 1994 to 1996. Neglected by a weak state and capricious president, many of the conditions for a coup attempt apparently were in place.

These conditions led many analysts, Russian and Western, to predict a coup was possible or even likely. October 1993, some argued, had "latin-americanized" the country and established the conditions for a coup. Others argued during the first Chechen war that the army's role in a civil war would lead them to seek sovereign power. Still others saw the financial crisis of August 1998, with the subsequent political shake-up, as presaging a coup attempt.[96]

In fact, to state the blindingly obvious, there was no military coup in Russia during Yeltsin's reign. Furthermore, after the October events the armed forces were not involved in any sovereign power issues. There

---

[95] Interview with Yevnevich, "Pust' sudyat politikov"; Vladimir Gavrilenko, "Nasha pamyat' i bol'," *KZ*, October 4, 1994, 1; Shaposhnikov, "Armiya v gorode."

[96] A complete citation of all the predictions of a military coup in Russia would run for an entire page. Some examples include Aleksandr Kuz'mishchev, "Import politicheskoy kul'tury," *NG*, November 3, 1993, 4; Thomas M. Nichols, "'An Electoral Mutiny?' Zhirinovsky and the Russian Armed Forces," *Armed Forces & Society*, 21, (1995), 327–347; Aleksandr Zhilin, "Chechnya's Spreading Impact on Kremlin Politics," *Prism: A Bi-Weekly on the Post Soviet States* (Jamestown Foundation electronic publication), July 21, 1995; Yegor Gaidar, *Liberation*, September 23, 1998 [FBIS-SOV-98-266]; Gennadiy Zyuganov, *Interfax*, November 10, 1998 [FBIS-SOV-98-314].

were two occasions when such military participation was a particularly strong possibility, but on both occasions the military leadership played no role. These two episodes were (a) the eve of the presidential elections in 1996 and (b) the government reshuffle in the aftermath of the August 1998 financial crisis. After briefly discussing these two issues, I reevaluate the opportunities and motives for military intervention for the period 1994–1999.

The presidential election of 1996 was the first such election since the collapse of the Soviet Union and the adoption of a new Constitution in December 1993. The election was seen by many as an important indicator of the success of Russia's rocky transition to democracy, yet in the early months of 1996 (the elections were held in June and July) there were considerable doubts as to whether they would be held at all. Some of Yeltsin's advisers, and particularly his influential bodyguard Korzhakov, urged Yeltsin to cancel the elections, believing that Yeltsin could not win a free election.[97]

A possible pretext for canceling the elections was the March 15 resolution of the Duma, the parliament that replaced the Supreme Soviet, repudiating the December 1991 decision on dissolving the Soviet Union. Yeltsin ordered his staff to prepare a decree on disbanding the Duma, banning the Communist Party, and postponing the presidential elections. He began consulting with security and law enforcement officials about methods for dealing with potential opposition from the Duma and society. Yeltsin, however, eventually decided not to go ahead with the plan due to opposition from several key officials. Not only did his main political advisers object to the plan, but his Interior Minister, Anatoliy Kulikov, did as well. Kulikov claims he was motivated both by the knowledge that Yeltsin's decision was unconstitutional and by his belief that the government lacked reliable forces to enforce the proposed measures.[98]

From our perspective, the most significant aspect of this story is that Defense Minister Grachev apparently was out of the loop on all of the plans and preparations. Yeltsin's brief account mentions a meeting with the "power ministers," but he does not mention Grachev by name. Other sources claim that Grachev was not summoned to the Kremlin that day, and reportedly he was only asked by Yeltsin over the phone in general terms if the army would assist the MVD in an emergency. Kulikov believed that the army could not

---

[97] Baturin et al., *Epokha Yel'tsina*, pp. 558–563; Yel'tsin, *Prezidentskiy marafon*, pp. 31–33; Remnick, *Resurrection*, pp. 331–333.

[98] Andrey Kamakin, interview with Anatoliy Kulikov, "Anatoliy Kulikov: 'Ya v avantyurakh ne uchastvuyu'," *NG*, July 23, 1999; Baturin et al., *Epokha Yel'tsina*, pp. 558–563; Yel'tsin, *Prezidentskiy marafon*, pp. 31–33; author's interview with Georgiy Satarov, September 30, 1999; Joel Ostrow interview with Yuriy Baturin, June 2000. I thank Dr. Ostrow for sharing his notes on this interview.

be relied on to help impose emergency measures, and it seems that Yeltsin shared these fears.[99]

Another period in which there was considerable speculation that the military would intervene in sovereign power issues was in the aftermath of the August 1998 financial crisis. Yeltsin sacked the Prime Minister at the time, Sergey Kiriyenko, and for several weeks Yeltsin and the Duma could not agree on the appointment of a successor. Many analysts warned of a potential repeat of the violence of October 1993, and polling showed that sixty-six percent of Russians thought this was a possible outcome. Papers warned of ominous military preparations.[100]

The military leadership showed no interest in being involved in resolving the conflict, however, and ultimately played no role. Defense Minister Igor Sergeyev came out for a quick end to the crisis and stated his hope that there would be no bloodshed, as there had been in October 1993. In the end a compromise prime ministerial candidate, Yevgeniy Primakov, was found who satisfied both Yeltsin and the Duma.[101]

Finally, it is worth noting that Yeltsin's transfer of power to his successor Vladimir Putin took place without army participation. Although the circumstances of the succession were strange, with Yeltsin's surprise resignation on the eve of the millennium on December 31, 1999, they were formally in line with the Constitution. Three months later, Putin was elected to the post of president. As was the case with most transfers of power since the early nineteenth century, the army was a passive bystander.

How can the armed forces' noninvolvement in sovereign power issues during this period be explained? The two-step model of opportunity and motive sheds light on this outcome. Although state weakness remained a fundamental problem throughout the 1990s, organizational structural barriers somewhat limited the opportunities for military intervention. Furthermore, although the corporate interest motives for a coup were probably as compelling as at any point in Russian history, the officer corps, for the most part, remained committed to an apolitical organizational culture.

[99] On Grachev's noninvolvement, in addition to the cites in the previous note, see Baranets, *Yel'tsin i ego generaly*, p. 262.

[100] "Poll Shows Russians Think Force May be Used Over Crisis," *Interfax*, September 4, 1998; "Defense Ministry Prepared for Trouble," *RFE/RL Newsline*, August 31, 1998; "Press on Power Ministries' Preparations," *RFE/RL Newsline*, September 2, 1998. Examples of speculation about a military coup include: Vladimir Klint, "The Last Days of Boris Yeltsin," *Forbes*, September 7, 1998; "Lebed Warns Military Is in 'Revolutionary Mood'," *International Herald Tribune*, September 1, 1998. For a good statement of the view that fears of a coup were unwarranted, see Richard Overy, "Why No Russian Franco?," *London Times*, September 15, 1998.

[101] Barry Renfrew, "Russian PM Outlines Economic Plans," *AP*, September 4, 1998; Yel'tsin, *Prezidentskiy marafon*, pp. 217–233.

Opportunity: Domestic Structure

The Russian state continued to be a weak actor throughout the 1990s. Whether conceived of in terms of its autonomy from other social forces, or its capacity to implement its decisions, there were serious grounds for believing that the state lacked the strength to resist a concerted coup attempt.

There was little change in any of the basic indicators of state strength discussed at the beginning of the chapter. Although national and local level elections continued to take place, the new constitutional order remained very young and there had been no turnover in executive power since the collapse of the Soviet Union. Political violence was outrageously high due to the civil war in Chechnya. The central state remained at loggerheads with many regions about contradictory laws and revenue transfers. The only political party that could consistently gain more than fifteen percent of the vote, and that was assured of outliving its leader, was the Communist Party. Most troublesome, perhaps, was the penetration of both big business and criminal structures into the state apparatus. Vadim Volkov argues that under Yeltsin the Russian state lacked one of the most fundamental characteristics of modern statehood: "the state has lost the monopoly of legitimate violence."[102]

The one domestic structure argument that has some merit for this period concerns the relationship between economic development and military coups. As discussed in Chapter 1, coups are more likely in poor countries, although coups have also taken place in more developed states. This pattern continued in the 1990s, when most coups occurred in relatively poor countries, such as Pakistan and the Ivory Coast. However, several countries at levels of development comparable to that of Russia based on GDP per capita figures, such as Venezuela and Thailand, did experience military intervention in the last decade. And, of course, Russia had a coup attempt in 1991 and two instances of military arbitration in the early 1990s. Russia's level of development, then, clearly was not a barrier in itself to military participation in sovereign power issues. Still, this domestic structure argument, unlike the political capacity one, may play some role in explaining Russian military passivity under Yeltsin.

---

[102] Vadim Volkov, "Violent Entrepreneurship in Post-Communist Russia," *Europe-Asia Studies*, 51 (1999), 752. See also Valerie Sperling, ed., *Building the Russian State: Institutional Crisis and the Quest for Democratic Governance* (Boulder, CO: Westview Press, 2000); Kathryn Stoner-Weiss, "Central Weakness and Provincial Autonomy: The Process of Devolution in Russia," *Program on New Approaches to Russian Security Policy Memo Series*, Memo 39, November 1998; Stephen E. Hanson and Jeffrey S. Kopstein, "The Weimar/Russia Comparison," *Post-Soviet Affairs*, 13 (1997), 271–277; Pauline Jones Luong, "The Current Economic Crisis in Russia Is Neither," *Program on New Approaches to Russian Security Policy Memo Series*, Memo 35, November 1998; Anatol Lieven, *Chechnya: Tombstone of Russian Power* (New Haven, CT: Yale University Press, 1998), pp. 150–185; Donald N. Jensen, "Is Russia Another Somalia?," *RFE/RL Newsline*, January 27, 1999; David Hoffman, "Yeltsin's Absentee Rule Raises Specter of a 'Failed State'," *Washington Post*, February 26, 1999, 1.

Opportunity: Organizational Structure

There continued to exist a number of alternative power structures that represented possible counterweights to military intervention. Indeed, in the mid-1990s several of these organizations expanded either their size or their areas of competency. Although these organizations had been on the same side as the army in August 1991 and October 1993, and the general weakness of the state raised questions about their ability to stop a concerted military challenge, they represented potential barriers to military intervention.

The most prominent possible counterbalancer remained the Internal Troops (VV) of the MVD. Several analysts claimed that the VV expanded in the mid-1990s under the tutelage of MVD head Kulikov. However, it appears that these troops also were downsized in the 1990s, just not as quickly as the regular army. The most important of these units for our purposes was the so-called Dzerzhinsky Division, numbering around 10,000 troops, located near Moscow; this grouping was involved both in the August 1991 coup attempt and in putting down the October 1993 uprising.[103]

Less well known, but perhaps more significant, were the forces of the Main Guards Directorate (GUO in Russian) and the Presidential Security Service (SBP). Together these organizations were responsible for the security of the president and other top governmental officials. Reportedly they numbered more than 20 thousand personnel, including the 5,000 strong Kremlin (Presidential) regiment and several special units. They also had links, and on occasion operational control, over several army units near Moscow.[104]

These and other forces of the so-called power ministries were believed by some analysts to be deliberately manipulated counterweights on the part of Yeltsin. Anatol Lieven maintains that President Boris Yeltsin pursued a strategy of "divide and rule" designed to reduce the threat of military intervention. Mark Galeotti argues that "an intricate balance of terror" has been created that prevents coup attempts.[105] The Federal Security Service (FSB), the successor to the KGB, also continued to place agents inside the army to monitor the officer corps.

Yeltsin's experience in October 1993 probably did lead him to devote more resources to these other agencies, particularly the GUO and SBP. In November 1993 he made the SBP a separate agency from the GUO, telling Korzhakov that he needed "my personal mini-KGB." Given that the Ministry

---

[103] Brian D. Taylor, "The Rise and Fall of the Russian Internal Troops?" *Program on New Approaches to Russian Security Policy Memo Series*, Memo 45, November 1998; Mark Galeotti, *The Kremlin's Agenda: The New Russia and Its Armed Forces* (Coulsdon, Surrey, UK: Jane's Information Group, 1995), pp. 111–117; Mark Galeotti, "Moscow's armed forces: a city's balance of power," *JIR*, 9, 2 (1997), 51–54.

[104] Nikolay Troitskiy, "Pretoriantsy tret'ego Rima," *Obshchaya gazeta*, January 12, 1995, 8; Galeotti, *The Kremlin's Agenda*, pp. 120–121; Galeotti, "Moscow's armed forces."

[105] Lieven, *Chechnya*, p. 289; Galeotti, "Moscow's armed forces."

of Security/FSB had proven itself largely useless in October 1993, this was not surprising.[106]

An equally plausible reason why agencies like the SBP and the MVD may have been favored by Yeltsin after October 1993 was not so much his fear that the army would intervene in sovereign power issues, but his concern about the exact opposite – that they would refuse to become involved in them on his behalf in the future. Retired Colonel Petr Romashkin, a military expert in the Duma, contends that the distaste of the army for playing an internal role in October led Yeltsin to give more resources to the MVD. Moreover, three of the Yeltsin government's top officials in defense and security policy – Yuriy Baturin (Defense Council secretary), Andrey Kokoshin (Security Council secretary), and Aleksandr Piskunov (Administrative Department of the Government, responsible for coordinating government decrees and laws pertaining to the power ministries) – all maintain that the MVD was not built up to counterbalance the army. Kokoshin notes that the break-up of the KGB into multiple agencies at the end of 1991 was clearly an attempt to weaken that agency, but that the changing fortunes of other power ministries was not a deliberate policy of Yeltsin. Piskunov concurs that this was not a deliberate policy.[107]

A more likely explanation than counterbalancing for the changing fortunes of the different power ministries in the 1990s was a combination of bureaucratic politics and rational decision. Aleksey Arbatov, Deputy Chair of the Duma Defense Committee, notes that among the political elite there was a general perception that current threats were more internal than external. Moreover, the army had a huge infrastructure left over from the Cold War that made it a more likely target for cuts. The war in Chechnya reinforced the view that the major threats were internal, and that the VV MVD had a larger role to play, particularly since many army officers were reluctant to use the armed forces in Chechnya because they considered it not their function. The cuts undertaken in the VV and several other power ministries starting in 1998 also suggest that bureaucratic politics is a better explanation for these agencies' shifting fortunes than a deliberate strategy. Finally, many MVD officers are former army generals, including several of the Internal Troops' commanders in the last decade, and would probably be very reluctant to take up arms against former comrades; the VV is thus an unlikely counterbalancer.[108]

[106] Korzhakov, *Boris Yel'tsin*, p. 404; Baturin et al., *Epokha Yel'tsina*, pp. 213–214.

[107] Author's interview with Colonel (Retired) Petr Romashkin [assistant to Duma Deputy Alexey Arbatov], June 8, 2000; Baturin et al., *Epokha Yel'tsina*, p. 216; Andrei Kokoshin presentation at Harvard University, June 19, 1998; Joel Ostrow interviews with Yuriy Baturin and Alexander Piskunov, June 2000. Again, my thanks to Dr. Ostrow.

[108] Author's interview with Aleksey Arbatov, August 13, 1997; Taylor, "Rise and Fall"; Author's interview with Vadim Solovyev [Managing Editor, *NVO*], June 16, 2000.

Strangely enough, despite his expressed concern about the possibility of a military coup, Yeltsin makes no mention in his memoirs of efforts he undertook to prevent them. He discusses four generals who were involved in politics, but none of them in the context of a potential coup. General Dzhokar Dudayev, the Chechen leader, was obviously not a candidate for such a role, and Yeltsin explicitly states that his first Minister of Defense, Grachev, "always avoided politics." General Korzhakov, his bodyguard, came from the secret police and not the armed forces and, as Yeltsin admits, acquired enormous power because Yeltsin let him. The fourth general he discusses, Aleksandr Lebed, was retired from the army when he ran for president and was subsequently appointed head of the Security Council by Yeltsin himself. Yeltsin states that members of his administration seriously discussed the "worst-case scenario" of Lebed attempting a military coup, but that it was clear to him that Lebed would never do such a thing "under any circumstances." Grachev, Korzhakov, and Lebed were all fired by Yeltsin in 1996 for various reasons and, despite much speculation about coups at the time, without any serious difficulty.[109]

The presence of other bodies capable of counterbalancing a coup certainly would complicate the planning of any potential plotter. Secret police monitoring also continues to exist.[110] In my view, however, both the extent and deliberateness of counterbalancing as a Yeltsin strategy has been overstated. To get a full picture of the reasons behind Russian military nonintervention, we also need to consider material and ideational motives.

Motives: Corporate Interest

The military's decline, which began under Gorbachev, accelerated under Yeltsin and continued apace until the end of Yeltsin's rule. The British journalist Anatol Lieven states flatly, "the Russian army today is weaker than it has been for almost four hundred years."[111]

These signs of weakness are diverse and wide-ranging. Two basic indicators of corporate interest, organizational size and budget, show clear evidence of an organization under threat. In the eight years after the collapse of the Soviet Union the size of the Russian armed forces dropped by almost two-thirds (Figure 7.1). Similarly, between 1992 and 1999 the military budget was slashed by sixty-two percent (Figure 7.2).[112]

---

[109] Yel'tsin, *Prezidentskiy marafon*, pp. 60–79. For an example of coup speculation on the eve of Lebed's firing, see, for example, Vitaliy Tret'yakov, "Rossiya prevratilas' v Afganistan," *NG*, October 9, 1996.

[110] Baranets, *Genshtab bez tayn*, Vol. II, p. 126.

[111] Anatol Lieven, "Russia's Military Nadir: The Meaning of the Chechen Debacle," *The National Interest*, 44 (1996), 24.

[112] The data used for these charts are from multiple issues of *The Military Balance*, published by The International Institute for Strategic Studies, London.

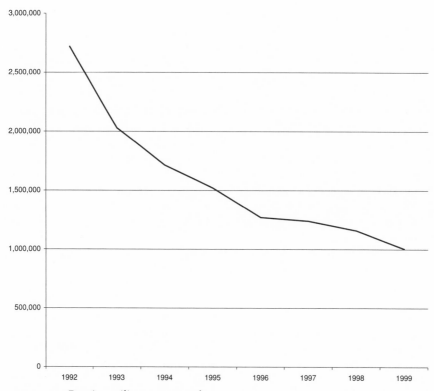

FIGURE 7.1. Russian military personnel.

If anything, these figures understate the extent of decline, particularly in terms of the budget. According to some estimates, Russian defense spending declined from 142 billion dollars in 1992 to four billion dollars in 1999, a ninety-eight percent decrease! Moreover, actual expenditures in the 1990s rarely, if ever, reached the budgeted amount. For example, in 1998 actual expenditures were only fifty-five percent of planned allocations.[113]

Across a range of issues the military was in a state of crisis, including housing, manpower, social support, training, and supplies. Over 125,000 officers and warrant officers did not have their own apartments. More than seventy percent of officers were regularly paid late, in many cases not receiving their salaries for months at a time. Military units had

[113] Nikolay Mikhaylov, "Nastalo vremya uchredit' kollektivnuyu otvetsvennost' za strategich-eskuyu bezopasnost'," *NVO*, February 4, 2000; Sergey Manyukov, "Mech krizisa nad voyennym byudzhetom," *Orientir*, No. 2, 1999, 5–6. See also U.S. Department of State, *Annual Report on Military Expenditures, 1998*; Sergey Rogov, *Military Reform and the Defense Budget of the Russian Federation* (Alexandria, VA: Center for Naval Analyses, August 1997); Alexei G. Arbatov, "Military Reform in Russia: Dilemmas, Obstacles, and Prospects," *International Security*, 22, 4 (1998), 94–99, 103–112.

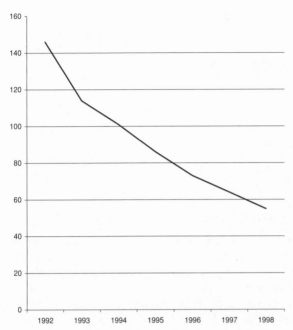

FIGURE 7.2. Russian military budget (billions of 1997 U.S. dollars).

electricity and telephone service cut off for lack of payment. Many units spent much of their time simply struggling to survive, not engaged in military training. In a poll conducted in June 2000, more than ninety percent of officers reported that conditions in the army were poor, and over eighty percent said they were dissatisfied with their life in the army.[114]

The situation in the Russian armed forces became so bad that in 1998 the Defense Ministry issued instructions on foraging for food in the forest, and some units were supplied with dog food. Allegedly some officers' wives, even in the relatively well-off Moscow region, worked as prostitutes to raise money for their families. The military leadership complained bitterly about the hardships inflicted upon a once-mighty army. On February 23, 1997, Armed Forces Day, then Defense Minister Igor Rodionov stated, "What sort of defense minister am I? I am the minister of a disintegrating army and dying

---

[114] "Kapitany Baltflota golodayut, no ne sdayutsya," *Izvestiya*, July 14, 1998; "Ofitsery neu-dovletvoreny svoyey zhizn'yu, no ostavlyat' armiyu ne toropyatsya," *Izvestiya*, July 14, 1998; Lev Rokhlin, "Vozdushnye zamki dlya zashchitnikov Otechestva," *Pravda-5*, February 21, 1998, 1–2; Andrey Korbut, "Armiya vse aktivnee vyrazhala delovol'stvo min-istrami," *NG*, March 27, 1998, 3; Anatole Shub, "Most Russian Officers Still Demoral-ized," *Opinion Analysis*, USIA M-123-00 (Washington, D.C.: Department of State Office of Research, July 28, 2000).

navy." General Lev Rokhlin, the former chair of the parliament's defense committee, remarking on the abysmal conditions in the armed forces, stated in February 1997 that "if this happened to the army of a well-to-do country, there would have been a military coup long ago."[115]

Rokhlin was not versed in civil–military relations theory, but he intuitively understood the claim made by much of the comparative, Soviet, and post-Soviet literature: Armies whose interests are consistently ignored will be inclined to intervene. The corporate interest approach, then, performs the worst of the four being considered; the Russian political leadership under Yeltsin did not cater to military interests, but the officer corps remained passive.

Motives: Organizational Culture

The dominant organizational culture of the Russian army continued to hold the view that intervention in sovereign power issues was illegitimate. Although Yeltsin was highly unpopular among the armed forces, praetorian sentiments remained the minority position.

One important public change in Russian organizational norms was the abandonment of the slogan "the army outside politics." After the October 1993 events the phrase came under attack from President Yeltsin and some of his close supporters, and it was therefore dropped from Grachev's lexicon. Many officers continued to adhere to it in some form in private, with qualifications. One retired colonel noted that it would make a nice "bumper sticker," saying he liked the slogan but in reality in all countries the army has a political role. Other officers adhered to the rationale used in Ministry of Defense training literature – that the army is the "object" of politics, but should not be its "subject." In other words, as a state institution the military fulfilled the decisions of civilian leaders. Other officers, such as one retired general, categorically rejected the slogan as "complete nonsense," but for the same rationale given by the supporters of it – that the army implemented orders of politicians, and was therefore, ipso facto, "in politics." Thus, Russian officers understood the distinction between defense politics, in which the army obviously played a role, and sovereign power issues, a sphere where the armed forces should not be involved.[116]

---

[115] Simon Saradzhyan, "Army Tells Soldiers to Forage for Food," *MT*, August 14, 1998; Baranets, *Poteryannaya armiya*, pp. 515–516; *Izvestiya*, February 25, 1997, 1; Sergei Shargorodsky, "Russians Blue in the Face over Ailing Red Army," *Salt Lake Tribune*, February 24, 1997.

[116] Author's interviews (the first two are the sources for the exact quotes): Colonel (ret.) Mikhail Pogorely, June 6, 2000; General (retired) Aleksandr Vladimirov, September 21, 1999; Major-General Slipchenko; Colonel Yushenkov; General Achalov; Major-General Tsal'ko; Marshal Evginiy Shaposhnikov, September 29, 1999; Major-General (retired) S. A. Tyushkevich, June 5, 2000; Colonel (retired) Vitaliy Tsygichko, June 9, 2000.

TABLE 7.3. *Approval or Disapproval of Using Armed Forces for Certain Roles*

	Approve	Disapprove
Fight against separatism in regions of Russia?	28	68
Fight organized crime?	38	60
Protect parliament?	45	52
Protect president?	47	50
Protect the Kurile Islands if attacked by Japan?	98	0.5

Source: Ball, "The Unreliability of the Russian Officer Corps."

Several major polls conducted between 1994 and 1999 provided further evidence of the Russian army's commitment to the norm of civilian supremacy. A major poll by the German Friedrich–Ebert Foundation was released in the fall of 1994. Seventy-one percent of officers thought that a military coup in the next two years was improbable, ten percent thought it was a certainty, and eleven percent thought it was probable. This scenario was considered the second least likely of twelve scenarios, falling only behind a "seizure of power by Russian fascist elements." Even full Russian membership in NATO by 1996 was considered more likely. Officers also expressed objections to most potential domestic uses of the army; the only three that officers approved were in case of natural disasters, the struggle against organized crime, and nuclear power accidents. They opposed being used to protect both the parliament and the president. Majorities also opposed being used against separatist movements, for construction and economic projects, for gathering the harvest, and to break strikes.[117]

The most comprehensive analysis of Russian officer corps opinion was conducted by Deborah Yarsike Ball in the summer of 1995. Ball arrived at a number of findings that are relevant to an assessment of officer corps organizational culture. She found that the majority of officers hold democratic views and do not support an authoritarian government. Furthermore, Russian officers continue to believe that the army's primary task is external defense of the state and to reject internal usage. More than eighty percent opposed using the army for public works and railroad construction and for harvesting crops. On the other hand, seventy percent approved of using the military in case of nuclear power plant accidents, and ninety-seven percent approved using the army to help in case of natural disasters. Officers also opposed using the armed forces for a variety of domestic policing missions (see Table 7.3).

[117] *The Military Elite in Russia 1994* (Munich/Moscow: Friedrich–Ebert Foundation, August 1994).

TABLE 7.4. *Would You Follow Orders to*
Put Down a Separatist Rebellion?

Response	Percent
Definitely follow orders	17
Probably follow orders	34
Probably not follow orders	24
Definitely not follow orders	15
Refused to answer	4
Undecided	6

Source: Ball, "How Reliable Are Russia's Officers?"

These results are very similar to those of the Ebert Foundation poll, with
the exception that a majority in the Ball survey also disapproved of using the
army against organized crime. Summarizing her results, Ball concludes, "the
military feels that internal troops should take care of the country's 'internal'
problems, and that the military should be responsible for protecting the
nation against external threats."[118]

Ball's data on the willingness of officers to follow orders are more disturbing, and they are similar to the polling data available for 1993 discussed
above. Large numbers of officers said that they would not follow orders to
be used internally against separatists (see Table 7.4).

Officers' responses reflect the institutional lessons embodied in the "Tbilisi
syndrome" and reinforced in August 1991 and October 1993: Officers' activities in the event of domestic usage are likely to be heavily scrutinized,
and one should be very cautious about fulfilling orders of dubious legality. It was this concern that prompted Grachev to insist on a written order
from Yeltsin on October 4, 1993. Ball also found that fifty-one percent of
officers stated that they would have disobeyed orders to storm the White
House in October 1993.[119] As far as is known, though, only a handful of
officers actually disobeyed direct orders in October 1993. It is easier to tell
a pollster that you would disobey an order than it is to actually do so when
the consequences could well be a dishonorable discharge from the armed
forces. Regardless, these data clearly do not demonstrate praetorian urges
on the part of the officer corps. This very hesitancy to follow questionable
orders would likely have doomed any attempt at intervention, and it may
have influenced Yeltsin's decision not to go ahead with the disbanding of the
Duma in March 1996.

---

[118] Deborah Yarsike Ball and Theodore P. Gerber, "The Political Views of Russian Field Grade
Officers," *Post-Soviet Affairs*, 12 (1996), 166; Deborah Yarsike Ball, "How Reliable are
Russia's Officers?" *JIR*, 8, 5 (1996), 204–207.
[119] Ball, "How Reliable are Russia's Officers?"

Another major survey of 1,200 active-duty officers conducted in May 1997 found that seventy-eight percent of those questioned maintained that the military should not be involved in domestic politics. Thus, throughout the period 1992–1997 there were strong majorities against military participation in sovereign power issues.[120]

Russian military behavior in a series of domestic and foreign events in the mid- and late 1990s led some to conclude that the army had serious political ambitions and were slipping out of civilian control. A full discussion of these issues is not possible here, but a brief discussion of two of them, the war in Chechnya and the sudden deployment of Russian troops to Kosovo in June 1999, shows that these fears are exaggerated.

Chechnya. There are two important civil–military relations issues about the first war in Chechnya (1994–1996): who made the decision to start the war and whether the government controlled the army's activity once the war had started. On the decision to start the war, it is clear that Yeltsin made the final decision. The decision was made at a Security Council meeting on November 29, 1994. Reportedly, Yeltsin instructed all those present to vote in favor of war. Much is murky about this decision, but it appears that Grachev at least initially was opposed, if not to the war in general, then at least to the accelerated tempo that Yeltsin demanded. Grachev did contribute to the decision by boasting, in a fit of bureaucratic one-upmanship, that a single paratroops regiment could take the capital of Chechnya, Grozny, in two hours. Yeltsin ignored the advice of his more liberal colleagues who opposed military action. Yeltsin's ultimate responsibility for the decision is clear from several decrees he signed at the time, including one in secret. In January 1995, in response to speculation that he was not in charge, Yeltsin stated publicly, "I strictly control the power structures, know every day the situation in Chechnya, and nothing serious there happens without me." He makes a similar claim in his memoirs.[121]

There was considerable opposition within the armed forces to the first war in Chechnya. In fact, the Main Military Collegium did not discuss the issue before the decision to invade was made by the Security Council. Three deputy

---

[120] Steven A. Grant, with the assistance of Maya DeHart, "Russian Officers Face Personal and Political Insecurities," *Opinion Analysis*, USIA M-113-97 (Washington, D.C.: USIA Office of Research and Media Reaction, July 14, 1997), 3.

[121] Baranets, *Genshtab bez tayn*, Vol. II, pp. 136–137; Baranets, *Yel'tsin i ego generaly*, pp. 209, 241; Baturin et al., *Epokha Yel'tsina*, pp. 595–634; Maria Eismont, "The Chechen War: How it All Began," *Prism: A Bi-Weekly on the Post Soviet States* (Jamestown Foundation electronic publication), March 8, 1996; Carlotta Gall and Thomas de Waal, *Chechnya: Calamity in the Caucasus* (New York: New York University Press, 1998), pp. 143–172; "Taynoye stanovitsya yavnym," *Novoye vremya*, No. 14, 1995, 6–7; ITAR-TASS, "Boris Yel'tsin o merakh po likvidatsii chechenskogo krizisa," *KZ*, January 19, 1995, 1; Yel'tsin, *Prezidentskiy marafon*, p. 67.

defense ministers (Boris Gromov, Georgiy Kondrat'ev, and Valeriy Mironov) were dismissed for opposition to the war. Gromov argued that the army's involvement in domestic politics "has not once produced positive results." Colonel-General Eduard Vorob'ev, the deputy commander of the Ground Forces, resigned rather than take command of the Chechen operation. The prominent General Aleksandr Lebed also was an outspoken critic of the war. Over 500 officers refused to go to Chechnya in the first few months of the war.[122]

As the war dragged on into 1995 and 1996, some analysts suggested that military units in Chechnya were out of control and that the country's civilian political leadership was unable to exercise oversight over military conduct. In August 1996 Yeltsin's newly appointed National Security Adviser, Aleksandr Lebed, who was in charge of Chechen peace negotiations, ostensibly faced down a local commander (Lieutenant-General Konstantin Pulikovskiy) who had given an ultimatum to the Chechen rebels, allegedly without official Moscow backing. Russian journalists differed both over whether the Russian armed forces favored an end to the war and whether Pulikovskiy was acting in accordance with Yeltsin's and Lebed's plans. Yeltsin's adviser on ethnic issues, Emil Pain, stated that Pulikovskiy's ultimatum had been approved by the country's leadership and that Lebed certainly knew of it. Regardless of the details of this episode, Lebed successfully completed a peace settlement with Chechnya and all Russian forces were withdrawn. Those who said that the army in Chechnya was out of control and that the political leadership could not enforce its will were wrong.[123]

When the war resumed in the fall of 1999, there were again reports of the army leadership dictating to President Yeltsin and Prime Minister Vladimir Putin. General Vladimir Shamanov, one of the commanders of the Chechnya operation, gained headlines with his assertion that if the war was stopped, there would be a huge exodus of officers from the army, which might push the country to the brink of civil war. Such a statement points to definite problems

---

[122] Colonel General Boris Gromov, interview by Aleksandr Zhilin, "Boris Gromov: 'Operatsiya gotovilas' v glubokoy tayne . . . ','" *MN*, January 8, 1995, 1, 5; Boris Gromov, "Sluzhba po sovesti – dolg soldata," *Obshchaya gazeta*, April 13, 1995, 1; *NTV*, April 7, 1995 [FBIS-SOV-95-068]; INTERFAX, January 19, 1995 [FBIS-SOV-95-013]; Remnick, *Resurrection*, pp. 269, 279–283; Unattributed, "Byvshiye podchinennye Valeriya Mironova uvazhayut," *KD*, April 8, 1995, 1; Baranets, *Yel'tsin i ego generaly*, pp. 40–41, 332–333.

[123] Vitaliy Tret'yakov, "Chechnya: kriticheskiy realizm," *NG*, April 24, 1996, 1; Michael Specter, "Aide to Yeltsin Disputes Orders Over Chechnya," *New York Times*, August 21, 1996, 1; Oleg Zhirnov, "Kto stoyal za Pulikovskim?," *Moskovskaya pravda*, August 23, 1996, 1; Pavel Fel'gengauer, "Voyna v Chechne i reforma armii nesovmestimy," *Segodnya*, August 22, 1996, 1; Yuriy Golotyuk, "Segodnya istek srok 'ul'timatuma general Pulikovskogo'," *Segodnya*, August 22, 1996, 1; Dmitriy Kamyshev, "48 chasov bez voyny," *KD*, August 22, 1996, 1, 3; Dmitriy Kamyshev, "Okazyvayetsya, eto byla shutka," *KD*, August 23, 1996, 1, 3.

with civil–military relations, but not to an army striving for political control. When queried about his statement, Shamanov noted that if an order to stop did come, "the army will fulfil its order, no one should doubt this." Yeltsin and his heir-apparent Putin made a calculated decision in the fall of 1999 to let the army conduct the Chechen campaign as it saw fit, wagering that a successful war would enhance Putin's standing before the elections. Although military influence did grow during this period, it was with Putin's blessing and under his control.[124]

Kosovo. The surprise deployment of a group of Russian paratroopers from Bosnia to Kosovo in June 1999, without prior consultation with NATO, also raised questions about civilian control in Russia. The confusion led observers to suggest that the army had acted without Yeltsin's approval. One of Russia's best known military analysts, Pavel Fel'gengauer, wrote afterwards that the effect of this operation may be very important for Russian politics, because "the military may figure that if they once again defy authority and move to oust Yeltsin, their armor will be drowned in flowers in Moscow, as it was last week in Pristina."[125]

In fact, there is considerable evidence that Yeltsin approved the plan in advance. U.S. Deputy Secretary of State Strobe Talbott was in Moscow at the time negotiating the nature of Russia's role in the Kosovo peace-keeping force. Talbott was at the Russian Ministry of Defense when the Russian paratrooper operation took place, and the Russian Minister of Defense, Igor Sergeyev, and the Chief of the General Staff, Anatoliy Kvashnin, excused themselves to consult with Yeltsin about two hours before the actual deployment. U.S. officials believe contingency plans had been worked out to deploy Russian forces as soon as NATO began to move peace-keepers into Kosovo, and Russian officials mistakenly believed that NATO troops were already crossing the border. An American official at Talbott's meeting offered this interpretation of events, and at least one Russian source confirms this version. Some Russian sources maintain that Kvashnin received permission from Yeltsin without Sergeyev being in the loop, and Talbott suggests that Kvashnin misled Sergeyev, Foreign Minister Igor Ivanov, and, ultimately, Yeltsin about the Russian operation. Talbott's own account, however, is consistent with other evidence that indicates that (a) the Russians genuinely thought that NATO was going to deploy troops

[124] Richard Pipes, "Russian Outrages in Chechnya," *IntellectualCapital.com*, October 28, 1999; Simon Saradzhyan, "Generals Tell Politicians: Hands Off," *MT*, November 5, 1999; Vladimir Gutnov, "Rossiya ne dolzhna opravdyvat'sya za svoye stremleniye pokonchit' s terrorizmom," *NG*, November 4, 1999; Mark Kramer, "Civil–Military Relations in Russia and the Chechnya Conflict," *Program on New Approaches to Russian Security Policy Memo Series*, Memo 99, December 1999.
[125] Pavel Felgenhauer, "Russia Shuns Unified Force," *MT*, June 17, 1999.

with or without Russian approval and (b) Yeltsin himself approved the operation.[126]

Thus, based again on polling data and military behavior, the dominant organizational culture of the Russian armed forces in the late 1990s remained committed to a norm of civilian supremacy. However, as in the beginning of the decade, this culture was not monolithic. As the polling data suggest, there was an organizational subculture (around ten to twenty percent of the officer corps) with a more praetorian stance.

One officer in this subgroup, Colonel Viktor Baranets, achieved momentary notoriety in Russia in February 1997 when he published excerpts from his diary in which he said he was so distraught about his living conditions that he fantasized about shooting a grenade out of his General Staff office window at Yeltsin's motorcade. Baranets was, not surprisingly, instantly sacked, particularly given that he worked as a press secretary for Minister of Defense Igor Rodionov at the time. Rodionov asked Baranets when he fired him, "I'm meeting with the president tomorrow. Am I supposed to tell him that the press secretary of the minister of defense intends to shoot you?" Baranets' defense that it was just a fantasy hardly excuses his actions.[127]

Baranets went on to publish a series of books about the Russian army in the 1990s. He contends that Yeltsin was extremely unpopular in the army, that officers were increasingly desperate due to their material conditions, and that discussions about possible actions, up to and including a coup, did take place. Ultimately he grows more and more disillusioned, although he still clings to the hope that spontaneous uprisings by desperate civilians and military personnel could bring down the government.[128]

A series of pretenders, with varying degrees of seriousness, put themselves forward as a Russian "man on horseback" who could pull Russia out of its misery. Most prominently, in the summer of 1997 General Rokhlin charged that Yeltsin was responsible for the collapse of the army, called on Yeltsin to resign, and announced that he was forming a Movement in Support of the Army that would rally the people and push Yeltsin from power.[129] Many observers took this threat seriously, but the movement had little support (it received .59 percent of the vote in December 1999 Duma elections) and

---

[126] Author's interview with anonymous U.S. government official; Strobe Talbott, *The Russia Hand: A Memoir of Presidential Diplomacy* (New York: Random House, 2002), pp. 332–349; Igor Korotchenko and Vladimir Mukhin, "Rossiyskiy desant operedil natovskiy kontingent," *NVO*, June 18, 1999; Author's interview with Dmitriy Trenin, September 13, 1999; Rosa Tsvetkova, "We Are Going into a War," *Vremya MN*, June 29, 1999, 1, 2 [*Defence & Security*, No. 76, July 2, 1999].

[127] Baranets, *Poteryannaya armiya*, pp. 523–524.

[128] See, for example, Baranets, *Yel'tsin i ego generaly*, pp. 27–28; Baranets, *Poteryannaya armiya*, p. 510; Baranets, *Genshtab bez tayn*, Vol. II, pp. 167–189.

[129] Lev Rokhlin, "My skoro poteryayem pravo nazyvat'sya grazhdanami Rossii," *Sovetskaya Rossiya*, August 14, 1997, 13.

Rokhlin himself was killed in the summer of 1998, although who was responsible remains a mystery. A 1999 U.S. State Department report concludes, "attempts to organize the armed forces into opposition movements... have fizzled after receiving little support from the armed forces and have had negligible impact on Russia's political order."[130]

Of course, creating a public movement is the opposite strategy to organizing a coup. To the extent that Russian officers have been involved in Russian domestic politics, it has been mainly to lobby for military interests within legally available channels. When Russian officers run for public office, for example, it implies an acceptance of the democratic process, not its rejection.[131]

Indeed, despite the claims by Baranets and others, the majority of observers believe that sentiment in the armed forces for intervention remained extremely low even in the worst years of Yeltsin's rule. Top Yeltsin aides Baturin and Satarov both stated that the Presidential Administration did not worry about coup attempts. In a series of conversations that I conducted with retired military officers, military journalists, and civilian analysts between 1993 and 2000, the vast majority contended that a military coup was not possible in Russia and such speculation was groundless. Similarly, a series of elite interviews by another Western scholar came to the same conclusion, noting that "it was felt that... this was too far outside of the military's history and tradition to be possible [and] that the Army is too politically divided and weak to manage it in any case." Thus, these analysts believed a combination of organizational culture and structure explained military passivity.[132]

Motives: Individual Self-Interest

The individual self-interest of officers, in particular the fear of failing or getting caught, often can inhibit coups. However, as pointed out in Chapter 1, this argument fails as a general account because it (a) ignores the many personal incentives to participate in coups and (b) cannot explain the hundreds of cases of military intervention around the world in the last several decades. Still, this factor undoubtedly played some role in Russia during Yeltsin's tenure.

---

[130] U.S. Department of State, *Annual Report on Military Expenditures, 1998*. For an overview of the many conspiracy theories about Rokhlin's murder, see Andrei Rogachevskii, "The Murder of General Rokhlin," *Europe-Asia Studies*, 52 (2000), 95–110.

[131] Although most Western democracies appropriately restrict active-duty officers from running for public office, this is not true in Russia. See also Ball and Gerber, "Political Views," 160.

[132] Ostrow interviews with Baturin and Satarov; Author's interviews; David Betz, *"If they are ordered 'Die of hunger!' they will die": Russian Defence Analysts Speak on Civil–Military Relations*, Glasgow Papers No. 2, 1999 (Glasgow: University of Glasgow, 1999), p. 21.

Several analysts argued that Yeltsin turned a blind eye to military corruption as a way of buying off top generals, who could provide for themselves materially without participating in risky coup schemes.[133] This argument provides a plausible explanation for the noncoup of top Russian
officers, but it is also somewhat ad hoc. First, in other countries, coups
often have been motivated by the desire of officers to gain access to the
rent-seeking opportunities provided by capturing state power. This has been
particularly true in countries that rely on raw material exports for their main
source of revenue.[134] In Russia, however, military officers did not attempt
to seize the state in order to turn themselves into economic "oligarchs,"
unlike their counterparts in countries such as Nigeria. Second, in many
countries, coups are not carried out by the high command, but instead by
disgruntled mid-level officers. There is abundant evidence, discussed earlier, of the material hardships faced by Russian officers at all levels. Although some officers undoubtedly lined their pockets, there were many
others who could have benefited substantially from participating in a successful coup. Finally, as argued in Chapter 1, an individual self-interest argument for military intervention is dependent on factors at other modes
and levels of analysis to determine whether the potential benefits of participating in a coup outweigh the costs. In Yeltsin's Russia, the presence
of counterbalancing institutions and the knowledge that most officers adhered to a norm of civilian supremacy were important deterrents to intervention that would have been a factor in the calculations of potential
praetorians.

CONCLUSION

The Russian military was dragged into one sovereign power dispute under
Boris Yeltsin, in October 1993. The weakness of the new Russian state is the
best explanation for the crisis. The army's hesitation to play an internal role,
and its ultimate subordination to the president's orders, is best explained by
the army's organizational culture.

Looking at the Yeltsin period as a whole, the opportunities for intervention were relatively high compared to most of the Soviet period. This fact
helps explain why the possibility of a coup was such a hot topic. Low state

---

[133] Pavel Fel'gengauer, "Novye russkie generaly," *Segodnya*, January 17, 1998; Kimberly
Marten Zisk, "Institutional Decline in the Russian Military: Exit, Voice, and Corruption,"
Program on New Approaches to Russian Security Policy Memo Series, Memo 67, September
1999; Author's interview with Solovyev.

[134] John Mukum Mbaku, "Military Coups as Rent-Seeking Behavior," *Journal of Political and
Military Sociology*, 22(1994), 241–284; Samuel Decalo, *Coups and Army Rule in Africa:
Motivations and Constraints*, 2nd ed. (New Haven, CT: Yale University Press, 1990);
Rosemary H. T. O'Kane, "A Probabilistic Approach to the Causes of Coups d'Etat," *British
Journal of Political Science*, 11, 3(July 1981), 287–308.

political capacity did make a military coup more of an option. On the other hand, organizational structure in its various forms, such as counterbalancing and penetration, did remain a potential barrier to army intervention. How robust these mechanisms would have proven in a crisis is difficult to say, but the chaos in the various power ministries in October 1993 suggests that the state's control over its own coercive apparatus was less robust than in the past.

The material motives for a military coup were about as high as one could imagine, given the fate of the army in the aftermath of Soviet collapse. Thus, the corporate interest approach performs the worst of the four alternatives. The Russian military suffered a multitude of blows to its interests under Yeltsin but showed little desire to try to defend them through extra-legal means. Moreover, in October 1993 the military did not try to play the two sides in the dispute against each other to promote its organizational interests, and ultimately the army sided with the contender for power who was less likely to promote the military's interests.

One reason these corporate interest motives for intervention did not translate into action was because of an apolitical organizational culture. Institutional lessons specific to the Russian armed forces greatly influenced officer corps behavior, both in October 1993 and in subsequent crises. Military attachment to a norm of civilian supremacy, although somewhat weakened during Yeltsin's reign, remained quite robust given the revolutionary changes in the country and in the army's political fortunes. The successful weathering of this period is also a cause for hope about the future of Russian civil–military relations.

8

Organizational Culture and the Future of Russian Civil–Military Relations

The fate of Russian democracy under Vladimir Putin remains highly uncertain. One clear message of this book, however, is that the Russian military is not a threat to democratization. At the end of this chapter I will take up this point more directly and will discuss some of the policy implications of my argument. Before turning to policy, however, we must return to history and political science. The three remaining tasks, then, are to summarize the evidence and my interpretation of it, to explore some theoretical issues raised by the book, and to discuss what policy implications follow from this analysis.

THE RUSSIAN MILITARY IN POLITICS

In the early Imperial period of Russian history, which starts with Peter the Great, the officer corps was heavily involved in leadership politics. Military men were responsible for the rise to power of Peter himself, Catherine the Great, Alexander I, and a slew of other monarchs in the eighteenth century. Imperial Russia had a problem with palace coups.

This pattern of praetorianism was sharply reversed in the nineteenth century. The failed Decembrist uprising of 1825 represented a key organizational lesson for the officer corps, and from this point forward the Russian army was much more cautious about becoming involved in sovereign power issues. This lesson was reinforced by civilian oversight efforts instituted by Tsar Nicholas I, and one of the mechanisms he created, secret police monitoring of the officer corps, persists to this day. Finally, the great Russian Defense Minister Dmitriy Milyutin instituted a series of reforms in the second half of the century that largely extracted the army from internal politics and administration and reoriented the military toward external defense.

In the twentieth century the Russian armed forces were involved in sovereign power issues during the two revolutionary periods that marked the creation and collapse of the Soviet Union. In both 1917 and 1991–1993 the army was a key player in domestic politics. Detailed analysis of these cases showed that the military was generally dragged into politics against its will by civilian power struggles and the prospect of state collapse. Additionally, these two brief periods of involvement represent a clear exception to the general pattern over the past two centuries, when the military has remained "outside politics."

I have argued in this book that the best way to explain Russian military behavior in sovereign power issues is through a two-step model composed of *opportunity* and *motive*, following Samuel Finer's classic *The Man on Horseback*. Opportunity is determined by the structural constraints imposed by state political capacity and by the degree of organizational cohesion (including penetration and counterbalancing by secret police and paramilitary bodies). Motives for military intervention can derive either from threats to the army's corporate interests or from officer beliefs about their proper role in sovereign power issues.

Throughout I have insisted that a monocausal theory of military intervention is unlikely to capture the diversity of army behavior. This has certainly proved true of events in Russia, and the considerable social science literature on civil–military relations points to a similar conclusion.

Three of the four theoretical approaches investigated – domestic structure, organizational structure, and organizational culture – all performed reasonably well as explanatory lenses for studying Russian military involvement in sovereign power issues. I believe that the detailed case analysis showed the particular importance of organizational culture as a factor shaping officer corps decisions, but a reasonable case also can be made for domestic structure as a significant factor.

I argue that the fourth perspective under consideration, corporate interest, proved to be a less useful guide. This conclusion is particularly striking given the prominence of this argument in both the Soviet studies and comparative civil–military relations literature. It is to this question, and to several related theoretical issues, that I now turn.

CIVIL–MILITARY RELATIONS THEORY REVISITED

In this section several important theoretical issues are discussed in greater detail. In addition to discussing the relative importance of the four approaches, I offer some thoughts on where cultures come from and how they change, an alleged weakness of cultural theories. Finally, I discuss the importance of building explanations of military involvement in sovereign power issues that emphasize multiple causality and the interaction of factors based on different modes and levels of analysis, as well as different types of involvement, such as arbitration.

TABLE 8.1. *Theory Performance*

	Intervention/No Intervention	
	Correct	Incorrect
Domestic Structure	8	2
Organizational Structure	7	3
Corporate Interest	6	4
Organizational Culture	7	3

	Arbitration		
	Correct	Incorrect	Mixed
Domestic Structure	3	1	1
Organizational Structure	1	4	0
Corporate Interest	1	3	1
Organizational Culture	3	1	1

Corporate Interest Revisited

On the face of it, corporate interest does not perform that badly in explaining Russian military behavior in twentieth-century sovereign power issues (see Table 8.1).[1] A corporate interest perspective correctly predicted intervention in 1917 and 1991, as well as nonintervention throughout much of the post-Stalin Soviet era. Although this approach was also wrong in four cases, including the Stalinist purges and the Yeltsin era, it was right more often than it was wrong.

The detailed case studies, however, showed that a corporate interest argument was often right for the wrong reasons. Both in 1917 and 1991, military intervention came about due to the imminent danger of state collapse. Although military interests obviously would be harmed by state collapse, it would be a serious distortion of both the theory and the cases to say that army corporate interests as conventionally understood were the cause of intervention.

If we look at the five cases of military arbitration in the twentieth century, the poor performance of the corporate interest argument becomes even more clear. Only in 1957, during Khrushchev's showdown with the "anti-party group," can the behavior of the military leadership, in particular Marshal Zhukov, be attributed to corporate interest concerns. In October 1917, December 1991, and October 1993, those officers in the arbiter position took the position more harmful to army material interests. High command behavior in February 1917 during the abdication of Nicholas II was more

---

[1] Table 8.1 was created based on Tables 3.1, 4.1, 5.1, 6.1, and 7.1, which should be consulted for further details about the predictions of the various approaches and the actual outcomes.

ambiguous, motivated primarily by concern about the war effort, something that clearly affected military interests but also was a much bigger issue than narrow organizational concerns.

Although I have argued that corporate interest approaches are a poor guide to understanding the behavior of the Russian armed forces in sovereign power disputes, this perspective may be quite useful in explaining the conduct of the Russian military in other domains of civil–military relations, or the propensity of armies to coup in other states. Roman Kolkowicz and Timothy Colton were right to argue that the Soviet armed forces pursued their organizational interests, in terms of power and resources, in policy decisions in the realm of defense politics.[2] They were wrong, however, to assume that this behavior would carry over to the sovereign power realm. There was no reason that civil–military conflict over military doctrine or spending, for example, would lead to a military coup, any more than similar conflicts in the United States lead to military intervention.

Corporate interest motives, then, must be considered with regard to structural and normative factors that also influence military behavior. When these other factors are considered, it becomes clear that there were multiple reasons why military intervention was unlikely throughout most of the Soviet period.

Organizational Culture Revisited

Throughout the book I have stressed the importance of organizational culture as an explanation for Russian military behavior. Yet Table 8.1 seems to suggest that domestic structure performs slightly better than organizational culture, and that organizational structure and corporate interest do a respectable job of explaining military intervention, although not arbitration. How do I justify my emphasis on organizational culture?

There are several reasons why I stress the utility of organizational culture arguments. First, this approach has been relatively neglected in the study of military coups, and thus a detailed demonstration of its usefulness is worth highlighting.[3] Second, and more important, the in-depth process tracing in the case studies shows that organizational culture can play a very important role even when its predictions are incorrect. Thus, if a corporate interest argument was often right for the wrong reasons, an organizational culture account was often wrong for the right reasons.

For example, although the Kornilov affair is coded as a coup, a full analysis of the case shows that the intervention only took place after a bizarre series

---

[2] Roman Kolkowicz, *The Soviet Military and the Communist Party* (Princeton, NJ: Princeton University Press, 1967); Timothy J. Colton, *Commissars, Commanders, and Civilian Authority: The Structure of Soviet Military Politics* (Cambridge, MA: Harvard University Press, 1979).

[3] The most important exception is the work of J. Samuel Fitch. See the discussion in Chapter 1.

of events provoked General Kornilov into open opposition with the Kerensky government. Furthermore, the rapid collapse of the revolt was at least partially due to the strength of a norm of civilian supremacy in the Russian officer corps, although organizational structure (in terms of officer-troop splits) and collective action problems (individual self-interest) also played a role. Similarly, in August 1991 General Dmitriy Yazov's participation in the coup attempt was half-hearted, and several of his key subordinates took steps that led directly to the putsch's failure. Thus, even when the Russian army did intervene in sovereign power issues due to the threat of state collapse, officer norms were a key factor contributing to the failure of these efforts.

Organizational culture also played an important role in determining officer behavior in cases of arbitration. During the Bolshevik takeover in October 1917, the collapse of the Soviet Union in December 1991, and the Yeltsin–Supreme Soviet showdown in October 1993, key officers evinced a clear unwillingness to take on the arbiter role. The high command was also an unenthusiastic participant in the events that led to Nicholas II's abdication.

Finally, it is worth pointing out that the two structural accounts benefit from fairly liberal interpretations of their core arguments. The domestic structure perspective traditionally has argued that low state capacity leads to military intervention. In fact, in many cases in Russia, state weakness has led not to intervention but to arbitration, but I gave this theoretical approach credit for getting these cases right. The organizational structure argument benefits from being interpreted consistently with a logical variant of the argument, which predicts nonintervention in the case of organizational splits, even though the existing empirical literature on coups shows that divided militaries are more likely, rather than less likely, to intervene. This approach also does poorly in predicting behavior in arbitration cases; in Russia, officers from different armed bodies have tended to cooperate rather than counterbalance or split into contending sides.

Nonetheless, these structural accounts focused on opportunity clearly add a great deal to an explanation of Russian military behavior. Indeed, one of the most interesting things about the cases is how explanations involving different modes and levels of analysis interact to affect outcomes. Before turning to this issue, however, we must examine the question of cultural change.

Cultural Origins and Change

Cultural arguments are frequently faulted for being unable to identify where culture comes from and how it changes. In this view, culture is an all too easily invoked residual variable that is itself an "uncaused cause" or, in Peter Hall's words, a *"deus ex machina* that is itself unexplainable."[4]

---

[4] Peter A. Hall, *Governing the Economy: The Politics of State Intervention in Britain and France* (New York: Oxford University Press, 1986), p. 34.

The problem of "uncaused causes," however, is a generic problem to any scientific research question. Unless one starts every research topic with the Big Bang and primordial ooze, there is a prehistory to the story any social scientist or historian has to tell. Not just culture and ideas, but also institutions and interests, have to be caused by something that is outside the scope of the topic at hand. It is just as valid for culturalists to take a snapshot approach to a question as it is for institutionalists or rational choice adherents to do so.

Nonetheless, there are good reasons to take a longer view in many social science accounts, including cultural ones.[5] In this book we have seen how an organizational culture can develop and change over a long period. In the nineteenth century the praetorian culture of the Russian army was transformed into an apolitical one that has persisted to this day. Revisiting that change, and comparing it to the theoretical literature on cultural change, can point to more general lessons.

Looking back at the change in Russian military culture in the nineteenth century, three issues stand out as particularly important:

1. The failed Decembrist uprising of 1825.
2. The reforms of Dmitriy Milyutin as Defense Minister from 1861 until 1881.
3. The strict discipline and political monitoring instituted by Tsar Nicholas I and continued by his successors.

These three factors worked together over a multidecade period to transform the organizational culture of the Russian officer corps. All three of these factors have found more general support in both the organizational culture and civil–military relations literature. The findings here, then, reinforce more general arguments about cultural change, thus underlining their importance. At the same time, a factor often stressed as important in explaining cultural change, external shock, was not important as a cause in the case of Russian military organizational culture.

Institutional Lessons. The sources of culture often can be found in the specific institutional experiences of an organization. Unique events in the life of the organization, the organizational culture literature argues, teach its members what behavior is appropriate.[6] More specifically, civil–military

---

[5] For a discussion of some of these issues, see Paul Pierson, "Not Just What, but *When*: Timing and Sequence in Political Processes," *Studies in American Political Development*, 14 (2000), 72–92, as well as the subsequent commentaries by Robert Jervis, Kathleen Thelen, Amy Bridges, and Paul Pierson, pp. 93–119.

[6] See, for example, James G. March, Lee S. Sproul, and Michal Tamuz, "Learning from Samples of One or Fewer," *Organization Science*, 2 (1991), 1–13; Daniel C. Feldman, "The Development and Enforcement of Group Norms," *Academy of Management Review*, 9 (1984), 51.

relations scholars have pointed to the effect that failed coups or disastrous periods of military rule have had in strengthening a norm of civilian supremacy in countries such as Argentina and Sri Lanka.[7] Conversely,
a history of successful coups may strengthen a praetorian organizational
culture.[8]

Organizational Leaders. An organization's founder plays an important role
in determining its culture, and subsequent leaders also have the ability to
bring about cultural change.[9] A perhaps extreme example of this influence from civil–military relations is seen in the case of Michel Le Tellier,
French Secretary of State for War from 1643 until 1677. David Ralston credits Le Tellier with establishing the basic parameters of the French military
"constitution" for the subsequent three centuries.[10] Arguably, Milyutin had
a similarly long-lasting effect in Russia. More recent leaders, although not
as significant as Milyutin, also have been very important. For example, the
stewardship of Yevgeniy Shaposhnikov and Pavel Grachev from 1991 to
1996, regardless of other flaws in their leadership, helped the armed forces
weather the transition from the Soviet to the post-Soviet period without the
spread of praetorianism among most officers.

External Control. Finally, external monitoring can shape the culture of organizations in general, and militaries in particular. The ability of civilian
leaders to fire officers out of step with their agenda is an important tool in establishing civilian supremacy. Samuel Huntington, for example, stresses the
importance of firing potentially disloyal officers and severely punishing coup
plotters. Such advice would be applauded by organizational theorists, who
note the importance of removing "deviants" as a way of reinforcing organizational culture. Civilians also should use their ability to monitor doctrine,
budgets, and military education to enforce a norm of civilian supremacy.
Although cultural theory tells us that changing a culture from the outside is
difficult, it is also the case, as Elizabeth Kier notes, that because armies are

---

[7] J. Samuel Fitch, *The Armed Forces and Democracy in Latin America* (Baltimore, MD: The Johns
Hopkins University Press, 1998), pp. 72–75; Donald L. Horowitz, *Coup Theories and Officers'
Motives: Sri Lanka in Comparative Perspective* (Princeton, NJ: Princeton University Press, 1980),
pp. 204–216.

[8] Douglas A. Hibbs, Jr., *Mass Political Violence: A Cross-National Causal Analysis* (New York:
John Wiley & Sons, 1973), pp. 106–107, 189.

[9] The classic statement is Philip Selznick, *Leadership in Administration: A Sociological Interpretation* (Berkeley, CA: University of California Press, 1957). See also J. Steven Ott, *The Organizational Culture Perspective* (Pacific Grove, CA: Brooks/Cole Publishing, 1989), pp. 81–82;
Pasquale Gagliardi, "The Creation and Change of Organizational Cultures: A Conceptual
Framework," *Organization Studies*, 7 (1986), 121, 129.

[10] David B. Ralston, ed., *Soldiers and States: Civil–Military Relations in Modern Europe* (Boston:
D. C. Heath, 1966), p. 23.

"total organizations" it may be easier for change to be imposed from the top than in other settings.[11]

External Shock. What is missing from this account of cultural change is a factor often highlighted by others: external shock.[12] Although "institutional lessons" as a source of cultural change can come from dramatic shocks, they need not do so. Moreover, at least in the case of the Russian armed forces, severe external shocks, such as the Russian Revolution and the collapse of the Soviet Union, did not change the norm of civilian supremacy in significant ways. This was because of three other factors stressed here: failed interventions in 1917 and 1991 reinforced existing norms, top officers were committed to perpetuating these norms, and civilian leaders took steps to ensure the loyalty and subordination of the officer corps. Although political crises in 1917 and 1991–1993 did lead to greater military involvement in domestic politics, this was due primarily to the weakness of the state and not to a more praetorian organizational culture. On the other hand, there are clear cases, such as in post-Nazi Germany, in which external shocks did have major affects on an army's organizational culture.[13]

Cultural change, like military coups, cannot be explained with a simple "golden-bullet" theory. On the other hand, several causes of cultural change uncovered in other environments and cases were found to be important in explaining the development of Russian military organizational culture. Thus, the significance of these "causal mechanisms" is further substantiated.[14]

Multicausality and Interaction Effects

Military involvement in sovereign power issues is best understood in terms of a two-step model of opportunity and motive. Assuming this argument is

[11] Barry R. Posen, *The Sources of Military Doctrine: France, Britain, and Germany Between the World Wars* (Ithaca, NY: Cornell University Press, 1984), pp. 53–59, 74–79; Peter D. Feaver, *Delegation, Monitoring, and Civilian Control of the Military: Agency Theory and American Civil–Military Relations* (Cambridge, MA: John M. Olin Institute for Strategic Studies, Harvard University, May 1996), pp. 29–30; Samuel P. Huntington, *The Third Wave: Democratization in the Late Twentieth Century* (Norman, OK: University of Oklahoma Press, 1991), pp. 251–252; Ott, *Organizational Culture Perspective*, p. 92; Elizabeth Kier, *Imagining War: French and British Military Doctrine Between the Wars* (Princeton, NJ: Princeton University Press, 1997), p. 161.

[12] Harry Eckstein, "A Culturalist Theory of Political Change," *The American Political Science Review*, 82 (1988), 789–904; Paul Kowert and Jeffrey Legro, "Norms, Identity, and Their Limits: A Theoretical Reprise," in Peter J. Katzenstein, ed., *The Culture of National Security* (New York: Columbia University Press, 1996), pp. 470–474.

[13] Donald Abenheim, *Reforging the Iron Cross: The Search for Tradition in the West German Armed Forces* (Princeton, NJ: Princeton University Press, 1988).

[14] On causal mechanisms versus general laws, see Jon Elster, *Nuts and Bolts for the Social Sciences* (Cambridge: Cambridge University Press, 1989), pp. 3–10.

accepted, the next and more challenging step would be to come up with a general theoretical account that predicts how multiple variables interact to produce particular outcomes. This is a demanding task, and the difficulty of creating a multidimensional theory that adequately encompasses both structure and agency may explain why monocausal, universalistic theories are so commonly advanced.

At several places in the book I have suggested how the four theoretical approaches under discussion may complement each other. For example, I argued that domestic and organizational structure co-vary in predictable ways, with strong states being better able to maintain robust counterbalancing mechanisms than weak states. At the same time, the military itself is more likely to be internally divided when the state is in crisis, which may explain why internally divided armies are as inclined to intervene as more unified ones.

The most interesting interactions for my argument are those involving organizational culture. The evidence from this book suggests several interesting combinations.

The Russian case fairly clearly demonstrates that militaries with a relatively apolitical culture will endure serious blows to their corporate interests without pulling a coup. Even with a relatively permissive opportunity structure, such as during the late Gorbachev and Yeltsin years, there was no effort to organize a coup in order to protect the army from severe organizational threats. Thus, corporate interest remains an important potential cause of military intervention, but only in those cases in which there is both opportunity and a more praetorian organizational culture that sees involvement in sovereign power issues as legitimate.

The organizational structure argument has been bedeviled throughout by the disjuncture between a logical form of the argument, which suggests that divided militaries would be less inclined to intervene in politics, and the empirical record, which seems to show the opposite. Organizational culture helps us resolve this seeming paradox. More praetorian armies are more likely to resolve serious differences both with civilian elites and within the military through the use of force. A dangerous cycle of coup and counter-coup can develop when there are strong normative motives for intervention in combination with a divided military. In contrast, when there is a well-entrenched norm of civilian supremacy, officers will be particularly careful to avoid situations, such as sovereign power disputes, when open splits or counterbalancing could occur and push the country to the brink of civil war.

Domestic structure is the most common explanation for military intervention, and it performs well in the Russian cases. But with the exception of the Russian civil war the officer corps sought to avoid involvement in sovereign power issues even during periods of extreme state weakness, and even during the civil war the majority of officers initially adopted a neutral stance.

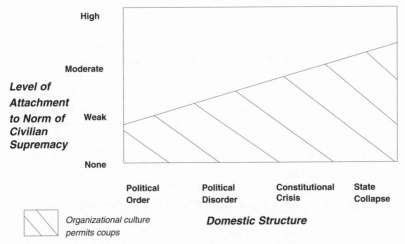

FIGURE 8.1. Organizational culture and domestic structure.

Organizational culture is likely to be a particularly important guide to be-havior when the opportunities for intervention are high, because structure is less constraining.

Thinking about how domestic structure and organizational culture ap-proaches may complement each other shows the importance of multicausal explanations. Figure 8.1 depicts a plausible hypothesis about how these two arguments may interact. In countries where the officer corps has a more praetorian organizational culture (i.e., little or no attachment to a norm of civilian supremacy), a coup can often come during periods of relative political stability and be provoked by relatively minor slights to corporate or personal interests. Thus Samuel Decalo, an expert on African militaries, has argued that coups are highly idiosyncratic events.[15] In countries where both structural and normative barriers to intervention are weak, this may well be true. In contrast, in Western Europe and North America the combination of these two variables is such that military involvement in sovereign power issues is now virtually unthinkable (although it was not that long ago that in countries like Spain and France the possibility of military intervention was very real).

In Russia what has varied most in the last century is not organizational culture but political stability and the power of the state. During constitutional crises, when the fundamental rules of the game are in question, the military has often been called on to play an arbiter role. It has taken on this role reluctantly, and with no desire to exploit the opportunity to seize power for itself. Only when the state was threatened with collapse did coup attempts

---

[15] Samuel Decalo, *Coups and Army Rule in Africa: Motivations and Constraints*, 2nd ed. (New Haven, CT: Yale University Press, 1990).

become possible, but without the requisite boldness to succeed that would come from a less apolitical army.

A review of the Russian historical experience thus demonstrates the importance of arbitration as a category of military involvement in sovereign power issues. The coup/no-coup dichotomy, although useful for large-N comparisons, does not really capture the diversity of ways in which the armed forces can play a role in sovereign power issues.[16] Arbitration remains the most likely method of Russian military involvement in sovereign power issues. Given the apolitical organizational culture of the Russian army, civilian decisions are at least as important as military ones in determining what role the military will play in domestic politics. Arbitration is also a possible route to military participation in politics in other states. For example, one can imagine a scenario in China where the military either assumes or is thrust into an arbiter role between contending factions of the political leadership.

Investigating the political behavior of a single army over a multicentury period allows us to see how complicated interactions among multiple possible causes play out. Some historians may well conclude that even the two-step, multicausal model put forward here does serious injury to the nuance and texture of the actual cases. But for those of us who believe that history is more than just "one damn thing after another," and see it as a possible source of general lessons about politics and society, then perhaps this book has yielded some conclusions that are of interest not only to social scientists but to policymakers as well.

DEMOCRATIZATION AND CIVIL–MILITARY RELATIONS

In recent decades, as part of a global trend toward greater democracy, there has been a general "return to the barracks" for the army in many countries. Military regimes no longer dominate the political landscape in Latin America – in fact, they are now completely absent from that region – and their presence has declined in Africa and Asia as well.

This is not to say that military rule is in danger of disappearing as a political phenomenon. In 1999, for example, Pakistan reverted to military rule, and the Ivory Coast actually experienced the first coup in its history.[17]

---

[16] For other theoretical discussions of military involvement in sovereign power issues that move beyond the coup/non-coup dichotomy, see S. E. Finer, *The Man on Horseback: The Role of the Military in Politics*, 2nd ed. (Harmondsworth, England: Penguin Books, 1975), pp. 77–78, 127–148; Martin Edmonds, *Armed Services and Society* (Boulder, CO: Westview Press, 1990), p. 103.

[17] Interestingly enough, the ousted civilian president in the Ivory Coast, Henri Konan Bédié, apparently believed that paramilitary police forces could counterbalance a coup attempt. As is often the case, once an army coup was underway, the paramilitaries stayed on the sidelines. See "Now where?," *The Economist*, January 8, 2000, 42.

We clearly have not seen the end of military coups. But in general the trend over the last several decades has been positive.

Interestingly enough, democratization in Russia has actually increased fears about military intervention in politics. With the collapse of Communist Party control, the argument goes, the army has become a potentially dangerous actor on the Russian political scene.[18] The evidence in this book suggests that, at a minimum, the history behind this common story is wrong. Civilian supremacy predates communist rule in Russia, and there were multiple factors that inhibited military intervention during the Soviet period, not just the power of the Party.

Before assessing the future of civil–military relations in Russia, it is worth pausing to consider what lessons we might draw about preventing coups from the history of Russian civil–military relations.

Strengthening Norms of Civilian Supremacy

Given that military coups are the product of multiple causes involving both opportunities and motives, civilian leaders have several choices about where to concentrate their efforts in trying to prevent coups. The extent to which these factors are manipulable, however, varies considerably. No political leader wants to preside over a weak state, but figuring out how to create a strong one is a difficult task. Advice to "strengthen the rule of law" or "fight corruption" simply invites further questions about how to accomplish these goals.

Other factors, however, are more manipulable. In the short run, various institutional and organizational strategies are the most direct methods of trying to prevent military intervention. In the long run, however, there is no substitute for the creation of an organizational culture committed to civilian supremacy.[19] Fortunately there are steps that can be taken that have both positive short-run and long-run effects.

Appointment and Dismissal. Perhaps the most important lever available to the civilian political leadership is that of appointment and dismissal. At the same time, civilians should resist the temptation to appoint top generals based on personal loyalty. This simply reinforces the view that the armed forces are an institution that may play an important role in sovereign power

---

[18] For two of the best statements of this view, see Eva Busza, "State Disfunctionality, Institutional Decay, and the Russian Military," in Valerie Sperling, ed., *Building the Russian State: Institutional Crisis and the Quest for Democratic Governance* (Boulder, CO: Westview Press, 2000), pp. 113–136; Lilia Shevtsova, "Russia's Fragmented Armed Forces," in Larry Diamond and Marc F. Plattner, eds., *Civil–Military Relations and Democracy* (Baltimore, MD: The Johns Hopkins University Press, 1996), pp. 110–133.

[19] On this point see also Jendayi Frazer, "Conceptualizing Civil–Military Relations During Democratic Transition," *Africa Today*, 42, Nos. 1–2 (1995), 40–41.

issues. What should matter in personnel decisions are the professional qualities of the officers and their commitment to a norm of civilian supremacy. To put it another way, leading officers should be loyal to certain principles, but not to particular politicians. Similarly, officers who reject apolitical values should be dismissed.

In some cases, particularly after a period of military rule, civilian leaders may have relatively limited control over military appointments. This is a weapon that the military must be persuaded to give up. Without control over the top positions, it is hard to control the armed forces in the short run or remake their organizational culture in the long run.

Institutional Barriers. Changing institutions may be harder for civilian leaders than changing commanders, but the long-run payoff of such changes is potentially huge. The goal of institutional reform is to wall off the armed forces from tasks and positions that are contrary to the spirit of civilian rule.

Alfred Stepan's concept of the "dimensions of military institutional prerogatives" is one of the most complete accounts of these institutional barriers. Stepan highlights eleven areas of institutional prerogatives. These eleven realms relate to the constitutional status of the armed forces and their formal and informal position relative to other state actors, such as the legislature, the judicial system, and other executive branch actors. For example, the principle of civilian supremacy is conveyed by the civilian leadership more strongly to the extent that the military has no constitutionally sanctioned independent role in the political system, the chief executive is both de jure and de facto commander-in-chief, and the police are separate from the army, with the army playing no role in domestic policing.[20]

Another important institutional barrier is the restriction of active-duty officers from holding elected office, such as in the legislature or in local government. This has been a problem in post-Soviet Russia, where the presence of officers in the parliament and even as governors of regions sends a signal that runs counter to the principle of civilian supremacy.[21] Of course, popular generals often have made a successful transition to the role of politician, such as Charles de Gaulle in France and Dwight Eisenhower in the United States. But officers who want to take this route should be forced to hang up their uniform first.

Often the institutional roles of the military are inherited from a previous period of authoritarian rule. For example, in the Soviet system the presence of officers in state and Communist Party bodies tended to reinforce military

---

[20] Alfred Stepan, *Rethinking Military Politics: Brazil and the Southern Cone* (Princeton, NJ: Princeton University Press, 1988), pp. 93–102.

[21] On this point, with an instructive comparison to Poland, see Eva Busza, "Transition and Civil–Military Relations in Poland and Russia," *Communist and Post-Communist Studies*, 29 (1996), 167–184.

subordination to civilian rule, in the form of the party. Even more problematic is when the position of the armed forces in state bodies is mandated, sometimes in the constitution, by a departing military government. These "reserved domains" are meant to protect the armed forces from political, legal, or budgetary challenges by subsequent civilian governments.[22]

These reserved domains can be quite difficult to challenge. For example, in Turkey the military continues to see itself as the guardian of secularism almost 20 years after the return to civilian rule. They maintain their political influence through the military-dominated National Security Council, which often dictates policy to the civilian Turkish leadership. Although civilian leaders occasionally make statements about curtailing the military's political role, the institutional structure of Turkish politics has not been changed to restrict the army's internal power.[23]

When civilian leaders should press for institutional limits on the military's power is a political question that must be answered within the specific country context. Obviously this is a more difficult undertaking after periods of military rule, particularly if the military established reserved domains when exiting power. In cases in which the military has a clearly demonstrated attachment to a norm of civilian supremacy, such as in Russia, there should be no reason that civilians should hold back on establishing firm institutional controls.

Military Education and Socialization. Political leaders should pay attention to the military education system and the process of officer socialization. What officers say to each other in their journals, textbooks, and seminars contributes to their outlook on sovereign power issues. In the past, Soviet military journals stressed the supremacy of the Communist Party; this was a good thing. It is an encouraging sign that now these very same journals publish the text of major legislation adopted by the parliament and the president.

It may be difficult for civilian outsiders to penetrate this domain if there is a weak history of civilian oversight. Thus, more fundamental institutional changes may have to take priority over this issue. But some civilian leaders have had success in this realm, and in the long run there is no substitute for more direct efforts to transform organizational culture. The socialization process in "total organizations" can be very powerful, so officer corps education must be made consistent with apolitical norms. Kier suggests

---

[22] On reserved domains, see: Juan J. Linz and Alfred Stepan, *Problems of Democratic Transition and Consolidation: Southern Europe, South America, and Post-Communist Europe* (Baltimore, MD: The Johns Hopkins University Press, 1996), pp. 67–69, 82. Similar ideas are developed in Stepan, *Rethinking Military Politics*, pp. 93–102; Huntington, *Third Wave*, pp. 238–241.

[23] For examples, see Stephen Kinzer, "Turkish Premier Confronts Military Over Islam," *The New York Times*, March 21, 1998, A4; Stephen Kinzer, "Turkish Generals Demand Curbs on Islamic Extremists," *The New York Times*, March 28, 1998, A3.

encouraging the placement of military officers in civilian universities and exchanges with foreign militaries as methods of exposing officers to different ideas.[24] Such approaches could be particularly helpful in promoting norms of civilian control.

Missions. The content of military organizational culture is influenced by the functions performed by the military. This relationship between the tasks performed by the army and the ideas held by its members is why limiting the political ambit of the armed forces is so crucial. In terms of military missions, trying to limit the application of internal violence to police and paramilitary bodies is often a wise strategy.

Of course, at times this may be impossible. Given Boris Yeltsin's political decision to use armed force against Chechnya, subsequently endorsed by his successor Vladimir Putin, it is hard to see how the military could have been left out of this mission. The Chechen example, however, also show some of the risks, in terms of army prestige and morale, of prolonged involvement in internal warfare. For this reason, prominent Russian generals turned politicians such as Aleksandr Lebed and Boris Gromov opposed the use of the armed forces in Chechnya.

A corollary of this prescription is the need to emphasize the external missions of the armed forces. For example, Spanish incorporation into NATO, a military alliance with a clear external orientation, helped solidify officer attachment to a norm of civilian supremacy. In cases where external threats are hard to come by, military participation in peacekeeping missions may be an appropriate substitute.[25]

Finally, civilian elites need to know the organizational culture of their armed forces as a prerequisite for making intelligent choices about changing this culture. In many cases the transition to democracy takes place after a period of military rule. In these circumstances it is almost inevitable that there will be civil–military negotiation about the prerogatives of the armed forces in the new political order. Concessions to the armed forces may be one of the prices of a successful transition. However, in cases where the armed forces have a tradition of subordination to civilian rule and commitment to the norm of civilian supremacy is high, it makes no sense to negotiate with the army over the conditions of the transition or to give them an expanded

[24] Huntington, *Third Wave*, pp. 244–245; Kier, *Imagining War*, pp. 160–164. For a critical evaluation of the military–military programs of the United States in post-Communist Central and Eastern Europe, see Marybeth Peterson Ulrich, *Democratizing Communist Militaries: The Cases of the Czech and Russian Armed Forces* (Ann Arbor, MI: University of Michigan Press, 1999).

[25] Huntington, *Third Wave*, pp. 245–248, 252; Michael C. Desch, "Threat Environments and Military Missions," in Diamond and Plattner, *Civil–Military Relations*, pp. 12–29; Condoleezza Rice, "The Military Under Democracy," *Journal of Democracy*, 3, 2 (1992), 39–40; Frazer, "Conceptualizing Civil–Military Relations," 45–46.

political role. An apolitical military is a substantial gift in the transition to democracy; the last thing one should do is ask the army to play a political role to which it is not accustomed and that it has no desire to play.

The Future of Russian Civil–Military Relations

The entire thrust of this book suggests that Russia is one of those "lucky" countries that has an apolitical military during an attempted transition to democracy. If democratization is faltering, as many observers suspect under President Vladimir Putin, it is not due to the threat of military intervention. In the sovereign power domain of civil–military relations, the situation in Russia is relatively good.

Military arbitration, however, remains a possibility in Russia. With a new political order still in the process of formation and consolidation, major political crises are by no means out of the question. If history is any guide, the Russian army is likely to try to avoid direct involvement in sovereign power issues and will certainly not try to seize power for itself.

However, this is not to suggest that all is well with Russian civil–military relations or with the organizational culture of the armed forces. In the domain of defense politics, and in other aspects of military organizational culture, there are several reasons for concern.

Many of the problems currently facing the Russian army are to some degree a by-product of the severe blows to its corporate interests over the last fifteen years. But some issues have deeper roots and therefore will be harder to eliminate. Rather than focusing on the unlikely possibility of military intervention, three other issues demand serious civilian attention: corruption, the undisciplined use of violence, and weak parliamentary influence on defense policy.

Corruption. Corruption, meaning the use of public office for private gain, is obviously not a phenomenon unique to the armed forces in Russia. As retired Colonel Vitaliy Tsygichko remarked, "corruption in the army is no less than corruption in the country as a whole."[26] But the ubiquitous nature of the problem in society hardly makes it less of a threat. And there are particular reasons to be concerned about corruption in the armed forces. As one of the fundamental agencies of state power, whose members are called to put state interests above their own, a corrupt army is potentially unreliable as a defender of the state.

Although corruption has a long history in the Russian and Soviet armed forces, the problem has become worse due to the dire economic situation of many officers and the weakness of the state as a law-enforcement body.[27]

---

[26] Author's interview, June 9, 2000.
[27] On corruption in the Imperial Russian and Soviet officer corps, see, respectively,

Multiple forms of corruption exist in the Russian armed forces today. Some of the more common varieties include accepting bribes to get young men out of military service, distributing military apartments to friends and relatives, and manipulating financial flows (by depositing money intended for salaries in a bank account for several months and collecting interest, for example). Both officers and soldiers have been guilty of selling weapons, fuel, and other supplies and materials on the black market. Officers have also hired out conscripts as cheap labor to businesspeople, in some cases basically selling conscripts as slaves.[28]

Eliminating corruption in the Russian armed forces requires, at a minimum, better standards of living for officers (i.e., higher salaries) and stronger legal and institutional mechanisms in the country at large. Corruption in the armed forces is thus another symptom of the weakness of the Russian state and is a problem that will not go away soon. Although it does not represent a threat to civilian supremacy, it does hinder efforts to reform the armed forces to make them less expensive, more effective, and more open to civilian oversight.

Violence. Officers, in Samuel Huntington's classic formulation, are specialists in the "management of violence." The key word here is not violence but management; using violence per se does not require professional expertise.[29] Too often, though, Russian officers use violence indiscriminately, particularly against their own soldiers, and also tolerate it against civilians in wartime.

This tendency to use violence against subordinates is hardly a new phenomenon, and to a certain degree it is present in many armies. Both the legacy of serfdom and the weak development of the rule of law in Russia tended to make the use of physical violence an acceptable disciplinary means in the Tsarist army, but Allen Wildman argues that physical discipline was

---

John Bushnell, "The Tsarist Officer Corps, 1881–1914: Customs, Duties, Inefficiency," *American Historical Review*, 86 (1981), 757–758; Roger R. Reese, *Stalin's Reluctant Soldiers: A Social History of the Red Army, 1925–1941* (Lawrence, KS: University Press of Kansas, 1996), pp. 116–118; William Odom, *The Collapse of the Soviet Military* (New Haven, CT: Yale University Press, 1998), pp. 42, 90.

[28] For examples, see Gul'chachak Khannanova, "Serzhant prodaval soldat chechentsam za geroin," *Kommersant daily*, July 23, 1999; Sergey Vladimirov, "The Generals steal on the same scale...," *Vremya MN*, August 6, 1999 [*Defence & security*, No. 92, August 9, 1999]; Eugenia Lentz, "The looting guards!," *Segodnya*, July 12, 2000 [*Defence & security*, No. 81, July 14, 2000]. Two overviews of crime in the military are: Vladimir Popov and Aleksandr Tuyurikov, "Sotsiologi preduprezhdayut," *Nezavisimoye Voyennoye Obozreniye*, September 22, 2000; Graham H. Turbiville, Jr., *Mafia in Uniform: The Criminalization of the Russian Armed Forces* (Fort Leavenworth, KS: Foreign Military Studies Office, United States Army, 1995).

[29] Samuel P. Huntington, *The Soldier and the State: The Theory and Politics of Civil–Military Relations* (Cambridge, MA: Belknap/Harvard University Press, 1957), pp. 11–14.

"not shockingly more cruel" than in Germany or France. Although the Soviet armed forces forbade corporal punishment, the use of violence against soldiers and lower-level officers by their superiors continued. For example, the former General and Krasnoyarsk Governor Aleksandr Lebed brags in his memoirs about an episode when, as a young Captain in Afghanistan, he knocked out eleven insubordinate soldiers in succession with a punch to the jaw. Violence among conscripts has also been a problem. The problem of *dedovshchina*, or the hazing of first-year conscripts by second-year soldiers, has been particularly severe.[30]

In wartime, Russian soldiers continue to direct indiscriminate violence and brutality at the civilian population, most recently in Chechnya. Anatol Lieven correctly points out that no Western state or army has clean hands in this respect, noting that both historically and relatively recently (France in Algeria, the United States in Vietnam) Western armies have at times engaged in brutal violence against innocent civilians. But the use of torture and rape as weapons of war in Chechnya cannot be justified because of the historical crimes of others, and is also self-defeating from the Russian point of view, given their goal of weakening Chechen desires for independence.[31] The behavior of the Russian armed forces in Chechnya demonstrates a darker aspect of Russian military organizational culture.

Changing these negative proclivities will require sustained civilian attention, rather than the hands-off and defensive stance generally displayed by the Russian government. Several reforms in particular recommend themselves, although it will take time to implement them. First, officer education needs to devote greater attention to the laws of war, such as the Geneva Convention. Second, a move toward a professional army, instead of relying on poorly educated, equipped, and trained conscripts, would in the long run improve both officers' relations with their subordinates and the behavior of Russian troops in battle. Third, and a logical corollary of adopting an all-volunteer structure, would be the creation of a professional noncommissioned officer (NCO) corps. Russia has never had a professional NCO structure, so such a change would have serious effects on the entire structure

---

[30] John L. H. Keep, *Soldiering in Tsarist Russia* (Colorado Springs, CO: United States Air Force Academy, 1986), pp. 7–8; Allan K. Wildman, *The End of the Russian Imperial Army: The Old Army and the Soldiers' Revolt*, Vol. I (Princeton, NJ: Princeton University Press, 1980), p. 34; Reese, *Stalin's Reluctant Soldiers*, p. 62; Aleksandr Lebed, *Za derzhavu obidno*...(Moskva: Moskovskaya pravda, 1995), pp. 74–75. A good discussion of *dedovshchina* is in Odom, *Collapse of the Soviet Military*, pp. 46–48, 286–289.

[31] Anatol Lieven, "Against Russophobia," *World Policy Journal*, 17, 4 (2000/2001) [at http://www.worldpolicy.org/]. For two good journalistic accounts of Russian human rights abuses in Chechnya, see Maura Reynolds, "War Has No Rules for Russian Forces Fighting in Chechnya," *Los Angeles Times*, September 17, 2000; Anna Politkovskaya, "How the heroes of Russia turned into the tormentors of Chechnya," *The Guardian*, February 27, 2001.

of the armed forces and the functions performed by junior and middle-level officers. It is certainly possible that adopting this reform at the time of a severe budget crunch would be difficult and could potentially discredit the very idea. But it is hard to avoid the conclusion that in the long run it will be difficult not only to solve problems such as *dedovshchina* and interarmy violence, but also to raise the fighting level of the army in general, without such a reform.[32]

Parliamentary Influence. The Russian armed forces are clearly under civilian control in the sovereign power domain of civil–military relations. Although not a central focus of this book, there is also considerable evidence that in the defense politics domain the influence of the armed forces is not unduly large. The Russian military, like the armed forces in all countries, lobbies for its policy preferences, but it remains ultimately subordinate to the civilian leadership.

The problem in the defense policy realm, then, is not *whether* the army is under civilian control, but *whose* control. The political system created in the last decade of democratization is sometimes referred to as "super-presidential" due to the considerable power vested in the office of the presidency.[33] This tendency to give the executive branch predominant influence is also true of defense policy.

Boris Yeltsin never had an interest in having a parliament that shared equally in governance, particularly in the area of defense and security policy. Civilian control of the armed forces for Yeltsin meant his personal control, assisted by the Presidential Administration and, at times, the Defense and Security Councils. Vladimir Putin seems to have similar feelings. At the same time, civilian control beyond the presidency is not nonexistent. The government, particularly the Administrative Department and the Ministry of Finance, plays important roles in working out laws and decrees that apply to the armed forces and in formulating the budget. Perhaps equally important is the role played by nongovernmental institutions, such as the press and organizations like the Council on Foreign and Defense Policy, in shining a spotlight on military affairs. Despite some progress, though, the degree of institutionalization of robust civilian control mechanisms is clearly

---

[32] On the need for a professional army, see Aleksandr Gol'ts, "Vo vsuyu ivanovskuyu," *Itogi*, April 2, 2001. On the historic absence of professional NCOs in the Russian and Soviet military, and some of the consequences, see Reese, *Stalin's Reluctant Soldiers*, pp. 120–121; Odom, *Collapse of the Soviet Military*, pp. 43–44, 286–288; Anatol Lieven, *Chechnya: Tombstone of Russian Power* (New Haven, CT: Yale University Press, 1998), pp. 290–293.

[33] M. Steven Fish, "The Executive Deception: Superpresidentialism and the Degradation of Russian Politics," in Sperling, *Building the Russian State*, pp. 177–192; Eugene Huskey, "Overcoming the Yeltsin Legacy: Vladimir Putin and Russian Political Reform," in Archie Brown, ed., *Contemporary Russian Politics: A Reader* (Oxford, England: Oxford University Press, 2001), pp. 82–96.

disappointing. Perhaps the biggest failure in this regard is the limited role the Duma plays in civilian oversight.[34]

The most important barrier to greater Duma participation in military affairs are the institutional limits on its power. The Duma plays no role in confirming the Minister of Defense or the other heads of the power ministries. Indeed, the Constitution does not grant the Duma oversight authority over executive branch structures. Thus, the very notion of parliamentary control of the military is arguably unconstitutional.[35]

The Duma does play a role in passing legislation and amendments that apply to the armed forces, such as the Law on Defense and the Law on the Status of Service Personnel. There are efforts underway to pass a law on civilian or parliamentary control of the armed forces. There are also proposals to establish a Duma representative responsible for monitoring military service questions, a position analogous to the Duma's human rights representative. Such efforts have been stymied in the past, however, both by divisions within the Duma itself and by opposition from the executive branch. The Duma has also battled for years for a more open military budget. Although some members of the Duma, particularly those on the Defense Committee, now have greater access to the budget, without public debate on these issues it will be difficult for parliament to gain greater control in this area.

To date, Duma influence has been largely due to the personal stature of some of its members, such as the current Defense Committee Chair, retired General Andrei Nikolayev. Although it would be unrealistic to expect that the Duma could achieve influence comparable to that of the U.S. Congress over defense policy – the United States is unique, even among developed democracies, in this respect – an expanded role for the Duma would be an important step in Russian civil–military relations.

An important corollary to such institutional change would be restrictions on the ability of active-duty military officers to seek elected office. Officer-politicians in Russia have not been particularly effective advocates for the armed forces, while at the same time they send the wrong signal about military participation in politics. Such restrictions would be consistent with President Putin's stated goal of "the demilitarization of society's life in Russia." Putin made this statement in March 2001 at the time of his appointment of a civilian defense minister, Sergei Ivanov, although Ivanov's background as a general in the Federal Security Service (FSB) makes him a not entirely "pure" civilian. The appointment of Ivanov was an important step because his background is outside the armed forces, but further

---

[34] Brian D. Taylor, "The Duma and Military Reform," *Program on New Approaches to Russian Security Policy Memo Series*, Memo No. 154, October 2000.

[35] This point was stressed to me by Colonel (Retired) Peter Romashkin, Legislative Assistant to Duma Deputy Aleksey Arbatov. Interview, June 8, 2000.

"demilitarization" of Russia's political life would see more civilians serving in the Ministry of Defense and fewer active-duty officers sitting in the Duma.[36]

Most of these deficiencies in Russian civil–military relations and military organizational culture are deeply rooted and will not be changed quickly. Fortunately, there are also highly positive aspects of Russian civil–military relations and military organizational culture that are also very entrenched, in particular a norm of civilian supremacy in sovereign power issues. It is worth remembering that establishing more democratic civil–military relations is always a protracted process, with both setbacks and advances. Given the political and economic collapse that accompanied the end of Communist rule in Russia, along with the disintegration of the Soviet Union itself, the rapid creation of well institutionalized democratic civil–military relations could hardly be expected. But with the fundamental basis of an apolitical military organizational culture in place, the potential for progressive and democratic change in Russian military affairs remains very much alive.

---

[36] On officer participation in Duma elections, see Robert V. Barylski, *The Soldier in Russian Politics: Duty, Dictatorship, and Democracy Under Gorbachev and Yeltsin* (New Brunswick, NJ: Transaction Publishers, 1998), pp. 274–275, 285, 335–364. For Putin's statement, see: "Statement by the President of the Russian Federation Vladimir Putin," *RTR Vesti Program*, 17:00, March 28, 2001 [Federal News Service (http://www.fednews.ru)]. For analysis of the Ivanov appointment, see: Gol'ts, "Vo vsuyu ivanovskuyu"; Oksana Antonenko, "Putin's 'new' national security team," *IISS Strategic Pointers*, March 29, 2001.

Index